Forensic Psychology
Second Edition

BPS Textbooks in Psychology

BPS Blackwell presents a comprehensive and authoritative series covering everything a student needs in order to complete an undergraduate degree in psychology. Refreshingly written to consider more than North American research, this series is the first to give a truly international perspective. Written by the very best names in the field, the series offers an extensive range of titles from introductory level through to final year optional modules, and every text fully complies with the BPS syllabus in the topic. No other series bears the BPS seal of approval!

Each book is supported by a companion website, featuring additional resource materials for both instructors and students, designed to encourage critical thinking, and providing for all your course lecturing and testing needs.

For other titles in this series, please go to www.bpsblackwell.co.uk

Forensic Psychology
Crime, Justice, Law, Interventions

Second Edition

EDITED BY

GRAHAM DAVIES
ANTHONY BEECH

The British Psychological Society | **BPS BLACKWELL**

This edition first published 2012 by the British Psychological Society and John Wiley & Sons Ltd

Copyright © 2012 the British Psychological Society and John Wiley & Sons Ltd

BPS Blackwell is an imprint of John Wiley & Sons Ltd

Cover photograph © Jess Hurd, photographer. Reproduced with kind permission of reportdigital.co.uk

Photographs on Part opening pages: Part I, p. 15 – © Franck Boston (used under licence from Shutterstock); Part II, p. 97 – © Brian A. Jackson (used under licence from Shutterstock); Part III, p. 227 – © Tupungato (used under licence from Shutterstock); Part IV, p. 305 – © Franck Boston (used under licence from Shutterstock).

All effort has been made to trace and acknowledge ownership of copyright. The publisher would be glad to hear from any copyright holders whom it has not been possible to contact.

Registered office

John Wiley & Sons Ltd, The Atrium, Southern Gate, Chichester, West Sussex, PO19 8SQ, United Kingdom

For details of our global editorial offices, for customer services and for information about how to apply for permission to reuse the copyright material in this book please see our website at www.wiley.com

The right of Graham Davies and Anthony Beech to be identified as the editors of this work has been asserted in accordance with the UK Copyright, Designs and Patents Act 1988.

Reprinted April 2013

Library of Congress Cataloging-in-Publication Data

Forensic psychology : crime, justice, law, interventions / edited by Graham
    Davies, Anthony Beech.—2nd ed.
      p. cm.
    Includes bibliographical references and index.
    ISBN 978-1-119-99195-3
      1. Forensic psychology. I.   Davies, Graham, 1943- II.   Beech, Anthony R.
  RA1148.F5565 2012
  614.15—dc23

                                                                    2011038988

A catalogue record for this book is available from the British Library.

Set in 11/12.5pt Dante MT by MPS Limited, a Macmillan Company, Chennai, India

Printed in Great Britain by TJ International Ltd, Padstow, Cornwall

The British Psychological Society's free Research Digest e-mail service rounds up the latest research and relates it to your syllabus in a user-friendly way. To subscribe go to www.researchdigest.org.uk or send a blank e-mail to subscribe-rd@lists.bps.org.uk

Commissioning Editor:	Andrew McAleer
Assistant Editors:	Georgia King and Katharine Earwaker
Marketing Managers:	Fran Hunt and Jo Underwood
Project Editor:	Juliet Booker

GD: For my family and *The Guardian* and Radio 4:
the crutches of my day.

AB: For my family, and Bon Iver, Richard Hawley,
and the Fleet Foxes, who have kept me going
through days of heavy editing.

Brief Contents

Contents

3   Contributions of Forensic Neuroscience   55

Anthony Beech, Benjamin Nordstrom and Adrian Raine

4   Effects of Interpersonal Crime on Victims   77

Catherine Hamilton-Giachritsis and Emma Sleath

Contributors

Anthony Beech
University of Birmingham, UK

Erica Bowen
University of Coventry, UK

Charles J. Brainerd
Cornell University, USA

Brian R. Clifford
University of Aberdeen and University of East London, UK

Graham Davies
University of Leicester and University of Birmingham, UK

Louise Dixon
University of Birmingham, UK

David P. Farrington
Institute of Criminology, Cambridge University, UK

Dawn Fisher
St. Andrews Healthcare, Birmingham, UK

Michelle Ginty
St. Andrews Healthcare, Birmingham, UK

Pär Anders Granhag
University of Gothenburg, Sweden

Catherine Hamilton-Giachritsis
University of Birmingham, UK

Leigh Harkins
University of Birmingham, UK

Maria Hartwig
John Jay College of Criminal Justice, City University of New York, USA

Ruth Hatcher
University of Leicester, UK

Robyn E. Holliday
University of Leicester, UK

Clive Hollin
University of Leicester, UK

Ulf Holmberg
Kristianstad University, Sweden

Joyce E. Humphries
University of Leicester, UK

William R. Lindsay
Castlebeck, Darlington and University of Abertay, Scotland

Lindsay C. Malloy
Florida International University, USA

Ruth Mann
Rehabilitation Services Group, National Offender Management Service, UK

James McGuire
University of Liverpool, UK

Amanda M. Michie
Lothian NHS Trust, Edinburgh, Scotland

Benjamin Nordstrom
Departments of Criminology, Psychiatry, and Psychology, University of Pennsylvania, USA

Emma J. Palmer
University of Leicester, UK

Adrian Raine
Departments of Criminology, Psychiatry, and Psychology, University of Pennsylvania, USA

Valerie F. Reyna
Cornell University, USA

Chelsea Rose
Victoria University of Wellington, New Zealand

Jagjit Sandhu
St. Andrews Healthcare, Birmingham, UK

Elin M. Skagerberg
The Tavistock and Portman National Health Service Foundation Trust, UK

Emma Sleath
University Of Leicester, UK

John L. Taylor
*Northumbria and Tyne & Wear NHS Foundation Trust
and Northumbria University, UK*

Max Taylor
University of St. Andrews, Scotland

Maria M. Ttofi
Institute of Criminology, Cambridge University, UK

Tim Valentine
Goldsmiths University of London, UK

Tony Ward
Deakin University, Melbourne, Australia

Jayson Ware
*Offender Services and Programs, Corrective Services,
NSW, Australia*

Helen L. Westcott
University of Leicester, UK

Jacqueline M. Wheatcroft
*Department of Applied Psychology, University of Liverpool,
UK*

Gwenda M. Willis
Victoria University of Wellington, New Zealand

Jessica Woodhams
University of Birmingham, UK

Daniel B. Wright
Florida International University, USA

Preface to Second Edition

Forensic psychology continues to grow, both as a profession for graduates and in terms of student interest. The media has also ensured that the topic enjoys considerable interest for the public at large, though as some of our authors are at pains to point out, there is frequently a sizable gap between myth and reality! In 2008, Graham Davies, with his Leicester colleagues Clive Hollin and Ray Bull, published *Forensic Psychology*, a briefer treatment of the topic for advanced undergraduate and postgraduate students, covering psychological contributions to investigative practice, courtroom procedures and work with offenders. In their preface they noted the predominance of texts that took as their norms the US system of justice, which differs quite radically from European and British models, and the book sought to rectify this imbalance. This second edition builds on the success of this earlier book, but with a new editorial team of Graham Davies and Anthony Beech, Professor in Criminological Psychology at the University of Birmingham.

The current text is very much more than simply an updated edition of the 2008 text. The book's ambition and scope has been greatly expanded, drawing upon extensive feedback from readers and teaching staff. The number of chapters has almost doubled, enabling coverage to be extended to new and growing areas of forensic practice. These new chapters include work with a variety of different types of offenders and offences. Some of the authors and their chapters from the original book have been retained, but all have been rigorously revised and updated to reflect the developments that have occurred in the area in the interim. In selecting contributors, the editors have continued to mix leading senior researchers with younger academics who have shown particular expertise in interesting and enthusing today's generation of students.

The new edition has been selected as the latest addition to the British Psychological Society's *Textbooks in Psychology* series published for the Society by Wiley. In keeping with its status, the text will have a dedicated website, containing links to other relevant forensic sites and student quiz questions linked to each of the chapters in the book. Case studies feature in all the chapters, together with topics for essays and class discussions, and additional recommended reading. There will also be a section of the site reserved for teaching staff containing possible examination questions and sample PowerPoint slides.

As before, the book is divided into four parts. Part I: *The Causes of Crime* looks at different theoretical approaches to crime, including both criminological and psychological perspectives. Notable additions are new chapters dealing specifically with developmental aspects of offending (criminal careers) and psychobiological approaches, both written by leading authorities in their field. Part II, devoted to *Investigating Crime* in addition to covering traditional topics like eyewitness testimony, interviewing and detecting deception, contains specialist treatments of stalking and domestic violence, offender profiling and crime analysis and the very contemporary issue of terrorism. Part III looks at psychological aspects of *The Trial Process*, including psychological aspects of decision-making by judges and juries, the pressures on witnesses, the special problems of identification evidence and the growing and still controversial use of psychologists as expert witnesses. Part IV contains a greatly expanded treatment of *Dealing with Offenders*. In addition to asking 'What Works?' and a survey of the range of risk assessment tools and behaviour programmes developed by psychologists, specialist chapters are devoted to treating offenders convicted of sexual and violent assaults, those with learning disabilities and the mentally disordered. A final chapter from one of the pioneers of the 'good lives' movement looks at the prospects for reform and rehabilitation for those who are convicted and sentenced by the courts.

We have been well served and supported by our colleagues at Wiley. Andrew McAleer provided the initial encouragement for a second edition and supported our ambitions for a larger and more comprehensive text. Georgia King has dealt with our many routine queries courteously and efficiently. Katharine Earwaker cheerfully took on the task of finding a cover design and appropriate illustrations. We hope they – and you – like the book.

Graham Davies and Anthony Beech

About the Editors

Graham Davies is Professor Emeritus of Psychology at the University of Leicester and an Honorary Professor of Forensic Psychology at the Universities of Birmingham and Coventry. His research interests focus on the testimony of children and adults and the support of vulnerable witnesses at court, on which topics he has published some 10 books and over 150 articles in scientific journals. He led the writing team responsible for the original version of *Achieving Best Evidence*, the standard guidance on interviewing victims and witnesses in the English courts, and has considerable experience as an expert witness in court cases where the testimony of children or other vulnerable witnesses is a focus of concern. He is a Fellow of the British Psychological Society and a former president of the Society for Applied Research in Memory and Cognition and of the European Association for Psychology and Law. He is the founding editor of the journal *Applied Cognitive Psychology* and co edits the *Wiley Series on Crime Policing and the Law*. In addition to his academic and professional work, he sits as a Magistrate on the Loughborough, Melton, Belvoir and Rutland bench.

Anthony Beech is Professor and Head of the Centre for Forensic and Criminological Psychology at the University of Birmingham, UK. He has worked extensively with the prison and probation services in the UK, and has a number of links with police agencies in the UK. He has authored over 140 peer-reviewed articles, 30 book chapters and five books in the area of forensic science / criminal justice. His particular areas of research interests are: risk assessment of offenders; reducing online exploitation of children; and increasing psychotherapeutic effectiveness of the treatment given to offenders. His particular speciality is around the assessment and treatment of sex offenders. In 2009 he received the Significant Achievement Award from the Association for the Treatment of Sexual Abusers in Dallas, Texas for recognition of his work in this area. He has extensive experience of forensic psychology in the UK. In 2005 he was made a Fellow of the British Psychological Society. In 2009 he was the recipient of the Senior Award from the Division of Forensic Psychology, British Psychological Society, for a significant lifetime contribution to forensic psychology.

GRAHAM DAVIES, ANTHONY BEECH AND CLIVE HOLLIN

CHAPTER OUTLINE

Forensic psychology is a broad and growing area of psychological research and practice. It embraces a variety of studies at the interface of psychology and the law, spanning both legal and criminological issues. Formally, the *legal aspect* of forensic psychology concerns the application of psychological knowledge and methods to the process of law, and the *criminological aspect* deals with the application of psychological theory and method to the understanding (and reduction) of criminal behaviour through interventions. More succinctly, the legal aspect deals with evidence, witnesses and the courts, while the criminological aspect focuses on crime and criminals. Among the range of tasks undertaken by forensic psychologists are:

- piloting and implementing treatment programmes for offenders;
- generating research evidence to support penal policy and practice;
- undertaking assessments of risk for violent and sexual offenders;
- domestic violence and family issues;
- treating offenders with drug or alcohol problems;
- writing reports and giving evidence in court;
- advising parole boards and mental health tribunals;
- crime analysis and offender profiling;
- conducting experimental and field studies on the reliability of witnesses;
- advising on interview techniques with suspects and vulnerable witnesses; and
- counter-terrorism policy and hostage negotiation.

The umbrella term *forensic psychology* is used to embrace both legal and criminological research and application, even though the term *forensic* strictly means the employment of scientific tests, or techniques, used in connection with the detection of crime. As the issue of crime and offending continues to grow in importance in society, it seems inevitable that policy makers will turn increasingly to psychology in general, and forensic psychology in particular, for answers to such questions as 'What makes a person offend?' and 'How can crime be reduced?' The aim of this book is to give a broad outline of current topics in psychology, ranging from causes of crime (Section 1) to the detection of crime (Section 2), legal processes (Section 3) and finally risk assessment and treatment of offenders (Section 4).

We will now give a brief background to the area in order to put the chapters that follow into context. Hence, to understand how forensic psychology emerged as the high profile psychological science it is today, it is useful to begin by examining briefly the roots of both *legal psychology* and *criminological psychology*. We will then describe the professional pathways into forensic psychology and the principal organisations and journals that support the discipline, followed by an overview of the structure and content of the book.

LEGAL PSYCHOLOGY

Legal psychology was one of the first areas of applied psychology to be explored by experimental psychologists. It then languished as a discipline until the 1970s, when there was a great resurgence of interest in research at the interface of psychology and law, which continues to this day. Legal psychology began in Europe around the turn of the 20th century (see Sporer, 1982). Prominent among these pioneers was the Austrian *Hans Gross* (1847–1915) who in his career claimed to have performed over 45,000 pre-trial examinations on witnesses. As a result of his experiences, he became sceptical about the accuracy of witnesses and developed tests to try to discriminate those who might prove reliable. He described his experiences in probably the first textbook of legal psychology, published in 1898.

One issue of concern to Gross was the suggestibility of witnesses under questioning. The French psychologist *Alfred Binet* (1857–1911) had conducted some of the earliest studies on suggestibility and conformity effects in children, described in his book *La Suggestibilité* (1900) and these ideas were taken up by the German psychologist *Louis William Stern* (1871–1938). It was Stern who, as part of his programme of research into what he termed the *Psychologie der Aussage* (the psychology of verbal reports), started the first journal devoted to witness psychology and introduced new methods such as the 'event test', a carefully rehearsed incident staged in front of onlookers who are subsequently asked to report the events in their own words and answer questions concerning details, a technique still in use today (Sporer, 1982). Suggestibility, particularly in relation to vulnerable witnesses and its impact on their testimony, remains a focus of contemporary research (see Chapters 5 and 6).

The *Aussage* movement continued to be active in Germany up until World War I, but the man credited with publicising the new science to the English-speaking world was Stern's friend, *Hugo Münsterberg* (1863–1916). Münsterberg moved from Germany to Harvard University in 1892 to accept an invitation from William James to set up their first experimental psychology laboratory. Münsterberg's interests in psychological aspects of the law went well beyond issues of testimony. In 1908, he published *On the Witness Stand*, a book aimed at publicising and promoting the value of psychology to law enforcement in general and the courts in particular. Among the topics discussed by Münsterberg were:

- the accuracy of witness testimony;
- the detection of deception;
- false confessions;
- suggestive questioning at court; and
- effective interviewing procedures.

Sadly, the emergence of Münsterberg's book did not usher in a new dawn for legal psychology. Its somewhat bombastic tone and casual generalisations alienated lawyers (he dismissed them as 'obdurate'), precisely the group to whom the implications of the book might most usefully have been directed. It drew from the distinguished American jurist *John H. Wigmore* (1863–1943) a majestic rebuke in the form of a satirical account of an imaginary trial in which Münsterberg's more specious and expansive statements were held up to ridicule (Wigmore, 1909). Wigmore did concede that while psychology had little to offer to the law at present, there might come a time when psychology would have matured sufficiently to make a significant contribution. This rejection of Münsterberg's ideas was followed by his death in 1916, which effectively ended the study of legal psychology in the United States. When interest in legal psychology revived in the 1970s, most of the topics Münsterberg had identified remained central to contemporary research, together with new themes arising from the stresses of contemporary society.

One of the principal motives for the renewed involvement of psychologists in legal matters was that of concerns around mistaken identification that had led to miscarriages of justice. In the UK, Lord Justice Devlin published a report in 1976 on a series of cases involving mistaken identity. The *Devlin Inquiry* into law and practice on identification was the first in the UK to take evidence from psychologists on perception and identification. One of its recommendations was that 'research should be directed as to establishing ways in which the insights of psychology can be brought to bear on the conduct of identification parades and the practice of the courts' (p.149). This led directly to Home Office funding of research into bodily and voice identification (Bull & Clifford, 1984; Shepherd *et al.*, 1982) and in turn to a more positive approach generally toward the value of psychological research as applied to the police and the law (Bull *et al.*, 1983). Research on identification issues remains a major strain in contemporary forensic research (see Chapter 14).

In the USA, the involvement of psychologists in identification issues took a rather different form. In the UK, psychologists with expertise in witness matters were not generally permitted to give evidence in criminal trials, with the exception of cases of alleged false confession (i.e. Gudjonsson, 2003). In the USA, *Elizabeth Loftus* and *Robert Buckhout* (1935–1990) were among the first psychologists permitted to testify as experts at trials regarding the reliability of eyewitness testimony in general and identification in particular. This testimony was routinely challenged at trial and this in turn led to a greater investment in research to better understand the processes that led to witness error (see Chapter 15). Here, an important distinction emerged between estimator and system variables (Wells, 1978):

- *Estimator* variables concerned the haphazard circumstances surrounding an initial observation of a perpetrator, such as lighting and distance from the witness.
- *System* variables covered those factors in control of law enforcement officials, such as how many persons were present on an identification parade and their degree of similarity to the suspect.

Much of this new research was summarised in Loftus's influential book *Eyewitness Testimony* (Loftus, 1979), which added to the growing interest among experimental psychologists in the legal process. Loftus's work had focused very much on the vagaries of witness testimony. It built on the findings of the *Aussage* movement by exploring the impact of 'post-event information': information that a witness to a crime read, saw or talked about after an incident and the adverse effect this might have on the reliability of their testimony at any subsequent trial (see Chapters 5 and 6). In the 1980s, universities in the USA launched the first joint doctoral programmes involving the study of both psychology and law ('JD/PhD programs'), which in turn led to research with a much wider focus on psychological aspects of legal procedure. Research in areas such as the wording and timing of legal pronouncements, and in particular jury decision-making (Hastie *et al.*, 1983), laid the foundations for a psychology of jurisprudence (see Chapter 12).

One of the earliest concerns of forensic psychologists was the reliability of child witnesses and this issue, too, sprang back into prominence in the 1980s. In the UK and the USA, children's evidence had traditionally been excluded or restricted by the courts because of concerns over *suggestibility*. However, there was increasing public concern that such restrictions effectively prevented most child complainants of abuse from seeking justice. New research, particularly by the US psychologist *Gail Goodman* (e.g. Rudy & Goodman, 1991), demonstrated that under appropriate circumstances children were capable of providing reliable testimony, and this increased the pressure for reform of the law and the introduction of such child-friendly measures at court as remote or video testimony (see Chapter 15; Davies, 1999).

The dangers of the uncritical acceptance of particularly very young children's testimony are demonstrated by such miscarriages of justice as the *Kelly Michaels* trial in the USA (Bruck *et al.*, 1998) and the *Shieldfield Nursery* affair in the UK (Webster & Woffindon, 2002). Research, particularly by the US developmental psychologist *Stephen Ceci*, has highlighted situations where children's testimony is likely to be more or less reliable. Official guidance written by psychologists for investigators charged with interviewing children is careful to take account of the vulnerabilities, as well as the strengths, of children's testimony (see Chapters 5 and 6).

Another concern dating from Münsterberg is the detection of *deception*. Psychologists have carefully researched the many assumptions surrounding 'lie-signs' and have cast a critical eye over the various devices, from the polygraph (the 'lie detector', Wilcox, 2009) to fMRI (functional magnetic resonance imaging) brain scanning (see Chapter 3 for a description of this technique), which have claimed infallibility in spotting lies (Vrij, 2008). In 2004, the British Psychological Society published a research review of all established methods to date and concluded that none had yet reached a point where their use in the courts for determining truth and falsity could be recommended.

The suggestibility and reliability of adult witnesses has been raised by the acrimonious debate over the status of *recovered memories*: memories of trauma, often recovered during the course of therapy, of which the person was previously unaware. This issue, too, came into prominence as a result of a trial, in this case a murder trial in which there was a clash of expert testimony. In California, George Franklin stood trial for the murder of a young girl, Susan Nason, some 20 years previously. The principal evidence against him was the eyewitness account of his daughter, who had recently recovered a vivid memory of her father carrying out the murder when she was a young child. The prosecution expert, psychiatrist *Lenore Terr*, argued that the repression of memories was commonplace among clinical patients and that Ms Franklin's memories fitted this pattern. For the defence, *Elizabeth Loftus* argued that Ms Franklin's testimony contained significant errors and that there was nothing in it that could not have been gleaned from local newspaper reports of the time; Ms Franklin was confusing real events with self-generated imagery, perhaps fuelled by suggestion in therapy. The jury found George Franklin guilty, but the sentence was reversed on appeal (Maclean, 1993). This reversal was due in part to the research evidence accumulated in the interim that recovered memories are often unreliable and *false memories* can be readily generated by established experimental techniques in the psychological laboratory. Cognitive and clinical psychologists continue to debate the circumstances in which recovered memories may be reliable or false (see Chapter 15).

In recent years, three high-profile areas of policing and detection have benefited from psychological input in a way that would no doubt have intrigued Münsterberg. Movies such as *The Silence of the Lambs* and television series like *Cracker* have glamourised the role of psychologists as offender profilers, though the reality of psychology's involvement in profiling and crime analysis inevitably falls short of the picture painted by the media (see Chapter 9). Stalking is another crime that is rarely out of the public eye, generally in the context of the obsessive following of celebrities by 'fans' (Meloy *et al.*, 2008); however, it is most often seen by the courts as a feature of intimate partner violence (see Chapter 10). Terrorism, too, is never too far from the news pages and psychologists are increasingly called upon by the state to understand the motivation of terrorists and thus ways of mitigating the risk and consequences of terrorist acts (see Chapter 11).

CRIMINOLOGICAL PSYCHOLOGY

Common law has long recognised the important link between psychology and criminal behaviour. It is embodied in the legal principle of *mens rea* or 'guilty mind', meaning that an individual cannot be guilty of a crime unless he or she carries out the act both wilfully, and intentionally. Early theories of criminal behaviour emphasised the heritability of criminal behaviour, reflected in the work of the Italian criminologist *Cesare Lombroso* (1835–1909). Lombroso also drew on ideas from physiognomy (i.e. the idea that human traits are reflected in the structure of the face and body type) to argue that criminals were born to offend and that this was reflected in their particular facial characteristics and build, which he believed were present among habitual criminals. Even though some would suggest that they know what a rapist or a murderer should look like (e.g. Goldstein *et al.*, 1984), there is little evidence that these stereotypes have any basis in fact. As early as 1913, the English physician *Charles Goring* (1880–1917) found no systematic differences in physiognomy, and other physical characteristics, between a large sample of criminals and a comparison group of soldiers.

The application of psychological theories, starting with the psychodynamic ideas of Sigmund Freud and his successors, has had a significant influence on conceptions of many aspects of everyday life, including crime. The psychologist, psychiatrist and psychoanalyst *John Bowlby* (1907–1990) argued that separation of mother and child during the second six months of life had permanent, damaging consequences for a child's later development and well-being (in terms of attachment to others and self) and could in a number of cases lead the individual to become a criminal in later life.

Attachment can be broadly defined as the process by which an infant has an inborn biological need to maintain close contact with its parents/primary carers (Bowlby, 1969; 1973; 1980). Intimate contact creates experiences of safeness, and impacts upon the soothing systems within the brain. Infants are not born with the capacity to self-soothe; therefore, it is the caregiver's response to distress signals (e.g. holding, caressing, smiling, feeding) that enables modulation and reduction of stress levels. Fonagy (2001) suggests that attachment patterns are shaped by a combination of genetic factors and social experiences. The predisposed style is shaped by early social experiences.

Therefore, an individual's attachment style can be seen as a set of enduring characteristics for making sense of one's life experiences and interactions (Young *et al.*, 2003), in that the relationship between infant and primary caregiver provides a model for future interpersonal and intimate relationships. This model is maintained irrespective of whether the relationship between the individual and their primary caregiver(s) in childhood was positive or negative, and hence a model for the individual's future social interactions is formed, whether this is primarily about approach or avoidance behaviours/interactions and, *in extremis*, criminal behaviours. These issues are discussed in more detail in Chapter 2, which considers the role of early attachment and its effect on later criminal behaviour, while Chapter 4 examines the physical and psychological effects of child maltreatment.

The behaviourist school has also had an important influence in criminological psychology, in terms of both understanding and changing antisocial behaviours through treatment. *Behaviourism* places a general emphasis upon the role of learning in shaping all human behaviour, whether normal or abnormal, through the mechanism of conditioning. In this context there are two broad lines of thought: Pavlovian/classical conditioning, and operant learning (this approach has largely mutated into Bandura's (1977) *social learning theory*).

Hans Eysenck (1916–1997) used the principles of conditioning described by *Ivan Pavlov* (1849–1936) to develop a general theory linking crime with personality. Eysenck (1977) incorporated biological and social factors into his theory, bringing them together as factors that determined an individual's personality. According to Eysenck, an individual's personality determines, in large part, their ability to learn from (or condition to) other people in their social environment. Thus, personality plays a fundamental role in the process of the child's socialisation, with certain configurations of personality more or less likely to behave in a manner that is antisocial or criminal. Eysenck's ideas encouraged psychological research with offenders and some support has been found for them, but they are now seen as overly mechanistic, biological and deterministic. Hence, while at the time it was an important landmark in the application of psychological theories to explain criminal behaviour, Eysenck's theory has not had lasting impact on the current understanding and rehabilitation of offenders (see Chapter 2).

Somebody who has probably had more of an influence is the American psychologist *B.F. Skinner* (1904–1990), who advanced Pavlovian theory with the development of the notion of *operant learning*. Put simply, Skinner suggested that an individual's behaviour acts (or *operates*) on the environment, so producing consequences for the individual. Behaviour that produces consequences (social or material) that the person finds rewarding is likely to be repeated, in which case Skinner would say that the behaviour is being *reinforced*; if the behaviour produces consequences that the person finds aversive then they are less likely to repeat that behaviour, in which case Skinner would say that the behaviour is being *punished*. Skinner's notion of operant conditioning was taken and applied to explain criminal behaviour (Jeffery, 1965). Further, Skinner's operant learning was applied, with some success, in working with offenders to reduce the likelihood that they will subsequently reoffend (Laws & Marshall, 2003; Milan, 2001).

In the late 20th century, the emergence of *cognitive psychology* encouraged the integration of *internal* processes, such as thoughts and emotions, into behaviourist learning theory. This integration is most clearly seen in the development of *social learning theory* (SLT) by the psychologist Albert Bandura (Bandura, 1977; 1986). SLT gave rise to interventions that aimed to change internal processes (i.e. cognitions) as well as overt behaviour, giving rise to the term *cognitive-behavioural treatment* (CBT) and the associated methods of therapy (see Chapters 16, 17 and 18 in particular for details of the CBT approach).

CBT interventions have become increasingly popular for use with offenders (e.g. Browne *et al.*, 2012; Ireland *et al.*, 2009). For example, the social psychologist *Raymond Novaco* (Novaco *et al.*, 2012) emphasises the central importance of anger in understanding some forms of violence. Hence, the use of anger control treatments has become widespread with violent offenders (see Chapter 18). Similarly, in sex offender treatment, CBT is the mainstay of such interventions (see Chapter 18; and Beech *et al.*, 2009), while a social learning/CBT approach has also been successfully adapted for the treatment of those with intellectual disability (see Chapter 19 for details of such initiatives with these offenders).

The critical importance of appropriate cognitive development was also emphasised by the American psychologist *Lawrence Kohlberg* (1927–1987), whose work was inspired by the ideas of the great developmental psychologist *Jean Piaget* (1896–1980). Kohlberg argued that in order to achieve full moral maturity it was necessary for children to pass through six distinct stages of moral development, starting from a morality based on the threat of punishment, to moral reasoning based on an appreciation of the social value of order and reciprocity (Power *et al.*, 1989). The link between the hypothesised stage an individual has reached and their actual behaviour has remained a source of controversy, but as a formal analysis of the development of moral judgment, Kohlberg's model remains influential in both understanding and working with offenders (see Chapter 2).

A different line of development also took place in the UK in the form of crime prevention measures based on *rational choice theory*. Cornish and Clarke (1986) proposed that crime results from rational choice to offend by the criminal, with the prime motivation being personal gain, while avoiding detection, when the opportunities arise. This theory led to measures known as *situational crime prevention* (Wortley & Mazerolle, 2008) in which the environment is changed, say, by using electronic alarms to minimise the opportunities for crime or increasing police patrols to maximise the chances of crime detection.

However, despite such developments in psychological theory and practice in the 1970s–1980s, the popular view was that 'nothing works' in offender rehabilitation (Martinson, 1974; though to be fair to him, Martinson's point was that treatment was better carried out in the community, rather than in prison settings). This view led politicians and policy makers in some parts of the world, including the UK, to the pessimistic consensus that the only answer to rising crime the criminal justice system could offer was to build more prisons (Hollin, 2001). However, building on decades of research, this view was challenged by several groups of psychologists, principally from Canada and the UK, who rallied under the banner of the *What Works* initiative (Andrews & Bonta, 1994; McGuire, 1995). These psychologists argued that the meta-analyses of the results of treatment trials with offenders showed that interventions, principally employing cognitive-behavioural methods, produce lower rates of recidivism compared to controls.

The idea of a 'criminal brain' continues to intrigue researchers (Johnson, 1998), but the pessimistic view that 'criminals are born not made' has been consistently challenged, and tested, by psychologists and psychiatrists from the beginning of the 20th century. However, it is still observed that there is a hard core of individuals who would seem very intractable in treatment. Of particular interest is the notion of what is happening in the brains of those with antisocial personality disorder (ASPD), as defined by the Diagnostic and Statistical Manual of Mental Disorders (DSM-IV-TR; American Psychiatric Association, 2000) and/or identified as being psychopaths (typically as identified using the Hare Psychopathy Checklist Revised (PCL-R; Hare, 1991; 2003). Figures would suggest (www.mentalhealth.com) that 80 to 85 per cent of incarcerated offenders can be diagnosed as having ASPD (which is hardly surprising given the tautology of this premise), while 20 per cent can be regarded as psychopaths (as compared to 1 per cent that can be identified in the general population; Hare, 1999). Here, it should be noted that psychopaths account for roughly half of all the most serious crimes committed, including half of all serial killings, and repeat rapes (www.mentalhealth.com), and 80 per cent of psychopaths released from prison commit another crime, usually within three years.

It is a moot point to what extent there is a genetic aspect to criminal behaviour, but evidence would suggest that monozygotic (identical) twins were concordant for criminal behaviour (52 per cent) compared to 22 per cent of the dizygotic (non-identical) twins in a sample of 3586 Danish twins (Christensen *et al.*, 1977); while Blonigen *et al.* (2003), reporting on 271 adult twins of self-reported psychopathic personality traits, found substantial evidence of genetic contributions to variance in the personality construct of psychopathy. Although there is a growing body of evidence to show that there is a strong genetic contribution to juvenile delinquency (Popma & Raine, 2006), and a number of genes have been shown to have an association with antisocial behaviour, no one gene seems to 'explain criminal behaviour' (Goldman & Ducci, 2007). Investigating the potential genetic basis for complex behaviours is inherently complicated as they are likely to involve multiple genes, in contrast to conditions where there is a single-gene effect, as in classic Mendelian genetics (Uhl & Grow, 2004).

Poor upbringing is equally likely to lead to subsequent crminal behaviour. For example, more than 60 years ago, Bowlby (1946) argued in *Forty-Four Juvenile Thieves* that in *all* cases he described in the book, the cause of the delinquency could be traced to such 'maternal deprivation'. More recently, a number of authors have noted that a problematic upbringing (in terms of coercive parent–child interactions and the absence of positive and affectionate attachment bonds between parent and child, neglect, inconsistent parenting and severity of punishments) can lead to the development of disruptive, aggressive and often violent behaviours (see Chapter 2 for a critique of Bowlby's ideas).

Chapter 4 examines some recent findings in the neuroscience area regarding brain scanning and other techniques that are looking at the structure and function of antisocial/psychopathic offenders; an understanding of how to assess the risk of such individuals for future offending, and how to treat them, is an important part of forensic psychology.

However, it is important not to lose sight of the fact that around 70 per cent of those in prison (both men and women) have mental health problems, in that there are many men, women and children in prison who need health care above all else (see Chapter 19 for a discussion around the issue of mentally disordered offenders). Certainly if you had to invent a way to deepen mental health problems and create a health crisis, overcrowded prisons (and particularly the bleak isolation of a segregation unit) is the way to do it! It is also of note that more than 30 per cent of prisoners are incarcerated for drug-related offences and that drug use would appear to be responsible for the great majority of some types of crime, such as shoplifting and burglary (85 per cent of shoplifting, 70 to 80 per cent of burglaries and 54 per cent of robberies), while more than a quarter (29 per cent) of robbery victims believed their attacker to be under the influence of drugs. Similarly, epidemiological studies show that around 55 per cent of those received into custody are problematic drug users.

As we move further into the 21st century, the emphasis placed by the *What Works* movement upon an evidence-based approach to penal policy within the criminal justice system has begun to find support among more pragmatic policy makers in Europe and North America. Tony Ward and colleagues eloquently outline where rehabilitation may be going in terms of a more holistic and positive approach to treatment, in terms of his *good lives model* (see Ward & Gannon, 2006, and Chapter 21 of this book for a fuller exposition of this approach) and the *desistance* model outlined by Richard Laws and Tony Ward (2011). We would also note that the correct application of drug rehabilitation strategies, and treatment of offenders with mental health problems, would take the burden of the penal systems to deal with such individuals and free up resources to deal with the more intractable personality-disordered individuals who carry out most serious and violent crimes.

We would also note that not much has been said specifically about female offenders in this volume. Men outnumber women in all major crime categories (between 85 and 95 per cent of offenders found guilty of burglary, robbery, drug offences, criminal damage and violence against the person are male); therefore, women's services tend to be the Cinderella of the criminal justice system. More women are sent to prison for the non-violent crimes of theft and handling of stolen goods than any other crimes. It is of note that, according to the Women in Prison website (www.womeninprison.org.uk/statistics.php):

- one in four women in prison has spent time in local authority care as a child;
- 70 per cent have two or more *diagnosable mental health problems*;
- 66 per cent of sentenced women in prison say they were either *drug dependent or drinking* to hazardous levels before custody;
- more than 50 per cent report suffering from intimate partner abuse (see Chapter 10);
- rates of self-harm/self-injury accounted for 48 per cent of all incidents between 2003 and 2007, even though the number of women in prison accounted for about 6 per cent of the total prison population; and
- more than 17,700 children are separated from their mothers by imprisonment, in that two-thirds of women in prison have children.

For those who want to know more about work specifically with female offenders, Barker (2009), Blanchette and Brown (2006) and Gannon and Cortoni (2010) provide some useful starting places, while Lart *et al.* (2008) provide a rapid assessment of the evidence for interventions aimed at reducing reoffending in female offenders. We will now examine the processes by which students can become practising forensic psychologists.

HOW TO BECOME A FORENSIC PSYCHOLOGIST

There is no universal route to a career in forensic psychology, but most countries have at least three requirements: a broad grounding in psychology as a science, typically provided by an honours degree in psychology (*academic background*); advanced study of forensic psychology (*specialised training*); and a period of supervised training within a forensic setting (*professional practice*). Most countries require forensic psychologists to be registered members of a professional organisation, which is there to encourage best practice and ensure adherence to ethical guidelines (see www.ap-ls.org/links/currentforensicguidelines.pdf for sample US guidelines).

In the UK:

- Students seeking to become forensic psychologists must complete a degree in psychology, accredited by the British Psychological Society (BPS), which confers the *Graduate Basis for Chartership* or GBC.

- Achieving the GBC membership of the BPS demonstrates the breadth and depth of the student's knowledge of psychology, and a valuable set of subject-specific and transferable skills. If the student achieves an upper second class honours degree and can demonstrate some relevant forensic experience (perhaps acting as a prison visitor or witness service volunteer, or having had a placement in a forensic setting), they are in a good position to apply for a postgraduate training course.

- A number of UK universities offer postgraduate training programmes (at master's and/or doctoral level) in forensic psychology accredited by the British Psychological Society. A master's course is one year in duration, while a doctoral course will normally last three years (see www.bps.org.uk/careers-education-training/careers-education-and-training for information on accredited forensic courses in the UK).

- On completion of the course, the student will need to complete a further two years of supervised practice in a forensic setting (doctoral degrees in forensic psychology normally include the two years of supervised practice within the overall programme), supervised by a chartered psychologist. Satisfactory completion of this stage will allow the student, too, to achieve *chartered psychologist* status within the BPS, be allowed to put *CPsychol* after their name and use the chartered psychologist logo.

- However, *forensic psychologist* is one of a number of professional titles protected by law, so any student who wants to use this title will need to register with the *Health Professions Council* (HPC). If the student has successfully completed all the earlier steps and kept within ethical guidelines, then there should be no bar to their registration.

- The Health Professions Council (www.hpc-uk.org/aboutus/contactus) exists to protect the public by ensuring the fitness to practise of those on its registers. It does not play a role in facilitating the development or promotion of the professions that it regulates; that role is undertaken by the British Psychological Society.

Achieving professional standing in forensic psychology in the UK is a long and rigorous process taking a minimum of six years, but no more so than in most other developed countries. Although details vary between states, Australia and Canada have broadly similar training requirements and require the same pattern of separate academic and professional accreditation. In the USA, academic training in forensic psychology is taken to doctoral level, with a further two years of supervised internship before the candidate is eligible for diploma status, which is only granted after a lengthy oral examination. However, professional life is rewarding in all senses: the Chartered Management Institute (CMI) estimates the lifetime economic benefit associated with holding professional qualifications and membership of a professional institute at £152,000.

PROFESSIONAL ORGANISATIONS FOR FORENSIC PSYCHOLOGISTS

- The **Division of Forensic Psychology (DFP)** of **The British Psychological Society (BPS,** www.bps.org.uk) was founded in 1977 as the Division of Criminological and Legal Psychology, and was renamed the Division of Forensic Psychology in 1999.

- The DFP represents the interests of those psychologists who work in criminal and civil justice systems. DFP membership includes forensic psychologists working in academic settings, prison services, health, education and social services. Members must first qualify to join the BPS prior to applying for the DFP, which has grades of membership. Full membership requires completion of both academic training and supervised practice (see How to Become a Forensic Psychologist, earlier in this introduction) but interested graduates in psychology may become general members. The official journal of the DFP is *Legal and Criminological Psychology*. The DFP's website can be found at http://dfp.bps.org.uk

- The **European Association of Psychology and Law (EAPL)** was formed in 1992 and is the principal European organisation for psychologists and lawyers who work at the interface of the two disciplines. The EAPL aims to promote and develop research, and hosts regular conferences in different parts of Europe, the proceedings of which are regularly published. Membership is open to all professionals with a qualification in psychology, law or a related discipline such as criminology or psychiatry. Full membership requires a university-level qualification or equivalent professional experience, but

---

BOX 1 USEFUL WEBSITES RELATED TO FORENSIC PSYCHOLOGY

Listed here are a few useful websites that will be helpful to a forensic (or potential forensic) psychologist.

- BBC brief guide to forensic psychology: www.bbc.co.uk/science/humanbody/mind/articles/psychology/psychology_6.shtml
- Centre for Crime and Justice Studies: www.crimeandjustice.org.uk
- Centre for Forensic and Criminological Psychology, University of Birmingham: http://cfcp.bham.ac.uk/main.php
- Correctional Services Of Canada (includes a number of useful resources): www.csc-scc.gc.ca
- Division of Forensic Psychology, British Psychological Society: http://dfp.bps.org.uk
- FBI: www.fbi.gov

- Forensic psychology resources: www.tncrimlaw.com/forensic/f_psych.html
- Home Office (this is the main site; the research and statistics pages are probably the most useful but there is also a range of crime-related information in other sections): www.homeoffice.gov.uk
- Ministry of Justice (useful for information about courts, criminal cases, probation and prison matters): www.justice.gov.uk

NHS (describes forensic careers within the NHS):

- www.nhscareers.nhs.uk/details/Default.aspx?Id=451
- Observer (links to articles on crime and justice): www.observer.co.uk/crimedebate
- Weblinks to sites relating to forensic psychology and law: www.oklahoma.net/~jnichols/forensic.html

---

students and those without formal qualifications may join as affiliates. The official journal of the EAPL is *Psychology, Crime and Law*. The EAPL's web site can be found at www.eapl.eu

- **The American Psychology–Law Society (AP–LS)**, Division 41 of the *American Psychological Association* (APA), is an interdisciplinary organisation devoted to scholarship, practice and public service in psychology and law. Members of AP–LS need not be members of the APA, although many members belong to both organisations. Recent activities have included collecting course syllabuses and teaching materials, surveying career opportunities in psychology and law, and studying the special ethical problems of expert testimony. It sponsors a science policy forum and holds regular meetings, often under the auspices of the APA. Membership is open to interested professionals and students in other disciplines beyond psychology. The official journal of AP–LS is *Law and Human Behavior*, and its website can be found at www.ap-ls.org

- A number of organisations for applied psychologists include a large membership of forensic psychologists. The **Society for Applied Research in Memory and Cognition (SARMAC)** was founded in 1994 and includes many researchers interested in psychology and law. It holds regular conferences, invariably with sessions devoted to legal themes, and its membership is open to graduate and undergraduate students in psychology or related

disciplines; other interested persons can join as affiliates. For many years, SARMAC's official journal was *Applied Cognitive Psychology* (http://onlinelibrary.wiley.com/journal/10.1002/(ISSN)1099-0720), although it plans to launch its own journal in 2012. SARMAC's website can be found at www.sarmac.org/society.html

- The **National Organisation for the Treatment of Abusers (NOTA) (www.nota.co.uk) and the Association for the Treatment of Sexual Abusers (ATSA)** (www.atsa.com) are the UK and US organisations, respectively, for the treatment of sexual offenders, and typically have a number of forensic psychologists as members who assess/treat sexual offenders. Their associated journals are the *Journal of Sexual Aggression* and *Sexual Abuse: A Journal of Research and Treatment*.

- Box 1 provides some useful websites for further information regarding forensic psychology.

STRUCTURE AND CONTENT OF THIS BOOK

This text attempts to introduce students to the core areas of forensic psychology. It is divided into four parts, each devoted to a different facet of the discipline, and attempts to explore the unfolding of criminal behaviour from causes to the treatment of offenders.

Part 1: The Causes of Crime. In *Chapter 1* Emma Palmer examines the principal social and psychological theories that have been proposed to explain criminal behaviour, exploring, in particular, the links between crime, mental illness, learning disability and personality disorder. In *Chapter 2*, David Farrington and Maria Ttofi examine the developmental origins of crime: which youngsters are particularly likely to become criminals as adults by reason of their family background and early experiences? A very different perspective on crime is offered by Anthony Beech, Benjamin Nordstrom and Adrian Raine in *Chapter 3*. They argue that emerging neurological evidence supports the view that certain individuals are predisposed to a life of crime by reason of genetic inheritance: in particular, certain brain areas are structurally and functionally different in persons with antisocial tendencies compared to others. In *Chapter 4*, Catherine Hamilton-Giachritsis and Emma Sleath shift the perspective towards the impact of crime on the lives of its victims, highlighting recent research that aims to identify factors in adults and children that will promote resilience in the face of crime.

Part 2: Investigating Crime. Despite dazzling advances in high-tech police science ('the CSI effect'), most investigations still begin with, and are resolved by, witness statements. In *Chapter 5*, Lindsay Malloy, Daniel Wright and Elin Skagerberg review some of the key findings and theories in memory research and apply these to interviewing adult and child witnesses. Robyn Holliday, Joyce Humphries, Charles Brainerd and Valerie Reyna (*Chapter 6*) continue to develop these themes, with special reference to vulnerable witnesses; they describe additional techniques developed by psychologists to maximise the amount of useful information from witnesses with the minimum of error. Ulf Holmberg (*Chapter 7*) switches the emphasis to the ethical interviewing of suspects in a way most likely to lead to a reliable confession of guilt. Suspects often lie at interview and in *Chapter 8* Pär Anders Granhag and Maria Hartwig review recent research on detecting lies and deception in police interviews.

In recent years, three high-profile areas of policing and detection have become associated with forensic psychology. In *Chapter 9*, Jessica Woodhams considers the reality of crime analysis and offender profiling and the use of behavioural and crime scene evidence to pinpoint serial offenders. Stalking is another crime that fascinates the media and in *Chapter 10*, Louise Dixon and Erica Bowen locate the mundane reality of most stalking as a feature of intimate partner violence; they describe the scope and variety of such violence and consider the implications for the assessment of risk of repetition. Terrorism too is never too far from the news pages, and Max Taylor in *Chapter 11* examines the process by which individuals become, remain and, equally importantly, disengage from terrorism.

Part 3: The Trial Process. In *Chapter 12*, Jacqueline Wheatcroft describes how courts operate, including the impact of different styles of questioning by advocates, pre-trial publicity and judicial pronouncements, and reviews findings on how judges and juries reach decisions on guilt or innocence. The actual giving of evidence and its examination in court can cause witnesses undue stress, particularly when they are vulnerable by reason of age or impairment. In *Chapter 13*, Helen Westcott and Graham Davies examine how witness's concerns and fears of the legal process can best be safeguarded. Some types of evidence continue to cause particular concern to judges and advocates alike. In *Chapter 14*, Tim Valentine looks at the reliability of identification evidence and innovations driven by psychological research, designed to make the practice more reliable. Finally, in *Chapter 15*, Brian Clifford considers the contentious role of the psychologist as an expert witness, with particular reference to the possibility of mistaken identification, the testimony of children and memories recovered after delay.

Part 4: Dealing with Offenders. James McGuire in *Chapter 16* examines the critical role of sentencing, and examines the impact of different regimes of punishment and rehabilitation on the likelihood of reoffending. In *Chapter 17*, Ruth Hatcher looks at modern treatment regimes for offenders and the important issue of *risk assessment*, which will determine when an offender can safely be released once again onto our streets. Two groups of offenders that cause particular concern to the public are those found guilty of offences involving violent or sexual crimes. In *Chapter 18*, Leigh Harkins, Jayson Ware and Ruth Mann review the most effective treatment regimes for such offenders, and their impact on the prevention or reduction of future harm for others. Offenders with intellectual impairments are disproportionately represented in the prison population. In *Chapter 19*, William Lindsay, John Taylor and Amanda Michie consider how interventions can best be tailored to their special needs to reduce the risk of future offending. Mentally disordered offenders are another significantly over-represented group of offenders and in *Chapter 20*, Dawn Fisher, Michelle Ginty and Jagjit Sandhu consider the emerging speciality of forensic mental health, and the different treatment regimes and risk assessment procedures it has encouraged. Finally, in the concluding chapter of the book (*Chapter 21*), Tony Ward, Chelsea Rose and Gwenda Willis look beyond punishment and retribution towards rehabilitation and the promotion of better, more productive lives for past offenders.

REFERENCES

American Psychiatric Association (2000). *Diagnostic and statistical manual of mental disorders, fourth edition, text revision (DSM-IV-TR)*. Washington DC: American Psychiatric Association.

Andrews, D. & Bonta, J. (1994). *The psychology of criminal conduct*. New Providence, NJ: LexisNexus.

Bandura, A. (1977). *Social learning theory*. New York: Prentice-Hall.

Bandura, A. (1986). *Social foundations of thought and action: A social-cognitive theory*. Englewood Cliffs, NJ: Prentice-Hall.

Barker, J. (Ed.) (2009), *Women and the criminal justice system: A Canadian perspective*. Toronto: Emond Montgomery.

Beech, A.R., Craig, L.A. & Browne, K.D. (2009). *Assessment and treatment of sex offenders: A handbook*. Chichester: John Wiley & Sons, Inc.

Binet, A. (1900). *La suggestibilité* [On suggestibility]. Paris: Schleicher.

Blanchette, K. & Brown, S.L. (2006), *The assessment and treatment of women offenders: An integrated perspective*. Chichester: John Wiley & Sons, Inc.

Blonigen, D.M., Carlson, S.R., Krueger, R.F. & Patrick, C.J. (2003). A twin study of self reported psychopathic personality traits. *Personality and Individual Differences, 35*, 179–197.

Bowlby, J. (1946). *Forty-four juvenile thieves*. London: Bailliere Tindall and Cox.

Bowlby, J. (1969). *Attachment and loss: Attachment*. New York: Basic Books.

Bowlby, J. (1973). *Attachment and loss: Separation, anxiety and anger*. New York: Basic Books.

Bowlby, J. (1980). *Attachment and loss: Loss, sadness and depression*. New York: Basic Books.

British Psychological Society (2004). *A review of the current scientific status and fields of application of the polygraphic deception detection*. Leicester: British Psychological Society.

Browne, K.D., Beech, A.R. & Craig (Eds.) (2012). *Handbook of forensic psychology practice*. Oxford: Wiley-Blackwell.

Bruck, M., Ceci, S.J. & Hembrooke, H. (1998). Reliability and credibility of young children's reports: From research to policy and practice. *American Psychologist, 53*, 136–151.

Bull, R., Bustin, R., Evans, P. & Gahagan, D. (1983). *Psychology for police officers*. (Reprinted, 1985.) Chichester: John Wiley & Sons, Inc.

Bull, R. & Clifford, B. (1984). Earwitness voice recognition accuracy. In G. Wells & E. Loftus (Eds.) *Eyewitness testimony: Psychological perspectives*. New York: Cambridge University Press.

Christensen, K., Holm, N.V., Mcgue, M., Corder, L. & Vaupel, J.W. (1977). A Danish population-based twin study on general health in the elderly. *Journal of Aging and Health, 11*, 49–64.

Cornish, D.B. & Clarke, R.V.G. (Eds.) (1986). *The reasoning criminal: Rational choice perspectives on offending*. New York: Springer-Verlag.

Davies, G.M. (1999). The impact of television on the presentation and reception of children's evidence. *International Journal of Law and Psychiatry, 22*, 241–256.

Devlin, P. (1976). *Report to the Secretary of State for the Home Department on the departmental committee on evidence of identification in criminal cases*. London: HMSO.

Eysenck, H.J. (1977). *Crime and personality* (3rd edn). London: Routledge and Kegan Paul.

Fonagy, P. (2001). The human genome and the representational world. The role of early mother-infant interaction in creating an inter personal interpretive mechanism. *Bulletin of the Menninger Clinic, 65*, 427–448.

Gannon, T.A. & Cortoni, F. (Eds.) (2010). *Female sexual offenders: Theory, assessment, and treatment*. Chichester: Wiley-Blackwell.

Goldman, D. & F. Ducci (2007). The genetics of psychopathic disorders. In A.R. Felthous & H. Sa (Eds.) *International handbook of psychopathic disorders and the law* (pp.149–169). Chichester: John Wiley & Sons, Inc.

Goldstein, A.G., Chance, J.E. & Gilbert, B. (1984). Facial stereotypes of good guys and bad guys: A replication and extension. *Bulletin of the Psychonomic Society, 22*, 549–552.

Gross, H. (1898). *Kriminalpsychologie* [Criminal Psychology]. Leipzig: Vogel. English translation available at http://manybooks.net/titles/grosshanetext98crmsy10.html (retrieved 31 August 2011).

Gudjonsson, G.H. (2003). *The psychology of interrogations and confessions: A handbook*. Chichester: John Wiley & Sons, Inc.

Hare, R.D. (1991). *The Hare Psychopathy Checklist – Revised (PCL–R)*. Toronto, Ontario: Multi-Health Systems.

Hare, R.D. (1999). *Without conscience: The disturbing world of the psychopaths among us*. New York: Guilford.

Hare, R.D. (2003). *The Hare Psychopathy Checklist – Revised (PCL–R)* (2nd edn). North Tonawanda, NY: Multi-Health Systems.

Hastie, R., Penrod, S.D. & Pennington, N. (1983). *Inside the jury*. Cambridge, MA: Harvard University Press.

Hollin, C.R. (Ed.) (2001). *Handbook of offender asssessment and treatment*. Chichester: John Wiley & Sons, Inc.

Ireland, J.L., Ireland, C.A. & Birch, P. (2009). Assessment, treatment and management of violent and sexual offenders (pp.97–131). Cullompton, Devon: Willan.

Jeffery, C.R. (1965). Criminal behavior and learning theory. *Journal of Criminal Law, Criminology, and Police Science, 56*, 294–300.

Johnson, M. (1998). Genetic technology and its impact on culpability for criminal actions. *Cleveland State Law Review, 46*, 443–470.

Lart, R., Pantazis, C., Pemberton, S., Turner, W. & Almeida, C. (2008). *Interventions aimed at reducing re-offending in female offenders: A rapid evidence assessment (REA)*. London: The Home Office. Retrieved 31 August 2011 from www.justice.gov.uk/publications/docs/intervention-reduce-female-reoffending.pdf

Laws, D.R. & Marshall, W.L. (2003). A brief history of behavioral and cognitive behavioral approaches to sexual offenders: Part 1. Early developments. *Sexual Abuse: A Journal of Research and Treatment, 15*, 75–92.

Laws, D.R. & Ward, T. (2011). Desistance from sexual offending: Alternatives to throwing away the keys. New York: Guilford Press.

Loftus, E.F. (1979) *Eyewitness testimony*. Cambridge, MA: Harvard University Press.

Maclean, H.N. (1993) *Once upon a time*. New York: Harper-Collins.

McGuire, J. (Ed.) (1995). *What works: Reducing reoffending*. Chichester: John Wiley & Sons, Inc.

Meloy, J.R., Sheridan, L. & Hoffmann, J. (Eds.) (2008). *Stalking, threatening, and attacking public figures: A psychological and behavioral analysis*. New York: Oxford University Press.

Milan, M.A. (2001). Behavioural approaches to correctional management and rehabilitation. In C.R. Hollin (Ed.) *Handbook of offender assessment and treatment* (pp.139–154). Chichester: John Wiley & Sons, Inc.

Martinson, R. (1974). What works? – Questions and answers about prison reform. *The Public Interest, 10*, 22–54.

Münsterberg, H. (1908). *On the witness stand: Essays on psychology and crime*. New York: McClure.

Novaco, R.W., Renwick, S. & Ramm, M. (2012). *Anger treatment for offenders*. Chichester: Wiley-Blackwell.

Popma, A. & Raine, A. (2006). Will future forensic assessment be neurobiologic? *Child and Adolescent Psychiatry Clinics of North America, 15*, 429–444.

Power, F.C., Higgins, A. & Kohlberg, L. (1989). *Lawrence Kohlberg's approach to moral education*. New York: Columbia University Press.

Rudy, L. & Goodman, G.S. (1991). Effects of participation on children's reports: Implications for children's testimony. *Developmental Psychology, 27*, 527–538.

Sporer, S.L. (1982). A brief history of the psychology of testimony. *Current Psychological Reviews, 2*, 323–340.

Uhl, G.R. & Grow, R.W. (2004). The burden of complex genetics in brain disorders. *Archives of General Psychiatry, 61*, 223–229.

Vrij, A. (2008). *Detecting lies and deceit: Pitfalls and opportunities*. Chichester: John Wiley & Sons, Inc.

Ward, T. & Gannon, T.A. (2006). Rehabilitation, etiology, and self-regulation: The comprehensive good lives model of treatment for sexual offenders. *Aggression and Violent Behavior, 11*, 77–94.

Webster, R. & Woffindon, B. (2002, 31 July). Cleared: The story of Shieldfield. *The Guardian (G2)*. Retrieved 31 August 2011 from www.richardwebster.net/cleared.html

Wells, G.L. (1978). Applied eyewitness testimony research: System variables and estimator variables. *Journal of Personality and Social Psychology, 36*, 1546–1557.

Wigmore, J.J. (1909). Professor Münsterberg and the psychology of evidence. *Illinois Law Review, 3*, 399–445.

Wilcox, D. (Ed.) (2009). *The use of the polygraph in assessing, treating and supervising sex offenders*. Chichester: John Wiley & Sons, Inc.

Wortley, R. & Mazerolle, L. (2008). *Environmental criminology and crime analysis*. Cullompton, Devon: Willan.

Young, J.E., Klosko. J.S & Weisharr, M.E. (2003). *Schema therapy: A practitioner's guide*. London: Guilford Press.

SUGGESTED READINGS IN FORENSIC PSYCHOLOGY

We suggest the following books would form the basis for a useful set of references to the field of forensic psychology.

Adler, J. & Gray, J. (Eds.) (2010). *Forensic psychology: Concepts, debates and practice* (2nd edn). Cullompton, Devon: Willan Publishing. *A useful and up-to-date set of reviews of contemporary issues in forensic psychology, written by leading researchers.*

Andrews, D. & Bonta, J. (2010). *The psychology of criminal conduct* (5th edn). New Providence, NJ: LexisNexus. *The latest edition of the seminal work on 'What Works' in offender rehabilitation by two of its main proponents.*

Blackburn, R. (2001). *The psychology of criminal conduct* (2nd edn). Chichester: John Wiley & Sons, Inc. *An updated version of one of the seminal books in forensic psychology.*

Brown, J. & Campbell, E. (Eds.) (2010). *The Cambridge handbook of forensic psychology*. Cambridge: CUP. *Useful synopsis of many topics in forensic psychology.*

Browne, K.D., Beech, A.R. & Craig (Eds.) (2012). *Handbook of forensic psychology practice*. Oxford: Wiley-Blackwell. *This book gives an up-to-date account of the issues when working with offenders.*

Bull, R. & Carson, C. (Eds.) (2003). *Handbook of psychology in legal contexts* (2nd edn). Chichester: John Wiley & Sons, Inc. *A comprehensive review of the contribution of psychology from a legal perspective, including both civil and criminal contexts.*

Flannery, D.J., Vazsonyi, A.T. & Waldman, I.D. (2007). *Cambridge handbook of violent behavior and aggression*. Cambridge: Cambridge Unversity Press. *Useful reference book regarding violent and aggressive behaviour.*

Gudjonsson, G.H. (2003). *The psychology of interrogations and confessions: A handbook*. Chichester: John Wiley & Sons, Inc. *Review of theories of suggestibility and cases of false confessions by the pioneer of the field.*

Hare, R.D. (1999). *Without conscience: The disturbing world of the psychopaths among us*. New York: Guilford. *This very readable book gives a valuable insight into the mind of the psychopath.*

Hollin, C (Ed.) (2003). *The essential handbook of offender assessment and treatment*. Chichester: John Wiley & Sons, Inc; and Ireland, J.L., Ireland, C.A. & Birch, P. (2009). (Eds). *Violent and sexual offenders: Assessment, treatment and management*. Cullompton, Devon: Willan. *These two books provide authoritative descriptions of working with dangerous offenders.*

Loftus, E.F. (1996). *Eyewitness testimony*. Cambridge, MA: Harvard University Press. (Original work published 1979). *Classic text on eyewitness research by the leading researcher in the field; readable and still relevant.*

Maruna, S. (2001) *Making good: How ex-convicts reform and rebuild their lives*. Washington, DC: American Psychological Association. *Maruna investigates the divergent lives and aspirations of offenders who desist from, or continue, offending. Provides an invaluable insight into desistence processes.*

Shepherd, J.W., Ellis, H.D. & Davies, G.M. (1982). *Identification evidence: A psychological evaluation*. Aberdeen: Aberdeen University Press.

Soothill, K., Rogers, P. & Dolan, M. (Eds.) (2008). *Handbook of forensic mental health*. Cullompton, Devon: Willan. *Comprehensive reference book on forensic mental health, provided by leading academics/researchers in the field of forensic mental health*

Vrij, A. (2008). *Detecting lies and deceit: Pitfalls and opportunities*. Chichester: John Wiley & Sons, Inc. *Comprehensive coverage of debates on deception and its detection in adults and juveniles.*

Ward, T., Polaschek, D. & Beech, A.R. (2006). *Theories of sexual offending*. Chichester: John Wiley & Sons, Inc. *Review of meta-theories, micro-theories and offence process explanations of sexual offending.*

Part I
The Causes of Crime

1 Psychological Approaches to Understanding Crime

Emma J. Palmer

KEY TERMS

• actusrea • BritishCrimeSurvey • electroencephalogram(EEG) • functionalanalysis • longitudinalstudy • mensrea • meta-analysis • neuroimaging • vicarious reinforcement/learning

CHAPTER OUTLINE

As a discipline, psychology has contributed a number of theories that help our understanding of crime, and why people offend. At the same time, it is important to state that crime cannot only be explained by psychology. There are a number of other disciplines that can contribute to our understanding of crime, including sociology, philosophy, medicine and biological sciences, and law. However, the specific theories and methodologies of psychology allow it to make a unique contribution to the important question of why people commit crime.

This chapter will, therefore, cover three areas. First, it will outline two contemporary psychological theories of crime: moral reasoning theory and the social information-processing approach to explaining crime. Second, theories of three types of serious offending will be considered: interpersonal violence, sexual offending and arson. Finally, the specific issue of mentally disordered offenders will be discussed. This section will cover the different types of mental disorder – mental illness, intellectual disability and personality disorder – and their association to offending, before considering issues relating to the psychopathic offender in more depth.

PSYCHOLOGICAL THEORIES

Moral reasoning theory

A body of literature is available that examines the relationship between moral reasoning and offending. Moral reasoning refers to how individuals reason about and justify their behaviour with respect to moral issues. By far the most well-known approach to moral reasoning within psychology is the cognitive-developmental approach initially proposed by Piaget (1932) and subsequently developed by Kohlberg (1969; 1984). Kohlberg's theory is composed of six stages of moral reasoning through which individuals progress, with reasoning becoming more abstract and complex. This theory has recently been revised by Gibbs (2003; 2010) into a theory of 'sociomoral reasoning' in which the roles of social perspective-taking and empathy are given a greater emphasis.

Gibbs' (2003) theory focuses only on the first four stages of Kohlberg's theory (see Table 1.1). The first two stages represent 'immature moral reasoning', during which time reasoning is superficial and egocentric. Stages 3 and 4 are 'mature moral reasoning' and show an understanding of interpersonal relationships and other people's needs and, at stage 4, societal needs. Gibbs emphasised the need for acquisition of social perspective-taking skills for reasoning at these two stages, in

TABLE 1.1 *Gibbs' stages of sociomoral reasoning.*

Immature moral reasoning
Stage 1: Unilateral and physicalistic Reasoning refers to powerful authority figures (e.g. parents) and the physical consequences of behaviour. Individuals show little or no perspective-taking.
Stage 2: Exchanging and instrumental Reasoning incorporates a basic understanding of social interaction. However, this is typically in terms of cost/benefit deals, with the benefits to the individual being of most importance.
Mature moral reasoning
Stage 3: Mutual and prosocial Reasoning reflects an understanding of interpersonal relationships and the norms/expectations associated with these. Empathy and social perspective-taking are apparent, along with appeals to one's own conscience.
Stage 4: Systemic and standard Reasoning reflects an understanding of complex social systems, with appeals to societal requirements, basic rights and values, and character/integrity.

order to allow for emotions such as empathy to play a part in motivation decisions about reasoning and behaviour (Hoffman, 2000).

There is now a sizable amount of evidence pertaining to the relationship between moral reasoning and offending (Palmer, 2003; 2007). Looking at Kohlberg's/Gibbs' theories, it is possible to morally justify offending behaviour at each of the stages:

- Stage 1 – offending is morally justified if punishment can be avoided.
- Stage 2 – offending is morally justified if the benefits to the individual outweigh the costs.
- Stage 3 – offending is morally justified if it maintains personal relationships.
- Stage 4 – offending is morally justified if it maintains society or is sanctioned by a social institution.

However, although offending can be justified at all stages, the circumstances in which it usually occurs reflects moral reasoning at the less mature stages. Research examining this relationship confirms this prediction (for reviews, see Blasi, 1980; Nelson *et al.*, 1990; Palmer, 2003; Stams *et al.*, 2006), although the majority of the research has been with adolescent samples.

Two studies have also shown that the moral immaturity of young offenders is consistent across different values, rather than only for those related to offending (Gregg *et al.*, 1994; Palmer & Hollin, 1998).

Gibbs (2003; 2010) has also investigated the role of cognitive distortions in the relationship between moral reasoning and offending. According to Gibbs, the main offence-supporting distortion is egocentric bias, which is both characteristic of immature moral reasoning and the thinking styles of offenders (Antonowicz & Ross, 2005; Ross & Fabiano, 1985). A number of secondary cognitive distortions are proposed to support egocentricity in contributing to offending. These are a hostile attributional bias, by which ambiguous events/social interactions are interpreted as hostile; blaming others or external factors rather than oneself for behaviour that harms other people; and minimising consequences/mislabelling one's own antisocial behaviour in order to reduce feelings of guilt and regret.

Research has provided evidence for these cognitive distortions among antisocial and delinquent adolescents (Barriga & Gibbs, 1996; Liau et al., 1998; Palmer & Hollin, 2000). Therefore, within the moral reasoning theory framework, offending behaviour is seen as a result of sociomoral development delay beyond childhood, accompanied by an egocentric bias. The secondary cognitive distortions then allow individuals to disengage from taking responsibility for their behaviour on a moral level.

Social information-processing theory

Models of social information-processing have been applied to explain aggression and delinquent behaviour, in order to examine individual differences in why some individuals will respond to a certain situation aggressively whereas others will not. Although a number of such theories exist, an influential one in this area is that of Crick and Dodge (1994). This is a six-step model of social information-processing that describes how individuals perceive their social world and process information about it, and the influence of previous experience on these processes. The six steps in the model are:

1. Encoding of social cues
2. Interpretation and mental representation of the situation
3. Clarification of goals/outcomes for the situation
4. Access or construction of responses for the situation
5. Choice of response
6. Performance of chosen response.

Although these steps occur in sequence for a given situation stimulus, Crick and Dodge (1994) suggest that individuals can simultaneously perform the different steps, allowing for feedback between processes. Therefore, the model is conceptualised as a circular, rather than a linear

process. At all steps, processing is influenced by social knowledge structures based on an individual's past experiences, such as social schema and scripts.

At the first stage, social cues are perceived and encoded. These are used at the second stage, along with social knowledge structures to interpret the situation and provide a mental representation of it. When interpreting the situation, attributions are made about the intent of other people and the causality of events. Throughout, these processes are influenced by previous experiences in the form of social schema and scripts, to provide cognitive shortcuts to help process information quickly.

At the third stage the individual chooses their preferred goals/outcomes for the situation. This is likely to be influenced by pre-existing goal orientations, and the modification of these in line with the social cues associated with this situation.

The fourth stage requires the individual to generate a range of possible responses to the situation. This may be achieved with reference to past experience in similar situations or by creating new responses. These responses are evaluated at the fifth stage in order to choose one to perform. This step has received increased attention in recent years in the response evaluation and decision (RED) model (Fontaine & Dodge, 2006). The RED model outlines a number of criteria used when evaluating responses, including the perceived efficacy and value (in terms of its moral/social qualities) of the response, and the perceived efficacy and value of the outcome behaviour. Finally, at stage 6, the chosen response is enacted, requiring the individual to have appropriate verbal and non-verbal social skills.

Social information-processing and criminal behaviour

There is now a large body of research showing that aggressive and delinquent individuals show distinct patterns of social information-processing across the six steps (for reviews, see Fontaine & Dodge, 2006; Palmer, 2003).

At the first two steps, research suggests aggressive individuals experience a range of problems in encoding and interpreting social cues, leading to an inaccurate representation of the situation. Aggressive individuals appear to perceive fewer social cues (Dodge & Newman, 1981), take more notice of aggressive cues (Gouze, 1987) and pay more attention to cues at the end of interactions (Dodge & Tomlin, 1987). Aggressive people rely more on internal schema when interpreting situations (Dodge & Tomlin, 1987), with these schema tending to be aggressive in content (Strassberg & Dodge, 1987).

A number of studies have reported that aggressive individuals have a hostile attributional bias, and so often misinterpret situations as hostile (Orobio de Castro et al., 2002;

FIGURE 1.1 *Aggressive individuals generate fewer responses, suggesting they have a limited repertoire of responses from which to draw.*

Source: © SakisPagonas. Used under licence from Shutterstock.

Slaby & Guerra, 1988). This tendency is exacerbated when individuals feel threatened (Dodge & Somberg, 1987) or react impulsively (Dodge & Newman, 1981). There is also a suggestion that aggressive people attribute greater blame to external factors (Fondacaro & Heller, 1990).

At the third step, research has found that aggressive individuals tend to have dominance- and revenge-based goals, rather than prosocial goals (Lochman *et al.*, 1993).

When generating responses, aggressive individuals generate fewer responses than non-aggressive people (Figure 1.1), suggesting they have a limited repertoire from which to draw (Slaby & Guerra, 1988). The content of these responses is more aggressive as compared to the prosocial responses generated by non-aggressive people (Bliesener & Lösel, 2001; Lösel *et al.*, 2007; Quiggle *et al.*, 1992).

At the fifth step, aggressive individuals also evaluate responses by different criteria, rating aggressive responses more positively than prosocial responses (Quiggle *et al.*, 1992) and having more positive outcome expectancies and perceptions of self-efficacy for aggression (Hart *et al.*, 1990). Thus, aggression is viewed as being more effective to achieve their goals.

Finally, social skills are important at step 6, and there is some evidence that aggressive individuals have poor social skills (see Howells, 1986). If the chosen response is successful, it will be evaluated positively and reinforced, a suggestion supported by longitudinal research by Fontaine *et al.* (2008).

Taken together, the distinctive patterns of processing that are associated with aggressive and antisocial behaviour suggest that social information-processing is influential in the development of juvenile delinquency and adult offending. Further, research also shows that the more steps at which individuals exhibit problems, the greater the level of aggressive and antisocial behaviour (Crick & Ladd, 1990; Lansford *et al.*, 2006; Slaby &

Guerra, 1988). These patterns have been found among quite young children (for a review, see Palmer, 2003) and, along with research showing the role of parenting, highlight the importance of early childhood experiences in the development of such behaviours.

THEORIES, EVIDENCE AND CRIME

Interpersonal violence

Media reports often give the impression that there are high levels of violent offending. However, in reality this is not the case. Recent statistics show that in the year October 2009 to September 2010, violent crime comprised 20.1 per cent of offences reported to the police and 21.5 per cent of offences in the **British Crime Survey**, and that the level of violent crime has remained stable for a number of years (Home Office, 2011). A range of crimes are included under the label of 'violence', including murder, manslaughter and robbery. Domestic violence is gaining recognition as a serious problem and will also be considered here.

As noted by Polaschek (2006), research into violent offenders' criminal behaviour has revealed that they tend not to be specialists but commit a wide range of offences. Indeed, specialist violence offenders are quite rare. Results from **meta-analyses** and **longitudinal studies** also show that violent offenders have an early onset of offending behaviour and show considerable continuity of aggression and violence throughout their lives (Moffitt *et al.*, 2002; Molero-Samuelson *et al.*, 2010).

There are a number of theories that attempt to provide explanations of violence and violent offending, including those that focus on the role of social factors in violent offending and cognitive theories of aggression. Both of these approaches are covered in Chapter 2 and so will be only briefly mentioned here.

British Crime Survey an annual survey that measures the amount of crime in England and Wales by asking a sample of the population about their experiences of crime in the preceding year.

meta-analysis a statistical technique that allows the combination of the results of several quantitative studies in the attempt to answer a research question.

longitudinal study a research design that involves repeated observations over a long period of time.

Cognitive-behavioural theory and violence

Cognitive-behavioural approaches focus on the role of cognitive appraisal and other internal processes in violence. One way of examining these processes is through Crick and Dodge's (1994) six-step model of social information-processing. As outlined above, aggressive individuals show a range of distinctive processing patterns across these steps. The hostile attributional bias is one of the strongest findings, with a meta-analysis of 41 studies concluding it had a very strong relationship with aggressive behaviour among children and adolescents (Orobio de Castro et al., 2002) and more recent research showing that this relationship holds into adulthood (Petitt et al., 2010). Empathy is another important factor, with a meta-analysis by Jolliffe and Farrington (2004) reporting a significant association between poor empathy and violent offending.

Emotional arousal can also impact on cognitive processes, with anger playing a significant role in understanding violence. Proponents of this approach view violence as resulting from being angry (i.e. 'violent acts' are 'angry behaviours', Howells, 2004, p.190). Novaco's work showing that there are reciprocal relationships between angry emotional arousal and cognitive processes is important here. Novaco (1975; Novaco & Welsh, 1989) proposes angry thoughts can be triggered by situational events; these angry thoughts then increase emotional arousal (including physiological and psychological components); and this arousal heightens the intensity of the angry thoughts. As this cycle continues, the level of cognition (angry thoughts) and affect increase in turn, with an increased risk of violence.

Social factors and violence

A range of social factors have been shown to predict violent offending, many of which are similar to those associated with general offending. Evidence for the importance of the role played by family structure and parenting style in the development of violent offending is also provided from longitudinal studies (e.g. Moffitt, 2003). Research also shows a clear link between violence, and severe abuse in childhood and witnessing family violence (Widom & Maxfield, 2001). This association appears to be mediated through the impact of abuse on children's psychological functioning, such as problem-solving and coping abilities. See Case Study 1.1.

Neuropsychological factors and violence

There is some evidence that violence is associated with brain damage or dysfunction. **Electroencephalogram (EEG)**

electroencephalogram (EEG) a procedure in which changes in the electrical potential of the brain are recorded.

and **neuroimaging** studies have provided evidence that there is an increased level of brain abnormality among violent offenders (see Plodowski et al., 2009). Research

suggests that damage and malfunctioning of the frontal and temporal lobes are most associated with violence. However,

neuroimaging scanning techniques used to examine brain anatomy and activity.

neuropsychological research suffers from various methodological problems. These include the need to establish cause and effect, the question of what constitutes an abnormality, inadequate control groups and the representativeness of samples. Therefore, results should be interpreted cautiously (see Chapter 3 and Raine, 2002).

In recent years, attention has turned to the role of neuropsychological factors in violence. This approach proposes that the development of violence results from an interaction of social, environmental, genetic and neurobiological factors (Loeber & Pardini, 2009). However, to date, there is a dearth of research that examines the role of both neurobiological factors and psychosocial variables, and the interaction between them (cf. Rutter, 2009).

Domestic violence

Domestic violence refers to violence within the family, typically inter-partner violence. Many explanations of domestic violence are based on a feminist perspective. These hold that society is patriarchal, with an implicit assumption that men control the lives of women and children, both within the family and through social institutions (see Chapter 10 and Stewart et al., 2001). Men are proposed to maintain women's subordination through physical violence, as well as psychological and economic coercion. Social learning theory has also been applied to domestic violence. This approach views domestic violence as a behaviour that is learnt, through experiencing rewards from it and observing and modelling similar behaviour (**vicarious learning**). Other approaches view domestic violence as caused by psychopathology among abusers (Dutton, 1995), or resulting from dysfunctional relationships (Geffner et al., 1995).

vicarious reinforcement/learning learning to behave in a certain way as a result of observing the reinforcing and punishing consequences of that behaviour for other people.

Sexual offending

The term 'sexual offences' covers a number of crimes, including rape, unlawful sexual intercourse, indecent assault, indecent exposure, and gross indecency with a child. Other non-sexual offences can also sometimes have a sexual element, such as sexually motivated murder. Due to problems of under-reporting of crimes, it is difficult to put a figure on the number of sexual offences committed. However, figures for the 12 months to September 2010 show there were 55,169 sexual offences recorded by the police in this period (Home Office, 2011).

There are six major theories of sexual offending. Three of these cover child sexual abuse, two relate to rape and one attempts to explain all types of sexual offending.

Finkelhor's (1984) four preconditions model proposes that there are four preconditions that a child molester must pass through prior to an offence. First, there must be a motivation to sexually abuse, such as sexual arousal to a child, emotional congruence with a child, or blockage of sexual expression with an adult. Second, internal inhibitions against offending must be overcome. These inhibitions can be overcome through distorted beliefs about child abuse, becoming disinhibited through the use of alcohol or drugs, or experiencing severe stress. Third, external factors must be overcome to allow the abuse to occur, for example gaining the trust of the child and their family, or the child being left alone. Fourth, the child's resistance must be overcome, through using force or grooming techniques.

A second theory of child sexual abuse is Hall and Hirschmann's (1992) quadripartite model. Like Finkelhor's model, this proposes there are four components necessary for an offence to take place: sexual arousal to children; attitudes and beliefs (cognitions) that justify child abuse; poor self-regulation; and personality problems. This theory suggests that vulnerability to committing child sexual abuse is caused by personality problems. Situational factors, including opportunity, determine when this vulnerability is triggered, leading to deviant arousal, emotional disturbance, and offence-permitting thinking. Subtypes of child molesters are also proposed, based on the relative level of each of these factors. Therefore, some child abusers have greater levels of deviant arousal, others have greater emotional disturbance and others have more distorted cognitions. Research examining the risk factors for child molesters supports the four areas outlined in this theory, providing some support for it.

The third theory is the pathways model set out by Ward and Siegert (2002), which proposes that four separate but interacting psychological mechanisms are involved in child sexual abuse. These are: intimacy/social deficits; distorted sexual scripts; cognitive distortions; and emotional dysregulation. The four components are involved in all sexual offences, but one component dominates each pathway into offending. Offenders with multiple dysfunctional mechanisms form a fifth pathway and are hypothesised to be the 'pure paedophiles'.

Turning to theories of rape, an interaction model of sexual aggression was proposed by Malamuth et al. (1993). Specifically, this model proposes that sexual aggression is the result of the interaction of two 'paths':

the hostile masculinity path and the sexual promiscuity path. The hostile masculinity path emphasises the role of aggressive intimate relationships and sexual conquest in the concept of masculinity, along with valuing power, risk-taking, dominance and competitiveness. The sexual promiscuity path focuses on the role of sexual behaviours in maintaining self-esteem and peer status, and the appeal of impersonal sex.

Malamuth et al. (1993) proposed that sexual promiscuity is more likely to lead to sexual aggression among men possessing a high level of the characteristics within the hostile masculinity pathway. This suggestion has been supported among non-offender samples using measures of self-reported sexual aggression. However, it remains to be validated on sexual offender samples.

Ward and Beech (2006) have developed an integrated theory of sexual offending that includes biological, neuropsychological and ecological factors, This theory proposes that sexual offending results from 'vulnerabilities' that predispose an individual to sexual offending. According to Ward and Beech (2006), these vulnerabilities arise from the influence of genetics, evolutionary processes and neurobiological processes on brain development. The interaction between these systems and social learning is proposed to lead to the characteristics of sex offenders – deviant sexual arousal, cognitive distortions and emotional dysregulation. However, to date there is little empirical research testing this theory.

The only theory to date that covers all types of sexual offending is Marshall and Barbaree's (1990) integrated theory. This approach takes account of biological, developmental, sociocultural and situational variables that lead to psychological vulnerabilities. Negative childhood experiences (e.g. poor parenting, abuse) are proposed to lead children to experience problems in forming social, emotional and sexual attachments with other people. During adolescence when hormonal changes occur, aggression and sex can become linked due to both drives originating from the same neural substrates. Poor social skills can lead to rejection of prosocial attempts to be sexually intimate, which results in anger and an increased likelihood of an aggressive response. If the individual experiences support for aggressive behaviour from sociocultural sources (e.g. peers, media), this will increase the likelihood of aggression. Other situational factors and emotional states, such as substance use, anger or sexual frustration, can also impact on the ability of the individual to inhibit antisocial behaviour. Taken together, all these factors can result in a sexual offence being committed.

A weakness of Marshall and Barbaree's theory is its breadth, meaning that it does not provide explanations for why different types of sexual offending occur.

CASE STUDY 1.1   GANG VIOLENCE BY YOUNG PEOPLE

Barely a week seems to go past without mention of stabbings or worse carried out by youth gangs (Figure 1.2). Recent cases where youth gangs have been implicated in murders include those of Jessie James and Rhys Jones. Both are young people who were senselessly murdered by groups of other young people. This case study considers some factors that might be responsible for this type of violent crime.

A good place to start is by considering the social backgrounds from which young gang members are more likely to come. It is undoubtedly true that gangs proliferate in inner city areas, with many of the media stories referring to cities such as London and Manchester. The areas within these cities that tend to be associated with gangs are usually those that are run down and socially deprived.

The young people from these socially deprived areas often face other associated problems. For example, families living in these areas often live in poverty, with parents either in low paid jobs or unemployed, which can put pressure on family life. These problems can be increased for lone parents. For example, if a lone parent works, young children are looked after by older siblings and teenagers are left unsupervised for periods of time.

For some young people, this can leave them vulnerable to pressure from their friends and peers, either to take part in antisocial behaviour or to commit offences. Where there is a gang culture, joining one of the groups can provide some protection from being victimised. This is illustrated by the fact that many young people admit they start carrying a knife (or other weapons) so they can defend themselves, rather than because they intend to use it. Being surrounded by a culture of violence often appears to lead to further violence through such incremental steps.

Schools in socially deprived areas are often also run down, and struggle with the behavioural and emotional problems of their pupils. Clearly, this can impact on the educational experience that students receive. Falling in with a bad group of friends can lead young people to stop valuing education – or rather, educational achievement is not seen as being 'cool' and respect is gained through other, more antisocial activities. For these young people, getting an ASBO is often valued more than obtaining GCSEs.

Unfortunately, the problems of social deprivation, poor education and family problems are difficult to address and require long-term solutions rather than a 'quick fix'.

FIGURE 1.2 *Violence by youth gangs is regularly reported in the news.*
Source: © Monkey Business Images. Used under licence from Shutterstock.

Research has also found that some aspects emphasised by this theory, such as aggressive behaviour and disinhibition, are not shown by all sexual offenders.

There are certain factors common to all of these theories of sexual offending. They all suggest that sexual offending results from a mixture of distorted cognitions that allow sexual abuse of others, deviant sexual arousal, poor emotional and impulse management, and problems in relating to other people. Developmental adversity is a likely cause of these problems. A more detailed coverage of these theories can be found in Hollin, Hatcher *et al.* (2010) and Hollin, Palmer *et al.* (2010).

Research into the characteristics of sexual offenders has provided further understanding of their offences. Beech *et al.* (2005) provide a summary of such research among rapists. Characteristics commonly found among rapists include sexual preoccupation, sexual interest in rape/violence against women, sexual entitlement, hostile masculinity and controlling sexual beliefs, distrust of women, lack of emotional intimacy with other adults, grievance schema, poor problem-solving, poor emotional control and lifestyle impulsiveness. Research with child sexual abusers has revealed some overlaps with these characteristics, including sexual preoccupation, sexual interest or preference for children, sexual entitlement, beliefs supportive of child sexual abuse, lack of emotional intimacy with adults, emotional congruence with children, poor problem-solving and personal inadequacy, such as poor self-esteem, emotional loneliness and personal distress (e.g. Bumby, 1996; Fisher *et al.,* 1999; Hanson & Bussière, 1998; Hanson & Morton-Bourgon, 2005).

Arson

A large number of major fires within the UK are a result of arson, with Home Office figures showing 43,100 arson incidents were recorded by the police in 2006/2007 (Nicholas *et al.,* 2007). Fire service records suggest an even higher rate of arson, with 72,545 deliberate primary fires in the UK in 2006 (Department for Communities and Local Government, 2008). *Arson* refers to deliberate setting of fire to property, whereas the term *firesetting* is a broader term often used when referring to young children, and does not necessarily imply intent. Geller (1992) proposed four categories of arson: arson associated with mental disorders; arson associated with medical or biological disorders; juvenile fireplay or firesetting; and arson not associated with any psychobiological factors. Geller included within this last category arsons committed for profit, to conceal a crime, for revenge, vanity or recognition, vandalism or political arson. The factors associated with arson and firesetting will be considered in more detail next. However, unlike other areas, such as sexual offending, there are no clearly articulated theories of arson (see Palmer *et al.,* 2010).

Adult arsonists

Among adults, the majority of research has focused on arson among psychiatric populations, even though they are responsible for a minority of arson incidents. This has raised questions as to the generalisability of findings to offenders within the criminal justice system. However, this literature suggests a number of factors that may be associated with arson.

Research with psychiatric populations suggests arson may be associated with a number of mental illnesses, including schizophrenia (Ritchie & Huff, 1999), personality disorders (Hurley & Monahan, 1969), depression (O'Sullivan & Kelleher, 1987) and bipolar affective disorders and mood disorders (Geller, 1992).

Although there is little research, there does not appear to be a relationship between arson and neurological disorders, such as epilepsy (Byrne & Walsh, 1989), other EEG abnormalities (Powers & Gunderman, 1978) or head trauma (Hurley & Monahan, 1969). While there is some evidence of a link with dementia, this is probably attributable to accidents and careless smoking (Cohen *et al.,* 1990).

More evidence exists for an association between arson and developmental disorders and intellectual disabilities (Murphy & Clare, 1996; Ritchie & Huff, 1999). It has been suggested that this relationship is due to a lack of awareness of the consequences of setting fires among these populations.

Functional analysis of arson behaviours has highlighted the importance of social and environmental stimuli in reinforcing arson (Swaffer, 1994), and the interaction of these stimuli with predispositions to committing antisocial behaviours (Fineman, 1995). Canter and his colleagues have attempted to understand the behavioural patterns of firesetting and arson. Canter and Fritzon (1998) used two facets to categorise arson: person-oriented vs. object-oriented arsons; and expressive vs. instrumental arsons. They argued that these two facets interact to give four types of arson: expressive person-oriented; expressive other-oriented; instrumental person-oriented; and instrumental other-oriented. With a sample of adult and juvenile firesetters, Canter and Fritzon reported that individuals in their four categories differed on a number of characteristics. This research has since been replicated by Santilla *et al.* (2003) and Almond *et al.* (2005).

> **Functional analysis** an approach to understanding behaviour that focuses on determining its function for the individual.

Juvenile firesetters

The research suggests that many of the characteristics of young firesetters overlap with those of general juvenile delinquent populations (for a review, see Kolko, 2001). Young firesetters are more likely to be male

FIGURE 1.3 *Young firesetters are more likely to be male.*
Source: © Vanessa Nel. Used under licence from Shutterstock.

(Figure 1.3), with a meta-analysis of 22 studies revealing that 82 per cent of young firesetters were male (Kolko, 1985). Firesetting in children is often associated with a range of other externalising behaviours. These include aggression, extreme antisocial behaviour and conduct disorder (Dadds & Fraser, 2006; Kolko, 1985; McCarty & McMahon, 2005). Other research has reported high levels of drug and alcohol abuse among firesetters (e.g. Repo & Virkkunen, 1997).

A range of psychological factors has been associated with firesetting in children and adolescents. These include poor interpersonal skills, such as impulsivity, poor assertion skills and inability to resolve conflicts (Harris & Rice, 1984). There is also evidence that psychiatric problems are more prevalent among firesetting populations (Kolko & Kazdin, 1988; Räsänen et al., 1995).

Parental and family functioning have also been implicated in firesetting. Factors include poor childrearing practices, such as a lack of supervision and lax or inconsistent discipline (Kolko & Kazdin, 1990). Child abuse, maltreatment and neglect are also prevalent among young firesetters. Firesetting has also been associated with parental relationship problems, conflict and violence, and parents who report experiencing personal difficulties and life stresses (Kolko & Kazdin, 1991;

McCarty & McMahon, 2005). Young firesetters have also been found to be more likely to have experienced the loss of the mother as compared to non-firesetters, with 40 per cent spending time in an orphanage, foster home or psychiatric facility (Ritvo et al., 1982). There are also increased levels of academic underachievement, school disruption and suspension/expulsions from school among young firesetters (Hollin et al., 2002).

One study comparing young firesetters with young delinquents who were not firesetters showed that firesetters have more problems than non-firesetters, with firesetting often used to obtain power over adults (Sakheim & Osborn, 1986). Kolko (2001) has also emphasised the role of children's exposure to fire materials and fire-competence when examining motivations for firesetting behaviour (see Chapter 19 for a discussion of the assessment and treatment of firesetters).

MENTALLY DISORDERED OFFENDERS

'Mentally disordered offenders' is a legal term that refers to those individuals who have a mental disorder and have also committed an offence. The types of mental disorder include mental illness (schizophrenia and depression), intellectual disabilities, and personality disorder, along with the special case of psychopathic offenders. There is a body of research examining the relationship between mental disorder and offending. There certainly appears to be some relationship, with an increased prevalence of mental disorder among criminal populations (Fazel & Danesh, 2002; Shaw, 2001; Steadman et al., 2009), particularly among women, older people and ethnic minority groups. This is mirrored by higher levels of offending among psychiatric populations as compared to the general population (Taylor, 2001).

Why are mentally disordered offenders a special case?

In the eyes of the law, for a person to be found guilty of an offence they have to be criminally responsible. This relates to the distinction in law between **actus rea** (bad act) and **mens rea** (guilty state of mind). For an individual to be found guilty, both actus rea and mens rea must be proved, i.e. (1) that the act is an offence and the defendant did commit the offence; and (2) that at the

actus rea
literally, a 'guilty act';
that a criminal act has
occurred.

mens rea literally,
'guilty mind'; that the
defendant is aware
of criminal intent and
responsible for their
actions.

time of the offence, the individual knew both (a) that what they were doing was bad and (b) that what they were doing was wrong (i.e. against the law). In the UK, the McNaughton Rule states that an individual is not criminally responsible if: '. . . at the time of committing the act, the party accused was labouring under such a defect of reason from a disease of the mind, as not to know the nature and quality of the act he was doing; or if he did know it, he did not know he was doing what was wrong'.

If the defence can prove that such a 'defect' or mental disorder existed at the time of the offence, then the person can be found 'not guilty' on the grounds that they are not criminally responsible.

Types of mentally disordered offender

The different types of mental disorder and their association with offending will be considered next.

Mental illness

The category of mental illness includes schizophrenia and depression, and these will be considered in turn.

Schizophrenia refers to a group of disorders characterised by disturbances of perception, thought, affect and actions. Individuals often experience hallucinations, delusions and/or paranoia (the psychotic symptoms of schizophrenia), and withdraw from others. The prevalence of schizophrenia in the general population is around 1 per cent. The figure is far higher among offenders, with offenders referred for psychiatric treatment often having committed a violent offence. In a systematic review of 62 studies of prisoners from 12 countries, Fazel and Danesh (2002) reported 4 per cent of male and female offenders had schizophrenia. A recent study in the USA reported that 14.5 per cent of male prisoners and 31 per cent of female prisoners had a current serious mental illness (Steadman et al., 2009). These figures lead to the question of whether schizophrenia somehow causes the offending, or if there is simply an association caused by other factors (see Douglas et al., 2009). It should also be noted that most of the research has examined the association of schizophrenia with violent offending.

When considering why schizophrenia may be associated with offending, three explanations have been proposed: first, that it *causes* offending; second, that it is a *consequence* of offending; or third, that it is *correlated* with offending and both result from other factors (Douglas et al., 2009). With respect to the first explanation, it has been suggested that paranoid ideas, command hallucinations and other delusions associated with schizophrenia may influence behaviour, although research shows that this is true in only a minority of cases (Monahan et al., 2001; Smith & Taylor, 1999).

For the explanation that schizophrenia is a consequence of offending, it has been proposed that schizophrenia may result from the associated stress and trauma brought about by committing an offence, particularly a violent offence. There is some support for this, with research showing that committing a violent offence is associated with suicide/self-harm and victimisation among people with schizophrenia (Hillbrand, 2001; Nicholls et al., 2006).

With respect to the third explanation, research shows that similar factors are associated with both schizophrenia and violent behaviour, such as negative life experiences relating to families, relationship problems, low socio-economic status, and loss of employment (Elbogen & Johnson, 2009; Walsh et al., 2002). Therefore, it has been suggested that experiencing stressful life events can lead to both schizophrenia and offending/violence for individuals with a predisposing vulnerability. The role of comorbid substance misuse has also been highlighted (Elbogen & Johnson, 2009; Taylor, 2001). Use of alcohol and drugs is likely to exacerbate the psychotic symptoms of schizophrenia, and may also lead to a reduced compliance with medication. Substance misuse is also associated with an elevated risk of offending in its own right (Mills et al., 2003). Offenders with a diagnosis of schizophrenia may also have other mental health problems, further complicating the picture.

Depression can be split into two types: unipolar (major) depression and bipolar depression. Major depression is characterised by a pervasive sad mood, feelings of guilt and self-blame, disturbed appetite, tiredness, lethargy and recurring thoughts of suicide. In bipolar depression, individuals experience alternating periods of mania and depression. Of the two types, major depression is the most common and affects 8 per cent of the general population, with bipolar experienced by about 1 per cent. In contrast, research among offenders has found the prevalence of depression to be higher (Brinded et al., 2001). For example, in Fazel and Danesh's (2002) review, the prevalence of major depression was 10 per cent among male prisoners and 12 per cent among women prisoners.

There are a number of ways in which depression and offending may be linked: first, an individual may offend because they are depressed; second, depression may be triggered by guilt after an offence; and third, an individual may be depressed when they committed an offence but the depression did not cause the offence. It is also possible that imprisonment for an offence may trigger depression.

Most attention has focused on the first and third explanations. The research suggests that the link between depression and offending is much weaker than for schizophrenia and personality disorder (e.g. Grann

CASE STUDY 1.2   A VIOLENT ACT: MENTAL ILLNESS OR SOCIAL ISOLATION?

In recent years, there has been a spate of mass killings by gunmen, particularly in the USA (Figure 1.4). A recent high profile case occurred at Virginia Tech University in April 2007, in which a 23-year-old student, Seung-Hui Cho, shot 32 other students and staff before killing himself. In the days following the shootings, it emerged that the gunman had experienced mental health problems and had shown suicidal tendencies since he was 13 years old. However, a closer look at his history reveals other issues that were implicated in what happened.

FIGURE 1.4 *In recent years, there has been a spate of mass killings by gunmen.*

Source: © Sascha Burkard. Used under licence from Shutterstock.

Cho's family had moved to the USA when he was 8 years of age. The fact that he didn't know much English led to social isolation, and even once his language skills improved he remained quiet, and even withdrawn. At age 12, he was diagnosed with social anxiety disorder, specifically selective mutism. He was prescribed antidepressants, which seemed to help, but was taken off these after about a year. Cho is reported as not having a good relationship with his father, and not speaking much to his parents. However, how much this was normal teenage behaviour rather than problematic is not clear.

At high school his teachers developed a programme to help him complete his school week and he continued to attend counselling. As a result, he graduated in 2003 with good grades. Although the school suggested he go to college close to home, he chose to apply to Virginia Tech. His counsellor gave Cho the name of someone at the university to call if he needed help; however, he never did so.

The first few years at college appeared to go fine, with Cho achieving good grades and being in regular contact with his family. However, in autumn 2005, problems started to appear. He stopped writing home and argued with his teachers, and there were complaints from female students who had received harassing emails, text messages and phone calls from him. As a result, he was referred to counselling. A roommate also reported that after one warning to stop contacting a woman, Cho said, 'I might as well kill myself now'. A psychiatric evaluation followed, along with a few brief phone calls with a counsellor.

Reviewing these facts, it would appear that Cho certainly had mental health problems. However, it is clear that his social isolation and lack of social skills were also contributory factors to what happened. The strong support system that acted as a safety net at high school was simply not there at university, and he gradually became more isolated. These environmental factors were clearly important in the deterioration in Cho's mental health and the associated increase in his antisocial behaviour – and provide a good example of the complex nature of the mental illness/offending relationship.

et al., 2008). With respect to the third explanation, it is also important to consider what factors may have triggered the depression. Social and environmental factors are often precursors to a depressive episode, such as losing a job, or relationship problems (Kendler *et al.*, 1999). As noted above, these factors are themselves also associated with an increased risk of offending.

Overall, for both schizophrenia and depression, the mental illness may not be the only factor to consider when explaining the link with offending. Account should also be taken of the complex interactions between the individual, their mental state, their predispositions, and social and environmental factors. The exacerbating influence of substance misuse should also not be ignored. Furthermore, the influence of each of these factors may vary for different people at different times. See Case Study 1.2.

Intellectual disabilities

Individuals with intellectual disabilities (ID) are characterised by impairments of intelligence and social functioning. While there are no legal criteria regarding IQ scores for ID, in clinical practice an IQ of 70 is normally seen as 'borderline'. When this is combined with below average social functioning, a diagnosis of LD is applied. An IQ of less than 50 represents a substantial amount of impairment. Intellectual disability can be present from birth or can result from hypoxia (lack of oxygen) at birth, serious illness or brain damage.

Within the general population, 2–2.5 per cent of people have an IQ of less than 70 (Holland, 2004). A recent systematic review by Fazel *et al.* (2008) of ten studies from four countries reported that between 0 per cent and 2.8 per cent of prisoners were diagnosed with intellectual disabilities, from which they concluded that the typical percentage of ID diagnosis was 0.5–1.5 per cent. However, this figure may be low due to offenders with intellectual disabilities receiving hospital orders under the Mental Health Act or being dealt with in the community, rather than being imprisoned. Other studies have examined the prevalence of offending among individuals known to services for intellectually disabled people. Again, these have shown low levels of offending, ranging from 2 per cent (Lyall *et al.*, 1995) to 5 per cent (McNulty *et al.*, 1995).

Notwithstanding these figures, it is not at all clear how intellectual disabilities and offending are linked. The term 'intellectual disability' covers a wide range of individuals who can differ on a number of characteristics. As a result there is no clear definition of the term, particularly within the borderline area. Research suggests that there are two groups of offenders with intellectual disabilities (Holland, 2004). First, there are offenders with a mild intellectual disability who are not known to services, often come from disadvantaged homes in which other family members are offenders and have many characteristics in common with general offenders. Second is a more heterogeneous group of offenders who are known to intellectual disability services. These offenders are thought to commit fewer offences, but these offences may be more dangerous.

While people with intellectual disabilities commit a variety of offences, there appears to be a disproportionate number convicted for sexual offences (Law *et al.*, 2000). However, there appear to be distinct differences between the sexual offences committed by offenders with intellectual disabilities and the general sexual offender population. As compared to the general sexual offender population, the sexual offences committed by offenders with intellectual disabilities involve less planning and the victim often does not know the offender. This has led to suggestions that sexual offences by offenders with intellectual disabilities may represent inappropriate and impulsive behaviour towards other people, rather than being deliberate acts of sexual aggression. It may be that the person with intellectual disabilities is not aware of the social rules governing acceptable behaviours in such situations, but lacks the social competence to express their feelings and the social skills required to make acceptable sexual approaches to people (Hudson *et al.*, 1999).

Similar explanations have been suggested with regard to offenders with intellectual disabilities who have committed violent offences. Here, it may be that the violent behaviour is a result of impulsivity or frustration, or a lack of social skills in dealing with provocative situations. Research has also shown aggression in samples of people with intellectual disabilities to be associated with poor self-concept (Jahoda *et al.*, 1998).

Personality disorders

A personality disorder is a persistent disorder that impacts on how the individual relates to themselves, others and their environment, leading to major problems in their social functioning. There are 10 personality disorders that are classified into three categories by the *DSM-IV* (American Psychiatric Association, 1994). Cluster A (odd-eccentric) includes paranoid, schizoid, and schizotypal personality disorders; Cluster B (dramatic-erratic-emotional) includes antisocial, borderline, histrionic, and narcissistic personality disorders; and Cluster C (anxious-fearful) includes avoidant, dependent, and obsessive-compulsive personality disorders.

Coid *et al.* (2006) reported a prevalence of 4.4 per cent for at least one personality disorder among adults in the general population in Great Britain (5.4 per cent of men and 3.4 per cent of women). The most prevalent was obsessive-compulsive personality disorder (2.6 per cent), with the least prevalent being dependent and schizotypal personality disorders. These figures are considerably higher in forensic settings. Findings from the Prisoner Cohort Study in England and Wales found that 72.9 per cent of male prisoners met the criteria for at least one personality disorder (Roberts *et al.*, 2008). Antisocial personality disorder (64.5 per cent) was the most prevalent, followed by paranoid personality disorder (21.7 per cent), with histrionic and dependent personality disorders the least prevalent (1.2 per cent and 0.7 per cent, respectively). Within the prisoner sample there were also considerable levels of comorbidity with other personality disorders and mental illness.

Research shows there to be some relationship between personality disorders and offending, especially antisocial personality disorder and violent offences (Hodgins *et al.*, 1996; Roberts & Coid, 2010). Less research has examined other personality disorders and offending, although Roberts and Coid (2010) report a number of relatively small correlations of other personality disorders with a range of offence types. While the exact nature of this relationship is not fully understood, there are a number of personality traits common to many personality disorders that are associated with offending (Hart, 2001). These traits include anxiety, emotional instability, insecure attachments, depressiveness, hostility, impulsivity and lack of empathy. Furthermore, being aggressive and having a history of antisocial behaviour are diagnostic criteria for antisocial personality disorder (McMurran, 2001). However, care should be taken when attributing causality of offending to personality disorder, as there may be other factors other than the personality disorder that increase the risk of offending, including comorbidity of substance abuse, other personality disorders and other mental illness.

In England and Wales, offenders suffering from personality disorders can be sentenced to prison or a probation order, or they can be dealt with under the Mental Health Act 1983. Within legislation, personality disorder comes under the legal classification of 'psychopathic disorder', which is defined as 'a persistent disorder or disability of the mind . . . which results in abnormally aggressive or seriously irresponsible conduct'. 'Psychopathic disorder' is not a clinical diagnosis, however, and, as is discussed below, although there are overlaps, psychopathy and personality disorder are not the same thing.

The special case of the psychopathic offender

The term 'psychopathic offender' refers to those offenders classified under the Mental Health Act 1983 as having a 'psychopathic disorder', defined as 'a persistent disorder or disability of the mind (whether or not including significant impairment of intelligence) which results in abnormally aggressive or seriously irresponsible conduct'. It is, therefore, a legal term, rather than a clinical diagnosis. Clinically, it appears that offenders detained under the term 'psychopathic disorder' exhibit traits similar to a personality disorder, specifically antisocial personality disorder (ASPD). However, this diagnosis does not necessarily fit all offenders within this category.

There have been attempts to describe psychopathic offenders, and to develop diagnostic criteria for psychopathy. Some of the most important work in this area is that of Cleckley (1976) and Hare (1980). This work highlighted a number of characteristics as defining psychopaths. These include a lack of guilt and remorse, impulsiveness, irresponsibility, pathological lying, manipulativeness, shallow affect, egocentricity, glibness, superficial charm and a failure to learn from experience. Hare went on to develop a clinical assessment tool, the Psychopathy Checklist–Revised (PCL-R, see Chapter 17 for details; also Hare, 1991; 2003). Research suggests that the test assesses three interrelated aspects of psychopathy: (1) an arrogant and manipulative interpersonal style; (2) affective deficits; and (3) an impulsive and irresponsible behavioural style (Cooke *et al.*, 2004; Cooke & Michie, 2001).

A large body of research exists showing that offenders with psychopathy (as assessed using the PCL-R) are persistent and serious offenders, with a particularly strong relationship between psychopathy and violence (see meta-analyses by Campbell *et al.*, 2009; Edens *et al.*, 2007; Leistico *et al.*, 2008). However, less is known about the mechanisms of this relationship. Three suggestions have been put forward by Hart (1998), relating to cognition, affect and behaviour. First, psychopaths exhibit a cognitive pattern that includes a hostile attributional bias, attentional deficits and beliefs that support the reinforcing nature of violence. Second, they show affective deficits in guilt, empathy and fear that can increase the likelihood of offending regardless of the consequences for the safety of themselves or other people. Third, psychopaths exhibit behavioural impulsiveness, often acting without thinking.

There are a number of problems with the legal term 'psychopathic disorder'. First, there is circularity in the diagnosis of 'psychopathic disorder' in that it is made on the basis of violent/very antisocial behaviour. Thus, no distinction is made between the psychiatric state of psychopathy and the behaviour that equals its symptoms. Therefore, it is perhaps no surprise that psychopathy is associated with violence. It is likely that there are people with psychopathic traits in the general population, who because they do not commit offences (or do not get caught) do not come to the attention of the criminal justice system. Second, research has shown that legally defined psychopaths and those identified using the PCL-R are not the same individuals. For example, Blackburn (1995) states that only a quarter of psychopaths in his research would be categorised as psychopaths by the PCL-R. Therefore, 'psychopathic disorder' and psychopathy do not represent the same construct. These issues have led to suggestions that psychopathy may actually be a severe personality disorder, or that it is not a mental disorder at all but an evolved lifestyle that is adaptive to certain situations (Rice, 1997). If the latter suggestion is the case, then psychopaths who commit violent acts may do so as a result of the same factors as other violent offenders (see Chapter 18 for a full discussion of treatment issues).

CONCLUSIONS

This chapter has considered how psychological theory and research has contributed to our understanding of offending. As has been shown, some theories, such as moral reasoning theory and social information-processing approaches, have been applied to general offending. Psychology has also been applied to the specific areas of violent offending, sexual offending and arson, in an attempt to provide a greater understanding of these more serious crimes.

Mentally disordered offenders provide another challenge to psychology, in that a range of individuals with different problems fall under this umbrella. Considering these offenders by types of mental disorder allows us to begin to understand the associations between these disorders and offending. This research provides some clarification of the question of whether mental disorder *causes* offending or if the association can be explained with reference to other factors. As has been shown, while it is true that an association does exist, it is often difficult to disentangle issues of causality.

Finally, the special case of the psychopathic offender was considered. This highlighted the problems with the legal definition of psychopathic disorder and its relationship to the concept of psychopathy as defined by Hare (1991).

Overall, it can be seen that psychology can make an important contribution to our understanding of why people offend. However, there remain a number of issues that we do not yet fully understand, and further research is required in these areas. Examples of these include the developmental precursors to sexual offending, a coherent theory of arson and firesetting, and the true nature of the link between mental disorder and offending. The importance of this knowledge lies in how it can be translated into practice with offenders, in terms of informing future developments in working with offenders to reduce their likelihood of reoffending.

SUMMARY

- **This chapter has considered how psychological theories and research has contributed to our understanding of offending.**

- **Theories such as Kohlberg's theory of moral reasoning and social information-processing approaches have been applied to offending behaviour.**

- **Psychology has also been applied to the specific areas of violent offending, sexual offending, and arson.**

- **'Mentally disordered offenders' covers a range of individuals with different problems. Considering these offenders by type of mental disorder has aided understanding of the associations between these disorders and offending.**

- **The research has also provided some clarification of the question of whether mental disorder *causes* offending or if the association can be explained with reference to other factors. While it is true that an association does exist between mental disorder and offending, it is often difficult to disentangle causality.**

- **Finally, the special case of the psychopathic offender was considered. This highlighted the problems with the legal definition of psychopathic disorder and its relationship to the concept of psychopathy as defined by Hare (1991).**

ESSAY/DISCUSSION QUESTIONS

1. What factors lead to criminal behaviour?

2. What might lead to offenders having distinctive patterns of social information-processing?

3. Compare and contrast the different theories of violent offending.

4. Is crime caused by mental illness?

REFERENCES

Almond, L., Duggan, L., Shine, J. & Canter, D. (2005). Test of the arson action system model in an incarcerated population. *Psychology, Crime and Law, 11*, 1–15.

American Psychiatric Association (1994). *Diagnostic and statistical manual of mental disorders, 4th edition (DSM-IV)*. Washington, DC: American Psychiatric Association.

Antonowicz, D.H. (2005). The reasoning and rehabilitation program: Outcome evaluations with offenders. In M. McMurran & J. McGuire (Eds.) *Social problem-solving and offending: Evidence, evaluation and evolution* (pp.163–181). Chichester: John Wiley & Sons, Inc.

Barriga, A.Q. & Gibbs, J.C. (1996). Measuring cognitive distortion in antisocial youth: Development and preliminary validation of the 'How I Think' questionnaire. *Aggressive Behavior, 22*, 333–343.

Beech, A., Oliver, C., Fisher, D. & Beckett, R. (2005). *STEP 4: The Sex Offender Treatment Programme in prison: Addressing the offending behaviour of rapists and sexual murders*. University of Birmingham: Centre for Forensic and Family Psychology.

Blackburn, R. (1995). Psychopaths: Are they bad or mad? In N.K. Clark & G.M. Stephenson (Eds.) *Criminal behaviour: Perceptions, attributions, and rationality. Issues in criminological and legal psychology, No. 22*. Leicester: British Psychological Society.

Blasi, A. (1980). Bridging moral cognition and moral action: A critical review of the literature. *Psychological Bulletin, 88*, 1–45.

Bliesener, T. & Lösel, F. (2001). Social information processing in bullies, victims, and competent adolescents. In G.B. Traverso & L. Bagnoli (Eds.) *Psychology and law in a changing world: New trends in theory, practice and research* (pp.65–85). London: Routledge.

Brinded, P.M.J., Simpson, A.I.F., Laidlaw, T.M., Fairley, N. & Malcolm, F. (2001). Prevalence of psychiatric disorders in New Zealand prisons: A national study. *Australian and New Zealand Journal of Psychiatry, 35*, 166–173.

Bumby, K. (1996). Assessing the cognitive distortions of child molesters and rapists: Development and validation of the RAPE and MOLEST scales. *Sexual Abuse: A Journal of Research and Treatment, 8*, 37–54.

Byrne, A. & Walsh, J.B. (1989). The epileptic arsonist. *British Journal of Psychiatry, 155*, 268–271.

Campbell, M.A., French, S. & Gendreau, P. (2009). The prediction of violence in adult offenders: A meta-analytic comparison of instruments and methods of assessment. *Criminal Justice and Behavior, 36*, 657–590.

Canter, D.V. & Fritzon, K. (1998). Differentiating arsonists: A model of fire-setting actions and characteristics. *Legal and Criminological Psychology, 3*, 73–96.

Cleckley, H. (1976). *The mask of sanity* (5th edn). St. Louis, MO: Mosby.

Cohen, M.A.A., Aladjem, A.D., Bremin, D. & Ghazi, M. (1990). Fire-setting by patients with the acquired immunodeficiency syndrome (AIDS). *Annals of International Medicine, 122*, 386–387.

Coid, J., Yang, M., Tyrer, P., Roberts, A. & Ullrich, S. (2006). Prevalence and correlates of personality disorder in Great Britain. *British Journal of Psychiatry, 188*, 423–431.

Cooke, D.J. & Michie, C. (1998). Predicting recidivism in a Scottish prison sample. *Psychology, Crime and Law, 4*, 169–211.

Cooke, D.J., Michie, C., Hart, S.D. & Clark, D. (2004). Reconstructing psychopathy: Clarifying the significance of antisocial and socially deviant behaviour in the diagnosis of psychopathic personality disorder. *Journal of Personality Disorders, 18*, 337–357.

Crick, N.R. & Dodge, K.A. (1994). A review and reformulation of social information processing mechanisms in children's social adjustment. *Psychological Bulletin, 115*, 74–101.

Crick, N.R. & Ladd, G.W. (1990). Children's perceptions of the outcomes of aggressive strategies: Do the ends justify being mean? *Developmental Psychology, 26*, 612–620.

Dadds, M.R. & Fraser, J.A. (2006). Fire interest, fire setting and psychopathology in Australian children: A normative study. *Australian and New Zealand Journal of Psychiatry, 40*, 581–586.

Department for Communities and Local Government (2008). *Fire statistics, United Kingdom 2006*. London: Department for Communities and Local Government.

Dodge, K.A. & Newman, J.P. (1981). Biased decision-making processes in aggressive boys. *Journal of Abnormal Psychology, 90*, 375–379.

Dodge, K.A. & Somberg, D.R. (1987). Hostile attributional biases among aggressive boys are exacerbated under conditions of threat to the self. *Child Development, 58*, 213–224.

Dodge, K.A. & Tomlin, A.M. (1987). Utilization of self-schemas as a mechanism of interpersonal bias in aggressive children. *Social Cognition, 5*, 280–300.

Douglas, K.S., Guy, L.S. & Hart, S.D. (2009). Psychosis as a risk factor for violence to others: A meta-analysis. *Psychological Bulletin, 135*, 679–706.

Dutton, D.G. (1995). *The domestic assault of women: Psychological and criminal justice perspectives*. Vancouver, Canada: UBC Press.

Edens, J.F., Campbell, J.S. & Weir, J.M. (2007). Youth psychopathy and criminal recidivism: A meta-analysis of the psychopathy checklist measures. *Law and Human Behavior, 31*, 53–75.

Elbogen, E.B. & Johnson, S.C. (2009). The intricate link between violence and mental disorder: Results from the national epidemiological survey on alcohol and related conditions. *Archives of General Psychiatry, 66*, 152–161.

Fazel, S. & Danesh, J. (2002). Serious mental disorder in 23,000 prisoners: A systematic review of 62 surveys. *Lancet, 359*, 545–550.

Fazel, S., Xenitidis, K. & Powell, J. (2008). The prevalence of intellectual disabilities among 12,000 prisoners: A systematic review. *International Journal of Psychiatry and Law, 31,* 369–373.

Fineman, K.R. (1995). A model for the qualitative analysis of child and adult fire deviant behaviour. *American Journal of Forensic Psychology, 13,* 31–60.

Finkelhor, D. (1984). *Child sexual abuse: New theory and research.* New York: Free Press.

Fisher, D., Beech, A.R. & Browne, K. (1999). Comparison of sex offenders to non-sex offenders on selected psychological measures. *International Journal of Offender Therapy and Comparative Criminology, 43,* 473–491.

Fondacaro, M.R. & Heller, K. (1990). Attributional style in aggressive adolescent boys. *Journal of Abnormal Child Psychology, 18,* 75–89.

Fontaine, R.G. & Dodge, K.A. (2006). Real-time decision making and aggressive behavior in youth: A heuristic model of response evaluation and decision (RED). *Aggressive Behavior, 32,* 604–624.

Fontaine, R.G., Yang, C., Dodge, K.A., Bates, J.E. & Pettit, G.S. (2008). Testing an individual systems model of response evaluation and decision (RED) and antisocial behavior across adolescence. *Child Development, 79,* 462–475.

Geffner, R., Barrett, J.J. & Rossman, B.B.R. (1995). Domestic violence and sexual abuse: Multiple systems perspectives. In R.H. Mikesell, D.-D. Lusterman & S.H. McDaniel (Eds.) *Integrating family therapy: Handbook of family psychology and systems theory* (pp.501–517). Washington, DC: APA.

Geller, J.L. (1992). Arson in review. *Clinical Forensic Psychiatry, 15,* 623–645.

Gibbs, J.C. (2003). *Moral development and reality: Beyond the theories of Kohlberg and Hoffman.* Thousand Oaks, CA: Sage Publications.

Gibbs, J.C. (2010). *Moral development and reality: Beyond the theories of Kohlberg and Hoffman* (2nd edn). Thousand Oaks, CA: Sage Publications.

Gouze, K.R. (1987). Attention and social problem solving as correlates of aggression in pre-school males. *Journal of Abnormal Psychology, 15,* 181–197.

Grann, M., Danesh, J. & Fazel, S. (2008). The association between psychiatric diagnosis and violent re-offending in adult offenders in the community. *BMC Psychiatry, 8,* 92.

Gregg, V.R., Gibbs, J.C. & Basinger, K.S. (1994). Patterns of developmental delay in moral judgment by male and female delinquents. *Merrill-Palmer Quarterly, 40,* 538–553.

Hall, G.C.N. & Hirschmann, R. (1992). Sexual aggression against children: A conceptual perspective of etiology. *Criminal Justice and Behavior, 19,* 8–23.

Hanson, R.K. & Bussière, M.T. (1998). Predicting relapse: A meta-analysis of sexual offender recidivism studies. *Journal of Consulting and Clinical Psychology, 66,* 348–362.

Hanson, R.K. & Morton-Bourgon, K.E. (2005). The characteristics of persistent sexual offenders: A meta-analysis of recidivism studies. *Journal of Consulting and Clinical Psychology, 73,* 1154–1163.

Hare, R.D. (1980). A research scale for the assessment of psychopathy in criminal populations. *Personality and Individual Differences, 1,* 111–119.

Hare, R.D. (1991). *The Hare Psychopathy Checklist – Revised (PCL–R).* Toronto, Ontario: Multi-Health Systems.

Hare, R.D. (2003). *The Hare Psychopathy Checklist – Revised (PCL–R)* (2nd edn). North Tonawanda, NY: Multi-Health Systems.

Harris, G.T. & Rice, M.E. (1984). Mentally disordered fire-setters: Psychodynamics versus empirical approaches. *International Journal of Law and Psychiatry, 7,* 19–34.

Hart, C.H., Ladd, G.W. & Burleson, B.R. (1990). Children's expectations of the outcomes of social strategies: Relations with sociometric status and maternal disciplinary styles. *Child Development, 61,* 127–137.

Hart, S.D. (1998). Psychopathy and risk for violence. In D.J. Cooke, A.E. Forth, J. Newman & R.D. Hare (Eds.) *Psychopathy: Theory research and implications for society* (pp.355–373). Netherlands: Kluwer Academic Publishers.

Hart, S.D. (2001). Forensic issues. In W.J. Livesley (Ed.) *Handbook of personality disorders: Theory, research, and treatment* (pp.555–569). New York: The Guilford Press.

Hillbrand, M. (2001). Homicide-suicide and other forms of co-occurring aggression against self and against others. *Professional Psychology: Research and Practice, 32,* 626–635.

Hodgins, S., Mednick, S.A., Brennan, P.A., Schulsinger, G. & Engberg, M. (1996). Mental disorder and crime: Evidence from a Danish birth cohort. *Archives of General Psychiatry, 54,* 489–496.

Hoffman, M.L. (2000). *Empathy and moral development: Implications for caring and justice.* Cambridge: Cambridge University Press.

Holland, A.J. (2004). Criminal behaviour and developmental disability: An epidemiological perspective. In W.R. Lindsay, J.L. Taylor & P. Sturmey (Eds.) *Offenders with developmental disabilities* (pp.23–34). Chichester: John Wiley & Sons, Inc.

Hollin, C.R., Epps, K.J. & Swaffer, T.J. (2002). Adolescent fire-setters: Findings from an analysis of 47 cases. *Pakistan Journal of Psychological Research, 17,* 1–16.

Hollin, C.R., Hatcher, R.M. & Palmer, E.J. (2010). Sexual offences against adults. In F. Brookman, M. Maguire, H. Pierpoint & T. Bennett (Eds.) *Handbook of crime* (pp.505–524). Cullompton: Willan Publishing.

Hollin, C.R., Palmer, E.J. & Hatcher, R.M. (2010). Sexual offences against children. In F. Brookman, M. Maguire, H. Pierpoint & T. Bennett (Eds.) *Handbook of crime* (pp.525–541). Cullompton: Willan Publishing.

Home Office (2011). *Crime in England and Wales: Quarterly update to September 2010.* London: Home Ofice.

Howells, K. (1986). Social skills training and criminal and antisocial behaviour in adults. In C.R. Hollin & P. Trower (Eds.) *Handbook of social skills training, volume 1: Applications across the life span.* Oxford: Pergamon.

Howells, K. (2004). Anger and its link to violent offending. *Psychiatry, Psychology and Law, 11,* 189–196.

Hudson, A., Nankervis, K., Smith, D. & Phillips, A. (1999). *Identifying the risks: Prevention of sexual offending amongst adolescents with an intellectual disability.* Melbourne: Research Unit, DisAbility Services Division, Victorian Department of Human Services.

Hurley, W. & Monahan, T.M. (1969). Arson: The criminal and the crime. *British Journal of Criminology, 9,* 145–155.

Jahoda, A., Pert, C., Squire, J. & Trower, P. (1998). Facing stress and conflict: A comparison of the predicted responses and self-concepts of aggressive and non-aggressive people with intellectual disability. *Journal of Intellectual Disability Research, 42,* 360–369.

Jolliffe, D. & Farrington, D.P. (2004). Empathy and offending: A systematic review and meta-analysis. *Aggression and Violent Behavior, 9,* 441–476.

Kendler, K.S., Karkowski, L.M. & Prescott, C.A. (1999). Causal relationship between stressful life events and the onset of major depression. *American Journal of Psychiatry, 156,* 837–841.

Kohlberg, L. (1969). Stage and sequence: The cognitive-developmental approach to socialization. In D.A. Goslin (Ed.) *Handbook of socialization theory and research* (pp.347–480). Chicago: Rand McNally.

Kohlberg, L. (1984). *Essays on moral development: The psychology of moral development.* San Francisco, CA: Harper and Row.

Kolko, D.J. (1985). Juvenile fire-setting: A review and methodological critique. *Clinical Psychology Review, 5,* 345–376.

Kolko, D.J. (2001). Fire-setters. In C.R. Hollin (Ed.) *Handbook of offender assessment and treatment* (pp.391–414). Chichester: John Wiley & Sons, Inc.

Kolko, D.J. & Kazdin, A.E. (1988). Prevalence of fire-setting and related behaviours among child psychiatric patients. *Journal of Consulting and Clinical Psychology, 56,* 628–630.

Kolko, D.J. & Kazdin, A.E. (1990). Matchplay and fire-setting in children: Relationship to parent, marital and family dysfunction. *Journal of Clinical Child Psychology, 19,* 229–238.

Kolko, D.J. & Kazdin, A.E. (1991). Motives of childhood fire-setters: Fire-setting characteristics and psychological correlates. *Journal of Child Psychology and Psychiatry, 32,* 535–550.

Lansford, J.E., Malone, P.S., Dodge, K.A., Crozier, J.C., Pettit, G.S. & Bates, J.E. (2006). A 12-year prospective study of patterns of social information processing problems and externalizing behaviors. *Journal of Abnormal Child Psychology, 35,* 715–724.

Law, J., Lindsay, W.R., Quinn, K. & Smith, A.H.W. (2000). Outcome evaluation of 161 people with mild intellectual disabilities who have offending or challenging behaviour. *Journal of Intellectual Disability Research, 45,* 130–138.

Leistico, A.-M.R., Salekin, R.T., DeCoster, J. & Rogers, R. (2008). A large-scale meta-analysis relating the Hare measures of psychopathy to antisocial conduct. *Law and Human Behavior, 32,* 28–45.

Liau, A.K., Barriga, A.Q. & Gibbs, J.C. (1998). Relations between self-serving cognitive distortions and overt vs. covert antisocial behavior in adolescents. *Aggressive Behavior, 24, 335–346.*

Lochman, J.E., Wayland, K.K. & White, K.J. (1993). Social goals: Relationship to adolescent adjustment and to social problem solving. *Journal of Abnormal Child Psychology, 21,* 135–151.

Loeber, R. & Pardini, D. (2009). Neurobiology and the development of violence: Common assumptions and controversies. In S. Hodgins, E. Viding & A. Plodowski (Eds.) *The neurobiological basis of violence: Science and rehabilitation* (pp.1–22). London: Oxford University Press.

Lösel, F., Bliesener, T. & Bender, D. (2007). Social information processing, experiences of aggression in social contexts, and aggressive behavior in adolescents. *Criminal Justice and Behavior, 34,* 330–347.

Lyall, I., Holland, A.J., Collins, S. & Styles, P. (1995). Incidence of persons with learning disability detained in police custody: A needs assessment for service development. *Medicine, Sciences and the Law, 35,* 61–71.

Malamuth, N.M., Heavey, C.L. & Linz, D. (1993). Predicting men's antisocial behavior against women: The interaction model of sexual aggression. In G.C.N Hall, R. Hirschman, J.R. Graham & M.S. Zaragoza (Eds.) *Sexual aggression: Issues in etiology, assessment and treatment* (pp.63–97). Washington DC: Taylor & Francis.

Marshall, W.L. & Barbaree, H.E. (1990). An integrated theory of sexual offending. In W.L. Marshall, D.R. Laws & H.E. Barbaree (Eds.) *Handbook of sexual assault: Issues, theories and treatment of the offender* (pp.257–275). New York: Plenum.

McCarty, C.A. & McMahon, R. (2005). Domains of risk in the developmental continuity of fire setting. *Behavior Therapy, 36,* 185–195.

McMurran, M. (2001). Offenders with personality disorders. In C.R. Hollin (Ed.) *Handbook of assessment and treatment* (pp.467–479). Chichester: John Wiley & Sons, Inc.

McNulty, C., Kissi-Deborah, R. & Newsom-Davies, I. (1995). Police involvement with clients having intellectual disabilities: A pilot study in South London. *Mental Handicap Research, 8,* 129–136.

Mills, J.F., Kroner, D.G. & Hemmati, T. (2003). Predicting violent behavior through a static-stable variable lens. *Journal of Interpersonal Violence, 18,* 891–904.

Moffitt, T.E. (2003). Life-course-persistent and adolescence-limited antisocial behavior: A 10-year research review and a research agenda. In B.B. Lahey, T.E. Moffitt & A. Caspi (Eds.) *Causes of conduct disorder and juvenile delinquency* (pp.49–75). New York: Guilford Press.

Moffitt, T.E., Caspi, A., Harrington, H. & Milne, B.J. (2002). Males on the life-course persistent and adolescence-limited pathways: Follow-up at age 26 years. *Development and Psychopathology, 14*, 179–207.

Molero-Samuelson, Y., Hodgins, S., Larsson, A., Larm, P. & Tengström, A. (2010). Adolescent antisocial behaviour as predictor of adverse outcomes to age 50: A follow-up study of 1,947 individuals. *Criminal Justice and Behavior, 37*, 158–174.

Monahan, J., Steadman, H.J., Silver, E., Appelbaum, P.S., Robbins, P.C., Mulvey, E.P., *et al.* (2001). *Rethinking risk assessment: The MacArthur study of mental disorder and violence.* New York: Oxford University Press.

Murphy, G.H. & Clare, I.C.H. (1996). Analysis of motivation in people with mild learning disabilities (mental handicap) who set fires. *Psychology, Crime and Law, 2*, 153–166.

Nelson, J.R., Smith, D.J. & Dodd, J. (1990). The moral reasoning of juvenile delinquents: A meta-analysis. *Journal of Abnormal Child Psychology, 18*, 231–239.

Nicholas, S., Kershaw, C. & Walker, A. (2007). *Crime in England and Wales 2006/07* (4th edn). London: RDSD.

Nicholls, T.L., Brink, J., Desmarais, S.L., Webster, C.D. & Martin, M. (2006). The Short-Term Assessment of Risk and Treatability (START): A prospective validation study in a forensic psychiatric sample. *Assessment, 13*, 313–327.

Novaco, R.W. (1975). *Anger control: Development and evaluation of an experimental treatment.* Lexington, KT: D.C. Heath.

Novaco, R.W. & Welsh, W.N. (1989). Anger disturbances: Cognitive mediation and clinical prescriptions. In K. Howells & C.R. Hollin (Eds.) *Clinical approaches to violence* (pp.39–60). Chichester: John Wiley & Sons, Inc.

Orobio de Castro, B., Veerman, J.W., Koops, W., Bosch, J.W. & Monshouwer, H. (2002). Hostile attribution of intent and aggressive behavior: A meta-analysis. *Child Development, 73*, 916–934.

O'Sullivan, G.H. & Kelleher, M.J. (1987). A study of fire-setters in the south-west of Ireland. *British Journal of Psychiatry, 151*, 181–823.

Palmer, E.J. (2003). *Offending behaviour: Moral reasoning, criminal conduct and the rehabilitation of offenders.* Cullompton: Willan Publishing.

Palmer, E.J. (2007). Moral cognition and aggression. In T.A. Gannon, T. Ward, A.R. Beech & D. Fisher (Eds.) *Aggressive offenders' cognition: Theory, research and practice* (pp.199–214). Chichester: John Wiley & Sons, Inc.

Palmer, E.J. & Hollin, C.R. (1998). A comparison of patterns of moral development in young offenders and non-offenders. *Legal and Criminological Psychology, 3*, 225–235.

Palmer, E.J. & Hollin, C.R. (2000). The inter-relations of sociomoral reasoning, perceptions of own parenting, and attribution of intent with self-reported delinquency. *Legal and Criminological Psychology, 5*, 201–218.

Palmer, E.J., Hollin, C.R., Hatcher, R.M. & Ayres, T.C. (2010). Arson. In F. Brookman, M. Maguire, H. Pierpoint & T. Bennett (Eds.) *Handbook of crime* (pp.380–392). Cullompton: Willan Publishing.

Pettit, G.S., Lansford, J.E., Malone, P.S., Dodge, K.A. & Bates, J.E. (2010). Domain specificity in relationship history, social-information processing and violent behaviour in early adulthood. *Journal of Personality and Social Psychology, 98*, 190–200.

Piaget, J. (1932). *The moral judgment of the child.* London: Routledge and Kegan Paul.

Plodowski, A., Gregory, S.L. & Blackwood, N.J. (2009). Persistent violent offending among adult men: A critical review of neuroimaging studies. In S. Hodgins, E. Viding & A. Plodowski (Eds.) *The neurobiological basis of violence: Science and rehabilitation* (pp.137–155). London: Oxford University Press.

Polaschek, D.L.L. (2006). Violent offenders: Concept, theory, and practice. In C.R. Hollin & E.J. Palmer (Eds.) *Offending behaviour programmes: Development, application, and controversies* (pp.113–154). Chichester: John Wiley & Sons, Inc.

Powers, P.S. & Gunderman, R. (1978). Kleine-Levin syndrome associated with fire setting. *Pediatrics and Adolescent Medicine, 132*, 786–792.

Quiggle, N.L., Garber, J., Panak, W.F. & Dodge, K.A. (1992). Social information processing in aggressive and depressed children. *Child Development, 63*, 1305–1320.

Raine, A. (2002). Biosocial studies of antisocial and violent behavior in children and adults: A review. *Journal of Abnormal Child Psychology, 30*, 311–326.

Räsänen, P., Hirvenoja, R., Hakko, H. & Vaeisaenen, E. (1995). A portrait of the juvenile arsonist. *Forensic Science International, 73*, 41–47.

Repo, E. & Virkkunen, M. (1997). Young arsonists: History of conduct disorder, psychiatric diagnosis and criminal recidivism. *Journal of Forensic Psychiatry, 8*, 311–320.

Rice, M.E. (1997). Violent offender research and implications for the criminal justice system. *American Psychologist, 52*, 414–423.

Ritchie, E.C. & Huff, T.G. (1999). Psychiatric aspects of arsonists. *Journal of Forensic Science, 44*, 733–740.

Ritvo, E., Shanock, S. & Lewis, D. (1982). Fire-setting and nonfire-setting delinquents: A comparison of neuropsychiatric, psychoeducational, experiential and behavioural characteristics. *Child Psychiatry and Human Development, 13*, 259–267.

Roberts, A., Yang, M., Zhang, T. & Coid, J. (2008). Personality disorder, temperament, and childhood adversity: Findings from a cohort of prisoners in England and Wales. *Journal of Forensic Psychiatry and Psychology, 19*, 460–483.

Roberts, A.D.L. & Coid, J.W. (2010). Personality disorder and offending behaviour: Findings from the national survey of male prisoners in England and Wales. *Journal of Forensic Psychiatry and Psychology, 21*, 221–237.

Ross, R.R. & Fabiano, E.A. (1985). *Time to think: A cognitive model of delinquency prevention and offender rehabilitation.* Johnson City, TN: Institute of Social Sciences and Arts.

Rutter, M. (2009). Introduction: The two-way interplay between neuroscience and clinical practice in the understanding of violence and its remediation. In S. Hodgins, E. Viding & A. Plodowski (Eds.) *The neurobiological basis of violence: Science and rehabilitation* (pp.*xi–xx*). London: Oxford University Press.

Sakheim, G.A. & Osborn, E. (1986). A psychological profile of juvenile fire-setting in residential treatment: A replication study. *Child Welfare, 45*, 495–503.

Santilla, P., Häkkänen, H., Alison, L. & Whyte, C. (2003). Juvenile fire-setters: Crime scene actions and offender characteristics. *Legal and Criminological Psychology, 8*, 1–20.

Shaw, J. (2001). *Prison healthcare.* NHS National Programme on Forensic Mental Health Research and Development. Department of Health.

Slaby, R.G. & Guerra, N.G. (1988). Cognitive mediators of aggression in adolescent offenders: 1. Assessment. *Developmental Psychology, 24*, 580–588.

Smith, A.D. & Taylor, P.J. (1999). Serious sex offending against women by men with schizophrenia. *British Journal of Psychiatry, 174*, 233–237.

Stams, G.J., Brugman, D., Dekovi, M., van Rosmalen, L., van der Laam, P. & Gibbs, J.C. (2006). The moral judgment of juvenile delinquents: A meta-analysis. *Journal of Abnormal Child Psychology, 34*, 697–713.

Steadman, H.J., Osher, F.C., Robbins, P.C., Case, B. & Samuels, S. (2009). Prevalence of serious mental illness among jail inmates. *Psychiatric Services, 60*, 761–765.

Stewart, L., Hill, J. & Cripps, J. (2001). Treatment of family violence in correctional settings. In L.L. Motiuk & R.C. Serin (Eds.) *Compendium 2000 on effective correctional programming.* Ottawa, Ontario: Ministry of Supply and Services.

Strassberg, Z. & Dodge, K.A. (1987). *Focus of social attention among children varying in peer status.* Paper presented at the annual meeting of the Association for the Advancement of Behavior Therapy, Boston, MA.

Swaffer, T.J. (1994). Predicting the risk of reoffending in adolescent fire-setters II: The key to success. In N.K. Clark & G.M. Stephenson (Eds.) *Rights and risks: The application of forensic psychology* (pp.64–67). Leicester: British Psychological Society.

Taylor, P.J. (2001). *Mental illness and serious harm to others.* NHS National Programme on Forensic Mental Health Research and Development. London: Department of Health.

Walsh, E., Buchanan, A. & Fahy, T. (2002). Violence and schizophrenia: Evaluating the evidence. *British Journal of Psychiatry, 180*, 490–495.

Ward, T. & Beech, A.R. (2006). An integrated theory of sexual offending. *Aggression and Violent Behavior, 11*, 44–63.

Ward, T. & Siegert, R.J. (2002). Toward a comprehensive theory of child sexual abuse: A theory knitting perspective. *Psychology, Crime, & Law, 8*, 319–351.

Widom, C.S. & Maxfield, M.G. (2001). *An update of the cycle of violence.* Washington, DC: National Institute of Violence.

ANNOTATED READING LIST

Hollin, C.R. (2007). Criminological psychology. In M. Maguire, R. Morgan & R. Reiner (Eds.) *The Oxford handbook of criminology* (4th edn) (pp.43–77). Oxford: Oxford University Press. *This chapter reviews psychological theories of criminal behaviour.*

Palmer, E.J., Hollin, C.R., Hatcher, R.M. & Ayres, T.C. (2010). Arson. In F. Brookman, M. Maguire, H. Pierpoint & T. Bennett (Eds.) *Handbook of crime* (pp.380–392). Cullompton: Willan Publishing. *This chapter provides a review of research on arson.*

Polaschek, D.L.L. (2006). Violent offenders: Concept, theory, and practice. In C.R. Hollin & E.J. Palmer (Eds.) *Offending behaviour programmes: Development, application, and controversies* (pp.113–154). Chichester: John Wiley & Sons, Inc. *A useful review of theories and treatment of violent offending, including domestic violence.*

Prins, H. (2005). *Offenders, deviants or patients?* (3rd edn). Hove: Routledge. *Highlights the complexity of the issues relating to mentally disordered offenders.*

Ward, T., Polaschek, D.L.L. & Beech, A.R. (Eds.) (2006). *Theories of sexual offending.* Chichester: John Wiley & Sons, Inc. *A good source on the theories of sexual offending.*

2 Developmental and Psychological Theories of Offending

David P. Farrington and Maria M. Ttofi

CHAPTER OUTLINE

developmental propensity theory a theory that aims to explain the factors in development that lead certain individuals to develop an underlying propensity for conduct disorder and juvenile delinquency.

interactional theory a theory that focuses on the factors that encourage antisocial behaviour at different ages and assume bidirectional effects (e.g. poor parental supervision causes antisocial behaviour and antisocial behaviour causes poor parental supervision).

social control theory a theory proposing that people are inhibited from offending according to the strength of their bonding to society.

In this chapter, we will first review four developmental theories of offending: the **developmental propensity theory** of Lahey and Waldman (2005), the adolescence-limited/life-course-persistent theory of Moffitt (1993), the **interactional theory** of Thornberry and Krohn (2005), and the age-graded informal **social control theory** of Sampson and Laub (2009). (For more details about these theories, see Farrington, 2005a.) Then we will review four psychological theories: the attachment theory of Bowlby (1969), the personality theory of Eysenck (1996), the **social learning theory** of Patterson (1982) and the **lifestyle theory** of Walters (2006). Finally, we will review the **integrated cognitive antisocial potential (ICAP) theory** (Farrington, 2005b).

surveys. Farrington has directed the **Cambridge Study in Delinquent Development**, which is a prospective longitudinal survey of over 400 London males from age 8 to age 48 (Farrington *et al.*, 2006; Farrington, Coid *et al.*, 2009). The main reason why developmental and life-course criminology became important during the 1990s was because of the enormous volume and significance of longitudinal research on offending that was published during this decade. Particularly influential were the three 'causes and correlates' studies originally mounted by the US Office of Juvenile Justice and Delinquency Prevention in Denver, Pittsburgh and Rochester (Huizinga *et al.*, 2003; Loeber *et al.*, 2003; Thornberry *et al.*, 2003). Other important longitudinal projects that came to prominence in the 1990s were the Seattle Social Development Project (Hawkins *et al.*, 2003), the Dunedin study in New Zealand (Moffitt *et al.*, 2001), the Montreal longitudinal-experimental study (Tremblay *et al.*, 2003), and the further analyses by Laub and Sampson (2003) of the classic study by Glueck and Glueck (1950).

integrated cognitive antisocial potential (ICAP) theory a theory primarily designed to explain offending by lower-class males, and influenced by the results obtained in the Cambridge Study.

prospective longitudinal surveys studies that follow a group of individuals (a cohort) over time, with repeated measures.

Cambridge Study in Delinquent Development a prospective longitudinal survey of 411 South London males first studied at age 8 in 1961, with the aim of advancing knowledge about conviction careers up to age 50 and life success up to age 48.

DEVELOPMENTAL THEORIES

social learning theory suggests that people learn from one another, via observation, imitation, and reinforcement. The theory has been described as a bridge between behaviourist and cognitive learning theories because it encompasses attention, memory, and motivation.

lifestyle theory seeks to redress the problems created by psychology's dependence on theoretical mini-models by offering an overarching conceptual framework that combines the insights of yesterday's grand theories with the methodological rigour of today's mini-models. It assumes that delinquency is part of a characteristic lifestyle.

Developmental and life-course criminology (DLC) is concerned mainly with three topics: (a) the development of offending and antisocial behaviour from the womb to the tomb; (b) the influence of risk and protective factors at different ages; and (c) the effects of life events on the course of development. Whereas traditional criminological theories aimed to explain between-individual differences in offending, such as why lower-class boys commit more offences than upper-class boys, DLC theories aim to explain within-individual changes in offending over time (Farrington *et al.*, 2002).

In conducting research on development, risk and protective factors, life events and DLC theories, it is essential to carry out **prospective longitudinal**

Lahey and Waldman: Developmental propensity theory

Lahey and Waldman (2005) aimed to explain the development of conduct disorder and juvenile delinquency, focusing particularly on childhood and adolescence. Their developmental propensity theory is influenced by data collected in the Developmental Trends Study (Loeber *et al.*, 2000). Lahey and Waldman do not address adult life events or attempt to explain desistance in the adult years. They assume that it is desirable to distinguish different types of people, but they propose a continuum of developmental trajectories rather than only two categories of adolescence-limited and life-course-persistent offenders, for example.

Their key construct is antisocial propensity, which tends to persist over time and has a wide variety of behavioural manifestations, reflecting the versatility and comorbidity of antisocial behaviour. The most important factors that contribute to antisocial propensity are low cognitive ability (especially verbal ability), and three dispositional dimensions: prosociality (including sympathy and empathy, as opposed to callous-unemotional traits); daring (uninhibited or poorly controlled); and negative emotionality (e.g. easily frustrated, bored, or annoyed). These four factors are said to have a genetic basis, and Lahey and Waldman discuss gene–environment interactions.

In an important empirical test of this theory, Lahey *et al.* (2006) analysed data collected in the Pittsburgh Youth Study and found that prosociality (negatively), daring and negative emotionality at age 7 independently predicted self-reported delinquency between ages 11 and 17. Furthermore, these predictions held up after controlling for major demographic predictors of delinquency such as family income, the mother's education and ethnicity. In a later test, Lahey *et al.* (2008) developed the Child and Adolescent Dispositions Scale (CADS) to measure the three dimensions and showed that these predicted conduct disorder in three samples in Georgia, Chicago and Pittsburgh.

Moffitt: Adolescence-limited versus life-course-persistent offending

Moffitt (1993) proposed that there are two qualitatively different categories of antisocial people (differing in kind rather than in degree), namely life-course-persistent (LCP) and adolescence-limited (AL) offenders (**adolescent-limited offending** and **life-course-persistent offending**). As indicated by these terms, the LCPs start offending at an early age and persist beyond their twenties, while the ALs have a short criminal career largely limited to their teenage years. The LCPs commit a wide range of offences including violence, whereas the ALs commit predominantly 'rebellious' non-violent offences such as vandalism. This theory aims to explain findings in the Dunedin longitudinal study (Moffitt *et al.*, 2001).

adolescent-limited offending describes delinquent/antisocial behaviour that occurs during an individual's teen years, but ceases when they become adults.

life-course-persistent offending) describes delinquent/antisocial behaviour that persists throughout an individual's lifetime, often starting in childhood.

The main factors that encourage offending by the LCPs are cognitive deficits, an undercontrolled temperament, hyperactivity, poor parenting, disrupted families, teenage parents, poverty and low socio-economic status (SES). Genetic and biological factors, such as a low heart rate, are important. There is not much discussion of neighbourhood factors, but it is proposed that the neuropsychological risk of the LCPs interacts multiplicatively with a disadvantaged environment. The theory does not propose that neuropsychological deficits and a disadvantaged environment influence an underlying construct such as antisocial propensity; rather, it suggests that neuropsychological and environmental factors are the key constructs underlying antisocial behaviour.

The main factors that encourage offending by the ALs are the 'maturity gap' (their inability to achieve adult rewards such as material goods during their teenage years) and peer influence (especially from the LCPs). Consequently, the ALs stop offending when they enter legitimate adult roles and can achieve their desires legally. The ALs can easily stop because they have few neuropsychological deficits. The theory assumes that there can be labelling effects of 'snares' such as a criminal record, incarceration, drug or alcohol addiction and (for girls) unwanted pregnancy, especially for the ALs. However, the observed continuity in offending over time is largely driven by the LCPs. The theory focuses mainly on the development of offenders and does not attempt to explain why offences are committed. However, it suggests that the presence of delinquent peers is an important situational influence on ALs, and that LCPs seek out opportunities and victims.

Decision-making in criminal opportunities is supposed to be rational for the ALs (who weigh likely costs against likely benefits) but not for the LCPs (who largely follow well-learned 'automatic' behavioural repertoires without thinking). However, the LCPs are mainly influenced by utilitarian motives, whereas the ALs are influenced by teenage boredom. Adult life events such as getting a job or getting married are hypothesised to be of little importance, because the LCPs are too committed to an antisocial lifestyle and the ALs desist naturally as they age into adult roles.

Possibly because it is arguably the earliest and most famous DLC theory, there has been more empirical research on this theory than on any others. Moffitt (2006) published a very impressive review of 10 years of research on her theory. While many of the predictions were confirmed, she discussed the need for additional categories of individuals: abstainers (who were overcontrolled, fearful, sexually timid and unpopular), low-level chronics (who were undercontrolled like the LCPs, with family adversity, parental psychopathology and low intelligence) and adult-onset offenders (whose existence was doubtful according to Moffitt). She argued that the abstainers in adolescence did not become adult-onset offenders, but Zara and Farrington (2009) found that adult-onset offenders in the Cambridge study tended to be nervous and to have few friends at age 8–10, as well as still being sexual virgins at age 18.

Thornberry and Krohn: Interactional theory

The interactional theory of Thornberry and Krohn (2005) particularly focuses on factors encouraging anti-social behaviour at different ages. It is influenced by findings in the Rochester Youth Development Study (Thornberry et al., 2003). Thornberry and Krohn do not propose types of offenders but suggest that the causes of antisocial behaviour vary for children who start at different ages. At the earliest ages (birth to 6), the three most important factors are neuropsychological deficit and difficult temperament (e.g. impulsiveness, negative emotionality, fearlessness, poor emotion regulation), parenting deficits (e.g. poor monitoring, low affective ties, inconsistent discipline, physical punishment) and structural adversity (e.g. poverty, unemployment, welfare dependency, a disorganised neighbourhood). They also suggest that structural adversity might cause poor parenting.

Neuropsychological deficits are less important for children who start antisocial behaviour at older ages. At ages 6–12, neighbourhood and family factors are particularly salient, while at ages 12–18 school and peer factors dominate (Figure 2.1). Thornberry and Krohn also suggest that deviant opportunities, gangs and deviant social networks are important for onset at ages 12–18. They propose that late starters (ages 18–25) have cognitive deficits such as low intelligence and poor school performance but that they have been protected from antisocial behaviour at earlier ages by a supportive family and school environment. At ages 18–25, they find it hard to make a successful transition to adult roles such as employment and marriage.

The most distinctive feature of this interactional theory is its emphasis on reciprocal causation. For example, it is proposed that the child's antisocial behaviour elicits coercive responses from parents and rejection by peers, and makes antisocial behaviour more likely in the future. The theory does not postulate a single key construct underlying offending but suggests that children who start early tend to continue because of the persistence of neuropsychological and parenting deficits and structural adversity. Interestingly, Thornberry and Krohn predict that late starters (ages 18–25) will show more continuity over time than earlier starters (ages 12–18) because the late starters have more cognitive deficits. In an earlier exposition of the theory, Thornberry and Krohn (2001) proposed that desistance was caused by changing social influences (e.g. stronger **family bonding**), protective factors (e.g. high intelligence and school success) and intervention programmes. Hence, they think that criminal justice processing has an effect on future offending.

family bonding activities that keep parents and children in harmony, ensuring they share the same goals and attitudes within the family.

FIGURE 2.1 *At ages 6–12, neighbourhood and family factors are particularly salient, while at ages 12–18 school and peer factors dominate.*

Source: © Elena Rostunova. Used under licence from Shutterstock.

Thornberry (2005) has also extended this theory to explain the intergenerational transmission of antisocial behaviour. He suggested that the parent's prosocial or antisocial bonding, structural adversity, stressors and ineffective parenting mediated the link between the parent's antisocial behaviour and the child's antisocial behaviour. Thornberry et al. (2009) tested these ideas in the Rochester Intergenerational Study and concluded that parental stress and ineffective parenting were the most important mediating factors.

Sampson and Laub: Age-graded informal social control theory

The key construct in Sampson and Laub's (2005) theory is age-graded informal social control, which means the strength of bonding to family, peers, schools and, later, adult social institutions such as marriages and jobs. Sampson and Laub primarily aimed to explain why people do not commit offences, on the assumption that why people want to offend is unproblematic (presumably caused by hedonistic desires) and that offending is inhibited by the strength of bonding to society. Their theory is influenced by their analyses of the Glueck and Glueck (1950) follow-up study of male delinquents and non-delinquents (Laub & Sampson, 2003; Sampson & Laub, 1993).

The strength of bonding depends on attachments to parents, schools, delinquent friends and delinquent siblings, and also on parental socialisation processes such as discipline and supervision. Structural background variables (e.g. social class, ethnicity, large family size, criminal parents, disrupted families) and individual difference factors (e.g. low intelligence, difficult temperament, early conduct disorder) have indirect effects on offending through their effects on informal social control (attachment and socialisation processes).

Sampson and Laub are concerned with the whole life course. They emphasise change over time rather than consistency, and the poor ability of early childhood risk factors to predict later life outcomes. They focus on the importance of later life events (adult turning points) such as joining the military, getting a stable job and getting married, in fostering desistance and 'knifing off' the past from the present. They also suggest that neighbourhood changes can cause changes in offending. Because of their emphasis on change and unpredictability, they deny the importance of types of offenders such as 'life-course persisters'. They suggest that offending decreases with age for all types of offenders (Sampson & Laub, 2003).

Sampson and Laub do not explicitly include immediate situational influences on criminal events in their theory, and believe that opportunities are not important because they are ubiquitous (Sampson & Laub, 1995). However, they do suggest that having few structured routine activities is conducive to offending. They focus on why people do not offend rather than on why people offend, and emphasise the importance of individual free will and purposeful choice ('human agency') in the decision to desist. They also propose that official labelling influences offending through its effects on job instability and unemployment. They argue that early delinquency can cause weak adult social bonds, which in turn fail to inhibit adult offending.

In a later exposition of their theory, Sampson and Laub (2009) again argue against offender typologies and in favour of 'noisy, unpredictable development'. They contend that long-term patterns of offending cannot be explained by individual differences or childhood or adolescent characteristics, and that childhood variables are 'modest prognostic devices'. They further argue against the concept of 'developmental criminology', which they take to mean a 'predetermined unfolding', and in favour of the idea of 'life-course criminology', which (they say) refers to the constant interaction between the individual and the environment.

Happily, Sampson and Laub's predictions can be tested empirically. Our view is that childhood risk factors are better than 'modest' predictors of later offending. For example, in the Cambridge study, the percentage of boys who were convicted increased from 20 per cent of those with no childhood risk factors to 85 per cent of those with five or six childhood risk factors (Farrington, Coid et al., 2009). Similarly, in predicting adult offending, Sampson and Laub might expect that childhood variables would not predict independently of adult variables, but Farrington, Ttofi et al. (2009) found several age 8–10 variables that predicted either onset or persistence in offending after age 21. More research is clearly needed, especially contrasting the polar opposite predictions of Moffitt (1993) and Sampson and Laub (2009).

CASE STUDIES: THE CAMBRIDGE STUDY IN DELINQUENT DEVELOPMENT

The following are two cases from the Cambridge Study in Delinquent Development. Case Study 2.1 is an example of a boy who offended infrequently over a long time period, while Case Study 2.2 is an example of a boy who offended frequently over a short time period. Both cases

CASE STUDY 2.1   BOY A

This boy's parents were both aged 24 when he was born. Neither parent was convicted. He had two younger brothers, one of whom was convicted. At age 7, his father was said to be paranoid, accusing his mother of being unfaithful, and was committed to a mental hospital. At age 8, the boy was said to be obstinate, aggressively outgoing, and wandering. He was 37th out of 39 in the class, and was easily hurt by teasing. At ages 8–10, he was rated as daring

(Continued)

and unpopular but not troublesome, with a nervous or psychiatrically treated father. At age 8, his mother was said to be harsh and erratic, nagging, quick-tempered, and not in control of the children. At age 10, the social worker noted that the boy's father did not have regular work, had occasional labouring jobs but most of the time sat at home doing nothing.

At age 12, the boy's father was in and out of mental hospitals for schizophrenia and the boy was living with his father's parents. At age 13, he was thrown out and taken into care. He was said to be apathetic and living in a dream world, which was attributed to his lack of sleep. At age 14 the school report said that he was underdeveloped, withdrawn, bullied, badly dressed and unwashed. At age 14 he was living in a hostel, and his father's whereabouts were not known. At age 15, his mother was the breadwinner,

working in the civil service by day and in a bingo hall at night. After leaving school at age 15, the boy had five short-term jobs in the next four years and was sacked from all of them. He got married at age 24, had two sons, and is still living with his wife.

At age 11, he stole a comic from a market stall and was caught by the police. At age 13, the police were called because he had an airgun in the street. He was first convicted at age 16, for being carried in a stolen car. At age 19, he was convicted for stealing copper piping from a derelict house. At age 20, he was convicted of criminal damage, vandalising a police cell after he was arrested for drunk driving. At age 35, he was convicted for receiving a stolen vehicle and finally, at age 43, he was convicted for possessing a firearm without a certificate. He was fined for his offences and never received a custodial sentence.

CASE STUDY 2.2   BOY B

This boy was the youngest of four children. His parents were aged 38 (father) and 40 (mother) when he was born, and neither was convicted. He had two older brothers and one older sister, all of whom were convicted. At age 8–10, he was rated as daring and troublesome, his test results revealed low intelligence, his parents were rated as disharmonious and his mother was rated as nervous or psychiatrically treated. At age 9, the social worker recorded a hostile family atmosphere and was of the opinion that the father was a 'dictator'. The father went out drinking a lot and the mother complained about the father. The mother had got into debt. The boy was described as a non-reader, generally backward, who hung around with a gang who were often in trouble for throwing milk bottles, and so on. The father described him as a 'happy wanderer' because he stayed out late and would not say where he had been. At age 12, the boy was said to mix with other boys outside school who misbehaved. The father had a good job as a printer and the family were comfortably off.

At age 14, the notes from the boy's approved school stated that the mother was overprotective and the father was strict and punitive. The boy was described as quiet, passive, nervous and withdrawn, with an IQ of 70. His offending was attributed to parental disharmony. At age 15, the social worker noted that the father was a heavy drinker and had a duodenal ulcer, while the mother was

fussy, nervous, depressed and neglected the home, which was dirty and smelly. She worked as a cleaner, and had summonsed the father in domestic court for persistent cruelty. The boy left school at age 15. At age 16, the boy said that he had violent arguments with his father and that his father sometimes hit his mother. His father then left home but his mother then could not pay the rent and the family was evicted. His mother suffered from nerves and had a period in hospital to calm her nerves. At age 18, the boy had a well-paid job as a roofer, and went to the pub most nights and often got drunk. He got married at age 18 to his pregnant girlfriend, had five sons, and is still living with his wife.

He was first convicted at age 10, for smashing the window of a car and attempting to steal a radio. He was convicted for similar offences at ages 11 and 12, and was given a probation order. At age 13 he burgled a house, and at age 14 he was convicted for possessing an offensive weapon (a knife), at which point he was sent to an approved school. At age 16, he was convicted for stealing car tyres and wheels, and then at ages 16, 17, 18 and 19 he was convicted for stealing cars. He was given a fine or probation for these offences. Finally, he was convicted at age 20 of robbery of a valuable case of jewellery (with an accomplice who had a sawn-off shotgun) and was sentenced to 18 months in prison. He had no further convictions.

show the typically deprived, disrupted and problematic family backgrounds of delinquents, combined with individual deviance and low school attainment.

PSYCHOLOGICAL THEORIES

Psychological theories aim to explain why some individuals become offenders rather than others. They always include postulates about psychological or individual difference factors such as impulsiveness, personality factors or intelligence, and about family factors such as parental supervision or discipline. They sometimes also include postulates about biological, peer, school, community, neighbourhood and **situational factors**. Chapter 1 reviewed some psychological theories; four more will be reviewed briefly here.

> **situational factors** factors within an individual's environment that influence his/her behaviour.

Bowlby: Attachment theory

Bowlby (1969) emphasised the importance of attachment between a child and a primary caretaker (usually the mother). He argued that it was very important for a child to have a continuous, warm, loving relationship with a mother figure during the first five years of the child's life, and especially during the first two years (Figure 2.2). He further argued that mother love in infancy and childhood was just as important for mental health as were vitamins and proteins for physical health. If a child suffered a prolonged period of maternal deprivation during the first five years of life (especially a 'broken home'), this was likely to have irreversible negative effects, including becoming a cold 'affectionless character' and a delinquent.

Bowlby's theory was greatly influenced by his empirical study of 44 juvenile thieves and 44 control children referred to the same clinic for emotional problems (Bowlby, 1951). He interviewed the parents of both groups of children and found that almost 40 per cent of the juvenile thieves had been separated from their mothers for more than six months during their first five years of life, compared with only two of the controls. One third of the juvenile thieves had an 'affectionless character', compared with none of the controls. However, by modern standards, this study was methodologically poor. For example, the numbers were small, there were no controls for other variables that might have influenced delinquency, many of the children from broken homes had been reared in institutions (so the active

FIGURE 2.2 *Bowlby argued that it was very important for a child to have a continuous, warm, loving relationship with a mother figure during the first five years of the child's life, and especially during the first two years.*

Source: © Balazs Justin. Used under licence from Shutterstock.

ingredient may have been institutional rearing and constantly changing caretakers rather than a broken home), and the parents were reporting retrospectively (so their reports may have been biased by the knowledge that their child had become a delinquent).

Most studies of broken homes have focused on the loss of the father rather than the mother, because the loss of a father is much more common. In prospective longitudinal studies, it is found that children who are separated from a biological parent are more likely to offend than children from intact families. For example, in the Newcastle (UK) Thousand Family birth cohort study, Kolvin *et al.* (1988) discovered that boys who experienced divorce or separation in their first five years of life had a doubled risk of conviction up to age 32 (53 per cent as opposed to 28 per cent). In the Cambridge study, 60 per cent of boys who had been separated from a parent by their 10th birthday were convicted up to age 50, compared with 36 per cent of the remainder (Farrington, Coid *et al.*, 2009). In the Dunedin study in New Zealand,

Henry *et al.* (1996) found that boys from single-parent families were particularly likely to be convicted.

McCord (1982) in Boston carried out an innovative study of the relationship between homes broken by loss of the biological father and later serious offending by boys. She found that the prevalence of offending was high for boys from broken homes without affectionate mothers (62 per cent) and for those from unbroken homes characterised by parental conflict (52 per cent), irrespective of whether they had affectionate mothers. The prevalence of offending was low for those from unbroken homes without conflict (26 per cent) and – importantly – equally low for boys from broken homes with affectionate mothers (22 per cent). These results suggest that it might not be the broken home that is criminogenic but the parental conflict that often causes it. They also suggest that a loving mother might in some sense be able to compensate for the loss of a father.

The importance of the cause of the broken home was also shown in the UK National Survey of Health and Development by Wadsworth (1979), in which over 5000 children were followed up from birth. Illegitimate children were excluded from this survey, so all the children began life with two married parents. Boys from homes broken by divorce or separation had an increased likelihood of being convicted or officially cautioned up to age 21 (27 per cent) in comparison with those from homes broken by death of the mother (19 per cent), death of the father (14 per cent) or from unbroken homes (14 per cent). Homes broken while the boy was between birth and age 4 especially predicted delinquency, while homes broken while the boy was between ages 11 and 15 were not particularly criminogenic. Remarriage (which happened more often after divorce or separation than after death) was also associated with an increased risk of delinquency, suggesting an undesirable effect of step-parents. The meta-analysis by Wells and Rankin (1991) also shows that broken homes are more strongly related to delinquency when they are caused by parental separation or divorce rather than by death, and a more recent meta-analysis confirmed the undesirable effects of divorce (Price & Kunz, 2003).

Much research suggests that frequent changes of parent figures predict offending by children (e.g. Krohn *et al.*, 2009). For example, in a longitudinal survey of a birth cohort of over 500 Copenhagen males, Mednick *et al.* (1990) found that divorce followed by changes in parent figures predicted the highest rate of offending by children (65 per cent), compared with divorce followed by stability (42 per cent) and no divorce (28 per cent). In the Dunedin study in New Zealand, Henry *et al.* (1993) reported that both parental conflict and many changes of the child's primary caretaker predicted the child's antisocial behaviour up to age 11. Also, in the Oregon Youth Study follow-up of over 200 boys, Capaldi and Patterson (1991) concluded that antisocial mothers caused parental transitions, which in turn caused child antisocial behaviour.

Explanations of the relationship between broken homes and delinquency fall into three major classes. Trauma theories (such as Bowlby's) suggest that the loss of a parent has a damaging effect on a child, most commonly because of the effect on attachment to the parent. Life-course theories focus on separation as a sequence of stressful experiences, and on the effects of multiple stressors such as parental conflict, parental loss, reduced economic circumstances, changes in parent figures and poor childrearing methods. Selection theories argue that disrupted families produce delinquent children because of pre-existing differences from other families in risk factors such as parental conflict, criminal or antisocial parents, low family income or poor childrearing methods.

Hypotheses derived from the three theories were tested in the Cambridge study (Juby & Farrington, 2001). In agreement with Bowlby's theory, loss of the mother was more damaging than loss of the father. However, while boys from broken homes were more delinquent than boys from intact homes, they were not more delinquent than boys from intact high-conflict families. Interestingly, this result was replicated in Switzerland (Haas *et al.*, 2004). Overall, the most important factor was the post-disruption trajectory. Boys who remained with their mother after the separation had the same delinquency rate as boys from intact low-conflict families. Boys who remained with their father, with relatives or with others (e.g. foster parents) had high delinquency rates. It was concluded that the results favoured life-course theories rather than trauma or selection theories.

Eysenck: Personality theory

Psychology assumes that behaviour arises from the interaction between the individual and the environment. Studies show that behaviour is remarkably consistent over time; or, to be more precise, the relative ordering of individuals is remarkably consistent over time (Roberts & Del Vecchio, 2000). It is assumed that this behavioural consistency depends primarily on the persistence of underlying tendencies to behave in particular ways in particular situations. These tendencies are termed 'personality traits', such as impulsiveness, excitement seeking, assertiveness, modesty and dutifulness. Larger personality dimensions, such as extraversion, refer to 'clusters' of personality traits.

Before 1990, the best-known research on personality and crime was undoubtedly that inspired by the

FIGURE 2.3 *Eysenck viewed offending as natural and even rational, on the assumption that human beings were hedonistic, sought pleasure and avoided pain.*

Source: © Monkey Business Images. Used under licence from Shutterstock.

Eysenck theory and the Eysenck personality question-naires (Eysenck, 1996). He viewed offending as natural and even rational, on the assumption that human beings were hedonistic, sought pleasure and avoided pain (Figure 2.3). He assumed that delinquent acts, such as theft, violence and vandalism, were essentially pleasurable or beneficial to the offender. In order to explain why everyone was not a criminal, Eysenck suggested that the hedonistic tendency to commit crimes was opposed by the conscience, which was viewed as a conditioned fear response.

Eysenck proposed that the conscience was built up in childhood. Each time a child committed a disapproved act and was punished by a parent, the pain and fear aroused in the child tended to become associated with the act by a process of classical (automatic) conditioning. After children had been punished several times for the same act, they felt fear when they next contemplated it, and this fear tended to stop them committing it. According to the theory, this conditioned fear response was the conscience, and it would be experienced subjectively as guilt if the child committed a disapproved act.

On the Eysenck theory, people who commit offences are those who have not built up strong consciences, mainly because they have inherently poor conditionability. Poor conditionability is linked to Eysenck's three dimensions of personality: extraversion (E), neuroticism (N) and psychoticism (P). People who are high on the E dimension build up conditioned responses less well, because they have low levels of cortical arousal. People who are high on the N dimension condition less well, because their high resting level of anxiety interferes with their conditioning. Also, since N acts as a drive, reinforcing existing behavioural tendencies, neurotic extraverts should be particularly criminal. Eysenck also predicted that people who are high on P would tend to be offenders, because the traits included in his definition of psychoticism (emotional coldness, low empathy, high hostility and inhumanity) were typical of criminals. However, the meaning of the P scale is unclear, and it might perhaps be more accurately labelled as psychopathy (discussed in Chapter 1). Zuckerman (1989) suggested that the P scale should be termed 'impulsive unsocialised sensation-seeking'.

A review of studies relating Eysenck's personality dimensions to official and self-reported offending concluded that high N (but not E) was related to official offending, while high E (but not N) was related to self-reported offending (Farrington *et al.*, 1982). High P was related to both, but this could have been a tautological result, since many of the items on the P scale are connected with antisocial behaviour or were selected because of their ability to discriminate between prisoners and non-prisoners. In the Cambridge study, those high on both E and N tended to be juvenile self-reported offenders, adult official offenders and adult self-reported offenders, but not juvenile official offenders. These relationships held independently of other criminogenic risk factors such as low family income, low intelligence and poor parental childrearing behaviour. However, when individual items of the personality questionnaire were studied, it was clear that the significant relationships were mainly caused by the items measuring impulsiveness (e.g. doing things quickly without stopping to think). Hence, it seems likely that research inspired by the Eysenck theory essentially reflects the link between impulsiveness and offending.

It is generally true that impulsiveness is the most crucial personality dimension that predicts offending. Unfortunately, there are a bewildering number of constructs referring to a poor ability to control behaviour. These include impulsiveness, hyperactivity, restlessness, clumsiness, not considering consequences before acting, a poor ability to plan ahead, short time horizons, low self-control, sensation-seeking, risk-taking and a poor ability to delay gratification.

There are also many different ways of operationally defining and measuring these constructs, including psychomotor tests such as the Porteus Mazes (which measure clumsiness, motor coordination and the ability to plan ahead), self-report questionnaires (including items such as 'I often do and say things without thinking'), ratings by parents, teachers and peers, and various psychological tests (e.g. where a child chooses between a small immediate reward and a large delayed one, in order to measure the ability to delay gratification). Virtually all these constructs, measured in different ways, are consistently related to measures of offending (Blackburn, 1993, pp.191–196; Jolliffe & Farrington, 2009).

In the Cambridge study, boys nominated by teachers as lacking in concentration or restless, those nominated by parents, peers or teachers as the most daring or risk-taking, and those who were the most impulsive on psychomotor tests at age 8–10 all tended to become offenders later in life. Later self-report measures of impulsiveness were also related to offending. Daring, poor concentration and restlessness all predicted both official convictions and self-reported delinquency, and daring was consistently one of the best independent predictors (Farrington, 1992).

The most extensive research on different measures of impulsiveness was carried out in another longitudinal study of males (the Pittsburgh Youth Study) by White et al. (1994). The measures that were most strongly related to self-reported delinquency at ages 10 and 13 were teacher-rated impulsiveness (e.g. 'acts without thinking'), self-reported impulsivity, self-reported undercontrol (e.g. 'unable to delay gratification'), motor restlessness (from videotaped observations) and psychomotor impulsivity (on the Trail Making Test). Generally, the verbal behaviour rating tests produced stronger relationships with offending than the psychomotor performance tests, suggesting that cognitive impulsiveness (based on thinking processes) was more relevant than behavioural impulsiveness (based on test performance). Future time perception and delay of gratification tests were less strongly related to self-reported delinquency.

There have been many theories put forward to explain the link between impulsiveness and offending. One of the most popular suggests that impulsiveness reflects deficits in the executive functions of the brain, located in the frontal lobes. Persons with these neuropsychological deficits will tend to commit offences because they have poor control over their behaviour, a poor ability to consider the possible consequences of their acts and a tendency to focus on immediate gratification. Executive functions include sustaining attention and concentration, abstract reasoning, concept formation, goal formulation, anticipation and planning, programming and initiation of purposive sequences of motor behaviour, effective self-monitoring and self-awareness of behaviour, and inhibition of inappropriate or impulsive behaviours (Moffitt & Henry, 1991; Morgan & Lilienfeld, 2000). Interestingly, in the Montreal longitudinal-experimental study, a measure of executive functioning based on tests at age 14 was the strongest neuropsychological discriminator between violent and non-violent boys (Seguin et al., 1995). This relationship held independently of a measure of family adversity (based on parental age at first birth, parental education level, broken family and low social class).

Patterson: Social learning theory

Patterson (1982) and Patterson et al. (1992) developed a version of social learning theory focusing on ideas of coercion, based on systematic observation of interactions between parents and children. Patterson found that parents of antisocial children were deficient in their methods of childrearing. These parents failed to tell their children how they were expected to behave, failed to monitor their behaviour to ensure that it was desirable, and failed to enforce rules promptly and unambiguously with appropriate rewards and penalties. The parents of antisocial children used more punishment (such as scolding, shouting or threatening) but failed to use it consistently or make it contingent on the child's behaviour.

The basic idea of social learning theory is very simple: actions that are rewarded are more likely to occur subsequently and actions that are punished are less likely to occur subsequently. Patterson especially emphasised the importance of coercive actions by parents and children. If a parent behaves coercively towards a child (for example, by shouting or threatening), the effect depends on the reaction of the child. If the child reacts coercively (for example by yelling or arguing), and if the parent then stops being coercive, the child learns to use hostile reactions to terminate hostile situations. The main idea is that children raised in coercive families learn to use coercive behaviour. In contrast, skilful parents use positive reinforcement (rewards) for desirable behaviours and ignore or use time out (sending the child to his/her room) for undesirable behaviours. According to the theory, consistent and contingent reactions by parents, and careful monitoring of children, are effective in preventing delinquency (Snyder *et al.*, 2003).

In agreement with this theory, research shows that many different types of childrearing methods predict offending. The most important dimensions of childrearing are supervision or monitoring of children, discipline or parental reinforcement, warmth or coldness of emotional relationships, and parental involvement with children. Parental supervision refers to the degree of monitoring by parents of the child's activities, and their degree of watchfulness or vigilance. Of all these childrearing methods, poor parental supervision is usually the strongest and most replicable predictor of offending (Smith & Stern, 1997). Many studies show that parents who do not know where their children are when they are out, and parents who let their children roam the streets unsupervised from an early age, tend to have delinquent children. For example, in McCord's (1979) classic Cambridge-Somerville study in Boston, poor parental supervision in childhood was the best predictor of both violent and property crimes up to age 45.

Parental discipline refers to how parents react to a child's behaviour. It is clear that harsh or punitive discipline (involving physical punishment) predicts offending (Haapasalo & Pokela, 1999). In their follow-up study of nearly 700 Nottingham children, John and Elizabeth Newson (1989) found that physical punishment at ages 7 and 11 predicted later convictions; 40 per cent of offenders had been smacked or beaten at age 11, compared with 14 per cent of non-offenders. Erratic or inconsistent discipline also predicts delinquency. This can involve either erratic discipline by one parent, sometimes turning a blind eye to bad behaviour and sometimes punishing it severely, or inconsistency between two parents, with one parent being tolerant or indulgent and the other being harshly punitive.

The classic longitudinal study by Robins (1979) in St Louis shows that poor parental supervision, harsh discipline and a rejecting attitude all predict delinquency. Similar results were obtained in the Cambridge study.

Harsh or erratic parental discipline, cruel, passive or neglecting parental attitudes and poor parental supervision, all measured at age 8, all predicted later juvenile convictions and self-reported delinquency (West & Farrington, 1973). Generally, the presence of any of these adverse family background features doubled the risk of a later juvenile conviction.

Patterson applied his theory by developing parent management training. He aimed to train antisocial parents in effective childrearing methods, namely noticing what a child is doing, monitoring behaviour over long periods, clearly stating house rules, making rewards and punishments contingent on behaviour, and negotiating disagreements so that conflicts and crises did not escalate. His treatment was shown to be effective in reducing child stealing and antisocial behaviour over short periods (Dishion *et al.*, 1992; Patterson *et al.*, 1982). Other types of parent training, such as those devised by Webster-Stratton (2000) in Seattle, and by Sanders *et al.* (2000) in Brisbane, Australia, are also effective in reducing child antisocial behaviour (see Piquero *et al.*, 2009).

Walters: Lifestyle theory

Walters (2006) proposed a theory that mainly aimed to explain the development of a criminal lifestyle and subsequent change and desistance processes. He defined the principal features of a criminal lifestyle as including social rule-breaking (e.g. offending), irresponsibility (e.g. in jobs and relationships), self-indulgence (e.g. in substance abuse, tattoos) and interpersonal intrusiveness (e.g. in violence). This lifestyle was linked to certain cognitions, self-beliefs, and thinking styles (Walters, 2002). His functional model explained how this lifestyle developed, focusing on hedonistic motivation, excitement-seeking, a desire for personal advantage, and constructive or defensive reactions to fears and threats. Defensive reactions include aggression, withdrawal, immobilisation and appeasement. Finally, his change model explained how people gave up the criminal lifestyle, focusing on changes in self-concept, taking responsibility, increases in self-confidence and understanding the impact of actions on other people.

Much research suggests that offending is one element of a larger constellation of social problems of males, termed 'the delinquent way of life' by West and Farrington (1977). They concluded (p.78):

Judging by their own accounts, delinquents are less conforming and less socially restrained than non-delinquents, and this difference shows up in all aspects of their lives. They are more immoderate in their smoking, drinking, gambling and sexual habits. They more often become violent after drinking. They drive more recklessly and are more likely to sustain injuries. They are more often spendthrifts. They show little interest in reading or in further education. Their work records are much less stable. They earn more per week, but are in jobs with poor prospects. They mix more with all-male groups of the kind that gets into trouble. They spend more of their leisure time away from home, and indulge more often in seemingly aimless 'hanging about'. They more often take prohibited drugs. They express more pro-aggressive and anti-establishment sentiments in response to an attitude questionnaire. They are more often in conflict with or alienated from their parental home. They are readier to adopt the dress styles and ornaments, notably tattoos, associated with anti-establishment attitudes. [Also] delinquents are more aggressive than non-delinquents in behaviour as well as in verbally expressed attitudes.

Much research on desistance is concordant with the Walters lifestyle theory (Kazemian & Farrington, 2010). For example, according to Gove (1985), desistance from crime is a result of five key internal changes: shifting from self-centredness to consideration for others; developing prosocial values and behaviour; increasing ease in social interactions; greater consideration for other members of the community; and a growing concern for the 'meaning of life'. Giordano et al. (2002) discussed the theory of cognitive transformation, which is defined as cognitive shifts that promote the process of desistance. They described four processes of cognitive transformations. First, the offender must be open to change. Second, through a process of self-selection, individuals expose themselves to prosocial experiences that will further promote desistance (e.g., employment, marriage). Third, the individual adheres to a new prosocial and noncriminal identity. Finally, there is a shift in the perception of the criminal lifestyle, so that the negative consequences of offending become obvious.

THE ICAP THEORY

The integrated cognitive antisocial potential (ICAP) theory (Figure 2.4) was primarily designed to explain offending by lower-class males, and it was influenced by results obtained in the Cambridge study (Farrington, 2005b). It integrates ideas from many other theories, including strain, control, learning, labelling and rational choice approaches (see Cote, 2002); its key construct is antisocial potential (AP) and it assumes that the translation from antisocial potential to antisocial behaviour

depends on cognitive (thinking and decision-making) processes that take account of opportunities and victims. Figure 2.4 is deliberately simplified in order to show the key elements of the ICAP theory on one page; for example, it does not show how the processes operate differently for onset compared with desistance or at different ages.

The key construct underlying offending is antisocial potential (AP), which refers to the potential to commit antisocial acts. 'Offending' refers to the most common crimes of theft, burglary, robbery, violence, vandalism, minor fraud and drug use, and to behaviour that in principle might lead to a conviction in Western industrialised societies such as the USA and the UK. Long-term persisting between-individual differences in AP are distinguished from short-term within-individual variations in AP. Long-term AP depends on impulsiveness, on strain, modelling and socialisation processes, and on life events, while short-term variations in AP depend on motivating and situational factors.

Regarding long-term AP, people can be ordered on a continuum from low to high. The distribution of AP in the population at any age is highly skewed; relatively few people have relatively high levels of AP. People with high AP are more likely to commit many different types of antisocial acts, including different types of offences. Therefore, offending and antisocial behaviour are versatile rather than specialised. The relative ordering of people on AP (long-term between-individual variation) tends to be consistent over time, but absolute levels of AP vary with age, peaking in the teenage years, because of changes within individuals in the factors that influence long-term AP (e.g. from childhood to adolescence, the increasing importance of peers and decreasing importance of parents).

In the interests of simplification, Figure 2.4 makes the ICAP theory appear static rather than dynamic. For example, it does not explain changes in offending at different ages. Since it might be expected that different factors would be important at different ages or life stages, it seems likely that different models would be needed at different ages. Perhaps parents are more important in influencing children, peers are more important in influencing adolescents, and spouses and partners are more important in influencing adults (Theobald & Farrington, 2009).

Long-term risk factors

A great deal is known about risk factors that predict long-term persisting between-individual differences in antisocial potential. For example, in the Cambridge study, the most important childhood risk factors for later offending were hyperactivity-impulsivity-attention deficit, low intelligence or low school attainment, family criminality,

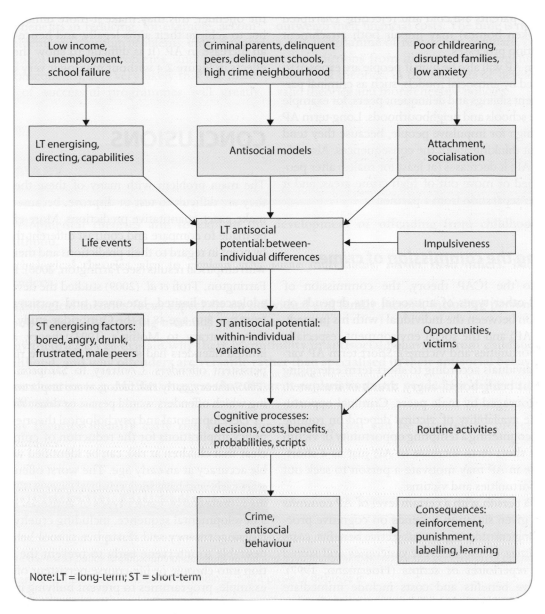

FIGURE 2.4 *The integrated cognitive antisocial potential (ICAP) theory.*

family poverty, large family size, poor childrearing and disrupted families (Farrington, 2003). Figure 2.4 shows how risk factors are hypothesised to influence long-term AP. This figure could be expanded to specify protective factors and study different influences on onset, persistence, escalation, de-escalation and desistance.

Following strain theory, the main energising factors that potentially lead to high long-term AP are desires for material goods, status among intimates, excitement and sexual satisfaction. However, these motivations only lead to high AP if antisocial methods of satisfying them are habitually chosen. Antisocial methods tend to be chosen by people who find it difficult to satisfy their needs legitimately, such as people with low income, unemployed

people and those who fail at school. However, the methods chosen also depend on physical capabilities and behavioural skills; for example, a 5-year-old would have difficulty in stealing a car. For simplicity, energising and directing processes and capabilities are shown in one box in Figure 2.4.

Long-term AP also depends on attachment and socialisation processes. AP will be low if parents consistently and contingently reward good behaviour and punish bad behaviour. (Withdrawal of love may be a more effective method of socialisation than hitting children.) Children with low anxiety will be less well socialised, because they care less about parental punishment. AP will be high if children are not attached to (prosocial) parents,

Farrington, D.P. (Ed.) (2005a). *Integrated developmental and life-course theories of offending*. New Brunswick, NJ: Transaction.

Farrington, D.P. (2005b). The Integrated Cognitive Antisocial Potential (ICAP) theory. In D.P. Farrington (Ed.) *Integrated developmental and life-course theories of offending* (pp.73–92). New Brunswick, NJ: Transaction.

Farrington, D.P. (2006). Building developmental and life-course theories of offending. In F.T. Cullen, J.P. Wright & K.R. Blevins (Eds.) *Taking stock: The status of criminological theory* (pp.335–364). New Brunswick, NJ: Transaction.

Farrington, D.P. (2007). Childhood risk factors and risk-focussed prevention. In M. Maguire, R. Morgan & R. Reiner (Eds.) *The Oxford handbook of criminology* (4th edn) (pp.602–640). Oxford: Oxford University Press.

Farrington, D.P., Biron, L. & LeBlanc, M. (1982). Personality and delinquency in London and Montreal. In J. Gunn & D.P. Farrington (Eds.) *Abnormal offenders, delinquency, and the criminal justice system* (pp.153–203). Chichester: John Wiley & Sons, Inc.

Farrington, D.P., Coid, J.W., Harnett, L., Jolliffe, D., Soteriou, N., Turner, R. & West, D.J. (2006). *Criminal careers up to age 50 and life success up to age 48: New findings from the Cambridge Study in Delinquent Development*. London: Home Office (Research Study No. 299).

Farrington, D.P., Coid, J.W. & West, D.J. (2009). The development of offending from age 8 to age 50: Recent findings from the Cambridge Study in Delinquent Development. *Monatsschrift für Kriminologie und Strafrechtsreform (Journal of Criminology and Penal Reform), 92*, 160–173.

Farrington, D.P., Loeber, R., Yin, Y. & Anderson, S.J. (2002). Are within-individual causes of delinquency the same as between-individual causes? *Criminal Behaviour and Mental Health, 12*, 53–68.

Farrington, D.P., Ttofi, M.M. & Coid, J.W. (2009). Development of adolescence-limited, late-onset and persistent offenders from age 8 to age 48. *Aggressive Behavior, 35*, 150–163.

Giordano, P.C., Cernkovich, S.A. & Rudolph, J.L. (2002). Gender, crime, and desistance: Toward a theory of cognitive transformation. *American Journal of Sociology, 107*, 990–1064.

Glueck, S. & Glueck, E.T. (1950). *Unraveling juvenile delinquency*. New York: Commonwealth Fund.

Gove, W. (1985). The effect of age and gender on deviant behavior: A biopsychological perspective. In A.S. Rossi (Ed.) *Gender and the life course* (pp.115–144). New York: Aldine.

Haapasalo, J. & Pokela, E. (1999). Child-rearing and child abuse antecedents of criminality. *Aggression and Violent Behavior, 1*, 107–127.

Haas, H., Farrington, D.P., Killias, M. & Sattar, G. (2004). The impact of different family configurations on delinquency. *British Journal of Criminology, 44*, 520–532.

Hawkins, J.D., Smith, B.H., Hill, K.G., Kosterman, R., Catalano, R.F. & Abbott, R.D. (2003). Understanding and preventing crime and violence: Findings from the Seattle Social Development Project. In T. P. Thornberry & M.D. Krohn (Eds.) *Taking stock of delinquency: An overview of findings from contemporary longitudinal studies* (pp.255–312). New York: Kluwer/Plenum.

Henry, B., Caspi, A., Moffitt, T.E. & Silva, P.A. (1996). Temperamental and familial predictors of violent and nonviolent criminal convictions: Age 3 to age 18. *Developmental Psychology, 32*, 614–623.

Henry, B., Moffitt, T.E., Robins, L., Earls, F. & Silva, P.A. (1993). Early family predictors of child and adolescent antisocial behaviour: Who are the mothers of delinquents? *Criminal Behaviour and Mental Health, 3*, 97–118.

Huesmann, L.R. (1997). Observational learning of violent behavior: Social and biosocial processes. In A. Raine, P.A. Brennan, D.P. Farrington & S.A. Mednick (Eds.) *Biosocial bases of violence* (pp.69–88). New York: Plenum.

Huizinga, D., Weiher, A.W., Espiritu, R. & Esbensen, F. (2003). Delinquency and crime: Some highlights from the Denver Youth Survey. In T.P. Thornberry & M.D. Krohn (Eds.) *Taking stock of delinquency: An overview of findings from contemporary longitudinal studies* (pp.47–91). New York: Kluwer/Plenum.

Jolliffe, D. & Farrington, D.P. (2009). A systematic review of the relationship between childhood impulsiveness and later violence. In M. McMurran & R. Howard (Eds.) *Personality, personality disorder, and violence* (pp.41–61). Chichester: John Wiley & Sons, Inc.

Juby, H. & Farrington, D.P. (2001). Disentangling the link between disrupted families and delinquency. *British Journal of Criminology, 41*, 22–40.

Kazemian, L. & Farrington, D.P. (2010). The developmental evidence base: Desistance. In G.J. Towl & D.A. Crighton (Eds.) *Forensic psychology* (pp.133–147). Oxford: Blackwell.

Kolvin, I., Miller, F.J.W., Fleeting, M. & Kolvin, P.A. (1988). Social and parenting factors affecting criminal-offence rates: Findings from the Newcastle Thousand Family Study (1947–1980). *British Journal of Psychiatry, 152*, 80–90.

Krohn, M.D., Hall, G.P. & Lizotte, A.J. (2009). Family transitions and later delinquency and drug use. *Journal of Youth and Adolescence, 38*, 466–480.

Lahey, B.B., Applegate, B., Chronis, A.M., Jones, H.A., Williams, S.H., Loney, J. & Waldman, I.D. (2008). Psychometric characteristics of a measure of emotional dispositions developed to test a developmental propensity model of conduct disorder. *Journal of Clinical Child and Adolescent Psychology, 37*, 794–807.

Lahey, B.B., Loeber, R., Waldman, I.D. & Farrington, D.P. (2006). Child socioemotional dispositions at school entry that predict adolescent delinquency and violence. *Impuls: Tidsskrift for Psykologi, 3*, 40–51.

Lahey, B.B. & Waldman, I.D. (2005). A developmental model of the propensity to offend during childhood and adolescence. In D.P. Farrington (Ed.) *Integrated developmental and life-course theories of offending* (pp.15–50). New Brunswick, NJ: Transaction.

Laub, J.H. & Sampson, R.J. (2003). *Shared beginnings, divergent lives: Delinquent boys to age 70*. Cambridge, MA: Harvard University Press.

Loeber, R., Farrington, D.P., Stouthamer-Loeber, M., Moffitt., T.E., Caspi, A., White, H.R., Wei, E.H. & Beyers, J.M. (2003). The development of male offending: Key findings from fourteen years of the Pittsburgh Youth Study. In T.P. Thornberry & M.D. Krohn (Eds.) *Taking stock of delinquency: An overview of findings from contemporary longitudinal studies* (pp.93–136), New York: Kluwer/Plenum.

Loeber, R., Green, S.M., Lahey, B.B., Frick, P.J. & McBurnett, K. (2000). Findings on disruptive behavior disorders from the first decade of the Developmental Trends Study. *Clinical Child and Family Psychology Review, 3,* 37–60.

McCord, J. (1979). Some child-rearing antecedents of criminal behavior in adult men. *Journal of Personality and Social Psychology, 37,* 1477–1486.

McCord, J. (1982). A longitudinal view of the relationship between paternal absence and crime. In J. Gunn & D.P. Farrington (Eds.) *Abnormal offenders, delinquency, and the criminal justice system* (pp.113–128). Chichester: John Wiley & Sons, Inc.

Mednick, B.R., Baker, R.L. & Carothers, L.E. (1990). Patterns of family instability and crime: The association of timing of the family's disruption with subsequent adolescent and young adult criminality. *Journal of Youth and Adolescence, 19,* 201–220.

Moffitt, T.E. (1993). Adolescence-limited and life-course-persistent antisocial behavior: A developmental taxonomy. *Psychological Review, 100,* 674–701.

Moffitt, T.E. (2006) Life-course persistent and adolescent-limited antisocial behavior. In D. Cicchetti & D.J. Cohen (Eds.) *Developmental psychopathology, Vol. 3: Risk, disorder, and adaptation* (pp.570–598). New York: John Wiley & Sons, Inc.

Moffitt, T.E., Caspi, A., Rutter, M. & Silva, P.A. (2001). *Sex differences in antisocial behaviour: Conduct disorder, delinquency, and violence in the Dunedin longitudinal study.* Cambridge: Cambridge University Press.

Moffitt, T.E. & Henry, B. (1991). Neuropsychological studies of juvenile delinquency and juvenile violence. In J.S. Milner (Ed.) *Neuropsychology of aggression* (pp.131–146). Boston: Kluwer.

Morgan, A.B. & Lilienfeld, S.O. (2000). A meta-analytic review of the relation between antisocial behavior and neuropsychological measures of executive function. *Clinical Psychology Review, 20,* 113–136.

Newson, J. & Newson, E. (1989). *The extent of parental physical punishment in the UK.* London: Approach.

Patterson, G.R. (1982). *Coercive family process.* Eugene, OR: Castalia.

Patterson, G.R., Chamberlain, P. & Reid, J.B. (1982). A comparative evaluation of a parent training program. *Behavior Therapy, 13,* 638–650.

Patterson, G.R., Reid, J.B. & Dishion, T.J. (1992). *Antisocial boys.* Eugene, OR: Castalia.

Piquero, A., Farrington, D.P., Welsh, B.C., Tremblay, R.E. & Jennings, W.G. (2009). Effects of early family/parent training programs on antisocial behavior and delinquency. *Journal of Experimental Criminology, 5,* 83–120.

Price, C. & Kunz, J. (2003). Rethinking the paradigm of juvenile delinquency as related to divorce. *Journal of Divorce and Remarriage, 39,* 109–133.

Roberts, B.W. & Del Vecchio, W.F. (2000). The rank order consistency of personality traits from childhood to old age: A quantitative review of longitudinal studies. *Psychological Bulletin, 126,* 3–25.

Robins, L.N. (1979). Sturdy childhood predictors of adult outcomes: Replications from longitudinal studies. In J.E. Barrett, R.M. Rose & G.L. Klerman (Eds.) *Stress and mental disorder* (pp.219–235). New York: Raven Press.

Sampson, R.J. & Laub, J.H. (1993). *Crime in the making: Pathways and turning points through life.* Cambridge, MA: Harvard University Press.

Sampson, R.J. & Laub, J.H. (1995). Understanding variability in lives through time: Contributions of life-course criminology. *Studies on Crime and Crime Prevention, 4,* 143–158.

Sampson, R.J. & Laub, J.H. (2003). Life-course desisters? Trajectories of crime among delinquent boys followed to age 70. *Criminology, 41,* 555–592.

Sampson, R.J. & Laub, J.H. (2005). A general age-graded theory of crime: Lessons learned and the future of life-course criminology. In D.P. Farrington (Ed.) *Integrated developmental and life-course theories of offending* (pp.165–181). New Brunswick, NJ: Transaction.

Sampson, R.J. & Laub, J.H. (2009). A life-course theory and long-term project on trajectories of crime. *Monatsschrift fur Kriminologie und Strafrechtsreform (Journal of Criminology and Penal Reform), 92,* 226–239.

Sanders, M.R., Markie-Dadds, C., Tully, L.A. & Bor, W. (2000). The Triple P – Positive Parenting Program: A comparison of enhanced, standard and self-directed behavioral family intervention for parents of children with early onset conduct problems. *Journal of Consulting and Clinical Psychology, 68,* 624–640.

Seguin, J., Pihl, R.O., Harden, P.W., Tremblay, R.E. & Boulerice, B. (1995). Cognitive and neuropsychological characteristics of physically aggressive boys. *Journal of Abnormal Psychology, 104,* 614–624.

Smith, C.A. & Stern, S.B. (1997). Delinquency and antisocial behavior: A review of family processes and intervention research. *Social Service Review, 71,* 382–420.

Snyder, J., Reid, J. & Patterson, G.R. (2003). A social learning model of child and adolescent antisocial behaviour. In B.B. Lahey, T.E. Moffitt & A. Caspi (Eds.) *Causes of conduct disorder and juvenile delinquency* (pp.27–48). New York: Guilford.

Theobald, D. & Farrington, D.P. (2009). Effects of getting married on offending: Results from a prospective longitudinal survey of males. *European Journal of Criminology, 6,* 496–516.

Thornberry, T.P. (2005). Explaining multiple patterns of offending across the life course and across generations. *Annals of the American Academy of Political and Social Science, 602,* 156–195.

Thornberry, T.P., Freeman-Gallant, A. & Lovegrove, P.J. (2009). Intergenerational linkages in antisocial behaviour. *Criminal Behaviour and Mental Health, 19*, 80–93.

Thornberry, T.P. & Krohn, M.D. (2001). The development of delinquency: An interactional perspective. In S.O. White (Ed.) *Handbook of youth and justice* (pp.289–305). New York: Plenum.

Thornberry, T.P. & Krohn, M.D. (2005). Applying interactional theory to the explanation of continuity and change in antisocial behavior. In D.P. Farrington (Ed.) *Integrated developmental and life-course theories of offending* (pp.183–209). New Brunswick, NJ: Transaction.

Thornberry, T.P., Lizotte, A.J., Krohn, M.D., Smith, C.A. & Porter, P.K. (2003). Causes and consequences of delinquency: Findings from the Rochester Youth Development Study. In T.P. Thornberry & M.D. Krohn (Eds.) *Taking stock of delinquency: An overview of findings from contemporary longitudinal studies* (pp.11–46). New York: Kluwer/Plenum.

Tremblay, R.E., Vitaro, F., Nagin, D., Pagani, L. & Seguin, J.R. (2003). The Montreal longitudinal and experimental study: Rediscovering the power of descriptions. In T.P. Thornberry & M.D. Krohn (Eds.) *Taking stock of delinquency: An overview of findings from contemporary longitudinal studies* (pp.205–254). New York: Kluwer/Plenum.

Ttofi, M.M. & Farrington, D.P. (2011). Effectiveness of school-based programs to reduce bullying: A systematic and meta-analytic review. *Journal of Experimental Criminology, 7*, 27–56.

Wadsworth, M. (1979). *Roots of delinquency.* London: Martin Robertson.

Walters, G.D. (2002). The Psychological Inventory of Criminal Thinking Styles (PICTS): A review and meta-analysis. *Assessment, 9*, 278–291.

Walters, G.D. (2006). *Lifestyle theory: Past, present and future.* New York: Nova Science Publishers.

Webster-Stratton, C. (2000). *The Incredible Years training series.* Washington, DC: Office of Juvenile Justice and Delinquency Prevention.

Wells, L.E. & Rankin, J.H. (1991). Families and delinquency: A meta-analysis of the impact of broken homes. *Social Problems, 38*, 71–93.

West, D.J. & Farrington, D.P. (1973). *Who becomes delinquent?* London: Heinemann.

West, D.J. & Farrington, D.P. (1977). *The delinquent way of life.* London: Heinemann.

White, J.L., Moffitt, T.E., Caspi, A., Bartusch, D.J., Needles, D.J. & Stouthamer-Loeber, M. (1994). Measuring impulsivity and examining its relationship to delinquency. *Journal of Abnormal Psychology, 103*, 192–205.

Zara, G. & Farrington, D.P. (2009). Childhood and adolescent predictors of late onset criminal careers. *Journal of Youth and Adolescence, 38*, 287–300.

Zuckerman, M. (1989). Personality in the third dimension: A psychobiological approach. *Personality and Individual Differences, 10*, 391–418.

ANNOTATED READING LIST

Cullen, F.T. & Wilcox, P. (Eds.) (2010). *Encyclopedia of criminological theory* (two volumes). Los Angeles, CA: Sage. *This exhaustive encyclopaedia includes entries on social learning theory, rational choice theory, crime and personality, the ICAP theory, biosocial theory, self-control theory, psychopathy, moral development theory, developmental propensity theory, developmental pathways, adolescence-limited versus life-course-persistent offending, age-graded informal social control, lifestyle theory, situational action theory and many other topics. It is hard to think of any criminological theory that is not described here!*

Farrington, D.P. (Ed.) (1994). *Psychological explanations of crime.* Aldershot: Dartmouth. *This book reviews theories focusing on individual factors (including the Eysenck personality theory, impulsiveness and low self-control), theories focusing on family factors (including Trasler's social learning theory) and theories focusing on peer, school and situational factors.*

Farrington, D.P (Ed.) (2005). *Integrated developmental and life-course theories of offending.* New Brunswick, NJ: Transaction. *This book presents accounts of eight major developmental and life-course theories of offending, by Lahey and Waldman, Piquero and Moffitt, Farrington, Catalano and colleagues, LeBlanc, Sampson and Laub, Thornberry and Krohn, and Wikstrom. It also includes an introduction and conclusion that provide more information about the theories and compare them.*

Farrington, D.P. & Welsh, B.C. (2007). *Saving children from a life of crime.* Oxford: Oxford University Press. *This book reviews what is known about individual, family, socio-economic, peer, school and community influences on offending, and then what is known about individual, family, peer, school and community prevention of offending.*

Lahey, B.B., Moffitt, T.E. & Caspi, A. (Eds.) (2003). *Causes of conduct disorder and delinquency.* New York: Guilford Press. *The chapters in this book present theories by Patterson, Moffitt, Lahey, Wikstrom and Sampson, together with chapters on the development of antisocial behaviour and physical aggression, cognitive factors, biological influences, and animal models of the causes of aggression.*

Wortley, R. (2011). *Psychological criminology.* London: Routledge. *This book reviews biological, personality, developmental, learning, cognition and situational theories of offending.*

3 Contributions of Forensic Neuroscience

Anthony Beech, Benjamin Nordstrom and Adrian Raine

KEY TERMS

- ACE model • conduct disorder (CD) • foetal alcohol syndrome (FAS) • monozygotic (MZ)/dizygotic (DZ) twins
- theory of mind (ToM) • traumatic brain injury (TBI)

CHAPTER OUTLINE

The aim of this chapter is to investigate the contribution of forensic neuroscience to the understanding of the aetiology of criminal behaviours. In the first section of this chapter we consider how disturbances in the neurobiological processes through which *prenatal* and *postnatal* risk factors, and *problematic upbringings*, sometimes in combination with *genetic* factors, can potentiate the probability of offending. Next we will examine in some detail such risk factors in antisocial disorders, which account for the majority of offending, such as *psychopathy* and *antisocial personality disorder* (ASPD). In this section we will also briefly examine *conduct disorder* (CD), which is often identified as a precursor of ASPD. Then, we will examine what effects the risk factors outlined in the first section of the chapter have on critical areas of the brain, particularly the *amygdala*, the *insular*, the *orbital prefrontal cortex* and the *anterior cingulate cortex,* and how problems in these areas may in part lead to psychopathy, antisocial personality disorder (ASPD), and conduct disorder (CD). Finally, we will examine some of the techniques that have been used to investigate problematic brain structure and functioning in offenders.

We will now examine such risk factors in more detail, broken down into those that arise during pregnancy (prenatal), those that arise during birth (perinatal) and environmental postnatal factors, as well as adverse upbringing. Case Study 3.1 is illustrative of the kind of risk factors observed in the histories of many dangerous offenders (see the next section).

DEVELOPMENTAL RISK FACTORS AND OFFENDING

Prenatal factors

These are subtle physical defects such as having a curved little finger, a single palmar crease, low-seated ears or a furrowed tongue, which are thought to arise from abnormalities in foetal development. These are also thought to serve as biomarkers for abnormalities in neural development. Such *minor physical anomalies* (MPAs) may have a genetic

CASE STUDY 3.1   D.P.

A young woman was brutally attacked in her own home in the USA while her roommates were out. After a brutal physical assault in which she was punched and slashed with a knife, her attacker tied her hands with a lamp cord in her bedroom and ransacked her house and car. He returned to her room where he raped her, slashed her throat and then stabbed her in the chest, killing her. Shortly after, he was apprehended by the police. The young woman's murderer was identified as D.P., a 24-year-old man with a prior history of violent crime. His defence team did not deny that he had committed the murder, but argued that the crime was impulsive and opportunistic. The prosecution argued that his crime was predatory and premeditated and amounted to first-degree murder, a capital crime in the US state where the offence occurred. After the jury found D.P. guilty of first-degree murder, information was provided at the sentencing portion of his hearing to try to mitigate the sentence in order to avoid execution by lethal injection. D.P.'s defence team continued to assert that his crimes were not premeditated and, thus, did not rise to the level of blameworthiness that would warrant execution. They further posited that executing someone for a brash, impulsive act 'lowered the bar' for execution and made capital punishment too available for future cases. The prosecution

advanced the case that D.P. was a cold-blooded, predatory murderer who should receive the most severe sanction possible.

Information from D.P.'s history showed that he had been born to a single, teenage mother. In the first two years of his life he was admitted to hospital emergency rooms five times, including for injuries related to having been shaken violently for crying too much. He was also noted to have eaten paint chips as a baby. His later childhood medical history revealed treatment for severe physical and sexual abuse. One medical appointment recorded his resting heart rate at 60 beats per minute, which put him in the third percentile for his age. School records showed a history of disruptive behaviour and poor performance. Social services records reported that his mother was frequently absent, and that he slept in abandoned buildings in a dangerous, inner-city environment. Neuropsychological testing revealed that he had notable executive functioning deficiencies and evidence of right hemispheric dysfunction. When a PET scan was performed it showed dramatic reductions in blood flow to his bilateral prefrontal cortices. Due to the combined influence of these biopsychosocial risk factors, D.P. was spared the death sentence and was instead given a life sentence.

basis, but they might also be due to anoxia, bleeding or infection (Guy *et al.*, 1983). Early studies have showed an increase in the prevalence of MPAs in school-aged boys exhibiting behavioural problems (Halverson & Victor, 1976). MPAs have also been shown to be correlated with aggressive behaviours in children as young as 3 years of age (Waldrop *et al.*, 1978). It has also been shown that MPAs identified at age 14 predict violence at age 17 (Arsenault *et al.*, 2002). Similarly, a study of 72 male offspring of psychiatrically ill parents found that those with both MPAs and family adversity had especially high rates of adult violent offending (Brennan *et al.*, 1997). Another study showed that the presence of MPAs significantly interacted with environmental risk factors (e.g. poverty, marital conflict) to predict conduct problems in adolescence (Pine *et al.*, 1997).

There is a significant body of evidence that demonstrates that *maternal smoking* during pregnancy predisposes children towards developing antisocial behaviour (Wakschlag *et al.*, 2002). Maternal prenatal smoking predicts externalising behaviours in childhood and criminal behaviour in adolescence (Fergusson *et al.*, 1998; Orlebeke *et al.*, 1997; Wakschlag *et al.*, 1997). Researchers have also identified a clear dose-dependent relationship between smoking and later criminal behaviour: the greater the amount of smoking by the mother during pregnancy, the greater the risk of criminality in later life for the child (Figure 3.1, Brennan *et al.*, 1999; Maughan *et al.*, 2004). Although the mechanism by which smoking produces these effects is unknown, basic science research has shown that the byproducts of smoking may affect the brain's dopaminergic and noradrenergic systems (Muneoka *et al.*, 1997) and glucose metabolism (Eckstein *et al.*, 1997). Smoking may also affect various brain structures including the basal ganglia, cerebral and cerebellar cortices, which are implicated in the deficits observed in violent offenders (Olds, 1997; Raine, 2002). There is also a great deal of evidence that *prenatal exposure to alcohol* predisposes individuals to antisocial behaviour (Fast *et al.*, 1999; Olson *et al.*, 1997; Streissguth *et al.*, 1996).

foetal alcohol syndrome (FAS) is not a uniform clinical picture, but a spectrum of disorders, varying in severity.

Foetal alcohol syndrome (FAS) does not arise in all children exposed to alcohol *in utero*, and evidence shows that children who do not display the full FAS syndrome can still have some of the functional deficits characteristic of the syndrome (Schonfeld *et al.*, 2005). Children who did not meet diagnostic criteria for FAS yet were exposed to high levels of alcohol *in utero* were at increased risk of antisocial behaviour (Roebuck *et al.*, 1999).

Perinatal risk factors

Obstetrical complications are untoward events that occur at the time of delivery and include: maternal pre-eclampsia

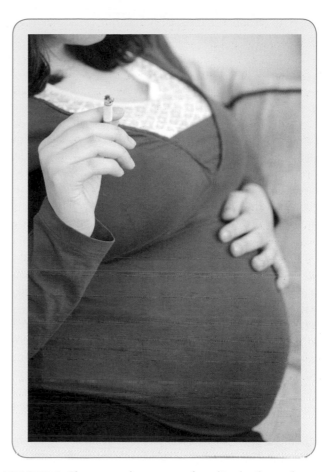

FIGURE 3.1 *The greater the amount of smoking by the mother during pregnancy, the greater the risk of criminality for the child in later life.*

Source: © Zurijeta. Used under licence from Shutterstock.

(a medical condition in which hypertension arises in pregnancy); premature birth; low birth weight; use of forceps in delivery; transfer to a neonatal intensive care unit; anoxia; and low Apgar scores (a measure of post-birth wellbeing for the baby). Maternal complications have been shown to have deleterious effects on neonatal brain function (Liu 2004; Liu & Wuerker, 2005). Newborn babies who suffer obstetrical complications are also more likely to exhibit externalising behaviours at age 11 than those without complications. Obstetrical complications were found to mediate the relationship between low IQ and externalising behaviours (Liu *et al.*, 2009).

Raine, Brennan *et al.* (1994) investigated a cohort of 4269 Danish men and found that obstetrical complications significantly interacted with *severe maternal rejection* (e.g. efforts to abort the pregnancy, reporting the pregnancy as unwanted, or attempting to give up custody of the baby) to predict violent crime in adolescence. These findings have since been replicated in the USA, Sweden, Finland, and Canada, and it has been repeatedly shown that birth complications interact with a number of psychosocial risk factors to produce antisocial behaviour (Hodgins *et al.*, 2001; Kemppainen *et al.*, 2001; Tibbetts & Piquero, 1999).

Postnatal risk factors

Poor nutrition has been investigated as a risk factor for criminal behaviour for some time (Breakey, 1997; Werbach, 1995). The exact mechanism by which malnutrition later affects antisocial behaviour is not well understood. It has been hypothesised that proteins, or minerals, may either regulate neurotransmitters and hormones, or ameliorate neurotoxins (Coccaro *et al.*, 1997; Liu & Raine, 2006). Studies have also shown that deficiencies in nutrients such as proteins, zinc, iron and docosahexaenoic acid (a component of omega 3 fatty acid) can lead to impaired brain functioning and a predisposition to antisocial behaviour in childhood and adolescence (Arnold *et al.*, 2000; Lister *et al.*, 2005; Rosen *et al.*, 1985).

Although most studies have focused on nutrition in the postnatal period, one study investigated the role of malnutrition in the prenatal period in producing antisocial behaviour (Neugebauer *et al.*, 1999). This group studied the offspring of women who were pregnant during the German food blockade of Dutch cities in World War II. The blockade produced near starvation and severe food shortages. The researchers found that the male offspring of women who were in the first and second trimesters (but not the third trimester) of pregnancy during this time had 2.5 times the rate of antisocial personality disorder than did the offspring of women who were not affected by food shortages. Another study of prenatal nutrition studied a sample of 11,875 pregnant women. Those women who ate less seafood (i.e. less than 340 grams a week), which is rich in omega 3 fatty acids, had offspring who demonstrated significantly lower scores on a number of neurodevelopmental outcomes, including prosocial behaviour, than the offspring of mothers who ate more seafood (Hibbeln *et al.*, 2007).

Longitudinal studies have also shown that malnutrition in infancy is associated with aggressive behaviour, and attentional deficits, in childhood (Galler *et al.*, 1983; Galler & Ramsey, 1989), while Liu and Raine (2006) found in a prospective longitudinal study that children with protein, iron or zinc deficiencies at age 3 had significantly more aggressive and hyperactive behaviour at the age of 8, more antisocial behaviour at age 11, and more excessive motor activity and conduct disorder at age 17, compared to controls. Significantly, this study also found a dose-dependent relationship between the extent of malnutrition and the extent of later behaviour problems.

traumatic brain injury (TBI) occurs when an external force traumatically injures the brain.

Traumatic brain injury (TBI) has also been implicated as a precursor of antisocial behaviour. One group of investigators found that half of the juvenile delinquents in their sample had a history of TBI, and a third of the delinquents with TBI were thought by their parents to have neuropsychological sequelae from their injuries (Hux *et al.*, 1998). Another study, which used more severe criteria in the definition of traumatic brain injury than the previous study, found that 27.7 per cent of the delinquents in their sample had a history of TBI (Carswell *et al.*, 2004). A number of large, longitudinal studies have repeatedly shown an increased incidence of delinquent behaviour among youth with a history of TBI (Asarnow *et al.*, 1991; McAllister 1992; Rivera *et al.*, 1994).

Adverse developmental histories leading to problematic interactions (attachment)

The concept of attachment can be broadly defined as the process by which an infant has an inborn biological need to maintain close contact with its main caretaker(s), and create experiences of safeness that impact upon affect and affect regulation (self-soothing) systems within the brain (Mitchell & Beech, 2011). Therefore, an individual's *attachment style* can be seen as a set of enduring characteristics for making sense of one's life experiences and interactions (Young *et al.*, 2003). This model is maintained irrespective of whether the relationship between the individual and their primary caregiver in childhood was positive or negative, and hence is a model for the individual's future social interactions and whether these are broadly negative or positive throughout their lifespan. *Secure* attachments give rise to internal working models of others as safe, helpful and supportive (Baldwin, 2005), while an *insecure* attachment style causes the individual to become highly socially ranked, and focused on the power of others to control or reject them (Gilbert, 2005). See Box 3.1 for an outline of the four attachment styles identified in adults – one is a secure style and the other three are insecure styles (dismissive, preoccupied, disorganised). Box 3.2 outlines very briefly the neurochemistry of attachment.

There have been indications in the general attachment literature regarding the relationship between insecure styles of attachment (due to problematic behaviours) and their link with subsequent offending. As early as the 1940s, Bowlby (1944) suggested that lack of care, and/or early separations from primary attachment figures (i.e. mother/father figures), predispose individuals to develop an *affectionless* style of interacting characteristic of psychopathy (see below). A number of authors have noted the role of coercive parent–child interactions and the absence of a positive and affectionate bond between parent and child, neglect, inconsistent parenting and severity of punishments (e.g. Frodi *et al.*, 2001; Greenberg *et al.*,

BOX 3.1 ATTACHMENT STYLES IN ADULTHOOD (FROM MAIN, 1995 AND MAINE & HESS, 1990)

Secure (*autonomous*) **attachment** is a style characterised by objective evaluations of attachment-related experiences, whether these are good or bad. This pattern is associated with sensitive and responsive parenting in childhood. Individuals with a secure attachment style, in childhood and adulthood, have been found to have high levels of self-esteem, view others as warm and accepting, and report high levels of intimacy in close adult relationships.

Dismissive **attachment** (*avoidant* **in childhood**) is a style characterised by an emphasis on achievement and self-reliance at the expense of intimacy. This pattern is associated with a rejecting or interfering parenting style, in that the parent has behaved in a remote, cold and controlling way. Hence, if parents are emotionally unavailable the child will tend to pull away from them and so develop a way of operating that minimises reliance on others for support, as a child and later in life. This leads to deactivation of *attachment mechanisms*, ultimately resulting in an adult who is emotionally autonomous and only ready to express self-preservative behaviours, at the expense of any warm, interpersonal interactions with others. By definition, such a person would be expected to show some antisocial characteristics from time to time, and will often be self-absorbed and unwilling to approach others for help and emotional support.

Preoccupied/anxious **attachment** (*resistant* **or** *ambivalent* **in childhood**) is a style characterised by the individual being enmeshed in past (typically childhood) attachment experiences, and having an inability to report a coherent view of interactions with others. This style has been found to be associated with the individual experiencing an inconsistent parenting style in childhood, where the parent(s) behave in ways that interfere with the child's autonomy or exploration, leading him or her to be uncertain of the quality of relationships, and to live in fear of rejection in later life. Hence, the person has a sense of confusion, especially when it comes to relational issues. Therefore, this style is associated with a heightened sense of rejection, feelings of general incompetence and inadequacy and, *in extremis*, *social withdrawal*.

Disorganised/unresolved) **attachment** (*disorganised/disoriented* **in childhood**) is the style most often associated with parental maltreatment (see Chapter 4), or where the primary caregivers have experienced an unresolved loss or trauma of their own. Here a parenting style that is frightening (or frightened) leads to the situation where the child is caught in a conflict where what should be their source of security becomes a source of fear. Individuals with this style may not be actively hostile in their interactions with others, but may behave in a *passive-aggressive* manner. We would also note that this attachment style is common in individuals with psychiatric disorders.

BOX 3.2 THE NEUROCHEMISTRY OF ATTACHMENT

- The process of attachment at a neurobiological level is primarily driven by the release of neuropetides *oxytocin* (OT) and *arginine vasopressin* (AVP) and their subsequent actions on the amygdala, the orbital prefrontal cortex and the anterior cingulated cortex. (See below for a description of these areas and how problems in these areas potentiate offending behaviours.)

- OT and AVP differ from each other at only two amino acid positions. They are synthesised by neurosecretory neurons in the hypothalamus and are shuttled to the pituitary for peripheral release or, alternatively, are released in other brain regions.

- OT and AVP are important hormones in the peripheral nervous system (upon release into the bloodstream by the posterior pituitary, OT affects uterine contraction and milk ejection in females, while AVP regulates water re-absorption and vasoconstriction).

- When released in the limbic system, particularly the amygdala, and the hippocampus, OT and AVP act like neurotransmitters.

- The central release of OT and AVP is associated with the emergence of social bonding, stress regulation, social communication and emotional reactivity.

(*Continued*)

- Release of OT and AVP can also occur as a consequence of socially pleasant sensory experiences, such as comforting touches and smells (Uvnas-Moberg, 1998; Wismer Fries *et al.*, 2005).

- Levels of OT and AVP are modulated by the actions of the neurotransmitters serotonin (5-hydroxytryptamine, 5HT) and dopamine.

- At birth, and during breastfeeding, the peripheral release of OT (acting systemically as a hormone) is often accompanied by the central synaptic release of OT.

- Similarly, large surges in OT, peripherally and centrally, are found in sexual climax and sexual 'afterplay' in

both human males and females (Blaicher *et al.*, 1999; Caldwell 2002), and hence can be seen as the 'love chemical'.

- AVP, also released into the brain during sexual activity, initiates and sustains patterns of activity that support the pair-bond between the sexual partners. In particular, AVP seems to induce the male to become aggressive towards other males in non-human species.

- Although the exact role that AVP release plays in human attachment behaviours is currently unclear it is assumed to be necessary for the consolidation of social memory.

FIGURE 3.2 *Prolonged separations from parents, combined with frightening threats from parents/caregivers, lead children to feel a dysfunctional level of anger.*

Source: © kondrytskyi. Used under licence from Shutterstock.

1993; Sampson & Laub 1990), while Craissati (2009) notes that violent criminals' lives are associated with extremely disturbed attachment representations, a history of abuse and a marked lack of empathy for others. (See Chapter 10 for a discussion of this in relationship to intimate partner violence offenders.)

As regards specific types of insecure attachment and their relationship to offending patterns generally, Dozier *et al.* (1999) note that prolonged separations from parents, combined with frightening threats from parents/caregivers, lead children to feel a dysfunctional level of anger, which often involves intense hate (Figure 3.2). Initially the anger may be directed towards the parents, but this would obviously be a dangerous strategy (given the level of potential threat from parents). For such individuals, the early absence of a strong attachment to the parent may have been masked by the adult's physical

capacity to control the child, such that delinquency only starts to express itself in adolescence, when the individual becomes more influenced by antisocial peers than by parental control (Craissati, 2009). Specifically, Lyons-Ruth *et al.* (1993) reported that *disorganised* attachment, together with maternal psychosocial problems, were highly predictive of hostile behaviours in young children. Finzi *et al.* (2001) found that physically abused children were characterised by an *avoidant* attachment style, and were aggressive and suspicious of others. Weinfield *et al.* (2008) note that children with *avoidant* or *disorganised* attachment styles were likely to show angry, aggressive behaviours with parents and peers, perhaps in response to rejection and insensitivity by the caregivers, or because of the situation of having a caregiver who is frightening or frightened; while Saltaris (2002) found that a history of abuse and extremely disturbed attachment representations led to a marked lack of empathy towards others and was associated with subsequent violent criminality.

We will now briefly examine how genetics predispositions can interact with the environmental risk factors outlined above.

Gene–environment interactions and offending

One way to investigate whether there is a genetic component to a syndrome is to compare the frequency with which there is co-occurence in siblings, particularly **monozygotic (MZ)/dizygotic (DZ) twins**. Blonigen *et al.* (2003), reporting on 353 adult twins of self-reported psychopathic

> **monozygotic (MZ)/ dizygotic (DZ) twins** MZ (identical) twins arise from a single ovum and have exactly the same genetic material. DZ (fraternal) twins arise from two separate ova, and like any siblings, share 50 per cent of the same genes.

personality traits, found substantial evidence of genetic contributions to variance in overall self-reported levels of psychopathy (see the section below on this concept) using the *Psychopathic Personality Inventory* (PPI; Lilienfield & Andrews, 1996) in MZ ($N = 165$; correlation effect size $r = .46$, $p < .05$) compared to DZ twins ($N = 106$; $r = -0.26$, non-significant result); and in all of the subscales of the PPI (including *Machievellianism, coldheartedness and impulsiveness*). Larsson *et al.* (2006) investigated the

ACE model used to examine the relative contributions of genetics and environment. Heritability is represented by the letter 'A', the common or shared environment by 'C' and environmental conditions by 'E'. Also known as 'non-shared environmental influences'.

genetic basis for psychopathy using the **ACE model** ('A' = genes; 'C' = shared family environment; 'E' = environmental risk factors unique to the individual, such as head injury). They found that 'A' (genes) accounted for 63 per cent of the variance; 'C' (the shared environment) accounted for 0 per cent; and 'E' (the unique environment) accounted for 37 per cent of the variance. In contrast, Miles and Carey (1997), examining aggression in a meta-analytic study, found that genes ('A') and shared environment ('C') were equally important in explaining aggressive behaviour. Rhee and Waldman (2002), in a meta-analytic study of over 100 behavioural genetic studies, found that 40–50 per cent of the variance of antisocial behaviour was due to genetic inheritance ('A'), 15–20 per cent to shared environmental influences ('C') and 30 per cent to unique environmental influences ('E')

Adoption studies are another mechanism for studying the genetic versus the environmental contributions to antisocial behaviour. In such studies, the characteristics of a child's biological and adoptive parents are considered relative to the child's own behaviour. In a large sample of adoptees in Denmark, Gabrielli and Mednick (1984) found strong evidence for a genetic propensity for criminal behaviour, while a study of 862 Swedish male adoptees found that genetic influences were the most significant contributor to later criminal behaviour (Cloninger *et al.*, 1982). In this study, the researchers also found that if a person had both a biological parent and an adoptive parent who were criminals, the person's likelihood of criminal behaviour was greater than the sum of the individual risks. In other words, there was a multiplicative effect of having a biological predisposition to crime and then being raised in a criminogenic environment.

Another large study of gene–environment interaction identified people who carried a genotype that conferred a low expression of monoamine oxidase-A (MAO-A) activity (Caspi *et al.*, 2002). (MAO-A is an enzyme that degrades neurotransmitters, such as dopamine, norepinephrine, and serotonin.) The researchers looked at the people with high versus low MAO-A activity and also

whether or not the individual had been abused as a child. They found evidence of a strong interaction between low MAO-A activity and childhood maltreatment and the likelihood of developing conduct disorder (see below for a description of this problem).

As for the development of attachment patterns outlined in Box 3.1, these are also shaped by a combination of genetic factors and social experiences (Fonagy, 2001). For example, recent molecular genetic studies have suggested that different attachment styles may reflect variations in the genes for the neurotransmitters, dopamine and serotonin (Gillath *et al.*, 2008). Hence, a particular form (polymorphism) of the DRD2 dopamine receptor gene is associated with an insecure style of attachment characterised by preoccupied/anxious attachment; while a polymorphism of the serotonin 5HT2A receptor gene is associated with an avoidant style of attachment (Gillath *et al.*, 2008). However, even though these candidate genes predispose a person to a certain style of social interactions, the predisposed style can either emerge or be modified by early social experience, and can either be active as a protective factor or potentiate antisocial behaviours.

Modifying risk factors

Obviously, not all risk factors for criminal behaviour (e.g. male gender, having a biological parent with a history of criminal behaviour) are modifiable. However, there are some risk factors (e.g. smoking, nutrition) that potentially can be modified. Some of these interventions are outlined in Box 3.3.

Later in the chapter, we will examine the actual effects on the brain. But first we will examine the impact of risk factors, particularly adverse developmental histories on particular types of antisocial disorders, specifically: *psychopathy* and *antisocial personality disorder*.

RISK FACTORS FOR ANTISOCIAL DISORDERS

Psychopathy

Psychopathy cannot readily be recognised by physical symptoms that are seen within other types of mental illness or disorder. For example, the *psychopath* does not experience hallucinations or even hear voices that tell her or him to act and behave in certain ways, unlike someone who is diagnosed with schizophrenia (see Chapter 20

BOX 3.3   MODIFYING ENVIRONMENTAL RISK FACTORS

- Successful interventions have been developed to reduce prenatal alcohol exposure (Chang *et al.*, 1999; 2005).

- Interventions have been designed to reduce smoking in pregnancy, but these have been less effective (Ershoff *et al.*, 2004).

- Other studies have sought to correct nutritional deficits. One randomised, double-blind, placebo-controlled study was performed in a sample of 486 state schoolchildren to see if a daily multivitamin and mineral supplement could reduce antisocial behaviour (Schoenthaler & Bier, 2000). The treatment group had a 47 per cent reduction in antisocial behaviour after four months, compared to controls.

- A randomised, double-blind, placebo-controlled trial of omega-3 fatty acid supplementation was carried out in a sample of 50 children. The intervention group had a 42.7 per cent reduction in conduct disorder problems (Stevens *et al.*, 2003), compared to controls.

- Other interventions address more than one risk factor at a time. For example, one highly successful intervention for prevention of later criminal and antisocial behaviour involved home nursing visits for pregnant and new mothers. Parenting, health and nutritional guidance were provided in the sessions (Olds *et al.*, 1998).

- Prenatal education on nutrition, health, and parenting has been found to lead to reductions in juvenile delinquency at age 15 (Lally *et al.*, 1988).

- A multidimensional intervention was tested in a randomised control trial, involving physical exercise, nutritional and educational enrichment in a sample of 3- to 5-year-olds. The intervention was found to significantly reduce antisocial behaviour at age 17, and criminal behaviour at age 23, and was especially effective for the subgroup of children who displayed signs of malnutrition at age 3, suggesting the nutritional aspect of the treatment was particularly beneficial (Raine *et al.*, 2003).

---

for a description of this disorder). Psychopathy cannot be easily identified by any distinctive clinical symptoms. It includes personality characteristics that can be broadly described as: *criminally minded; glib/superficially charming; manipulative; lack of remorse or guilt/conscience; pathological lying; lack of emotional depth; irresponsibility and impulsiveness; callous parasitic lifestyle; poor behavioural controls; promiscuous sexual behaviour* and *a history of childhood (antisocial) problems.* Psychopaths also show emotional empathy deficits, although **theory of mind (ToM)** abilities appear to be relatively unaffected (Blair, 2005), with only the moral interpretation of events being absent in this group. Obviously this mix of personality traits and behaviours makes it highly likely that such individuals will commit crimes. The demographics of psychopathy are shown in Box 3.4.

theory of mind (ToM) the ability to attribute mental states (i.e. beliefs, intents, desires, pretending, knowledge) to oneself and others and to understand that others have beliefs, desires and intentions that are different from one's own.

As for risk factors and psychopathy, Lang *et al.* (2002) reported a relationship between victimisation as a child and later violence, as evidenced by the frequency of psychopaths having alcoholic or antisocial fathers (Figure 3.3). Also, the fact that such individuals often report evidence of severe childhood abuse, extensive neglect, early foster placements and institutionalisation suggests a possible link. Psychopathic traits seen in adults have been

reported to be present in childhood before the age of 8 (Blair, 2005; Blair *et al.*, 2006). Hence, it is plausible that such risk factors could foster the development of psychopathic traits.

Blair *et al.* (2005), for example, note that an adverse upbringing can lead to poor attachment, disrupting the development of morality. Such neglect/trauma would therefore be expected to exert a deep and enduring impact on attachment style and future attachment formation strategies. Frodi *et al.* (2001), in a study of 26 criminal offenders, found that most reported a dismissing attachment style, with the rest reported as 'unclassifiable' in terms of attachment. Taylor (1997) found that dismissive attachment, in a sample of women, was correlated with psychopathy. The relationship found in these studies does not necessarily suggest that psychopathy evolves from dismissive attachment (Beech & Mitchell, 2009). However, the seeming unfamiliarity in these samples with the concept of attachment, clearly suggests a link.

A developmental model of psychopathic behaviours is also supported by two neurological case studies reported by Anderson and colleagues (Anderson *et al.*, 1999; 2000), in which damage to the ventromedial prefrontal cortex was incurred during very early childhood. The traumatic brain damage in these two cases resulted in a syndrome, which can be termed 'pseudopsychopathy', which persisted into adulthood. These cases did not exhibit all the features of psychopathy, but their moral reasoning was

BOX 3.4   DESCRIPTION OF PSYCHOPATHY
(SEE WWW.MENTALHEALTH.COM/DIS/P20-PE04.HTML)

- It occurs in roughly 1 per cent of the population.

- 20 per cent of incarcerated criminals probably qualify as psychopaths (Hare, 1999).

- Psychopaths have committed roughly half of all crimes.

- Psychopathy is a very good predictor of recidivism (i.e. committing another offence of a similar nature).

- Incarcerated psychopaths have committed an average of four violent crimes by the age of 40.

- 80 per cent of psychopaths released from prison commit another crime, usually within three years, compared to 50 per cent of the general prison population.

- The disorder is most commonly assessed on the basis of the Psychopathy Checklist – Revised (PCL–R; Hare, 1991; 2003), which is a 20-item checklist (described in Chapter 17, Table 17.4).

FIGURE 3.3 *It could be anyone … the lack of easily recognisable symptoms mean that it is very difficult to tell who is a psychopath.*
Source: © gemphotography. Used under licence from Shutterstock.

extremely limited, they were verbally and physically abusive, had an inability to plan, never expressed guilt or remorse for their behaviour, and were not responsive to verbal or physical punishment. This traumatic brain damage, we would argue, mirrors some of the neuronal changes that result from early psychological trauma as reported by Solomon and Heide (2005). See Case Study 3.2 for a 19th-century case description of acquired psychopathy.

Antisocial personality disorder (ASPD)

ASPD is described in the *Diagnostic and Statistical Manual of Mental Disorders* (DSM-IV-TR; American Psychiatric Association, 2000, p.706) as a 'pervasive pattern of disregard for and the violation of the rights of others' and can include a disregard for social norms, deceitfulness, impulsivity, irritability/aggressiveness, reckless disregard for the safety of others, irresponsibility, and a failure

CASE STUDY 3.2　PHINEAS GAGE

One famous case that can illuminate the neuroanatomical correlates of antisocial behaviour is that of Phineas Gage (Damasio *et al.*, 1994). Gage was a hard-working foreman for the Rutland & Burlington Railroad in America. He was highly regarded in his community for being morally upright, and was a model man of his times. He was always on time for work, never swore, and abstained from tobacco and alcohol use. On the afternoon of 13 September 1848, he was supervising the blasting of some rock near Cavendish, Vermont, to clear the way for more rail track to be laid. A hole had been drilled into the stone and gunpowder was poured in. As a last step prior to blasting, a long-handled tamping iron was used to pack down the powder. Tragically, the tamping iron scraped the side of the hole and generated a spark, which ignited the powder before Gage could get clear. The tamping iron shot out of the hole like a missile and passed straight through Gage's skull then high into the air, landing some 80 feet away from him. Gage surprised everyone by regaining consciousness and talking, even sitting up and walking to the horse-drawn cart that took him to seek medical attention.

Although Gage miraculously survived the incident, he was noted to be a dramatically changed man. Where once he was punctual, pious and well-mannered, after his injury he became irascible, unreliable and profane. Although he survived over a decade after his injury, he was noted by his friends to bear no resemblance to the man they knew before the accident. Damasio *et al.* (1994) reconstructed his skull from previously taken measurements and showed that Gage had suffered from damage to his left and right prefrontal cortices. By damaging the parts of the brain that affect emotional processing and executive functioning, Gage became a famous case of 'acquired psychopathy'.

BOX 3.5　CRITERIA FOR ASPD (FROM DSM-IV-TR)

- Must be at least 18 years old
- Three or more of the following:
  - Conduct disorder before the age of 15
  - Disregard for the rights of others
  - Impulsive, irresponsible behaviour
  - Deceitfulness
  - Irritability and aggressiveness
  - Reckless disregard for the safety of others

- Lack of remorse
- Low tolerance for frustration and boredom

The prevalence of ASPD is 3.6 per cent in the general population (5.5 per cent in men, and 1.9 per cent in women.) Figures would suggest that 80–85 per cent of incarcerated offenders can be reliably diagnosed as having ASPD (www.mentalhealth.com/dis/p20-pe04 .html), which is hardly surprising given the tautology of this premise.

---

to show remorse. The DSM-IV-TR criteria for ASPD are shown in Box 3.5.

Evidence for the association between problematic developmental histories and ASPD comes from, among others, Zanarini *et al.* (1989), who found that 89 per cent of individuals in their sample who met DSM criteria for ASPD reported experiencing prolonged separations from a parent/caregiver at some point during their childhood, specifically through divorce or separation (Robins, 1996). McCord (1979) found that ASPD was the most likely outcome when the individual's mother was unaffectionate and did not provide adequate supervision, and when their father was 'deviant'. Zanarini *et al.* (1989) also reported that many of those diagnosed with ASPD had experienced physical abuse, or harsh discipline, in childhood.

Conduct disorder (CD) is often the precursor of ASPD; however, many young people with CD do not develop ASPD. CD is defined in DSM-IV-TR (American Psychiatric Association, 2000) as a repetitive, and persistent, pattern of behaviour in which the basic rights of others, or societal conventions are flouted, and is often seen as a precursor of later antisocial behaviours. Many individuals

conduct disorder (CD) in childhood is a repetitive, and persistent, pattern of behaviour in which the basic rights of others, or societal conventions, are flouted. Many individuals with CD show little empathy and concern for others, and may frequently misperceive the intentions of others as being more hostile and threatening than is actually the case.

with CD show little empathy and concern for others, and may frequently misperceive the intentions of others as being more hostile and threatening than is actually the case. Avoidant attachment has been found to be related to CD by Rosenstein and Horowitz (1996).

THE NEUROBIOLOGY OF SOCIAL/ANTISOCIAL BEHAVIOURS

Social behaviours are underpinned by neurobiological action (particularly in the *amygdala*, the *orbital prefrontal cortex* and *[anterior] cingulate gyrus*) and although a great deal has been written about the neurobiology/neurochemistry of the 'social brain', relatively less has been written about these in relationship to offending. In this section we will examine the neurobiology of these functions.

The most important area of the midbrain that is associated with the social brain is the *limbic system*. This area is a loosely defined collection of brain structures that play crucial roles in the control of emotions and motivation. The principal limbic structures involved are the amygdala and the anterior cingulated, along with the orbital prefrontal cortex and an associated area of the brain: the *insular*. We will now briefly examine these (see Mitchell & Beech, 2011, for a more in-depth review of this topic).

The *amygdala* is a set of interconnected nuclei (large clusters of neurons) found deep within the temporal lobes. Its functions are related to arousal; the control of autonomic responses associated with fear; emotional responses; and emotional memory; and it is therefore centrally involved in attention, learning and affect. The amygdala can be split into two major subdivisions: the *basolateral complex*, which is made up of the lateral and basal nuclei; and the *centromedial complex*. The basolateral complex can roughly be thought of as being the principal input region of the amygdala with afferents (incoming projections) arising principally from the prefrontal cortex, limbic cortex and hippocampus, and exerts potent effects upon sexual behaviours. These neural structures enable conditional associations to be made between neutral stimuli and sexual reinforcers. The basal nuclei, in conjunction with the lateral nuclei, also play a role in reinforcement more generally. The *central nuclei* of the centromedial complex are involved in responding to fearful stimuli. The sensory inputs to the central nuclei, which drive these fear responses, arise principally from cortical and thalamic projections to the lateral nuclei of the amygdala. These sensory inputs form synapses,

which have a high degree of plasticity. This enables the encoding of conditioned emotionally significant stimuli, and thus enables the amygdala to play a central role in aversive conditioning (LeDoux, 2000). The *medial nuclei* of the centromedial complex are positioned at the heart of the neural circuitry, which directs and organises sexual behaviours.

The *insular cortex* is a long-neglected brain region that has emerged as crucial to understanding what it feels like to be human. It is suggested that it is the source of social emotions, like lust, disgust, pride and humiliation, guilt and shame. It helps give rise to moral intuition, empathy and the capacity to respond emotionally.

The *orbital prefrontal cortex* (OPFC) can be considered as the apex of the neural networks of the social brain and is critical to the adaptation of behaviour in response to predicted changes in reinforcement. It bridges the cognitive analysis of complex social events taking place within the cerebral cortex, and emotional reactions mediated by the amygdala and the autonomic nervous system. The OPFC therefore acts as a 'convergence zone' with its connections to the hypothalamus allowing it to integrate internal and external information. Its inhibitory role in autonomic functioning (via the amygdala and other subcortical regions) means that it is critically involved in emotional regulation. It has been suggested that another role of the OPFC is to generate an expectation of the reaction of others, which is used to direct behaviour.

The *anterior cingulate cortex* (ACC) first appeared in animals demonstrating maternal behaviour. Therefore the ACC appears to provide the basic circuitry for communication, cooperation and empathy, being involved in the simultaneous monitoring of personal, environmental information and allocation of attention to the most pertinent information in the environment and a particular moment in time. The ACC can be subdivided into affective and cognitive parts and integrates emotional and attentional processing. The ACC also becomes activated when individuals, or particularly those they have a close emotional bond to, experience pain or social stress. Damage to this area can include decreased empathy, emotional instability and inappropriate social behaviour (Brothers, 1996).

Neurobiological problems and offending

Early deprivation and other suboptimal rearing conditions, as outlined above, are associated with severe problems in social and emotional functioning that potentially endure throughout life. It could be predicted that these early experiences would be reflected in long-term changes in the underlying neurobiology and the neuro-chemistry of attachment/social brain systems. The ensuing atypical morphological organisation could result in social withdrawal, pathological shyness, explosive and inappropriate emotionality, and an inability to form normal emotional attachments (Joseph, 2003).

A number of lines of evidence associate impaired structure and function in areas of the social brain (i.e. the amygdala, the OPFC and the ACC) and in other associated areas. These, it is argued, lead to increases in violence and instrumental aggression and, *in extremis*, ASPD and psychopathic behaviours. Table 3.1 shows the techniques that have looked at structures of these and other brain areas. Table 3.2 outlines techniques that have been used to examine the functional aspects of such brain structures.

TABLE 3.1 *Techniques used to examine the structural integrity of different areas of the brain.*

Computerised axial tomography (CAT)	CAT scans are produced using a series of X-rays taken along the axis of the body. The X-rays pass unevenly through tissues of different densities, allowing for distinctions between fluid, bone and brain tissue to be made. A computer then assembles these slices into a sequence of cross-sectional images.
Magnetic resonance imaging (MRI)	MRI scans are created by using powerful magnetic fields to orient all of the hydrogen atoms (primarily found in water molecules) in the brain in the same direction. A radio frequency electromagnetic field is introduced, which produces a signal that is detected by the MRI scanner's receiver. These signals are then assembled into high-resolution images that can distinguish the grey from the white matter of the brain. MRI scans do not use radiation and produce more detailed pictures than do CAT scans, but they also take much longer to obtain and are much more expensive. That said, both types of imaging produce images of brain structures that can then be measured and studied.
Diffusion tensor imaging (DTI)	A relatively new technique, allowing images to be taken of the structural integrity of the white matter tracts connecting various parts of the brain.

TABLE 3.2 *Techniques used to examine the functional aspects of different areas of the brain.*

Electroencephalogram (EEG)	In an EEG, the subject has electrodes placed in specific points over the scalp. These electrodes detect the brain's electrical impulses, which are then recorded and analysed by a computer. The frequency and amplitude of the resultant signals can then be interpreted. Increasing frequency is associated with increasing arousal, and lower frequency is associated with lower arousal.
Event-related potential (ERP)	This is a measure of the magnitude of change of brain activity after the presentation of specific stimuli. The change, or deflection, may be positive or negative in direction, and occurs within milliseconds of the onset of the stimulus. Typically, an ERP is measured a number of times, and the average of all the trials is taken, for example. *P300* is a positive waveform that typically occurs approximately 300 milliseconds after the presentation of a stimulus. It reflects processes involved in stimulus evaluation or categorisation (i.e. it is related to the engagement of attention).
Functional magnetic resonance imaging (fMRI)	This measures changes in blood oxygen in regions of interest in the brain before and after cognitive tasks are undertaken. These *blood oxygen level dependent* (BOLD) signals are used as a proxy for how active a region of the brain is. By comparing groups of interest with matched controls, the patterns of activation, or inactivation, in their brains can be studied to learn how the functioning of various brain regions relates to the condition in question.
Photon emission tomography (PET)	This technique relies on injecting subjects with a radioactively labelled substance, such as glucose. Images of their brains can then be obtained, showing areas of higher radioactive signal due to glucose metabolism, which indicates level of neural activity.
Single photon emission tomography (SPECT)	This form of imaging also involves the injection of a radioactive tracer. The camera detects the amount of radiation coming from different parts of the brain. These differences are due to differences in *regional cerebral blood flow* (rCBF) and reflect different levels of activity in various parts of the brain.

Structural evidence of problems in offenders

Raine *et al.* (2000) studied 21 individuals with ASPD, and compared them to a matched group of substance users, and non-offending controls. They found an 11 per cent reduction in the grey matter of the OPFC of the ASPD group compared to the other two matched groups. Other researchers have found that, compared to normal controls, persons with ASPD have smaller temporal lobes (Dolan *et al.*, 2002; Laakso *et al.*, 2002), as well as reductions in their dorsolateral, medial frontal and the OPFC (Laakso *et al.*, 2002). Laakso and colleagues (Laakso *et al.*, 2000; 2001) found that, for a group of violent offenders with alcoholism and ASPD, the smaller the posterior hippocampus (an area that is associated with fear conditioning) and the hippocampus (a structure linked to learning and memory), the higher the PCL–R score (Hare, 1991, 2003).

Huebner *et al.* (2008) found smaller grey matter volumes in the OPFC and temporal lobes of children with CD, compared to normal controls. Sterzer *et al.* (2005) found reduced grey matter volumes in the amygdala and the insular of adolescents with CD compared to normal controls. Kruesi *et al.* (2004) report that diminished right temporal lobe volume (which includes the amygdala) is associated with CD, and reduced temporal lobe, but not prefrontal volumes, in incarcerated psychopaths.

Functional evidence of problems in offenders

Blair *et al.* (2006), and Mitchell *et al.* (2002), have argued that the psychological/behavioural characteristics identified in psychopathy reflect abnormal functioning in the neural circuitry involving the amygdala and the OPFC. Birbaumer *et al.* (2005) found that psychopaths show no significant activity in the limbic-prefrontal circuit (amygdala, OPFC, insula and the ACC), using fMRI, during tasks involved in verbal and autonomic conditioning. The lack of recognition of fear in psychopaths, due to a measurable lack of amygdala function, would suggest that this would make it easier to offend, as a key component of committing interpersonal violence towards others is the requirement to not recognise or understand the mental state of the other (the potential victim).

In a PET study, Raine, Buchsbaum *et al.* (1994) found that a sample of murderers demonstrated reduced glucose metabolism in the anterior medial prefrontal, OPFC, and superior frontal cortices compared to a normal comparison group, after a continuous performance task. A follow-up study with a larger sample using a similar methodology found the same pattern of reduced glucose metabolism in the anterior frontal cortices, and in the amygdalas and hippocampi as well (Raine, Buchsbaum *et al.*, 1997).

Sterzer *et al.* (2005) employed fMRI to examine patterns of brain activation in CD adolescent males, and 14 matched controls, as they looked at neutral pictures and pictures with a strong negative affective valence. It was found that when the CD youths viewed the distressing pictures they had significantly reduced activity to their left amygdalae compared to the controls. Another group using a similar methodology studied 12 children and adolescents with callous-unemotional traits and either oppositional defiant disorder or CD, 12 with attention deficit hyperactivity disorder, and 12 comparison controls. All looked at photographs of neutral, angry or fearful faces. Compared to the other two groups, the group with callous-unemotional traits demonstrated significantly reduced amygdala activation on viewing the fearful (but not the angry or neutral) faces (Marsh *et al*, 2008). Further, on a functional connectivity analysis, the callous-unemotional children showed reduced connectivity between the ventromedial prefrontal cortex and the amygdala. The degree of reduction in this connectivity was negatively correlated with the score on a scale that measured the degree of callous-unemotional traits. Similar findings have been described in adult populations (Kiehl *et al.*, 2004; Muller *et al.*, 2003).

Slower EEG activity in children and adolescents has been found to be associated with later criminal behaviour (Mednick *et al.*, 1981; Petersen *et al.*, 1982). Raine *et al.* (1990) demonstrated that, compared to their peers with higher arousal, 15-year-old boys with lower arousal as measured by resting EEG were more likely to become criminals at age 24. Children with externalising and antisocial behaviours have been noted to demonstrate abnormal patterns of EEG asymmetry in their frontal lobes (Ishikawa & Raine, 2002; Santesso *et al.*, 2006). It has been noted that dominant EEG frequencies increase with age (Dustman *et al.*, 1999). The EEG abnormalities noted with respect to criminal behaviour have been hypothesised to be due to cortical immaturity (Volavka, 1987). It has been suggested that abnormal frontal EEG asymmetry might belie language and analytic reasoning deficits, thus impairing emotion regulation (Santesso *et al.*, 2006).

A meta-analysis of studies of ERP in antisocial populations found that, in general, antisocial individuals have smaller P300 amplitudes and longer latencies (Gao & Raine, 2009). Early onset of drug abuse and criminal behaviour have also been shown to be related to smaller P300 amplitudes (Iacono & McGue, 2006). Other studies have demonstrated that greater negative amplitude at 100 milliseconds (N100) (elicited by any unpredictable stimulus in the absence of task demands) and faster P300 latency at age 15 predict criminal behaviour at age 24 (Raine *et al.*, 1990).

Neuropsychological tests provide another method for testing the functional level of various brain areas. One of the most consistent findings in the neuropsychological aspects of criminality is that antisocial populations have lower verbal IQs compared to non-antisocial groups (Brennan *et al.*, 2003; Déry *et al.*, 1999; Teichner & Golden, 2000). Researchers have found that verbal deficits on testing at age 13 predict delinquency at age 18 (Moffitt *et al.*, 1994). A number of authors have also found evidence that such neuropsychological deficits show interactive effects when they are present in children with social risk factors as well (Aguilar *et al.*, 2000; Brennan *et al.*, 2003; Raine 2002).

Executive functioning is another neuropsychological function of interest in criminology (Moffitt, 1990; 1993). A meta-analysis of 39 studies incorporating data from 4589 individuals examined the relationship between executive dysfunction and antisocial behaviour (Morgan & Lilienfeld, 2000). These authors found significant effect sizes ($d = 0.86$ for juvenile delinquency and $d = 0.46$ for conduct disorder) for executive dysfunction. Other neuropsychological tests have focused on how antisocial populations respond to *affectively charged* stimuli. Loney *et al.* (2003) found that juveniles with callous-unemotional traits showed slower reaction times after being presented with emotionally negative words, while those with impulsive traits showed faster reaction times to such stimuli. Adult psychopaths have been found to have deficits in passive-avoidance learning tasks (Newman & Kosson, 1986) and adolescent psychopaths have been shown to demonstrate hyper-responsivity to rewards (Scerbo *et al.*, 1990). Taken together, these data suggest that psychopathic individuals will be less sensitive to punishment and more sensitive to the possibility of rewards as a consequence of their behaviour. Also, given the executive function literature, they may be less able to plan, act in a rationally self-interested fashion, control their impulses and respond flexibly to the various problems encountered in everyday life. We will now examine other psychophysiological correlates of offending.

Other psychophysiological evidence

A number of psychophysiological studies have found biological correlates of criminal behaviour. These studies include *heart rate* and *skin conductance*. We will now briefly examine some of the findings in these areas.

Low resting heart rate
In longitudinal studies, low resting heart rate has been shown accurately to identify individuals who are at risk

for later developing antisocial behaviour. Low resting heart rate is also the best-replicated biological correlate of antisocial behaviour in juvenile samples (Ortiz & Raine, 2004). In a meta-analytic review of 29 samples, the average effect size was 0.56. This effect was demonstrated in both genders and irrespective of measurement technique (Raine, 1996). In the Cambridge Study in Delinquent Development (see Chapter 2), a series of six regression analyses were used to identify the best independent risk factors of violence (Farrington, 1997). Only two risk factors – low resting heart rate and poor concentration – were found, independently of all other risk factors, to predict violence.

The same study found evidence of an interaction between low resting heart rate and several environmental risk factors (e.g. coming from a large family, having a teenage mother, being of low socio-economic status) in producing violent behaviour. This finding is specific for antisocial behaviour (Rogeness *et al.*, 1990) and has not been shown in other psychiatric syndromes. The finding that low resting heart rate predicts later crime has been replicated in many countries (Farrington 1997; Mezzacappa *et al.*, 1997; Moffitt & Caspi, 2001; Raine, Venables *et al.*, 1997). Lastly, it has been shown that having a high resting heart rate is negatively correlated with later violent behaviour (i.e. a high resting heart rate is a protective factor against developing criminality; Raine *et al.*, 1995).

Skin conductance
Low skin conductance has been shown to be associated with conduct problems (Lorber, 2004). Boys with CD have been shown to have reduced fluctuations in skin conductance and impairments in conditioned fear responses (Fairchild *et al.*, 2008; Herpertz *et al.*, 2005). Longitudinal studies have demonstrated that reduced skin conductance arousal at age 15 has been associated with criminal offending at age 24 (Raine *et al.*, 1995) and that low skin conductance at age 11 predicts institutionalisation at age 13 (Kruesi *et al.*, 1992). Impaired fear conditioning as measured by skin conductance at age 3 has been shown to predict aggression at age 8 and criminal behaviour at age 23 (Gao *et al.*, 2010). Low sympathetic reactivity has been shown in psychopathy-prone adolescents and in children with conduct disorder and callous-unemotional traits (Anastassiou-Hadjichara & Warden 2008; Kimonis *et al.*, 2006; Loney *et al.*, 2003). At age 3, having an abnormal skin conductance response to unpleasant stimuli is a risk factor for displaying psychopathy in adulthood (Glenn *et al.*, 2007).

SUMMARY

- In this chapter we have sought to clarify how these biological aspects of the self can be used to understand, identify and, hopefully, predict individuals who criminally offend. Specifically, we provided an overview of the risk factors that can lead to such problems, such as prenatal, perinatal, postnatal and developmental histories, which can set the scene for future offending.

- We have also attempted briefly to outline the relationship between genetic and environmental factors and their relationship to offending.

- Then we have looked at how these risk factors can have effects upon particular parts of the brain, and have described some of the techniques that have been used to examine such problematic brain areas in terms of structure and function.

- Understanding these processes, we would suggest, is the first step in being able to modify risk factors (some examples are shown in Box 3.3), or target at-risk individuals for services designed to attenuate their criminal propensity, as outlined in Part IV of this book.

ESSAY/DISCUSSION QUESTIONS

1. Is poor attachment to parents a necessary or sufficient cause of antisocial behaviour?

2. Name two prenatal risk factors and two postnatal risk factors for the development of crime. Are any risk factors modifiable and, if so, what public policy remedies can you suggest that could reduce criminal behaviour?

3. Describe the difference between structural brain imaging studies and functional brain imaging studies.

4. What do ACE models studies tell us about the contributions of genetic and environmental influences on crime?

5. Could brain imaging information be used in criminal trials and, if so, how?

REFERENCES

Aguilar, B., Sroufe, A., Egeland, B. & Carlson, E. (2000). Distinguishing the early-onset/ persistent and adolescent-onset antisocial behavior types: From birth to six years. *Development and Psychopathology, 12*, 109–132.

American Psychiatric Association (2000). *Diagnostic and statistical manual of mental disorders, fourth edition, text revision (DSM-IV-TR)*. Washington DC: American Psychiatric Association.

Anastassiou-Hadjichara, X. & Warden, D. (2008). Physiologically-indexed and self-perceived affective empathy in conduct-disordered children high and low on callous-unemotional traits. *Child Psychiatry and Human Development, 39*, 503–517.

Anderson, S.W., Bechara, A., Damasio, H., Tranel D. & Damasio A.R. (1999). Impairment of social and moral behavior related to early damage in human prefrontal cortex. *Nature Neuroscience, 2*, 1032–1037.

Anderson, S.W., Damasio, H., Tranel, D. & Damasio, A.R. (2000). Long-term sequelae of prefrontal cortex damage acquired in early childhood. *Developmental Neurospychology, 18*, 281–296.

Arnold, L.E., Pinkham, S.M. & Votolato, N. (2000). Does zinc moderate essential fatty acid and amphetamine treatment of attention-deficit/ hyperactivity disorder? *Journal of Child and Adolescent Psychopharmacology, 10*, 111–117.

Arsenault, L., Tremblay, R.E., Boulerice, B. & Saucier, J.F. (2002). Obstetrical complications and violent delinquency: Testing two developmental pathways. *Child Development, 73*, 496–508.

Asarnow, R., Satz, P., Light, R. & Neumann, E. (1991). Behavior problems and adaptive functioning in children with mild and severe closed head injury. *Journal of Pediatric Psychology, 16*, 543–555.

Baldwin, M.W. (2005). *Interpersonal cognition*. New York: Guilford.

Beech, A.R. & Mitchell, I.J. (2009). Attachment difficulties. In M. McMurran & R. Howard (Eds.) *Personality, personality disorder and risk of violence* (pp.213–228). Chichester: John Wiley & Sons, Inc.

Birbaumer, N., Viet R., Lotze M., Erb, M., Hermann, C., Grodd, W., *et al.* (2005). Deficient fear conditioning in psychopathy – A functional magnetic resonance imaging study. *Archives of General Psychiatry, 62*, 799–805.

Blaicher, W., Gruber, D., Bieglmayer, C., Blaicher, A.M., Knogler, W. & Huber, J.C. (1999). The role of oxytocin in relation to female sexual arousal. *Gynecologic and Obstetric Investigation, 47*, 125–126.

Blair, R.J.R. (2005). Applying a cognitive neuroscience perspective to the disorder of psychopathy. *Development and Psychopathology, 17*, 865–891.

Blair, R.J.R., Mitchell, D. & Blair, K. (2005). *The psychopath: Emotion and the brain.* Oxford: Blackwell.

Blair, R.J.R., Peschardt, K.S., Budhani, S., Mitchell, D.G.V. & Pine, D.S. (2006). The development of psychopathy. *Journal of Child Psychology and Psychiatry, 47*, 262–275.

Blonigen, D.M., Carlson, S.R., Krueger, R.F. & Patrick, C.J. (2003). A twin study of self reported psychopathic personality traits. *Personality and Individual Differences, 35*, 179–197.

Bowlby, J. (1944). Forty-four juvenile thieves: Their characters and home-life. *International Journal of Psychoanalysis, 25*, 19–53.

Breakey, J. (1997). The role of diet and behaviour in childhood. *Journal of Paediatrics and Child Health, 33*, 190–194.

Brennan, P.A., Grekin, E.R. & Mednick, S.A. (1999). Maternal smoking during pregnancy and adult male criminal outcomes. *Archives of General Psychiatry, 56*, 215–219.

Brennan, P.A., Hall, J., Bor, W., Najman, J.M. & Williams, G. (2003). Integrating biological and social processes in relation to early-onset persistent aggression in boys and girls. *Development and Psychopathology, 39*, 309–323.

Brennan, P.A., Mednick, S.A. & Raine, A. (1997). Biosocial interactions and violence: A focus on perinatal factors. In A. Raine, P. Brennan, D. Farrington & S.A. Mednick (Eds.) *Biosocial basis of violence* (pp.163–174). New York: Plenum Press.

Brothers, L. (1996). Brain mechanisms of social cognition. *Journal of Psychopharmacology, 10*, 2–8.

Caldwell, J.D. (2002). A sexual arousability model involving steroid effects at the plasma membrane. *Neuroscience and Biobehavioral Reviews, 26*, 13–30.

Carswell, K., Maughan, B., Davis, H., Davenport, F. & Goddard, N. (2004). The psychosocial needs of young offenders and adolescents from an inner city area. *Journal of Adolescence, 27*, 415–428.

Caspi, A., McClay, J., Moffitt, T.E., Mill, J., Martin, J., Craig, I.W., *et al.* (2002). Role of genotype in the cycle of violence in maltreated children. *Science, 297*, 851–854.

Chang, G., McNamara, T.K., Orav, E.J. & Wilkins-Haug, L. (2005). Brief intervention for prenatal alcohol use:. A randomized trial. *Obstetrics and Gynecology, 10*, 991–998.

Chang, G., Wilkins-Haug, L., Berman, S. & Goerz, M.A. (1999). Brief intervention for alcohol use in pregnancy: A randomized trial. *Addiction, 94*, 1499–1508.

Cloninger, C.R., Sigvardsson, S., Bohman, M., & von Knorring, A. (1982). Predisposition to petty criminality in Swedish adoptees. II. Cross-fostering analysis of gene-environment interaction. *Archives of General Psychiatry, 39*, 1242–1247.

Coccaro, E.F., Bergeman, C.S., Kavoussi, R.J. & Seroczynski, A.D. (1997). Heritability of aggression and irritability: A twin study of the Buss-Durkee aggression scales in adult male subjects. *Biological Psychiatry, 41*, 273–284.

Craissati, J. (2009). Attachment problems and sex offending. In A.R. Beech, L.E. Craig & K.D. Browne (Eds.) *Handbook of assessment and treatment of sexual offenders* (pp.13–38). Chichester: John Wiley & Sons, Inc.

Damasio, H., Grabowski, T., Frank, R., Galaburda, A.M. & Damasio, A.R. (1994). The return of Phineas Gage: Clues about the brain from the skull of a famous patient. *Science, 264*, 1102–1105.

Déry, M., Toupin, J., Pauzé, R., Mercier, H. & Fortin, L. (1999). Neuropsychological characteristics of adolescents with conduct disorder: Association with attention-deficit-hyperactivity and aggression. *Journal of Abnormal Child Psychology, 27*, 225–236.

Dolan, M., Deakin, J.F.W., Roberts, N. & Anderson, I.M. (2002). Quantitative frontal and temporal structural MRI studies in personality-disordered offenders and control subjects. *Psychiatry Research Neuroimaging, 116*, 133–149.

Dozier, M., Stovall, K.C. & Albus, K. (1999). Attachment and psychopathology in adulthood. In J. Cassidy & P.R. Shaver (Eds.) *Handbook of attachment theory and research* (pp.497–519). New York: Guilford Press.

Dustman, R.E., Shearer, D.E. & Emmerson, R.Y. (1999). Life-span changes in EEG spectral amplitude, amplitude variability and mean frequency. *Clinical Neurophysiology, 110*, 1399–1409.

Eckstein, L.W., Shibley, I.J., Pennington, J.S., Carver, F.M. & Pennington, S.N. (1997). Changes in brain glucose levels and glucose transporter protein isoforms in alcohol- or nicotine- treated chick embryos. *Brain Research and Developmental Brain Research 15*, 383–402.

Ershoff, D.H., Ashford, T.H. & Goldenberg R.L. (2004). Helping pregnant women quit smoking. An overview. *Nicotine and Tobacco Research, 6*, S101–S105.

Fairchild, G., Van Goozen, S.H.M., Stollery, S.J. & Goodyer, I.M. (2008) Fear conditioning and affective modulation of the startle reflex in male adolescents with early-onset or adolescence-onset conduct disorder and health control subjects. *Biological Psychiatry, 63*, 279–285.

Farrington, D.P. (1997). The relationship between low resting heart rate and violence. In A Raine, P. Brennan, D. Farrington & S.A. Mednick (Eds.) *Biosocial basis of violence* (pp.89–106). New York: Plenum Press.

Fast, D.K., Conry, J. & Loock, C.A. (1999). Identifying Fetal Alcohol Syndrome among youth in the criminal justice system. *Journal of Developmental and Behavioral Pediatrics, 20*, 370–372.

Fergusson, D.M., Woodward, L.J. & Horwood L.J. (1998). Maternal smoking during pregnancy and psychiatric adjustment in late adolescence. *Archives of General Psychiatry, 55*, 721–727.

Finzi, R., Ram, A, Har-Even D., Shnitt, D. & Weizman, A. (2001). Attachment styles and aggression in physically abused and neglected children. *Journal of Youth and Adolescence, 30*, 769–786.

Fonagy, P. (2001). The human genome and the representational world: The role of early mother-infant interaction in creating an interpersonal interpretive mechanism. *Bulletin of the Menninger Clinic, 65*, 427–448.

Frodi, A., Dernevik, M., Sepa, A., Philison, J. & Bragesjö, M. (2001). Current attachment representations of incarcerated offenders varying in degree of psychopathy. *Attachment and Human Development, 3*, 269–283.

Gabrielli, W.F. & Mednick, S.A. (1984). Urban environment, genetics, and crime. *Criminology, 22*, 645–652.

Galler, J.R. & Ramsey, F. (1989). A follow-up study of the influence of early malnutrition on development. *Journal of the American Academy of Child and Adolescent Psychiatry, 26*, 254–261.

Galler, J.R., Ramsey, F., Solimano, G. & Lowell, W.E. (1983). The influence of early malnutrition on subsequent behavioral development. II. Classroom behavior. *Journal of the American Academy of Child and Adolescent Psychiatry, 22*, 16–22.

Gao, Y. & Raine, A. (2009). P3 event-related potential impairments in antisocial and psychopathic individuals: A meta-analysis. *Biological Psychiatry, 83*, 199–210.

Gao, Y., Raine, A., Venables, P.H., Dawson, M.E. & Mednick, S.A. (2010). Poor childhood fear conditioning predisposes to adult crime. *American Journal of Psychiatry, 167*, 56–60.

Gilbert, P. (2005). Compassion and cruelty: A biopsychosocial approach. In P. Gilbert (Ed.) *Compassion: Conceptualisations, research and use in psychotherapy* (pp.9–74). London: Routledge.

Gillath, O., McCall, C., Shaver, P.R., Baek, J.M. & Chun, D.S. (2008) Genetic correlates of adult attachment style. *Personality and Social Psychology Bulletin 34*: 1396–1405.

Glenn, A.L., Raine, A., Mednick, S.A. & Venables, P. (2007). Early temperamental and psychophysiological precursors of adult psychopathic personality. *Journal of Abnormal Psychology, 116*, 508–518.

Greenberg, M.T., Speltz, M.L. & DeKlyen, M. (1993). The role of attachment in the early development of disruptive behavior problems. *Development and Psychopathology, 5*, 191–213.

Guy, J.D., Majorski, L.V., Wallace, C.J. & Guy, M.P. (1983). The incidence of minor physical anomalies in adult male schizophrenics. *Schizophrenia Bulletin, 9*, 571–582.

Halverson, C.F. & Victor, J.B. (1976). Minor physical anomalies and problem behavior in elementary schoolchildren. *Child Development, 47*, 281–285.

Hare, R.D. (1991). *The Hare Psychopathy Checklist – Revised.* Toronto: Multi-Health Systems.

Hare, R.D. (1999). *Without conscience: The disturbing world of the psychopaths among us.* New York: Guilford.

Hare, R.D. (2003). *The Hare Psychopathy Checklist – Revised: Second Edition.* Toronto: Multi-Health Systems.

Herpertz, S.C., Mueller, B., Qunaibi, M., Lichterfeld, C., Konrad, K. & Herpertz-Dahlmann, B. (2005). Response to emotional stimuli in boys with conduct disorder. *American Journal of Psychiatry, 162*, 1100–1107.

Hibbeln, J.R., Davis, J.M., Steer, C., Emmett, P., Rogers, I., Williams, C., et al. (2007). Maternal seafood consumption in pregnancy and neurodevelopmental outcomes in childhood (ALSPAC study): An observational cohort study. *Lancet, 369*, 578–585.

Hodgins, S., Kratzer, L. & McNeil, T.F. (2001). Obstetric complications, parenting, and risk of criminal behavior. *Archives of General Psychiatry, 58*, 746–752.

Huebner, T., Vloet,T.D., Marx, I., Konrad, K., Fink, G.R., Herpertz, S.C., et al. (2008). Morphometric brain abnormalities in boys with conduct disorder. *Journal of the American Academy of Child and Adolescent Psychiatry, 47*, 540–547.

Hux, K., Bond, V., Skinner, S., Belau, D. & Sanger, D. (1998). Parental report of occurences and consequences of traumatic brain injury among delinquent and non-delinquent youth. *Brain Injury, 12*, 667–681.

Iacono, W.G. & McGue, M. (2006). Association between P3 event-related brain potential amplitude and adolescent problem behavior. *Psychophysiology, 43*, 465–469.

Ishikawa, S.S. & Raine, A. (2002). Psychophysiological correlates of antisocial behavior: A central control hypothesis. In J. Glicksohn. (Ed.) *The neurobiology of criminal behavior* (pp.187–229). Boston, MA: Kluwer.

Joseph, R. (2003). Environmental influences on neural plasticity, the limbic system, emotional development and attachment: A review. *Child Psychiatry and Human Development, 29*, 189–208.

Kemppainen, L., Jokelainen, J., Jarvelin, M.R., Isohanni, M. & Rasanen, P. (2001). The one-child family and violent criminality: A 31-year follow-up study of the Northern Finland 1966 birth cohort. *American Journal of Psychiatry, 158*, 960–962.

Kiehl, K., Smith, A.M., Mendrek A., Forster B.B., Hare R.D. & Liddle P.F. (2004). Temporal lobe abnormalities in semantic processing by criminal psychopaths as revealed by functional magnetic resonance imaging. *Psychiatry Research Neuroimaging, 130*, 27–42.

Kimonis, E.R., Frick, P.J., Fazekas, H. & Loney, B.R. (2006). Psychopathy, aggression, and the processing of emotional stimuli in non-referred girls and boys. *Behavioral Sciences and the Law, 24*, 21–37.

Kruesi, M.J.P., Casanova, M.V., Mannheim, G. & Johnson-Bilder, A. (2004). Reduced temporal lobe volume in early-onset conduct disorder. *Psychiatry Research Neuroimaging, 132*, 1–11.

Kruesi, M.J.P., Hibbs, E.D., Zahn, T.P., Keysor, C.S., Hamberger, S.D., Bartko, J.J., et al. (1992). A 2-year prospective follow-up study of children and adolescents with disruptive behavior disorders. Prediction by cerebrospinal fluid 5-hydroxyindoleacetic acid, homovanillic acid, and autonomic measures? *American Journal of Psychiatry, 49*, 429–435.

Laakso, M.P., Gunning-Dixon, F., Vaurio, O., Repo-Tiihonen, E., Soininen, H. & Tiihonen, J. (2002). Prefrontal volume in habitually violent subjects with antisocial personality disorder and Type 2 alcoholism. *Psychiatry Research Neuroimaging, 114*, 95–102.

Laakso, M.P., Vaurio, O., Koivisto, E., Savolainen, L., Eronen, M., Aronen, H.J., et al. (2001). Psychopathy and the posterior hippocampus. *Behavioral Brain Research, 118*, 187–193.

Laakso, M.P., Vaurio, O., Savolainen, L., Repo, E., Soininen, H., Aronen, H.J. & Tiihonen, J. (2000). A volumetric MRI study of the hippocampus in Type 1 and 2 alcoholism. *Behavioral Brain Research, 109*, 117–186.

Lally, J.R., Mangione, P.L. & Honig, A.S. (1988). Long-range impact of an early intervention with low income children and their families. In D.R. Powell (Ed.) *Parent education as early childhood intervention* (pp.79–104). Norwood, NJ: Ablex.

Lang, S., Klinteberg, B. & Alm, P.O. (2002). Adult psychopathy and violent behavior in males with early neglect and abuse. *Acta Psychiatrica Scandinavica, 106*, Supplement 412, 93–100.

Larsson, H., Andershed, H. & Lichtenstein, P. (2006). A genetic factor explains most of the variation in the psychopathic personality. *Journal of Abnormal Psychology, 115*, 2211–2230.

LeDoux, J.E. (2000) Emotion circuits in the brain. *Annual Review of Neuroscience, 23*, 155–184.

Lilienfeld, S.O. & Andrews, B.P. (1996). Development and preliminary validation of a self-report measure of psychopathic personality traits in noncriminal populations. *Journal of Personality Assessment, 66*, 488–524.

Lister, J.P., Blatt, G.J., DeBassio, W.A., Kemper, T.L., Tonkiss, J., Galler, J.R., et al. (2005). Effect of prenatal protein malnutrition on numbers of neurons in the principal cell layers of the adult rat hippocampal formation. *Hippocampus, 15*, 393–403.

Liu, J. (2004). Childhood externalizing behavior. Theory and implications. *Journal of Child and Adolescent Psychiatric Nursing, 17*, 93–103.

Liu, J. & Raine, A. (2006). The effect of childhood malnutrition on externalizing behaviors. *Current Opinion in Pediatrics, 18*, 565–570.

Liu, J., Raine, A., Wuerker, A., Venables, P.H. & Mednick, S.A. (2009). The association of birth complications and externalizing behavior in early adolescents. *Journal of Research on Adolescence, 19*, 93–111.

Liu, J. & Wuerker, A. (2005). Biosocial bases of aggressive and violent behavior – implications for nursing studies. *International Journal of Nursing Studies, 42*, 229–241.

Loney, B.R., Frick, P.J., Clements, C.B., Ellis, M.L. & Kerlin, K. (2003). Callous-unemotional traits, impulsivity and emotional processing in adolescents with antisocial behavior problems. *Journal of Clinical Child and Adolescent Psychology, 32*, 66–80.

Lorber, M.F. (2004). Psychophysiology of aggression, psychopathy, and conduct problems: A meta-analysis. *Psychological Bulletin, 130*, 531–552.

Lyons-Ruth, K., Alpern, L. & Repacholi, B. (1993). Disorganized infant attachment classification and maternal psychosocial problems as predictors of hostile aggressive behavior in the preschool classroom. *Child Development, 64*, 572–585.

Main, M. (1995). Recent studies in attachment. In S. Goldberg, R. Muir & J. Kerr (Eds.) *Attachment theory: Social, developmental and clinical perspectives* (pp.407–474). Hillsdale: NJ: Analytic Press.

Main, M. & Hesse, E. (1990). Parent's unresolved traumatic experiences are related to infant disorganization status: Is frightened and/or frightening behavior the linking mechanism? In M.T. Greenberg, D. Cicchetti & E.M. Cummings (Eds.) *Attachment in the pre-school years* (pp.161–182). Chicago, IL: University of Chicago Press.

Marsh, A.A., Finger, E.C., Mitchell, D.G.V., Reid, M.E., Sims, C., Kosson, D.S., et al. (2008). Reduced amygdala response to fearful expressions in children and adolescents with callous-unemotional traits and disruptive behavior disorders. *American Journal of Psychiatry, 165*, 712–720.

Maughan, B., Taylor, A., Caspi, A. & Moffitt, T.E. (2004). Prenatal smoking and early childhood conduct problems. Archives of General Psychiatry, 61, 836–843.

McAllister, T. (1992). Neuropsychiatric sequelae of head injuries. *Psychiatric Clinics of North America, 15*, 661–665.

McCord, J. (1979). Some child-rearing antecedents of criminal behavior in adult men. *Journal of Personality and Social Psychology, 37*, 1477–1486.

Mednick, S.A., Volavka, J., Gabrielli, W.F. & Itil, T. (1981). EEG as a predictor of antisocial behavior. *Criminology, 19*, 219–229.

Mezzacappa, E., Tremblay, R.E., Kindlon D.J., Saul J.P., Arsenault L, Seguin, J.R., et al. (1997). Anxiety, antisocial behavior and heart rate regulation in adolescent males. *Journal of Child Psychology and Psychiatry, 38*, 457–468.

Miles, D.R. & Carey, G. (1997). Genetic and environmental architecture of human aggression. *Journal of Personality and Social Psychology, 72*, 207–217.

Mitchell, D.G.V., Colledge, E., Leonard, A. & Blair, R.J.R. (2002). Risky decisions and response reversal: Is there evidence of orbitofrontal cortex dysfunction in psychopathic individuals? *Neuropsychologia, 40*, 2013–2022.

Mitchell, I.J. & Beech, A.R (2011). Towards an attachment related neurobiological model of offending. *Clinical Psychology Review, 31*, 872–882.

Moffitt, T.E. (1990). Juvenile delinquency and attention-deficit disorder. Developmental trajectories from age 3 to 15. *Child Development, 61*, 893–910.

Moffitt, T.E. (1993). Adolescence-limited and life-course-persistent antisocial behavior. A developmental taxonomy. *Psychological Review, 100,* 674–701.

Moffitt, T.E. & Caspi, A. (2001). Childhood predictors differentiate life-course persistent and adolescence-limited antisocial pathways among males and females. *Development and Psychopathology, 13,* 355–375.

Moffitt, T.E., Lynam, D.R. & Silva, P.A. (1994). Neuropsychological tests predicting persistent male delinquency. *Criminology, 32,* 277–300.

Morgan, A.B. & Lilienfeld, S.O. (2000). A meta-analytic review of the relationship between antisocial behavior and neuropsychological measures of executive function. *Clinical Psychology Review, 20,* 113–136.

Muller, J.L., Sommer, M., Wagner, V., Lange, K., Taschler, H., Röder, C.H., *et al.* (2003). Abnormalities in emotion processing within cortical and subcortical regions in criminal psychopaths: Evidence from a functional magnetic imaging study using pictures with emotional content. *Psychiatry Research Neuroimaging, 54,* 152–162.

Muneoka, K., Ogawa, T., Kamei, K., Muraoka, S., Tomiyoshi, R., Mimura, Y., *et al.* (1997). Prenatal nicotine exposure affects the development of the central serotonergic system as well as the dopaminergic system in rat offspring. Involvement of route of drug administrations. *Brain Research and Developmental Brain Research, 102,* 117–126.

Neugebauer, R., Hoek, H.W. & Susser, E. (1999). Prenatal exposure to wartime famine and development of antisocial personality disorder in early adulthood. *Journal of the American Medical Association, 4,* 455–462.

Newman, J.P. & Kosson, D.S. (1986). Passive avoidance learning in psychopathic and non-psychopathic offenders. *Journal of Abnormal Psychology, 95,* 252–256.

Olds, D. (1997). Tobacco exposure and impaired development: A review of the evidence. *Mental Retardation and Developmental Disabilities Research Reviews, 3,* 257–269.

Olds, D., Henderson, C.R.J., Cole, R., Eckenrode, J., Kitzman, H., Luckey, D., *et al.* (1998). Long-term effects of nurse home visition on children's criminal and antisocial behavior: 15-year follow-up of a randomized controlled trial. *Journal of the American Medical Association, 280,* 1238–1244.

Olson, H.C., Streissguth, A.P., Sampson, P.D., Barr, H.M., Bookstein, F.L. & Thiede, K. (1997). Association of prenatal alcohol exposure with behavioral and learning problems in early adolescence. *Journal of the American Academy of Child and Adolescent Psychiatry, 36,* 1187–1194.

Orlebeke, J.F., Knol, D.L. & Verhulst, F.C. (1997). Increase in child behavior problems resulting from maternal smoking during pregnancy. *Archives of Environmental Health, 52,* 317–321.

Ortiz, J. & Raine A. (2004). Heart rate level and antisocial behavior in children and adolescents: A meta analysis. *Journal of American Academy of Child and Adolescent Psychiatry, 43,* 154–162.

Petersen, K.G.I., Matousek, M., Mednick, S.A., Volavka, J. & Pollock V. (1982). EEG antecedents of thievery. *Acta Psychiatrica Scandanavia, 65,* 331–338.

Pine, D.S., Shaffer, D., Schonfield, I.S. & Davies, M. (1997). Minor physical anomolies. Modifiers of environmental risks for psychiatric impairment? *Journal of the American Academy of Child and Adolescent Psychiatry, 36,* 395–403.

Raine, A. (1996). Autonomic nervous system activity and violence. In D.M. Stoff & R.B. Cairns (Eds.) *Neurobiological approaches to clinical aggression research* (pp.145–168). Mahwah, NJ: Lawrence Erlbaum.

Raine, A. (2002). Biosocial studies of antisocial and violent behavior in children and adults: A review. *Journal of Abnormal Child Psychology, 304,* 311–326.

Raine, A., Brennan, P. & Mednick, S.A. (1994). Birth complications combined with early maternal rejection at age 1 year predispose to violent crime at age 18 years. *Archives of General Psychiatry, 51,* 984–988.

Raine, A., Buchsbaum, M., Stanley, J., Lottenberg, S., Abel, L. & Stoddard, S. (1994). Selective reductions in prefrontal glucose metabolism in murderers. *Biological Psychiatry, 36,* 365–373.

Raine, A., Buchsbaum, M. & LaCasse, L. (1997). Brain abnormalities in murderers indicated by positron emission tomography. *Biological Psychiatry, 42,* 495–508.

Raine, A., Lencz, T., Bihrle, S., LaCasse, L. & Colletti, P. (2000). Reduced prefrontal gray matter volume and reduced autonomic activity in antisocial personality disorder. *Archives of General Psychiatry, 57,* 119–127.

Raine, A., Mellingen, K., Liu, J., Venables, P., Sarnoff, A. & Mednick, S.A. (2003). Effects of environmental enrichment at ages 3–5 years on schizotypal personality and antisocial behavior at ages 17 and 23 years. *American Journal of Psychiatry, 160,* 1627–1635.

Raine, A., Venables, P.H. & Mednick, S.A. (1997). Low resting heart rate age 3 years predisposes to aggression at age 11 years. Evidence from the Mauritius Child Health Project. *Journal of American Academy of Child and Adolescent Psychiatry, 36,* 1457–1464.

Raine, A., Venables, P.H. & Williams, N. (1990). Relationships between CNS and ANS measures of arousal at age 15 years as protective factors against criminal behavior at age 29 years. *American Journal of Psychiatry, 152,* 1595–1600.

Raine, A., Venables, P.H. & Williams, N. (1995). High autonomic arousal and electrodermal orienting at age 15 years as protective factors against criminal behavior at age 29 years. *American Journal of Psychiatry, 152,* 1595–1600.

Rhee, S.H. & Waldman, I.D. (2002). Genetic and environmental influences on antisocial behavior: A meta-analysis of twin and adoption studies. *Psychological Bulletin, 128,* 490–529.

Rivera, J., Jaffee, K., Polissar, N.L., Fay, G.C., Martin, K.M., Shurtleff, H.A., *et al.* (1994). Family functioning and children's academic performance and behavior problems in the year following brain injury. *Archives of Physical Medicine and Rehabilitation, 75,* 369–379.

Robins, L. (1996). *Deviant children grown up.* Baltimore, MD: Williams & Wilkins.

Roebuck, T.M., Mattson, S.N. & Riley, E.P. (1999). Behavioral and psychosocial profiles of alcohol-exposed children. *Alcoholism. Clinical and Experimental Research, 23,* 1070–1076.

Rogeness, G.A., Cepeda, C., Macedo, C.A., Fischer, D. & Harris, W.R. (1990). Differences in heart rate and blood pressure in children with conduct disorder, major depression and separation anxiety. *Psychiatry Research, 33,* 199–206.

Rosen, G.M., Deinard, A.S., Schwartz, S., Smith, C., Stephenson, B. & Grabenstein, B. (1985). Iron deficiency among incarcerated juvenile delinquents. *Journal of Adolescent Health Care, 6,* 419–423.

Rosenstein, D.S. & Horowitz, H.A. (1996). Adolescent attachment and psychopathology. *Journal of Consulting and Clinical Psychology, 64,* 244–253.

Saltaris, C. (2002). Psychopathy in juvenile offenders: Can temperament and attachment be considered as robust developmental precursors. *Clinical Psychology Review, 22,* 729–752.

Sampson, R.J. & Laub, J.H. (1990). Crime and deviance over the life course: The salience of adult social bonds. *American Sociological Review, 55,* 609–627.

Santesso, D.L., Reker, D.L., Schmidt, L.A. & Segalowitz, S.J. (2006). Frontal electroencephalogram activation asymmetry, emotional intelligence, and externalizing behaviors in 10-year-old children. *Child Psychiatry and Human Development, 36,* 311–328.

Scerbo, A., Raine, A., O'Brien, M., Chan, C.J., Rhee, C. & Smiley, N. (1990). Reward dominance and passive avoidance learning in adolescent psychopaths. *Journal of Abnormal Child Psychology, 18,* 451–463.

Schoenthaler, S.J. & Bier, I.D. (2000). The effect of vitamin-mineral supplementation on juvenile delinquency among American schoolchildren: A randomized double blind placebo-controlled trial. *Journal of Alternative and Complementary Medicine, 6,* 19–29.

Schonfeld, A.M., Mattson, S.N. & Riley, E.P. (2005). Moral maturity and delinquency after prenatal alcohol exposure. *Journal of Studies on Alcohol, 6,* 19–29.

Solomon, E.P. & Heide, K.M. (2005). The biology of trauma. *Journal of Interpersonal Violence, 20,* 51–60.

Sterzer, P., Stadler, C. Krebs, A., Kleinschmidt, A. & Poustka, F. (2005). Abnormal neural responses to emotional visual stimuli in adolescents with conduct disorder. *Biological Psychiatry, 57,* 7–15.

Stevens, L., Zhang, W., Peck, L., Kuczek, Y., Grevstad, N. & Mahon, A. (2003). EFA supplementation in children with inattention, hyperactivity, and other disruptive behaviors. *Lipids, 38,* 1007–1021.

Streissguth, A.P., Barr, H.M., Kogan, J. & Bookstein, F.L. (1996). *Understanding the occurrence of secondary disabilities in clients with fetal alcohol syndrome (FAS) and fetal alcohol effects (FAE). Technical Report No. 96–06.* Seattle, WA: University of Washington, Fetal Alcohol and Drug Unit.

Taylor, C. (1997). *Psychopathy and attachment in a group of incarcerated females.* Unpublished doctoral dissertation. San Francisco, CA: California School of Professional Psychology, Alliant International University.

Teichner, G. & Golden, C.J. (2000). The relationship of neuropsychological impairment to conduct disorder in adolescence: A conceptual review. *Aggression and Violent Behavior, 5,* 509–528.

Tibbetts, S.G. & Piquero, A.R. (1999). The influence of gender, low birth weight, and disadvantaged environment in predicting early onset of offending. A test of Moffitt's interactional hypothesis. *Criminology, 37,* 843–878.

Uvnas-Moberg, K. (1998) Oxytocin may mediate the benefits of positive social interaction and emotions. *Psychoneuroendocrinology 23,* 819–835.

Volavka, J. (1987). Electroencephalogram among criminals. In S.A. Mednick, T.E. Moffitt & S. Stack (Eds.) *The causes of crime. New biological approches.* (pp.137–145). Cambridge: Cambridge University Press.

Wakschlag, L.S., Lahey, B.B., Loeber, R., Green, S.M., Gordon, R.A. & Leventhal B.L. (1997). Maternal smoking during pregnancy and the risk of conduct disorder in boys. *Archives of General Psychiatry, 54,* 670–676.

Wakschlag, L.S., Pickett, K.E., Cook, E., Benowitz, N.L. & Leventhal, B.L. (2002). Maternal smoking during pregnancy and severe antisocial behavior in offspring: A review. *American Journal of Public Health, 92,* 966–974.

Waldrop, M.F., Bell, R.Q., McLauglin, B. & Halverson, C.F. (1978). Newborn minor physical anomalies predict short attention span, peer aggression, and impulsivity at age 3. *Science, 199,* 563–564.

Weinfield, N.S., Sroufe, A., Egeland, B. & Carlson, E. (2008). Individual differences in infant-caregiver attachment: Conceptual and empirical aspects of security. In J. Cassidy & P.R. Shaver (Eds.) *Handbook of attachment: Theory, research, and clinical applications* (2nd edn) (pp.78–101). New York: Guilford.

Werbach, M. (1995). Nutritional influences on aggressive behavior. *Journal of Orthomolecular Medicine, 7,* 45–51.

Wismer Fries, A.B., Ziegler, T.E., Kurain, J.P., Jacoris, S. & Pollack, S.D. (2005). Early experience in humans is associated with changes in neuropeptides critical for regulating social behavior. *Proceedings of the National Academy of Sciences, 102,* 17237–17240.

Young, J.E., Klosko. J.S. & Weisharr, M.E. (2003). *Schema therapy: A practitioner's guide.* London: Guilford Press.

Zanarini, M.C., Gunderson, J.G., Marino, M.F., Schwartz, E.O. & Franenber, F.R. (1989). Childhood experiences of borderline patients. *Comprehensive Psychiatry, 30,* 18–25.

ANNOTATED READING LIST

Bartol, C.R. & Bartol, A.M. (2008). *Criminal behavior* (8th edn). Upper Saddle River, NJ: Pearson. *This text has several good chapters on biological risk factors of criminal behaviour. The information is lucidly presented and is presented at a basic level.*

Cassady, J. & Shaver, P.R. (Eds.) *Handbook of attachment; Theory research and clinical applications* (2nd edn). New York: Guilford Press. *This provides a good background to the concept of attachment.*

Feinberg, T.E. (2001). *Altered egos: How the brain creates the self.* New York: Oxford University Press. *This book is recommended to anyone who found the story of Phineas Gage (in Case Study 3.2) interesting. Feinberg's writing is highly readable and he describes how injuries to different parts of the brain can lead to unusual neuropsychiatric syndromes. While the book does not focus on crime, it does beautifully describe how the brain creates personality.*

Hare, R.D. (1999). *Without conscience: The disturbing world of the psychopaths among us.* New York: Guilford Press. *This very readable book gives a valuable insight into the mind of the psychopath.*

Hodgins, S., Viding, E. & Plodowski, A. (2009). *The neurobiological basis of violence: Science and rehabilitation.* Oxford: Oxford University Press. *Good overview of the neorobiology of violence, by leading researchers in the area.*

Volavka, J. (2002). *Neurobiology of violence* (2nd edn). Washington, DC: American Psychiatric Publishing, Inc. *This is an excellent comprehensive, if somewhat advanced, text about the neurobiology of violence. It includes an excellent chapter on drugs of abuse and how these affect the risk for violence.*

4 Effects of Interpersonal Crime on Victims

CATHERINE HAMILTON-GIACHRITSIS AND EMMA SLEATH

KEY TERMS

• Child Protection Plan • cognitive processing therapy • comorbidity • control behaviours • dysregulation of the emotion and stress pathways • executive functioning • externalising behaviours/symptoms • familial trauma • gender role • indirect victimisation • intergenerational cycle of maltreatment • internalising symptoms • intimate partner violence • longitudinal study • maladaptive beliefs • prolonged exposure therapy • resilience • sociocultural factors • stress inoculation training • suicidality • symptomology

CHAPTER OUTLINE

Sadly, for too many people, violent and sexual victimisation begins in childhood, but many adult women and men are also victims of interpersonal crimes, such as rape and **intimate partner violence** (IPV). The effects of such victimisation can be seen in both the short and long term in a variety of domains, including physical, psychological, social and interpersonal relationships, and even at the community level through the financial cost and indirect impacts on society. Negative effects in childhood have been shown to include mental health difficulties, educational disengagement, behavioural difficulties and increased risk of further victimisation and/or perpetration against others. In adulthood, victimisation is associated with poorer physical and mental health outcomes, both in the short and long term, which can severely impact on the function and quality of victims' lives. This chapter will briefly review the definition and extent of interpersonal crime, followed by discussion of the short- and long-term effects of victimisation in childhood (i.e. physical, sexual and emotional maltreatment) and adulthood (i.e. rape and intimate partner violence).

> **intimate partner violence** physical, sexual, psychological aggression and/or controlling behaviours used against a current or past intimate partner of any sex.

CHILDHOOD VICTIMISATION

One of the key difficulties in assessing interpersonal crime is in gaining accurate estimates of such events,

due to differences in sources of data and methodological variations (e.g. definition used, sampling strategy, measurement tools), as well as whether victims perceive themselves to be a victim of crime and/or feel able to report it. For example, a national study in the Netherlands found that only 12.6 per cent of cases of victimisation were reported to child protection services (Euser et al., 2010), with other studies showing similar findings (Fallon et al., 2010). Similarly, definitional differences impact on the rates of maltreatment recorded; in a sample of 303 maltreated children in the USA, neglect was found to have occurred in 70.1 per cent of cases but only to have been recognised by child protection professionals in 41 per cent of cases (Mennen et al., 2010). Thus, consideration of data needs to account for the methodological difficulties inherent in this area of work.

Definitions and measurement

Physical, sexual and emotional abuse and neglect (see Table 4.1) can occur either within or outside the family. Maltreatment definitions vary according to the era, cultural context and profession using them (Cicchetti & Toth, 1995). In recent years the effects of witnessing intimate partner violence, often referred to as a form of emotional abuse, has become embedded in definitions.

Rates of maltreatment are usually reported in one of two ways: incidence and prevalence. Incidence refers to the number of cases reported or detected within a set

TABLE 4.1 *Definitions of childhood maltreatment.*

Physical abuse	Hitting, shaking, throwing, poisoning, burning or scalding, drowning, suffocating or otherwise causing physical harm to a child or failing to protect a child from that harm. Physical harm may also be caused when a parent or carer fabricates the symptoms of, or deliberately induces illness in, a child.
Sexual abuse	Forcing or enticing a child or young person to take part in sexual activities, including prostitution, whether or not the child is aware of what is happening . . . May include non-contact activities, such as involving children in looking at, or in the production of, pornographic material or watching sexual activities, or encouraging children to behave in sexually inappropriate ways.
Emotional abuse	The persistent emotional maltreatment of a child such as to cause severe and persistent adverse effects on the child's emotional development . . . It may involve seeing or hearing the maltreatment of another . . . Some level of emotional abuse is involved in all types of maltreatment of a child, though it may occur alone.
Neglect	The persistent failure to meet a child's basic physical and/or psychological needs, likely to result in the serious impairment of the child's health or development . . . Neglect may occur during pregnancy as a result of maternal substance abuse. Once a child is born, neglect may involve . . . failing to protect a child . . . or the failure to ensure access to appropriate medical care or treatment. It may also include neglect of, or unresponsiveness to, a child's basic emotional needs.

Source: Working Together to Safeguard Children (Department for Education and Skills, 2006). Reproduced with permission.

period, usually one year, whilst prevalence is the number of individuals who retrospectively report experiencing maltreatment during childhood (usually aged 0–18 years for child maltreatment).

> **Child Protection Plan** details areas of concern, planned action and monitoring for a child who is considered to be in need of protection from physical, sexual and/or emotional abuse and/or neglect.

In terms of incident rates, at 31 March 2010, there were 39,100 children in England who were subject to a **Child Protection Plan** or CPP (3.55 per 1,000), with 44,300 children over the whole year, 13.4 per cent of whom were subject to a plan for a second time (Department for Education, 2010). For breakdown by type of maltreatment, see Table 4.2. The greatest risk is to babies, with the highest rate of registration in England and Wales for children under 1 year (5.6 per 1,000), accounting for 13 per cent of the total number of registered children (Department for Children, Schools and Families, 2008). A comparison of UK, European and American rates shows some similarities (Denmark and UK) but inclusion of concern about a child from any professional (such as in national incidence studies) tends to lead to higher rates of referral (Table 4.3).

Prevalence data usually comes from self-report but rates are highly dependent on methodology, which can make comparisons between different studies difficult (Gilbert *et al.*, 2009). In the UK, May-Chahal and Cawson (2005) found that 16 per cent of 2,869 18–24 year olds surveyed reported having experienced intra- or extrafamilial maltreatment in childhood. In a review of rates of child sexual abuse in studies up to 2007, overall mean prevalence rates ranged from 34.4 per cent for Africa ($N = 2,357$) compared to 15.8 per cent for America ($N = 47,369$), 10.1 per cent for Asia ($N = 7,110$) and 9.2 per cent for Europe ($N = 35,974$; Pereda *et al.*, 2009). In general, rates for women were significantly higher than for men with the exception of South Africa, which was very high for both sexes (43.7 per cent females and 60.9 per cent males), but also France (0.9 per cent females, 0.6 per cent males) and Portugal (2.7 per cent females, 2.6 per cent males), where the rate was very low for both.

Despite this, some research suggests that some forms of maltreatment (i.e. sexual and physical abuse) have declined in prevalence from 2003 to 2008 in the USA, but that caregiver physical abuse and neglect, as well as witnessing sibling victimisation, have increased (Finkelhor *et al.*, 2010).

TABLE 4.2 *Children under 18 years subject to a Child Protection Plan in England in the year to 31 March 2010.*

	N	*%*
Neglect	19,300	43.5
Emotional abuse	12,300	27.8
Physical abuse	6,300	14.2
Sexual abuse	2,500	5.6
Multiple or not recommended	4,000	9.0

Source: Adapted with permission from Department for Education, 2010.

Effects of childhood maltreatment

Negative effects of childhood maltreatment are found both in childhood (Table 4.4) and ongoing into adulthood (Table 4.5). However, it is also acknowledged that some children are able to emerge from maltreatment experiences showing functional, adaptive behaviour in their day-to-day life (Goldstein & Brooks, 2005).

The most extreme outcome following childhood maltreatment is, unfortunately, death and/or disability. In the UK and USA, most such fatalities occur in children

TABLE 4.3 *Incidence rates in UK, Europe and USA*.*

	Rate per 1000 children	*Sample*	*Source*
UK	3.5	Children subject of a Child Protection Plan, 0–17 years	Department for Education, 2010
Denmark	2.7	0–17 years	Riis *et al.*, 1997
Netherlands	6.9	National Incidence Study 0–18 years	Euser *et al.*, 2010
USA	17.1	National Incidence Study 0–18 years	Sedlak *et al.*, 2010
USA	43.1 (range by State: 15.4–104.3)	National referral rate (not accounting for substantiation or duplication)	US Department of Health and Human Services *et al.*, 2010

*Methodological differences in samples, criteria and definitions.

TABLE 4.4 *Effects of maltreatment in childhood.*

Death
Physical and mental disability
Mental health difficulties (e.g. post-traumatic stress, eating disorders, self-injurious behaviour)
Physical health difficulties (e.g. sleep disorders, enuresis, encopresis, stress)
Emotional difficulties (e.g. low self-esteem, poor self-worth)
Behavioural difficulties (e.g. antisocial behavioural, criminal acts, substance misuse)
Educational difficulties and failure
Impact on social and interpersonal functioning (e.g. relationships with others, attachment difficulties)
Risk of further victimisation

TABLE 4.5 *Long-term effects in adulthood following childhood sexual abuse found in a review of 25 meta-analyses.*

Symptom	Effect size range (Pearson's correlations coefficient; r)
Alcohol problems	.07
Anger	.18
Anxiety	.13–.20
Borderline personality disorder	.28
Depression	.12–.22
Dissociation	.09–.19
Eating disorders	.06–.10
Hostility	.11
Interpersonal sensitivity	.10
Interpersonal problems	.19
Obsessive-compulsive symptomatology	.10–.17
Paranoia	.11
Phobia	.12
Post-traumatic stress disorder	.20
Psychological adjustment problems	.10–.27
Psychotic symptoms	.11
Self-esteem impairments	.04–.17
Self-mutilation	.20
Sexual adjustment	.09–.18
Sexual promiscuity	.14
Social adjustment	.07
Somatisation	.09–.17
Substance misuse	.20
Suicidal ideation and behaviour	.09–.22
Traumatic stress symptoms	.25

Source: Adapted from Hillberg *et al.,* 2011 with permission from SAGE publications.

under the age of 5 years, with the greatest percentage of deaths in infants under 1 year old, with head injury, physical battering and/or severe neglect the most common causes (Kleevens & Leeb, 2010; Sidebotham *et al.,* 2011). The UK rate between 2005 and 2009 was 0.63 cases per 100,000 children per year (aged 0–17); the most common cause of death was severe physical assault (Figure 4.1), with severe neglect present in at least 40 per cent of cases but less likely to be the direct cause of death (Sidebotham *et al.,* 2011). The median age of the children was 16 months, with boys more likely to experience physical assault, girls more likely to experience severe neglect and older children more likely to be victims of overt homicide. Of those children who have died from maltreatment, only about one third were known to child protection agencies. In the USA, the rate in 2009 was 2.34 deaths per 100,000 children (US Department of Health and Human Services *et al.,* 2010). Relatives (mainly maternal and paternal caregivers) are generally deemed to be responsible in over 80 per cent of cases (Lee & Lathrop, 2010).

One of the most identified effects of child maltreatment is the association with mental health and emotional/behavioural difficulties. Perhaps the most prominent of these are depression and other internalising disorders (Kim & Cicchetti, 2006). These can include eating disorders (Nygaard Christoffersen & DePanfilis, 2009), psychological distress (Newcomb *et al.,* 2009), anxiety (Cougle *et al.,* 2010) and depression (Bennett *et al.,* 2010), as well as self-injurious or suicidal behaviour, addiction and low self-esteem (see Gilbert *et al.,* 2009 for a review). Whilst all forms of maltreatment have been found to have an effect, some studies suggest that psychological maltreatment or emotional abuse has the most negative impact (Nygaard Christoffersen & DePanfilis, 2009).

After controlling for stressors (family conflict, parental personal difficulties, external constraints in home and community), socio-economic status and child gender,

FIGURE 4.1 *Whilst all forms of maltreatment have been found to have an effect, some studies suggest that psychological maltreatment or emotional abuse has the most negative impact.*

Source: © Sean Bolt. Used under licence from Shutterstock.

externalising behaviours/symptoms these refer to problems that are manifested in outward behaviour and reflect a child's negative reactions to her/his environment, including aggression, delinquency and hyperactivity. Other terms used include *conduct problems* and *antisocial*.

internalising symptoms emotional and behavioural difficulties within an individual, such that the individual tries to over-control internal anxieties and worries (e.g. anxiety/depression).

indirect victimisation feeling victimised through witnessing someone else being victimised, such as watching another person being bullied or parent(s) being violent to each other.

child maltreatment alone is predictive of internalising and/or externalising difficulties in adolescents (Herrenkohl & Herrenkohl, 2007). Early studies also tended to show that boys were more likely to develop **externalising symptoms** such as aggressive behaviour and conduct disorders (Figure 4.2) and girls **internalising symptoms** such as depression (Feiring *et al.*, 2002). Later studies show a more complex picture, as outlined below. One study has found an association between every form of child maltreatment and the likelihood of victims experiencing at least 8 out of 10 adolescent health risks, including depression, regular alcohol use, binge drinking, marijuana or alcohol and inhalant use, and serious fights (Hussey *et al.*, 2006).

When the definition of victimisation is extended to include bullying and **indirect victimisation**, it is found that children who experience multiple victimisation

exposures are more likely to show negative outcomes (Turner *et al.*, 2009). In a **longitudinal study**, it was found that children who experienced intentional harm (i.e. maltreatment by an adult or bullying by another child) were significantly more likely to show psychotic symptoms at age 12 years even after controlling for confounding variables (such as socio-economic deprivation, lower IQ and genetic vulnerabilities; Arseneault *et al.*, 2011).

There is substantial evidence to suggest that one key outcome of maltreatment is the increased risk of subsequent maltreatment, which in turn leads to more serious outcomes (Barnes *et al.*, 2009). Re-referral rates for a child range from 8–13 per cent in four years (Fryer & Miyoshi, 1994) to 43.2 per cent of maltreated infants followed up for 11–15 years (Thompson & Wiley, 2009). Family re-referral rates range from 1–2 per cent (low risk) to over 50 per cent (high risk families) in five years, but may go up to 85 per cent over 10 years (DePanfilis & Zuravin, 1998). However, the risk is highest in the first 12 months following referral (Hindley *et al.*, 2006), with the risk doubling once a child has been referred on two occasions (Hamilton & Browne, 1999). The presence of other risk factors can compound this. When IPV and child maltreatment co-occur, a higher number of prior referrals for both forms of family violence and greater severity of IPV have been found (Browne & Hamilton, 1999), and re-referrals occur quicker (Casanueva *et al.*, 2009).

FIGURE 4.2 *Early studies showed that boys were more likely to develop externalising symptoms, such as aggressive behaviour and conduct disorders, while girls were more likely to develop internalising symptoms such as depression.*

Source: © Lynne Carpenter. Used under licence from Shutterstock.

Over 20 years ago, Widom (1989) noted that there was an increased risk of involvement in criminal activity following child maltreatment, which was then supported by other studies (for a review, see Falshaw *et al.*, 1996). Even then, however, it was also acknowledged that most do not go on to commit crimes (Widom, 1991). Those who experience recurrent forms of maltreatment are most at risk of committing violent crimes (Hamilton *et al.*, 2002). Thus, it is important to consider factors related to outcome.

Factors related to outcome

Age (stage of development), gender, type, relationship to perpetrator, frequency and severity of maltreatment have all been linked to outcome (Gilbert *et al.*, 2009). Externalising behaviour has been associated with higher frequency of incidents and developmental timing, but impairments of social functioning are more associated with the distribution of incidents over time, suggesting that the child may have time to show resilience in maltreatment-free phases (English *et al.*, 2005). Furthermore,

the presence of a supportive caregiver reduces the likelihood of long-term negative effects (Alexander & Lupfer, 1987), yet because the majority of child maltreatment is perpetrated by family members, friends or acquaintances, the likelihood of a supportive family environment is reduced.

Research has begun to investigate the mechanisms of this. For example, **familial trauma** (compared to non-familial trauma or no trauma) is associated with poorer performance on **executive functioning** (e.g. working memory, processing speed) even after accounting for socio-economic status, anxiety and possible brain injury exposure, which may lead to difficulties academically but also with social and interpersonal functioning (DePrince *et al.*, 2009). In addition, those children who experienced physical and sexual abuse before the age of 5 years and showed internalising symptoms were found to have **dysregulation of the emotion and stress pathways**, via cortisol production (Cicchetti *et al.*, 2010). The authors postulated that genes may be one reason why some children who experience early sexual or physical abuse develop internalising symptoms and others do not, but note that this requires further investigation. Overall, while the associations with negative long-term outcomes have been shown, the pathways by which this occurs continue to require investigation.

> **familial trauma** abuse or neglect perpetrated by a family member.

> **executive functioning** brain processes responsible for higher order cognitive tasks, such as planning, abstract reasoning and problem solving. *Executive dysfunction* involves impairments with, for example, impulse control, self-regulation, sustained attention, planning and problem-solving.

> **dysregulation of the emotion and stress pathways** relatively poor regulation of emotion and stress due to physiological responses.

Negative effects of child maltreatment in adulthood

In adulthood, long-term effects of child maltreatment have been demonstrated on mental and physical health, as well as social and emotional functioning (see Table 4.5). Perhaps unsurprisingly, many of the difficulties found in childhood remain in adulthood. The impact on enduring personality features is also more apparent (Kim *et al.*, 2009). Long-term effects even extend as far as increasing risk of premature death in family members (i.e. under 65 years), possibly as a result of chaotic family environments, with the highest risks occurring in families characterised by physical neglect, substance misuse and criminality (Anda *et al.*, 2009).

Individuals who have been maltreated in childhood may have an increased risk of further victimisation in adulthood through sexual victimisation and/or intimate partner violence (Gilbert *et al.*, 2009) or engagement in criminal behaviour (known as the 'victim to offender cycle'; Farrington *et al.*, 2001). One widely debated effect is the risk of maltreated children becoming familial abusers

intergenerational cycle of maltreatment maltreated children becoming familial abusers themselves.

themselves (the **intergenerational cycle of maltreatment** or ICM). Some argue the rate is as high as 30 per cent (+/−5 per cent; Kaufman & Zigler, 1987); other evidence suggests that in a short-term (13-month) follow-up, the rate is as low as 6.7 per cent (Dixon, Browne *et al.*, 2005). The most significant risk factors for the abused parent group were a parent under 21, history of mental illness or depression and the presence of a violent adult in the household. These risk factors, combined with poor parenting styles (such as unrealistic expectations, poor quality of interaction and negative attributions), more fully mediated the ICM (Dixon, Hamilton-Giachritsis *et al.*, 2005). Notably, the presence or absence of social support and financial security distinguished cycle-breakers from maintainers (i.e. those who continued the ICM) and initiators (i.e. non-abused parents who maltreated their children; Dixon *et al.*, 2009; see Figure 4.3). This confirms previous studies that have identified the importance of emotional and social support as protective factors for adults with a background of abuse and the absence of support as a risk factor for all parents (Cerezo *et al.*, 1996; Egeland, 1988; Ertem *et al.*, 2000).

Resilience

Childhood maltreatment has a variety of negative long-term outcomes, as highlighted in Case Study 4.1. However, some individuals show resilience and adaptive functioning. Current research is attempting to more clearly define the mechanisms through which different outcomes occur, moving from identifying key factors to the mechanisms through

resilience no agreed definition, but usually taken to mean the absence of psychopathology and successful functioning over a number of domains.

which they work and the implications for interventions (Masten & O'Dougherty Wright, 2010). Resilience is a difficult concept to define and is varyingly taken as the absence of psychopathology or successful functioning over a number of domains (Luthar, 2003). Rates of resilience also differ according to the time frame over which they are assessed. However, the key message is that resilience has repeatedly been demonstrated by individuals, following both childhood and/or adulthood maltreatment.

VICTIMISATION IN ADULTHOOD

There are many crimes that occur within society that result in an adult becoming a victim of crime. This section will focus on two particular crimes: intimate partner

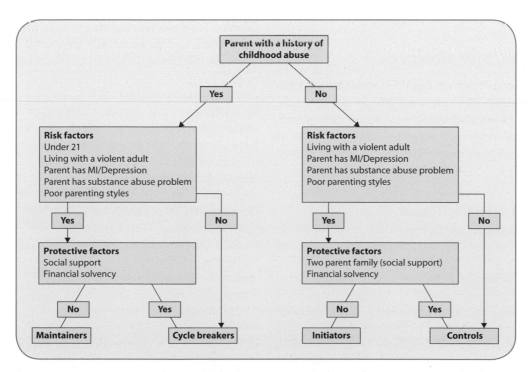

FIGURE 4.3 *Conceptual model discriminating child-maltreating and non-child-maltreating families.*

Source: Taken from Dixon, Browne & Hamilton-Giachritsis, 2009. Reproduced with permission of Springer.

CASE STUDY 4.1   RECURRENT VICTIMISATION AND THE INTERGENERATIONAL CYCLE OF MALTREATMENT

Sharon is a single mother in her early thirties. She has three children. Her early experiences were both abusive and neglectful, with the maltreatment covering many aspects of her life. Sharon's mother was an alcoholic and was emotionally abusive towards her; her father was physically violent to Sharon and her mother, as well as some other siblings who all left home as quickly as they could. Sharon and one sister were taken in and out of care due to maternal drinking, severe physical violence and abandonment of the children with their maternal grandfather. Sharon disclosed sexual abuse by a half-brother. Nobody protected Sharon, removed her from the situation or ensured that her half-brother stayed away from her. At school, Sharon was also bullied by other children because of her physically neglected appearance. Thus, there were many negative experiences with few protective factors. From adolescence, Sharon began to show both internalising (i.e. depression) and externalising (i.e. aggressive behaviour, risk-taking behaviour, drinking) consequences. In turn, this made Sharon vulnerable to further victimisation and she was subject to sexual assaults in her teens and early twenties. As an adult, Sharon has difficulties with substance misuse, self-harming behaviour, depression and aggressive behaviour. She has also been victimised by her partners. Sadly, her relationship with all three of her children appears to be quite emotionally neglectful and physically abusive. They have been exposed to repeated episodes of Sharon's self-harming and the subsequent attendance of medical professionals and/or the police at the house. She admits she does not show them much love, but does give them material belongings. Notably, the children are beginning to show similar behaviour and the pattern is being repeated again.

violence; and rape and sexual victimisation. In doing so, it will examine in more depth the impact of victimisation, discussing both the physical and psychological effects on the victim. Females are most at risk of becoming victims of these crimes; however, it is important that male victims of this crime are not ignored. Therefore, the experiences of both female and male victims of these types of violence will be assessed.

Intimate partner violence

This interpersonal violence can encompass many different types of abusive behaviours. Within the literature, the effects of physical abuse, sexual abuse, power/control behaviours and verbal abuse have all been shown to impact negatively upon the victim's wellbeing (Coker et al., 2002).

Definitional/labelling issues

In defining this crime, the violence that can occur within relationships has been described alternatively as intimate partner violence (IPV) or domestic violence, with the victims being described as battered men/women. Some preference has been expressed for the term IPV, particularly in North America, as it may more clearly identify the violence as being experienced between partners (McCaw et al., 2007). In this section, this is the term that will be used, as the violence that is discussed will relate solely to that which occurs between partners or ex-partners.

Impact on physical health

IPV victims can present to the healthcare system suffering from a range of physical injuries, most commonly to the face, neck and arms (Tjaden & Thoennes, 2000; Williamson, 2000). However, IPV can also have a significant impact on the long-term physical health of the victim (see Table 4.6). Campbell (2002) suggests that many of these health issues (e.g. irritable bowel syndrome) are associated with stress, which may explain why some of these health problems are prevalent amongst victims of IPV.

Impact on mental health

In addition to the physical impact of IPV, it is also important to consider the effects that this violence can have on the mental health of the victim (see Table 4.7). Victims of IPV are at an increased risk of suffering from mental health problems such as depression, post-traumatic stress disorder (PTSD), **suicidality** and substance misuse (Golding, 1999). In addition, **comorbidity**, by which victims suffer from more than one mental health issue, has also been reported (Nixon et al., 2004).

> **suicidality** thoughts or behaviours associated with suicide.

> **comorbidity** the diagnosis of a second (or more) disorder in addition to the initial diagnosis of a disorder.

Depression has been significantly associated with experiencing IPV (Wong et al., 2011), with levels of prevalence in samples of IPV victims significantly above those reported in national statistics of depression (e.g. Singleton et al., 2001). Depressive

TABLE 4.6 *Reported injuries and physical health complaints associated with IPV.*

Injuries	Physical health complaints
• Cuts	• Chronic pain (including neck pain, headaches, migraines, pelvic pain)
• Abrasions	• Central nervous system problems (fainting, seizures)
• Bruising	• Gastrointestinal symptoms (loss of appetite, nausea)
• Fractures	• Gastrointestinal disorders (irritable bowel syndrome)
• Sprains	• Cardiac symptoms (hypertension, chest pain)
• Broken teeth	• Urinary symptoms (pain, bladder/kidney infections)
• Bites	• Sexual dysfunction
• Unconsciousness	

Source: Adapted with permission from Campbell, 2002; Ellsberg et al., 2008; Williamson, 2000.

symptoms in IPV victims have, in particular, been associated with the severity of the psychological abuse endured and also with being a victim of childhood abuse (Koopman *et al.*, 2007). Women who have experienced both childhood abuse and IPV have been found to be twice as likely to suffer depressive symptoms compared to non-abused women (e.g. Fogarty *et al.*, 2008).

A smaller proportion of IPV victims also report substance misuse problems. Estimates of the number of victims suggest approximately 10 per cent report harmful alcohol or drug use (Coker *et al.*, 2002; Gerlock, 1999). In a sample of women enrolled in an alcohol addiction

TABLE 4.7 *Prevalence of mental health problems in IPV victims.*

	Prevalence (%)	
	Mean	Range
Depression	47.6	17.5–60.6
Suicidality (include attempts and ideation)	17.9	4.6–77.0
Post-traumatic stress disorder	63.8	31.0–84.4
Alcohol dependence	18.5	6.6–44.0
Drug dependence	8.9	7.0–25.0

Source: Adapted with permission from Golding, 1999.

treatment programme, more than two thirds reported experiencing IPV in the previous year (Chase *et al.*, 2003). A longitudinal study by Temple *et al.* (2008) also found that women who drank alcohol often ($M = 0.50$) were more likely to experience physical IPV compared to women who drank occasionally ($M = 0.25$), rarely ($M = 0.22$) or negligibly ($M = 0.24$). In relation to establishing the causation of substance misuse problems, Bennett and O'Brien (2007) propose a reciprocal relationship between IPV and substance misuse in which each factor increases the risk of experiencing the other. Therefore, women with a substance misuse problem are at greater risk of suffering IPV and women who suffer IPV are at a greater risk of developing a substance misuse problem (Kilpatrick *et al.*, 1997).

Type of abuse

As noted above, IPV can constitute a number of different behaviours. Bonomi *et al.* (2006) found more significant health problems in women who had experienced both physical and/or sexual IPV compared to women who had experienced non-physical IPV. Similarly, Coker *et al.* (2002) found that lifetime experience of physical violence and controlling IPV behaviours were associated with current poor health. In relation to depressive symptoms, Coker *et al.* (2002) found a significant relationship with all forms of IPV (physical, control and verbal) but stronger associations were found for controlling IPV behaviours compared to verbal abuse. Also, Mechanic *et al.* (2008) found that PTSD was predicted by harassing behaviour, emotional and verbal abuse, and minor injuries, but not physical abuse. For depression, this was predicted by harassing behaviour and emotional and verbal abuse, but not physical injury or physical abuse.

Male victims of intimate partner violence

Lifetime prevalence levels suggest that 5.8 per cent of men will experience physical IPV, 0.2 per cent will experience sexual IPV and 17.3 per cent will experience psychological IPV (Coker *et al.*, 2002). Physical injuries sustained by male victims are similar to those sustained by female victims, with reports of being kicked, pushed, grabbed and punched as well as more serious attacks involving choking (22.2 per cent) and being stabbed (1.9 per cent). However, male victims have been found to be less likely to suffer physical injuries than female victims, potentially because of gender differences in physical size and strength (Holtzworth-Munroe, 2005). **Control behaviours** by female perpetrators have also been reported by male victims (95 per cent) with a range of behaviours

control behaviours behaviours performed by the partner of an individual to restrain their freedom or control how that individual can act or behave, e.g. controlling how often they are allowed out of the family home.

CASE STUDY 4.2   INTIMATE PARTNER VIOLENCE AND ITS EFFECTS

Mary is a 36-year-old woman who has been married to her husband for five years. Mary has a previous history of being a victim of childhood physical and sexual abuse. She left school after college (aged 18 years) and has previously worked in full-time employment but has not worked for the last seven years and lists her occupation as housewife. She has one daughter who is 3 years old. During the last four years, Mary has been a victim of IPV carried out by her husband. Mary's husband controls many aspects of Mary's life, which means that Mary is not allowed to leave the house without her husband's permission. This has meant that Mary has very few friends and no strong social support network. Mary's husband has also physically assaulted her approximately seven times over the last year. These attacks have varied in severity. She has been left bruised by the attacks and once had to seek medical help for a cut on her face. In addition to the physical violence, her husband has raped her on several occasions. Mary has thought about suicide several times this year but does not want to leave her child in the care of her husband. She experiences flashbacks from these attacks, which lead her to have panic attacks. Mary has thought about calling the police but does not because she worries that her child will be taken away from her and that she would have nowhere to live and no money to live on. Mary has told nobody about the violence that she endures at home.

such as threats (77.6 per cent), emotional abuse (74.1 per cent) and intimidation (63.3 per cent) (Hines *et al.*, 2007). However, control behaviours have been found to be more common amongst female victims, with Robinson and Rowlands (2009) demonstrating that control behaviours affected six times as many female victims as male victims.

Given the similar experience of IPV for male victims compared to female victims, it is logical that the impact on physical and mental health is also very similar. Male victims report a number of psychological effects such as emotional hurt, fear, helplessness, anger, depression and distress (Hines & Malley-Morrison, 2001). In relation to post-traumatic symptoms, Hines (2007) found that, for men, the level of violence suffered within relationships was a significant predictor of post-traumatic stress symptoms. Affifi *et al.* (2009) demonstrated that amongst male victims, IPV was associated with a greater likelihood of suffering from psychiatric comorbidity (two or more psychiatric disorders), a disruptive disorder and a substance misuse problem.

Coker *et al.* (2002) compared the victimisation of men and women and found that many of the negative effects on health occurred similarly in both male and female victims of IPV. However, Carbone-Lopez *et al.* (2006) showed that men and women experienced IPV in a very similar pattern but that women were more likely to experience poor physical and mental health as a result of victimisation. Similarly, Affifi *et al.* (2009) found that male victims experienced a narrower range of poor mental health outcomes compared to female victims of IPV. This meant that male victims had an increased likelihood of suffering only externalising disorders (e.g. disruptive behaviour disorders and substance misuse problems), whereas female victims were at an increased risk of suffering both internalising (e.g. anxiety disorders) and externalising disorders in addition to suicide ideation. This suggests that the effects of IPV may be exhibit themselves differently for male and female victims.

Recovery and involvement with the criminal justice system

Our knowledge and understanding of the process of recovery from IPV is still limited (Smith, 2003). Blasco-Ros *et al.* (2010) showed that IPV victims can recover from its effects although this recovery can be affected by the type of abuse suffered. Factors associated with recovery are social support and a cessation of abuse (Beeble *et al.*, 2009). Interventions to help IPV victims have demonstrated some effects by treating post-traumatic symptoms (Johnson & Zlotnick, 2009), although evaluations of their long-term effectiveness are rare (Stover *et al.* 2009). Allen and Wozniak (2011) evaluated an intervention with a small sample of victims, delivered over 10 weeks, which subsequently showed significant improvements in the post-traumatic symptomology of the victims following the intervention. The process of recovery was linked with several themes such as the victims' creation of a safe living environment, establishing autonomy in their lives, taking pride in their appearance, reclamation of self, developing a more peaceful existence and rejoining the community. However, victims can still experience post-traumatic symptoms many years after they have left the abusive environment (Smith, 2003).

As shown in Case Study 4.2, many IPV victims have significant difficulties in help-seeking, with obstacles such as personal and family safety, economic dependence, psychological factors such as attachment and commitment,

sociocultural factors factors within both society and cultures that guide the thoughts and behaviour of people.

sociocultural factors, and legal factors (Hien & Ruglass, 2009). An involvement with criminal justice processes offers IPV victims the opportunity to engage in help-seeking and access legal resources, which may potentially play an important role in their recovery (Bell *et al.*, 2011). In terms of accessing formal and informal support, Barrett and St. Pierre (2011) showed that two thirds of victims will access formal support and over 80 per cent will access informal support. However, this leaves a significant number of IPV victims who do not access any support. Contacting the police or a court based programme were the least accessed routes of help-seeking (Wolf *et al.*, 2003). Walby and Allen (2004) found that approximately one third of female victims and two thirds of male victims had never told anyone about their victimisation. Reasons for this were varied, ranging from stating that the crime was too trivial or that it was a private matter, to a reported fear of revictimisation. As Walby and Allen noted, even when a case was reported to the police, it very rarely progressed to court.

Rape and sexual victimisation

This next section reviews the impact of victimisation in relation to rape, again assessing the impact on both physical and mental health. As with IPV, the focus of the majority of the literature is on female rape victims, but it is important that the occurrence of male rape is not neglected.

Impact on physical health

Although rape is a violent crime, a number of studies have demonstrated that approximately two thirds of victims do not sustain physical injury requiring medical attention (Feist *et al.*, 2007). This is not true for all studies, as Kelly *et al.* (2005) found that 70 per cent of their sample was injured by the incident. Of those victims who were injured, Myhill and Allen (2002) found that 52 per cent were slightly injured (bruising or a black eye), 30 per cent were moderately injured (extensive bruising) and 10 per cent were severely injured (cuts or broken bones), with the final 9 per cent designated as receiving 'other' injury. Baker and Sommers (2008) showed that 62.8 per cent of their sample suffered genital injuries, with a range of 1 to 24 different injuries in the genital area. However, victims are more likely to be injured non-genitally than genitally (Sommers *et al.*, 2001).

In relation to the physical health of victims, being a victim of rape has been associated with a significant

TABLE 4.8 *Summary of reported physical health conditions for victims of sexual assault.*

Symptom
• Gastrointestinal symptoms (including nausea, stomachache, colitis, indigestion, lack of appetite)
• Pain (including pelvic, back, joint, muscle ache, headache)
• Cardiopulmonary symptoms (palpitations, shortness of breath)
• Neurologic symptoms (fainting, dizziness, blurred vision)
• Sexual/reproductive symptoms (premenstrual symptoms, menstrual irregularities, pain during intercourse)

Source: Adapted with permission from Chandler *et al.*, 2006; Clum *et al.*, 2001; Golding, 1994.

range of physiological conditions (see Table 4.8). In particular, sustaining injury from the rape has been associated with higher reports of pain, more days in bed due to disability, and more functional disability than victims who were not injured (Leserman *et al.*, 1997). Unsurprisingly, these reports of physical health complaints are linked with rape victims having a significantly lower perception of their health (Goodman *et al.*, 1993). However, social support has been shown to mitigate this effect, with rape victims with higher levels of social support reporting better self-ratings of health post-assault (Kimerling & Calhoun, 1994).

Impact on mental health

As with other forms of interpersonal violence, rape has been associated with PTSD, depression, sleep disturbances, anxiety and fear, substance misuse, and social adjustment problems (Clum *et al.*, 2001; Tjaden & Thoennes, 2006). As with IPV victims, comorbidity is also a frequent occurrence (Kilpatrick & Acierno, 2003). Rape victims may also be more prone to suffering from PTSD than other victims of traumatic events (Kilpatrick *et al.*, 2007). The prevalence of PTSD amongst rape victims can vary from sample to sample although approximately one third of all rape victims demonstrate post-traumatic symptomology. Kilpatrick and Acierno found that 32 per cent of their sample had lifetime PTSD and 12.4 per cent had current (past six months) diagnosis of PTSD.

Certain victim-related factors have also been demonstrated to increase the likelihood that rape victims will develop PTSD post-assault, such as suffering from a prior history of depression and prior alcohol misuse (Acierno *et al.*, 1999). In addition, self-blame and **maladaptive beliefs** have also been linked with

maladaptive beliefs beliefs that demonstrate a pattern of thinking that does not show positive adaptation (e.g. self-blame is associated with poorer physical health).

poorer health outcomes; in particular, characterological blame (blame attributed to the character of the victim) was found to be highly distressing and harmful to health (Koss *et al.*, 2002). Similarly, negative social reactions from others have been strongly related to greater PTSD severity. In particular, receiving negative or stigmatising responses have been most strongly related to PTSD severity (Ullman & Filipas, 2001a). However, some factors can function to be protective against PTSD severity, with the education level of the victim, older age of the victim and disclosing the assault in more detail associated with less PTSD severity (Ullman & Filipas, 2001a).

Acknowledged and unacknowledged rape victims

There is considerable debate in examining whether victims who do not label their victimisation as rape can be or are as traumatised by this experience as victims who do label their experience as rape (Conoscenti & McNally, 2006). Estimates suggest that, of women who have been victims of rape, 42–73 per cent do not label their victimisation as rape (Littleton *et al.*, 2007). Botta and Pingree (1997) found that acknowledged rape victims reported less emotional problems than victims who were not sure that they had been raped, suggesting that acknowledgment may be a positive step for victims. However, Conoscenti and McNally (2006) found that acknowledged and unacknowledged rape victims did not differ in their levels of PTSD but acknowledged rape victims did report more intense health complaints than unacknowledged victims. Layman *et al.* (1996) found that acknowledged rape victims reported more PTSD symptoms and rape-related stress than unacknowledged rape victims. These findings were supported by Littleton and Henderson (2009), who again found that acknowledged rape victims reported more PTSD symptomology than unacknowledged victims, but that acknowledgement of the assault did not predict PTSD symptomology. Similarly, using path analysis, Harned (2004) showed that the distress that victims suffer stems from the assault itself, rather than the labelling of the experience. These findings tentatively suggest that acknowledgement status may not predict the impact of victimisation but the research in this area is still developing.

Characteristics of the assault

Most assault characteristics have not been found to be related to PTSD **symptomology** (e.g. victim–offender relationship). However, the victim's perceived life threat has been associated with more severe post-traumatic symptoms (Ullman *et al.*, 2007). Increased levels of PTSD symptomology have also been found in multiply

symptomology
symptoms and syndromes associated with a particular condition or phenomenon.

victimised women compared to single incident victims (Wilson *et al.*, 1999). More recent research has focused upon potential differences between forcible rape (where force, injury or threat of either is involved), incapacitated rape (involves voluntary intoxication of drugs/alcohol by the victim) and drug-assisted rape (involves deliberate intoxication of the victim using drugs/alcohol by the perpetrator) (Zinzow, Resnick, McCauley *et al.*, 2010). These findings have demonstrated that victims of forcible rape have the highest risk for PTSD and a major depressive episode, being three times more likely than non-victims to meet the criteria for both disorders. When compared with incapacitated rape and drug-assisted rape, forcible rape victims (OR = 3.46) were at a higher risk of PTSD than incapacitated rape victims (OR = 1.37) and, secondly, were at a higher risk of a major depressive episode (OR = 3.65) than both incapacitated rape (OR = 1.30) and drug-assisted rape victims (OR = 1.30) (Zinzow, Resnick, Amstadter *et al.*, 2010; Zinzow, Resnick, McCauley *et al.*, 2010). Further research will need to confirm these trends but it does appear that type of rape may have affected mental health outcomes in victims.

Male victims of rape

Men are more often viewed as the perpetrators of sexual crime than the victims (Mezey & King, 2000). However, a change in rape legislation in 1994 in England and Wales broadened the definition of a rape to encompass men as victims of rape. The Sexual Offences Act 2003 therefore defines rape as a crime that both men and women can be a victim of but that only men can perpetrate (as penetration is defined as penetration by a penis). Walker *et al.* (2005a) found that a third of their sample of 14 male rape victims sought medical attention for their injuries, but only five disclosed the sexual context of the assault. However, Weiss (2010) found that 9 per cent of male rape victims reported sustaining physical injury from the assault.

Psychological effects of victimisation are similar to those of female victims, with reports of depression, anxiety, substance misuse and suicide attempts (Walker *et al.*, 2005b). Male victims also report issues with sexuality and masculinity such that victims felt a perceived loss of masculinity in being subjected to the rape (Figure 4.4; Walker *et al.*, 2005a). Davies and Rutland (2007) suggest that many male rape victims are distrustful of seeking help because of the reactions they may encounter, foreseeing homophobic attitudes (even when the victim is not homosexual) and stereotypical views of the masculine **gender role**. The perception of men and their physical strength often means that a male rape victim may choose not to disclose their assault to anyone, increasing their sense of isolation (Willis, 2009).

gender role the adoption of socially proscribed behaviours and norms that are appropriate for each gender.

FIGURE 4.4 *As with other forms of interpersonal violence, rape has been associated with PTSD, depression, sleep disturbances, anxiety and fear, substance misuse, and social adjustment problems.*

Source: © Edw. Used under licence from Shutterstock.

Monk-Turner and Light (2010) found that anal penetration reduced the likelihood of male victims seeking counselling for their victimisation.

Recovery and involvement in the criminal justice system

Kimerling and Calhoun (1994) found that 75 per cent of their sample met the diagnosis for depression, ranging from mild to severe effects. However, by one year after the assault, this number had reduced to 26 per cent, suggesting that a significant number of rape victims do recover from the negative effects of the rape. Similar reductions in PTSD symptomology from 94 per cent at two weeks post-assault to 64 per cent one month afterward were reported by Rothbaum *et al.* (1992). However, rates of recovery from victimisation may be slower for sexual assault victims compared to nonsexual assault victims (Gilboa-Schectman & Foa, 2004). There may also be differences in the processes of seeking help for the effects of victimisation. Amstadter *et al.* (2010) found

that help-seeking amongst rape victims was associated with PTSD symptoms, but not depression or substance misuse. Interventions have been shown to be effective in treating much of the symptomology associated with rape victimization, such as depression and PTSD. Vickerman and Margolin (2009) suggest that cognitive behavioural programmes have demonstrated effectiveness in improving symptomology, along with some support for **cognitive processing therapy**, **prolonged exposure therapy** and **stress inoculation training**.

Reporting a rape to the police can be a challenging experience for rape victims and is a step that many do not choose to complete (HMCPSI/HMIC, 2007). Known as *secondary victimisation* (Campbell *et al.*, 1999), a significant number of rape victims have reported the police to be an unhelpful source of support (Ullman & Filipas, 2001b). Kaukinen and DeMaris (2009) found that police reporting seemed to exacerbate the impact of sexual assault, increasing the levels of depression reported. Other studies have linked increased PTSD symptomology with negative social reactions, which may often be received from formal help sources such as the police (e.g. Filipas & Ullman, 2001). However, these relationships must be interpreted cautiously because certain types of rape are more likely to be reported to the police (Du Mont *et al.*, 2003). It may be that these types of rape are associated with more significant long-term effects (Kaukinen & DeMaris, 2009).

Campbell *et al.* (2001) found that contact with the legal system was considered hurtful by half of the victims in their sample; however, a third did consider this contact to be healing. Victims whose cases were not prosecuted were more likely to consider this contact with the legal system to be hurtful.

cognitive processing therapy a form of therapy for post-traumatic stress disorder.

prolonged exposure therapy a cognitive-behavioural form of therapy for post-traumatic stress disorder.

stress inoculation training a form of therapy for post-traumatic stress disorder that attempts to inoculate the individual from future stressful situations.

SUMMARY

- Both male and female victims of childhood maltreatment and adulthood IPV and rape have been shown to suffer significant physical and psychological effects as result of their victimisation. These effects may manifest themselves differently in male and female victims. This may be particularly true in IPV, where males have been shown to exhibit a narrower range of effects from victimisation compared to females, who may suffer from externalising and/or internalising disorders.

- Recovery from these effects is possible with engagement in effective interventions, including treatments that combine both cognitive and behavioural approaches (for example, cognitive processing therapy for adult victims diagnosed with PTSD).

- It is important to acknowledge that many individuals do not show these negative long-term consequences, but research methodology has meant that the focus until recently was on more negative outcomes.

- There has been a growing interest in children and adults who show 'resilience', coming from the recognition that many individuals lead successful lives following maltreating experiences.

- It is important to investigate the pathways by which different outcomes occur, in order to establish interventions and prevention programmes to reduce suffering and the impact on individuals in childhood and adulthood, as well as on their families, the community and society.

ESSAY/DISCUSSION QUESTIONS

1. Critically evaluate the evidence that children who have been abused or neglected are at increased risk of negative long-term outcomes in both childhood and adulthood.
2. Discuss the risk and protective factors associated with the intergenerational cycle of maltreatment.
3. Critically evaluate the relationship between substance misuse (including alcohol) and intimate partner violence.
4. Discuss the psychological effects of adult victimisation, comparing and contrasting the effects between victims of IPV and victims of rape.

REFERENCES

Acierno, R., Resnick, H., Kilpatrick, D.G., Saunders, B. & Best, C.L. (1999). Risk factors for rape, physical assault and posttraumatic stress disorder in women: Examination of differential multivariate relationships. *Journal of Anxiety Disorders, 13,* 541–563.

Affifi, T.O., MacMillan, H., Cox, B.J., Asmundson, G.J.G., Stein, M.B. & Sareen, J. (2009). Mental health correlates of intimate partner violence in marital relationships in a nationally representative sample of males and females. *Journal of Interpersonal Violence, 24,* 1398–1417.

Alexander, P.C. & Lupfer, S.L. (1987). Family characteristics and long-term consequences associated with sexual abuse. *Archives of Sexual Behaviour, 16,* 235–245.

Allen, K.N. & Wozniak, D.F. (2011). The language of healing: Women's voices in healing and recovering from domestic violence. *Social Work in Mental Health, 9,* 37–55.

Amstadter, A.B., Zinzow, H.M., McCauley, J.L., Strachan, M., Ruggiero, K.J., Resnick, H.S. & Kilpatrick, D.G. (2010). Prevalence and correlates of service utilisation and help seeking in a national college sample of female rape victims. *Journal of Anxiety Disorders, 24,* 900–902.

Anda, R.F., Dong, M., Brown, D.W., Felitti, V.J., Giles, W.H., Perry, G.S., Valerie, E.J. & Dube, S.R. (2009). The relationship of adverse childhood experiences to a history of premature death of family members. *BMC Public Health, 9,* 106.

Arseneault, L., Cannon, M., Fisher, H.L., Polanczyk, G., Moffitt, T.E. & Caspi, A. (2011). Childhood trauma and children's emerging psychotic symptoms: A genetically sensitive longitudinal cohort study. *American Journal of Psychiatry, 168,* 65–72.

Baker, R.B. & Sommers, M.S. (2008). Relationship of genital injuries and age in adolescent and young adult rape survivors. *Journal of Obstetric, Gynecologic, and Neonatal Nursing, 37,* 282–289.

Barnes, J.E., Noll, J.G., Putnam, F.W. & Trickett, P.K. (2009). Sexual and physical revictimization among victims of severe childhood sexual abuse. *Child Abuse and Neglect, 33,* 412–420.

Barrett, B.J. & St. Pierre, M. (2011). Variations in women's help seeking in response to intimate partner violence: Findings from a Canadian population based study. *Violence against Women, 17,* 47–70.

Beeble, M.L., Bybee, D., Sullivan, C.M. & Adams, A.E. (2009). Main, mediating, and moderating effects of social support on the well-being of survivors of intimate partner violence across 2 years. *Journal of Consulting and Clinical Psychology, 77,* 718–729.

Bell, M.E., Perez, S., Goodman, L.A. & Dutton, M.A. (2011). Battered women's perceptions of civil and criminal court helpfulness: The role of court outcome and process. *Violence against Women, 17,* 71–88.

Bennett, D.S., Wolan Sullivan, M. & Lewis, M. (2010). Neglected children, shame-proneness, and depressive symptoms. *Child Maltreatment, 4,* 305–314.

Bennett, L. & O'Brien, P. (2007). Effects of coordinated services for drug-abusing women who are victims of intimate partner violence. *Violence Against Women, 13,* 395–411.

Blasco-Ros, C., Sanchez-Lorente, S. & Martinez, M. (2010) Recovery from depressive symptoms, state anxiety and post-traumatic stress disorder in women exposed to physical and psychological but not to psychological intimate partner violence: A longitudinal study. *BMC Psychiatry, 98.* Retrieved 17 August 2011 from www.biomedcentral.com/1471–244X/10/98

Bonomi, A.E., Thompson, R.S., Anderson, M. & Reid, R.J. (2006). Intimate partner violence and women's physical, mental and social functioning. *American Journal of Preventive Medicine, 30,* 458–466.

Botta, R.A. & Pingree, S. (1997). Interpersonal communication and rape: Women acknowledge their assaults. *Journal of Health Communication, 2,* 197–212.

Browne, K.D. & Hamilton, C. (1999). Police recognition of links between spouse abuse and child abuse. *Child Maltreatment, 4,* 136–147.

Campbell, J.C. (2002). Health consequences of intimate partner violence. *The Lancet, 359,* 1331–1336.

Campbell, R., Sefl, T., Barnes, H.E., Ahrens, C.E., Wasco, S.M. & Zaragoza-Diesfield, Y. (1999). Community services for rape survivors: Enhancing psychological well-being or increasing trauma. *Journal of Consulting and Clinical Psychology, 67,* 847–858.

Campbell, R., Wasco, S.M., Ahrens, C.E., Sefl, T. & Barnes, H.E. (2001). Preventing the 'second rape': Rape survivors' experiences with community services providers. *Journal of Interpersonal Violence, 16,* 1239–1259.

Carbone-Lopez, K., Kruttschnitt, C. & MacMillan, R. (2006). Patterns of intimate partner violence and their associations with physical health, psychological distress, and substance use. *Public Health Reports, 121,* 382–392.

Casanueva, C., Martin, S.L. & Runyan, D.K. (2009). Repeated reports for child maltreatment among intimate partner violence victims: Findings from the National Survey of Child and Adolescent Well-Being. *Child Abuse and Neglect, 33,* 84–93.

Cerezo, M.A., D'Ocon, A. & Dolz, L. (1996). Mother-child interactive patterns in abusive families versus nonabusive families: An observational study. *Child Abuse and Neglect, 20,* 573–587.

Chandler, H.K., Ciccone, D.S. & Raphael, K.G. (2006). Localisation of pain and self-reported rape in a female community sample. *Pain Medicine, 7,* 344–352.

Chase, K.A., O'Farrell, T.J., Murphy, C.M., Fals-Stewart, W. & Murphy, M. (2003). Factors associated with partner violence among female alcoholic patients and their male partners. *Journal of Studies on Alcohol, 64,* 137–149.

Cicchetti, D., Rogosch, F.A., Gunnar, M. & Toth, S.L. (2010). The differential impacts of early physical and sexual abuse and internalizing problems on daytime cortisol rhythm in school-aged children. *Child Development, 81,* 252–269.

Cicchetti, D. & Toth, S.L. (1995). A developmental psychopathology perspective on child abuse and neglect. *Journal of the American Academy of Child and Adolescent Psychiatry 34,* 541–563.

Clum, G.A., Nishith, P. & Resick, P.A. (2001). Trauma-related sleep disturbance and self-reported physical health symptoms in treatment-seeking female rape victims. *Journal of Nervous and Mental Disease, 189,* 618–622.

Coker, A.L., Davis, K.E., Arias, I., Desai, S., Sanderson, M., Brandt, H.M. & Smith, P.H. (2002). Physical and mental health effects of intimate partner violence for men and women. *American Journal of Preventive Medicine, 23,* 260–268.

Conoscenti, L.M. & McNally, R.J. (2006). Health complaints in acknowledged and unacknowledged rape victims. *Anxiety Disorders, 20,* 372–379.

Cougle, J.R., Timpano, K.R., Sachs-Ericsson, N., Keough, M.E. & Riccardi, C.J. (2010). Examining the unique relationships between anxiety disorders and childhood physical and sexual abuse in the National Comorbidity Survey-Replication. *Psychiatry Research, 177,* 150–155.

Davies, M. & Rutland, F. (2007). Male rape: The scope of the problem. *Forensic Update, 89,* 29–32.

Department for Children, Schools and Families. (2008). *Referrals, assessments and children and young people who are the subject of a child protection plan or are on the child protection registers: year ending 31 March 2007.* London: Department for Children, Schools and Families.

Department for Education and Skills. (2006). *Working together to safeguard children.* London: The Stationery Office.

Department for Education. (2010). *Referrals, assessments and children who were the subject of a child protection plan (2009–10 Children in Need census, final).* London: Department for Education.

DePanfilis, D. & Zuravin, S.J. (1998). Rates, patterns and frequency of child maltreatment recurrences among families known to CPS. *Child Maltreatment, 3,* 27–42.

DePrince, A.P., Weinzierl, K.M. & Combs, M.D. (2009). Executive function performance and trauma exposure in a community sample of children. *Child Abuse and Neglect, 33,* 353–361.

Dixon, L., Browne, K.D. & Hamilton-Giachritsis, C.E. (2005). Risk factors of parents' abused as children: a mediational analysis of the intergenerational continuity of child maltreatment (Part I). *Journal of Child Psychology and Psychiatry, 46,* 47–57.

Dixon, L., Browne, K.D. & Hamilton-Giachritsis, C.E. (2009). Patterns of risk and protective factors in the intergenerational cycle of maltreatment. *Journal of Family Violence, 24,* 111–122.

Dixon, L., Hamilton-Giachritsis C.E. & Browne, K.D., (2005). Behavioural measures of parents' abused as children: a mediational analysis of the intergenerational continuity of child maltreatment (Part II). *Journal of Child Psychology and Psychiatry, 46,* 58–68.

Du Mont, J., Miller, K.-L. & Myhr, T.L. (2003). The role of 'real rape' and 'real victim' stereotypes in the police reporting practices of sexually assaulted women. *Violence against Women, 9,* 466–486.

Egeland, B. (1988). Breaking the cycle of abuse: implications for prediction and intervention. In K.D. Browne, C. Davies & P. Stratton (Eds.) *Early prediction and prevention of child abuse* (pp.87–102). Chichester: John Wiley & Sons, Inc.

Ellsberg, M., Jansen, H., Heise, L., Watts, C.H. & Garcia-Moreno, C. (2008). Intimate partner violence and women's physical and mental health in the WHO multi-country study on women's health and domestic violence: an observational study. *The Lancet, 371,* 1165–1172.

English, D.J., Graham, J.C., Litrownik, A.J., Everson, M. & Bangdiwala, S.I. (2005). Defining maltreatment chronicity: Are there differences in child outcomes? *Child Abuse and Neglect, 29,* 575–595.

Ertem, I.O., Leventhal, J.M. & Dobbs, S. (2000). Intergenerational continuity of child physical abuse: how good is the evidence? *The Lancet, 356,* 814–819.

Euser, E.M., van IJzendoorn, M.H., Prinzie, P. & Bakermans-Kranenburg, M.J. (2010). Prevalence of child maltreatment in the Netherlands. *Child Maltreatment, 15,* 5–17.

Fallon, B., Trocmé, N., Fluke, J., MacLaurin, B., Tonmyr, L. & Yuan, Y-Y. (2010). Methodological challenges in measuring child maltreatment. *Child Abuse and Neglect, 34,* 70–79.

Falshaw, L., Browne, K.D. & Hollin, C.R. (1996). Victim to offender: A review. *Aggression and Violent Behavior, 1,* 389–404.

Farrington, D.P., Jolliffe, D., Loeber, R., Stouthamer-Loeber, M. & Kalb, L.M. (2001). The concentration of offenders in families and family criminality in the prediction of boys delinquency. *Journal of Adolescence, 24,* 579–596.

Feiring, C., Taska, L. & Chen, K. (2002). Trying to understand why horrible things happen: Attribution, shame, and symptom development following sexual abuse. *Child Maltreatment, 7,* 26–41.

Feist, A., Ashe, J., Lawrence, J., McPhee, D. & Wilson, R. (2007). Investigating and detecting recorded offences of rape. Home Office online report 18/07. Retrieved 17 August 2011 from www.homeoffice.gov.uk/rds/pdfs07/rdsolr1807.pdf

Filipas, H.H. & Ullman, S.E. (2001). Social reactions to sexual assault victims from various support sources. *Violence and Victims, 16,* 673–392.

Finkelhor, D., Turner, H., Ormrod, R. & Hamby, S.L. (2010). Trends in childhood violence and abuse exposure: Evidence from 2 national surveys. *Archives of Pediatrics and Adolescent Medicine, 164,* 238–242.

Fogarty, C.T., Fredman, L., Heeren, T.C. & Liebschutz, J. (2008). Synergistic effects of child abuse and intimate partner violence on depressive symptoms in women. *Preventive Medicine, 46,* 463–469.

Fryer, G.E. & Miyoshi, T.J. (1994). A survival analysis of the revictimization of children: the case of Colorado. *Child Abuse & Neglect, 18,* 1063–1071.

Gerlock, A.A. (1999). Health impact of domestic violence. *Issues in Mental Health Nursing, 20,* 373–385.

Gilbert, R., Spatz-Widom, C., Browne, K.D., Fergusson, D., Webb, E. & Janson, S. (2009). Burden and consequences of child maltreatment in high-income countries. *The Lancet, 373,* 68–81.

Gilboa-Schechtman, E. & Foa, E.B. (2004). Patterns of recovery from trauma: The use of intraindividual analysis. *Journal of Abnormal Psychology, 110,* 392–400.

Golding, J.M. (1994). Sexual assault history and physical health in randomly selected Los Angeles women. *Health Psychology, 13,* 130–138.

Golding, J.M. (1999). Intimate partner violence as a risk factor for mental disorders: A meta-analysis. *Journal of Family Violence, 14,* 99–132.

Goldstein, S. & Brooks, R.B. (Eds.) (2005). *Handbook of resilience in children.* NY: Kluwer Academic/Plenum Publishers.

Goodman, L.A., Koss, M.P. & Russo, N.F. (1993). Violence against women: Physical and mental health effects. Part I: Research findings. *Applied and Preventive Psychology, 2,* 79–89.

Hamilton, C.E. & Browne, K.D. (1999). Recurrent maltreatment during childhood: A survey of referrals to police child protection units. *Child Maltreatment, 4,* 275–286.

Hamilton, C.E., Falshaw, L. & Browne, K.D. (2002). The links between recurrent maltreatment and offending behaviour. *International Journal of Offender Therapy and Comparative Criminology, 46,* 75–94

Harned, M.S. (2004). Does it matter what you call it? The relationship between labelling unwanted sexual experiences and distress. *Journal of Consulting and Clinical Psychology, 72,* 1090–1099.

Herrenkohl, T.I. & Herrenkohl, R.C. (2007). Examining the overlap and prediction of multiple forms of child maltreatment, stressors, and socioeconomic status: A longitudinal analysis of youth outcomes. *Journal of Family Violence, 22,* 553–562.

Hien, D. & Ruglass, L. (2009). Interpersonal partner violence and women in the United States: An overview of prevalence rates, psychiatric correlates and consequences and barriers to help seeking. *International Journal of Law and Psychiatry, 32,* 48–55.

Hillberg, T., Hamilton-Giachritsis, C.E. & Dixon, L. (2011). Critical review of meta-analyses on the association between child sexual abuse and adult psychopathology. *Trauma, Violence, & Abuse, 12,* 38–49.

Hindley, N., Ramchandani, P.G. & Jones, D.P.H. (2006). Risk factors for recurrence of maltreatment: a systematic review. *Archives of Diseases of Childhood, 91,* 744–752.

Hines, D. (2007). Posttraumatic stress symptoms among men who sustain partner violence: An international multisite study of university students. *Psychology of Men and Masculinity, 8*, 225–239.

Hines, D.A., Brown, J. & Dunning, E. (2007). Characteristics of caller to the domestic abuse helpline for men. *Journal of Family Violence, 22*, 63–72.

Hines, D.A. & Malley-Morrison, K. (2001). Psychological effects of partner abuse against men: A neglected research area. *Psychology of Men and Masculinity, 2*, 75–85.

HMCPSI/HMIC. (2007). *Without consent: A report on the joint review of the investigation and prosecution of rape offences.* London: Home Office.

Holtzworth-Munroe, A. (2005). Male versus female intimate partner violence: Putting controversial findings into context. *Journal of Marriage and Family, 67*, 1120–1125.

Hussey, J.M., Chang, J.J. & Kotch, J.B. (2006). Child maltreatment in the United States: Prevalence, risk factors, and adolescent health consequences. *Pediatrics, 118*, 933–942.

Johnson, D.M. & Zlotnick, C. (2009). HOPE for battered women with PTSD in domestic violence shelters. *Professional Psychology: Research and Practice, 40*, 234–241.

Kaufman, J. & Zigler, E. (1987). Do abused children become abusive parents? *American Journal of Orthopsychiatry, 57*, 186–192.

Kaukinen, C. & DeMaris, A. (2009). Sexual assault and current mental health: The role of help-seeking and police response. *Violence against Women, 15*, 1331–1357.

Kelly, L., Lovatt, J. & Regan, L. (2005). *A gap or a chasm? Attribution in reported rape: Home Office Research Study, 293.* London: Home Office.

Kilpatrick, D.G. & Acierno, R. (2003). Mental health needs of crime victims: Epidemiology and outcomes. *Journal of Traumatic Stress, 16*, 119–132.

Kilpatrick, D.G., Acierno, R., Resnick, H.S., Saunders, B.E. & Best, C.L. (1997). A 2-year longitudinal analysis of the relationships between violent assault and substance use in women. *Journal of Consulting and Clinical Psychology, 65*, 834–847.

Kilpatrick, D.G., Amstadter, A.B., Resnick, H.S. & Ruggiero, K.J. (2007). Rape-related PTSD: Issues and interventions. *Psychiatric Times, 24*, 50–58.

Kim, J. & Cicchetti, D. (2006). Longitudinal trajectories of self-system and depressive symptoms among maltreated and nonmaltreated children. *Child Development, 77*, 624–639.

Kim, J., Cicchetti, D., Rogosch, F.A. & Manly, J.T. (2009). Child maltreatment and trajectories of personality and behavioural functioning: Implications for the development of personality disorder. *Developmental Psychopathology, 21*, 889–912.

Kimerling, R. & Calhoun, K.S. (1994). Somatic symptoms, social support, and treatment seeking among sexual assault victims. *Journal of Consulting and Clinical Psychology, 62*, 333–340.

Kleevens, J. & Lieb, R. (2010). Child maltreatment fatalities in children under 5: Findings from the National Violence Death Reporting System. *Child Abuse & Neglect, 34*, 262–266.

Koopman, C., Ismailji, T., Palesh, O., Gore-Felton, C., Narayanan, A., Saltzman, K.M., Holmes, D. & McGarvey, E.L. (2007). Relationships of depression to child and adults abuse and bodily pain among women who have experienced intimate partner violence. *Journal of Interpersonal Violence, 22*, 438–455.

Koss, M.P., Figuredo, A.J. & Prince, R.J. (2002). Cognitive mediation of rape's mental, physical and social health impact: Tests of four models in cross-sectional data. *Journal of Consulting and Clinical Psychology, 70*, 926–941.

Layman, M.J., Gidycz, C.A. & Lynn, S.J. (1996). Unacknowledged versus acknowledged rape victims: Situational factors and posttraumatic stress. *Journal of Abnormal Psychology, 105*, 124–131.

Lee, C.K. & Lathrop, S.L. (2010). Child abuse-related homicides in New Mexico: A 6-year retrospective review. *Journal of Forensic Sciences, 55*, 100–103.

Leserman, J., Li, Z., Drossman, D.A., Toomey, T.C., Nachman, G. & Glogau, L. (1997). Impact of sexual and physical abuse dimensions on health status: Development of an abuse severity measure. *Psychosomatic Medicine, 59*, 152–160.

Littleton, H. & Henderson, C.E. (2009). If she is not a victim, does that mean that she was not traumatised? Evaluation of predictors of PTSD symptomology among college rape victims. *Violence against Women, 15*, 148–167.

Littleton, H.L., Rhatigan, D.L. & Axsom, D. (2007). Unacknowledged rape: How much do we know about the hidden rape victim? *Journal of Aggression, Maltreatment, & Trauma, 14*, 57–74.

Luthar, S. (2003). *Resilience and vulnerability: Adaptation in the context of childhood adversities.* Cambridge: Cambridge University Press

Masten, A.S. & O'Dougherty Wright, M. (2010). Resilience over the lifespan: Developmental perspectives on resistance, recovery and transformation. In J. Reich, A.J. Zautra & J.S. Hall (Eds.) *Handbook of adult resilience* (pp.213–237). NY: Guildford Press.

May-Chahal, C. & Cawson, P. (2005). Measuring child maltreatment in the United Kingdom: a study of the prevalence of child abuse and neglect. *Child Abuse & Neglect, 29*, 969–984.

McCaw, B., Golding, J.M., Farley, M. & Minkoff, J.R. (2007). Domestic violence and abuse, health status, and social functioning. *Women & Health, 45*, 1–23.

Mechanic, M.B., Weaver, T.L. & Resick, P.A. (2008). Mental health consequences of intimate partner abuse: A multidimensional assessment of four different forms of abuse. *Violence Against Women, 14*, 634–654.

Part II
Investigating Crime

5 Eyewitness Evidence

Lindsay C. Malloy, Daniel B. Wright and Elin M. Skagerberg

KEY TERMS

• encoding • episodic • misinformation effect • misinformation paradigm • PEACE model of interviewing • rapport

CHAPTER OUTLINE

Human cognitive abilities are incredible. Consider the task faced by an eyewitness who is present during a street crime. The cognitive system allows the witness to transform characteristics of the light reflected towards her eyes into visual information and characteristics of perturbations in the air made by the culprit's vocal system into auditory information. The person synchronises these sources of information (and sometimes smells, tastes and tactile information) with a highly functional knowledge-base of past experiences. At later points in time, the witness is able to use this continually adapting knowledge-base to bring that distant information into the present. The witness may even be able to travel back to the past mentally to relive the event – what is

episodic relating to a specific episode or event.

called **episodic** memory (Tulving, 1985). As amazing as these cognitive abilities are, they are not perfect. Information is forgotten and distorted, and the past century of memory research has revealed some systematic patterns for these deficits. Eyewitness memory errors are arguably the leading cause of false imprisonment in the UK.

The purpose of this chapter is to discuss the reliability of memory in situations of particular relevance to forensic and legal psychology. We review some of the key findings and theories in memory research and apply these to interviewing adult cooperative witnesses and child cooperative witnesses. The area of eyewitness testimony is vast (see Toglia *et al.*, 2006, for a two-volume review), and thus our chapter is selective. In addition, we make various recommendations for both forensic practice and future research. We do not cover identification parades ('line-ups' in American English), where an eyewitness has the opportunity to choose the culprit from a group of people. This is covered in Chapter 14 and Brewer and Wells (2011).

To understand how findings from memory research can be applied to a forensic context, it is necessary to understand how memory science works. Within a criminal context, eyewitness memory is a tool that, if reliable, should be diagnostic of guilt or innocence. By this we mean that presenting eyewitness evidence should usually make guilty people seem more likely to be guilty, and innocent people seem more likely to be innocent. To be reliable, evidence does not have to always be correct, but it should usually be correct. In the US Supreme Court's *Daubert* (1993) ruling, the court argued that, for scientific evidence to be presented, there should be a known error rate (see Chapter 15 for further discussion on the legal admissibility of psychological research). The courts do not state what the maximum error rate (or the minimum reliability) should be to allow evidence to be presented in court because this threshold would likely depend on the type of evidence and could depend on peculiarities of an individual case. One of the main goals for eyewitness

researchers is to estimate this error rate and show how it varies by different factors.

Ultimately, to estimate the reliability of any forensic tool as complex and context-dependent as eyewitness memory, it is necessary to understand how the system works. If a scientist was trying to determine the reliability of a tool to detect, for example, explosive material from a body-scan device, the scientist would have the advantage that humans created the device, so the scientist could look at the blueprints. This gives him or her a head start in understanding the device. It is more difficult to understand the human cognitive system because it is the ongoing product of ad hoc engineering, a process of trial and error called evolution. As such, cognitive psychologists have had to use 'reverse engineering' to figure out how eyewitness memory works. Psychologists have ideas about how humans might work by watching their behaviour, and then they use a variety of methods to enrich the understanding of the human mind and create models for human cognition. The two most popular methods are: observing people in a somewhat natural environment and trying to deduce what mechanisms are in operation; and presenting people with cleverly designed situations that, depending on how people behave, differentiate among potential (often causal) mechanisms. These two approaches are described in more detail in relation to eyewitness testimony in Wright (2006). A third approach often used in cognitive science is to create a detailed model of the system, instantiate it in a computer program, and examine how the system works when presented with different types of input and how varying different aspects of the system affects its behaviour. This approach is used less in eyewitness research than in many other areas of cognitive psychology.

In a nutshell, those are the methods that eyewitness researchers have used to understand eyewitness processes and to estimate the reliability of memory in different situations. In this chapter, we describe research on these related pursuits by focusing on interviewing adult cooperative witnesses and interviewing child witnesses. Before doing this, it is worth describing some general issues about human memory that relate to both of these topics.

GENERAL ISSUES ABOUT HUMAN MEMORY

Going beyond lay theories of memory

One of the main conclusions of this chapter is that people – including jurors, police and teachers – weight eyewitness evidence too highly. We use metaphors to understand the complex worlds in which we live (Lakoff & Johnson, 1980); Roediger (1980; see also Draaisma, 2001) describes a number of the metaphors that people have used for memory. A popular metaphor is that memory works like a tape recorder (ask your oldest professor what this is) or an iPod. You store lots of information (songs would be like event memories) and then when you want to retrieve them you have to press some buttons and, if you find the desired memory, what is retrieved is accurate. According to this metaphor, memory errors occur because you cannot find the right file (and sometimes choose the wrong file) but if the right file is chosen, while it might be incomplete or slightly degraded over time, the information reported will essentially be accurate.

Consider the Hollywood courtroom eyewitness identification: the traumatised victim points his finger of justice at the defendant, who scowls behind her beady eyes. The eyewitness then describes the defendant's 'wicked glare' while she committed the crime! How could this testimony be in error? According to this metaphor, the witness has downloaded a file and is recounting the crime with the defendant as the assailant.

The metaphor of the iPod is so engrained in popular culture that it seems to be common sense and *de facto* true. However, while retrieval is an important part of memory, and some memory errors are due to faulty retrieval, the iPod metaphor is inappropriate. A good way for a lawyer to counter this myth would be to slam a human brain on the table. How could a juror possibly believe that the object that made the *thud* on the table and squirted really gross stuff across the courtroom is capable of accurately transporting information through time with great accuracy? A brain is about the size and texture of a peeled grapefruit, and even Hollywood does not believe grapefruits have grand intellectual skills.

Human brains can produce more accurate and complete memories than grapefruits and less accurate and complete memories than iPods (although brains can do lots of things iPods cannot do). It would be better to have a metaphor that falls somewhere between these. Neisser (1967; see also Hebb, 1949, p.47) described an alternative metaphor, that of a paleontologist who reconstructs a dinosaur from a few fossils and theories about dinosaurs. Neisser argued that memory was largely reconstructing the past from knowledge of the past and for purposes of the present. It is important to realise that metaphors do not say *exactly* how something works – no one believes that we each have a small paleontologist in our head – but the processes that a paleontologist uses may be analogous to some of the mental processes that are operating in memory.

Theories like Bartlett's (1932) *schema*, Schank and Abelson's *scripts* (1977) and Minsky's *frames* (1975) describe possible organisations for event knowledge and computational procedures that allow structures to guide the encoding of events that people encounter in such a manner that aspects of them can be used for reconstructing the events in the future. Schema, scripts, and frames are categories of events that allow both processing of information on new events of this type and activation of memory for past events of the same type. Humans are much more flexible than iPods and much better able to cope with and learn from the uncertainties we experience in everyday life. In most situations throughout human evolution, pristine memory is not that important. We take shortcuts, or heuristics, to process information quickly and to learn to associate events. This means our memory is dynamic in systematic ways.

One of the most important sets of studies about reconstructive memory began in the 1970s. Elizabeth Loftus (2005, for a review) showed both the reconstructive nature of memory and the circumstances in which information encountered after an event (called *post-event information* or PEI) is most likely to influence the reconstruction of the memory for the original event. Besides being important for theories of memory, this set of studies and the personal efforts by Loftus (1986) allowed memory research to be applied to US legal cases. Consider one of her classic studies. Loftus and Palmer (1974; experiment 2) showed participants a film clip of an automobile accident and then asked them how fast the cars were being driven when they either 'smashed' or 'hit' into each other (Figure 5.1). The average speed estimates were higher when the question implied a more violent crash (i.e. the verb 'smashed' was used rather than the less violent 'hit'). Interestingly, the people who were asked to estimate the speed when the cars 'smashed' were later more likely erroneously

FIGURE 5.1 *Loftus and Palmer (1974; experiment 2) showed participants a film of an automobile accident, then asked them how fast the cars were being driven when they 'smashed' or 'hit' into each other.*

Source: © Evgeny Murtola. Used under licence from Shutterstock.

CASE STUDY 5.1   A REMARKABLE WITNESS

The B9002 Cabrach to Lumsden road winds its way through some of the most lonely and inhospitable moorland in Scotland. On 23 June 1986, a tourist venturing along this road was surprised to come across a 10-year-old girl, dazed, bleeding and half-naked, standing beside a culvert. The girl was rushed to hospital in Aberdeen where she was found to have multiple fractures of the skull, cheek and jaw consistent with being hit repeatedly with a large stone. She had also been sexually assaulted.

A police officer stayed with the girl day and night as she slowly recovered and began to tell of her ordeal. She told police she had been abducted at knife-point and driven to the lonely spot where she was found, where she had been attacked and left for dead. Shortly before the incident, the girl's teacher had told her class always to try and remember the appearance of strangers who approached them in suspicious circumstances. Within two days, the police officer had elicited enough information to issue a description: 'A well-built man, about 5 ft 7 ins tall, clean-shaven, with dark, centre-parted greasy hair'. The girl also reported that he had worn a sweatshirt with a distinctive oil rig logo on the pocket, and gave a very precise description of the seat covers of the car, which police were able to link to a mud-flap, tyre marks and paint fragments found at the scene to identify the vehicle concerned. It was a mass-produced Datsun saloon, but the child's description of the seats marked it out as one of just 700 special edition models imported to the UK, of which just nine were registered locally.

The first vehicle checked belonged to Colin Findlay, an oil rig worker, currently working offshore. In his drive was a Datsun saloon missing a mud-flap. In his wardrobe the police found a sodden bundle of clothing, including the sweatshirt with the distinctive logo. Within a week of the crime, police flew out to an oil platform in the North Sea to arrest Findlay, who pleaded guilty at trial to attempted rape and assault of the young girl.

Talking point: The critical role of the police officer who stayed with the young girl as she recovered from her ordeal. What questions might you have asked and how would you have framed them so as to elicit the maximum amount of useful and accurate information?

Adapted from Davies *et al.*, 1998.

FIGURE 5.4 *The tone and content of forensic interviews with children are of critical importance, and the burden is on adults involved in the legal system to ensure that interviews are conducted according to best practice guidelines.*
Source: © Lisa F. Young. Used under licence from Shutterstock.

interviewers with structured guidelines to assist them with adhering to best practice. The NICHD protocol is based on research evidence concerning child development (e.g. memory, language) and was designed with practical needs and legal requirements in mind. The protocol has undergone extensive and international field-testing.

The NICHD Investigative Interview Protocol

The NICHD Investigative Interview Protocol consists of two primary parts – the *presubstantive phase* and the *substantive phase*. Within the presubstantive phase, there are several key phases. During the *introductory phase*, several features prepare children for their role as 'information providers'. For example, children are told that it is okay to say 'I don't know' and that they should not guess when providing answers. This instruction is included because research evidence shows that children tend simply to answer questions rather than admit or even notice that they have misunderstood (e.g. Memon & Vartoukian, 1996; Waterman *et al.*, 2000). Due to legal requirements in many jurisdictions, the protocol next advises that developmentally appropriate questions assess whether children understand the difference between the concepts of 'truth' and 'lies' (i.e. whether they can demonstrate 'truth–lie competency'). Children may not be able to articulate the definitions of abstract concepts, so questions that ask them to define 'truth' or 'lies' (e.g. 'What does it mean to tell the truth?') may not allow them to demonstrate their conceptual understanding. However, young children (even 4-year-olds) can demonstrate adequate truth–lie understanding when questioned in an age-appropriate manner using more concrete questions and examples (e.g. 'If I said that my shoes were red, would that be the truth or a lie?') (Lyon *et al.*, 2011; Lyon, Carrick, & Quas, 2010).

During the *rapport building phase*, children practice describing neutral event memories (e.g. what they did yesterday or for a recent holiday). This 'episodic memory practice' conveys the level of detail that will be expected of children later in the substantive phase of the interview while allowing them to practice responding to open-ended questions. In a sense, it gives children a chance to 'warm up' by providing narrative practice and allowing them to spend time becoming comfortable with the interviewer. Finally, this phase gives interviewers an opportunity to practice asking appropriate questions to elicit free-recall reports from children. The rapport building phase was designed in light of research showing that a supportive environment is beneficial in terms of children's willingness to cooperate and their reporting capabilities (e.g. Bottoms *et al.*, 2007; Hershkowitz *et al.*, 2006; Quas *et al.*, 2005; Roberts *et al.*, 2004).

Next, interviewers carefully transition into the *substantive phase* where substantive issues are discussed – typically, suspected abuse of the child interviewee. Interviewers begin by asking open-ended invitations to identify the target event(s), such as 'Tell me why you are here today'. Interviewers may need to ask more focused prompts to identify the target event(s) (e.g. 'I understand that something may have happened to you. Tell me everything that happened from the beginning to the end'). If the child makes an allegation, interviewers progress from open-ended invitations to more focused questions. Information obtained via free-recall prompts is more likely to be accurate than information derived from other question types (e.g. Dale *et al.*, 1978; Dent, 1986; Goodman *et al.*, 1991). Thus, focused questions are used only if necessary, as the goal is to elicit as much information as possible in the form of free-recall narratives that are provided in response to open-ended invitations and follow-up 'cued invitations' (e.g. 'Then what happened?'; 'Earlier you mentioned a [person/object/action]. Tell me everything about that'). Cued invitations are also free of interviewer contamination because they only enquire about aspects of the event that children have already mentioned.

When children are unable to provide any more information via free-recall prompts, interviewers may need to ask some direct questions that request information in specific categories. These are often in the form of 'wh–' questions. So for instance, if a child has mentioned a car, they might be asked, 'What colour was that car?' If important details are still missing from a child's report, an interviewer may progress to asking limited option-posing questions, typically in the form of yes/no or forced choice questions, such as 'Was the touch over or under your clothes?'.

Suggestive questions include those that bring up details that children have not mentioned (e.g. 'Where did he touch you?' if the child has not mentioned being touched) or communicate to children an expected response (e.g. 'He hit you, didn't he?'). Suggestive questions should always be avoided because they may contaminate memory reports and diminish credibility. Research studies demonstrate that suggestive interviewing procedures, especially if they are repeated, can lead young children to provide seriously distorted accounts of events they have witnessed (see Case Study 5.2).

When interviewed, young children typically say less than older children, especially in response to general open-ended invitation, but even 4-year-olds can provide information about their memories in response to free-recall prompts (e.g. Lamb *et al.*, 2003). Although they typically provide sparse accounts that leave out many details, free-recall narratives from young children are no less accurate than narratives provided by older children.

CASE STUDY 5.2   SAM STONE PAYS A VISIT TO THE NURSERY

In a now-classic study, Leichtman and Ceci (1995) investigated the effects of suggestive questioning and stereotyping on young children's reports of an event, when a man named 'Sam Stone' paid a brief visit to the children's day centre (nursery). The children were aged between 3 and 6 and were allocated to one of four groups: first, a *control* group, in which the children were not given any information about his visit beforehand; and second, a *stereotype* group, in which the children were read repeated stories illustrating the supposed clumsiness of Sam Stone, in the weeks leading up to his visit. Both of these groups were subsequently interviewed about Sam's visit in a non-suggestive way, four times over the next 10 weeks. In a third *suggestion* group, the children were not given any stereotype information about Sam's clumsiness and were again interviewed four times in the 10 week period, but with suggestive questions that implied that Sam had ripped a book and soiled a teddy bear. In a fourth, *stereotype and suggestion* group, the children were read the stereotypic stories beforehand *and* interviewed four times with suggestive questions. In the final phase, all the children received a fifth interview in which they were, first, asked to give a free recall about what had happened and, second, asked specific but neutral questions by a trained interviewer concerning whether Sam had damaged the book or the teddy bear.

Those in the *control* group gave generally highly accurate accounts and did not implicate Sam in damaging either the book or the teddy. In the *stereotype* only group, no children spontaneously reported damage by Sam to the book or teddy, but some 42 per cent of the youngest children agreed that he had when questioned, with 11 per cent maintaining this claim when gently challenged; the figures for the 5- to 6-year-olds were roughly half those of the younger participants. For the *suggestion*

only group, some 52 per cent of the 3- to 4-year-olds and 38 per cent of the 5- to 6-year-olds agreed, when questioned, that Sam had damaged the book and/or the teddy bear and again 12 per cent of the youngest group continued to maintain this claim when challenged (compared to 10 per cent for the older children). However, it was the combination of *stereotype* and *suggestion* that proved the most lethal to accuracy. Here, some 72 per cent of the youngest group claimed that Sam had damaged the book or teddy, and 21 per cent continued to insist that he had committed one of these misdeeds, even when they were gently challenged. The figures for the 5- to 6-year-olds were more accurate but, when challenged, 11 per cent still continued to maintain that the misbehaviour had taken place. Many children in this condition did not stop at acceding to the suggestions but also spontaneously embellished their responses with false details (Sam took the teddy into the bathroom and soaked it in hot water before smearing it with crayon).

Talking point: What are the potential implications of this study for investigators involved in assessing allegations of child sexual or physical abuse?

Finally, Leichtman and Ceci showed videotapes of the children describing Sam's actions to various groups of child protection professionals to see if they could distinguish between the accurate and inaccurate accounts on the basis of the child's statements alone. Performance in this informal test was essentially at chance; overall, the professionals rated the accurate account as the least credible and the inaccurate account as the most credible!

Talking point: What questions, if any, could the experts have asked the children to try to establish more accurately which children were telling the truth and which were relying on false memories?

However, younger children will usually require more cues and prompts to report more details (Hamond & Fivush, 1991; Lamb *et al.*, 2003). Around the world, field studies have shown the value of the NICHD protocol in improving the quality of investigative interviews; open-ended invitations increase, and focused and suggestive questions decrease when the protocol is used (Cyr & Lamb, 2009; Lamb *et al.*, 2008; Orbach *et al.*, 2000; Sternberg *et al.*, 2001). In these international field studies, most of the details and initial abuse disclosures were provided in response to open-ended invitations. Implementation of

the NICHD protocol has also had positive implications for case evaluation and prosecution (Hershkowitz *et al.*, 2007; Pipe *et al.*, 2008), meaning that its forensic value extends beyond the interview room.

Special care must be taken when conducting forensic interviews with children. However, awareness of children's developmental capacities and limitations does not end with the forensic interview itself. Researchers and practitioners are also concerned with how children's evidence is presented and used in the courtroom. There are several innovative ways that the legal system may try to lessen the stress associated with children's participation as eyewitnesses. For example, in some jurisdictions, children may participate in a preparation programme, or they may have a support person available to help them cope with the legal process (see Malloy *et al.*, 2006). One innovative measure borrowed from other arenas – closed circuit television (CCTV) – was implemented with child witnesses to reduce their stress by allowing them to testify from outside the courtroom. From a separate room, the child can respond to direct and cross-examination and avoid facing the defendant, while the testimony is played live in the courtroom. Theoretically, CCTV should serve multiple purposes, benefiting both child witnesses and the legal system. That is, CCTV should simultaneously reduce children's stress and negative consequences associated with legal involvement (Goodman *et al.*, 1992; Quas, Goodman *et al.*, 2005) and facilitate children's coping 'on the stand' so that they have more cognitive resources available for retrieving and reporting accurate and detailed information about potentially traumatic events.

Although there are several innovative measures aimed at facilitating children's effective participation in the legal system, CCTV represents one of the most researched reforms. CCTV appears to reduce children's stress: when interviewed via CCTV, children are rated as more relaxed by observers (see Chapter 13 and Davies & Noon, 1991; 1993) and rated as more confident, consistent and happy by legal professionals (Davies & Noon, 1993) than children who provide testimony in open court. In a laboratory analogue study, Goodman *et al.*(1998) found that when a 'defendant' committed a mock crime, children who testified via CCTV were less anxious about testifying than children who testified in 'open court'. Goodman *et al.* also noted that children were more accurate (e.g. in response to direct questions) when interviewed via CCTV (also see Orcutt *et al.*, 2001). Unfortunately, children's credibility appears somewhat diminished when testifying via CCTV compared to when testifying in the more traditional manner. However, in Goodman *et al.*'s study, use of CCTV did not affect whether jurors could determine the truthfulness of children's responses. Importantly, CCTV did not lead jurors to assume that the defendant was guilty. This is critical, as CCTV is used rarely in the USA because the Confrontation Clause of the Sixth Amendment of the Constitution provides defendants with the right 'to be confronted with the witnesses against him'. In contrast, CCTV is more common in the UK where those interested in facilitating children's legal participation are not constrained by any Confrontation Clause, and much of the field work has been conducted in the UK as a result (see Chapter 13 for more discussion on ways of facilitating children's testimony at court).

In sum, while we know that children are less communicatively competent and more suggestible than adults, we also know that even pre-school children can provide accurate reports about their experiences, including stressful or abusive experiences. Legal and forensic professionals must be aware and mindful of children's capabilities and limitations so that they ask questions and talk about concepts in ways that are developmentally appropriate. Investigative interview protocols specifically designed for use with children (like the NICHD protocol) can help interviewers and others who work with children in forensic contexts to achieve best practice. Other measures such as CCTV may be able to further enhance or facilitate children's testimony and well-being.

Finally, it is important to remember that when eyewitnesses (children and adults alike) are interviewed about a crime, more than memory is at work. For a successful interview, witnesses must be willing to reveal their experiences and motivated to discuss them. Most of the research conducted over the last few decades has focused on how to interview cooperative witnesses, and we have reviewed some key findings in this chapter. Although much of the research has focused on children's risk for false allegations, there is also a risk for false denials, long delays to disclosure, and recantation (Goodman-Brown *et al.*, 2003; Malloy *et al.*, 2007; Pipe *et al.*, 2007). The legal system should be wary of false allegations and false denials because both can have tragic consequences (see also Chapter 13).

Because children's statements are crucial for the discovery of maltreatment, failure to disclose, delayed disclosure and recantation may prevent prosecution and intervention (Myers, 1992). London *et al.* (2005; 2008) reviewed the literature concerning the disclosure of child sexual abuse. They concluded that a majority of children delay disclosure of child sexual abuse for long periods of time – with many delaying until adulthood. Although the extent to which children recant (retract or take back) true abuse allegations is more controversial than delayed disclosure, recent research suggests that at least some abused children recant sexual abuse allegations after disclosing. Malloy *et al.* (2007) found that 23 per cent of alleged child sexual abuse victims recanted their allegations during an investigation. Recantation was more common among younger children, children alleging abuse against parent figures, and children who lacked support from non-offending caregivers (typically their mothers). Recantation even occurred in cases for which there was medical or other evidence supporting the allegations. Other studies have linked social or motivational factors (e.g. child–perpetrator relationship, expectation of negative consequences) with children's willingness to disclose abuse promptly (Goodman-Brown *et al.*, 2003; Hershkowitz *et al.*, 2007; Malloy *et al.*, 2011).

CONCLUSIONS

People tend to value and trust eyewitness evidence too much. A quick glance at the statistics in the United States' Innocence Project database (www.innocenceproject.org) reveals that faulty eyewitness testimony played a role in more than 75 per cent of wrongful convictions. Human memory capabilities, while remarkable in some ways, are imperfect. The last few decades of research have advanced understanding of the reconstructive nature of memory and the circumstances in which errors are more likely (e.g. when people encounter misleading post-event information or suggestive questions; when eyewitnesses discuss their memories with each other).

It is important that forensic and legal practices recognise the characteristics of human memory, including its malleability. One way in which they can do so is by adopting and consistently adhering to empirically-based best practice interviewing methods for eliciting eyewitness testimony. This is particularly critical with child eyewitnesses because they are more suggestible than adults and have other characteristics (e.g. developing language skills) that make them more prone to err. The burden is on forensic interviewers and law enforcement to use appropriate methods to ensure that the most accurate evidence is gathered. Furthermore, researchers should continue to investigate new ways to improve existing interview protocols (e.g. eye closure; see Box 5.2).

Several questions remain unanswered and continued debates concern, for example, how to appropriately address some children's reluctance to disclose maltreatment without being suggestive in forensic interviews. Future research will continue to address practical issues and problems in the legal system while attempting to identify the underlying theoretical principles at work. Collaborations, open-mindedness and mutual respect between researchers and practitioners are vital for making advancements in the field of eyewitness testimony. We encourage scientists and practitioners to learn from and listen to each other and to work together to promote the use of empirically-based techniques and, as such, the pursuit of justice.

SUMMARY

- In general, people overvalue eyewitness evidence. It is important for all (including legal professionals and jurors) to recognise the imperfect nature of human memory.

- Memory is a reconstructive process: it can be influenced by post-event information such as misleading suggestions or by discussing events with other eyewitnesses (memory conformity).

- Memory can be divided into three stages, *encoding, storage* and *retrieval,* and memory is malleable at each of these stages (e.g. weapon focus effect during encoding; post-event information effects during retrieval).

- Even eyewitnesses who are confident may be incorrect when recounting an event that they witnessed or experienced.

- The cognitive interview (CI) is a well-established and commonly used method for interviewing cooperative adult witnesses. It is based on cognitive psychological theory and research evidence, and uses mnemonic devices to aid in retrieval.

- Children's developmental status and characteristics present certain challenges when they provide eyewitness testimony. However, even pre-school children can provide accurate accounts when they are interviewed appropriately.

- The most discussed investigative interview protocol designed for interviewing children is the National Institute of Child Health and Human Development (NICHD) Investigative Interview Protocol. The NICHD protocol is based on knowledge about child development and provides interviewers with structured guidelines to assist them with adhering to best practice.

- It is critical that legal and forensic professionals adopt and consistently adhere to empirically-based best practice interviewing methods and that researchers and practitioners continue to work together to improve techniques for obtaining eyewitness evidence.

ESSAY/DISCUSSION QUESTIONS

1. Eyewitness memory accuracy can be affected during all stages of memory. Describe these stages, giving examples of factors that can influence the accuracy of eyewitness memory at each stage.

2. Consider the strengths and vulnerabilities of children's eyewitness testimony.

3. Scientists claim that human memory is a 'reconstructive process'. What does this mean?

4. Discuss how investigative interview protocols (the cognitive interview for adults and the NICHD Investigative Interview Protocol for children) take into account the capabilities and limitations of eyewitnesses.

REFERENCES

Bartlett, F.C. (1932). *Remembering: An experimental and social study.* Cambridge: Cambridge University Press.

Bottoms, B., Quas, J. & Davis (2007). The influence of interviewer-provided social support on children's suggestibility, memory, and disclosures. In M.E. Pipe, M.E. Lamb, Y. Orbach & A. Cederborg (Eds.) *Child sexual abuse: Disclosure, delay and denial* (pp.135–157). Mahwah, NJ: Lawrence Erlbaum Associates.

Brewer, N. & Wells, G.L. (2011). Eyewitness identification. *Current Directions in Psychological Science, 20,* 24–27.

Bruck, M., Ceci, S.J. & Principe, G.F. (2006). The child and the law. In K.A. Renninger, I.E. Sigel, W. Damon & R.M. Lerner (Eds.) *Handbook of child psychology* (6th edn) Vol. 4 (pp.776–816). Hoboken, NJ: John Wiley & Sons, Inc.

Cyr, M. & Lamb, M.E. (2009). Assessing the effectiveness of the NICHD investigative interview protocol when interviewing French-speaking alleged victims of child sexual abuse in Quebec. *Child Abuse & Neglect, 33,* 257–268.

Dale, P.S., Loftus, E.F. & Rathbun, L. (1978). The influence of the form of the question of the eyewitness testimony of preschool children. *Journal of Psycholinguistic Research, 74,* 269–277.

Davies, G. & Noon, E. (1991). *An evaluation of the live link for child witnesses.* London: Home Office.

Davies, G. & Noon, E. (1993). Video links: Their impact on child witness trials. *Issues in Criminological & Legal Psychology, 20,* 22–26.

Davies, G., Stevenson-Robb, Y. & Flin, R. (1988). Tales out of school: Children's memory for an unexpected event. In M.M. Gruneberg, R.N. Sykes & P. Morris (Eds.) *Practical aspects of memory: Vol. I. Memory in everyday life* (pp.122–127). Chichester: John Wiley & Sons, Inc.

Deffenbacher, K.A., Bornstein, B.H., Penrod, S.D. & McGorty, E.K. (2004). A meta-analytic review of the effects of high stress on eyewitness memory. *Law & Human Behavior, 28,* 687–706.

Dent, H.R. (1986). Experimental study of the effectiveness of different techniques of questioning child witnesses. *British Journal of Social and Clinical Psychology, 18,* 41–51.

Draaisma, D. (2001). *Metaphors of memory.* Cambridge: Cambridge University Press.

Evans, J.R., Schreiber Compo, N. & Russano, M. (2009). Intoxicated witnesses and suspects: Procedures and prevalence according to law enforcement. *Psychology, Public Policy & Law, 15,* 194–221.

Fisher, R.P. & Geiselman, R.E. (1992). *Memory-enhancing techniques in investigative interviewing: The cognitive interview.* Springfield, IL: C.C. Thomas.

Fisher, R.P., Milne, R. & Bull, R. (2011). Interviewing cooperative witnesses. *Current Directions in Psychological Science, 20,* 16–19.

Gabbert, F., Hope, L. & Fisher, R.P. (2009). Protecting eyewitness evidence: Examining the efficacy of a self-administered interview tool. *Law and Human Behavior, 33,* 298–307.

Goodman, G.S., Bottoms, B.L., Schwartz-Kenney, B.M. & Rudy, L. (1991). Children's testimony about a stressful event: Improving children's reports. *Journal of Narrative and Life History, 1,* 69–99.

Goodman, G.S., Pyle-Taub, E., Jones, D.R.H., England, P., Port, L.P., Rudy, L & Prado, L. (1992). Emotional effects of criminal court testimony on child sexual assault victims. *Monographs of the Society for Research in Child Development, 57* (Serial No. 229).

Goodman, G.S., Toby, A.E., Batterman-Faunce, J.M., Orcutt, H., Thomas, S., Shapiro, C. & Sashsenmaier, T. (1998) Face to face confrontation: Effects of closed circuit technology on children's eyewitness testimony and jurors' decisions. *Law and Human Behavior, 22,* 165–203.

Goodman-Brown, T.B., Edelstein, R.S., Goodman,G.S., Jones, D.P.H. & Gordon, D.S. (2003). Why children tell: A model of children's disclosure of sexual abuse. *Child Abuse & Neglect, 27,* 525–540.

Hamond, N.R. & Fivush, R. (1991). Memories of Mickey Mouse: Young children recount their trip to Disney World. *Cognitive Development, 6,* 433–448.

Hasel, L.E. & Kassin, S.M. (2009). On the presumption of evidentiary independence: Can confessions corrupt eyewitness identifications? *Psychological Science, 20,* 122–126.

Davies, G.M. & Dalgleish, T. (Eds). (2001). *Recovered memories: Seeking the middle ground.* Chichester: John Wiley & Sons, Inc. *A useful discussion of the recovered memories topic which considers all sides of the debate.*

Lamb, M.E., La Rooy, L., Malloy, L.C. & Katz, C. (Eds.) (2011). *Children's testimony: A handbook of psychological research and forensic practice* (2nd edn). Chichester: John Wiley & Sons, Inc. *This book is a fully up-to-date resource covering a range of issues concerning children's testimony and children's ability to provide reliable testimony about experienced or witnessed events, including abuse.*

Loftus, E.F. (1996). *Eyewitness testimony* (2nd edn). Harvard: Harvard University Press. *Although published a number of years ago, this book is still a very accessible introduction to many of the themes discussed in this chapter.*

Milne, R. & Bull, R. (1999). *Investigative interviewing: Psychology and practice.* Chichester: John Wiley & Sons, Inc. *This book focuses on psychological research on how to interview suspects, victims and witnesses to achieve the best quality evidence.*

6 Interviewing Vulnerable Witnesses

Robyn E. Holliday, Joyce E. Humphries, Charles J. Brainerd and Valerie F. Reyna

KEY TERMS

Achieving Best Evidence ● blended memories ● change order ● change perspective ● context reinstatement ● familiarity ● fuzzy-trace theory ● interviewer bias ● long-term memory ● Memorandum of Good Practice ● misinformation effect ● rapport ● report all ● retrieval interference ● source monitoring errors ● suggestibility ● trace-alteration ● transfer of control ● working memory

CHAPTER OUTLINE

The number of vulnerable witnesses testifying in the courts has increased significantly in most Western countries in recent years. The most publicised are probably children, frequently testifying in cases of alleged sexual abuse, but other vulnerable witness groups are also increasingly seen and heard in court, notably the elderly and witnesses with learning disabilities. The appearance of such witnesses reflects the need to ensure that all groups in society have the opportunity to have their 'day in court' to have their testimony heard and tested and to ensure offenders are successfully prosecuted (see Chapter 13). 'Eyewitness testimony is the most damning of all evidence that can be used in a court of law' (Loftus, 1991). Reliable eyewitness testimony depends on accurate memory for the witnessed or experienced event. Psychological science and the legal system have become closely intertwined. The courts have taken notice of groundbreaking research on the eyewitness testimony of vulnerable witnesses, and this research is now routinely applied to actual cases. The contribution of psychological science has not been peripheral. Rather, research has changed the outcomes of important cases involving long prison terms and lifetime labelling of individuals as sex offenders, sometimes absolving and sometimes implicating the accused (see Ceci & Bruck, 1995, for actual cases).

This chapter begins by examining how memory operates and the strategies that must be employed in order to encode, store and later retrieve material accurately from memory. This leads on to a discussion of what causes failures of memory, particularly the role of **suggestibility** and **misinformation** in producing memories that are false, but nonetheless confidently held. Such *false memories* are particular areas of difficulty for some vulnerable witnesses. The chapter then goes on to consider the special interviewing techniques that have been developed to enable such witnesses to provide the police and the

> **suggestibility** *see* **misinformation effect**.

courts with the maximum amount of accurate information with the minimum of error.

HOW DO EXPERIENCES GET TURNED INTO INFORMATION IN THE BRAIN?

Information-processing theories

Such theories view the brain as a complex symbol-manipulating system through which information flows – a computer metaphor (see also Chapter 5). There is not a single information-processing theory but rather an account of the processes by which information passes in and out of the brain. It is widely accepted that what we remember is a combination of verbatim memory (exact details, which rapidly become inaccessible) along with reconstruction, two processes that are largely independent. **Fuzzy-trace theory** (e.g. Brainerd & Reyna, 1995; 1998) proposes that *verbatim memories* (exact details, i.e. 'red car') and *gist memories* (i.e. semantic and relational information; 'car' in this instance is vaguely specified – it could be any colour) are encoded, stored and retrieved in parallel. When asked to remember information, for instance during a police interview or in identifying a perpetrator from a line-up, remembering a verbatim memory is made on the basis of an *exact* match between the target details (e.g. a line-up face) and the details held in memory. In contrast, remembering a gist memory is made on the basis of the *similarity* between the target details (e.g. a line-up face) and the details held

> **fuzzy-trace theory** dual-processes model of memory; verbatim and gist traces are encoded for each detail.

in memory (Brainerd *et al.*, 1999). Fuzzy-trace theory proposes that the bulk of false memories are spontaneous products of understanding the gist of experience and that this tendency is increased when repeated, connected events have occurred, as in repeated abuse (Holliday *et al.*, 2011; Reyna *et al.*, 2007). However, this biasing tendency to spontaneously connect related events is lower in children than adults (Brainerd & Reyna, 2007).

MEMORY STRATEGIES FOR ENCODING, STORING AND RETRIEVING INFORMATION

Memory strategies

Such strategies are deliberate mental activities used to hold details in **working memory**, to store information, and to transfer information to **long term memory** and existing knowledge. In other words, memory strategies are cognitive or behavioural activities that are under the deliberate control of an individual, which are typically employed so as to enhance memory performance (see also Chapter 5).

> **working memory** a temporary memory system that permits the simultaneous storage and manipulation of information prior to possible storage in long-term memory. Working memory is needed for complex tasks such as reasoning, comprehension and learning.

> **long-term memory** stores personally significant information over time. Some of this information is fairly easy to recall, while other memories are much more difficult to access. Long-term memory is susceptible to forgetting, but some memories last a lifetime.

Information from the environment must be encoded, for example details of a suspect such as clothing, hair and eye colour, age, height and build. Once information is encoded, it must be stored within our brains. Encoded details are transferred from short-term memory to long-term memory. A number of memory storage strategies such as rehearsal, elaboration and organisation are employed to store details. This newly stored information is integrated into our existing knowledge base. For example, we might use a rehearsal memory strategy of repeating information when trying to learn a phone number, or remember a list of items to buy at the supermarket or the license plate of a car (Figure 6.1). We might make meaning connections between to-be-remembered details by the elaboration strategy. For example, in order to remember the words 'elephant', 'pin' and 'trunk', we could put the words into a memorable sentence such as 'the elephant had a pin in his trunk', or memorise the first letter of each word, 'e, p, t'.

FIGURE 6.1 *We might use a rehearsal memory strategy of repeating information when trying to learn a phone number.*
Source: © Ilya Genkin. Used under licence from Shutterstock.

How do the contents of memory get out of our brains?

Just as there are strategies for storing information in our brain, there are memory strategies for retrieving information. Retrieval strategies are deliberate operations designed to access information from long-term memory and move information to short-term memory ready for use. Using the example above, the encoded information about a suspect must be recollected when required, such as in a police interview. Recognition is the simplest and easiest method for such recollections. Asking a witness to identify the individual from a series of mug shots or a police line-up is easier for them than asking them to recall details, because the mug shot or line-up serve as retrieval cues (see Chapter 14). Recall is the hardest memory task because it requires generating memory information about an absent stimulus in order to recall it. Importantly, the accuracy of witness testimony can be affected at the encoding, storage and retrieval stages.

CHILDREN AND MEMORY STRATEGIES

Memory strategy use develops; there are age differences in the type, number and efficiency of strategy use (Bjorklund, 2005). Employment of strategies starts to emerge during pre-school years but is not very successful at first. During mid-childhood, usage of memory strategies increases dramatically.

Storage strategies

Rehearsal

Seminal research on this topic was reported by Flavell *et al.* (1966). These researchers presented 5-, 7- and 10-year-old children with pictures of objects to remember. Results showed a clear increase with age in the spontaneous use of verbal rehearsal as a memory encoding strategy and a resultant increase in levels of recall.

Organisation

Grouping information into meaningful chunks, for example when you learn a phone number, you may typically chunk the digits into groups of three digits. In a classic piece of research, Miller (1956) reported that adults can hold in memory an average of seven random numbers or letters (+ or −2). Moely *et al.* (1969) investigated children's use of the organisation strategy. Children aged 5, 6, 8, 10 and 11 years were allowed two minutes in which they were free to move around and touch pictures of objects from different categories (e.g. animals), which they recalled later. Moely *et al.* were interested in the number of times children sorted the pictures (e.g. lion, dog) into categories (e.g. animals). The oldest group spontaneously sorted the pictures into categories whilst the youngest children rarely did so. This, in turn, was linked to improved recall.

Elaboration

Creating a relationship between two items, for example in order to remember the words 'pig' and 'mud', the words could be included in a sentence: 'The mud swallowed the pig'. Beuhring and Kee (1987) investigated the use and efficacy of such a strategy in 5th and 12th grade participants. These researchers found that performance on a paired-associate learning task was improved to a greater extent by instructions in elaboration techniques in the older participants. So, efficient use of elaboration strategies appears late in development (late adolescence). Indeed, university students often need to be taught to use effortful elaboration because adults typically use this strategy inconsistently (for a review, see Bjorklund, 2005).

Retrieval strategies

As with storage strategies, use of retrieval strategies varies developmentally. The contents of memory are retrieved more accurately if the context in which the material was learned is reinstated. Using our earlier example, returning a witness to the location in which the suspect was seen committing the crime has positive benefits on recollection. Context is particularly important for young children (Bjorklund, 2005). On memory tests, young children perform better on recognition tests due in part to the representation of the original retrieval cues (e.g. a word or picture). Kobasigawa (1974) reported evidence of an age-related increase in the efficient employment of available retrieval cues (i.e. cue cards) from 5–6 to 10–11 years. The younger children encoded as much information as the older children but did not spontaneously use the available retrieval cues to assist with recall.

THE MISINFORMATION PARADIGM

The contents of our memories are subject to interference from a number of sources (e.g. parents, friends, the media and photographs). Arguably, the most important factor influencing accurate eyewitness testimony, however, is suggestibility.

The notion of memory reconstruction (i.e. gap filling – cf. Bartlett, 1932) is at the heart of research on the reliability of eyewitness testimony. Elizabeth Loftus is a recognised pioneer in the investigation of eyewitness testimony in the laboratory. Loftus and her colleagues (Loftus *et al.*, 1978) introduced the misinformation paradigm in which participants witness an event, are then misled about some aspects of the original event, and then try to recollect the original event. In Loftus (1977), for example, college students were shown a series of coloured slides of a road traffic accident. A red Datsun car knocked down a pedestrian. This was witnessed by the driver of a *green* car, who did not stop. Subjects were misinformed that this latter car was *blue*. Misled participants were more likely than controls to select a blue or a bluish-green colour (from an array of colours) for the car that did not stop. In other words, witnesses showed evidence of **blended memories** for this car; a blend of green (the colour in the witnessed event) and blue (the colour suggested).

blended memories a mix of initial and post-event memory details.	

When asked to choose between the original event and the post-event misleading details, research with adults (Loftus *et al.*, 1978; 1989) and children (Ceci *et al.*,

TABLE 6.1 *The standard and modified testing paradigms.*

Experimental condition	Phase 1 Original detail	Phase 2 Post-event misinformation	Standard test	Modified test
Control	(e.g. red ball)	(e.g. ball)	(e.g. red ball vs. green ball)	(e.g. red ball vs. blue ball)
Misled	(e.g. red ball)	(e.g. green ball)	(e.g. red ball vs. green ball)	(e.g. red ball vs. blue ball)

1987; Holliday *et al.*, 1999; Lampinen & Smith, 1995) has consistently found that misled participants are significantly more likely than controls (who have not been misled) to mistakenly select the misleading suggestions. This paradigm has come to be termed the 'standard test' of recognition memory in both the adult and child misinformation literature.

McCloskey and Zaragoza (1985) developed a 'modified test' that resembles the standard test except that at test the misled item is replaced by a new item (see Table 6.1). In the final phase of the standard test, participants choose between the original and the misled item (e.g. *red* ball vs. *green* ball). In the modified test condition, the misled alternative is replaced by a previously unseen novel item (e.g. *blue* ball). McCloskey and Zaragoza argued that if misinformation impairs original memories, participants in a misled condition would choose the original event detail (e.g. *red* ball) less often than those in a control condition. In a series of experiments using modified recognition tests with adults, McCloskey and Zaragoza found no significant differences in recognition accuracy between misled and control groups, providing evidence against the memory impairment view. They concluded that misinformation effects detected in the 'standard' testing paradigm were, in all likelihood, due to demand factors and/or response biases, and did not reflect true memory alteration.

A number of researchers have replicated McCloskey and Zaragoza's (1985) finding that the modified test eliminates the misinformation effect (e.g. Belli *et al.*, 1994; Bowman & Zaragoza, 1989). Others, however, have found a reduced but reliable misinformation effect on modified tests (e.g. Belli *et al.*, 1992; Holliday *et al.*, 1999; Schreiber & Sergent, 1998; for reviews of this literature, see Holliday *et al.*, 2002; Reyna *et al.*, 2002).

CHILD WITNESSES AND VICTIMS

Historically, in many countries children have been regarded by legal practitioners and other concerned professionals as unreliable eyewitnesses (Figure 6.2). Indeed, prior to the

FIGURE 6.2 *Historically, children have been regarded as unreliable eyewitnesses.*

Source: © Alexander Smushkov. Used under licence from Shutterstock.

1980s, children were believed to be poor witnesses, prone to making things up, highly suggestible and not able to distinguish fantasy from reality – in essence, second-class witnesses (see Chapter 13). At the turn of the 20th century, one of the most influential pioneers in memory and intelligence testing, the French developmental psychologist, Alfred Binet (1857–1911) published his classic book *La Suggestibilité* (1900). Binet proposed that auto-suggestion (the influence of a prominent thought) that originates inside an individual was the primary factor underlying suggestibility (Ceci & Bruck, 1995). Binet presented children aged 7 to 14 years with a number of lines that steadily increased in length, followed by a series of target lines that were equal in length to the last line in the study phase. Each child then drew each target line one at a time. Binet reported that children drew progressively longer lines (as they had seen in the study phase) even though each target line was the same length.

In 1910, a German psychologist, William Stern (1871–1938) asked children, adolescents and young adults (7- to 18-year-olds) to recall the details of a picture they had studied a few minutes earlier. Next the participants responded to questions, some of which were about the picture and some of which were misleading questions. In a prelude to modern research on false memories and suggestibility, Stern reported that the misleading questions produced the most errors, free recall produced the least amount of errors and the youngest children were more suggestible than the adolescents and young adults (Ceci & Bruck, 1995). In 1911, another German psychologist, Otto Lipmann (1880–1933) proposed that children encode details of a witnessed event differently from adults. He also noted that children were more compliant than adults in response to questions posed by an adult authority figure. Lipmann's views on child testimony and suggestibility, that is, the role of both cognitive (internal) and social (external) factors, remain the focus of contemporary research (e.g. Bruck & Ceci, 1999).

The last two decades have seen an explosion in eyewitness research, including many studies involving child witnesses (Brainerd & Reyna, 2005; Ceci & Bruck, 1995). Such research is timely because: (1) expert witnesses began providing the courts with opinions about the reliability of eyewitness testimony (e.g. see Loftus & Ketcham, 1991); (2) the societal beliefs of the 1960s and 1970s were rapidly changing, with increasing numbers of instances of child abuse being reported (refer to Case Studies 6.1 and 6.2); (3) few cases of child abuse were successfully prosecuted; and (4) in a growing number of countries the admissibility of child testimony and the abolition of legal constraints on children's evidence is known as the corroboration rule (i.e. the statements given to juries regarding the risk of convictions solely on the basis of a child's evidence; see Chapters 5 and 13).

FACTORS AFFECTING CHILDREN'S TESTIMONY

How reliable is a 6-year-old child's memory for an experienced or witnessed event? The answer is, it very much depends on a number of factors. Young children tend to forget information faster than older children (Brainerd et al., 1990; Howe, 1991), so the time delay between the witnessed event and testifying is critical. Young children report fewer details than older children and adults. However, the information that they do recollect is typically quite accurate (Holliday, 2003a). In 1981, Nelson and Gruendel published a study that evaluated pre-schoolers' verbal reports about routine and familiar events such as going to McDonald's. They found that children as young as 3 years accurately remembered details of events if such events were experienced a number of times. However, young children tend to provide adult questioners with the

details that they think the adult wants to hear (Holliday et al., 1999) and sometimes confuse the source of their memories – a child who has experienced an event and has received false information about that event may subsequently confuse memories of the event with memories of the false information. We will now consider a range of factors that impact on children's testimony.

Cognitive factors

Memory

Young children's free recall accounts tend to be accurate but less complete than those of older children. Hence, an interviewer must probe for detail with specific questions. Questioning increases the amount of information recollected but such information is often less accurate than that obtained with a free recall request, especially in young children (Brainerd et al., 2002; Holliday, 2003a). Open-ended questions (e.g. 'Can you tell me what happened?') are generally answered more accurately than specific questions (e.g. 'What colour was the man's hat?') but this ability improves with age (Holliday, 2003a; Poole & White, 1995).

Event-based knowledge

An important source of variability in children's true and false memory is prior knowledge (Bruck et al., 1997; Reyna et al., 2002). Studies examining children's event-relevant knowledge focus on the beneficial effects on accurate memory of prior knowledge that is consistent with experience (e.g. Chi, 1978; Goodman & Quas, 1997; Schneider et al., 1989), and on memory errors when children are asked to remember information that is inconsistent with prior knowledge (e.g. Ceci et al., 1981; Pillemer et al., 1994; Welch-Ross & Schmidt, 1996). Ornstein et al. (1998) examined the influence of prior knowledge on children's immediate and delayed recall of their memory for a physical examination and found that their knowledge of such an event had both positive and negative effects on recall, indicating that children confuse experience and expectation.

Language

Children's comprehension and production skills affect their susceptibility to misinformation acceptance. Children may fail to understand the questions (Waterman et al., 2002). Interviewers may misinterpret children's answers and jump to conclusions about the meaning of a child's statement. Of particular relevance for eyewitness testimony are the concepts of time, date and height, all of which are gradually acquired throughout childhood. Indeed, estimation of the height of an alleged perpetrator is quite difficult for children to make (and for some adults, too). Accurate estimations of when and for how long an abusive incident took place are not likely to be accomplished until around 10 years of age (Saywitz & Camparo, 1998).

Social factors

Compliance

Children's compliance to adult authority figures who question them (e.g. police officers, judges and social workers) also affects their vulnerability to misinformation acceptance. Young children are very aware of the high status of these people and are likely to report the suggested information because they view adult authority figures as credible sources of information (Ceci et al., 1987; Lampinen & Smith, 1995; Toglia et al., 1992). For example, in Ceci et al.'s (1987) study, suggestibility effects were reduced but not eliminated in the youngest children (4-year-olds) when another (7-year-old) child provided the misinformation. Hence, for these very young children, suggestibility effects were in part influenced by a stronger belief in information provided by adult authority figures.

Interviewer bias

Allegations of **interviewer bias** – that an interviewer had shaped the course of the interview to maximise disclo-

> **interviewer bias**
> where an interviewer shapes the course of the interview to maximise disclosures that are consistent with what they believe a child witnessed or experienced.

sures that were consistent with what he/she believed a child witnessed or experienced – were a common feature of several prominent trials during the 1980s and 1990s (e.g. Ceci & Bruck, 1995; Garven et al., 1998; Guilliatt, 1996; Pendergrast, 1996). It appeared that interviewers only sought details that confirmed what they believed had happened. In their discussions of a series of US day-care cases of the 1980s and 1990s (e.g. Little Rascals, Kelly Michaels and Country Walk), Ceci and Bruck (1995) highlight evidence of blatant interviewer biases: 'blind pursuit of a single hypothesis, and failure to test alternate, equally believable explanations of the children's behaviour' (p.99).

Repeated interviews and questions

In many countries, children are typically interviewed several times by different professionals and family members before a case comes to court. However, in other countries video recording the first professional interview has replaced multiple interviewing (see Chapter 13). Laboratory research suggests that repeated requests for information *within* an interview may signal to a child

that their earlier answer was incorrect. Young children, especially, are prone to change their answers when questioned repeatedly and are often reluctant to say 'I don't know' (although repeated questioning can sometimes improve recall; Reyna & Titcomb, 1997). This reluctance is particularly pertinent when yes/no questions are asked (Poole & White, 1991; see also Bruck et al., 1995).

The misinformation effect

Researchers continue to identify the conditions under which children are adversely affected by the implantation of misinformation after a witnessed event. Initial research interest in this area was precipitated by increased participation of young children in the legal system. In the UK, several legislative changes were introduced to promote inclusion of child witnesses, including abolition of the corroboration requirement, court evidence given via closed-circuit television (CCTV – see Chapters 5 and 13), video-recorded interviews as evidence and relaxation of the competency requirement (see Chapter 13). If the sole witness is a child, the credibility of that child's testimony is crucial in determining the outcome of the case (Reyna et al., 2002). One of the key issues affecting the reliability of children's reports in such cases is suggestive questioning. Such questioning can be seen in high profile cases involving claims of sexual assaults made by young children in the 1980s to 1990s in a number of countries including the UK (see Ceci & Bruck, 1995; Guilliatt, 1996; Pendergrast, 1996). In this chapter we have adopted a broad definition of the *suggestibility* or *misinformation effect* that incorporates social (acquiescence) and psychological (memory) factors that affect 'children's encoding, storage, retrieval, and reporting of events' (Ceci & Bruck, 1993, p.404). Children are vulnerable to misinformation effects yet the nature of the underlying mechanisms responsible for these effects continues to be debated (Brainerd & Reyna, 2005; Holliday et al., 2002).

In a widely cited series of studies, Ceci et al. (1987) found evidence of misinformation effects in children aged 3 to 12 years, with the magnitude of these effects largest in the 3- and 4-year-olds. Zaragoza (1987; 1991) found evidence of suggestibility effects only when children aged 3 to 6 years were tested with the standard (Loftus) memory test. Zaragoza concluded that social demand factors and response biases inherent in the standard test were responsible for suggestibility effects in children rather than changes in their memory of the target event. Holliday et al. (1999) investigated the relationship between memory trace strength of the original event and post-event misinformation, when 5- and 9-year-old children responded on either a standard or a modified test. Suggestibility effects were found on both types of

CASE STUDY 6.1   OLD CUTLER PRESBYTERIAN DAY CARE CENTRE

In *State v. Fijnje* [1991], Robert Fijnje was accused of sexually abusing a large number of pre-school children who attended a church-sponsored day care centre in Miami, Florida over a two-year period. At the time of the alleged abuse, Fijnje, a teacher's assistant at the Old Cutler Presbyterian day care centre, was between 11 and 13 years old.

'The initial disclosure came from a 3-year-old child who was in therapy for regressive toileting practices, nightmares, and refusal to attend the church day care. When questioned by her therapist during the initial session as to why she did not want to attend the day care, the young child said that there was a boy who played too roughly, tossing her into the air and catching her. (It was subsequently confirmed by the staff that the defendant did indeed do this, ignoring protests by the children that he was tossing them too high.) Despite an absence of any disclosures of sexual abuse by the child during that session or any physical or corroborative evidence, the therapist appears to have held the hypothesis from the very first session that sexual abuse was at the root of the child's difficulties, because she made her beliefs known after the initial therapy session and soon after she made her first report to the state's Hotline for Abuse.'

Ceci & Bruck, 1995, pp.13–14

'After approximately three more months of therapy, with the assistance of anatomical dolls, the child disclosed the first details of her alleged sexual molestation. Over the course of the following seven months, she named a number of other children and adults who she claimed were present during the abuse.'

Ceci & Bruck, 1995, p.14

Fijnje was arrested soon after his 14th birthday. After spending two years in a youth offender facility, he was acquitted on all charges.

Further study: This case involved therapy-induced false memory reports in very young children, many of whom did not disclose sexual abuse until several months into therapy. Moreover, the first child who disclosed was recalling an incident that had occurred at least six months before disclosure. How reliable would this child's account be, at age three, for abuse that allegedly occurred when she was two-and-a-half years old? None of the children testified in court. Instead, each child's therapist gave evidence on the child's behalf (hearsay).

In your further study, find a case or cases of alleged sexual and/or ritual abuse and look for any examples of interviewer or confirmatory bias, compliance to authority, peer pressure, and leading and suggestive questioning.

---

tests, implying that both memory and social factors are responsible for suggestibility effects in children (see also Holliday & Hayes, 2001; for reviews see Bruck & Ceci, 1999; Holliday *et al.*, 2002; Reyna *et al.*, 2002).

Dual memory processes and suggestibility in children

Is suggestibility a process of which we are consciously aware? Or is it an unconscious process? Is it both? These are important questions because if suggestibility is for the most part a conscious process it might be possible to devise methods to minimise its negative effects on memory. Such questions have been addressed in a series of studies conducted in Holliday's laboratory over the last

decade (e.g. Holliday, 2003b; Holliday & Albon, 2004; Holliday & Hayes, 2000; 2001; 2002).

Holliday and Hayes (2000) showed that misinformation effects in children were due to two memory processes – *recollection* (intentional acceptance of suggestions) and **familiarity** (automatic acceptance of suggestions). (For a related approach, see Brainerd *et al.*, 1998.) Five- and eight-year-old children were read a story, followed by misleading post-event details and then completed a final recognition memory test. Holliday and Hayes established that both recollection and familiarity were implicated in children's reporting of misinformation but the relative roles of these processes were affected by the method of encoding of misinformation. A larger recollection component was found for self-generated

> **familiarity** a feeling that a detail has previously been experienced in the absence of contextual details.

misinformation than for misinformation that was simply read aloud. Such findings accord with the view that misinformation effects in children can be influenced by social demand factors such as compliance (Zaragoza, 1991). In general, however, misinformation effects were more often due to familiarity than recollection. A large familiarity component to suggestibility is predicted by **trace alteration** (post-event suggestions automatically overwriting initial memory details) (Loftus *et al.*, 1978), **retrieval interference** (post-event suggestions blocking retrieval of initial memory details) (Morton, 1991) and *source-monitoring theories* (individuals adopt a

trace alteration misinformation that overwrites or amends the memory trace of the initially experienced event.

retrieval interference refers to the fact that more recently encoded or stronger information blocks access to the memory trace of an initially experienced event.

response criterion of familiarity, reporting the misinformation because it was the most recently presented, without considering the source of their memories, which implies that, for the most part, **source-monitoring errors** reflect automatic memory processes) (Johnson *et al.*, 1993). However, theories that propose *both* recollection and familiarity, such as fuzzy-trace theory (Brainerd & Reyna, 1998), provide the closest fit to these data. The results reported in Holliday and Hayes' (2000) findings were replicated in subsequent studies with children aged 4 to 10 years (Holliday, 2003b; Holliday & Albon, 2004; Holliday & Hayes, 2001; 2002) and in a real-life event (Memon *et al.*, 2006). Importantly, familiarity-based suggestibility *decreased* from 4–5 years to 10 years.

source-monitoring error incorrect attribution of the source of a memory (e.g. confusing internal thoughts with physical reality).

CASE STUDY 6.2 CAN THE CHILDREN BE BELIEVED?

'On 2nd August 1988 Margaret Kelly Michaels, a 26-year-old nursery school teacher, was convicted of sexually abusing children in the Wee Care Nursery School in Maplewood, New Jersey (*State v. Michaels* [1988]). Kelly was said to have licked peanut butter off children's genitals, played the piano while nude, made children drink her urine and eat her faeces, raped and assaulted children with knives, forks, spoons, and Lego blocks. She was accused of performing these acts during regular school hours over a period of 7 months. None of the alleged acts were noticed by staff or reported by children to their parents, nor did any of the parents notice any signs of strange behaviour or genital soreness in their children, or smell urine or faeces on them when they collected them from school at the end of the day.'

Ceci & Bruck, 1995, pp.11–12

The major premise behind the explosion of allegations of sexual abuse made by very young children in the 1980s and early 1990s at their day care centres was that children never fabricate such details and, on the contrary, children are often reluctant to disclose such things (the child sexual abuse accommodation syndrome; see Summit, 1983).

Bruck and colleagues published research in 1995 that had far-reaching implications for all these cases. Bruck *et al.*

found quite the opposite: that 3-year-old children do make up tales of being touched on their genitals.

- Bruck *et al.* (with permission) installed hidden cameras in a doctor's office and filmed individual 3-year-old children's routine medical examination, during which half the participants were gently touched by the pediatrician on their genitals and bottom.

- Immediately after this examination, each child was taken to the room next door and asked whether the doctor had touched them. (The experimenter pointed to the genitals of an anatomically detailed doll. Extensive use was made of these dolls in interviews conducted in the USA by social workers and psychiatrists.)

- More than half the children gave inaccurate descriptions of their examinations.

- Many showed, on the doll, genital and anal touching that did not occur.

- Nearly 60 per cent of the children used the dolls in a sexualised or aggressive manner.

Further study: What are the strengths and weaknesses surrounding the use of other methods, for example, props (toys, models) and drawing in forensic interviews of children? Are these other methods more reliable than the anatomically detailed dolls (see Chapter 15)?

Implications for children's eyewitness testimony

Holliday and colleagues' research suggests that questioning techniques that inadvertently encourage children to generate an incorrect detail themselves may be even more detrimental to the accuracy of subsequent testimony than the overt provision of a (wrong) suggestion by the questioner (Reyna *et al.*, 2002). Similarly, researchers have found that generating a mental image of events that did *not* occur in their childhood (e.g. breaking a window) increased the likelihood that the child would report that such events had actually occurred (Garry *et al.*, 1996).

In the day care cases discussed earlier, children were frequently subjected to therapeutic interventions (e.g. imagery induction) and investigative techniques that directed them to speculate or 'think hard' about events that *might* have happened to them (Ceci & Bruck, 1995). In the McMartin preschool case, for example, these techniques were most often employed when alternative means failed to result in allegations of abuse. Researchers have reported that young children who are repeatedly encouraged to imagine or visualise false events come to believe that such events actually occurred and provide elaborate descriptions of the contextual and emotional details surrounding these events (e.g. Ceci, Huffman *et al.*, 1994; Ceci, Loftus *et al.*, 1994).

Stereotype induction and suggestibility

Leichtman and Ceci (1995) evaluated the effect of stereotypes on 3- to 6-year-old children's memories of a subsequent visit by an adult male, Sam Stone. At weekly intervals before Sam's visit, children were read stories that portrayed Sam as a good-hearted but awkward person. Ten weeks after Sam's visit, children were given an interview that included two leading questions about actions that Sam did not perform (destroying a book, dirtying a teddy bear). Significantly, 30 per cent of the children falsely reported that Sam performed at least one of these actions. Children's false reports were thus likely to have been based on their negative stereotypes of Sam induced before he visited the school (see also Chapter 5).

In the forensic context, the impact of negative stereotypes on children's recollections can be seen in the Little Rascals day care and McMartin preschool cases, and in the 1987 death row case of Frederico Macias in Texas (Ceci & Bruck, 1995). In the Macias case, it was possible that the child's false testimony could have been influenced by negative information about Macias supplied to the child by her parents *prior* to the episode the child was alleged to have witnessed. Recent research by Memon *et al.* (2006) showed that young children were less able to reject misinformation presented prior to a classroom visit by an adult male when that misinformation was positive. An applied analogy can be made to the murders of two British schoolgirls in the summer of 2003, known as the Soham murders. Both the murderer, Ian Huntley, and his girlfriend, Maxine Carr (who was found guilty of conspiracy to pervert the course of justice), were known to the girls through their connections with local schools. Indeed, Huntley pretended to assist in early searches for the girls and even appeared on television during the days after the girls' disappearance. It is possible that witnesses did not come forward at first with information about Huntley and Carr's movements and behaviours because they held positive images of them.

VULNERABLE ADULTS

Elderly eyewitnesses

Older adults represent a special group of witnesses (Figure 6.3). The fact that in some countries growing numbers of older adults remain active in the community makes it likely that some will witness or be the victim of a crime. Elder abuse (physical, psychological, financial, sexual and neglect) is being reported with increasing frequency. Adults over 75 years of age are particularly vulnerable, and men and women are equally affected (Action on Elder Abuse, 2004). Obtaining eyewitness testimony that is forensically relevant, from young-old and oldest-old individuals, is now becoming a major concern to policy makers and professionals (see Chapter 13).

Only a handful of laboratory studies have evaluated older adults' recall accuracy in an eyewitness context. In

FIGURE 6.3 *Older adults represent a special group of witnesses.*
Source: © Steshkin Yevgeniy. Used under licence from Shutterstock.

general, recall is less complete and less accurate (in comparison to young adults), whether the event is a slide show (Yarmey & Kent, 1980), a video clip (Holliday *et al.*, in press; List, 1986) or a live staged event (Yarmey, 1993). Similar age-related differences are evident when memory is tested immediately, minutes or days after the to-be-remembered event (Brimacombe *et al.*, 1997; List, 1986; Yarmey, 1993).

Witnesses with learning disabilities

Individuals with learning disabilities (LD) are another group of eyewitnesses who are regarded in the criminal justice system as vulnerable witnesses. Such adults are typically reported as slower than normal developing adults to encode, store and retrieve details of an event (Milne & Bull, 2001). This is not to say that what they recollect is inaccurate; on the contrary, the number of details recollected is fewer, but just as accurate as for other adult witnesses.

With regard to people with LD, studies have shown they are particularly susceptible to the negative effects of social demand factors. Indeed, Kebbell and Hatton (1999) reviewed the research literature and reported that adults with LD are more likely to respond yes to questions irrespective of the content of such questions. Adults with LD are also more likely than other adults to make up answers in response to questioning. Given these characteristics it is not surprising that adults (and children) with LD can be highly suggestible, depending on how well they are questioned/interviewed. Caution must be taken when interviewing these most vulnerable witnesses.

Adults with LD may have particular problems with retrieving information from memory. Indeed, given that these witnesses have been found to be highly suggestible (e.g. Cardone & Dent, 1996; Milne *et al.*, 1999), it is of major importance that adults with LD, like other groups of vulnerable witnesses, be questioned appropriately and non-suggestively. Some of the special protocols that have been developed for interviewing vulnerable witnesses are described in the next section.

FORENSIC INTERVIEW PROTOCOLS

The cognitive interview

The *original cognitive interview* protocol was devised by Geiselman and colleagues (1984) for use with adult witnesses. Memory trace retrieval is usually enhanced when there is an overlap between the encoding and retrieval environments (i.e. encoding specificity; Tulving & Thomson,

1973). This overlap is achieved by **context reinstatement**: mental reconstruction of the physical and personal contexts surrounding the event to be recalled. A second instruction is to **report all**: relate all details regardless of their perceived relevance. Individual memory traces may also be accessed via several different retrieval paths, minimising reliance on prior knowledge and expectations. Varied retrieval (Tulving, 1974) is facilitated by a **change perspective** instruction (recall the event from several relevant perspectives) and a **change order** instruction (recall the event in a different temporal order, e.g. backwards).

The *revised cognitive interview* (Fisher & Geiselman, 1992) retains the four cognitive mnemonics. However, it also stresses the importance of social and communication factors (e.g. **rapport**, **transfer of control** of the interview to the interviewee). *Social factors* also play a role in determining the extent to which memory performance is influenced by advancing age. For example, older adults' accuracy on memory tests was reduced if they were first read a statement that portrayed a negative stereotype about memory in old age (e.g. ageing is detrimental for memory) (Hess & Hinson, 2006). Such stereotypes probably make older adults overly cautious about reporting information. A cognitive interview may ameliorate this, in part because it stresses the importance of reporting any detail, regardless of its perceived relevance ('report all' instruction); and it emphasises that the witness is the expert about the to-be-remembered event ('transfer of control' instruction). For practitioners, shortened modified interview protocols that facilitate accurate recollections are important given the potential problems surrounding interviewing vulnerable witnesses (limited attention span, faster forgetting) and pressures on police and other professionals to obtain maximum information as soon as possible after a crime (see Chapter 5 for further details).

Misinformation effects and the cognitive interview

A few studies have examined whether cognitive interview memory-jogging methods minimise the impact of

context reinstatement a cognitive interview prompt to reinstate mentally the surrounding context of the initial event.

report all cognitive interview prompt to tell everything about the incident under investigation.

change perspective cognitive interview prompt to recall the initial event from another perspective.

change order cognitive interview prompt to recall the initial event in a different order (e.g. backwards).

transfer of control cognitive interview instruction designed to pass control of an interview to the interviewee.

misleading questions on school-aged child witnesses. In Memon *et al.*'s (1996) study, for example, 8- and 9-year-olds watched a short film, then 12 days later were given misleading and neutral questions before and after a cognitive interview employing only two of the cognitive interview mnemonics, *context reinstatement* and *report all*. Memon et al. (1996) found no differences in responding to pre-interview questions. When children were questioned post-interview, however, those given a prior cognitive interview gave more correct responses to misleading questions than those given a structured (control) interview (for similar findings see Milne & Bull, 2003). Hayes and Delamothe (1997) reported that the *context reinstatement* and *report all* mnemonics failed to reduce 6- and 10-year-old children's acceptance of misleading information if presented *before* the interview. It is clear that the timings of the misinformation and the forensic interview are the keys to these disparate findings. Indeed, Holliday (2003b) evaluated this proposition and reported that 5- and 8-year-old children's reporting of misinformation during interviews and on subsequent recognition memory tests was significantly reduced if they had been interviewed with a developmentally modified cognitive interview before they were asked for a free recall narrative and before they were given a memory test. Importantly, these findings only held for misinformation that was self-generated in response to cues given by the experimenter in the post-event misinformation phase.

Which cognitive interview mnemonics improve children's recollection?

Given the findings outlined above, the next step in Holliday's programme of research was to see whether a shorter version of the modified cognitive interview could be as effective at reducing suggestibility. Given the brief attention span of very young children, a short version of Holliday's (2003b) modified cognitive interview would be advantageous.

Hence, Holliday and Albon (2004) examined the effects of several variations of a cognitive interview on 4- and 5-year-old children's correct recall and subsequent reporting of misinformation. Children viewed an event followed by misinformation that was read or self-generated, before completing a cognitive interview. Developmentally modified cognitive interviews elicited significantly more correct details than control interviews. As Holliday (2003b) found, a cognitive interview presented after misleading information reduced children's

reporting of misinformation during the interview and reduced reporting of self-generated misinformation on memory tests. Crucially, however, just two cognitive interview mnemonics – report all and context reinstatement in combination – offered some protection against the negative effects of misinformation on memory (see also Verkampt & Ginet, 2010). The implication of this research is that a developmentally appropriate interview comprising these two cognitive interview mnemonics would take approximately 70 per cent of the time of a full cognitive interview.

The cognitive interview with adults with learning disabilities

A small handful of researchers have tested cognitive interview protocols with adults with LD. For example, Brown and Geiselman (1990) reported a one-third increase in correct details in a cognitive interview in comparison to a control interview. (Adults with LD recalled fewer correct details than other adults, which did not vary by interview condition.)

In Milne *et al.*'s (1999) study, adults with mild LD and typically developed adults watched a short film of an accident and were interviewed the next day with either a cognitive interview or a structured (control) interview (see Köhnken, 1993 for structured interview). An increase in correct details was found for those given a cognitive interview. Unfortunately, however, adults with LD in the cognitive interview condition reported more confabulated details about the witnessed persons in the video than adults with LD in a structured interview (Milne & Bull, 2001). Clearly, there is a great need for more research attention to be given to these vulnerable witnesses and victims.

The Memorandum of Good Practice and Achieving Best Evidence

Since 1989, following the recommendations of an official committee headed by Justice Pigot, video-recorded interviews have been used as a substitute for live examination-in-chief at trial in cases of child witnesses (Figure 6.4). The Criminal Justice Act 1991 incorporated the admissibility of video-recorded interviews as evidence-in-chief and courts have followed this law, leading to a significant increase in the number of cases in which children give evidence at court (see Chapter 13).

Given the evidential status of the recommended interviews, the Pigot Committee recommended that

FIGURE 6.4 *Since 1989, video-recorded interviews have been used for child witnesses instead of live examination at trial.*

Source: © Lisa F. Young. Used under licence from Shutterstock.

ABE was written for all vulnerable witnesses, including the elderly and people with learning disabilities. Both protocols were developed with substantial input from psychologists with expertise in interviewing and eyewitness testimony.

The MOGP and ABE make the following recommendations:

INITIAL PHASE

- Develop rapport with the child.
- Interview the child as soon as possible after the crime/abuse.
- Conduct interviews in an informal setting with trained interviewers.
- Explain the purpose and process of the interview.
- Establish the ground rules for responding to questions; tell the child that not every question must be answered, nor has every question a right or wrong answer. This minimises social demand suggestibility; tell the child to answer 'don't know' when necessary.

FREE NARRATIVE PHASE

- Encourage free narrative.

QUESTIONING PHASE OF THE INTERVIEW

- Employ a *phased approach* in questioning; begin with open-ended questions (e.g. 'Can you please tell me in your own words what happened?'), followed by specific questions (e.g. 'What colour was his shirt?') and non-leading questions (e.g. 'Where was your sister when this was happening?'), then closed questions (e.g. 'Do you remember anything about his clothing?') and leading questions only when necessary (e.g. 'What happened after he took you into the bathroom?' when the child has not mentioned being taken into the bathroom); avoid repeated questions.
- Minimise or avoid forced-choice questions (e.g. 'Was the shirt red or blue?'). Minimise or avoid multi-part questions (e.g. 'Did he ask you to go upstairs with him and did you then go into the bedroom?').

CLOSURE

- At the end of the interview summarise what the child has said (in the child's own words) and invite questions.

Memorandum of Good Practice (MOGP) original official guidance introduced in 1992 for police officers and social workers in England and Wales conducting video-recorded investigative interviews with child witnesses for possible criminal proceedings. Subsequently superseded by *Achieving Best Evidence*.

Achieving Best Evidence (ABE) from 2001, the official guidance in England and Wales for all parties (e.g. legal personnel; police officers; social workers) and covering all vulnerable witnesses, from the initial interview through to court appearance.

specific guidance should be prepared to ensure that interviews were conducted in a manner acceptable to the courts with the minimum of suggestion or misinformation. The Criminal Justice Act 1991 also established that police officers and social workers should have joint responsibility for conducting such interviews with children involved in cases of alleged abuse. Interviewers must follow the guidance first outlined in the **Memorandum of Good Practice** on *Video Recorded Interviews with Child Witnesses for Criminal Proceedings* (MOGP; Home Office & Department of Health, 1992) and then incorporated into **Achieving Best Evidence** in *Criminal Proceedings: Guidance for vulnerable or intimidated witnesses, including children* (ABE; Home Office & Department of Health, 2001; see Chapter 13 for more information and subsequent revisions). While the MOGP was specifically designed for child witnesses,

How effective has the Memorandum of Good Practice *been in practice?*

Davies *et al.* (2000) evaluated a number of MOGP interviews conducted by police officers with children aged 4 to 14 years in the context of alleged sexual abuse. Davies *et al.* found that the length of the interviews varied considerably from 20 to 90 minutes (the MOGP recommended no longer than 60 minutes). Little time (on average less than 10 minutes) was spent developing rapport. Specific questions produced more information in the young children; open-ended questions were more effective in the oldest children.

Likewise, Sternberg *et al.* (2001) evaluated the quality of 119 video-recorded MOGP interviews in which children aged 4 to 13 years appeared to allege abuse. The police interviewers employed forced-choice questions much more often than open-ended questions. Indeed, Sternberg *et al.* found that more than a third of the details reported by the children were in response to forced-choice and leading questions. As a result of such findings, Lamb *et al.* (2007) developed an alternative interviewing procedure, the NICHD protocol, used by some police forces in the UK. This is fully described in Chapter 5.

Guidance on interviewing child witnesses in Scotland

In 2003, the Scottish Executive published *Guidance on Interviewing Child Witnesses in Scotland*, a set of investigative interview protocols for use with children and other vulnerable witnesses such as adults with learning disabilities and elderly adults. The Steering Committee was headed by Professor Amina Memon and her colleague Lynn Hulse from the University of Aberdeen. This comprehensive document is very similar to ABE.

Which works best – a cognitive or a memorandum-type interview?

Researchers have reported mixed results concerning the effectiveness of the cognitive interview with children. An important finding is that, in general, a cognitive interview elicits more correct information than standard or structured interviews without compromising accuracy in children aged 7 to 12 years (Geiselman & Padilla, 1988; Granhag & Spjut, 2001; Holliday, 2003a; 2003b; McCauley & Fisher, 1996; Saywitz *et al.*, 1992). Nonetheless, some researchers (e.g. Hayes & Delamothe, 1997; McCauley & Fisher, 1995; Memon *et al.*, 1997) have found a concomitant increase in reporting of incorrect and/or confabulated details.

Researchers have also examined the types of details that are enhanced by a cognitive interview. Milne and Bull (2003), for example, reported that 8- to 9-year-old children recalled more correct person and action details in a cognitive interview than in a structured interview. Granhag and Spjut (2001) and Memon *et al.* (1997), on the other hand, found no such differences in reporting of person details in school-aged children. More correct information was reported in a cognitive interview with 5- to 12-year-olds than a control interview based on the MOGP and ABE (Granhag & Spjut, 2001; McCauley & Fisher, 1996; Saywitz *et al.*, 1992).

Holliday (2003b) compared two interview techniques, a modified cognitive interview based on the revised protocols developed by Fisher and Geiselman (1992) and an interview modelled on the MOGP. The study found that children's reports were more complete and they recalled 27 per cent more correct information during a modified cognitive interview than in a MOGP interview. Importantly, a cognitive interview enhanced reporting of correct details in children as young as 4 and 5 years. Of forensic relevance were the findings that a modified cognitive interview produced more pieces of person, action and object information relative to a MOGP interview.

A study conducted by Wright and Holliday (2007a) evaluated older witnesses' recall of a short film using either the MOGP or a revised cognitive interview. Recall was less complete and less accurate for older than for young adults. There was a trend for correct recall of person, action and object details to be improved using a revised (i.e. shortened) cognitive interview irrespective of age (see also Wright & Holliday, 2007b).

New research by Holliday *et al.* (in press) reported that cognitive interviews can reduce misinformation effects in elderly witnesses. Young and old adults viewed a film clip of a staged crime followed the next day by misinformation. They were then interviewed with either a modified cognitive interview or a control interview followed by a memory test. Young adults recalled three times the number of correct details than the old adults. Yet, both age groups' recollections of correct information increased when interviewed with a modified cognitive interview. Significantly, misinformation effects in the old adults were eliminated if they had previously been interviewed with a modified cognitive interview.

SUMMARY

- Vulnerable witnesses and victims of a crime include children, the elderly, and people with learning disabilities.

- Such witnesses present special difficulties in ensuring that they give their best evidence.

- Interview procedures need to be based on knowledge of how memory operates.

- The stages of memory-encoding, storage and retrieval are strategies employed to ensure material is accurately retained and retrieved from memory.

- Factors that could produce unreliable evidence in vulnerable witnesses, especially young children, include interviewer bias, knowledge, compliance to adult authority figures, and memory.

- Processes underlying children's suggestibility and theoretical explanations of such processes.

- Interview protocols have been especially developed for children and other vulnerable witnesses. These include the cognitive interview, the various guidance documents produced by the Home Office and Department of Health (MOGP and ABE) and the NICHD protocol.

- Research has evaluated the relative effectiveness of some of these procedures with different groups of vulnerable witnesses.

ESSAY/DISCUSSION QUESTIONS

1. Compare and contrast the trace-alteration and trace-blocking theories of the misinformation effect.

2. How does fuzzy-trace theory explain age differences in suggestibility in children?

3. Is a cognitive interview viable with young children?

4. Discuss the impact of compliance on children's memories for events in which they have been witnesses or participants.

REFERENCES

Action on Elder Abuse. (2004). *Hidden voices: Older people's experience of abuse.* London: Help the Aged.

Bartlett, F. (1932). *Remembering: A study in experimental and social psychology.* Cambridge: Cambridge University Press.

Belli, R.F., Lindsay, D.S., Gales, M.S. & McCarthy, T.T. (1994). Memory impairment and source misattribution in postevent misinformation experiments with short retention intervals. *Memory & Cognition, 22,* 40–54.

Belli, R.F., Windschitl, P.D., McCarthy, T.T. & Winfrey, S.E. (1992). Detecting memory impairment with a modified test procedure – manipulating retention interval with centrally presented event items. *Journal of Experimental Psychology: Learning, Memory, & Cognition, 18,* 356–367.

Beuhring, T. & Kee, D.W. (1987). Developmental relationships among metamemory, elaborative strategy use, and associative memory. *Journal of Experimental Child Psychology, 44,* 377–400.

Binet, A. (1900). *La* Suggestibilite. Paris: Schleicher.

Bjorklund, D.F. (2005). *Children's thinking* (4th edn). CA: Wadsworth/ Thomson.

Bowman, L.L. & Zaragoza, M.S. (1989). Similarity of encoding context does not influence resistance to memory impairment following misinformation. *The American Journal of Psychology, 102,* 249–264.

Brainerd, C.J. & Reyna, V.F. (1998). Fuzzy-trace theory and children's false memories. *Journal of Experimental Child Psychology, 71,* 81–129.

Brainerd, C.J. & Reyna, V.F. (2005). *The science of false memory.* New York: Oxford University Press.

Brainerd, C.J. & Reyna, V.F. (2007). Explaining developmental reversals in false memory. *Psychological Science, 18,* 442–448.

Brainerd, C.J., Reyna, V.F. & Forrest, T.J. (2002). Are young children susceptible to the false-memory illusion? *Child Development, 73,* 1363–1377.

Brainerd, C.J. Reyna, V.F., Howe, M.L. & Kingma, J. (1990). *The development of forgetting and reminiscence. Monographs of the Society for Research in Child Development, 55.*

Brainerd, C.J., Reyna, V.F. & Mojardin, A.H. (1999). Conjoint recognition. *Psychological Review, 106,* 160–179.

Brainerd, C.J., Stein, L. & Reyna, V.F. (1998). On the development of conscious and unconscious memory. *Developmental Psychology, 34,* 342–357.

Brimacombe, C.A., Quinton, N., Nance, N. & Garrioch, L. (1997). Is age irrelevant? Perceptions of young and old adult eyewitnesses. *Law and Human Behaviour, 21,* 619–634.

Brown, C.L. & Geiselman, R.E. (1990). Eyewitness testimony of mentally retarded: Effect of the Cognitive Interview. *Journal of Police & Criminal Psychology, 6,* 14–22.

Bruck, M. & Ceci, S.J. (1999). The suggestibility of children's memory. *Annual Review of Psychology, 50,* 419–439.

Bruck, M., Ceci, S.J., Francoeur, E. & Renick, A. (1995) Anatomically detailed dolls do not facilitate preschoolers' reports of a pediatric examination involving genital touching. *Journal of Experimental Psychology: Applied, 1,* 95–109.

Bruck, M., Ceci, S.J. & Melnyk, L. (1997). External and internal sources of variation in the creation of false reports in children. *Learning and Individual Differences, 9,* 289–316.

Cardone, D. & Dent, H. (1996). Memory and interrogative suggestibility: The effects of modality of information presentation and retrieval conditions upon the suggestibility scores of people with learning disabilities. *Legal and Criminological Psychology, 1,* 165–177.

Ceci, S.J. & Bruck, M. (1993). Suggestibility of the child witness: An historical review and synthesis. *Psychological Bulletin, 113,* 403–439.

Ceci, S.J. & Bruck, M. (1995). *Jeopardy in the courtroom: A scientific analysis of children's testimony.* Washington, DC: American Psychological Association.

Ceci, S.J., Caves, R.D. & Howe, M.J.A. (1981). Children's long-term memory for information that is incongruous with their prior knowledge. *British Journal of Psychology, 72,* 443–450.

Ceci, S.J., Huffman, M.L.C., Smith, E. & Loftus, E.F. (1994a). Repeatedly thinking about a non-event: Source misattributions among preschoolers. *Consciousness and Cognition, 3,* 388–407.

Ceci, S.J., Loftus, E.F., Leichtman, M.D. & Bruck, M. (1994b). The possible role of source misattributions in the creation of false beliefs among preschoolers. *International Journal of Clinical and Experimental Hypnosis, 42,* 304–320.

Ceci, S.J., Ross, D.F. & Toglia, M.P. (1987). Suggestibility of children's memory: Psycho-legal implications. *Journal of Experimental Psychology: General, 116,* 38–49.

Chi, M.T. (1978). Knowledge structures and memory development. In R.S. Siegler (Ed.) *Children's thinking: What develops?* (pp.73–96). Hillsdale, NJ: Erlbaum.

Davies, G.M., Westcott, H.L. & Horan, N. (2000). The impact of questioning style on the content of investigative interviews with suspected child sexual abuse victims. *Psychology, Crime & Law, 6,* 81–97.

Fisher, R.P. & Geiselman, R.E. (1992). *Memory-enhancing techniques for investigative interviewing: The cognitive interview.* Springfield, IL: Charles C. Thomas.

Flavell, J., Beach, D.R. & Chinsky, J. M. (1966). Spontaneous verbal rehearsal in a memory task as a function of age. *Child Development, 37,* 283–299.

Garry, M., Manning, C.G., Loftus, E.F. & Sherman, S.J. (1996). Imagination inflation: imagining a childhood event inflates confidence that it occurred. *Psychonomic Bulletin & Review, 3,* 208–214.

Garven, S., Wood, J.M., Malpass, R.S. & Shaw, J.S. (1998). More than suggestion: The effect of interviewing techniques from the McMartin preschool case. *Journal of Applied Psychology, 83,* 347–359.

Geiselman, R.E., Fisher, R.P., Firstenberg, I., Hutton, L.A., Sullivan, S., Avetissian, I. & Prosk, A. (1984). Enhancement of eyewitness memory: An empirical evaluation of the cognitive interview. *Journal of Police Science and Administration, 12,* 74–80.

Geiselman, R.E. & Padilla, J. (1988). Cognitive interviewing with child witnesses. *Journal of Police Science and Administration, 16,* 236–242.

Goodman, G.S. & Quas, J.A. (1997). Trauma and memory: Individual differences in children's recounting of a stressful experience. In N.L. Stein, P.A. Ornstein, B. Tversky & C. Brainerd (Eds.) *Memory for everyday and emotional events* (pp.267–294). Mahwah, NJ: Erlbaum.

Granhag, P.A. & Spjut, E. (2001). Children's recall of the unfortunate fakir: A further test of the enhanced cognitive interview. In R. Roesch, R.R. Corrado & R. Dempster (Eds). *Psychology in the courts* (pp.209–222). London: Routledge.

Guilliatt, R. (1996). *Talk of the devil: Repressed memory and the ritual abuse witch-hunt.* Melbourne: Text Publishing.

Hayes, B.K. & Delamothe, K. (1997). Cognitive interviewing procedures and suggestibility in children's recall. *Journal of Applied Psychology, 82,* 562–577.

Hess, T.M. & Hinson, J.T. (2006). Age-related variation in the influences of aging stereotypes. *Psychology and Aging, 3,* 621–625.

Holliday, R.E. (2003a). The effect of a prior cognitive interview on children's acceptance of misinformation. *Applied Cognitive Psychology, 17,* 443–457.

Holliday, R.E. (2003b). Reducing misinformation effects in children with Cognitive interviews: Dissociating recollection and familiarity. *Child Development, 74,* 728–751.

Holliday, R.E. & Albon, A.J. (2004). Minimising misinformation effects in young children with cognitive interview mnemonics. *Applied Cognitive Psychology, 18*, 263–281.

Holliday, R.E., Brainerd, C.J. & Reyna, V.F. (2011). Developmental reversals in false memory: Now you see them, now you don't! *Developmental Psychology, 47*, 442–447.

Holliday, R.E., Douglas, K. & Hayes, B.K. (1999). Children's eyewitness suggestibility: Memory trace strength revisited. *Cognitive Development, 14*, 443–462.

Holliday, R.E. & Hayes, B.K. (2000). Dissociating automatic and intentional processes in children's eyewitness memory. *Journal of Experimental Child Psychology, 75*, 1–42.

Holliday, R.E. & Hayes, B.K. (2001). Automatic and intentional processes in children's eyewitness suggestibility. *Cognitive Development, 16*, 617–636.

Holliday, R.E. & Hayes, B.K. (2002). Automatic and intentional processes in children's recognition memory: The reversed misinformation effect. *Applied Cognitive Psychology, 16*, 1–16.

Holliday, R.E., Humphries, J.E., Milne, R., Memon, A., Houlder, L., Lyons, A. & Bull, R. (in press). Reducing misinformation effects in older adults with Cognitive Interview mnemonics. *Psychology & Aging*.

Holliday, R.E., Reyna, V.F. & Hayes, B.K. (2002). Memory processes underlying misinformation effects in child witnesses. *Developmental Review, 22*, 37–77.

Home Office & Department of Health. (1992). *Memorandum of good practice on video recorded interviews with child witnesses for criminal proceedings*. London: HMSO.

Home Office & Department of Health. (2001). *Achieving best evidence in criminal proceedings: Guidance for vulnerable or intimidated witnesses, including children*. London: HMSO.

Howe, M.L. (1991). Misleading children's story recall: Forgetting and reminiscence of the facts. *Developmental Psychology, 27*, 746–762.

Johnson, M.K., Hashtroudi, S. & Lindsay, D.S. (1993). Source monitoring. *Psychological Bulletin, 114*, 3–28.

Kebbell, M. & Hatton, C. (1999). People with mental retardation as witnesses in court: a review. *Mental Retardation, 37*, 179–187.

Kobasigawa, A. (1974). Utilization of retrieval cues by children in recall. *Child Development, 45*, 127–134.

Köhnken, G. (1993). *The structured interview: A step-by-step introduction*. Unpublished manuscript.

Lamb, M.E., Orbach, Y., Hershkowitz, I.,, Esplin, P.W. & Horowitz, D. (2007). Structured forensic interview protocols improve the quality and informativeness of investigative interviews with children: A review of research using the NICHD Investigative Interview Protocol. *Child Abuse & Neglect, 31*, 1201–1231.

Lampinen, J.M. & Smith, V.L. (1995). The incredible (and sometimes incredulous) child witness: Child eyewitnesses' sensitivity to source credibility cues. *Journal of Applied Psychology, 80*, 621–627.

Leichtman, M. D. & Ceci, S. J. (1995). The effects of stereotypes and suggestions on preschoolers' reports. *Developmental Psychology, 31*, 568–578.

List, J.A. (1986). Age and schematic differences in the reliability of eyewitness testimony. *Developmental Psychology, 22*, 50–57.

Loftus, E.F. (1977). Shifting human color memory. *Memory & Cognition, 5*, 696–699.

Loftus, E.F., Donders, K., Hoffman, H.G. & Schooler, J.W. (1989). Creating new memories that are quickly accessed and confidently held. *Memory & Cognition, 17*, 607–616.

Loftus, E.F. & Ketcham, K. (1991). *Witness for the defense: The accused, the eyewitness and the expert who puts memory on trial*. New York: St Martin's Press.

Loftus, E.F., Miller, D.G. & Burns, H.J. (1978). Semantic integration of verbal information into visual memory. *Journal of Experimental Psychology: Human Learning and Memory, 4*, 19–31.

McCauley, M.R. & Fisher, R.P. (1995). Facilitating children's eyewitness recall with the revised cognitive interview. *Journal of Applied Psychology, 80*, 510–516.

McCauley, M.R. & Fisher, R.P. (1996). Enhancing children's eyewitness testimony with the cognitive interview. In G. Davies, S. Lloyd-Bostock, M. McMurran & C. Wilson (Eds) *Psychology, law, and criminal justice* (pp.127–133). Berlin: de Gruyter.

McCloskey, M. & Zaragoza, M. (1985). Misleading postevent information and memory for events: Arguments and evidence against memory impairment hypotheses. *Journal of Experimental Psychology: General, 114*, 1–16.

Memon, A., Holley, A., Wark, L., Bull, R. & Köhnken, G. (1996). Reducing suggestibility in child witness interviews. *Applied Cognitive Psychology, 10*, 503–518.

Memon, A., Holliday, R.E. & Hill, C. (2006). Pre-event stereotypes and misinformation effects in young children. *Memory, 14*, 104–114.

Memon, A., Wark, L., Bull, R. & Köhnken, G. (1997). Isolating the effects of the cognitive interview techniques. *British Journal of Psychology, 88*, 179–197.

Miller, G.A. (1956). The magical number seven, plus or minus two: Some limits on our capacity for processing information. *Psychological Review, 63*, 81–97.

Milne, R. & Bull, R. (2001). Interviewing witnesses with learning disabilities for legal purposes. *British Journal of Learning Disabilities, 29*, 93–97.

Milne, R. & Bull, R. (2003). Does the cognitive interview help children to resist the effects of suggestive questioning? *Legal and Criminological Psychology, 8*, 21–38.

Milne, R., Clare, I.C.H. & Bull, R. (1999) Using the cognitive interview with adults with mild learning disabilities. *Psychology, Crime and Law*, 5, 81–101.

Moely, B.E., Olson F.A., Halwes, T.H. & Flavell, J.H. (1969). Production deficiency in young children's clustered recall. *Developmental Psychology*, 1, 26–34.

Morton, J. (1991). Cognitive pathologies of memory: A headed records analysis. In W. Kessen, A. Ortonly & F. Craik (Eds) *Memories, thoughts, and emotions: Essays in honor of George Mandler*. (pp.199–210). Hillsdale, NJ: Erlbaum.

Nelson, K. & Gruendel, J. (1981). Generalised event representations: Basic building blocks of cognitive development. In M.E. Lamb & A.L. Brown (Eds.) *Advances in developmental psychology* (vol. 1, pp.131–158). Hillsdale, NJ: Lawrence Erlbaum.

Ornstein, P.A., Merritt, K.A., Baker-Ward, L., Furtado, E., Gordon, B. & Principe, G. (1998). Children's knowledge, expectation, and long-term retention. *Applied Cognitive Psychology*, 12, 387–405.

Pendergrast, M. (1996). *Victims of memory*. London: Harper Collins.

Pillemer, D.B., Picariello, M.L. & Pruett, J.C. (1994). Very long-term memories of a salient preschool event. *Applied Cognitive Psychology*, 8, 95–106.

Poole, D.A. & White, L.T. (1991). Effects of question repetition on the eyewitness testimony of children and adults. *Developmental Psychology*, 27, 975–986.

Poole, D.A. & White, L.T. (1995). Tell me again and again: Stability and change in the repeated testimonies of children and adults. In M. Zaragoza, J.R. Graham, G.N.N. Hall, R. Hirschman & Y.S. Ben-Porath (Eds.) *Memory, suggestibility, and eyewitness testimony in children and adults*. Thousand Oaks, CA: Sage.

Reyna, V.F. & Brainerd, C.J. (1995). Fuzzy-trace theory: An interim synthesis. *Learning and Individual Differences*, 7, 1–75.

Reyna, V.F., Holliday, R.E. & Marche, T. (2002). Explaining the development of false memories. *Developmental Review (Special Issue on Developmental Forensics)*, 22, 436–489.

Reyna, V.F., Mills B., Estrada, S. & Brainerd, C.J. (2007). False memory in children: Data, theory, and legal implications. In M. Toglia & D. Read (Eds.) *The handbook of eyewitness psychology, Volume 1: Memory for events* (pp 473–510). Mahwah, NJ: Erlbaum.

Reyna, V.F. & Titcomb, A.L. (1997). Constraints on the suggestibility of eyewitness testimony: A fuzzy-trace analysis. In D.G. Payne & F.G. Conrad (Eds). *A synthesis of basic and applied approaches to human memory* (pp.157–174). Hillsdale, NJ: Erlbaum.

Saywitz, K. & Camparo, L. (1998). Interviewing child witnesses. A developmental perspective. *Child Abuse and Neglect*, 22, 825–843.

Saywitz, K.J., Geiselman, R.E. & Bornstein, G.K. (1992). Effects of cognitive interviewing and practice on children's recall performance. *Journal of Applied Psychology*, 77, 744–756.

Schreiber, T. & Sergent, S. (1998). The role of commitment in producing misinformation effects in eyewitness memory. *Psychonomic Bulletin and Review*, 5, 443–448.

Scottish Executive. (2003). *Guidance on interviewing child witnesses in Scotland*. Edinburgh: Scottish Executive.

Sternberg, K.J., Lamb, M.E., Davies, G.M. & Westcott, H.L. (2001). The Memorandum of Good Practice: Theory versus application. *Child Abuse Neglect*, 26, 669–681.

Summit, R.C. (1983). The child sexual abuse accommodation syndrome, *Child Abuse and Neglect*, 7, 177–193.

Toglia, M.P., Ross, D.F., Ceci, S.J. & Hembrooke, H. (1992). The suggestibility of children's memory: A social-psychological and cognitive interpretation. In M.L. Howe, C.J. Brainerd & V.F. Reyna (Eds.) *Development of long-term retention* (pp.217–241). New York: Springer-Verlag.

Tulving, E. (1974). Cue dependent forgetting. *American Scientist*, 62, 74–82.

Tulving, E. & Thomson, D.M. (1973). Encoding specificity and the retrieval processes in episodic memory. *Psychological Review*, 80, 352–373.

Verkampt, F. & Ginet, M. (2010). Variations of the cognitive interview: Which one is the most effective in enhancing children's testimonies. *Applied Cognitive Psychology*. 24, 1279–1296.

Waterman, A., Blades, M. & Spencer, C. (2002). How and why do children respond to nonsensical questions? In H.L. Westcott, G.M. Davies & R.H.C. Bull (Eds.) *Children's testimony*. Chichester: John Wiley & Sons, Inc.

Schneider, W., Korkel, J. & Weinert, F.E. (1989). Domain-specific knowledge and memory performance: A comparison of high- and low-aptitude children. *Journal of Educational Psychology*, 81, 306–312.

Wright, A.M. & Holliday, R.E. (2007a). Enhancing the recall of young, young-old and old-old adults with the cognitive interview and a modified version of the cognitive interview. *Applied Cognitive Psychology*, 21, 19–43.

Wright, A.M. & Holliday, R.E. (2007b). Interviewing cognitively impaired older adults: How useful is a cognitive interview? *Memory*, 15, 17–33.

Yarmey, A.D. (1993). Adult age and gender differences in eyewitness recall in field settings. *Journal of Applied Social Psychology*, 23, 1921–1932.

Yarmey, A.D. & Kent, J. (1980). Eyewitness identification by elderly and young adults. *Law and Human Behavior*, 4, 359–371.

Zaragoza, M.S. (1987). Memory, suggestibility, and eyewitness testimony in children and adults. In S.J. Ceci, M. Toglia & D. Ross (Eds.) *Children's eyewitness memory* (pp.53–78). NY: Springer-Verlag.

Zaragoza, M.S. (1991). Preschool children's susceptibility to memory impairment. In J. Doris (Ed.) *The suggestibility of children's recollections: Implications for eyewitness testimony* (pp.27–39). Washington, DC: American Psychological Association.

ANNOTATED READING LIST

Ceci, S.J. & Bruck, M. (1995). *Jeopardy in the courtroom: A scientific analysis of children's testimony.* Washington, DC: American Psychological Association. *Essential reading. Includes detailed accounts of day care cases discussed in the case studies in this chapter; also very good for misinformation theories.*

Bjorklund, D.F. (2005). *Children's thinking* (4th edn). CA: Wadsworth/ Thomson. *Very good coverage of issues such as memory strategies and memory theories.*

Garven, S., Wood, J.M., Malpass, R.S. & Shaw, J.S. (1998). More than suggestion: The effect of interviewing techniques from the McMartin preschool case. *Journal of Applied Psychology, 83,* 347–359. *Covers the interviewing methods used in this important case.*

Holliday, R.E. (2003). Reducing misinformation effects in children with cognitive interviews: Dissociating recollection and familiarity. *Child Development, 74,* 728–751. *Latest research on evaluating the usefulness of cognitive interview protocols with children.*

Holliday, R.E., Douglas, K. & Hayes, B.K. (1999). Children's eyewitness suggestibility: Memory trace strength revisited. *Cognitive Development, 14,* 443–462. *Evaluation of memory trace strength theory of suggestibility.*

Reyna, V.F., Holliday, R.E. & Marche, T. (2002). Explaining the development of false memories. *Developmental Review, 22,* 436–489. *A review article covering suggestibility, misinformation, and memory Illusions in children.*

ULF HOLMBERG

Continued on Page A1.

KEY TERMS

● coerced-compliant false confession ● coerced-internalised false confession ● conversation management (CM) ● factual approach ● false confession ● guilt-presumptive process ● interrogation manuals ● investigative interviewing ● PEACE model of interviewing ● Police and Criminal Evidence Act 1984 ● voluntary false confession

CHAPTER OUTLINE

Imagine two men on a street, arguing loudly. The shouting gets louder and then one of the men hits the other in the face. The one who is hit falls backwards and smashes his head against the kerb so badly that he dies. Now, imagine you are the judge, and having to determine whether the action was performed with or without an intent to kill. You have a suspect, but is he a murderer or did unexpected circumstances cause the death? Is the suspect the aggressor or did he simply defend himself? Neither fingerprints nor DNA give the answer to such questions, and many others about when, where, what with, who by and why a certain crime has been committed. According to the UN Convention on Human Rights, a suspect must be given an opportunity to express and explain his or her perspective regarding an accusation. Thus, a police interview with the suspect remains the key feature in a criminal investigation.

The following three convicted criminals' experiences of police interviews will give the reader a glimpse of what really happens during police interviews with suspects. In the first interview (example A), with a suspect accused of murder, the police officer repeatedly asked the same questions about what the suspect had been doing during the previous 24 hours. This confession-seeking police interview resulted in conflict. As the police officer continually asked the same kinds of question, it forced the suspect to conclude that the officer was just trying to 'grill' him and so the suspect remained silent (Holmberg et al., 2007, p.357). Such a confrontational approach can create external pressures that lead to suspects displaying 'avoidance' during the interview (Gudjonsson & Petursson, 1991; Gudjonsson & Sigurdsson, 1994).

In the second interview (example B), a man convicted of rape described his encounter with a police officer who recognised his needs and emotions. In his own words he said:

> …then I got some questions and I started to talk, she [the police officer] was quite, quite broad-minded. She showed respect for me, I felt that it was something more than just a job for her, like 'now interrogation – bang boom' and nothing more – but she might possibly talk about it.
>
> *Holmberg et al., 2007, p.361*

In the third case (example C), a convicted rapist's description of his police interview indicates that the police interview may 'open doors' as well as 'shut doors':

> It was easier for me to talk to people who acted properly because people who interview people, they should not punish you, but they can do so just that by their way of talking, showing their hate for me as a human being, and at that moment you turn around and return their hate.
>
> *Holmberg, 1996, p.37*

Obviously, one of the most important parts of a crime investigation, the interview with the suspect, may be conducted and experienced in different ways and in this chapter I will discuss different kinds of police interview. As an introduction, let us begin with a brief examination of the recommendations found in **interrogation manuals**. This throws light on the confession culture, the assumption that most suspects are liars and the emphasis is upon psychologically coercive tactics. This view probably emanated from investigators who lacked knowledge of what research actually has shown. It might even be that an accusatory, confession-seeking behaviour by a police interviewer is a reflection of a society's need for revenge for such a heinous crime. The next section describes the effects on a police officer's behaviour while interrogating and questioning a suspect according to the guidance embodied in such manuals. One possible consequence of a confession-seeking interrogation is a **false confession** and the impact of this, as well as other explanations as to why some people falsely confess to a crime, will be discussed in the third part. Finally, I take a step from interrogation to investigative interviewing and give an account of what research has found regarding interviewing suspects. In other words, what could work from a human rights perspective that could also increase a suspect's readiness to talk (with the added hope that this might be a first step toward rehabilitation and a life without crime).

> **interrogation manuals** books, memoranda or other printed recommendations principally written by police officers, detectives or former staff members of scientific crime laboratories. The methods are often confession-seeking procedures based on uncritical/subjective use of psychological knowledge.

> **false confession** any confession or any admission to a criminal act that the confessor did not commit.

INTERROGATION MANUALS: WHAT ARE POLICE OFFICERS TOLD TO DO?

In almost any profession, there are manuals available providing guidelines as to how people should go about their work. Policing, and the interrogation of suspects, is no exception. A close look at 20 interrogation manuals and handbooks published in English reveals some concerns regarding strategy and an apparent neglect of human rights issues. A review of these manuals raises several issues and a crucial question about whether police interviews with suspects are about eliciting information or obtaining confessions.

One of the more obvious differences between the manuals is how they portray the very purpose of interrogation. Manuals from the US totally dominate the market (18 out of 20 in this review) and lay great emphasis on how to obtain a confession from a suspect. Several of them appear to have been strongly influenced by the *Reid technique* (Inbau *et al.*, 2001; see Table 7.1). This involves a nine-step interrogation process, during which the suspect's resistance to confess is gradually broken down.

Several manuals (e.g. Inbau *et al.*, 2001; Palmiotto, 2004; Royal & Schutt, 1976) promote the idea that an interrogation is to be preceded by an interview. Thus, the spokespersons for this approach make a distinction between the interview and the interrogation, and argue that the purpose of the interview is to obtain information and facts in order to establish whether the suspect is guilty or not. According to Buckley (2006), the interview step or phase should be non-accusatory, during which the suspect may volunteer useful information and reveal behaviour that the interviewer should evaluate in depth to make assessments of the suspect's credibility (Kassin, 2006).

The founders of the Reid technique claim that interviewers can be trained to detect lies at an 85 per cent level of accuracy (which exceeds the success rate found in any lie detection experiment in published research). Thousands of people, all over the world, have been tested in lie detection studies and these psychological studies have found that individuals cannot detect lies at levels much above chance (see Chapter 8; also Kassin, 2006; Vrij, 2000). According to Buckley (2006), when the interviewer believes that the suspect has not revealed the truth, the suspect is ready to be interrogated. This second step or phase urges the interrogator to provide at least 95 per cent of the conversation and not to ask any questions. Weinberg (2002) argues that if the interrogator

asks questions, this reveals insecurity regarding the guilt of the suspect, which is not regarded as a good strategy.

The sole purpose of the interrogation appears to be to obtain a confession, and for some suspects it means being persuaded to tell the truth (Buckley, 2006). You must ask, whose truth? Here the advocates of the Reid technique have the investigators, the police officers, in mind. However, some innocent people may be being interrogated without evidence of their involvement, but solely on the basis of a police hunch (Kassin, 2006). This means that the interrogation is a **guilt-presumptive process** where biases affect police officers' behaviour, instead of it being an objective, information-gathering process. (Later in this chapter, guilt-presumptions, and how such presumption may affect an interviewer's behaviour, will be discussed.)

> **guilt-presumptive process** style of interviewing that assumes the guilt of the suspect.

A confession is, of course, very valuable for the police, provided it is not a false one. It can make it easier to recover goods, lead to compensation and satisfaction for the victims and enable other culprits to be pursued, and may result in a conviction at trial. However, an interrogation technique with the sole purpose of obtaining confessions breaks one of the cardinal principles of investigative policing: the presumption of innocence (UN General Assembly, 1966, article 14:2). If the investigation and the initial interview conclude that the suspect is guilty, then the suspect who denies their guilt during the interrogation will naturally be considered a liar. Under these circumstances the interrogator will see no need to consider the suspect's credibility any further.

One of the techniques for obtaining a confession is *theme-building*. This is one of the nine steps in the Reid technique and the idea is to give the suspect a morally justifiable way out, given that the way out also includes an admission of guilt. The idea is that the suspect is unwilling to admit to the crime because her/his deeds are morally objectionable, an admission that would disturb the self-image. The interrogator then constructs a theme, a fake story, which is consistent with the known details of the crime. The story relieves the suspect of guilt, but if he or she agrees to the story, the individual simultaneously admits to the crime. It could be something like 'Okay, the money was taken; you might have borrowed it, just in order to pay for food for your family. You wanted to pay it back, didn't you?' Other methods are the use of fake evidence or the introduction of evidence that does not exist, all to persuade the suspect that he/she has been caught and might as well admit to the crime. One of the problems with this is that innocent but suggestible suspects might confess to a crime they did not commit, especially if they are influenced into believing that an admission might result in leniency from the

TABLE 7.1 *The nine steps of the Reid technique.*

Direct positive confrontation
Theme development
Handling denials
Overcoming objections
Procurement and retention of suspect's attention
Handling suspect's passive mood
Presenting an alternative question
Having suspect orally relate various details of offence
Converting an oral confession into a written confession

justice system. Thus, in some cultures, police interrogation methods can be problem-makers rather than problem-solvers for the criminal justice system.

The distinction between 'interrogation' and 'interviewing' in manuals

One confusing circumstance is how the different manuals use the words *interrogation* and *interview*. Commonly, the interview phase is understood as being an information-seeking conversation. Several manuals (e.g. Benson, 2000; Butterfield, 2002; Rutledge, 2001) do not describe methods for conducting the interview phase but those that do normally emphasise the importance of good communication. They generally advise establishing rapport with the suspect and actively seeking information with an open mind. Unfortunately, some manuals advise the police not to reveal any suspicions to the suspect at this point (e.g. Bristow, 1964; Inbau *et al.*, 2001; Yeschke, 2003). This is highly questionable according to the UN Covenant on Civil and Political Rights (UN General Assembly, 1966, article 9), which states that suspects have the right to be informed immediately about the reasons for an arrest and the accusations made against them (Figure 7.1).

FIGURE 7.1 *The UN Covenant on Civil and Political Rights states that suspects have the right to be informed immediately about the reasons for an arrest and the accusations made against them.*
Source: © Mark William Richardson. Used under licence from Shutterstock.

The *interrogation phase* is normally described as a confrontational process, the sole purpose of which is to obtain a confession. Twelve of 20 manuals contain methods that are highly questionable or actually illegal under international law (e.g. Benson, 2000; Inbau *et al.*, 2001; Starrett, 1998). These are mainly methods involving trickery and/or deceit, but some manuals (e.g. Butterfield, 2002) advocate methods very close to actual torture, as defined by the UN Universal Declaration of Human Rights article 5 (UN General Assembly, 1948). When coercive interrogation techniques, trickery and deceit are applied by the interrogator, other legal conflicts will arise with the principles of voluntariness and the presumption of innocence in the UN Covenant on Civil and Political Rights (UN General Assembly, 1966, article 14). A majority of the manuals seem to contain implicit contradictions that can confuse their readers. The contradictions mainly concern whether one is supposed to act with a humane attitude and establish rapport with the suspect, or if it is more effective to be rough and coercive. Some manuals (e.g. Inbau *et al.*, 2001) discuss the influence of interview stress and its impact on correct assessments of credibility. A stressed suspect is supposed to give away more clues to deception; hence the creation of stress within a suspect is argued to be good. Now, stress does not promote rapport or a working alliance, so in the context of **conversation management (CM)**, stress is often discouraged. Here it should be noted with regard to the interview phase that use of the stereotypical clues to deception is very ineffective and sometimes directly counterproductive when it comes to detecting deception accurately (Chapter 8; also DePaulo *et al.*, 2003; Granhag & Hartwig, this volume; Vrij, 2000).

> **conversation management (CM)** an interview technique, proposed by Shepherd, that emphasises the police officer's awareness and management of the interview, both verbally and non-verbally.

Inconsistency in manuals regarding the use of evidence

Several manuals are also inconsistent in their advice concerning the use of evidence known to the police (e.g. Inbau *et al.*, 2001; Starrett, 1998). They may have a well-reasoned strategy about the late disclosure of evidence, but usually contradict themselves in another chapter. This comes from the persistent promotion of the **factual approach**. This method encourages a direct disclosure of all available evidence to the suspect, sometimes even false information. This is promoted as likely to lead to a quick confession, as the suspect immediately sees

> **factual approach** the disclosure by the interviewer of all available evidence to the suspect, sometimes even false information, with the presumption that this will to lead to a quick confession.

that he or she has been caught and that further resistance is useless. There is research supporting the notion that strong (and valid) evidence encourages a guilty suspect to confess (e.g. Gudjonsson & Bownes, 1992; Gudjonsson & Petursson, 1991). Thus, it is not very surprising that it is a preferred technique among interrogators to use all the evidence available at the beginning of the interrogation. Unfortunately, many intelligent suspects then choose to make up a deceptive story, now including all the disclosed evidence. It doesn't have to be entirely credible, provided it raises sufficient doubt in the mind of the investigator.

Presenting all available evidence at the beginning of the interview is problematic in several ways. First, if all the evidence is disclosed, the investigator has given away any possibility of checking the correctness of the information provided by the suspect. If the evidence is not disclosed, the suspect can provide information about certain things that would be known only to the perpetrator and to the investigator from the evidence collected. Moreover, withholding the evidence and inviting the denying suspect to talk about the criminal event may, so long as the suspect does not choose to remain silent, lead to the disclosure of details that are palpably untrue in the light of the evidence available to the investigator. In the (guilty) suspect's efforts to show his or her innocence, the suspect creates a story that approximates the truth, but differs in critical details from the evidence available to the investigator, and must therefore be false.

The use of delayed and strategic disclosure of police information to the suspect is a central feature of the strategic use of evidence (SUE) technique (see Chapter 8 for further information on this technique). It must be emphasised that the SUE technique is rather more than simply withholding evidence early in the interview. By not disclosing the existing evidence, the SUE technique encourages suspects to reveal all possible explanations for their own behaviour in relation to the crime, which can then be compared to the evidence known to the interviewer. This gives the SUE technique twin advantages: it enables the investigator to judge the truthfulness or otherwise of the suspects' statements by judging what they say against what is known, and also encourages suspects to give their own accounts of their behaviour rather than simply denying their guilt.

Research has demonstrated that compared with untrained interviewers, SUE-trained interviewers asked more specific questions relating to evidence known only to the investigator, without disclosing the source. Furthermore, SUE-trained interviewers were significantly better in detecting deceptions than were untrained interviewers. The SUE technique has been shown to improve the detection of deception compared to early disclosure of the evidence by interviewers (see Chapter 8 and Hartwig, 2006; Hartwig et al., 2005a; 2005b; 2006).

Moreover, truth-telling suspects interviewed with the SUE technique experienced greater optimism that they would be seen as truthful, an important factor in influencing the overall interview climate (Hartwig et al., 2007).

In conclusion, there are many manuals available and they are of varying quality concerning their evidence base, utility, effectiveness of the guidelines given, adherence to the law and consistency. A majority of the manuals have serious shortcomings concerning conflict with research findings, risk of false confessions, voluntariness and presumption of innocence, and some of them are in direct conflict with basic human rights issues such as the principle of protection against torture. To some extent, these manuals explain why some police officers endorse a confession-seeking approach to interviewing. Another more likely explanation may be the development of beliefs about a suspect's guilt that affect the behaviour of the police interviewer.

EFFECTS ON INTERVIEWER BEHAVIOUR

Returning to example A cited at the beginning of this chapter, where the suspect was exposed to a coercive and confession-seeking interrogation that came to nothing more than conflict, the suspect felt himself coerced under external pressure and thus perceived the situation as the police officer attempting to 'grill' him, which in turn led to the suspect's conclusion that he would say no more and stay silent. Example C provides an explanation of the possible effects of police officers' behaviour while interviewing suspects. The man in this example argued that it was easier to talk about the crime he had committed when the interviewer acted 'properly', compared to when the interviewer adopted an aggressive and punitive approach. The suspect noted that when a police officer shows hate towards a suspect it is likely that the suspect will return the hate towards the police officer. From the investigative perspective, such a suspect is seen as resistant and not cooperative. However, this attitude may actually reflect the behaviour of the police officer.

Having analysed 400 video recordings and 200 audio recordings of UK police interviews, Baldwin (1992; 1993) emphasised the need for professionalism. Some officers adopted a confession-seeking approach and tried to persuade suspects to accept a predetermined description of their alleged crimes. These interviewers did not listen to what the suspects said, but instead continually interrupted them. Such interviewers occasionally became unduly flustered, aggressive and provocative. Some used a 'macho' style and were incapable of recognising how counter-productive this was. Baldwin was critical of such confession-seeking approaches.

Moston and Engelberg (1993) analysed 118 taped police interviews that involved a wide range of offences and a wide variety of suspects. They found that a common interviewing style was one that was confrontational and confession-seeking, which in turn created a major problem. When such interviewers directly accused suspects of having committed crimes and simply asked them to confirm the allegations, many suspects denied involvement, showed resistance or exercised their right to remain silent. Interviewees can show resistance through verbal or non-verbal blocking behaviours that obstruct interviewers' efforts to establish rapport and create appropriate communication. Unwillingness often stems from interviewees' psychological blocks such as anxiety, fear, depression, anger and antipathy (Shepherd, 1993). Such unwillingness may appear when the interviewer fails to orientate suspects sufficiently towards the purpose of the interview: suspects need to know the 'route map' if they are to deal in realities. Resistance may also be a reaction to the interviewer's disruptive talk, inappropriate listening and inappropriate pacing of the interview where, after the interviewee's response, the interviewer immediately asks another question or makes a comment, filling pauses and allowing no time for reflection.

In their study of confession-seeking approaches, Stephenson and Moston (1993) studied 1067 interviews and found that in 73 per cent of these cases the police interviewers seemed sure of the guilt of the suspect. In a widely cited article, Kassin and Gudjonsson (2004) reviewed in detail the literature on confessions. They describe interrogation as a guilt-presumptive process in which the police officer, affected by a strong prior belief concerning the guilt of the suspect, behaves accordingly. The officer's success is measured by whether the suspect confesses or denies. Beliefs about guilt may influence a police officer's interaction with a suspect, explaining why police officers adopt a confession-seeking interrogating approach (Mortimer & Shepherd, 1999). Psychological research has found that when people have formed a belief they become selective when seeking and interpreting new information (see e.g. Kassin et al., 2003). In this distorted, selective process, people strive for information to verify their belief. This process of cognitive confirmation bias may make a police officer's beliefs resistant to change, even in the presence of contradictory facts (Nickerson, 1998).

How bias affects questioning style

Innes (2002) argued that during crime investigations police officers may be overwhelmed by the amount of evidence in a case, leading the officer not to search for new facts that might reveal the whole truth. The officer may search for an amount of evidence that is sufficient to construct a satisfying internal representation of the criminal event and, in such a construction, gaps (without evidence) may be filled by imagination and conjecture to fashion a coherent story. Such a construction may feed into a presumption of the suspect's guilt, which in turn may shape the police officer's interviewing behaviour. Kassin et al. (2003) conducted an experiment that used students as interrogators to test the hypothesis that guilt presumption affects interviewers' behaviour. This study showed that when interviewers adopted a presumption of guilt rather than innocence, they asked more guilt-oriented questions and used more techniques and pressure in order to elicit a confession. This prior belief sets into motion a confession-seeking process of behavioural confirmation that affects the behaviour of the interviewer as well as the suspect, as in example A above, in which the suspect perceived that the police officer was just trying to 'grill' him.

In their study of confession-seeking procedures, Stephenson and Moston (1993; 1994) distinguish between accusatorial strategies and information-gathering strategies. When the evidence was judged as strong, the interviewer used an accusatorial approach, accusing the suspect early on in the interview. Thus, police officers' perceptions that the evidence is strong may promote a presumption of guilt, where the officer acts in a coercive and dominant manner, which in turn can elicit resistance and denials from the suspect. Such an analysis is supported by Holmberg and Christianson's (2002) study of 83 convicted murderers' and sexual offenders' experiences of their police interviews. They found that these men perceived the interview as either *dominant* or *humanitarian*. In the dominant experience, these offenders perceived their interviewers as impatient, rushing, aggressive, brusque, nonchalant, unfriendly, deprecating and condemning. The dominant experience was also associated with the offenders' feelings of anxiety and tendency to deny the alleged crime. Thus, a police officer who shows a dominant, coercive and confession-seeking approach may be seen as an anti-therapeutic agent because such behaviour may be counterproductive not only for the crime investigation but also for offenders' rehabilitation. This approach is clearly an example of the external pressure that convicted criminals experience when police officers use a confession-seeking approach (Gudjonsson & Petursson, 1991; Gudjonsson & Sigurdsson, 1999).

The danger with asking too many questions

A serious problem with a question-based approach to seeking information is that asking too many questions can be counterproductive. First, human beings have limited mental resources to process information (Baddeley, 1998). Imagine yourself in a rapid-fire interview concerning what you ate for lunch the previous week, where and with whom. Think about three, four and six days ago and imagine someone asking several hard-hitting questions about where you were sitting and with whom, as well as exactly what you had on your plate. The questions shift between different days and aspects of the events. It is likely that when you try to recall you will need some time to remember. In a situation where an interviewer asks many questions, perhaps jumping between different phases in the course of events, the interviewee needs time to recover detail. In such a situation, the interviewee's mental resources will be overloaded by the rain of questions to which he or she can only provide superficial answers.

Without the knowledge that psychologists have regarding the effects of limited mental resources, a police officer might wrongfully interpret the interviewee's pauses and hesitations as a reluctance to tell the truth, rather than a situation created by the police officer's rapid-fire questions. Interviewees need time to think and time to remember.

Second, the information contained in questions may affect a suspect's memory, because all remembering is constructive, meaning that an interviewee may subsequently incorporate information provided in the questions to construct an incorrect, fabricated account (see Chapter 6 for the same process operating with witness testimony). Thus, an interviewer who asks lots of questions may distort a suspect's memories of his or her criminal conduct (for a more detailed description of offenders' memories, see Christianson, 2007).

Thus, following the advice of the manuals described above and using a confession-seeking procedure will not only generate suspect resistance, but may also lead to confessions, some of which are false.

CASE STUDY 7.1   FALSE CONFESSION, A PRECURSOR OF A MISCARRIAGE OF JUSTICE

On Monday 30 March 1998, the journalist Jan Hoffman published an article on the front page of *The New York Times* entitled 'Police refine methods so potent, even the innocent have confessed' (Figure 7.2). In his article, Hoffman argued that American interrogators use tricks, deceptions and lies to extract confessions from suspects and that these techniques were so powerful that even innocent people confessed to the crime. Describing a case involving a false confession, Hoffman reported that the innocent man had said what they (the interrogators) wanted to hear. This was a man, suspected of the murder of a local shop owner, who falsely confessed after insisting on his innocence for nearly nine hours. During these nine hours, seven police officers had handled the questioning. The officers lied and told the suspect that they had found his fingerprints and hair at the crime scene, and that he had not passed the lie detector test. After these many hours of interrogation, the innocent man had given up the hope that telling the truth would give him his freedom back. With the hope of being released to go home, he told the police officers what they wanted to hear.

FIGURE 7.2 *The journalist Jan Hoffman criticised interrogation methods leading to false confessions.*

Even an innocent person may confess to a crime

Is it possible for an innocent person to confess to a crime that he or she has not committed? Yes, and it is not a new phenomenon. Munsterberg wrote about false confession as early as 1908, and described it as a normal reaction to the emotional shock of being arrested and interrogated. Historically, there are many examples of voluntary false confessions; for example, about 200 people confessed to the kidnapping of Charles Lindbergh's son in 1932. One of the most well-known confessors in the 1980s was Henry Lee Lucas, who confessed to hundreds of unsolved murders. In Sweden, more than a hundred individuals have been investigated after falsely confessing to the murder of former Prime Minister Olof Palme in 1986. These false confessions have been so detailed that the police could not easily dismiss them (Detective Superintendent Per-Olof Palmgren, personal communication, October 2007). Gudjonsson and Sigurdsson (1994) describe a self-report study of 229 Icelandic prison inmates of whom 27 (12 per cent) revealed that they had sometimes made false confessions to the police. In a similar study on 509 Icelandic prison inmates, Sigurdsson and Gudjonsson (1996) found that the same number of inmates (12 per cent) reported that they had made one or more false confessions to the police at some time in the past. The most frequent motives for making a false confession were to protect somebody else (50 per cent), to escape from police coercion (48 per cent) or to avoid detention (42 per cent). (Respondents could choose more than one category, which explains the overlaps between the motives reported.)

voluntary false confession a false confession offered by the suspect without any coercion from the investigator.

coerced-compliant false confession a false confession given in the face of coercion by the investigator, but only to appease the investigator and not accepted by the suspect.

coerced-internalised false confession a false confession given in the face of coercion by the investigator, which becomes fully accepted as the truth by the suspect.

There are several other documented cases of false confessions and the numbers are growing, showing that false confessions are a reality that may well lead to miscarriages of justice and, for that reason, it is important to understand the mechanisms underlying them (see Case Study 7.1). Research suggests that false confessions can be provoked by a number of different causes (Kassin & Gudjonsson, 2004). Gudjonsson (2003) distinguishes between **voluntary false confession, coerced-compliant false confession and coerced-internalised false confession.**

Sometimes it happens that a person, without any external pressure, voluntarily makes a self-incriminating statement and falsely confesses to a crime he or she has not committed. This situation can occur when the person knows the culprit and tries to protect him or her from being sentenced for the offence. Obviously, the reasons why innocent people make a *voluntary false confession* are full of nuances; it may be that they have a pathological desire for notoriety, which may be stimulated by media reports about high profile cases. Other explanations might be the person's inability to separate his or her fantasy from reality and fact; or their need to satisfy a desire for self-punishment based on feelings of guilt over previous offences or sins; or it could be the result of mental illness. Voluntary false confessions originate entirely from the confessor without any influence from the police, which is not the situation regarding the next type of false confession.

When a police officer interrogates a suspect and exposes them to pressure or coercion, a *coerced-compliant false confession* can arise (see Case Study 7.2). In such a situation, the suspect gives in to explicit coercion in the expectation of receiving some kind of immediate instrumental gain or favour (Gudjonsson, 2003; Kassin & Gudjonsson, 2004). The confessor is completely aware of his or her innocence and the confession is an act of compliance. The motive for making a coerced-compliant false confession may be to avoid a threatening situation from which the confessor is desperate to escape. Another reason for a confession of this type may be that it is based on a sound promise, an expectation or a hope of a reward.

The third type is the *coerced-internalised false confession* that may occur when a suspect, often a vulnerable person, temporarily or more persistently, comes to believe that he or she must have committed the crime in question (Gudjonsson, 2003; Kassin & Gudjonsson, 2004). Importantly, in such cases the suspect may have no memories of the alleged event (through, for example, drink or drugs) and this lack of memory may sometimes make him or her more likely to confabulate a false memory. In major investigations, the suspect may be exposed to several long interviews and he or she may start to doubt his or her own denials. Such a situation may occur without any tricks, deceit or pressure from the police officer. The person is cooperative, tries to remember and, without memories, may come to believe that he or she must have committed the crime. For the police interviewer, it is extremely important not to continue with questions that might introduce false memories. Instead, the interviewer must close the interview because the interviewee (likely innocent in the scenario described) is highly vulnerable, and particularly vulnerable to suggestion. Otherwise, there is a high risk for a coerced-internalised false confession as a result of memory distrust syndrome (MDS) (Gudjonsson, 2003). A person with MDS is especially vulnerable to suggestive cues, especially those implicit in questions, and the presence of an authority figure like a

CASE STUDY 7.2   COERCED-COMPLIANT FALSE CONFESSION

In 1989, a female jogger was found brutally beaten, raped and left for dead in Central Park in New York City, but she survived (Kassin & Gudjonsson, 2004). Within two days, the police had arrested five African-American and Hispanic-American boys aged between 14 and 16 as suspects for the attack. The brutal crime became a high-profile case for the national news media. The police aggressively interrogated the boys and they confessed to the crime. Four of these resultant confessions were then video-recorded and presented during the trial so that a successful conviction was almost inevitable. The videotapes showed the four boys describing in detail how they attacked the female jogger and carried out the crime; during the trial, one of the boys even expressed remorse and assured the court that he would not commit such a crime again. While there was no forensic evidence or physical traces linking the boys to the crime, they were all found guilty and sentenced to long terms of imprisonment. However, in many ways the boys' descriptions of the brutal crime were erroneous. Thirteen years later,

a man sentenced for a murder and three rapes committed at the time of the jogger attack, revealed on his own initiative that he was the one, and the only one, who had attacked and raped the female jogger. The subsequent investigation showed that the new suspect had unique and corroborated knowledge of the crime and the crime scene. In this investigation, a DNA test also showed that the semen samples found on the victim excluded the boys as perpetrators but incriminated the new suspect. In December 2002 and after 13 years in prison, the five boys' convictions based on their false confessions were withdrawn. The boys explained that when they confessed, they believed and expected that they would be released and allowed to go home once they had confessed. These confessions show specific motives for this kind of compliance, for example, being allowed to go home, sleep and make a phone call. Police officers' desire to end an interview and solve a crime may be extremely coercive for young people, especially those who are desperate, or phobic of being locked up in custody.

police officer might add to the likelihood of the person creating false memories. The creation of false memories occurs because the individual doubts his or her own autobiographical memory and is in a heightened state of suggestibility. He or she is cooperative, may be socially isolated and puts trust in the police officer who, deliberately or unintentionally, offers hints and cues that lead to false memories. The source of the memory becomes confused, the reality becomes distorted and a fertile base for internalised false confession is created.

To prevent false confessions, Davis and Leo (2006) suggest that the police should interrogate a person as a suspect only where there is sufficient grounds to support a presumption of guilt. The authors also suggest that the police should organise education for their officers about the risk and causes of false confessions, which would include education about how confirmatory bias may affect the work of a criminal investigator. Police officers should be aware of and avoid practices that may promote false confessions (e.g. not use confession-seeking tactics). That means that police officers need to acquire knowledge of, and be sensitive to, the psychological vulnerabilities that make some suspects particularly susceptible to such influences, and to adjust their interviewing techniques accordingly. In many countries, the concept of *interrogation* is seen as synonymous with single-minded confession-seeking, whereas the concept

of *interviewing* is seen as a much wider notion involving both the giving and receiving of information. The latter will be the focus in the final section of this chapter.

FROM INTERROGATION TO INVESTIGATIVE INTERVIEWING

The term *interrogation* has given way in the UK to *investigative interviewing* (Milne & Bull, 2003), which has emphasised and promoted the importance of changing attitudes towards the police interview. In order to understand the historical connections between police information-gathering techniques, the public and research, a brief review of the evolution of interrogation into investigative interviewing will be provided.

From antiquity to the first half of the 20th century, some interrogators have used acts of cruelty to discover criminal facts. Suspects have tried to hide their knowledge by silence or lies and, historically, the method chosen to obtain confessions has been the use of physical and mental coercion. Münsterberg (1908/1923) argued that threats and torture have been used all over the world for thousands of years to force suspects to confess. The term 'third degree' was introduced in 1900 to describe interrogating a prisoner by means of mental or physical torture to extract a confession (Merriam-Webster, 2004). Münsterberg (1908/1923) described the 'third degree' as including the use of dazzling light, the cold-water hose and secret blows that left few marks and he maintained that it was still in regular use by the police in some countries in the early decades of the 20th century. Public opinion was firmly against such methods, the public not being convinced that the 'third degree' was effective in bringing out the real truth from suspects. Up until the early 1930s and perhaps later, police interview tactics in some countries were generally characterised by coercion (Leo, 1992).

In Sweden, Hassler (1930) argued that the police interview should be inquisitorial, marked by coercive questioning. The suspect should, in the absence of inflicted pain, threat or deceit, be induced to provide a voluntary confession. Peixoto (1934), from a Brazilian standpoint, argued that the 'third degree' was coercive and of doubtful value. In the 1930s and 1940s, the use of coercive interviewing methods began to decline (Leo, 1992). Swedish police officers were recommended to try to win the interviewee's trust and then let the interviewee provide a free account before the police officer began to ask open-ended questions (Leche & Hagelberg, 1945). Leche and Hagelberg also emphasised the necessity for police officers to understand people's emotions and reactions, to have knowledge about how human memory functions, and to understand how a statement could be affected by different tactics adopted by the interviewer.

In order to secure the truth and to judge a witness's veracity, Gerbert (1954) stressed the need for understanding an interviewee's personality. Gerbert stated that some tense interviewees, who appeared to be guilty, were actually reacting to the interview, and became relaxed only when they were assured that the interview would be conducted in a fair and impartial way. However, in the 1960s, police deceptive techniques, tactics and stratagems became commonplace in interviews with suspects. These methods were, as discussed above, based on an uncritical and subjective use of psychological knowledge.

Conversation management

The psychologist Dr Eric Shepherd trained police officers from the City of London Police in the early 1980s. Shepherd developed a script for managing conversations with anybody a police officer would be likely to meet. In the context of this training, Shepherd coined the term *conversation management* (CM) (Figure 7.3) for this technique, which means that the police officer must

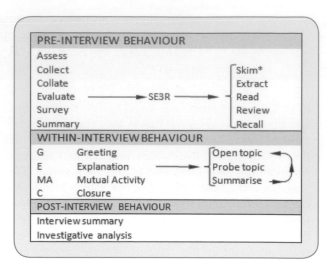

FIGURE 7.3 *Conversation management.*

Source: Reproduced from Milne & Bull (1999), *Investigative. Interviewing: Psychology and Practice,* p.57, Figure 4.1, by permission of John Wiley & Sons, Ltd.

* Instead of 'skim', Shepherd (2007) uses the word 'survey', which may have a wider meaning.

be aware of and manage the communicative interaction, both verbally and non-verbally (Milne & Bull, 1999). Conversation management comprises three phases: *pre-, within-* and *post-interview behaviour.*

In the pre-interview phase the officer has to work objectively and without any biases. He or she analyses the case in detail and develops questions to be answered, that is, to prepare and plan the interview. Shepherd (2007) describes this process as the 'systematic cycle of investigation', designated as 'ACCESS', a mnemonic specifying the six investigative processes: *assess, collect, collate, evaluate, survey* and *summarise.* In the first step, the investigator must *assess* the situation, the available information and the information needed. In the *collect* and *collate* steps, the investigator gathers all the information and combines all the details. The purpose of the *evaluate* phase is to put the details together and analyse the emergent investigative picture. In the survey phase, a methodical and comprehensive appraisal of the analysis is conducted. The cycle is completed in the *summarise* phase, where the investigator reviews what has been learned to date, and is ready to enter the systematic cycle of investigation again.

The challenge in all crime investigation is the systematic analysis of written and spoken text, and for that purpose Shepherd (2007) has developed the method known as SE3R. The aim of SE3R is to help the investigator to capture, identify, analyse and register all the information rapidly, even fine-grain details, from interviews and written statements. This, as Shepherd describes it, is a 'catch all' method that also provides the investigator with the opportunity to reflect upon certain features of the evidence that require to be explored at interview. The five steps are *survey, extract, read, review* and *respond*. In the *within-interview* phase, the interviewer is encouraged to pay attention to four sub-phases: *greeting, explanation, mutual activity* and *closure,* abbreviated as GEMAC. The greeting phase involves an appropriate introduction of the interviewer, which means establishing rapport. In the *explanation* phase, the interviewer must set out the aims and objectives, and develop the interview further. *Mutual activity* concerns the elicitation of narrative from the interviewee and clarifying questions from the interviewer. *Closure* is the important phase in which the interviewer attempts to create a positive end to the interview, aiming at mutual satisfaction with the content and performance of the session.

Police and Criminal Evidence Act 1984 known as PACE; Act introduced in England and Wales in 1984 governing the conduct of police investigations and interactions with suspects.

CM was consistent with the **Police and Criminal Evidence Act 1984** (known as PACE) introduced in England and Wales. PACE can be seen as a reaction, from the public, researchers and, to some extent, the police, to criticism of the existing methods used to interrogate suspects (Bull, 1999). The advent of PACE encouraged further research into police interviewing techniques in England and Wales.

Ethical interviewing vs. a confrontational approach

To facilitate the communicative interaction between a police interviewer and a suspect, Shepherd (1991) emphasised the importance of the interviewer showing human feeling towards suspects, and advocated ethical interviewing (EI). Shepherd argued that the EI approach lends itself to professional investigations. It also improves investigative equality, leading to a greater degree of success in crime prevention, detection and conviction of the guilty. This approach rests on ethical principles, signifying that individuals show mutual respect and treat each other as equal human beings with the same rights to dignity, self-determination and free choice. It also emphasises empathy, which means treating each other with a degree of mutual understanding. However, specialist investigative interviewers have been found to rate showing empathy and compassion amongst the least important interviewing skills (Cherryman & Bull, 2001).

As stated above, Baldwin's (1992; 1993) observation of video and audio recordings of police interviews emphasised the need for professionalism, and he called for the use of the basic rules of sound interviewing practice. Such professionalism provides for a fair and calm interview in which suspects may express their own point of view. Additionally, professional police interviewers must also pay attention to the suspects' responses, and avoid harrying tactics and coercion. Thus, an open-minded interviewer gives suspects time for reflection and the opportunity to express their own position. Professional interviewers establish rapport and listen actively to the suspects' responses. However, Baldwin observed that many officers showed difficulties in creating rapport with suspects, adopted a confession-seeking approach and tried to persuade suspects to accept a predetermined description of the event.

Baldwin concluded in the early 1990s that the competence of the police interviewers was unacceptably low. Moston and Engelberg's (1993) analysis of taped police interviews showed that the police used *confrontational* and *confession-seeking* approaches that were problematic. In their analysis of a large number of interviews, Stephenson and Moston (1993; 1994) found that, where the evidence against the accused was perceived as strong, police interviewers invariably assumed their guilt and adopted a confession-seeking approach. However, when the evidence was perceived as weak, they employed an information-gathering strategy. The latter approach increased the probability of obtaining a suspect's own account of the event.

Consistent with Stephenson and Moston's results, Williamson (1993) identified four interviewing styles that different police officers sought to adopt with suspects. Williamson's study used a questionnaire that was completed by 80 detectives. Two of these interviewing styles were characterised as *confession-seeking procedures* and the other two as *searches for securing evidence*. The first confession-oriented approach was conceptualised as *collusive*, implying that the interviewer acts in a cooperative, paternalistic, helpful and problem-solving way. The second confession-oriented style was the dominant one, in which the investigators adopted a *confrontational* approach, displayed impatience and showed their emotions towards the suspects. The third style, which involved a strategy of securing evidence, was labelled as *counselling*, and comprised a cooperative, unemotional and non-judgmental demeanour. The fourth style, in which again the interviewer tried to secure evidence, was labelled as *businesslike* and marked by a confrontational, brusque, factual and formal demeanour. Williamson's research revealed that interviewers who obtained many true confessions showed a positive attitude towards suspects. They also manifested sympathetic and cooperative behaviour. Dominant interrogators, on the other hand, kept up pressure on suspects through quick questioning. These police officers were regarded as unsympathetic and confrontational towards the suspects, who in turn often responded with resistance and denials. Considering

investigative interviewing a broader term than interrogation, describing a fair, dualistic and open-minded communication to obtain accurate and reliable information conducted within the framework of national law and the UN agreements on human, civil and political rights.

his findings, Williamson found the results congruent with the concept of **investigative interviewing**.

The PEACE model

Investigative interviewing was developed in the early 1990s under the aegis of the Home Office and Association of Chief Police Officers, and was incorporated into the *PEACE model of interviewing* (Milne & Bull, 2003; Figure 7.4). It arose partly as a response to the shortcomings researchers had revealed with existing approaches and followed an outcry from the public and the media over such methods. The mnemonic PEACE denotes: *planning and preparation; engage and explain; account, clarification and challenge; closure;* and *evaluation,* which are seen as important phases in a good interview (Bull, 1999; Bull & Milne, 2004; Milne & Bull, 1999; 2003).

In the PEACE model, interviewers are first obliged to plan and prepare themselves carefully before the interview. Both experienced police officers and researchers have repeatedly shown the benefits of being well prepared prior to an interview. They underline the importance of the planning and preparation phase as cost effective, and one of the most fundamental and crucial skills upon which the interview outcome is dependent. The *planning and preparation* phase not only includes reading the case file and being familiar with the facts; it also encourages police officers to seek out knowledge about the individual to be interviewed, in particular aspects that might complicate or facilitate the interview (e.g. vulnerabilities, religious and cultural aspects, addiction, physical and environmental circumstances).

Armed with knowledge about the specific case and the individual concerned, police officers are now in a position to plan how to conduct the interview with the suspect in question. *Engage and explain* is the first phase in the real interview, where interviewers inform the suspect about the allegation, their rights and the procedure to be followed in the interview. Here, it is also most important for interviewers to build rapport, engage suspects and try to motivate them to provide their perspective on the key events. The aim of this introduction to the interview is to provide suspects with a 'route map' for a fair and just interview of which they are going to be a part.

In the *account, clarification and challenge* phase, suspects are invited to give their account of what happened during the event in question. Interviewers then ask questions about aspects of the suspect's account that need to be clarified, and challenge any inconsistencies. The *closure* phase involves interviewers summing up what has been said and checking with suspects that everything has been correctly understood. It is also important to inform suspects, as far as is possible, about the next steps in the investigation, and bring the interview to an end on a positive note. The positive closure may prepare the way for a further interview.

The final phase of the PEACE model, *evaluation,* requires officers to evaluate the facts revealed in the interview and relate these to pre-existing information and to the aims of the interview. Additionally, it is important for interviewers to evaluate how they have conducted the interview and reflect on how the interview could have been improved. The aim of the PEACE model is to obtain correct and reliable evidence and to discover the truth in a crime investigation. This model emphasises ethical principles, which differentiates this method from other coercive and persuasive approaches to interviewing suspects described earlier. After examining 142 suspect interviews, Walsh and Bull (2010) concluded that the PEACE model works, and that following each stage carefully led to a better interview outcome: a full account, which included more confessions.

As regards the humanitarian experience, Holmberg and Christianson's (2002) study of convicted murderers' and sexual offenders' experiences of police interviews revealed that some offenders perceived their interviewers as cooperative, accommodating, positive, empathic, helpful and engaging. Experience of a humanitarian interview related significantly to the offenders' own perception of being respected by the interviewers. This study also found a significant positive relation between the humanitarian interviewing style and the offenders' admissions of crime. Kebbell *et al.* (2006) reported similar findings. In their first study, they interviewed 19 sexual offenders about their feelings during their most recent police interview and their reasons for confessing or denying the crime in question. In the second study, 44 convicted sexual offenders completed a questionnaire regarding their perceptions of police interviews and what they perceived as effective police interview practices.

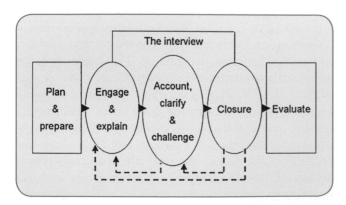

FIGURE 7.4 *The five phases of the PEACE model. In the interview phases, it may be necessary to go back to a previous phase to develop something more and then continue the interview.*

From the outcomes of these two studies, Kebbell *et al.* suggested that in order to maximise the likelihood of genuine confessions, police officers should be open-minded, act according to ethical principles and show humanity.

Moreover, interviewers' communication skills may affect how interviews are conducted. It can be argued that the development of an understanding relationship with the interviewee – that is, rapport as a communicative skill – is influenced by the interviewing style chosen. In line with this, Vanderhallen *et al.* (2010) found that a humanitarian interviewing style encouraged rapport and a better working alliance between the interviewer and interviewee (Figure 7.5). Walsh and Bull (2010) emphasised the importance of rapport-building in the PEACE model of compatible interviewing. They examined the impact of interviewing style on interview outcomes, ranging from no comments to a full account or a confession, and in terms of interviewers' skills. Rapport-building had the largest single impact and effect size when interview quality and outcomes were considered.

The reported effects and conclusion of Holmberg and Christianson (2002) and Kebbell *et al.* (2006) and other similar studies rely on correlational data that suggest a relation between two or more variables. Correlational studies cannot be used to draw conclusions about causal relationships, for example that a certain interviewing behaviour leads to a certain response. To reach a conclusion about a causal relationship it is necessary to conduct experiments in which there is strict control of the variables involved – that is, what actually happens in the process. For instance, Holmberg and Madsen (2010) conducted an experiment to investigate possible causal relations between the interviewing style employed and interview outcome, in terms of memory performance. Compared with a dominant style, this study revealed a significant causal relationship between a humanitarian interviewing style and better memory performance. Thus, an interviewee interviewed in a humanitarian style provides more information than an interviewee interviewed in a dominant style.

Investigative interviewing and therapeutic jurisprudence

Therapeutic jurisprudence is a growing movement within the philosophy of law and within the legal and judicial practice areas. Its roots can be found in the American legal realism movement, which developed in the first half of the 20th century. Therapeutic jurisprudence focuses on human problems and conflicts, and encourages police officers, prosecutors and other legal parties to understand that conflicts produce social and psychological effects on the individuals involved. It sees the law and its procedures as therapeutic agents because the law and its execution can have both therapeutic and anti-therapeutic consequences (Petrucci *et al.*, 2003).

The purpose of therapeutic jurisprudence is to develop legal procedures that promote the social and psychological well-being of the individual involved in a juridical action. The idea is that legal actors can use theories and empirical knowledge from the behavioural sciences to influence the practice of the law. In this way, jurisprudence can be seen as a therapeutic tool to promote psychological well-being in legal practice. The suspects who had felt themselves highly respected in Holmberg and Christianson's (2002) study showed significantly higher psychological well-being compared to those who felt themselves less respected (Holmberg *et al.*, 2007). Even those offenders who admitted their crimes showed significantly higher psychological well-being than those who did not. Admissions of guilt should not only be seen from an investigative and legal perspective: it is likely that admissions in the context of therapeutic jurisprudence may also enable the offender to work through the crime committed. Such admissions may enhance the suspect's memory for the crime as well as promoting their psychological well-being, which in turn may prevent offending in the future.

FIGURE 7.5 *Extending a hand and meeting the suspect is necessary for building rapport and the creation of a working alliance.*

Source: © Alberto Zornetta. Used under licence from Shutterstock.

SUMMARY

- Most manuals on police information-gathering techniques embody a concept of interrogation that is characterised by confession-seeking, often violating basic human rights legislation.

- These manuals, implicitly or explicitly, encourage a presumption of the suspect's guilt that in turn may prevent a fair investigation and may lead to a miscarriage of justice.

- Police officers' presumption of guilt and coercive questioning of suspects often leads to resistance from the suspect and can lead to a false confession and miscarriage of justice.

- Gudjonsson (2003) distinguishes between voluntary false confessions, coerced-compliant false confessions and coerced-internalised false confessions.

- Recent innovations, such as the PEACE interview, encourage establishing proper rapport with the suspect and free responding, and emphasise establishing facts rather than assuming guilt.

- Such an approach is characterised by a regard for justice and human rights and may minimise the risk of a miscarriage of justice.

ESSAY/DISCUSSION QUESTIONS

1. What tactics do interrogation manuals recommend for interviewing suspects and how do these accord with human rights legislation?

2. In what ways may a police interviewer be biased and how might such biases influence an interviewer's behaviour?

3. Describe three types of false confession and consider their causes.

4. Apart from investigative advantages, discuss at least two other advantages possibly promoted by a suspect freely making admissions.

REFERENCES

Baddeley, A. (1998). *Human memory: Theory and practice*. Boston, MA: Allyn & Bacon.

Baldwin, J. (1992). *Video taping police interviews with suspects – An evaluation. Police Research Series: Paper No. 1*. London: Home Office Police Department.

Baldwin, J. (1993). Police interview techniques: Establishing truth or proof? *The British Journal of Criminology, 33*, 325–352.

Benson, R. (2000). *Ragnar's guide to interviews, investigations, and interrogations*. Boulder CO: Paladin Press.

Bristow, A.P. (1964). *Field interrogation* (2nd edn). Springfield, IL: Charles C Thomas Publisher Ltd.

Buckley, J.P. (2006). The Reid Technique of interviewing and interrogation. In T. Williamson (Ed.) *Investigative interviewing: Rights, research, regulation*. Cullompton: Willan Publishing.

Bull, R. (1999). Police investigative interviewing. In A. Memon & R. Bull (Eds.) *Handbook of the psychology of interviewing*. Chichester: John Wiley & Sons, Inc.

Bull, R. & Milne, R. (2004). Attempts to improve police interviewing of suspects. In G.D. Lassiter (Ed.) *Interrogations, confessions and entrapment* (pp.181–196). New York: Kluwer.

Butterfield, R. (2002). *The official Guide to interrogation*. Philadelphia: Xlibris Corporation.

Cherryman, J. & Bull, R. (2001). Police officers' perceptions of specialist investigative skills. *International Journal of Police Science and Management, 3*, 199–212.

Christianson, S.A. (2007). *Offenders' memories of violent crimes*. Chichester: John Wiley & Sons, Inc.

Davis, D. & Leo, R. (2006). Strategies for preventing false confessions and their consequences. In M.R. Kebbell & G.M. Davies (Eds.) *Practical psychology for forensic investigations and prosecutions* (pp.121–149). Chichester: John Wiley & Sons, Inc.

DePaulo, B.M., Lindsay, J.J., Malone, B.E., *et al.* (2003). Cues to deception. *Psychological Bulletin, 129*, 74–118.

Gerbert, K. (1954). The psychology of expression and the technique of criminal interrogation. *Jahrbuch für Psychologie und Psychotherapie, 2*, 85–98.

Gudjonsson, G.H. (2003). *Psychology of interrogations and confessions: A handbook*. Chichester: John Wiley & Sons, Inc.

Gudjonsson, G.H. & Bownes, I. (1992). The reasons why suspects confess during custodial interrogation: Data from Northern Ireland. *Medicine, Science and the Law, 32*, 204–212.

Gudjonsson, G.H. & Petursson, H. (1991). Custodial interrogation: Why do suspects confess and how does it relate to their crime, attitude and personality? *Personality and Individual Differences, 12*, 295–306.

Gudjonsson, G.H. & Sigurdsson, J.E. (1994). How frequently do false confessions occur? An empirical study among prison inmates. *Psychology, Crime and Law, 1*, 21–26.

Gudjonsson, G.H. & Sigurdsson, J.E. (1999). The Gudjonsson Questionnaire–Revised (GCQR): Factor structure and its relationship with personality. *Personality and Individual Differences, 27*, 953–968.

Hassler, A. (1930). *Föreläsningar över den Svenska kriminalprocessen, I* (Lectures on the legal process in Sweden, I). Stockholm: A.B. Nordiska Bokhandeln i Distribution.

Hartwig, M. (2006). *Interrogating to detect truth and deception: Effects of strategic use of evidence*. Göteborg: Göteborg University.

Hartwig, M., Granhag, P.A. & Strömwall, L.A. (2007). Guilty and innocent suspects' strategies during police interrogations. *Psychology, Crime & Law, 13*, 213–227.

Hartwig, M, Granhag, P.A., Strömwall, L.A. & Kronkvist, O. (2006). Strategic use of evidence during police interviews: When training to detect deception works. *Law and Human Behavior, 30*, 603–619.

Hartwig, M., Granhag, P.A., Strömwall, L.A. & Vrij, A. (2005a). Detecting deception via strategic disclosure of evidence. *Law and Human Behavior, 29*, 469–484.

Hartwig, M., Granhag, P.A., Strömwall, L.A. & Vrij, A. (2005b). Strategic disclosure of evidence to detect deception: Towards a new research agenda. In A. Czerederecka, T. Jaskiewicz-Obydzinska, R. Roesch & J. Wójcikiewicz (Eds.) *Forensic psychology and law, facing the challenges of a changing world* (pp.219–232). Krakow: Institute of Forensic Research Publishers.

Hoffman, J. (1998, 30 March). Police refine methods so potent, even the innocent have confessed. *The New York Times*, p.1.

Holmberg, U. (1996). *Sexualbrottsförövares upplevelser av polisförhör* (Sexual offenders' experiences of police interviews). Report series 1996:7. Kristianstad: Kristianstad University.

Holmberg, U. & Christianson, S.Å. (2002) Murderers' and sexual offenders' experiences of police interviews and their inclination to admit or deny crimes. *Behavioural Sciences and the Law, 20*, 31–45.

Holmberg, U., Christianson, S.Å. & Wexler, D. (2007). Interviewing offenders: A therapeutic jurisprudential approach. In S.Å. Christianson (Ed.) *Offenders' memories of violent crimes* (pp.355–371). Chichester: John Wiley & Sons, Inc.

Holmberg, U. & Madsen, K. (2010, June). *Humanity and dominance in police interviews: Causes and effects*. Paper presented at the 4th International Investigative Conference, Brussels.

Inbau, F.E., Reid, J.E., Buckley, J.P. & Jayne, B.C. (2001). *Criminal interrogation and confessions* (4th edn). Sudbury: Jones & Bartlett.

Innes, M. (2002). The 'process structure' of police homicide investigations. *British Journal of Criminology, 42*, 669–688.

Kassin, S.M. (2006). A critical appraisal of modern police interrogations. In T. Williamson (Ed.) *Investigative interviewing: Rights, research, regulation*. Cullompton: Willan Publishing.

Kassin, S.M., Goldstein, C.J. & Savitsky, K. (2003). Behavioral confirmation in the interrogation room: On the dangers of presuming guilt. *Law and Human Behavior, 27*, 187–203.

Kassin, S.M. & Gudjonsson, G.H. (2004). The psychology of confessions: A review of the literature and issues. *Psychological Science in the Public Interest, 5*, 33–67.

Kebbell, M., Hurren, E. & Mazerolle, P. (2006). An investigation into the effective and ethical interviewing of suspected sex offenders. *Trends and Issues in Crime and Criminal Justice*, No. 327. Canberra: Australian Institute of Criminology.

Leche, E. & Hagelberg, V. (1945). *Förhör i brottmål* (Interrogation in criminal cases). Stockholm: P.A. Nordstedt & Söners Förlag.

Leo, R.A. (1992). From coercion to deception: The changing nature of police interrogation in America. *Crime, Law and Social Change, 18*, 35–59.

Merriam-Webster (2004). *Merriam-Webster online dictionary*. Retrieved 20 August 2011 from www.merriam-webster.com

Milne, R. & Bull, R. (1999). *Investigative interviewing: Psychology and practice*. Chichester: John Wiley & Sons, Inc.

Milne, R. & Bull, R. (2003). Interviewing by the police. In D. Carson & R. Bull (Eds.) *Handbook of psychology in legal contexts* (pp.111–125). Chichester: John Wiley & Sons, Inc.

Mortimer, A. & Shepherd, E. (1999). Frames of mind: Schemata guiding cognition and conduct in the interviewing of suspected offenders. In A. Memon & R. Bull (Eds.), *Handbook of the psychology of interviewing* (pp.293–315). Chichester: John Wiley & Sons, Inc.

Moston, S. & Engelberg, T. (1993). Police questioning techniques in tape-recorded interviews with criminal suspects. *Policing and Society, 3*, 223–237.

Munsterberg, H. (1908/1923). *On the witness stand*. Garden City, NY: Doubleday.

Nickerson, R.S. (1998). Confirmation bias: A ubiquitous phenomenon in many guises. *Review of General Psychology, 2*, 175–220.

Palmiotto, M.J. (2004). *Criminal investigation* (3rd edn). Lanham: Rowman & Littlefield.

Peixoto, A. (1934). The interrogation and confessions in the judiciary process. *Revista de Criminologia Buenos Aires, 21*, 383–395.

Petrucci, C.J., Winick, B.J. & Wexler, D.B. (2003). Therapeutic jurisprudence: An invitation to social scientists. In D. Carson & R. Bull (Eds.) *Handbook of psychology in legal contexts* (pp.579–601). Chichester: John Wiley & Sons, Inc.

Royal, R.E. & Schutt, S.R. (1976). *The gentle art of interviewing and interrogation: A professional manual and guide.* Upper Saddle River, NJ: Pearson Prentice Hall.

Rutledge, D. (2001). *Criminal interrogation, law and tactics* (4th edn). Boston: Wadsworth Publishing.

Shepherd, E. (1991). Ethical interviewing. *Policing, 7,* 42–60.

Shepherd, E. (1993). Resistance in interviews: The contribution of police perception and behaviour. *Issues in Criminal and Legal Psychology, 18,* 5–12.

Shepherd, E. (2007). *Investigative interviewing: The conversation management approach.* Oxford: Oxford University Press.

Sigurdsson, J.E & Gudjonsson, G.H. (1996). Psychological characteristics of 'false confessors': A study among Icelandic prison inmates and juvenile offenders. *Personality and Individual Differences, 20,* 321–329.

Starrett, P. (1998). *Interview and interrogation for investigations in the public or private sector.* San Clementine CA: Law Tec Publishing Co. Ltd.

Stephenson, G.M. & Moston, S.J. (1993). Attitudes and assumptions of police officers when questioning criminal suspects. *Issues in Criminological and Legal Psychology, 18,* 30–36.

Stephenson, G.M. & Moston, S.J. (1994). Police interrogation. *Psychology, Crime and Law, 1,* 151–157.

UN General Assembly. (1948). *UN universal declaration of human rights, article 5.*

UN General Assembly. (1966). *UN covenant on civil and political rights, article 9, 14:2 (presumption of innocence).*

Vanderhallen, M., Vervaeke, G. & Holmberg, U. (2010, June). *The working alliance in police interviewing.* Paper presented at the 4th International Investigative Conference, Brussels.

Vrij, A. (2000). *Detecting lies and deceit.* Chichester: John Wiley & Sons, Inc.

Walsh, D. & Bull, R. (2010). What really is effective in interviews with suspects? A study comparing interviewing skills against interviewing outcomes. *Legal and Criminal Psychology, 15,* 305–21.

Weinberg, C.D. (2002). *Effective interviewing and interrogation techniques.* San Diego CA: Academic Press.

Williamson, T.M. (1993). From interrogation to investigative interviewing: Strategic trends in police questioning. *Journal of Community and Applied Psychology, 3,* 89–99.

Yeschke, C.L. (2003). *The art of investigative interviewing* (2nd edn). Burlington: Butterworth-Heineman.

ANNOTATED READING LIST

Bartol, C.R. & Bartol, A.M. (2010). *Criminal behavior: A psychological approach.* NJ: Prentice Hall, Pearson Higher Education. *Offers detailed analysis of suspects and considers the behavioural, emotional and cognitive aspects of criminals.*

Bull, R., Valentine, T. & Williamson, T. (2009). *Handbook of psychology of investigative interviewing: Current developments and future directions.* Chichester: Wiley-Blackwell. *This comprehensive handbook explores current developments in investigative interviewing, which plays a vital role in criminal investigations.*

Christianson, S.Å. (2007). *Offenders' memories of violent crimes.* Chichester: John Wiley & Sons, Inc. *To conduct investigative interviewing, interviewers need knowledge of how memory and memory distortion function, which this textbook provides.*

Gudjonsson, G.H. (2003). *The psychology of interrogation and confessions.* Chichester: John Wiley & Sons, Inc. *Gudjonsson offers a comprehensive description of false confessions and the suggestibility of suspects.*

Kebbell, M.R. & Davies, G.M. (2006). *Practical psychology for forensic investigations and prosecutions.* Chichester: John Wiley & Sons, Inc. *A comprehensive, practicable guide to investigative interviewing, making decisions to prosecute, and enhancing the quality of evidence presented at court.*

Memon, A. & Bull. R. (2000). *Handbook of the psychology of interviewing.* Chichester: John Wiley & Sons, Inc. *Provides a genuine text on the psychology of interviewing, reviewing diagnosis and assessment in several contexts (e.g. forensic and social).*

Williamson, T. (2006). *Investigative interviewing: Rights, research, regulation.* Cullompton, Devon: Willan. *Together with researchers and practitioners, Williamson reviews the position of investigative interviewing in a variety of different countries, with different types of criminal justice systems.*

Williamson, T., Milne, B. & Savage, S. (2009). *International developments in investigative interviewing.* Cullompton, Devon: Willan. *Examines international developments in investigative interviewing, addressing in particular the moves that are being made away from a traditional interrogation model with its emphasis on persuading suspects to confess, to an approach where the emphasis is on a search for truth and the collection of complete, accurate and reliable information.*

8 Detecting Deception

Pär Anders Granhag and Maria Hartwig

CHAPTER OUTLINE

To define the topic under investigation is often a good point of departure. However, to define 'deception' is a far from easy task, and the conceptualisations offered in the literature are many. For the present context we define deception as an act 'intended to foster in another a belief or understanding which the deceiver considers to be false' (Zuckerman *et al.*, 1981, p.3). Thus, to unintentionally misremember is not to lie. Furthermore, it is possible to make distinctions between falsifications (everything being told is contrary to the truth), distortions (the truth is altered to fit the liar's goal) and concealments (the liar holds back the truth).

In the field of deception detection, the most frequently studied situation is that in which a person, frequently referred to as a 'target', provides a statement about the past that is either truthful or deceptive. An electronic recording, typically a videotape of the statement, is then shown to observers, sometimes referred to as 'lie-catchers'. The task of these lie-catchers is to make a judgment of whether the target is lying or telling the truth. For some four decades now, researchers have spent considerable effort studying human deception and its detection.

In this chapter, we will provide an overview of this extensive body of work. First, we will discuss the characteristics of deceptive and truthful behaviour. Our discussion will be guided by the different theoretical perspectives offered within the field. In relation to this, we will report what strategies people commonly apply when attempting to assess veracity, and to what extent these strategies have been shown to be successful.

Second, we will turn to methods focusing on verbal content, that is, methods designed to map differences between liars' and truth tellers' statements. In this section we describe several different methods – all focusing on analyses of the verbal content – and make clear which methods have scientific support, and which do not.

Third, we will provide an overview of findings from studies on psychophysiological detection of deception, simply put, the research surrounding the **polygraph**. This section describes the most frequently used test methods and research on their respective validity, as well as some of the applications of polygraph testing.

polygraph sometimes called a 'lie detector'. A machine that measures, typically, galvanic skin response, cardiovascular activity and breathing patterns in suspects under questioning.

Fourth, we will focus on some of the new directions within the field of deception detection. Specifically, we will discuss to what extent deception detection can be improved by brain scanning (such as fMRI), and by different training programmes. Finally we will discuss two future directions; the first is ways to interview to elicit diagnostic cues to deception, and the second is the emerging topic on how to discriminate between true and false intent.

FOUR APPROACHES

What cognitive and emotional processes can we expect to be at play during deception? And how might these processes cause liars' behaviour to differ from that of truth-tellers? Answers to these questions can be sought by four different approaches: the emotional approach, the cognitive load approach, the attempted control approach and the self-presentational perspective (DePaulo & Morris, 2004).

1. The emotional approach

The emotional approach states that lying causes emotions that differ from those experienced while telling the truth (Ekman, 2001). For example, a liar may experience fear of being judged as not being truthful. The consequences of being judged as a liar and, hence, the fear of apprehension, may differ depending on the context. For example, being judged as deceptive when suspected of having committed a serious crime could have serious consequences, which can create a great deal of fear. According to the emotional approach, experiencing emotions when lying can have behavioural consequences. It is predicted that fear of apprehension will cause liars to experience stress and arousal, causing the pitch of voice to rise and increasing blushing, sweating and the amount of speech errors, while feelings of guilt will cause liars to avert their gaze. According to the approach, the stronger the emotions experienced by the liars, the more likely that these emotions will leak, leaving visible traces in demeanour (Ekman, 2001).

2. The cognitive load approach

The cognitive load approach is based on the notion that lying may be more mentally demanding than telling the truth (Vrij *et al.*, 2008). Lying can be a more difficult task than telling the truth, in that a liar must provide a story consistent with the facts known by the interviewer, detailed enough to appear based on something self-experienced, but simple enough to be remembered if one is asked to repeat the story later on (Burgoon *et al.*, 1995). Research has shown that cognitively demanding tasks can result in gaze aversion (Ekman, 2001), since it can be distracting to look at the conversation partner.

Moreover, this approach predicts that engaging in a cognitively demanding task will result in fewer body movements (Ekman & Friesen, 1972) and long pauses within a statement, as well as between the interviewer's question and the reply.

3. The attempted control approach

The attempted control approach suggests that liars may be aware that internal processes (such as emotions) could result in cues to deception; consequently, they may try to minimise such cues in order to avoid detection (Vrij, 2004). Paradoxically, attempting to control one's behaviour in order to prevent leakage of deceptive cues may in itself result in cues to deception (DePaulo & Kirkendol, 1989). For example, trying to inhibit movements caused by nervousness and arousal may result in overcontrol, creating an unnaturally stiff impression.

4. The self-presentational perspective

The above approaches describe lying as an activity that differs qualitatively from telling the truth. In contrast to these approaches stands the self-presentational perspective (DePaulo, 1992; DePaulo et al., 2003), in which similarities between liars and truth-tellers are emphasised. Self-presentation has been defined as regulating one's own behaviour to create a particular impression on others (DePaulo, 1992). Liars and truth-tellers are seen as having a mutual goal: to appear honest. The major difference between liars' and truth-tellers' claims of honesty is that truth-tellers have grounds for their claims, and that they stay within the boundaries of the truth. As a consequence of this, liars and truth-tellers are predicted to differ cognitively and behaviourally in two important ways. First, deceptive statements could be less embraced by the communicator than are truthful ones. Liars are aware that their claims of honesty are illegitimate, which may result in more negative feelings, making them appear less pleasant and more tense (DePaulo et al., 2003). Moreover, since liars may be less familiar with the events or domains that their stories concern, they may provide less information.

Liars and truth-tellers are predicted to differ in a second way. Liars provide stories that they know depart from the truth, which may result in a deliberate attempt to seem credible. In contrast to providing an account based on a self-experience, liars are likely to experience acting in a more effortful way (DePaulo et al., 1991). Liars' attempts to control their behaviours, as well as their feelings of deliberateness, may cause their actions to appear less convincing, less involved and more tense, and may make them seem to hold back.

OBJECTIVE CUES TO DECEPTION

The above predictions were assessed in an extensive meta-analysis, which focused on objective cues to deception, that is, behavioural differences between liars and truth-tellers (DePaulo et al., 2003; see also DePaulo & Morris, 2004). The majority of the studies covered in the analysis included college students as participants, and were carried out in laboratory settings. The studies included people lying or telling the truth about personal opinions, about an event they had witnessed and about mock transgressions (i.e. a **mock crime**).

mock crime a technique much used in forensic psychology in which unsuspecting observers are exposed to a realistic but contrived criminal act.

The most important results from this meta-analysis were that (a) reliable cues to deception are scarce, and (b) behaviours that are actually related to deception lack strong predictive value. Liars seem to be somewhat more tense than truth-tellers. This is shown in that their pupils are more dilated and their pitch of voice is higher. People who are asked to rate the appearance of liars and truth-tellers (without knowing that some of them are lying while others are telling the truth) tend to perceive liars as being more tense and nervous. Liars are also perceived as less cooperative than truth-tellers (however, for a contrasting finding, see Vrij, 2005b) and their faces are perceived as less pleasant.

There are a few indications that liars' stories differ from those of truth-tellers. Liars talk for a shorter time and include fewer details compared to truth-tellers. Also, liars' stories make less sense in that they are less plausible, less logically structured and more ambivalent. Liars also sound more uncertain, and appear less vocally and verbally immediate, meaning that observers perceive liars to be less direct, relevant and personal in their communication. There are some differences in terms of specific details between deceptive and truthful accounts: liars spontaneously correct themselves and admit not remembering to a lesser extent than truth-tellers, indicating that liars' stories may lack some of the so-called ordinary imperfections of truthful accounts (this is in line with findings from research on **statement validity analysis (SVA)**, which will be described later in this chapter). Taken together, to some extent the results supported the self-presentational perspective, the cognitive load approach and the attempted control approach.

statement validity analysis (SVA) technique for assessing the veracity of a child's statement on the basis of verbal content, involving: a semi-structured interview; a criteria-based content analysis (CBCA) of the statements; and (c) an evaluation of the CBCA outcome.

LIE-CATCHERS' PERFORMANCE

There is a huge body of research investigating human deception detection accuracy. With few exceptions, accuracy levels fall between 45 per cent and 60 per cent (Vrij, 2008). In a meta-analysis, an average accuracy level of 54 per cent was found (Bond & DePaulo, 2006). Keeping in mind that the level of chance is 50 per cent, this is hardly an impressive performance. However, considering the scarcity and weakness of valid cues to deception, the result is not surprising.

Not only lay people, but also presumed lie experts – such as police officers, judges and customs officers – have participated in studies on deception detection. It could be assumed that these groups are more skilled at assessing veracity, since they face this task in their working life (Mann *et al.*, 2004). Also, police officers themselves seem to believe that they are better lie detectors than the average person (Inbau *et al.*, 2001; Vrij, 2004). The studies conducted so far on police officers' ability to detect deception indicate that this notion is incorrect (for an overview, see Vrij, 2005a). In these studies, accuracy rates tend to fall between 45 and 60 per cent; in other words, very similar to rates observed for lay people (for an exception, see Mann *et al.*, 2004). More generally, there is little support for individual differences in deception detection ability (Bond & DePaulo, 2008). In sum, that deception detection accuracy is mediocre is a robust phenomenon.

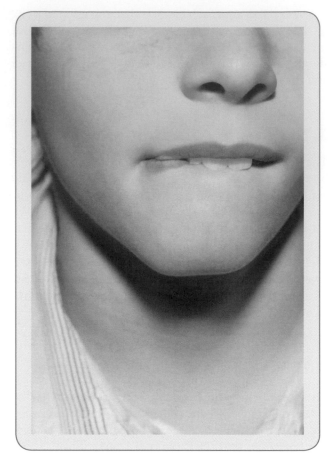

FIGURE 8.1 *People tend to associate lying with an increase in smiling and self-manipulations, such as hand/finger and leg/foot movements – behaviours that are indicative of nervousness.*
Source: © AISPIX. Used under licence from Shutterstock.

Misconceptions about deceptive behaviour

It has been argued that people's poor lie detection ability is partly due to wrongful beliefs about the characteristics of deceptive behaviour. Survey research of both lay people and presumed lie experts (e.g. police officers) has supported this by showing a lack of overlap between objective (i.e. actual) and subjective cues to deception (behaviours that people associate with deception) (Strömwall *et al.*, 2004). For example, people frequently express the belief that liars are prone to gaze aversion (a decrease in eye contact). People also tend to associate lying with hesitations, a slower speech rate, longer and more frequent pauses, and an increase in smiling and movements such as **self-manipulations**, for example hand/finger and leg/foot movements (Vrij, 2008). Generally, these behaviours are indicative of

self-manipulations hand/finger and leg/foot movements popularly believed to be associated with deception.

nervousness (Figure 8.1). However, liars are not necessarily more nervous than truth-tellers (Köhnken, cited in Vrij & Semin 1996); see Case Study 8.1.

A limitation of the survey research on subjective cues to deception is that it relies on self-reports. It has long been argued that people cannot necessarily self-report on their cognitive processes, as such processes may lie partly or wholly outside the realm of conscious awareness (Nisbett & Wilson, 1977). In line with this, a recent meta-analysis of behavioural correlates of deception judgments found that people do not necessarily rely on the cues they self-report (Hartwig & Bond, 2011). That is, while they self-report relying on gaze aversion and nervous behaviours, these cues are far from the strongest actual correlates of lie judgments. Contrary to survey research, this meta-analysis showed a rather strong overlap between subjective and objective cues to deception, suggesting that poor lie detection accuracy is more likely due to weaknesses in cues to deception rather than lie-catchers' misconceptions about deceptive behaviour.

CASE STUDY 8.1   WHEN TRAINING TO DETECT DECEPTION FAILS

As will be discussed later in this chapter, there have been several attempts to improve people's deception detection accuracy by providing various types of training. A training study of a slightly different nature was carried out by Kassin and Fong (1999). Instead of providing a training programme predicted to increase accuracy levels, the training consisted of recommendations on how to detect deception taken from a highly influential police interrogation manual.

In the study, 16 participants committed either one of four mock crimes such as vandalism or shoplifting, or a non-criminal act. They were all asked to deny involvement in the crime, creating a sample of both false denials (statements from guilty participants) and true denials (statements from innocent participants). Subsequent interrogations with the participants were videotaped, and used as stimulus materials. A sample of 40 lay people acted as lie-catchers, who were randomly allocated to either a training condition or a naïve condition. The training was based on parts of the interrogation manual *Criminal Interrogation and Confessions* by Inbau, Reid and colleagues (most recently Inbau *et al.*, 2001). The manual and the techniques described in it (referred to as the *Reid manual* and the *Reid technique*) have received fierce criticism for the heavy emphasis on manipulative and psychologically coercive elements (Gudjonsson, 2003), and lately also for the provision of cues to deception that completely lack diagnostic value (Vrij, 2003). In the study, lie-catchers in the training condition watched two videotape segments taken from a training seminar produced by Reid and colleagues. The first segment concerned cues to deception to be found in the verbal content, and described truthful statements as 'direct', 'spontaneous' and 'unqualified', and truth-tellers' denials as 'unequivocal' (Inbau *et al.*, 2001). In contrast, deceptive statements were said to be 'hesitant', 'general', 'evasive' and 'unspecific'. The second segment concerned nonverbal cues to deception, which were said to include gaze aversion, slouching in one's seat, covering of the eyes and mouth, and self-manipulations such as grooming gestures. It should be noted that the authors of the manual have much faith in the value of these cues: they state that using them can result in deception detection accuracy rates exceeding 80 per cent.

The results from the study by Kassin and Fong (1999) contradict the bold statements from the interrogation manual. Not only did the training group fail to outperform the naïve group (who achieved an accuracy level of nearly 56 per cent), they actually performed *worse* (nearly 46 per cent accurate judgments). However, the group who received training were more confident than the naïve group that they had made an accurate judgment of veracity. The trained group of lie-catchers also reported more reasons for their judgment, and a large proportion of these reasons were related to cues recommended in the training material. Taken together, the study shows that exposure to and use of the cues recommended in the Reid manual is not only inefficient but also directly counterproductive in improving accuracy in detecting deception and truth. Unfortunately, more than 500,000 people working in law enforcement and other agencies, as well as private companies, have already been trained in the technique (Reid & Associates, 2011) and it is likely that many more legal professionals have access to the manual in their everyday work life. The results directly point to the problems associated with relying on empirically unsupported methods when making judgments of veracity, and indirectly to the need for scientifically sound and empirically validated approaches to the detection of deception and truth.

Realism in deception detection studies

The external validity of deception detection research has been questioned. The most important and persistent criticism has concerned two aspects: first, the realism in the target material (the statement to be assessed by the lie-catchers); and second, the realism of the situation in which the lie-catchers are put (Hartwig, 2011). The targets in the paradigmatic deception detection experiment provide either a true or a false statement regarding their opinions or feelings, or about their involvement in some past event (sometimes a mock crime). This could be characterised as a *low-stake situation*, in that failing to give a credible impression has little or no consequences (low-stake lies). This does not mirror the *high-stake situations* encountered in the legal system, for example when a suspect is assessed in order to determine the likelihood of guilt. Failing to act in a credible way in such a situation can have severe and far-reaching consequences. It could be argued that deceptive behaviour may be different in low- and high-stake situations and that it thus would be premature to draw conclusions

low-stake lies lies that have trivial consequences; typically, the lies told by participants in laboratory studies of deception.

high-stake lies lies, the effectiveness of which are critical to the freedom of the liar; typically lies told by a suspect during a police interview.

about, for example, police officers' ability to detect **high-stake lies** (Miller & Stiff, 1993). Aldert Vrij and his colleagues have taken an important step in investigating real-life high-stake lies and truths in a police interrogation (e.g. Mann *et al.*, 2004). Although the pattern is not entirely clear, these studies indicate that realistic target materials slightly improve people's ability to detect lies.

The second part of the criticism of the realism in deception detection studies concerns the context in which the assessment occurs. In the typical study, participants watch a video clip of the target. Hence, they are restricted to passively watching the suspects, without any background information and without the possibility to ask questions as they find necessary in order to form the basis for a veracity assessment (Hartwig *et al.*, 2004). This is very different from the situation in which police officers normally make judgments of veracity. Instead, they often make judgments on the basis of their background information, and on their own interaction with the suspect. It could be argued that one reason for the modest accuracy rates often found in studies on police officers' deception detection ability is that they are unfamiliar with catching lies from passive observation. Research has disproven this notion. For example, it has been shown that experienced criminal investigators fail to assess veracity accurately even when they have the chance to plan and conduct an interrogation in a manner of their own choice (Hartwig *et al.*, 2004).

DETECTING DECEPTION FROM VERBAL CONTENT

Is it possible to detect deception on the basis of what is being said? If so, what should one listen for; and is it better to use human coders or computer programs? Or are you better off totally ignoring the verbal content, instead using special equipment in order to analyse the speaker's voice? Below we will address these questions by describing a number of deception detection methods, and (where possible) report on each method's discriminative power.

Statement validity analysis

Statement validity analysis (SVA) is the most widely used technique for assessing veracity on the basis of verbal content. It was originally developed in Germany and Sweden for assessing children's accounts of alleged

sexual abuse (Trankell, 1963; Undeutsch, 1967). Underlying the technique is the **Undeutsch hypothesis**, which states that if a child's statement is based on the memory of an actual experience, it will differ in content and quality from a statement based on fabrication (Steller & Köhnken, 1989). A full SVA is a four-stage procedure (Köhnken, 2004). The first stage consists of a thorough analysis of the case-file, which, in turn, forms the basis for the generation of hypotheses about the source of the statement. Second, a semi-structured interview is conducted, where the child tells his or her own story. The interview is audio-taped and transcribed. Third, the statement is assessed in terms of credibility, using a **criteria-based content analysis (CBCA)**. The CBCA is based on a list of 19 criteria, for example 'logical structure', 'descriptions of interactions' and 'self-deprecation'. For the full list and an in-depth discussion of each criterion, see Köhnken (2004). Finally, by using a **validity checklist**, alternative explanations to the CBCA outcome are considered (Steller & Köhnken, 1989).

The CBCA constitutes the core of the SVA. Its 19 criteria are grouped into five categories: (i) general characteristics; (ii) specific contents; (iii) peculiarities of content; (iv) motivation-related contents; and (v) offence-specific elements. The presence of each of the 19 criteria is rated (for example, using a 3-point scale, where '0' = absent, '1' = present, and '2' = strongly present). In essence, the more criteria present and the stronger the presence of each criterion, the stronger the support for the hypothesis that the statement is based on a genuine personal experience.

To what extent can CBCA discriminate between genuine and fabricated accounts? Before attempting to answer this question, one needs to consider that, although the CBCA is widely used in court in some countries (Vrij, 2008), it is problematic to use real-life cases in order to assess the diagnostic value of the technique. In most cases where the technique is used, there is no other evidence than the statement itself. In such cases, we simply do not know whether the accounts are based on genuine or fabricated experiences (i.e. the **ground truth** is unknown).

Undeutsch hypothesis hypothesis, first enunciated by Udo Undeutsch, that if a child's statement is based on the memory of an actual experience, it will differ in content and quality from a statement based on fabrication.

criteria-based content analysis (CBCA) method for analysing children's statements in terms of indices that are believed to reflect truthfulness. Comprises 19 criteria. Part of *statement validity analysis*.

validity checklist The final stage of the *statement validity analysis (SVA)*, in which alternative hypotheses are considered concerning a child's statement.

ground truth the reality of what actually occurred in a given event. Sometimes impossible to establish in criminal investigations on the basis of witness statements alone.

In order to get information on the technique's diagnostic value, laboratory studies are needed. Vrij (2005a) reviewed the 37 first studies from laboratory settings. The majority of these studies focused on adults' statements, which is not considered problematic as the Undeutsch hypothesis is not limited to children's statements (Köhnken, 2004). Vrij's review showed an overall accuracy rate of 73 per cent, and the technique proved to be equally good for detecting truthful and fabricated accounts (see Chapter 15 for further discussion of CBCA from an expert witness perspective).

Reality monitoring

reality monitoring (RM) the process by which people distinguish memories of real events from memories of imagined events. The distinction is based on such considerations as contextual information concerning time and place, and semantic information.

The term **reality monitoring (RM)** has been used in basic memory research for many years, and refers to people's ability to discriminate between self-experienced and imagined events (Johnson & Raye, 1981). Research on RM supports the notion that real experiences are products of perceptual processes, whereas imagined events are products of reflective processes. As a consequence, memories of real events tend to differ from memories of imagined events. Specifically, memories of real events tend to contain more perceptual information (e.g. details concerning taste, touch, smell) and contextual information (i.e. spatial and temporal details) than memories of imagined events. Memories of imagined events tend to contain more cognitive operations (e.g. 'I must have been tired, because it was late') than do memories of real events.

The Spanish psychologist Maria Alonso-Quecuty (1992) was the first to suggest that RM could be used as a tool not only for distinguishing between *one's own* real and imagined events, but also between *other people's* real and imagined events, thus framing RM as a tool for distinguishing between truthful and deceptive accounts. Many researchers have since picked up on her idea (Sporer, 2004), and the list of RM criteria is now slowly finding its final form.

Jaume Masip and his colleagues (2005) presented the first systematic overview of RM studies conducted within the deception detection framework. Overall accuracy was 75 per cent, and the technique proved to be about equally accurate in detecting truths and lies. Interestingly, the technique seemed to work equally well for children's and adults' statements. In sum, considering that the technique rests upon a well-established theoretical framework, and that the criteria are relatively easy to learn, the RM technique is a rather interesting complement (or alternative) to the CBCA.

Scientific content analysis

scientific content analysis (SCAN) a technique originally developed by Sapir, based on the assumption that a statement based on a memory of an actual experience differs in content from a statement based on invention.

The **scientific content analysis (SCAN)** technique was developed by Sapir, a former Israeli polygraph examiner. Similarly to SVA and RM, the underlying assumption of SCAN is that a statement based on memory of an actual experience differs in content from a statement based on invention. SCAN uses written statements, preferably statements that are handwritten by the examinee (to ensure that the examinee's own words are produced). The list of SCAN criteria is extensive, and includes 'denial of allegations', 'emotions' and 'change in language'. For a list of the 12 most commonly used criteria, see Vrij (2008) and Smith (2001). Compared to the CBCA and RM, a SCAN is much less standardised in terms of coding.

To date, there has been very little research on the diagnostic value of SCAN. To our knowledge there are only four published studies on the SCAN, two laboratory studies and two field studies. The two laboratory studies showed that truthful and deceptive statements did not differ with regard to the SCAN criteria tested (Nahari et al., in press; Porter & Yuille, 1996), and for both field studies the ground truth is unknown (Driscoll, cited in Vrij, 2008; Smith, also cited in Vrij, 2008). In sum, while the name of the method implies scientific status, one should be aware that the scientific evidence supporting the technique is very meagre (Shearer, 1999).

Computer-based linguistic analysis

Yet another approach to the detection of deception is to examine the linguistic structure of statements. Scientific studies based on this approach had already started to appear in the late 1960s, and the basic idea is easy to grasp: people's choice of words may reveal more about their underlying mental states than the actual message (Pennebaker & King, 1999). There are several methods for conducting a linguistic analysis (basically, decomposing text, based on natural language, to word level) but we will restrict our discussion to one recent method.

Linguistic inquiry and word count (LIWC)

linguistic inquiry and word count (LIWC) a computer-based technique that creates linguistic profiles by categorising words into different classes.

Linguistic inquiry and word count (LIWC) is a computer-based technique that creates linguistic profiles by means of categorising words into different classes, such as (a) standard language dimensions (e.g. pronouns and articles);

(b) psychological processes (e.g. emotional and sensory processes); and (c) relativity (e.g. space and time).

By using LIWC it has been found that some words are less frequent in deceptive statements (e.g. first-person pronouns), whereas other words are more frequent in deceptive statements (e.g. negative emotional words). An examination of the hit rates reveals room for improvement, even if the LIWC has proven to discriminate between deceptive and truthful statements at a rate better than chance. For example, Newman and colleagues (2003) found an average hit rate (over three studies) of 67 per cent. Interestingly, recent research shows that an automatic coding of RM criteria of liars' and truth-tellers' statements utilising the LIWC software programme resulted in fewer verbal cues to deception than a manual coding of the very same criteria (Vrij et al., 2007). Finally, and importantly, by decomposing text to word level, one loses context. Since the context of a statement is important in forensic settings (e.g. the statement's development over time), it may render linguistic analysis limited in legal contexts.

Computer analysis of voice stress

voice stress analysis belief that by measuring the activity in the muscles responsible for producing speech, it may be possible to infer the speaker's mental state (e.g. experiences of stress).

Another approach to deception detection is to analyse the voice itself, and neglect the verbal content. We will discuss two such approaches: **voice stress analysis (VSA)** and **layered voice-stress analysis (LVA)**.

Voice stress analysis (VSA)

This is sometimes called the **psychological stress evaluator (PSE)**. The basic assumption behind the technique is

layered voice-stress analysis (LVA) a lie detection technique that uses highly sophisticated technology to analyse for speech errors that are very difficult for the human ear to detect but, it is argued, can be measured by more refined methods.

psychological stress evaluator (PSE) alternative name for *voice stress analysis*.

rather straightforward: by measuring the activity in the muscles responsible for producing speech, it may be possible to infer the speaker's mental state (e.g. experiences of stress). The main phenomena of interest are what are called 'micro tremors' – weak, involuntary muscle activities that can be detected with electrodes. It is well established that such tremors occur in larger groups of muscles, for example the biceps. Unfortunately, there is very little scientific evidence for the existence of tremors in the muscles that produce speech (Shipp & Izdebski, 1981). In brief, if there is no tremor

in the muscles that produce speech, there is no tremor to measure in the voice. Also, even if it was possible to show tremor in the voice, a major challenge remains: to find scientific support for an association between (a) a certain type of tremor and lying, and (b) another type of tremor and telling the truth. Taken together, the VSA seems to suffer from problems related to both reliability and validity. For a similarly sceptical view of this technique, see the evaluation conducted by the National Research Council (2003).

Layered voice-stress analysis (LVA)

Layered voice-stress analysis is a more recent method, and its advocates claim that the method rests upon highly sophisticated technology. The LVA uses a computer program to analyse a digitised raw signal (sound) to identify errors in speech. These errors are very difficult for the human ear to pick up, but it is argued that they can be measured by more refined methods. Such errors are not exclusive to the human voice, and can be found for any type of sound (e.g. a clock ticking or a washing machine). The LVA offers statistical output on two such errors, and uses these to calculate a 'truth value'. Experts on forensic phonetics have equated the diagnostic value of the LVA to flipping a coin (Eriksson & Lacerda, 2007).

PSYCHOPHYSIOLOGICAL DETECTION OF DECEPTION

Previously in this chapter, we have discussed cues to deception in demeanour and in the verbal content of a statement. The third major branch of research on deception detection focuses on differences in psychophysiological patterns, which are typically measured using the polygraph.

Development of psychophysiological detection of deception

Physiological deception detection approaches have a long history. In China, suspected transgressors were forced to chew rice powder and spit it out. If the rice powder was still dry, the suspect was deemed to be guilty (Sullivan, 2001). Underlying such a technique is the assumption that liars and truth-tellers differ in terms of physiological responses. In the case of the rice powder technique, a decrease in saliva production was interpreted as a result of fear of being caught lying. The same assumption

FIGURE 8.2 *The modern polygraph measures at least three physiological systems, typically galvanic skin response (sweating from the palm), cardiovascular activity such as systolic and diastolic blood pressure (measured by a cuff on the upper arm) and breathing patterns (measured by sensors attached around the chest).*

Source: ©The University of Birmingham, UK. Reproduced with permission.

was the foundation for late 19th century attempts by Lombroso and others to measure changes in blood volume during an interrogation with a suspect (Grubin & Madsen, 2005).

The polygraph in its present form is an instrument built to measure the same physiological processes as Lombroso and the Chinese both attempted to tap. Although the modern polygraph is more technically sophisticated, the basic function of the polygraph is the same today as it was almost 100 years ago (Grubin & Madsen, 2005). The modern polygraph (Figure 8.2) measures at least three physiological systems, all governed by the autonomic nervous system (Fiedler *et al.*, 2002), typically, galvanic skin response (sweating from the palm); cardiovascular activity such as systolic and diastolic blood pressure (measured by a cuff on the upper arm); and breathing patterns (measured by sensors attached around the chest).

Although it is difficult to give exact information about how and where the polygraph is used, it is safe to say that it is used in a vast number of contexts in all parts of the world. In the USA, polygraph testing occurs in many parts of law enforcement (Honts, 2004), and polygraph tests play a role in the legal systems of, among others, Belgium, Canada, Israel, Japan, Korea,

Mexico, Thailand and Turkey (Honts, 2004; Pollina *et al.*, 2004; Vrij, 2008). Its use in these countries varies; in Japan, polygraph evidence is generally admissible (Hira & Furumitsu, 2002), while most countries are restrictive with the use of polygraph tests in court (Vrij, 2008). Traditionally, the use of the polygraph in the UK has been limited. However, in the 1980s, the Geoffrey Prime spy scandal sparked the British government's interest in the polygraph (Segrave, 2004). A working group was appointed to evaluate the reliability, validity and ethical aspects of the polygraph, and its use in criminal investigations and for employment evaluations (Grubin & Madsen, 2005). The working group came to the conclusion that the empirical support for the use of the polygraph was limited, and that some aspects might be inconsistent with the British Psychological Society's codes of conduct (British Psychological Society, 1986). The report of a more recent working group concurred with the earlier report, and concluded that the body of ecologically valid research on the polygraph is limited, and that there are a number of problems related to its use as a lie detector (British Psychological Society, 2004). Nevertheless, British researchers have recently explored the possibilities of using the polygraph for sex offender monitoring and treatment. So far, such attempts have shown promising results (Grubin & Madsen, 2006).

The control question test

There are two main types of polygraph test. The most frequently used is the **control question test (CQT),** sometimes referred to as the *comparison question test* (Honts, 2004), which is widely applied in law enforcement in the USA, Canada and Israel (Ben-Shakhar *et al.*, 2002).

> **control question test (CQT)**   a method of polygraph testing that compares reactions to control questions concerning past transgressions to questions relevant to the crime under investigation; a guilty person should react more strongly to the relevant questions.

The CQT is administered in several stages (Lykken, 1998). In the introductory phase, rapport is established, basic information is obtained and the subject is invited to provide free recall. Questions are then formulated, and the subject and the polygraph examiner discuss these questions. The first reason for this is that the examiner wants to establish that the subject has understood all the questions. The second reason is that the examiner wants to be sure that the subject will respond to the questions with 'yes' or 'no' (Vrij, 2008). After this, the question phase commences. This phase is run several times, and the responses are averaged across the different test occasions. Subjects are asked a number of questions belonging to one of three categories. The first category is *irrelevant questions* or *neutral questions* ('Is your last name Morris?'; 'Do you live in the United States?'); these questions are not included in the analysis of the results. The second category is *relevant questions*, which directly concern the crime being investigated ('Did you break into the house on Stanley Street?'; 'Did you shoot Mr. Philip?'). The third category is *control questions*, which concern transgressions in the past, unrelated to the event under scrutiny ('Before the age of 25, did you ever take something that did not belong to you?'). These questions are designed to force everyone to give a deceptive response, both because they are vague enough to cover the most frequent transgressions (such as lies for social purposes) and because the subject has been steered into denying such transgression during the introductory phase of the test. The purpose of the control questions is to establish a deception baseline, to which responses to the relevant questions are compared. Simply put, it is the difference in physiological responses between the relevant questions and the control questions that determines the outcome of the test. The idea is that a guilty subject will react more strongly to the relevant questions than to the control questions,

while the opposite pattern is expected for innocent people (Fiedler *et al.*, 2002).

Validity of the CQT

The polygraph has been evaluated using both field and laboratory approaches. Field studies show that the CQT is rather good at classifying guilty suspects. In an overview by Vrij (2008), it was concluded that more than 80 per cent of the guilty suspects failed the test. However, the accuracy rates are lower for innocent suspects. This indicates that the test has a tendency for false positive errors, which poses a problem in the legal system, where false positives (classifying innocent suspects as guilty) are considered more severe mistakes than false negatives (classifying guilty suspects as innocent). The results of field studies must, however, be interpreted with caution. The main problem associated with these studies is being able to establish ground truth – to know whether the subject is actually guilty or not. In some of the studies, a main source of information leading to classifications is confession evidence. It is a well-known fact within the scientific community that innocent people sometimes confess to crimes they have not committed (see Chapter 7 and Kassin, 2004).

In laboratory studies, the ground truth is not problematic. Rather, the challenge is to create externally valid situations, taking into account, among other things, the high-stake nature of polygraph tests in the investigative context. One problem with giving an overall accuracy figure for laboratory-based studies on the polygraph is variability in the criteria for deciding whether a study is externally valid. Honts (2004) lists three criteria for categorising studies as high quality. However, these criteria are not absolute; for example, one of the criteria is that the instrumentation and testing should be as similar as possible to those applied in the field setting. There could be different opinions about whether the testing is similar to that of the field setting. A second problem with estimating overall accuracy is that some reviews exclude inconclusive results (arguing that they are not decisions, e.g. Honts, 2004), while others include these outcomes. Hence, estimates of accuracy might vary. The review by Vrij (2008) showed a hit rate of between 74 and 82 per cent for guilty suspects, but with a pronounced error rate for innocent suspects. In an overview by Honts (2004), the average accuracy rate was 91 per cent, with no prominent tendency for either false negatives or false positives. A third summary of studies produced an overall accuracy of 86 per cent (National Research Council, 2003). In conclusion, although it is difficult to provide an exact figure, field and laboratory studies indicate that the CQT has some discriminative value.

Problems with the CQT

For decades, the CQT has been the target of harsh criticism (Ben-Shakhar & Furedy, 1990; Lykken, 1998). There is no room in this chapter to fully discuss this criticism, but we will briefly present some core arguments against the use of the CQT. Perhaps most importantly, a central assumption of the CQT is that innocent suspects will give more aroused responses to control questions than to relevant questions. Ekman (2001) argues that such an assumption is far from safe. For example, it is conceivable that innocent suspects would react more strongly to the details of the crime they are being falsely accused of (the relevant questions) than to a control question about a rather mild transgression in the past.

The guilty knowledge test

The second type of polygraph test is the **guilty knowledge test (GKT)** (Furedy & Heslegrave, 1991; Lykken, 1959; 1960). The basic idea behind the GKT is straightforward: it aims to detect concealed knowledge that only the guilty suspect has. This is done by presenting a question together with a number of answer alternatives, one of which is correct (e.g. 'What weapon was used to kill Mr. Sylvester? Was it a knife? A dagger? A pair of scissors?' and so on). The assumption is that a guilty suspect, who will recognise the correct answer, will experience more physiological arousal when the correct alternative is presented, compared to the incorrect alternatives. In contrast, an innocent suspect will react on average similarly to all alternatives, since they lack the 'guilty knowledge' (MacLaren, 2001).

> **guilty knowledge test (GKT)** a method of polygraph testing. Suspects are given multiple-choice questions about the crime; a guilty suspect should experience more physiological arousal to a correct choice that only a guilty person would know.

Validity of the GKT

The same methodological problems with field and laboratory studies with the CQT also apply to studies evaluating the validity of the GKT, and will not be repeated. In contrast to the CQT, the GKT seems to be slightly more accurate in classifying innocent than guilty suspects. In an overview by Vrij (2008), well over 90 per cent of innocent suspects and around 80 per cent of guilty suspects were correctly classified in laboratory studies. A review of 20 such studies showed somewhat lower figures, with 83 per cent of innocent suspects and 76 per cent of guilty suspects correctly classified (MacLaren, 2001). Results from real-life studies (cf. Elaad, 1990; Elaad et al., 1992) support the asymmetric pattern and, in a summary of field studies (Vrij, 2008), 96 per cent of innocent suspects were found to be cleared by the test, while only 59 per cent of the guilty suspects failed it.

Problems with the GKT

A survey showed that 75 per cent of a sample of both general psychologists and psychophysiologists considered the GKT to be based on scientifically sound principles, while only 33 per cent considered this to be true for the CQT (Iacono & Lykken, 1997). Despite this, there are problems with the GKT, of which we will address two. First, the validity of the test can be seriously challenged if the correct alternative stands out in any way. Such transparency could make the reaction pattern of innocent suspects look like that of guilty ones. One could partly solve that problem by presenting the answer alternatives to a group of naïve subjects, but Honts (2004) notes that this does not protect against idiosyncratic biases in individuals.

The second type of criticism concerns the applicability of the GKT. If the test is to be used, innocent suspects *must not* know the correct alternatives, otherwise an innocent suspect might give 'guilty' responses because of having been exposed to the critical information, for example, via the media. Moreover, the guilty suspect *must* know the answer. If a guilty person failed to perceive a certain detail at the crime scene, the guilty person might give innocent responses to questions about the detail because of lack of knowledge. These conditions drastically affect the applicability of the technique. For example, it has been estimated that the technique can be applied to less than 10 per cent of FBI cases (Podlesny, cited in Honts, 2004).

Countermeasures

There has been some debate in the research field concerning the extent to which it is possible for subjects to influence the outcome of polygraph tests. Any attempts with such a purpose are called *countermeasures*. The aim would be (during a CQT) to purposely enhance reactions to control questions or (during a GKT) to purposely provide similar responses to all answer alternatives. It has consistently been shown that people's spontaneous countermeasures are not effective in producing false negative outcomes (Honts & Amato, 2002). However, coaching subjects in countermeasures before the test occasion is a more serious threat to the polygraph. In experimental research, subjects who received training in countermeasures managed to impair the accuracy of the CQT. The countermeasures were both physical, such as biting the tongue or pressing the toes to the floor (Honts et al., 1985), and cognitive, such as counting backwards

(Honts *et al.*, 1994). For a classification and discussion on different types of countermeasures, see Honts and Amato (2002).

NEW DIRECTIONS IN DECEPTION DETECTION RESEARCH

Brain scanning

There are many methods for scanning the human brain (Figure 8.3); one of the more common is called **functional magnetic resonance imaging (fMRI)**. This method enables monitoring of neural activity during, for example, cognitive operations. During recent years fMRI has been used for many different purposes, among them to study the brain activity taking place during deception. The findings from this research indicate that the neural activity during lying may be different compared to the activity during telling the truth (Spence *et al.*, 2006). Specifically, fMRI studies show an increased activity in the prefrontal cortex during deception (i.e. the 'executive' part of the brain, supporting complex human behaviour such as speech and problem solving). These studies can be taken to indicate that lying is more cognitively demanding than telling the truth (Vrij *et al.*, 2006).

> **functional magnetic resonance imaging (fMRI)** technique of imaging activity with widespread uses in psychology, including searching for neural correlates of deception.

FIGURE 8.3 *There are many methods for scanning the human brain.*

Source: © giorgiomtb. Used under licence from Shutterstock.

The use of fMRI as a deception detection tool has received extensive media coverage. Indeed, the studies on neural correlates of deception are intriguing, and the findings reported are (so far) promising. Importantly though, this does not mean that the deception enigma is solved once and for all. Besides the facts that the fMRI equipment is extremely expensive and immobile, and demands that the target remains still, the studies conducted so far are very few. It still remains to be shown whether the fMRI is diagnostic for deception in situations of high forensic relevance. It is probably safe to assume that studies using fMRI will shed some light on the cognitive processes taking place during deception, but we will refrain from speculating on potential future applications of these techniques in forensic settings.

Interviewing to elicit cues to deception

Research suggests that lack of valid cues is a critical reason for the typically mediocre lie detection accuracy rates (DePaulo *et al.*, 2003; Hartwig & Bond, 2011). It is therefore interesting to note that there is a new wave of research where the aim is to elicit diagnostic cues to deception by actively interviewing in strategic ways (Vrij, Granhag *et al.*, 2010). This line of research can be viewed in contrast to the more passive set-up used in the paradigmatic deception study. It is possible to identify several different approaches within this new wave of research (Vrij *et al.*, 2011), and below we will briefly review three of these.

First, research based on the assumption that lying may be more demanding than truth-telling has attempted to increase cues to deception by placing targets under additional cognitive load. The assumption is that liars would be more hampered by such tasks, as their resources are already preoccupied with the cognitive challenge of lying. For example, in one study, liars and truth-tellers were asked to tell their story in reverse order. It was found that behavioural differences between liars and truth-tellers were more pronounced when the story was told in reverse order, compared to a control condition in which the story was told in chronological order (Vrij *et al.*, 2008). In another study, targets were instructed to maintain eye contact, which previous research has found to be mentally taxing (Beattie, 1981). Again, cues to deception were more pronounced in this condition compared to a control condition in which no instruction to maintain eye contact was given (Vrij, Mann *et al.*, 2010).

A second approach is to ask unanticipated questions. The core of this approach is that liars often prepare themselves before an interview (Strömwall *et al.*, 2006), and that this planning will pay off if the liar is only asked questions that he or she has anticipated. The idea is therefore to ask questions that are unanticipated; and the reasoning is that truth-tellers will be able to answer these by drawing on their memory, whereas liars will have a much more difficult time. This approach was foreshadowed by Colwell and his colleagues using mnemonics from the cognitive interview, and showing that cues to deception became more pronounced when liars and truth-tellers were questioned using memory-enhancing techniques (Colwell *et al.*, 2007). This approach was recently refined by Vrij and colleagues (2009), showing that it was possible to elicit diagnostic cues to deception by asking pairs of liars and truth-tellers to answer in an unanticipated format. That is, when asked to make a drawing of a layout of a restaurant (where the liars claimed to have been, in order to produce an alibi) more cues to deception emerged compared to when the same lying pairs provided verbal descriptions of the restaurant. In short, research shows that it is possible to elicit cues to deception by asking unanticipated questions, but also by asking the suspect to answer an anticipated question in an unanticipated format.

Yet another 'interviewing to detect deception' approach is the research programme on the *strategic use of evidence (SUE) technique*. This technique is applicable to situations where the interviewer has some sort of evidence pointing to the suspect's guilt. The technique rests on the theoretically-driven assumption that liars and truth-tellers will have different counter-interrogation strategies (Granhag & Hartwig, 2008). Specifically, theoretical notions applicable to the psychology of guilt and innocence predict that guilty suspects will use much more aversive strategies with respect to possibly self-incriminating information (Strömwall *et al.*, 2006), whereas innocent suspects will use much more straightforward strategies (Kassin, 2005). For example, innocent people may volunteer that they were at the crime scene, while guilty people tend to omit or deny such information. Importantly, recent work shows that these basic assumptions are empirically supported. In brief, guilty mock-suspects have been found to avoid mentioning possibly self-incriminating information more often (Strömwall *et al.*, 2006), and deny holding possibly self-incriminating information (Hartwig *et al.*, 2006), compared to innocent suspects.

A full-scale use of the SUE technique demands extensive pre-interview planning, which includes a multidimensional assessment of the evidence at hand and tactical considerations with respect to both the questions asked and the potential disclosure of the evidence. However, at the core of the technique is to encourage the suspect to tell his story (in order to open up for 'avoidance') and – in the next phase – closing in on the critical information by asking open and specific questions (in order to open up for 'denials'). There is now a series of empirical studies showing that if the basics steps of the SUE technique are used, it is possible to elicit diagnostic cues to deception (for further detail see Chapter 7 and Clemens *et al.*, 2010; Hartwig *et al.*, 2005; 2011). In essence, guilty suspects' statements tend to be less consistent with the available evidence compared to innocent suspects' statements.

CASE STUDY 8.2 WHEN TRAINING TO DETECT DECEPTION WORKS

Hartwig and her colleagues (2006) showed that it is possible to train police trainees to become better at detecting deception. Their study set out to investigate the effects of the *strategic use of evidence technique* (the *SUE* technique). The study was carried out at a police academy in Sweden, and a total of 82 police trainees participated. In the first phase of the study (day 1), half of the trainees received a three-hour training session in the SUE technique, while the other half received no such training. In the second phase of the study (day 2), a group of 82 university students acted as mock suspects, and half of these committed a mock theft by stealing a wallet from a briefcase in a bookstore (guilty suspects). The other half visited the same bookstore, searched for a particular item but committed no mock theft (innocent suspects). Later on the same day, each suspect (whether guilty or innocent) was interviewed by one police trainee (whether trained or untrained). The trained and untrained police trainees were given exactly the same case file, containing pieces of evidence pointing to the suspect's guilt (e.g. information that the suspect's fingerprints had been found on the briefcase). This evidence was 'true' for all suspects, in that all guilty suspects had to touch the briefcase in order to steal the wallet, and all innocent suspects had to touch the briefcase in order to properly search a particular box for a paper punch. The trained trainees were asked to interview in line with the SUE technique, and the untrained trainees were free to interview as they wished. By providing the police trainees with background information, and allowing them to interview the suspect (instead of passively watching a

(Continued)

videotaped interview), the design of this study was very different from all previous training studies.

The results showed that the trained interviewers did indeed use the SUE technique, whereas the untrained interviewers did not. Furthermore, the analysis showed that (a) guilty suspects avoided mentioning incriminating information during the free recall phase of the interview (whereas innocent suspects showed a much less avoidant strategy) and (b) guilty suspects denied holding incriminating information when asked specific questions addressing this information (whereas innocent suspects showed much less denial). This boiled down to the fact that guilty suspects interviewed by trained interviewers produced statements that were much more inconsistent with the existing evidence, than did guilty suspects interviewed by untrained interviewers. Specifically, the more statement–evidence inconsistency, the more likely were the trained interviewers to assess the suspect as guilty. (The same association did not prove significant for untrained interviewers.) In brief, by using the SUE technique, the trained interviewers created and used a diagnostic cue to deception: statement–evidence inconsistency. The overall deception accuracy was 85.4 per cent for trained interviewers and 56.1 per cent for untrained interviewers. The accuracy score for the trained interviewers is one of the highest in the scientific literature, whereas the accuracy score for the untrained is in line with most other groups tested (Bond & DePaulo, 2006).

Case Study 8.2 shows that the SUE technique can be taught and that it can improve deception detection accuracy. In relation to this, we think a few words on training to detect deception is warranted. Workshops on 'deception detection' are very popular and some of these workshops offer to train the participants in becoming better lie-catchers. The effectiveness of these training programmes is rarely evaluated, therefore we know little about this.

Turning to scientific studies on the effect of training – that is, controlled attempts to train people to become better at distinguishing between liars and truth-tellers – a few things should be noted. First, such studies have been conducted for quite some time (for summaries of this line of research, see Bull, 1989; 2004). Second, the methodologies used in order to train the participants vary extensively over the different studies. Some programmes have included information about cues to deception (e.g. Fiedler & Walka, 1993), whereas others have included both information on cues to deception and outcome feedback about one's own deception detection performance (e.g. Porter et al., 2000). Third, the effects of training are generally small. A meta-analysis by Frank and Feeley (2003), based on 20 training vs. no training comparisons (extracted from 11 published studies), showed a very small overall effect in terms of deception detection accuracy (the positive effect was significant, but added only 4 per cent advantage for trained participants).

Discriminating between true and false intent

Recently, researchers have begun to acknowledge that attempts to deceive are not always about the past, but that some situations call for an assessment of whether a particular statement made about the future is truthful or not (Granhag, 2010). Differently put, sometimes it is of crucial importance to be able to discriminate between true and false intent. So far, there are very few studies on this theme, but considering that many of (for very good reasons) are occupied with the threat of tomorrow, we predict that 'false intent' will be an interesting avenue for future research. The very first psycho-legal study on true and false intent was carried out at an international airport in the UK (Vrij et al., 2011), showing that passengers lying about their intentions (activities at their final destination) told statements that were less plausible than, but equally detailed as, the statements told by truth-telling passengers. Taking a different approach on the same theme Granhag and Knieps (2011) departed from the concept of *episodic future thought (EFT)*, which represents the ability to mentally pre-experience a one-time personal event that may potentially occur in the future (see e.g. Szpunar, 2010). It was predicted and found that a significantly higher proportion of truth-telling (vs. lying) suspects would agree that they had evoked a mental image while planning their future actions. In essence, the combined empirical evidence of the study strongly supported the assumption that EFT is a helpful concept for illuminating the differences that may occur when forming true and false intentions.

CONCLUSIONS

Research on deception detection has exploded over the past years, and the current zeitgeist tells us that this sub-area of forensic psychology will continue to grow. In an era of threat, violence and terrorism, a premium is placed on research dealing with security and control.

We believe that research on deception detection has an important role to play in the struggle for justice and a safer society. However, in order for research to make significant contributions, and to have a fair chance of reaching the desks of policy makers, several tough challenges must be dealt with. In short, it is not enough to debunk the 'foolproof way to detect deception' claims flourishing in the media and in pseudoscience; researchers also need to pay close attention to their own activities. It is true that the field offers many new and intriguing problems (e.g. deception over the internet), as well as a number of old problems still awaiting solutions (e.g. how to train people to become better lie-catchers). In order to properly address these problems, the ecological validity of the overall research agenda must be increased. For example, researchers must come up with creative designs that better mirror the interactive processes at play in most real-life interview situations. On a positive note, it is possible to discern a paradigmatic shift in research focus, from studies mapping people's judgment errors and wrongful beliefs, toward studies with an aim of enhancing people's deception detection performance, by, for example, interviewing in a strategic manner (Vrij, Granhag *et al.*, 2010). This is indeed promising, but our conclusion is that much significant work on deception has yet to be conducted.

SUMMARY

- In order to predict liars' and truth-tellers' behaviour, four different approaches have been suggested: the *emotional approach*, the *cognitive load approach*, the *attempted control approach* and the *self-presentational perspective.*

- Research shows that people are poor at detecting deception. The main reasons are that cues to deception are very scarce (*objective cues*) and that people's beliefs about cues to deception (*subjective cues*) are incorrect.

- *Statement validity analysis* and *reality monitoring* are two methods for analysing a statement's verbal content in order to detect deception. Scientific evaluation shows that neither of these methods is perfect, but that they can be of help when assessing veracity.

- There is reason to be sceptical towards alternative methods such as *scientific content analysis*, *voice stress analysis* and *layered voice-stress analysis*, as these methods rest on a very weak theoretical ground, and lack empirical support.

- The *control question test (CQT)* and the *guilty knowledge test (GKT)* are the two most common tests within the domain of psychophysiological detection of deception. While both tests have been heavily criticised, they have both proven to have some discriminative value.

- It is possible to identify a new wave of research where the aim is to find strategic ways to interview in order to actively elicit diagnostic cues to deception. This new wave of research can be viewed in contrast to the traditional way of examining passive observers' deception detection performance.

ESSAY/DISCUSSION QUESTIONS

1. The area of deception detection is not very well developed in terms of theory. However, a number of approaches have been suggested in order to predict behavioural differences between liars and truth-tellers. Name and describe four such approaches, and reflect on their similarities and differences.

2. Research shows that people's deception detection performance is rather poor. How can this result be explained?

3. It is possible to identify two main techniques for analysing a statement's verbal content in order to detect deception. Describe these two methods and their reliability and accuracy.

4. Broadly speaking, there are two types of polygraph test. Describe each type and their similarities and differences. Is either test a reliable instrument for detecting deception by offenders?

REFERENCES

Alonso-Quecuty, M.L. (1992). Deception detection and reality monitoring: A new answer to an old question? In F. Lösel, D. Bender & T. Bliesener (Eds.) *Psychology and law: International perspectives* (pp.328–332). Berlin: Walter de Gruyter.

Beattie, G.W. (1981). A further investigation of the cognitive interference hypothesis of gaze patterns during conversation. *British Journal of Social Psychology, 20,* 243–248.

Ben-Shakhar, G., Bar-Hillel, M. & Kremnitzer, M. (2002). Trial by polygraph: Reconsidering the use of the Guilty Knowledge Technique in court. *Law and Human Behavior, 26,* 527–541.

Ben-Shakhar, G. & Furedy, J.J. (1990). *Theories and applications in the detection of deception: A psychophysiological and international perspective.* New York: Springer-Verlag.

Bond Jr, C.F. & DePaulo, B.M. (2006). Accuracy of deception judgments. *Personality and Social Psychology Review, 10,* 214–234.

Bond, C.F. Jr. & DePaulo, B.M. (2008). Individual differences in judging deception: Accuracy and bias. *Psychological Bulletin, 134,* 477–492.

British Psychological Society. (1986). The report of the working group on the use of the polygraph in criminal investigations and personnel screening. *Bulletin of the British Psychological Society, 39,* 81–94.

British Psychological Society (2004). *A review of the current scientific status and fields of application of polygraphic deception detection.* Final Report from the BPS Working Party. London: British Psychological Society.

Bull, R. (1989). Can training enhance the detection of deception? In J. Yuille (Ed.) *Credibility assessment.* Deventer: Kluwer Academic.

Bull, R. (2004). Training to detect deception from behavioural cues: Attempts and problems. In P.A. Granhag & L.A. Strömwall (Eds.) *The detection of deception in forensic contexts* (pp.251–268). Cambridge: Cambridge University Press.

Burgoon, J.K., Buller, D.B. & Guerrero, L.K. (1995). Interpersonal deception IX: Effects of social skills and nonverbal communication on deception success and detection accuracy. *Journal of Language and Social Psychology, 14,* 289–311.

Clemens, F., Granhag, P.A., Strömwall, L.A. Vrij, A., Landström, S., Roos af Hjelmsäter, E. & Hartwig, M. (2010). Skulking around the dinosaur: Eliciting cues to children's deception via strategic disclosure of evidence. *Applied Cognitive Psychology, 24,* 925–940.

Colwell, K., Hiscock-Anisman, C., Memon, A., Taylor, L. & Prewett, J. (2007). Assessment Criteria Indicative of Deception (ACID): An integrated system of investigative interviewing and detecting deception. *Journal of Investigative Psychology and Offender Profiling, 4,* 167–180.

DePaulo, B.M. (1992). Nonverbal behavior and self-presentation. *Psychological Bulletin, 111,* 203–243.

DePaulo, B.M. & Kirkendol, S.E. (1989). The motivational impairment effect in the communication of deception. In J.C. Yuille (Ed.) *Credibility assessment* (pp.51–70). Dordrecht, The Netherlands: Kluwer.

DePaulo, B.M., LeMay, C.S. & Epstein, J.A. (1991). Effects of importance of success and expectations for success on effectiveness at deceiving. *Personality and Social Psychology Bulletin, 17,* 14–24.

DePaulo, B.M., Lindsay, J.J., Malone, B.E., Muhlenbruck, L., Charlton, K. & Cooper, H. (2003). Cues to deception. *Psychological Bulletin, 129,* 74–118.

DePaulo, B.M. & Morris, W.L. (2004). Discerning lies from truths: Behavioral cues to deception and the indirect pathway of intuition. In P.A. Granhag & L.A. Strömwall (Eds.) *The detection of deception in forensic contexts* (pp.15–40). Cambridge: Cambridge University Press.

Ekman, P. (2001). *Telling lies: Clues to deceit in the marketplace, politics and marriage.* New York: Norton.

Ekman P. & Friesen, W.V. (1972). Hand movements. *Journal of Communication, 22,* 353–374.

Elaad, E. (1990). Detection of guilty knowledge in real-life criminal investigations. *Journal of Applied Psychology, 75,* 521–529.

Elaad, E., Ginton, A. & Jungman, N. (1992). Detection measures in real-life criminal guilty knowledge tests. *Journal of Applied Psychology, 77,* 757–767.

Eriksson, A. & Lacerda, F (2007). Charlatanry in forensic speech science: A problem to be taken seriously. *International Journal of Speech, Language and the Law, 14,* 169–193.

Fiedler, K., Schmid, J. & Stahl, T. (2002). What is the current truth about polygraph lie detection? *Basic and Applied Social Psychology, 24,* 313–324.

Fiedler, K. & Walka, I. (1993). Training lie detectors to use nonverbal cues instead of global heuristics. *Human Communication Research, 20,* 199–223.

Frank, M.G. & Feeley, T.H. (2003). To catch a liar: Challenges for research in lie detection training. *Journal of Applied Communication Research, 31,* 58–75.

Furedy, J.J. & Heslegrave, R.J. (1991). The forensic use of the polygraph: A psychophysiological analysis of current trends and future prospects. In J.R. Jennings, P.K. Ackles & M.G. Coles (Eds.) *Advances in psychophysiology,* Vol. 4 (pp.157–189). Greenwich, CT: JAI Press.

Granhag, P.A. (2010). On the psycho-legal study of true and false intentions: Dangerous waters and some stepping stones. *Open Criminology Journal, 3,* 37–43.

Granhag, P.A. & Hartwig, M. (2008). A new theoretical perspective on deception detection: On the psychology of instrumental mind reading. *Psychology, Crime and Law, 14,* 189–200.

Granhag, P.A. & Knieps, M. (2011). Episodic future thought: Illuminating the trademarks of forming true and false intentions. *Applied Cognitive Psychology, 25,* 274–280.

Grubin, D. & Madsen, L. (2005). Lie detection and the polygraph: A historical review. *The Journal of Forensic Psychiatry and Psychology, 16,* 357–369.

Grubin, D. & Madsen, L. (2006). Accuracy and utility of post-conviction polygraph testing of sex offenders. *British Journal of Psychiatry, 188,* 479–483.

Gudjonsson, G.H. (2003). *The psychology of interrogations and confessions: A handbook.* Chichester: John Wiley & Sons, Inc.

Hartwig, M. (2011). Methods in deception research. In B. Rosenfeld and S. Penrod (Eds.) *Research methods in forensic psychology.* Chichester: John Wiley & Sons, Inc.

Hartwig, M. & Bond, C.F., Jr. (2011). Why do lie-catchers fail? A lens model meta-analysis of human lie judgments. *Psychological Bulletin, 137,* 643–659.

Hartwig, M., Granhag, P.A., Strömwall, L.A., Wolf, A., Vrij, A. & Roos af Hjelmsäter, E. (2011). Detecting deception in suspects: Verbal cues as a function of interview strategy. *Psychology, Crime, & Law, 17,* 643–656.

Hartwig, M., Granhag, P.A. & Strömwall, L.A. (2007). Guilty and innocent suspects' strategies during police interrogations. *Psychology, Crime & Law, 13,* 213–227.

Hartwig, M., Granhag, P.A., Strömwall, L.A. & Kronkvist, O.(2006). Strategic use of evidence during police interviews: When training to detect deception works. *Law and Human Behavior, 30,* 603–619.

Hartwig, M., Granhag, P.A., Strömwall, L.A. & Vrij, A. (2004). Police officers' lie detection accuracy: Interrogating freely vs. observing video. *Police Quarterly, 7,* 429–456.

Hartwig, M., Granhag, P.A., Strömwall, L.A. & Vrij, A. (2005). Detecting deception via strategic disclosure of evidence. *Law and Human Behavior, 29,* 469–484.

Hira, S. & Furumitsu, I. (2002). Polygraphic examinations in Japan: Application of the guilty knowledge test in forensic investigations. *International Journal of Police Science and Management, 4,* 16–27.

Honts, C.R. (2004). The psychophysiological detection of deception. In P.A. Granhag & L.A. Strömwall (Eds.) *The detection of deception in forensic contexts* (pp.103–123). Cambridge: Cambridge University Press.

Honts, C.R. & Amato, S. (2002). Countermeasures. In M. Kleiner (Ed.) *Handbook of polygraph testing* (pp.251–264). London: Academic.

Honts, C.R., Hodes, R.L. & Raskin, D.C. (1985). Effects of physical countermeasures on the physiological detection of deception. *Journal of Applied Psychology, 70,* 177–187.

Honts, C.R., Raskin, D.C. & Kircher, J.C. (1994). Mental and physical countermeasures reduce the accuracy of polygraph tests. *Journal of Applied Psychology, 79,* 252–259.

Iacono, W.G. & Lykken, D.T. (1997). The validity of the lie detector: Two surveys of scientific opinion. *Journal of Applied Psychology, 82,* 426–433.

Inbau, F.E., Reid, J.E., Buckley, J.P. & Jayne, B.C. (2001). *Criminal interrogation and confessions.* Gaithersburg: Aspen Publishers.

Johnson, M.K. & Raye, C.L. (1981). Reality Monitoring. *Psychological Review, 88,* 67–85.

Kassin, S.M. (2004). True or false: 'I'd know a false confession if I saw one'. In P.A. Granhag & L.A. Strömwall (Eds.) *The detection of deception in forensic contexts* (pp.172–194). Cambridge: Cambridge University Press.

Kassin, S.M. (2005). On the psychology of confessions: Does innocence put innocent at risk? *American Psychologist, 60,* 215–228

Kassin, S.M. & Fong, C. (1999). 'I'm innocent!': Effects of training on judgments of truth and deception in the interrogation room. *Law and Human Behavior, 23,* 499–516.

Köhnken, G. (2004). Statement validity analysis and the 'detection of the truth'. In P.A. Granhag & L.A. Strömwall (Eds.) *The detection of deception in forensic contexts* (pp.41–63). Cambridge: Cambridge University Press.

Lykken, D.T. (1959). The GSR in the detection of guilt. *Journal of Applied Psychology, 44,* 385–388.

Lykken, D.T. (1960). The validity of the guilty knowledge technique: The effects of faking. *Journal of Applied Psychology, 44,* 258–262.

Lykken, D.T. (1998). *A tremor in the blood: Uses and abuses of the lie detector.* New York: Plenum Press.

MacLaren, V.V. (2001). A quantitative review of the Guilty Knowledge Test. *Journal of Applied Psychology, 86,* 674–683.

Mann, S., Vrij, A. & Bull, R. (2004). Detecting true lies: Police officers' ability to detect suspects' lies. *Journal of Applied Psychology, 89,* 137–149.

Masip, J., Sporer, S.L., Garrido, E. & Herrero, C. (2005). The detection of deception with the Reality Monitoring approach: A review of the empirical evidence. *Psychology, Crime & Law, 11,* 99–122.

Miller, G.R. & Stiff, J.B. (1993). *Deceptive communication.* Newbury Park: Sage Publications.

Nahari, G., Vrij, A. & Fisher, R.P. (in press). Does the truth come out in the writing? SCAN as a lie detection tool. *Law and Human Behavior.*

National Research Council. (2003). *The polygraph and lie detection.* Washington, DC: National Academy Press.

Newman, M.L., Pennebaker, J.W., Berry, D.S. & Richards, J.M. (2003). Lying words: Predicting deception from linguistic styles. *Personality and Social Psychology Bulletin, 29,* 665–675.

Nisbett, R.E. & Wilson, T.D. (1977). Telling more than we can know: Verbal reports on mental processes. *Psychological Review, 84,* 231–259.

Pennebaker, J.W. & King, L.A. (1999). Linguistic styles: Language use as an individual difference. *Journal of Personality and Social Psychology, 77,* 1296–1312.

Pollina, D.A., Dollins, A.B., Senter, S.M., Krapohl, D.J. & Ryan, A.H. (2004). Comparison of polygraph data obtained from individuals involved in mock crimes and actual criminal investigations. *Journal of Applied Psychology, 89,* 1099–1105.

Porter, S., Woodworth, M. & Birth, A. (2000). Truth, lies and videotape: An investigation of the ability of federal parole officers to detect deception. *Law and Human Behavior, 24,* 643–658.

Porter, S. & Yuille, J.C. (1996). The language of deceit: An investigation of the verbal clues to deception in the interrogation context. *Law and Human Behavior, 20,* 443–458.

Reid, J.E. & Associates. (2011). *The Reid technique of interviewing and interrogation.* Retrieved 20 August 2011 from www.reid.com

Segrave, K. (2004). *Lie detectors: A social history.* Jefferson, NC: McFarland and Company.

Shearer, R.A. (1999). Statement analysis: SCAN or scam? *Skeptical Inquirer, 23,* 40–43.

Shipp, T. & Izdebski, K. (1981). Current evidence for the existence of laryngeal macrotremor and microtremor. *Journal of Forensic Science, 26,* 501–505.

Smith, N. (2001). *Reading between the lines: An evaluation of the scientific content analysis technique (SCAN).* London: Home Office Policing and Reducing Crime Unit.

Spence S.A., Hunter, M.D., Farrow, T.F.D., Green R.D., Leung, D.H., Hughes, C.J. & Ganesan, V. (2006). A cognitive neurobiological account of deception: Evidence from functional neuroimaging. In S. Zeki & O. Goodenough (Eds.) *Law and the brain* (pp.169–182). Oxford: Oxford University Press.

Sporer, S.L. (2004). Reality monitoring and detection of deception. In P.A. Granhag & L.A. Strömwall (Eds.) *The detection of deception in forensic contexts* (pp.64–102). Cambridge: Cambridge University Press.

Steller, M. & Köhnken, G. (1989). Criteria-Based Content Analysis. In D.C. Raskin (Ed.) *Psychological methods in criminal investigation and evidence* (pp.217–245). New York, NJ: Springer-Verlag.

Strömwall, L.A., Granhag, P.A. & Hartwig, M. (2004). Practitioners' beliefs about deception. In P.A. Granhag & L.A. Strömwall (Eds.) *The detection of deception in forensic contexts* (pp.229–250). Cambridge: Cambridge University Press.

Strömwall, L. A., Hartwig, M. & Granhag, P. A. (2006). To act truthfully: Nonverbal behavior and strategies during a police interrogation. *Psychology, Crime & Law, 12,* 207–219.

Sullivan, E. (2001). *The concise book of lying.* New York: Picador.

Szpunar, K.K. (2010). Episodic future thought: An emerging concept. *Perspectives on Psychological Science, 5,* 142–162.

Trankell, A. (1963). *Vittnespsykologins arbetsmetoder* (Methods of eyewitness psychology). Stockholm: Liber.

Undeutsch, U. (1967). Beurteilung der Glaubhaftigkeit von Aussagen (Assessing credibility of statements). In U. Undeitsch (Ed.) *Handbuch der Psychologie Vol. 11: Forensische Psychologie* (Handbook of psychology Vol. 11: Forensic psychology) (pp.26–181). Göttingen: Hogrefe.

Vrij, A. (2003). We will protect your wife and child, but only if you confess. In P.J. van Koppen & S.D. Penrod (Eds.) *Adversarial versus inquisitorial justice: Psychological perspectives on criminal justice systems* (pp.55–79). New York, NJ: Kluwer Academic.

Vrij, A. (2004). Why professionals fail to catch liars and how they can improve. *Legal and Criminological Psychology, 9,* 159–181.

Vrij, A. (2005a). Criteria-based content analysis: The first 37 studies. *Psychology, Public Policy and Law, 11,* 3–41.

Vrij, A. (2005b). Cooperation of liars and truth tellers. *Applied Cognitive Psychology, 19,* 39–50.

Vrij, A. (2008). *Detecting lies and deceit: Pitfalls and opportunities* (2nd edn). New York, NY: John Wiley & Sons, Inc.

Vrij, A., Fisher, R., Mann, S. & Leal, S. (2006). Detecting deception by manipulating cognitive load. *Trends in Cognitive Science, 10,* 141–142.

Vrij, A., Granhag, P.A., Mann, S. & Leal, S. (2011). Outsmarting the liars: Toward a cognitive lie detection approach. *Current Directions in Psychological Science, 20,* 28–32.

Vrij, A., Granhag, P.A. & Porter, S. (2010). Pitfalls and opportunities in nonverbal and verbal lie detection. *Psychological Science in the Public Interest, 11,* 89–121.

Vrij, A., Leal, S., Granhag, P.A., Mann, S., Fisher, R.P., Hillman, J., *et al.* (2009). Outsmarting the liars: The benefit of asking unanticipated questions. *Law and Human Behavior, 33,* 159–166.

Vrij, A., Mann, S., Fisher, R.P., Leal, S., Milne, R. & Bull, R. (2008). Increasing cognitive load to facilitate lie detection: The benefit of recalling an event in reverse order. *Law and Human Behavior, 32,* 253–265.

Vrij, A., Mann, S., Kristen, S. & Fisher, R.P. (2007). Cues to deception and ability to detect lies as a function of police interview styles. *Law & Human Behavior, 31,* 499–518.

Vrij, A., Mann, S., Leal, S. & Fisher, R.P. (2010). 'Look into my eyes': Can an instruction to maintain eye contact facilitate lie detection? *Psychology, Crime & Law, 16,* 327–348.

Vrij, A. & Semin, G.R. (1996). Lie experts' beliefs about nonverbal indicators of deception. *Journal of Nonverbal Behavior, 20,* 65–80.
Zuckerman, M., DePaulo, B.M. & Rosenthal, R. (1981). Verbal and nonverbal communication of deception. In L. Berkowitz (Ed.) *Advances in experimental social psychology* (Vol. 14, pp.1–59). New York: Academic Press.

ANNOTATED READING LIST

DePaulo, B.M., Lindsay, J.J., Malone, B.E., Muhlenbruck, L., Charlton, K. & Cooper, H. (2003). Cues to deception. *Psychological Bulletin, 129*, 74–118. *Most recent and comprehensive meta-analysis of the research on cues to deception, highlighting how few cues are consistently reliable.*

Ekman, P. (2001). *Telling lies: Clues to deceit in the marketplace, politics and marriage.* New York: Norton. *Classic analysis of the process of deception written by an internationally acknowledged pioneer of the field.*

Granhag, P.A. & Strömwall, L.A. (2004). *The detection of deception in forensic contexts.* Cambridge: Cambridge University Press. *Collection of papers by an international group of experts on various aspects of lying and deception.*

Vrij, A. (2008). *Detecting lies and deceit: Pitfalls and opportunities* (2nd edn). Chichester: John Wiley & Sons, Inc. *Aldert Vrij's book is probably the most comprehensive treatment of the research literature on lie detection.*

Vrij, A., Granhag, P.A. & Porter, S. (2010). Pitfalls and opportunities in nonverbal and verbal lie detection. *Psychological Science in the Public Interest, 11*, 89–121. *A recent, extensive and easy-to-access summary of the field, which looks at the topic from an applied angle.*

9 Offender Profiling and Crime Linkage

Jessica Woodhams

KEY TERMS

• acquisitive crime • behavioural distinctiveness • behavioural investigative advisors • cognitive-affective personality system (CAPS) • crime linkage • crime linkage practitioner • evidence-based practice • geographical proximity • homology assumption • indicators of series membership • offender consistency hypothesis • offender profiling • serial murder • serial offenders • shoemark evidence

CHAPTER OUTLINE

It is a truism in criminology that a minority of offenders commit the majority of crime. These prolific or chronic offenders are also responsible for more serious forms of crime. The actual percentage of offenders and the percentage of crimes for which they are believed responsible vary across countries but the core finding is the same (Bennett & Davis, 2004; Farrington & West, 1993; Wolfgang *et al.*, 1972). Some prolific offenders are classified as **serial offenders**, criminals who commit two or more crimes of the same type against different victims on different occasions (Federal Bureau of Investigation, 2008). These offenders cause harm to many victims and therefore they are costly to our society, both in human and financial terms. In terms of finance, the average monetary cost to society of a sexual assault in the UK has been calculated as approximately £31,000, with the cost to the victim being approximately £27,000 (Home Office, 2007). The resources available to the police to investigate crime are inevitably limited and recent years have seen a move towards intelligence-led policing aimed at targeting those offenders who commit a disproportionate number of crimes (Innes *et al.*, 2005).

> **serial offenders** offenders who have committed more than one offence against different victims. This term can be applied to specific crime types (e.g. *serial rape*, *serial murder*, or *serial burglary*).

Although physical evidence, such as DNA or fingerprints, is one of the most objective ways of identifying a suspect for a crime and for identifying multiple crimes committed by the same offender, it is not always left at a crime scene (Davies, 1991). This can be due to the circumstances of the offence, for instance, an attempted rape that is not completed due to third-party disturbance. Also, greater awareness of forensic techniques can mean that some criminals take precautions to avoid leaving behind such evidence (Durnal, 2010; Pye & Croft, 2004). Processing physical evidence is also time-consuming and costly (Santtila *et al.*, 2005). If there is no physical evidence at the crime scene, or if the processing of such evidence is too expensive, is there other evidence from the crime scene that could be used to assist in detecting the offender and determining the extent of his/her offending? **Offender profiling** and **crime linkage**, the subjects of this chapter, are two psychological procedures that have the *potential* to assist in identifying perpetrators.

> **offender profiling** in its narrowest sense, refers to making predictions about offenders' characteristics from the way they behaved during a crime.

> **crime linkage** an analytical technique whereby potential crime series are identified through the analysis of the offender's crime scene behaviour.

Before going further it is necessary to consider what we mean by 'crime linkage' and 'offender profiling'. *Crime linkage* is 'a form of behavioural analysis used to identify crimes committed by the same offender, through their behavioural similarity' (Woodhams, Hollin *et al.*, 2007, p.233) and sometimes their geographical or temporal proximity. It is also called *case linkage*, *linkage analysis* and *comparative case analysis*.

Offender profiling is also known by many names, including *psychological profiling*, *criminal profiling*, *investigative profiling*, *crime scene analysis* and *criminal investigative advice*.

Definitions of offender profiling also vary from the relatively narrow definition of deducing an offender's personality and characteristics from a detailed analysis of his/her crime scene behaviour (Ainsworth, 2000) to a much broader conception including estimating an offender's future level of threat, providing the police with advice regarding how to interview a suspect, and crime linkage analysis (Copson, 1995). This variation is in part due to the range of services that profilers have provided to the police and also reflects a concerted effort to move away from talking about 'offender profilers', as they are portrayed in the popular media, to referring instead to **behavioural investigative advisors** (Alison *et al.*, 2010) who provide police with a broader range of investigative support (Rainbow, 2008). For the sake of clarity, in this chapter the term 'offender profiling' refers to the practice of inferring an offender's characteristics or personality from crime scene behaviour. Behavioural investigative advice will be returned to later in the chapter, in the section tracing the evolution of offender profiling.

> **behavioural investigative advisors** experts who are employed by or consulted by the police, and who provide behavioural advice for police investigations.

Both crime linkage and offender profiling have most often been applied to serious forms of crime such as **serial murder** and *rape* and, as explained by Canter (2000), it was for the motiveless stranger crime and serial murders that psychological advice was first sought by criminal investigators. Indeed, there has been some disagreement in the literature as to which forms of crime profiling can or should be applied (Canter, 2000; Crabbe *et al.*, 2008). The opinions proffered include that it should only be applied to violent crimes, crimes where the offender expresses his/her personality, or where there is suggestion of mental dysfunction or psychopathology. In contrast, others argue that it should have a broader application. Recently, Goodwill and Alison (2007) have proposed that even within one crime type (e.g. within robberies or within rapes), some crimes will be more 'profilable' than others. The range of crime types that have been the subject of offender profiling and crime linkage research is further illustrated below.

> **serial murder** refers to a series of murders that may have been committed by the same individual(s).

CRIME LINKAGE

Although rarely mentioned in popular dramatisations of forensic psychology, crime linkage is conducted in many countries, including the USA, Canada, Australia, the UK, South Africa and New Zealand. It is practised by police employees, such as crime analysts, behavioural investigative advisors and police officers, and by consultants, such as academic psychologists. It aims to identify crimes that have been committed by the same offender. Typically, this analysis is limited to a specific type of crime, for example, searching for a series of stranger rapes committed by the same offender.

To be able accurately to identify crimes that have been committed by the same offender from crime scene behaviour requires offenders to behave in a similar way each time they commit a crime of that type. This is called the **offender consistency hypothesis** (Canter, 1995). Recently, investigations have begun as to whether offenders are consistent across crimes of different types too (Tonkin *et al.*, 2011). In the future it may therefore be possible to identify serial offenders who are versatile in their offending, committing crimes of different types (e.g. two rapes, four robberies), as well as serial offenders who specialise in crimes of the same type (e.g. six robberies). It is important to note here that offenders do not have to commit their crimes in a perfectly consistent manner for the crimes of one offender to be distinguished from the crimes of his/her peers (Bennell *et al.*, 2009). In

> **offender consistency hypothesis** the assumption that offenders will commit their crimes in a relatively consistent manner. This means that their crimes should be similar in terms of the behaviour they display.

fact, in practice, it would be very unlikely for offenders to be perfectly consistent in their crime scene behaviour because of the effect of changing environment (Davies, 1992) and the interpersonal nature of some crimes, such as rape, robbery and murder (Santtila *et al.*, 2005).

As well as needing offenders to be relatively consistent in the way they commit their crimes, it is also necessary that offenders have a degree of distinctiveness in their style of offending. If burglars committed their burglaries in exactly the same way, it would not be possible to tell one burglary series from another. This requirement of crime linkage is referred to as **behavioural distinctiveness** (Woodhams, Hollin *et al.*, 2007) or *discrimination* (Bennell & Canter, 2002): there is an implicit assumption that intra-individual behavioural variation will be less than inter-individual behavioural variation (Alison *et al.*, 2002).

> **behavioural distinctiveness** the principle that offenders commit their crimes in different ways to one another.

Identifying crimes that have been committed by the same serial offender has several advantages, including the efficient deployment of limited police resources and the pooling of witness descriptions and physical evidence from different crime scenes (Grubin *et al.*, 2001). Some crime types, such as sex offences, are notoriously difficult to prosecute and victim credibility can be pivotal in the successful prosecution of a case (Ellison, 2005). With such cases crime linkage has a further advantage. If, through crime linkage, an offender can be prosecuted for a series of offences, each victim gains credibility from the others (Davies, 1992). Crime linkage analysis has been presented in legal proceedings in the USA, Australia, the UK, South Africa and New Zealand (see Case Studies 9.1 and 9.2 for details of two cases).

CASE STUDY 9.1   THE NEWCASTLE MURDER SERIES (LABUSCHAGNE, 2006)

From February 2004 to January 2005 in the town of Newcastle in the KwaZulu-Natal province of South Africa, two young heterosexual couples were attacked by a lone male offender in the same park, whereby the female victims were raped and the male victims murdered. During the same time period, the bodies of two males were also recovered from the same area. There was no DNA evidence linking the four rapes and murders; however, the surviving rape victims from the first two crimes identified the accused during identity

parades and the accused confessed his involvement in the murders to a witness. Themba Anton Sukude was arrested following this confession to the witness. Evidence of behavioural similarity was used to support charging the accused for the third and fourth murders. Some of the similar and dissimilar behaviours identified by Brigadier Labuschagne in his linkage analysis can be seen in Table 9.1. Labuschagne's linkage analysis report was used as evidence during the trial and the accused was found guilty of all charges.

(Continued)

TABLE 9.1 *Similar and dissimilar behaviours identified by Brigadier Labuschagne in the Newcastle murder series (see Case Study 9.1).*

Crime 1 Murder and rape	Crime 2 Murder and rape	Crime 3 Murder	Crime 4 Murder
Occurred at night	Occurred at night	Occurred at night	Occurred at night
Female rape victim threatened with knife	Female rape victim threatened with knife		
Male victim killed with rock (from scene)	Male victim killed with rock (from scene)	Male victim killed with rock (from scene)	Male victim killed with rock (from scene)
Blitz (sudden) attack	Blitz (sudden) attack	Blitz (sudden) attack	Blitz (sudden) attack
Rape of female	Rape of female	Male victim found undressed (potential female rape victim?)	
No property stolen	Property stolen (telephones, purse)		No property stolen

Source: Labuschagne, 2006.

CASE STUDY 9.2   STEVEN FORTIN (HAZELWOOD & WARREN, 2003)

Steven Fortin was tried for the murder of Melissa Padilla on several occasions (Meyer, 2007). He was finally convicted and sentenced to life imprisonment without parole for her murder in June 2010. In his first trial, retired FBI profiler, Roy Hazelwood, presented evidence of behavioural similarity between the actions of the perpetrator who murdered Melissa Padilla and the behaviour displayed during a sexual offence in the state of Maine for which Steven Fortin had been convicted. Fifteen similarities in modus operandi behaviour (behaviour necessary to commit the offence) were iden-

tified, which included characteristics of the victims, the environment in which they were attacked, the use of force and the injuries they sustained as a result. In addition, five ritual behaviours, which reflect motive, were highlighted as being common to both crimes: both victims were brutally beaten about the face, manually strangled from the front, raped anally, and bitten on the chin and breast. Roy Hazelwood concluded that the 15 shared modus operandi behaviours alongside the five shared ritual behaviours formed a unique signature across the two crimes.

As noted earlier in the chapter, crime linkage also involves noting differences between the crimes under analysis and considering whether they are meaningful in terms of invalidating an opinion of linkage. In Case Study 9.2, Roy Hazelwood identified 11 differences that included the locations of the offences, the time/weekday on which they occurred, and physical characteristics of the victims (e.g. their height and weight). He explains in his article with Janet Warren (Hazelwood & Warren, 2003) that these differences can be attributed to the opportunistic nature of the crimes and the attack in Maine being disturbed by a third party, and therefore they 'pose no threat to the signature opinion' (p.316).

Crime linkage, like offender profiling, involves the detailed study of the crime scene and, where these

are available, reports from victims or witnesses as to how the offender behaved. Often it is conducted in a reactive manner (Woodhams, Bull, *et al.*, 2007) in response to a request from a police force that believe it has identified a series (through similar crime scene behaviour or through DNA matches), whereby the crime linkage practitioner might be asked to investigate whether there are other crimes that form part of the same series. Also, the police may request crime linkage analysis because they are investigating a single, very serious, offence for which they think a serial offender might be responsible.

crime linkage practitioner a person employed by the police, or who is consulted by the police, who conducts crime linkage analysis.

Where the crime linkage practitioner suspects they have identified two or more crimes that might have been committed by the same offender, they conduct a detailed analysis of the behaviour displayed at each crime scene. They identify behaviours that are common to the crimes and they consider how the behaviour displayed might differ. Where repeated behaviours are identified, the practitioner must also consider how rare these behaviours are. To do this, the practitioner needs to know how often a given behaviour is displayed by all offenders. For example, if within a series of stranger rapes the offender always ties up the victim, the practitioner would need to consider how often this behaviour occurs in all stranger rapes. This relates to the assumption of crime linkage that offenders must be relatively distinctive in their offending styles. If a behaviour is relatively rare and it occurs across all offences in the potential series, the practitioner can be more confident that these crimes were committed by the same offender and therefore represent a series. The practitioner would, however, take more than one behaviour into account when arriving at such a decision.

The practitioner might also consider the geographical locations of the offences and their closeness, as well as how closely clustered the offences are in time. The **geographical proximity** of offences is thought to be a more

geographical proximity the closeness of two (crime) locations in space.

reliable indicator of whether crimes are committed by the same offender, because offenders commit their offences within well-defined areas with which they are familiar (Bennell & Jones, 2005). If the geographical areas in which offenders commit their crimes don't overlap a great deal, crimes by the same offender should be located close together as well as being a distance away from the crimes of different offenders.

In some countries, there are large-scale police databases (Figure 9.1) that hold information about the crime scene behaviour displayed by the offender, geographical location and time/date of each crime in the database. These can be used to support crime linkage analysis since the database can be searched for crimes that are close together in time and space, and similar in crime scene behaviour. This can be done in a reactive way, following a request from an investigating officer, or in a proactive way (Woodhams, Bull et al., 2007).

Evidence-based practice

The use of crime linkage analysis to support decision-making in police investigations, as well as its use in legal proceedings, means that the implications of incorrectly linking crimes are significant (Grubin et al., 2001). Psychologists' professional practice guidelines emphasise

FIGURE 9.1 *In some countries, there are large-scale police databases that hold information about the crime scene behaviour displayed by the offender.*

Source: © Nicholas Moore. Used under licence from Shutterstock.

evidence-based practice psychological practice that is informed by the best theory and/or the best evidence available at that time.

the importance of engaging in **evidence-based practice** and using the best research evidence (e.g. American Psychological Association, 2007; Health Professions Council, 2009). It is therefore important that the principles underpinning crime linkage are demonstrated to be empirically supported and that research findings continue to inform how crime linkage is conducted in practice. As stated above, crime linkage rests on two assumptions; those of behavioural consistency and distinctiveness. Research studies have been accumulating since the 1970s (Green *et al.*, 1976) to the present day on the consistency and distinctiveness of criminal behaviour and a considerably larger body of research spanning many decades exists regarding the *consistency* and *distinctiveness* of non-criminal behaviour (Pervin, 2002).

Empirical evidence

The study of (non-criminal) behavioural consistency and distinctiveness has a long history, which has been characterised by fierce debates as to whether people were consistent across situations or not, and whether behaviour was the product of personality or the situation (van Mechelen & de Raad, 1999). Modern models of person-

cognitive-affective personality system (CAPS) a model of personality devised by Mischel and Shoda (1995).

ality recognise that behaviour is a product of personality *and* the situation (e.g. the **cognitive-affective personality system (CAPS)**, Mischel & Shoda, 1995). According to these models, psychological features of situations activate or inhibit mental representations (such as goals, beliefs, expectations, plans and memories) producing behaviour. Situations with similar psychological features are hypothesised to produce similar behaviour because they will trigger similar mental representations (Mischel, 1999). Personality systems, such as the CAPS, develop over time, particularly during childhood and adolescence (Pervin, 2002), and are unique to the individual in terms of the patterns and strengths of associations between mental representations (Zayas & Shoda, 2009). These models predict behavioural consistency under certain conditions (when encountering psychologically-similar situations), but also inter-individual variation in behaviour. Also, as explained by Zayas and Shoda (2009), when in a situation where two people interact, one actor's behaviour becomes the other actor's situation (see Figure 9.2). Psychologists have tested these hypotheses and predictions and have found evidence of behavioural consistency in situations of psychological similarity as well as different behaviour produced by different people in the same situation (Shoda *et al.*, 1994).

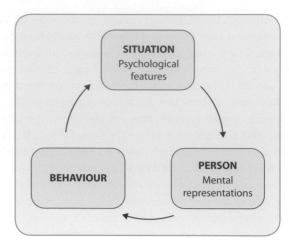

FIGURE 9.2 *The interaction between the situation and the person in producing behaviour (e.g. the cognitive affective personality system).* Source: Mischel & Shoda (1995). Reproduced with permission of APA.

In comparison to the volume of research conducted on the consistency and distinctiveness of non-criminal behaviour, the research on the consistency and distinctiveness of criminal behaviour is in its infancy. A range of crime types have been investigated by researchers, including interpersonal types of crime such as murder (e.g. Bateman & Salfati, 2007), sexual offences (e.g. Bennell *et al.*, 2009) and robbery (Woodhams & Toye, 2007); and acquisitive forms of crime, such as burglary (e.g. Bennell & Jones, 2005) and car theft (Tonkin *et al.*, 2008). Arson has also been studied (Santtila, Fritzon *et al.*, 2004). Broadly speaking, studies of **acquisitive crime** have found only limited evidence for consistency and distinctiveness in crime scene behaviour within series. In contrast, studies of interpersonal types

acquisitive crime types of crime that involve property being stolen or acquired fraudulently.

of crime report being able to identify, with a good degree of accuracy, crimes from the same series using similarity in crime scene behaviour. This provides support for the two underlying assumptions of crime linkage with interpersonal types of crime. This doesn't mean that offenders who commit acquisitive forms of crime are not consistent and distinctive too. Instead, it is possible that they are but that the information that the police have about how they behave during the offence is too limited. This is not surprising when you consider that car theft or burglary often happens without a witness being present who can subsequently describe the offender's behaviour to the police. Instead, the behaviours engaged in by the offender have to be inferred from what's left at the crime scene.

For acquisitive forms of crime, crimes from the same series can be identified most accurately using geographical and temporal proximity (e.g. Goodwill & Alison, 2006; Markson *et al.*, 2010). These variables are also good at predicting whether crimes belong to the same series for interpersonal forms of crime (Woodhams & Toye, 2007). However, the effectiveness of geographical proximity for linking varies for different crimes. Bennell and Jones (2005) found it to be more effective for residential burglaries than commercial burglaries. As reported above, geographical proximity will best identify series when the geographical areas in which criminals offend overlap the least (the distinctiveness element of crime linkage). As explained by Bennell and Jones, commercial properties tend to be clustered together, therefore the spaces in which commercial burglars commit their crimes overlap to a greater degree.

There are several reasons for the success of geographical proximity when linking crimes. One suggestion is that crime location data is objective and less open to interpretation when compared to crime scene behaviour (Alison et al., 2001). It is also routinely collected by police officers when investigating a crime (Tonkin et al., 2008). A further explanation is that the decision of where to commit a crime is under the offender's control and therefore is less likely to be distorted by situational factors than, say, a behaviour such as the type of property stolen, which can depend on what is available in the premises (Bennell & Canter, 2002).

Returning to the issue of evidence-based practice, it is too early in the research process to make firm recommendations for conducting crime linkage. However, what researchers have found so far suggests that for acquisitive forms of crime, geographical proximity (and to a lesser extent, temporal proximity) should be used for deciding if crimes form part of the same series. The research findings for interpersonal forms of crime, at least in terms of robbery and sexual offences, are more promising in terms of using crime scene behaviour to identify crime series. In addition to offending in relatively specific areas, robbers and sex offenders also seem to show a degree of consistency and distinctiveness in their crime scene behaviour.

Evaluations of the effectiveness of crime linkage

The existing research suggests that crime linkage may be effective, provided appropriate **indicators of series membership** are used. However, it is important to note that the way in which crime linkage is researched does not necessarily reflect how it is conducted in practice. There has been no large-scale systematic study of the effectiveness of crime linkage in practice. To do this would require the predictions of series membership by practitioners to be recorded and followed up after a specified time period to determine if the crimes were indeed committed by the same offender, as predicted,

> **indicators of series membership** features of a crime, which could be behavioural, spatial or temporal, which suggest that it belongs to a crime series.

or not. Clearly, to assess this requires serial offenders to be detected and convicted and with some crime types the low detection/conviction rate would make this difficult. This is not unlike the research on risk assessment whereby practitioners make predictions about offenders' risk of re-offending and after a specified time period the criminal records of the offenders are checked to see if they did or did not re-offend in the time period.

Anecdotal reports and case studies of the success of crime linkage do exist (e.g. Collins et al., 1998; Labuschagne, 2006). In addition, two experimental studies have assessed the relative performance of experts and novices on a crime linkage task (Bennell et al., 2010; Santtila, Korpela et al., 2004). Santtila, Korpela et al. (2004) tested the ability of experienced car crime investigators, experienced investigators of other crime types, novice investigators and naive participants to link series of car theft. The experienced car crime investigators were the most accurate. They used fewer features when making decisions about series membership and the features they focused on represented behaviours that would be under the offender's control, such as type of vehicle and the time and location of the offence. Bennell et al. (2010) investigated how accurately university students and police professionals could link burglary series. This time the novices (students) performed better at the linking task than the police professionals. From the comments made by some of the professionals, this might be because they were relying on behaviours that research suggests are less effective for identifying series (e.g. how the premise was selected, how it was entered and what was stolen). (It is important to note that Santtila, Korpela et al. (2004) distinguished between experts in linking car theft and experts in linking other crime types in their study, whereas Bennell et al. (2010) did not differentiate their professionals in this way. This might account for the differences in findings.) Interestingly, training based on the empirical research on linking burglaries improved performance in both groups.

Conclusions on crime linkage

Identifying crime series has several advantages to the police and can benefit society. However, if a crime linkage practitioner gives the police or the courts inaccurate advice, the consequences are significant. It is therefore important that crime linkage is assessed and shown to be a valid practice. Studies testing the principles of case linkage are accumulating and suggest that accurate crime linkage may be possible if appropriate indicators of series membership are attended to. However, these vary depending on the crime type being investigated. Two experimental studies of experts' performance at a crime linkage task have produced conflicting results but indicate the scale of the errors that can stem from using inappropriate behaviours to link crimes. This, and Bennell *et al.*'s (2010) finding that training improved performance on a linking task, highlights the importance of disseminating research findings regarding crime linkage to practitioners. What this area of forensic psychology is lacking at present is a real-world assessment of crime linkage whereby predictions about series membership are made and systematically followed up to determine accuracy.

OFFENDER PROFILING

In contrast to crime linkage, offender profiling is the topic of a considerable number of scholarly articles and book chapters, as well as forms of popular media (Figure 9.3). It is a contentious area and strong opinions exist. As you will see, 'offender profiling' does not refer to a uniform practice and how it is conducted has evolved over time, and continues to evolve. In researching it, we often have to use data that is held and collated by police forces, which presents its own difficulties in terms of the quality of the data (Alison *et al.*, 2001). If you are considering studying this field, the sheer volume of literature to get

FIGURE 9.3 *The contentious area of offender profiling is the topic of a considerable number of scholarly articles as well as popular media, including TV series such as Cracker.*

Source: © ITV / Rex Features. ITV Archive Poster with Robbie Coltrane, used for *Cracker* – 2006. Reprinted with permission.

to grips with can be quite daunting. While it is an exciting area to research and study, it is also challenging.

Quite a lot of the debate within this field relates to whether offender profiling is, or should be, an art or a science. As psychologists, it is important that our practice is evidence-based and therefore empirical research of the underpinnings of offender profiling is crucial. Before considering this empirical research, the history of offender profiling and some of the major ways in which it has developed will be briefly outlined.

The roots of offender profiling have been traced back to Dr Thomas Bond, who provided the UK police with an opinion regarding Jack the Ripper's physical appearance, likely dress, state of mind and motivation for a series of murders in London in 1880 (Canter, 2004). However, as Canter (2004) explains, it was through the activities of the FBI in the USA that offender profiling gained its fame. The use of offender profiling (and behavioural investigative advice) to guide police investigations has since spread to other countries including Australia, Canada, Finland, Germany, Sweden, the Netherlands and Singapore (Alison *et al.*, 2010; Davis & Bennett, 2006; Snook *et al.*, 2008). In 1995, Copson reported that in the previous decade some type of offender profiling advice had been sought (including crime linkage analysis) in more than 200 British police investigations.

Offender profilers come from a variety of professional backgrounds. A study in 1995 in the UK of 184 instances of profiling advice reported that the advice had been sought from forensic, clinical and academic psychologists, forensic and clinical psychiatrists, police officers and police scientists (Copson, 1995). A recent international review of the admittance of expert evidence on offender profiling and crime scene analysis in the courts (Bosco *et al.*, 2010) produced similar results: criminologists, psychiatrists, psychologists and FBI special agents had all served as expert witnesses regarding offender profiling. The three main areas on which they had testified were motivation for the crime, whether the behaviour of an offender corresponded with particular personal characteristics, and evidence of linkage between crimes.

With such a long history, we might expect offender profiling to have been the subject of a considerable body of scientific research. Recently, two literature reviews have been conducted on offender profiling to determine the nature of its underpinning literature (Dowden *et al.*, 2007; Snook *et al.*, 2007). From a literature search spanning 31 years, Dowden *et al.* (2007) identified a sizable literature regarding offender profiling, some 132 articles; however, most articles were 'discussion pieces' with only the minority of articles reporting inferential statistics. Similarly, a narrative review by Snook *et al.* (2007) of 130 articles on criminal profiling concluded that most writing on the subject used 'common sense' rationales rather than empirically-based rationales. This lack of empirical research is a cause for concern in light of psychological principles of evidence-based practice. As Dowden *et al.* (2007) argue, empirical research is needed for offender profiling to be seen as a 'legitimate field of study within the behavioral sciences' (p.52). The few empirical studies of the principles underpinning offender profiling will be returned to below.

Schools of thought in offender profiling

When talking about the history of offender profiling, it is often categorised into three different schools of thought (Alison *et al.*, 2010):

- the *criminal investigative approach* (also called the *FBI approach*, *criminal investigative analysis* or *crime scene analysis*);
- the *clinical-practitioner approach* (also known as *diagnostic evaluation*); and
- the *statistical approach* (sometimes known as *investigative psychology*).

A very brief and simplified outline of each approach is given below. The key difference between these three approaches is the *knowledge base* used by the offender profiler to make inferences about an offender's characteristics from his/her crime scene behaviour. Other approaches that are referred to are *crime action profiling* (Kocsis, 2007) and *behavioural evidence analysis* (Turvey, 2008). These are not discussed further here but the interested reader can find out more from the cited sources.

The criminal investigative approach

The criminal investigative approach to profiling is informed by the investigator's extensive knowledge developed from exposure to a large number of cases and their experience of criminal investigations (Canter, 2004). In addition, the FBI conducted interviews with incarcerated rapists and murderers, from which typologies of offenders were developed (Wilson *et al.*, 1997). For example, in-depth interviews with 36 convicted sexually-motivated serial murderers were incorporated with the extensive investigative experience of members of the FBI Behavioral Science Unit to produce a typology of murderers (Jackson & Bekerian, 1997) to determine from crime scene behaviour whether a murderer could be classified as organised, disorganised or mixed. An organised murderer would show evidence of having planned the crime, of having committed the crime in a controlled manner, leaving few or no clues and with a stranger as a target (Jackson & Bekerian, 1997). In developing the typology, offender characteristics were

---

> ## BOX 9.1   THE FBI APPROACH TO PROFILING
>
> According to Jackson and Bekerian (1997), the steps followed in constructing an offender profile according to the FBI approach are:
>
> - *Data assimilation* – at this stage the profiler must collate all available information about the crime. This can include written materials (e.g. victim or witness statements, autopsy reports) or visual materials (e.g. CCTV or photographs).
> - *Crime classification* – the crime is classified into a type using the collated information.
> - *Crime reconstruction* – hypotheses about how the crime unfolded are developed in terms of the sequence of events, the behaviours of the different parties (e.g. victim, offender(s)).
> - *Profile generation* – the profile is generated including hypotheses about the offender's sociodemographic characteristics, and his/her habits and personality. According to Jackson and Bekerian (1997), the profiles produced tend to be written in a standardised manner.

associated with each classification and thus, in practice, predictions could be made about an offender's characteristics by classifying the murder into one of three types based on an examination of their crime scene behaviour. For example, an organised murder would be committed by someone who lived an orderly life, was of average to high intelligence, socially competent and likely to be engaged in skilled employment (Canter *et al.*, 2004).

The clinical approach

Several authors have noted that there is no one approach to 'clinical profiling' (Mullen, 2000; Wilson *et al.*, 1997). Some clinical profilers (Copson *et al.* 1997) have likened their approach to that of the original FBI profilers, interpreting the offender's motive and drawing on psychological literature (e.g. personality theory, Boon, 1997) to make predictions about the offender's characteristics. Boon (1997) has stressed that the aim of clinical profiling is not to solve a case, but to provide 'insight into the nature of both the case and the offender(s)' (p.46). Like the criminal investigative approach, as well as using psychological theory, clinical profilers draw on their accrued experience. Rather than this being experience of criminal investigations, clinical profilers draw on their experience of working with clients in a forensic mental health setting that can be applied to the case under investigation (Alison *et al.*, 2004). Predictions about an offender's personality or characteristics are made by drawing on 'multiple observations of single cases' (Bekerian & Jackson, 1997, p.210).

According to Boon (1997) and Copson et al. (1997), the clinical profiler begins by collating all information available about the crime, including details of the victim, the crime scene and the circumstances of the offence. This might include visiting the crime scene itself. From this, the profiler must identify the 'crime type at a fundamental level (e.g. murder) and then move on to be more specific about its character' (Boon, 1997, pp.45–46), in terms of the weapons used, the nature and extent of the victim's injuries, and so on. The profiler must attempt to understand what happened, how (in detail) and to whom, and thereby reconstruct the criminal event (Copson et al., 1997). Copson et al. (1997) explain that the clinical profiler will be looking for evidence of emotion, desires, moods and psychopathology in the case material. Having identified the salient elements of the offence, the profiler selects a personality theory, or theories, which will help explain the offence in question as well as being appropriate to the operational needs of the police investigation (Boon, 1997). The psychological literature is drawn upon to understand the offender's motive and suggest offender characteristics (Copson et al., 1997).

The statistical approach

The statistical approach to profiling, attributed to Professor David Canter and his colleagues, 'is primarily based on the multivariate analysis of behavioural and other information found at the crime scene to infer an offender's characteristics and psychological processes' (Alison et al., 2010, p.118). Canter (2000) sees offender profiling as being firmly rooted in the discipline of psychology and argues that offender profiling is similar to other areas of psychology. In occupational psychology, for example, psychologists try to predict someone's future behaviour in the workplace based on what we know about their characteristics (as ascertained from psychometric tests). Canter (2000) argues that this is not dissimilar to what the offender profiler is trying to achieve, whereby they are attempting the reverse: to predict someone's likely characteristics based on what we know of their behaviour.

In constructing his/her profile, the statistical profiler will use statistically-derived relationships between crime scene behaviour and offender characteristics that have been generated from databases of similar solved crimes and apprehended criminals, to make predictions about the characteristics of the suspect in question (Snook et al., 2007). The statistical approach to profiling is therefore a research-oriented approach to profiling, and many studies exist that have tried to identify bivariate relationships between single crime scene behaviours and single

offender characteristics (e.g. Davies et al., 1998; House, 1997) or that have clustered together crime scene behaviours to identify styles of offending, with the aim of investigating whether particular offender characteristics are more often associated with a particular style of offending (e.g. Canter & Fritzon, 1998; Canter & Heritage, 1990). For example, several studies of different crime types, including rape, paedophilic sex offences and homicides, have reported similar 'modes of interpersonal transaction' (Canter, 2000, p.37) between the offender and the victim. These modes are the offender treating the victim as a *person* (where there are attempts at building rapport or a relationship), as an *object* (where the victim is used and controlled for the offender's gain) and as a *vehicle* for the offender's emotional state. The statistical profiler could therefore make predictions about an offender's characteristics based on the observation of him/her displaying one or more single crime scene behaviours (e.g. the use of bindings or the use of gloves) or they could determine the offender's dominant style of offending, or mode of interaction, and refer to the research literature regarding the common characteristics found to be associated with this style or mode.

The dominant schools of thought in offender profiling that have evolved differ from one another in terms of their incorporation of research findings to justify the predictions being made in the offender profile, and the emphasis they place on psychological theory and/or practitioner experience. In 1997, Bekerian and Jackson expressed concern that the offender profiling field might become fractured, and argued that offender profiling would better develop as a field if consideration were given to 'hybrid profiling techniques' incorporating both the statistical analysis of large databases as well as experience of salient case studies. To an extent, this is being realised; according to Alison et al. (2010), such divisions are less relevant nowadays due to the emergence of 'a more pragmatic, interdisciplinary practitioner–academic model' (p.115).

The assumptions of offender profiling

As was mentioned earlier in this chapter, literature reviews have highlighted the lack of empirical research on offender profiling. One area where empirical research has been conducted, although it is limited, is the investigation of the assumptions of offender profiling. Offender profiling shares two assumptions with crime linkage, those of offender behavioural consistency and distinctiveness, and thus the empirical research on these assumptions has already been described above. In addition, offender profiling assumes that there is a relationship between the way someone behaves at a crime scene and their characteristics/personality. This has been called the A(ctions) → C(haracteristics) relationship (Canter, 1995). If such relationships exist, it follows that offenders who behave in a similar way when committing their offences should be similar to one another in terms of their characteristics or personality, or conversely that offenders with different offending styles should be different in their characteristics/personality. This has been termed the **homology assumption** (Mokros & Alison, 2002). A recent review (Doan & Snook, 2008) outlined six studies of the homology assumption. These had sampled arsons, rapes and robberies. Little supporting evidence for the homology assumption was found.

homology assumption the assumption that, because there is a relationship between crime scene actions and offender characteristics, offenders with similar crime scene behaviour will share similar characteristics.

As explained by Goodwill and Alison (2007), one reason for the failure of studies to find evidence for the homology assumption might be because researchers have considered all crime scene behaviours to be equally effective in predicting offender characteristics. Rather, this may be 'dependent on the extent to which the behaviors enacted are influenced by situational, psychological or interpersonal factors' (Goodwill & Alison, 2007, p.824). The role of the interaction between the person and the situation in producing behaviour was referred to earlier and is something that offender profiling researchers have been highlighting as an area in need of research for some time (Alison et al., 2002).

Further, there needs to be a theoretical framework that explains why we would expect certain sociodemographic variables to be associated with certain crime scene behaviours (Mokros & Alison, 2002; see Figure 9.4). The offender characteristics tested in studies of the homology assumption (e.g. age, ethnicity, employment, education, marital status, criminal history and journey-to-crime distance) were selected because they are commonly predicted in offender profiles (Mokros & Alison, 2002). However, it has been questioned whether, based on models of personality, we should expect relationships between crime scene behaviour and demographic characteristics. Instead, relationships between crime scene behaviour and someone's developmental history (e.g. past learning experiences) or how they act in non-criminal situations are more likely (Woodhams & Toye, 2007).

Recently, theories from evolutionary psychology, consumer psychology, social psychology and criminology were used to explain why we might expect to find relationships between the cost of footwear worn to the crime scene by burglars (as ascertained from **shoemark evidence** left at the scene) and their characteristics (age and

shoemark evidence physical forensic evidence left at a crime scene, consisting of an impression of the shoe/footwear worn by the offender.

FIGURE 9.4 The roots of offender profiling have been traced back to Dr. Thomas Bond who provided the UK police with an opinion regarding Jack the Ripper's physical appearance, likely dress, state of mind and motivation for a series of murders in London in 1880.
Source: © Anelina. Used under licence from Shutterstock.

gender, employment status, relative deprivation of his/her residence) (Tonkin et al., 2009). The homology assumption was tested in terms of assessing (1) whether offenders who wore footwear of a similar cost were of a similar age and lived in a residence of similar deprivation; and (2) whether offenders of different genders and different employment status wore footwear of a significantly different cost. Support for the homology assumption was found for the offenders' employment status and the deprivation of their residences. Other theoretically-informed investigations of the homology assumption might also be fruitful.

In addition, it has been argued that it's naïve to expect crime scene actions to map onto offender characteristics in a simple manner and instead we should develop our understanding of the processes (e.g. personality) that underlie the relationship between criminal actions and characteristics (Youngs, 2004). Similarly, Goodwill and colleagues (Goodwill & Alison, 2007; Goodwill et al., 2009) have called for studies that investigate variables that moderate our ability to predict characteristics from crime scene behaviour. For example, in their study, Goodwill and Alison (2007) demonstrated that it was possible to predict offender age from victim age, but only where the offender had engaged in planning and where excessive violence was used.

It might therefore be possible to predict *some* offender characteristics from *some* crime scene behaviours, where we have a theoretical framework that accounts for such a relationship, and perhaps only in certain circumstances. This shifts the focus onto individual crime scene behaviours, which also better reflects how some practitioners conduct profiling: Ter Beek *et al.* (2010) recently highlighted that when conducting offender profiling in the Netherlands, practitioners focus on individual crime scene behaviours rather than classifying offenders into types (i.e. offending styles or interactional modes).

Evaluations of offender profiles

The content of offender profiles is another area that has been the recipient of scrutiny and subsequent criticism. In 2003, Alison *et al.* analysed 21 offender profiles written from 1992 to 2001 by profilers from the USA, the UK and other European countries where the offender had subsequently been convicted. The three main schools of thought (i.e. statistical, criminal investigative and clinical) were all represented in the sample. The profiles contained nearly 880 claims about offenders' characteristics. These reports came under criticism because Alison *et al.* (2003) found that over half of the claims made could not be verified post-conviction because, for example, they pertained to how the offender was feeling at the time of the offence. More than 20 per cent of claims were vague or open to interpretation, and for more than 80 per cent of the claims the profiler failed to provide any justification for the advice offered.

In 2007, Almond *et al.* conducted a similar analysis of 45 reports written in 2005 by behavioural investigative advisors employed by the National Policing Improvement Agency (NPIA). These reports pertained to predictions of offender characteristics, the veracity of victim allegations, linkage analysis and geographical profiling. The reports contained 805 claims. Ninety-six per cent of the claims were accompanied by some form of justification, but only 34 per cent were formally supported. Seventy per cent of the claims were verifiable, 43 per cent were falsifiable, and only 8 per cent were ambiguous.

In the UK at least, the reports of offender profilers who are approved by the Association of Chief Police Officers (ACPO) or who are employed by the NPIA are audited and evaluated for their quality (Rainbow, 2008). In addition, interpretations and investigative suggestions made within the reports produced by ACPO and NPIA offender profilers must be supported by evidence and/or

a rationale, and if the reports are not of a sufficient quality, ACPO-approved status can be revoked

In summary, whilst criticisms have been made regarding the content of offender profiles, steps are being taken to establish professional standards and assessments suggest the quality of some offender profiling reports are improving. For published examples of actual offender profiling reports, the interested reader is referred to Alison *et al.* (2004) and Alison (2005).

Evaluations of the effectiveness of offender profiling

Within the popular literature on offender profiling, one does not have to look far to find reports of the effectiveness of offender profiling. Several authors have highlighted that there is a 'plethora' of positive anecdotes about the use of offender profiling but that empirical support for these claims is lacking (Snook *et al.*, 2008; Woskett *et al.*, 2007). Snook *et al.* (2008) also caution that these anecdotes can be misleading, for example, where profilers report the *number* of correct predictions made rather than the *proportion* (which would take account of incorrect predictions). They illustrate this point with an example where authors of a profile reported that they made 11 correct predictions; however, Snook *et al.* (2008) note that the profile was actually only 38 per cent accurate when the 18 incorrect predictions were also taken into account.

Several assessments of offender profiling advice from the perspectives of the users also exist, which have been conducted in different countries including the UK and the Netherlands. In 1995, Copson surveyed 126 detectives in the UK who had received offender profiling advice from 29 different profilers. This advice included predicting the characteristics of unknown offenders, advice regarding interviewing strategy and linkage analysis. Over 50 per cent of the detectives felt that the advice had provided them with new information but it was uncommon for the detectives to act on the advice directly or for the advice to assist in solving the case. Despite this, 69 per cent of the detectives said they would seek the advice of a profiler again. Similar findings were reported by Jackson *et al.* (1997) following their survey of 20 detective teams in Belgium and the Netherlands who had received offender profiling advice. The range of advice was similar to that reported by Copson (1995). Of the 42 evaluations made, only two were entirely negative. In only six cases did the advice relate to predicting offender characteristics. For these six cases, one evaluation was negative, three were intermediate and two were positive; however, an offender was not apprehended as a direct result in any of these cases.

As well as seeking the views of the users (Copson, 1995), Gudjonsson and Copson (1997) were able to assess the accuracy of the claims made in 50 offender profiles where the offender had subsequently been apprehended. Of the items of advice that could be assessed for accuracy, 68 per cent of the items of advice offered by 'statistical profilers' and 74 per cent by 'clinical profilers' were judged to be accurate. Like the more recent studies of the content of profiles (Alison *et al.*, 2003; Almond *et al.*, 2007), Gudjonsson and Copson (1997) criticised the vague nature of some claims that were made. Whilst the users of offender profiling advice seem content with the service received and that a number of the claims made have been found to be correct, such evaluations are not without their critics. Canter (2000), for example, criticised them for being premature, bearing in mind the limited evidence for the underlying assumptions of offender profiling.

SUMMARY

- Both offender profiling and crime linkage can be of great benefit in detecting offenders, but equally both can divert police investigations down the 'wrong track' if the advice given is incorrect (Goodwill *et al.*, 2009; Grubin *et al.*, 2001).

- The linking together of crimes to form a series based on behavioural similarity is called *crime linkage analysis*. It is widely practiced but is rarely discussed in the popular media.

- The prediction of offender characteristics or personality from crime scene behaviour is referred to as *offender profiling* but its practice is not as uniform as this definition would suggest.

- Several schools of thought regarding how a person's characteristics should be profiled from crime scene behaviour have developed; however, these are making way for a more integrated approach to profiling.

- A broader range of *behavioural investigative advice* is now offered to the police, which incorporates offender profiling and crime linkage analysis.

- Both crime linkage and offender profiling have been evaluated against the principle of *evidence-based practice*. Whilst the behavioural consistency and distinctiveness assumptions of offender profiling (in its narrowest sense) and crime linkage have received support from psychological research, these studies have their limitations and do not yet reflect the reality of the task faced by practitioners. Investigations of the *homology assumption* have been less successful.

- The importance of the situation in producing behaviour through its interaction with the person has long been recognised in psychological research of non-criminal behaviour. This suggests that a more complex view of the relationship between criminal actions and offender characteristics is needed.

ESSAY/DISCUSSION QUESTIONS

1. How does the media portrayal of offender profiling differ from actual practice?

2. Critically evaluate the empirical evidence for the assumptions underpinning crime linkage and offender profiling.

3. How do the different schools of thought in offender profiling differ from one another?

4. If you received funding to conduct a research project on offender profiling or crime linkage, what study would you choose to conduct and why? You should critique the scope and quality of the previous research in arriving at your answer.

REFERENCES

Ainsworth, P.B. (2000). *Psychology and crime: Myths and reality.* Harlow, England: Longman.

Alison, L.J. (Ed.) (2005). *The forensic psychologist's casebook: Psychological profiling and criminal investigation.* Abington, Oxford: Willan.

Alison, L.J., Bennell, C., Mokros, A. & Ormerod, D. (2002). The personality paradox in offender profiling: A theoretical review of the processes involved in deriving background characteristics from crime scene actions. *Psychology, Public Policy and Law, 8,* 115–135.

Alison, L.J., Goodwill, A., Almond, L., van den Heuvel, C. & Winter, J. (2010). Pragmatic solutions to offender profiling and behavioural investigative advice. *Legal and Criminological Psychology, 15,* 115–132.

Alison, L.J., Smith, M. & Morgan, K. (2003). Interpreting the accuracy of offender profiles. *Psychology, Crime and Law, 9,* 185–195.

Alison, L.J., Snook, B. & Stein, K.L. (2001). Unobtrusive measurement: Using police information for forensic research. *Qualitative Research, 1,* 241–254.

Alison, L., West, A. & Goodwill, A. (2004). The academic and the practitioner: Pragmatists' views of offender profiling. *Psychology, Public Policy and Law, 10,* 71–101.

Almond, L., Alison, L. & Porter, L. (2007). An evaluation and comparison of claims made in behavioural investigative advice reports compiled by the National Policing Improvement Agency in the United Kingdom. *Journal of Investigative Psychology and Offender Profiling, 4,* 71–83.

American Psychological Association (2007). *Guidelines for psychological practice with girls and women.* Retrieved 22 August 2011 from www.apa.org/practice/guidelines/girls-and-women.pdf

Bateman, A.L. & Salfati, C.G. (2007). An examination of behavioral consistency using individual behaviors or groups of behaviors in serial homicide. *Behavioral Sciences and the Law, 25,* 527–544.

Bekerian, D.A. & Jackson, J.L. (1997). Critical issues in offender profiling. In J.L. Jackson & D.A. Bekerian (Eds.) *Offender profiling: Theory, research and practice* (pp.209–220). Chichester: John Wiley & Sons, Inc.

Bennell, C., Bloomfield, S., Snook, B., Taylor, P.J. & Barnes, C. (2010). Linkage analysis in cases of serial burglary: Comparing the performance of university students, forensic professionals, and a logistic regression model. *Psychology, Crime, and Law, 16,* 507–524.

Bennell, C. & Canter, D. (2002). Linking commercial burglaries by *modus operandi:* Tests using regression and ROC analysis. *Science and Justice, 42,* 1–12.

Bennell, C. & Jones, N.J. (2005). Between a ROC and a hard place: A method for linking serial burglaries by *modus operandi. Journal of Investigative Psychology and Offender Profiling, 2,* 23–41.

Bennell, C., Jones, N.J. & Melnyk, T. (2009). Addressing problems with traditional crime linking methods using receiver operating characteristic analysis. *Legal and Criminological Psychology, 14,* 293–310.

Bennett, D. & Davis, M.R. (2004, November). *The Australian forensic reference group: A multidisciplinary collaborative approach to profiling violent crime.* Paper presented at the Australian Institute of Criminology International Conference, Melbourne, Australia.

Boon, J.C.W. (1997). The contribution of personality theories to psychological profiling. In J.L. Jackson & D.A. Bekerian (Eds.) *Offender profiling: Theory, research and practice* (pp.43–59). Chichester: John Wiley & Sons, Inc.

Bosco, D., Zappala, A. & Santtila, P. (2010). The admissibility of offender profiling in the courtroom: A review of legal issues and court opinions. *International Journal of Law and Psychiatry, 33,* 184–191.

Canter, D. (1995). Psychology of offender profiling. In R. Bull & D. Carson (Eds.) *Handbook of psychology in legal contexts* (pp.343–355). Chichester: John Wiley & Sons, Inc.

Canter, D. (2000). Offender profiling and criminal differentiation. *Legal and Criminological Psychology, 5,* 23–46.

Canter, D. (2004). Offender profiling and investigative psychology. *Journal of Investigative Psychology and Offender Profiling, 1,* 1–15.

Canter, D., Alison, L, Alison, E. & Wentink, N. (2004). The organized/disorganized typology of serial murder: Myth of model? *Psychology, Public Policy and Law, 10,* 293–320.

Canter, D. & Fritzon, K. (1998). Differentiating arsonists: A model of firesetting actions and characteristics. *Legal and Criminological Psychology, 3,* 73–96.

Canter, D. & Heritage, R. (1990). A multivariate model of sexual offences behavior: Developments in offender profiling. *Journal of Forensic Psychiatry, 1,* 185–212.

Collins, P.I., Johnson, G.F., Choy, A., Davidson, K.T. & Mackay, R.E. (1998). Advances in violent crime analysis and law enforcement: The Canadian Violent Crime Linkage Analysis System. *Journal of Government Information, 25,* 277–284.

Copson, G. (1995). *Coals to Newcastle? Part 1: A study of offender profiling* (Special Interest Series Paper 7). London: Home Office.

Copson, G., Badcock, R., Boon, J. & Britton, P. (1997). Editorial: Articulating a systematic approach to clinical crime profiling. *Legal and Criminological Psychology, 7,* 13–17.

Crabbe, A., Decoene, S. & Vertommen, H. (2008). Profiling homicide offenders: A review of assumptions and theories. *Aggression and Violent Behavior, 13,* 88–106.

Davies, A. (1991). The use of DNA profiling and behavioural science in the investigation of sexual offences. *Medicine, Science & Law, 31,* 95–101.

Davies, A. (1992). Rapists' behaviour: A three aspect model as a basis for analysis and the identification of serial crime. *Forensic Science International, 55*, 173–194.

Davies, A., Wittebrood, K. & Jackson, J.L. (1998). *Predicting the criminal record of the stranger rapist* (Special Interest Series Paper 12). London: Home Office

Davis, M. & Bennett, D. (2006) Criminal investigative analysis in the Australian context. *InPsych, October.*

Doan, B. & Snook. B. (2008). A failure to find empirical support for the homology assumption in offender profiling. *Journal of Police and Criminal Psychology, 23*, 61–70.

Dowden, C., Bennell, C. & Bloomfield, S. (2007). Advances in offender profiling: A systematic review of the profiling literature published over the last three decades. *Journal of Police and Criminal Psychology, 22*, 44–56.

Durnal, E.W. (2010). Crime scene investigation (as seen on TV). *Forensic Science International, 199*, 1–5.

Ellison, L. (2005). Closing the credibility gap: The prosecutorial use of expert witness testimony in sexual assault cases. *The International Journal of Evidence and Proof, 9*, 239–268.

Farrington, D.P. & West, D.J. (1993). Criminal, penal and life histories of chronic offenders: Risk and protective factors and early identification. *Criminal Behaviour and Mental Health, 3*, 492–523.

Federal Bureau of Investigation. (2008). *Serial murder: Multi-disciplinary perspectives for investigators.* Washington, DC: US Department of Justice.

Goodwill, A. & Alison, L. (2006). The development of a filter model for prioritizing suspects in burglary offences. *Psychology, Crime and Law, 12*, 395–416.

Goodwill, A. & Alison, L. (2007). When is profiling possible? Offense planning and aggression as moderators in predicting offenders' age from victim age in stranger rape. *Behavioral Sciences and the Law, 25*, 823–840.

Goodwill, A.M., Alison, L.J. & Beech, A.R. (2009). What works in offender profiling? A comparison of typological, thematic and multivariate models. *Behavioral Sciences and the Law, 27*, 507–529.

Green, E.J., Booth, C.E. & Biderman, M.D. (1976). Cluster analysis of burglary M/O's. *Journal of Police Science and Administration, 4*, 382–388.

Grubin, D., Kelly, P. & Brunsdon, C. (2001). *Linking serious sexual assaults through behavior.* Home Office Research Study 215. London: Home Office.

Gudjonsson, G.H. & Copson, G. (1997). The role of the expert in criminal investigation. In J.L. Jackson & D.A. Bekerian (Eds.) *Offender profiling. Theory, research and practice* (pp.61–76). Chichester: John Wiley & Sons, Inc.

Hazelwood, R.R. & Warren, J.I. (2003). Linkage analysis: Modus operandi, ritual, and signature in serial sexual crime. *Aggression and Violent Behavior, 8*, 587–598.

Health Professions Council (2009). *Standards of proficiency: Practitioner psychologists.* London: The Health Professions Council.

Home Office (2007). *Crime in England and Wales 2006/7.* London: Home Office.

House, J.C. (1997). Towards a practical application of offender profiling: The RNC's criminal suspect prioritization system. In J.L. Jackson & D.A. Bekerian (Eds.) *Offender profiling: Theory, research and practice* (pp.177–190). Chichester: John Wiley & Sons, Inc.

Innes, M., Fielding, N. & Cope, N. (2005). The appliance of science? The theory and practice of criminal intelligence analysis. *British Journal of Criminology, 45*, 39–57.

Jackson, J.L. & Bekerian, D.A. (1997). Does offender profiling have a role to play? In J.L. Jackson & D.A. Bekerian (Eds.) *Offender profiling: Theory, research and practice* (pp.1 7). Chichester: John Wiley & Sons, Inc.

Jackson, J.L., van Koppen, P.J. & Herbrink, J.C.M. (1997). *Does the service meet the needs? An evaluation of the consumer satisfaction with specific profile analysis and investigative advice as offered by the Scientific Research Advisory Unit of the National Criminal Intelligence Division (CRI) – The Netherlands.* Leiden, The Netherlands: NSCR.

Kocsis, R.N. (2007). Schools of thought related to criminal profiling. In R.N. Kocsis (Ed.) *Criminal profiling: International theory, research and practice* (pp.393–404). Totowa, NJ.: The Humana Press Inc.

Labuschagne, G.N. (2006). The use of linkage analysis as evidence in the conviction of the Newcastle serial murderer, South Africa. *Journal of Investigative Psychology and Offender Profiling, 3*, 183–191.

Markson, L., Woodhams, J. & Bond, J. (2010). Linking serial residential burglary: Comparing the utility of modus operandi behaviors, geographical proximity and temporal proximity. *Journal of Investigative Psychology and Offender Profiling, 7*, 91–107.

Meyer, C.B. (2007). Criminal profiling as expert evidence? An international case law perspective. In R.N. Kocsis (Ed.) *Criminal profiling: International perspectives in theory, practice and research* (pp.207–248). Totowa, NJ.: The Humana Press Inc.

Mischel, W. (1999). Personality coherence and dispositions in a cognitive-affective personality system (CAPS) approach. In D. Cervone & Y. Shoda (Eds.) *The coherence of personality: Social-cognitive bases of consistency, variability and organisation* (pp.37–60). London: Guilford Press.

Mischel, W. & Shoda, Y. (1995). A cognitive-affective system theory of personality: Reconceptualising situations, dispositions, dynamics and invariance in personality structure. *Psychological Review, 102*, 246–268.

Mokros, A. & Alison, L.J. (2002). Is offender profiling possible? Testing the predicted homology of crime scene actions and background characteristics in a sample of rapists. *Legal and Criminological Psychology, 7*, 25–43.

Mullen, D.A. (2000). Criminal profiling: Real science or just wishful thinking. *Homicide Studies, 4*, 234–264.

Pervin, L.A. (2002). *Current controversies and issues in personality* (3rd edn). New York: John Wiley & Sons, Inc.

Pye, K. & Croft, D.J. (2004). Forensic geoscience: introduction and overview. In K. Pye & D.J. Croft (Eds.) *Forensic geosciences: Principles, techniques and applications. Geological Society, London, Special Publications, 232*, 1–5.

Rainbow, L. (2008). Taming the beast: The UK approach to the management of behavioural investigative advice. *Journal of Police and Criminal Psychology, 23*, 90–97.

Santtila, P., Fritzon, K. & Tamelander, A.L. (2004). Linking arson incidents on the basis of crime scene behavior. *Journal of Police and Criminal Psychology, 19*, 1–16.

Santtila, P., Junkkila, J. & Sandnabba, N.K. (2005). Behavioral linking of stranger rapes. *Journal of Investigative Psychology and Offender Profiling, 2*, 87–103.

Santtila, P., Korpela, S. & Häkkänen, H. (2004). Expertise and decision-making in linking of car crime series. *Psychology, Crime and Law, 10*, 97–112.

Shoda, Y., Mischel, W. & Wright, J.C. (1994). Intraindividual stability in the organization and patterning of behavior: Incorporating psychological situations into the idiographic analysis of personality. *Journal of Personality and Social Psychology, 67*, 674–687.

Snook, B., Cullen, R.M., Bennell, C., Taylor, P.J. & Gendreau, P. (2008). The criminal profiling illusion: What's behind the smoke and mirrors? *Criminal Justice and Behavior, 35*, 1257–1276.

Snook, B., Eastwood, J., Gendreau, P., Goggin, C. & Cullen, R.M. (2007). Taking stock of criminal profiling: A narrative review and meta-analysis. *Criminal Justice and Behavior, 34*, 437–453.

Ter Beek, M., van den Eshof, P. & Mali, B. (2010). Statistical modelling in the investigation of stranger rape. *Journal of Investigative Psychology and Offender Profiling, 7*, 31–47.

Tonkin, M., Bond, J.W. & Woodhams, J. (2009). Fashion conscious burglars? Testing the principles of offender profiling with footwear impressions recovered at domestic burglaries. *Psychology, Crime and Law, 15*, 327–345.

Tonkin, M., Bull, R., Woodhams, J., Bond, J. & Palmer, E. (2011). Linking different types of crime using geographical and temporal proximity. *Criminal Justice and Behavior, 38*, 1069–1088.

Tonkin, M., Grant, T. & Bond, J. (2008). To link or not to link: A test of the case linkage principles using serial car theft data. *Journal of Investigative Psychology and Offender Profiling, 5*, 59–77.

Turvey, B.E. (2008). *Criminal profiling: An introduction to behavioral investigative analysis* (3rd edn). Burlington, MA: Academic Press.

van Mechelen, I. & de Raad, B. (1999). Editorial: Personality and situations. *European Journal of Personality, 13*, 333–336.

Wilson, P.R., Lincoln, R. & Kocsis, R. (1997). Validity, utility and ethics of profiling for serial violent and sexual offenders [electronic version]. *Psychiatry, Psychology and Law, 1*, 1–11. Retrieved 22 August from http://epublications.bond.edu.au/hss_pubs/24

Wolfgang, M.E., Figlio, R.M. & Sellin, T. (1972). *Delinquency in a birth cohort*. Chicago: University of Chicago Press.

Woodhams, J., Bull, R. & Hollin, C.R. (2007). Case linkage: Identifying crimes committed by the same offender. In R.N. Kocsis (Ed.) *Criminal profiling: International perspectives in theory, practice and research* (pp.117–133). Totowa, NJ: The Humana Press Inc.

Woodhams, J., Hollin, C.R. & Bull, R. (2007). The psychology of linking crimes: A review of the evidence. *Legal and Criminological Psychology, 12*, 233–249.

Woodhams, J. & Toye, K. (2007). An empirical test of the assumptions of case linkage and offender profiling with serial commercial robberies. *Psychology, Public Policy & Law, 13*, 59–85.

Woskett, J., Coyle, I.R. & Lincoln, R. (2007). The probity of profiling: Opinions of Australian lawyers on the utility of criminal profiling in Court. *Psychiatry, Psychology and Law, 14*, 306–314.

Youngs, D. (2004). Personality correlates of offence style. *Journal of Investigative Psychology and Offender Profiling, 1*, 99–119.

Zayas, V. & Shoda, Y. (2009). Three decades after the personality paradox: Understanding situations. *Journal of Research in Personality, 43*, 280–281.

ANNOTATED READING LIST

Alison, L.J., Goodwill, A., Almond, L., van den Heuvel, C. & Winter, J. (2010). Pragmatic solutions to offender profiling and behavioural investigative advice. *Legal and Criminological Psychology, 15*, 115–132. *A good outline of behavioural investigative advice and how 'offender profiling' has evolved.*

Alison, L., West, A. & Goodwill, A. (2004). The academic and the practitioner: Pragmatists' views of offender profiling. *Psychology, Public Policy and Law, 10*, 71–101. *Proposes the need for integration of the different 'factions' within offender profiling and outlines principles for constructing an offender profile with reference to a real case.*

Boon, J.C.W. (1997). The contribution of personality theories to psychological profiling. In J.L. Jackson & D.A. Bekerian (Eds.) *Offender profiling: Theory, research and practice* (pp.43–59). Chichester: John Wiley & Sons, Inc. *Using case studies, this chapter illustrates how personality theory can be associated with salient case details to generate hypotheses about offender characteristics.*

Canter, D., Alison, L, Alison, E. & Wentink, N. (2004). The organized/disorganized typology of serial murder: Myth of model? *Psychology, Public Policy and Law, 10,* 293–320. *A detailed critique and empirical test of the organised/disorganised typology.*

Herndon, J.S. (2007). The image of profiling: Media treatment and general impressions. In R.N. Kocsis (Ed.) *Criminal profiling: International theory, research and practice* (pp.303–323). Totowa, NJ: Humana Press. *A review of how offender profiling has been portrayed in a variety of popular media.*

Rainbow, L. (2008). Taming the beast: The UK approach to the management of behavioural investigative advice. *Journal of Police and Criminal Psychology, 23,* 90–97. *An article written by one of the UK's behavioural investigative advisors about the work they conduct.*

Woodhams, J., Bull, R. & Hollin, C.R. (2007). Case linkage: Identifying crimes committed by the same offender. In R.N. Kocsis (Ed.) *Criminal profiling: International perspectives in theory, practice and research* (pp.117–133). Totowa, NJ: The Humana Press. *Contains a description of how case linkage is conducted in practice and considers how case linkage fares when assessed against criteria for the admittance of expert evidence in court.*

10 Intimate Partner Violence and Stalking

Louise Dixon and Erica Bowen

CHAPTER OUTLINE

'Stalker guilty of stabbing ex-girlfriend to death in "brutal" attack', reads the London Evening Standard news headline (Bailey, 2010). This article goes on to describe how Gemma Doorman, 24, was stabbed to death by her ex-partner Vikramgit Singh in July 2008, as she left a restaurant in south-west London. The 'frenzied attack' occurred after months of stalking and harassment, which Miss Doorman had previously reported to the police.

This is just one example of many worldwide media headlines that depict stories of relationships that have culminated in the murder of one partner. While not all cases of partner homicide are characterised by **stalking** and harassment, most victims of stalking know their perpetrator, and in a large proportion of stalking cases the target is an ex-intimate partner (Spitzberg, 2002). Such murder cases provoke questions about why the fatality occurred and whether this arguably foreseeable event could have been prevented. These are questions that many academics and practitioners in the field have endeavoured to answer.

> **stalking** a range of unwanted and repeated actions directed towards a specific individual that induce fear or concern for safety, or that induce feelings of harassment.

In order to understand why the most severe cases of **intimate partner violence (IPV)** happen, it is necessary to understand the nature and aetiology of the violence that can occur in intimate relationships. It is beyond the scope of this chapter to give a comprehensive account of these issues. The aim of this chapter is to provide readers with an overview of the IPV and stalking literatures, through which reference will be made to the most influential research in order to provide a firm foundation for further investigation. The chapter will examine definitions, rates, theories and typologies of IPV and stalking, before considering the implications that such knowledge has for risk assessment. See also Chapter 4 for a further discussion of this topic.

DEFINITIONS AND TERMINOLOGY

In order for professionals to respond to IPV and stalking in an accurate and consistent manner, agreement must be reached about what each term refers to. Definitions determine what an agency will class as IPV or stalking and therefore who they will provide services to, or include in official statistics that guide policy and practice (Bowen, 2011a; Dixon & Graham-Kevan, 2011).

Intimate partner violence

IPV has increasingly been understood as a public matter and social problem since the 1970s (Figure 10.1; Dutton,

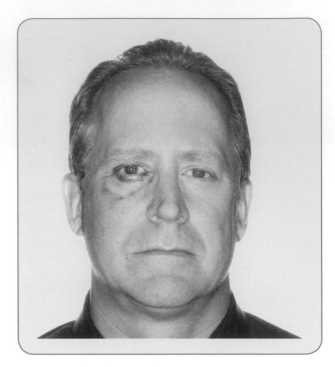

FIGURE 10.1 *Intimate partner violence (IPV) has been increasingly understood as a public matter and social problem since the 1970s. Source:* © Suzanne Tucker. Used under licence from Shutterstock.

2006). It takes place between members of a couple, regardless of their social group, ethnicity, gender or educational background and as such cannot be said to be associated with one particular sub-section of the population. Definitions of IPV (of which numerous exist within the literature) share some reference to the different forms of aggression it can encompass. Typically, definitions provide some reference to physical, psychological and sexual aggression, emphasising that IPV should be understood as more than just physical violence. Some definitions also acknowledge that more subtle 'controlling behaviours' should be included in any definition (examples of each form of IPV are provided in Table 10.1). The importance of recognising controlling behaviours has been shown by research that has demonstrated that these behaviours may be a precursor to physical aggression and are likely to co-occur with it; that some women report them to be more damaging than physical aggression; and that they are unlikely to diminish over time (Graham-Kevan, 2007).

In any definition, particular attention should be paid to the terminology that describes the relationship status and gender of the couple involved in the violence. Much empirical research has determined that violence can occur in dating relationships in young couples (e.g. Bowen, 2011c; Ko *et al.*, 2008), in estranged couples (e.g. Dutton & Kerry, 1999) and in same sex relationships (e.g. Nowinski & Bowen, in revision; Renzetti & Miley, 1996). A broad definition should therefore include current and former marital, dating and cohabiting relationships and heterosexual and same

TABLE 10.1 *Examples of the different forms of intimate partner violence.*

Form of intimate partner violence	Explanation	Examples of behavioural acts
Physical aggression/coercion	To make physical contact with the intent to cause pain or injury to another, or to coerce that person into doing something against their will	Pushing, slapping, grabbing, biting, punching, pulling hair, kicking, hitting with an object, choking, using a weapon against person
Sexual aggression/coercion	To use physical force or verbal coercion to make sexual contact with a person against their will	Indecent assault, using physical force to force other into sexual intercourse, using verbal threats or intimidation to coerce other in sexual intercourse
Psychological aggression	To expose an individual to behavior that may cause psychological harm (i.e. harm to intellectual or mental capacity that results in impairment of a person's ability to function; Browne & Herbert, 1997)	Insults, name calling, humiliation tactics, threats to harm the other person or their loved ones, destroying property
Controlling behaviours	Behaviour enacted with the aim of controlling or monitoring another person's actions. While all of the above categories may be described as controlling behaviours, often more subtle behaviours are overlooked – examples here are concerned with such subtle behaviours	Controlling another's money, telling the other they are confused or have 'got it wrong' when they have not, following another person without their consent, checking another person's email or telephone calls without their consent, making the other jealous on purpose, limiting another's access to friends and family, monitoring another's movements and contact with others in some way

sex couples. Hence, terminology should be inclusive of all relationship types and be gender neutral in description.

The adjectives used to describe the violence must also be given consideration in any definition. Words that allude to severe and chronic violence (such as 'battering') apply to only a minority of all cases and therefore exclude less severe and frequent assaults. The spectrum of acts recognised as IPV will be limited where such restrictive terms are used in a definition. Academics working in the field of aggression research have suggested that distinct terms should be used to coin the different severity of acts, with *aggression* used to refer to acts that are less likely to result in injury (e.g. slapping) and *violence* used to highlight acts more likely to result in injury (e.g. choking and stabbing) (Archer, 1994; 2000).

For the purpose of consistency, this chapter will use the term 'IPV' to refer to acts of aggression or violence that take place between intimate partners. The definition of this term is understood to be '...any form of aggression and/or controlling behaviours used against a current or past intimate partner of any gender or relationship status' (Dixon & Graham-Kevan, 2011, p.1) to reflect that this problem can occur between people of any gender and in any relationship status, and can be of varying forms and severity.

Stalking

The term 'stalking' is a colloquial term adopted as a consequence of a number of high profile cases in which individuals experienced repeated criminal behaviour and/or harassment (Budd & Mattinson, 2000). Implied by the term 'stalking' are predatory pursuit behaviours (Westrup & Fremouw, 1998), and while following may constitute a proportion of the behaviours identified as stalking, the actual range of behaviours that fall within this term is much broader. Sheridan and Davies (2004) suggest that an infinite array of behaviours may be defined as stalking because definition of the phenomenon is in fact driven by victim perceptions. Indeed, this is one reason why there are alternative terms used within the literature. For example, 'obsessional harassment' (Zona *et al.*, 1993) and 'harassment' and 'obsessional following' (Meloy & Gothard, 1995) are frequently used to refer to a range of behaviours, which might include, but are not limited to, pursuit or following behaviours.

Contention surrounds the use of the word 'obsessional', which suggests that it is the presence of repeated intrusive thoughts about the target that ultimately directly causes stalking behaviour. This assumption is yet to be scientifically scrutinised. It has also been argued that both terms 'stalking' and 'following' do little to differentiate between a range of behaviours and one specific action (Westrup & Fremouw, 1998). The term 'harassment' is also used within the literature to reflect persistent unwanted behaviours that may or may not elicit feelings of fear, which is identified by some as the defining feature of stalking behaviour.

A final term within the literature that has been inaccurately used to refer to these behaviours is 'erotomania'. Erotomania is a psychiatric disorder that is classified within the *Diagnostic and Statistical Manual of Mental Disorders* (DSM-IV-TR, American Psychiatric Association, 2000) as a subtype of delusional disorder in which the patient has 'delusions that another person, usually of higher status, is in love with the individual' (American Psychiatric Association, 2000, p.329). However, as many individuals who are diagnosed as erotomanic also have other psychiatric conditions, it is unclear the extent to which erotomania actually leads an individual to engage in stalking behaviour. Indeed, few stalkers are ever diagnosed as erotomanics, and fewer erotomanics engage in stalking, which directly challenges the relevance of this disorder to the phenomenon of stalking (Westrup & Fremouw, 1998).

In the British Crime Survey 2004/05, stalking was defined as 'two or more incidents that caused distress, fear or alarm of obscene/threatening unwanted letters or phone calls, waiting or loitering around home or workplace, following or watching or interfering with or damaging personal property by any person including a partner or family member' (Finney, 2006, p.v). This definition is very broad, and shows that the majority of stalking behaviours would not be unwanted within different contexts. For example, in some contexts having someone wait for you outside your home would not be viewed as fear-provoking. In addition, the definition emphasises that for stalking behaviour to occur, the victim must feel fearful as a result.

Consequently, this definition highlights the extremely subjective nature of stalking that makes it unlike any other form of crime (Fox *et al.*, 2011). Individual perceptions of what constitutes threatening and fear-inducing behaviour will differ; consequently, if a target does not formally recognise they are being stalked, then stalking is not actually happening. However, research indicates that there is considerable consistency in people's perceptions of what does and does not constitute stalking behaviour (e.g. Sheridan *et al.*, 2000; 2001; 2002). These difficulties aside, across the terms and definitions of stalking offered in the literature, it is generally agreed that stalking constitutes a range of unwanted and repeated actions directed towards a specific individual that induce fear or concern for safety or that induce harassment (Figure 10.2; Cupach & Spitzberg, 2000; Sheridan & Davies, 2001; Westrup & Fremouw, 1998). Consequently, this is how stalking will be defined for the purpose of this chapter.

FIGURE 10.2 *Stalking constitutes a range of unwanted and repeated actions directed towards a specific individual that induce fear or concern for safety or that induce harassment.*
Source: © Steven Frame. Used under licence from Shutterstock.

Lifetime and 12-month prevalence rates of intimate partner violence and stalking

Typically, surveys around the world have attempted to determine lifetime and 12-month rates of IPV and stalking by asking a representative sample of a community to self-report their experiences of victimisation. Accurate prevalence rates for a country can only be determined by surveying nationally representative community samples (Gelles, 1990), as this approach is more stringent than using official police arrest or conviction records, which notoriously underreport actual figures (Bowen, 2011a). However, this methodology is not without its problems.

Intimate partner violence (IPV)

Results from surveys with nationally representative samples show IPV to be an international social problem of significant magnitude (e.g. World Health Organization, 2005). However, while many surveys utilise nationally representative samples, their design is informed by a feminist perspective, which assumes that IPV constitutes men's violence to women (not women's violence to men; see the section on 'Risk Factors and Theories' for a more in-depth description of the feminist perspective). Consequently, surveys designed from this perspective necessarily only ask females about their victimisation (e.g. Moracco et al., 2007; World Health Organization, 2005). This one-sided approach limits knowledge to female victimisation, and prevents learning about male victimisation, female perpetration and reciprocal aggression (where both partners aggress against one another).

Crime surveys typically identify rates of victimisation in nationally representative samples via self-report methods. The British Crime Survey identifies victimisation rates of different types of crime for large samples of men and women aged between 16–59 resident in households in England and Wales. The British Crime Survey gathers information about incidents that are not reported to the police, which is particularly important for intimate violence as this is notoriously underreported to the authorities (Bowen, 2011a). Since 2004, the British Crime Survey has consistently included a module on 'intimate violence', which respondents complete alone. Approximately 25,000 respondents completed the module in the British Crime Survey 2008/09. Findings showed that around 13 per cent of men and 24 per cent of women reported they had been a victim once or more of any 'partner abuse' (non-physical, threats, force, sexual assault or stalking) since the age of 16. Furthermore, around 3 per cent of men and 5 per cent of women reported this had happened in the previous 12 months (Smith et al., 2010).

Figures from crime surveys typically show higher rates of female victimisation, which are often taken as support for a feminist explanation of IPV. However, the context of crime surveys must be considered. People, particularly men, do not typically interpret relationship aggression as a criminal behaviour or view their experiences as violent (Povey et al., 2008; Straus, 1999). Thus, cueing respondents to think about IPV as a crime is not conducive to accurate reporting and, hence, crime survey figures should be interpreted with caution.

Surveys that ask representative community samples of men and women about their experiences in the context of conflict in relationships are scarce (Santovena & Dixon, 2011). One exemplar survey that adopted this methodology was the National Family Violence Survey (NFVS; see Straus et al., 1980; Straus & Gelles, 1985). The NFVS was conducted in 1975 and again in 1985, with representative US community samples. The surveys measured rates and severity of partner aggression using a systematic measure, the Conflict Tactics Scale (CTS), which is a self-report tool initially developed in the late 1970s and which has since been revised to the CTS2 (see Straus et al., 1996). Importantly, the CTS/CTS2 set IPV in the context of conflict in the relationship (rather than crime or violence), which is arguably more conducive to honest reporting than the aforementioned contexts (Straus, 1999). Respondents are simply asked to report on a range of predetermined behavioural acts in which both they and their partner have engaged during times of conflict with each other.

The CTS2 contains five subscales that distinguish rationale tactics, physical assault, psychological aggression, sexual coercion and injury. Furthermore, minor acts of physical and psychological aggression, sexual coercion and injury are differentiated from more severe forms of these acts, hence less severe acts of physical assault that might not otherwise be considered as constituting IPV (e.g. slapping, pushing, grabbing) are also measured. The behavioural acts listed form clearly defined behavioural categories. Therefore, results can be systematically compared within and across samples. Indeed, this tool allowed the systematic collection of large data sets from which international prevalence and incidence rates have been calculated. This methodology found approximately equal rates (around 12 per cent) of physical partner aggression perpetrated by both sexes in a 12-month period, across time. In terms of lifetime prevalence, 28 per cent of respondents reported physical victimisation in 1975 and 22 per cent in 1985.

Assessment of stalking behaviours

A range of methodologies have been employed to assess stalking (Fox et al., 2011) and, akin to the issues previously discussed in relation to estimates of IPV prevalence, considerable variations in prevalence have arisen even when survey methods have been used. For example, according to the British Crime Survey 2004/05, 23 per cent of women and 15 per cent of men reported having experienced stalking since the age of 16. However, when based on reported victimisation in the previous year, the previously identified gender differences disappeared, with 9 per cent of both men and women reporting such experiences. As mentioned previously, stalking was defined through a range of repeated explicitly identified behaviours.

Based on experience since age 16, 33 per cent of women and 25 per cent of men reported that they had been stalked by a partner; 5 per cent of men and women reported being stalked by a family member; 34 per cent of women and 35 per cent of men reported being stalked by someone else known to them; and 42 per cent of women and 48 per cent of men reported being stalked by a stranger. Percentages add to more than 100, due to multiple stalking experiences within the sample.

These data show that women are more likely than men to report experiencing stalking perpetrated by an intimate partner, whereas men are more likely to have been stalked by other acquaintances or strangers. In general, though, stalking by a stranger seems to be most common for both genders, although women are most likely to be victims overall.

Data from North America present prevalence estimates that are markedly lower than those reported by the British Crime Survey. Estimates from the Injury Control and Risk Survey of stalking prevalence between 2000 and 2003 (Basile et al., 2006) revealed that 4.5 per cent of adults reported ever having been stalked. Women were more likely than men to report this experience (7 per cent vs. 2 per cent). The low prevalence rates reported are likely due to the definition of stalking used. Participants were asked: 'Have you ever had someone besides bill collectors or sales people follow or spy on you, try to communicate with you against your will, or otherwise stalk you for more than one month?'. If respondents said yes, they were then asked to select whether the most recent experience was 'nothing to be concerned about, annoying, somewhat dangerous or life-threatening' (Basile et al., 2006, p.173). Only respondents who selected the latter two options were then classified as victims of stalking (Basile et al., 2006) in order to reflect behaviours that were both unwanted and fear-provoking.

These data broadly support the findings of an earlier meta-analysis of 103 studies by Spitzberg (2002) who found that the average prevalence of stalking was 23.5 per cent for women and 10.5 per cent for men and, on average, the stalking occurred over a two-year period. The majority of victims across studies were women (75 per cent) and the majority of perpetrators were men (79 per cent). In just under half of cases (49 per cent) the stalking occurred within the context of an intimate relationship. These findings must be qualified by the possibility of response and reporting bias associated with gender, which also affects estimates of stalking victimisation and perpetration in the same way that it affects estimates of partner violence. That is, men are less likely to report their own victimisation, as they are possibly less likely to feel the necessary extent of threat in order for such experiences to be valid (Sheridan et al., 2002; White et al., 2002).

Intimate partner stalking

Within the international literature, it has been claimed that victims of stalkers are most likely to be current or former intimates or spouses (Melton, 2000). Although the British Crime Survey 2008/09 suggests that this is not necessarily the most frequently cited form of stalking in general, the apparent gendered nature of intimate

partner stalking appeals to researchers of violence against women more broadly. Intimate partner stalking has been isolated as a 'special case' of stalking for five main reasons (Logan & Walker, 2009), as shown in Box 10.1.

Researchers vary in the methodology they employ in conducting surveys to determine rates of IPV and stalking. It is therefore difficult to compare rates across surveys, countries and time. Consequently, it is important to consider the methodology used in studies carefully before generalising figures to represent the population at large. Agreed definitions and terms, and consistency in methodological approach, will allow researchers to produce comparable studies and resultant prevalence and incidence rates. However, considering large-scale self-report community studies (e.g. the National Family Violence Survey, Straus & Gelles, 1990), it seems likely that an estimate of between 20 per cent and 30 per cent for the lifetime prevalence rate for all men and women experiencing *physical* violence is a sensible approximation (Dixon & Graham-Kevan, 2010), and between 10 per cent and 35 per cent for the lifetime prevalence, for all men and women, of stalking. In addition, the evidence suggests considerable overlap between these two phenomena.

RISK FACTORS AND THEORIES

Theories serve to explain how it is that a phenomenon occurs, and identify the circumstances and factors that lead to its occurrence (i.e. risk factors). A broad range of risk factors have been implicated in IPV and stalking, and are typically identified through comparing the characteristics of individuals who engage in the behaviour of interest, to those who do not. In contrast to the empirical evidence base relating to IPV, the stalking literature is less comprehensive, and our knowledge about the characteristics of stalkers arises either through sampling clinical groups of those who have been arrested and are likely to have greater levels of psychopathology, or university students.

A useful heuristic framework within which to consider the role of risk factors is that provided by the nested ecological model (Dutton, 1985), adapted from Bronfenbrenner's (1979) ecological developmental model. Within this framework, risk factors are identified by their relative proximity to the individual. As such, risk factors are conceptualised as occurring at one of four levels: *macrosystem* (broad societal/cultural influences); *mesosystem* (social group influences, such as church/school); *microsystem* (interpersonal relationship influences); and *ontogenetic* (individual developmental/internal influences). Table 10.2 provides examples of identified risk factors for IPV and stalking within each level of this model.

BOX 10.1   STALKING WITHIN THE CONTEXT OF AN INTIMATE RELATIONSHIP

- Relationships in which stalking arises are characterised by a range of violent and abusive behaviours (e.g. Cupach & Spitzberg, 2000; Davis *et al.*, 2000). Indeed, Douglas and Dutton (2001) have even gone so far as to suggest that the stalking of current or former intimate partners, incorporating psychological and/or controlling behaviours as outlined in Table 10.1, is a form of IPV itself. In a study of 120 male IPV perpetrators, it was found that 30 per cent reported also having stalked their partners (Burgess *et al.*, 1997). In addition, it has been found that between 30 per cent and 65 per cent of stalkers had engaged in violence towards the intimate partners they had more recently stalked (e.g. Kienlen *et al.*, 1997).

- When stalking is in the context of an intimate relationship, it enables the perpetrator to draw upon a wider range of stalking tactics that are influenced by their intimate knowledge of the victim, in particular their knowledge of specific fears, concerns and vulnerabilities (Mohandie *et al.*, 2006; Sheridan & Davis, 2001).

- When stalking is in the context of an intimate relationship, it increases the likelihood that perpetrators will both threaten the victim and use violence (James & Farnham, 2003; Rosenfeld, 2004). In addition, it has been found that violence is more likely to be used by stalkers who first threaten to use it than by those who do not (Brewster, 2000). As typified in the case from the *London Evening Standard* that opened this chapter (Bailey, 2010), stalking is also a risk factor for intimate partner homicide. For example, McFarlane *et al.* (1999) reported that 76 per cent of partner homicide victims had been stalked prior to being killed.

- Such stalking is likely to have been initiated during the course of the relationship rather than once the relationship has terminated (Mullen *et al.*, 2000). Depending on the study, between 25 per cent and 80 per cent of female intimate partner stalking victims reported that the stalking started during the relationship (e.g. Hackett, 2000; Logan, Cole *et al.*, 2006; Melton, 2007). Stalking during a relationship has been found to lower the likelihood of a woman leaving (Logan, Cole *et al.*, 2006). In addition, however, there is evidence that being stalked after the cessation of a relationship may place a victim at increased risk of ongoing and increased severity violence (Logan *et al.*, 2004; Melton, 2007).

- The occurrence of stalking has been found to be associated with greater psychological distress for victims, ranging from symptoms of anxiety and post-traumatic stress disorder (Logan, Walker *et al.*, 2006) to symptoms of psychiatric diagnoses and severe depression (Blaauw *et al.*, 2002). Moreover, should stalking occur within a previously violent intimate relationship, this has been found to further compound the emotional distress caused to the victim (e.g. Brewster, 2002).

Table 10.2 shows that a very broad range of factors have been implicated in both IPV and stalking, and that these two behaviours appear to be indicated by some common risk factors, which is not surprising given the occurrence of stalking within intimate, and previously violent intimate relationships. Despite the implication of multiple risk factors, the most popular theoretical explanations of IPV have traditionally focused on the role of single factors (see Bowen, 2011a for a more in-depth examination of relevant theories of IPV).

Feminist theories have to date been most influential in accounting for IPV, despite the fact that little empirical support currently exists for this position. This perspective views IPV as predominantly acted out by men towards their female partner, caused by societal rules that support male dominance and female subordination (Dobash & Dobash, 1979; Yllö, 2005). Hence, 'patriarchy' is viewed as a direct cause of men's violence towards their female partner (Bell & Naugle, 2008). While it is accepted by the feminist position that some women may be violent to their male partner, this is purported to occur predominantly out of self-defence or in retaliation to the male's aggression (Dobash & Dobash, 2004; Respect, 2008). Consequently, violence towards women is viewed as special, unrelated to other forms of violence or crime (Dixon, Archer *et al.*, 2011). Therefore, in the long term feminism seeks to change the root cause of men's violence to women, by overturning patriarchal social structures, to eradicate violence to women (Dutton, 2006). Despite these admirable aims, there is little empirical support for the expected strong relationship between patriarchy and IPV (e.g. Stith *et al.*, 2004; Sugarman & Frankel, 1996).

In fact, research that tests the hypothesis that either gender may be perpetrators and/or victims of IPV has found that men and women engage in violent acts at approximately equal rates. This gender symmetry is shown in the results of the National Family Violence Survey (Straus *et al.*, 1980; Straus & Gelles, 1985), described above, and in other gold standard pieces of research, such as Archer's (2000) meta-analysis. Archer examined gender differences in the perpetration of heterosexual IPV in 82 independent studies that examined rates of physical violence by men and women. In total, a combined data set of 64,487 people was produced for analysis. Results showed that women were

TABLE 10.2 *Examples of risk factors associated with male perpetration of intimate partner violence and stalking.*

Ecological levels	Intimate partner violence risk factors	Stalking risk factors
Macrosystem	• Patriarchal values/systems	
Mesosystem	• Unemployment • Peer group has pro-violence norms	• Unemployment
Microsystem	• High relationship conflict • Low relationship satisfaction • Controlling behaviours within intimate relationship	• Unstable personal relationships • End of relationship • High relationship conflict • Psychological abuse of partner prior to break-up • Controlling behaviours within intimate relationships • Social isolation
Ontogenetic	• Witnessing IPV as a child • Child abuse • Borderline personality traits • Antisocial personality traits • Drug use/abuse • Alcohol use/abuse • Pro-violence attitudes • Social problem-solving deficits • Negative attitudes towards women • Jealousy • Poor impulse control	• Substance abuse • Schizophrenia • Borderline personality traits • Narcissistic personality traits • Attachment • Erotomanic delusions • Low empathy • High trait anger • Jealousy • High education • Poor impulse control

slightly more likely than men to use physical aggression against a partner (Cohen's d = −0.05), yet overall women were slightly more likely to be injured (d = +0.15) and require medical treatment for their injuries than men (d = +0.08). He also reported that the sample studied was an important moderator of effect size, with younger and non-clinical samples more likely to be in the female direction. For example, studies using shelter samples produced very high effect sizes in the male direction, while community and student samples were slightly more likely to be in the female direction. Such research findings highlight that men *and* women can be both aggressors and victims of physical violence within their intimate relationships, which undermines the feminist perspective as a complete explanation for IPV.

An equally popular theory that has been applied to understanding IPV is social learning theory (SLT, Bandura, 1977). According to SLT, violent and abusive behaviours and pro-violence beliefs are learned during childhood through either the direct experience or the observation of these behaviours and attitudes modelled by others, most typically parents. The likelihood that such behaviours will be exhibited depends on whether they are perceived to be reinforced. Woodin and O'Leary (2009) note that behavioural learning is deemed to occur through processes of both classical and operant conditioning, and also through cognitive mediational processes (p.46). At its

most basic, then, an SLT account of IPV predicts that violence between parents, observed by their children, leads their children to use violence in intimate relationships. This is known as the 'intergenerational transmission of violence', which is the most widely tested assumption of the SLT account of IPV. However, the resulting empirical evidence suggests that this association is not straightforward.

For example, in a 20-year prospective study of 582 youths and their mothers, Ehrensaft *et al.* (2003) examined the prospective role of childhood disruptive behaviour disorders, childhood neglect and abuse, parenting practices and inter-parental violence as risk factors for adult IPV. It was found that a diagnosis of childhood conduct disorder was the single most important risk factor for IPV, increasing the odds of it occurring by seven times. However, exposure to inter-parental violence and childhood abuse both remained significant predictors even when childhood conduct disorder was entered as a predictor in the model, although conduct disorder partially mediated the effect of child abuse. The results of this and other prospective longitudinal studies (e.g. Capaldi & Clark, 1998; Lussièr *et al.*, 2009; Magdol *et al.*, 1997; White & Widom, 2003) confirm that the relationship between exposure to violent models during childhood and adult IPV is weak, and is influenced by a range of additional factors, most notably childhood conduct disorder and antisocial personality behaviours such as crying, clinging and seeking contact lead to the development of attachments or emotional bonds between the child and parent (Goodwin, 2003) and serve to attain proximity to the caregiver in times of fear, anxiety and stress. Romantic attachment patterns have been proposed to hold particular promise in the study of IPV, as attachment regulates proximity and distance in intimate relationships (Hazan & Shaver, 1987). Box 10.2 describes the four adult attachment styles that have been identified (Bartholomew & Horowitz, 1991).

It has been theorised by Dutton (1995; 1998; 1999) that adult IPV reflects insecure attachment styles (dismissive, preoccupied, fearful) developed during childhood, and is associated with abandonment anxiety and anger. Indeed, there is evidence that IPV men are more likely to be characterised by insecure than secure attachment styles (e.g. Dutton et al., 1994).

In addition, several personality constructs and styles of interpersonal functioning consistent with insecure attachment characteristics have also been found to be prevalent in samples of IPV perpetrators. For example, Dutton et al. (1994) found that fearful attachment styles were related to anger, jealousy and trauma symptoms. Murphy et al. (1994) found that maritally violent men reported higher levels of interpersonal dependency, dependency on their intimate partner, and lower self-esteem than did maritally distressed but non-violent, and maritally satisfied and non-violent men. Holtzworth-Munroe et al. (1997) found violent men to be more likely characterised by preoccupied and disorganised attachment patterns, jealousy and higher levels of dependency on their partners than non-violent men. Studies have also identified that insecurely attached violent men are also more likely to engage in controlling behaviours, and that this combination predicts the frequency and severity of violence used (e.g. Mauricio & Gormley, 2001).

Given the description of stalking behaviour, its association with IPV and the identified risk factors in Table 10.2, it is perhaps not surprising that stalking has been conceptualised as a form of attachment behaviour. Indeed, an attachment framework is the only coherent theoretical account of stalking to emerge within the literature to date, although others have argued for a feminist account due to the high rate of controlling behaviours associated with intimate stalking, and indeed the purported use of stalking as a means of control (e.g. Melton, 2000). Meloy (1996) first argued that obsessional following was 'proximity seeking toward an angry or frightened object that usually responds adversely to the act of pursuit' (Meloy, 1996, p.150), which uses explicit attachment terminology. There is evidence that stalking behaviours among university students are associated with anxious (preoccupied) attachment, although this seems to be mediated by anger-jealousy (Davis et al., 2000). A more recent study

FIGURE 10.3 *The relationship between exposure to violent models during childhood and adult intimate partner violence is weak, and is influenced by a range of additional factors, most notably childhood conduct disorder and antisocial personality traits.*

Source: © AFH. Used under licence from Shutterstock.

traits (Figure 10.3). Along with feminist theories, SLT has been a major influence on the skills-based components of treatment programmes, and many current programmes combine feminist ideology with cognitive-behavioural skills training to a greater or lesser degree (Bowen, 2011a).

attachment theory a well-developed theory of early development, which focuses on the formation of early relationships and the implications of how these relationships are formed for later childhood and adult functioning.

Attachment theory is a well-developed theory of early development, which focuses on the formation of early relationships, and the implications of how these relationships are formed for later childhood and adult functioning. In particular, the attachment model proposes the need for infants to have a secure base in the form of one or more preferred caregivers, from which they can safely explore the world, and to which they can return for safety if required (Bowlby, 1988). As a consequence, during healthy development, attachment

BOX 10.2   ATTACHMENT STYLES IN BRIEF

Attachment reflects two underlying dimensions: *positivity/negativity about oneself*; and *positivity/negativity about others*, resulting in four adult attachment styles (Bartholomew & Horowitz, 1991):

- Those with a **secure attachment style (positive view of self and positive view of others)** are theorised to be comfortable with intimacy and are also autonomous in intimate relationships.
- Those with a **dismissing attachment style (positive view of self and negative view of others)** are compulsively self-reliant and typically minimise the importance of intimate relationships.
- Those with a **preoccupied attachment style (negative view of self and positive view of others)** exhibit high levels of dependency on others, and are preoccupied with the importance of intimate relationships from which they gain a sense of self-esteem.
- Those with a **fearful attachment style (negative view of self and negative view of others)** are afraid of rejection, which manifests itself as a fear of intimacy. Consequently, these individuals avoid social interactions and intimate relationships.

has confirmed the association with both anxious (preoccupied) attachment style and anger (Patton *et al.*, 2010). Although an attachment approach makes intuitive sense when explaining stalking within the context of intimate relationships, Patton *et al.* (2010) also argue that attachment insecurity may play a role when stalking occurs generally in circumstances where proximity to the target is desired, regardless of whether the target is previously known to the perpetrator.

The benefit of these theories over the feminist perspective is that they do not assume the gender of perpetrator or victim; rather it is possible for men or women to be victims or perpetrators. Hence, surveys and empirical research that are influenced by such a gender inclusive approach may feasibly set out to test a two-tailed hypothesis about the gender of perpetrators. Empirical research suggests that various theories can account for variance in the aetiology of IPV and stalking and that, collectively, several theories can offer a better explanation, rather than any one theory in isolation (O'Leary *et al.*, 2007).

SUBTYPES OF PERPETRATORS

Intimate partner violence

Empirical research has repeatedly demonstrated the presence of different types of offender, each with different aetiology. In their review of the literature, Holtzworth-Munroe and Stuart (1994) proposed a hypothetical typology of IPV men living in the community. They proposed that three dimensions of marital violence could differentiate between three types of perpetrator. These were: the severity of marital violence; generality of violence;

and psychopathology/personality disorder. These were named the generally violent/antisocial, dysphoric/borderline and family only perpetrators and were proposed to account for 25 per cent, 25 per cent, and 50 per cent of male IPV perpetrators in the community respectively. These three types are shown in Box 10.3.

The typology has gathered support from several empirical studies that find evidence for some or all of the proposed subtypes (e.g. Boyle *et al.*, 2008; Chase *et al.*, 2001; Huss & Langhinirichsen-Rohling, 2006; Holtzworth-Munroe *et al.*, 2000). Limited research has examined whether similar typologies of female perpetrators exist. However, work that has examined this has found similarities in both US and UK non-lethal female offenders (e.g. Babcock *et al.*, 2003; Dixon, Fatania *et al.*, 2011). Further research into female perpetration is warranted.

Stalking

Given the previous discussion of the application of attachment theory to stalking behaviours, it is not surprising that stalking within intimate relationships has been identified as falling into the **dysphoric/borderline** subgroup of IPV perpetrators (Dutton & Kerry, 1999) (see Box 10.3). However, despite the potential relevance of anxious (preoccupied) attachment to all forms of stalking, considerable attempts have also been made to identify subtypes of stalkers. In contrast to those identified within the IPV literature, stalker subtypes are typically identified by the characteristics of their victims. A potentially useful typology has been refined by Zona *et al.* (1998). They identified three stalking types, as shown in Box 10.4.

Classifications of stalkers, as shown in Box 10.4, have been criticised in the literature, due to the vagueness with which subtypes are identified (e.g. Westrup, 1998)

BOX 10.3 HOLTZWORTH-MUNROE AND STUART (1994) IPV SUBTYPES

- The **generally violent/antisocial** perpetrator has multiple risk factors that increase the likelihood they will act with moderate to severe levels of violence within and outside their family unit. They have the highest levels of exposure to violence in their childhood; have extensive involvement with deviant peers; have high impulsivity, substance abuse, criminality, antisocial personality and narcissism; have negative attitudes towards women; have attitudes supportive of violence in general; lack conflict resolution skills in a wide variety of situations; and have a dismissive attachment style. They display low levels of empathy, and psychological distress and depression, alongside moderate levels of anger. They are likely to engage in violence to a partner in situations where they feel the need to keep or regain control, for example if they feel disrespected or rejected (see Case Study 10.1).

- The **dysphoric/borderline** perpetrator may also act out moderate to severe violence, primarily aimed at family members. They will most probably have experienced some family violence in childhood and involvement with deviant peers; demonstrate the highest levels of psychological distress, emotional volatility, depression and anger; hold moderate attitudes supportive of violence, and hostility to women; display low to moderate levels of empathy, criminality and substance abuse; display moderate impulsivity; and display low marital communication skills. They display characteristics of borderline personality and preoccupied or fearful attachment. As such, they will likely react with anger if they feel rejected, abandoned or slighted. Estrangement or threats of separation may result in stalking or harassment in attempts to maintain or re-establish the intimate relationship (see Case Study 10.2).

- The **family-only** perpetrator is violent to family members and acts out with low severity and frequency. He demonstrates the least criminal behaviour and psychopathology, and evidences similar risk to non-violent men. Their violence is likely to result from a accumulation of low level risk factors such as some exposure to family violence in childhood, poor communication skills with their partner; mild impulsivity; dependency on their partner, alcohol and drug abuse.

CASE STUDY 10.1 INTIMATE PARTNER VIOLENCE

David, a 23-year-old man, was convicted and sentenced for the attempted murder of his girlfriend, Heather. A prison psychologist has met with David in order to understand the aetiology of his offending in more detail.

In terms of risk factors, David was unemployed at the time of the offence, and describes a childhood with an absent mother and abusive and rejecting father. He explains that he did not care that his mother was not around, as 'women are useless, in fact there are only a couple of things women are good for – cooking and sex' (indicating negative attitudes about women). He explains that he spent a lot of time on the streets from a young age, mixing with his peers on the local estate. They would steal cars, commit burglary and set fires, among other antisocial acts (deviant peer group). David has abused alcohol and drugs intermittently from a young age (substance abuse) and has a long list of criminal convictions for offences such as robbery, drug dealing, burglary, violence to intimate partners, acquaintances and strangers, affray and criminal damage. His file reports that a psychiatrist diagnosed him with conduct disorder in adolescence and that he has attitudes supportive of violence.

David had been cohabiting with Heather for three months. He was very controlling over Heather's movements, restricting her from seeing friends, controlling all her earnings and displaying persistent jealousy over her friendships with other people, especially men (controlling behaviours). Heather had previously confided in a police officer that she thought David was going to kill her.

On the day in question, David had been drinking heavily. He found out that Heather had left the house without his permission. He reports that he was angry with her for daring to disrespect him in this way, and that he remembers thinking, 'I will show her who's boss'. The police statements report that he punched her repeatedly in the face and body, and stamped on her head. A neighbour heard Heather's initial screams for help, and called the police. Heather was hospitalised in intensive care for three weeks. Immediately after the assault, David left the house and returned to the pub to continue drinking. He reports feeling no remorse for his actions and states that he was angry that she had put him in prison and that she had 'better watch her step when he gets out'. He also reports that she 'deserved it' and that he is glad that he has taught her a lesson not to mess with him.

The prison psychologist has concluded that David evidences characteristics similar to a **generally violent/antisocial** offender.

CASE STUDY 10.2   STALKING

Simon, a 36-year-old man, was convicted and is awaiting sentence for the harassment of and threats to kill his ex-girlfriend, Sarah. The probation psychologist has met with Simon in order to understand the aetiology of his offending in more detail, to inform the judge's sentencing decision.

In terms of risk factors, Simon was employed at the time of the offence, and describes a childhood during which he experienced prolonged physical abuse from his mother and sexual abuse from his father. In addition, Simon reports that his father was also abusive towards his mother, and that he frequently witnessed these incidents. He explains that for many years he experienced flashbacks concerning these incidents, and that such was his fear of his parents he would frequently wet the bed as a young child (trauma symptoms). He ran away from home at the age of 13, and was subsequently placed in local authority care after reporting his experiences. Simon has spent much of his life in intimate relationships but reports that he has difficulty trusting anyone, particularly women. He reports that even when relationships seem to be going well, he believes that his partner is unfaithful and cannot trust them when he can't see what they are doing. Simon claims that these feelings preoccupy him constantly and that, regardless of what his partner says

or does to try and reassure him, nothing seems to make him feel better. Simon has a criminal record, which mainly comprises of convictions for harassment and criminal damage, all of which focus on partners or ex-partners.

Simon had been cohabiting with Sarah for three years before Sarah ended their relationship some five years ago. When they were together Simon was very controlling over Sarah's movements, needing to know exactly where she was going and who she was going to be with. He also displayed persistent jealousy over her friendships with other people, especially men (controlling behaviours). Sarah had never made any complaints to the police about Simon's behaviour.

Sarah has been gathering evidence regarding her harassment by Simon over the course of the last five years, since their relationship ended. The evidence under consideration indicates that Sarah had received more than fifty threatening letters, hundreds of seemingly anonymous threatening emails and, for the last six months, a wreath of roses once a month with a doctored photograph attached to it depicting her violent death and a 'date of execution' highlighted.

The probation psychologist concluded that David evidenced characteristics similar to a **dysphoric/borderline** offender.

and their basis in clinical samples that are unlikely to be representative. However, taken together, such evidence about the heterogeneity of IPV and stalking perpetration supports the need for a multifactor framework to guide understanding of these problems. Indeed, this is important, as some research suggests different types of men will benefit from different types of intervention (e.g. Saunders, 1996).

IMPLICATIONS FOR PRACTICE: RISK ASSESSMENT

Risk assessments are undertaken in many walks of life to determine the level of risk that an identified threat poses. In the case of IPV, risk assessments are carried out

BOX 10.4   STALKING TYPOLOGY (ZONA *ET AL.*, 1998)

- **Erotomanic** stalking is conducted by individuals who hold the delusional belief that the victim, who is unattainable to them, loves them. The stalking behaviours are therefore used as extreme attention-seeking behaviours in order to make the target aware of the perpetrator's existence. Typically this occurs when the target is a member of the perpetrator's social network, and it is more likely to occur in female stalkers who pursue high status males with whom they have had no previous relationship.

- **Simple obsessional** stalking typically arises either from an intimate relationship or from an acquaintance known through work or a professional setting.

   Motives within the two subcategories above have been identified as either the desire to maintain or restart an intimate relationship, or vengeance for a perceived act of mistreatment (which Simon from Case Study 10.2 clearly fits).
- **Love-obsessional** stalking occurs when the target is known to the stalker but there is no previous intimate relationship between them. Such a target might include public figures with power and/or status, or celebrities.

by numerous types of professional (e.g. police, psychologists, social workers, independent domestic violence advocates) to understand the risk of harm (usually categorised at high, medium or low risk levels) that an individual perpetrator poses to their current or ex-intimate partner. Such assessments are useful in a number of domains, such as safety planning for victims or other family members, developing a treatment plan and evaluating post treatment risk. The validity and reliability of risk assessments is therefore of importance if professionals are to predict the likelihood of harm posed to a victim with a good degree of accuracy.

Risk assessment has been attempted using various methods of clinical, actuarial and structured professional judgement. A clinical approach to risk assessment relies on the professional's experience only; it is not guided by any framework and as such has been found to be open to many biases and less accurate than actuarial approaches that derive risk factors through empirical methods and use cut-off scores to indicate risk levels. However, the actuarial method is not without criticism; for example, it has a heavy reliance on static factors that cannot change over time, resulting in a perpetrator being unable to reduce their assigned risk level as such structured professional judgement tools have been offered as a compromise. This method provides a guide or framework, developed from the empirical literature, which professionals can systematically follow to draw conclusions about risk (see Bowen, 2011b; Nicholls *et al.*, 2007 for a detailed discussion).

This evidence base has been instrumental in developing risk assessment tools that can estimate risk of harm or lethality from an intimate partner. Various actuarial and structured professional judgement tools exist; examples of these are the *Spousal Assault Risk Assessment* (Kropp *et al.*, 1999); *Brief Spousal Assault Form for the Evaluation of Risk* (Kropp *et al.*, 2004); *Ontario Domestic Assault Risk Assessment* (Hilton *et al.*, 2004); and *Domestic Violence Screening Inventory* (Williams & Houghton, 2004). The *Danger Assessment – Revised* (Campbell *et al.*, 2009) has been developed specifically to identify women who are at risk of very severe and lethal partner violence. Only one formal assessment of risk for stalking – the guidelines for *Stalking Assessment and Management* (Kropp *et al.*, 2006) – has been published, and this draws upon the structured professional judgement approach to risk assessment (detailed in Bowen, 2011b).

While the majority of risk assessment tools are developed from studies that have examined men's aggression to a female partner (and not female heterosexual or same sex aggression), they do all assess the presence of multiple factors in a perpetrator's or victim's life and, as such, have drawn on the evidence derived from different theoretical perspectives rather than reliance on one perspective. This allows for a comprehensive and thorough risk assessment, which is necessary if the cause of the problem is to be understood properly and the type of perpetrator identified, which will necessarily inform treatment and/or management strategies.

SUMMARY

- It is evident that IPV and stalking are international social problems of significant magnitude that can occur independently or co-occur. Regardless of the survey design used to estimate prevalence rates it is clear that this violence negatively affects a considerable percentage of those examined.

- Consensus on the magnitude of the problems and which sex is primarily affected remains uncertain to date, due to differences in understanding about the nature and aetiology of the problems. However, the evidence base shows a gender-inclusive approach to investigating both is needed.

- Research into the risk profiles of perpetrators shows that multiple factors provide an explanation for both IPV and stalking and that subtypes with different profiles of aetiological risk are evident, although further investigations into typologies of IPV women and stalking are clearly needed.

- Collectively, the body of empirical evidence discussed here has led researchers to develop tools that can aid the comprehensive assessment, prediction and prevention of IPV and stalking. Such systematic approaches are necessary if the prevention of fatalities, such as that described in the introduction of this chapter, are to be achieved.

ESSAY/DISCUSSION QUESTIONS

1. 'Multifactor theories provide the best explanation for the aetiology of intimate partner violence and most accurately inform risk assessment.' Critically discuss this statement using the evidence base.

2. 'Intimate partner violence and stalking are heterogeneous crimes and this should be taken into account during assessment and/or treatment of offenders.' Critically discuss.

3. Critically evaluate the claim that erotomania is the basis of all stalking behaviours.

4. Critically evaluate the claim by Douglas and Dutton (2001) that stalking should be considered a form of domestic violence.

REFERENCES

American Psychiatric Association. (2000). *Diagnostic and statistical manual of mental disorders* (4th edn, text revision). Washington, DC: American Psychiatric Association.

Archer, J. (1994). Introduction. In J. Archer (Ed.) *Male violence* (pp.1–20). London: Routledge.

Archer, J. (2000). Sex differences in aggression between heterosexual partners: A meta-analytic review. *Psychological Bulletin, 126*, 651–680.

Babcock, J.C., Miller, S.A. & Siard, C. (2003). Toward a typology of abusive women: Differences between partner-only and generally violent women in the use of violence. *Psychology of Women Quarterly, 27*, 153–161.

Bailey, B. (2010, March 16). Stalker guilty of stabbing ex-girlfriend to death in brutal attack. *London Evening Standard*. Retrieved 22 August 2011 from www.thisislondon.co.uk/standard/article-23815878-stalker-guilty-of-stabbing-ex-girlfriend-to-death-in-frenzied-attack.do

Bandura, A. (1977). *Social learning theory*. Oxford, England: Prentice-Hall.

Bartholomew, K. & Horowitz, L.M. (1991). Attachment styles among young adults: A test of a four category model. *Journal of Personality and Social Psychology, 61*, 226–244.

Basile, K., Swahn, M., Chen, J. & Saltzman, L. (2006). Staling in the United States: Recent national prevalence estimates. *American Journal of Preventive Medicine, 31*, 172–175.

Bell, K.M. & Naugle, A.E. (2008). IPV theoretical considerations: Moving towards a contextual framework. *Clinical Psychology Review, 28*, 1096–1107.

Blaauw, E., Winkel, F., Arensman, E., Sheridan, L. & Freeve, A. (2002). The toll of stalking: The relationship between features of stalking and psychopathology of victims. *Journal of Interpersonal Violence, 17*, 50–63.

Bowen, E. (2011a). *The rehabilitation of partner-violent men*. Chichester: Wiley-Blackwell.

Bowen, E. (2011b). Prevalence and experiences of dating violence in early adolescence. *Journal of Adolescent Health*. Manuscript submitted for publication.

Bowen, E. (2011c). An overview of IPV risk assessment and the potential contributions of victim appraisals. *Aggression and Violent Behavior, 16*, 225–241.

Bowlby, J. (1988). *A secure base: Parent-child attachment and healthy human development*. New York: Basic Books.

Boyle, D.J., O'Leary, D.O., Rosenbaum, A. & Hassett-Walker, C. (2008). Differentiating between generally and partner-only violent subgroups: Lifetime antisocial behaviour, family of origin violence and impulsivity. *Journal of Family Violence, 23*, 47–55.

Brewster, M. (2000). Stalking by former intimates: Verbal threats and other predictors of physical violence. *Violence and Victims, 15*, 41–54.

Brewster, M. (2002). Trauma symptoms of former intimate stalking victims. *Women & Criminal Justice, 13*, 141–161.

Bronfenbrenner, U. (1979). *The ecology of human development: Experiments by nature and design*. Cambridge, MA: Harvard University Press.

Browne, K.D. & Herbert, M. (1997). *Preventing family violence*. Chichester: John Wiley & Sons, Inc.

Budd. T. & Mattinson, J. (2000). *Stalking findings from the 1998 British Crime Survey. Home Office Research Findings 129*. London: Home Office.

Burgess, A.W., Baker, T., Greening, D., Hartman, C.R., Burgess, A.G., Douglas, J.E., *et al.* (1997). Stalking behaviours within domestic violence. *Journal of Family Violence, 12*, 389–403.

Campbell, J.C., Webster, D.W. & Glass, N.E. (2009). The danger assessment: Validation of a lethality risk assessment instrument for intimate partner femicide. *Journal of Interpersonal Violence, 24*, 653–674.

Capaldi, D.M. & Clark, S. (1998). Prospective family predictors of aggression toward female partners for at-risk young men. *Developmental Psychology, 37*, 61–73.

Chase, K.A., O'Leary, K.D. & Heyman, R.E. (2001). Categorizing partner-violent men within the reactive-proactive typology model. *Journal of Consulting and Clinical Psychology, 69*, 567–572.

Cupach, W. & Spitzberg, B. (2000). Obsessive relational intrusion: Incidence, perceived severity and coping. *Violence and Victims, 15,* 357–372.

Davis, K., Ace, A. & Andra, M. (2000). Stalking perpetrators and psychological maltreatment of partners: Anger-jealousy, attachment insecurity, need for control and break-up context. *Violence and Victims, 15,* 407–425.

Dixon, L., Archer, J. & Graham-Kevan, N. (2011). *Perpetrator programmes for partner violence: Are they based on ideology or evidence?* Manuscript submitted for publication.

Dixon, L., Fatania, R. & Howard, P. (2011). *Classifying female perpetrated intimate partner aggression.* Manuscript submitted for publication.

Dixon, L. & Graham-Kevan, N. (2010). Spouse abuse. In B.S. Fisher & S.P. Lab (Eds.) *Encyclopaedia of victimology and crime prevention.* Thousand Oaks. Sage.

Dixon, L. & Graham-Kevan, N. (2011). Understanding the nature and aetiology of IPV and implications for practice: A review of the evidence base. *Trauma, Violence and Abuse.* Manuscript submitted for publication.

Dobash, R.P. & Dobash, R.E. (1979). *Violence against wives: A case against the patriarchy.* New York: The Free Press.

Dobash, R.P. & Dobash, R.E. (2004). Women's violence to men in intimate relationships. *British Journal of Criminology, 44,* 324–349.

Douglas, K.S. & Dutton, D.G. (2001). Assessing the link between stalking and domestic violence. *Aggression and Violent Behavior, 6,* 519–546.

Dutton, D.G. (1985). An ecologically nested theory of male violence towards intimates. *International Journal of Women's Studies, 8,* 404–413.

Dutton, D.G. (1995). *The domestic assault of women.* Vancouver, BC: UBC Press.

Dutton, D.G. (1998). *The abusive personality.* New York: The Guilford Press.

Dutton, D.G. (1999). Limitations of social learning models in explaining intimate aggression. In X.B. Arriaga & S. Oskamp (Eds.) *Violence in intimate relationships* (pp.73–87). Thousand Oaks, CA: Sage.

Dutton, D.G. (2006). *Rethinking domestic violence.* Vancouver: UBC Press.

Dutton, D.G. & Kerry, G. (1999). Modus operandi and personality disorder in incarcerated spousal killers. *International Journal of Law and Psychiatry, 22,* 287–299.

Dutton, D.G., Saunders, K., Starzomski, A. & Bartholomew, K. (1994). Intimacy-anger and insecure attachment as precursors of abuse in intimate relationships. *Journal of Applied Social Psychology, 24,* 1367–1387.

Ehrensaft, M.K., Cohen, P., Brown, J., Smailes, E., Chen, H. & Johnson, J.G. (2003). Intergenerational transmission of partner violence: A 20-year prospective study. *Journal of Consulting and Clinical Psychology, 71,* 741–753.

Finney, A. (2006). *Domestic violence sexual assault and stalking: Findings from the 2004/05 British Crime Survey. Home Office Online Report No12/06.* London: Home Office.

Fox, K.A., Nobles, M.R. & Fisher, B.S. (2011). Method behind the madness: An examination of stalking measures. *Aggression and Violent Behavior,* in press.

Gelles, R.J. (1990). Methodological issues in the study of family violence. In M.A. Straus & R.J. Gelles (Eds.) *Physical violence in American families, risk factors and adaptations to violence in 8145 families.* (pp.17–28). New Brunswick: Transaction Publishers.

Goodwin, I. (2003). The relevance of attachment theory to the philosophy, organization and practice of adult mental health care. *Clinical Psychology Review, 23,* 35–56.

Graham-Kevan, N. (2007). Power and control in relationship aggression. In J. Hamel & T.L. Nicholls (Eds.) *Family interventions in domestic violence: A handbook of gender inclusive theory and treatment.* (pp.87–108). New York: Springer.

Hackett, K. (2000). Criminal harassment. *Juristat, 20,* 1–16.

Hazan, C. & Shaver, P. (1987). Romantic love conceptualised as an attachment process. *Journal of Personality and Social Psychology, 52,* 511–524.

Hilton, N.Z., Harris, G.T., Rice, M.E., Lang, C., Cormier, C.A. & Lines, K.J. (2004). A brief actuarial assessment for the prediction of wife assault recidivism: The Onrario Domestic Assault Risk Assessment. *Psychological Assessment, 16,* 267–275.

Huss, M.T. & Langhinrichsen-Rohling, J. (2006). Assessing the generalization of psychopathy in a clinical sample of domestic violence perpetrators. *Law and Human Behavior, 30,* 571–586.

Holtzworth-Munroe, A., Meehan, C., Herron, K., Rehman, U. & Stuart, G.L. (2000). Testing the Holtzworth-Munroe and Stuart (1994) batterer typology. *Journal of Consulting and Clinical Psychology, 68,* 1000–1019.

Holtzworth-Munroe, A. & Stuart, G.L. (1994). Typologies of male batterers: Three subtypes and the differences among them. *Psychological Bulletin, 116,* 476–497.

Holtzworth-Munroe, A., Stuart, G.L. & Hutchinson, G. (1997). Violent versus nonviolent husbands: Differences in attachment patterns, dependency and jealousy. *Journal of Family Psychology, 11,* 314–331.

James, D. & Farnham, F. (2003). Stalking and serious violence. *Journal of the American Academy of Psychiatry and Law, 31,* 432–439.

Kienlen, K.K., Birmingham, D.L., Solberg, K.B., O'Regan, J.T. & Meloy, J.R. (1997). A comparative study of psychotic and nonpsychotic stalking. *Journal of the American Academy of Psychiatry and Law, 25,* 317–334.

Ko Ling, C., Straus, M.A., Brownridge, D.A., Tiwari, A. & Leung, W.C. (2008). Prevalence of dating IPV and suicidal ideation among male and female university students worldwide. *Journal of Midwifery and Women's Health, 53,* 529–537.

Kropp, P.R., Hart, S.D. & Belfrage, H. (2004). *Brief Spousal Assault Form for the Evaluation of Risk (B–SAFER). User manual.* Vancouver: British Columbia Institute on Family Violence.

Kropp, P.R., Hart, S.D. & Lyon, D.R. (2006). *Guidelines for Stalking Assessment and Management (SAM).* Vancouver, BC: Proactive Resolutions.

Kropp, P.R., Hart, S.D., Webster, C.D. & Eaves, D. (1999). *Manual for the spousal assault risk assessment guide* (3rd edn). Toronto, Ontario, Canada: Multi-Health Systems.

Logan, T., Cole, J., Shannon, L. & Walker, R. (2006). *Partner stalking: How women respond, cope and survive.* New York: Springer.

Logan, T.K. & Walker, R. (2009). Partner stalking: Psychological dominance or 'business as usual'? *Trauma, Violence and Abuse, 10,* 247–270.

Logan, T., Walker, R., Jordan, C. & Campbell, J. (2004). An integrative review of separation and victimisation among women: Consequences and implications. *Violence, Trauma, & Abuse, 5,* 143–193.

Logan, T., Walker, R., Jordan, C. & Leukefeld, C.G. (2006). *Women and victimization: Contributing factors, interventions and implications.* Washington, DC: APA.

Lussier, P., Farrington, D.P. & Moffitt, T.E. (2009). Is the antisocial child father of the abusive man? A 40-year prospective longitudinal study of the developmental antecedents of intimate partner violence. *Criminology, 47,* 741–780.

Magdol, L., Moffitt, T.E., Caspie, A., Fagan, J. & Silva, P.A. (1997). Gender differences in partner violence in a birth cohort of 21 year olds: Bridging the gap between clinical and epidemiological approaches. *Journal of Consulting and Clinical Psychology, 65,* 68–78.

Mauricio., A.M. & Gormley, B. (2001). Male perpetration of physical violence against female partners. *Journal of Interpersonal Violence, 16,* 1066–1081.

McFarlane, J., Campbell, J.C., Wilt, S., Sachs, C., Ulrich, Y. & Xu, X. (1999). Stalking and intimate partner femicide. *Homicide Studies, 3,* 300–316.

Meloy, J.R. (1996). Stalking (obsessional following): A review of some preliminary studies. *Aggression and Violent Behavior, 1,* 147–162.

Meloy, J.R. & Gothard, S. (1995). Demographics and clinical comparison of obsessional followers and offenders wtih mental disorders. *Journal of Forensic Science, 45,* 147–152.

Melton, H. (2000). Stalking: A review of the literature and direction for the future. *Criminal Justice Review, 25,* 246–262.

Melton, H. (2007). Predicting the occurrence of stalking in relationships characterised by domestic violence. *Journal of Interpersonal Violence, 22,* 3–25.

Mohandie, K., Meloy, J., McGowan, M. & Williams, J. (2006). The RECON typology of stalking: Reliability and validity based upon a large sample of North American stalkers. *Journal of Forensic Science, 51,* 147–155.

Moracco, K.E., Runyan, C.W., Bowling, J.M. & Earp, J.A.L. (2007). Women's experiences with violence: A national study. *Women's Health Issues, 2,* 3–12.

Mullen, P., Pathe, M. & Purcell, R. (2000). *Stalkers and their victims.* New York: Cambridge University Press.

Murphy, C.M., Meyer, S.L. & O'Leary, K.D. (1994). Dependency characteristics of partner assaultive men. *Journal of Abnormal Psychology, 103,* 729–735.

Nicholls, T.N., Desmarais, S.L., Douglas, K.S. & Kropp, P.R. (2007). Violence risk assessments with perpetrators of intimate partner abuse. In J. Hamel & T.L. Nicholls (Eds.) *Family interventions in domestic violence: A handbook of gender-inclusive theory and treatment.* (pp.275–301). New York: Springer.

Nowinski, S. & Bowen, E. (in revision). IPV against men in heterosexual and homosexual intimate relationships: Prevalence and correlates. *Aggression and Violent Behavior.*

O'Leary, K.D., Smith Slep, A.M. & O'Leary, S.G. (2007). Multivariate models of men's and women's partner aggression. *Journal of Consulting and Clinical Psychology, 75,* 752–764.

Patton, C.L., Nobles, M.R. & Fox, K.A. (2010). Look who's stalking: Obsessive pursuit and attachment theory. *Journal of Criminal Justice, 38,* 282–290.

Povey, D., Coleman, K., Kaiza, P., Hoare, J. & Jansson, K. (2008). *Homicide, firearms and intimate violence 2006/07 (Home Office Statistical Bulletin 03/08).* London: Home Office.

Renzetti, C. & Miley, C.H. (Eds.) (1996). *Violence in lesbian and gay partnerships.* New York: Haworth Press.

Respect. (2008). *Respect position statement: Gender and domestic violence.* Retrieved 22 August 2011 from www.respect.uk.net/data/files/respect_gender__dv_position_satatement.doc

Rosenfeld, B. (2004). Violence risk factors in stalking and obsessional harassment: A review and preliminary meta-analysis. *Criminal Justice and Behavior, 31,* 9–36.

Santovena, E.E. & Dixon, L. (2011). Investigating the true rate of physical intimate partner violence: A review of nationally representative surveys. *Aggression and Violent Behavior.* Manuscript submitted for publication.

Saunders, D.G. (1996). Feminist-cognitive-behavioral and process-psychodynamic treatments for men who batter: Interaction of abuser traits and treatment models. *Violence and Victims, 11,* 393–414.

Sheridan, L. & Davies, G.M. (2001). Stalking: the elusive crime. *Legal and Criminological Psychology, 6,* 133–147.

Sheridan, L. & Davies, G. (2004). Stalking. In J.R. Adler (Ed.) *Forensic psychology: Concepts, debates and practice* (pp.197–216). Cullompton: Willan.

Sheridan, L., Davies, G.M. & Boon, J.C.W. (2001). Stalking: Perceptions and prevalence. *Journal of Interpersonal Violence, 16,* 151–167.

Sheridan, L., Gillett, R. & Davies, G.M. (2000). Stalking: Seeking the victim's perspective. *Psychology, Crime & Law, 6,* 267–280.

Sheridan, L., Gillett, R. & Davies, G.M. (2002). Perceptions and prevalence of stalking in a male sample. *Psychology, Crime & Law, 8,* 289–310.

Smith, K., Flatley, J., Coleman, K., Osborne, S., Kaiza, P. & Roe, S. (2010). *Homicides, firearm offences and intimate violence 2008/09. Home Office Statistical Bulletin 01/10.* London: Home Office.

Spitzberg, B.H. (2002). The tactical topography of stalking victimization and management. *Trauma, Violence and Abuse, 3,* 261–288.

Stith, S.M., Smith, D.B., Penn, C.E., Ward, D.B. & Tritt, D. (2004). Intimate partner physical abuse perpetration and victimization risk factors: A meta-analytic review. *Aggression and Violent Behavior: A Review Journal, 10,* 65–98.

Straus, M.A. (1999). *Characteristics of the National Violence Against Women Study that might explain the low assault rate for both sexes and the even lower rate for assaults by women.* Retrieved 22 August 2011 from www.batteredmen.com/straus22.htm

Straus, M.A. & Gelles, R.J. (1985). *Is family violence increasing? A comparison of 1975 and 1985 national survey rates.* Paper presented at the American Society of Criminology, San Diego. In D.G. Dutton (2007). *Rethinking domestic violence* (p.42). Vancouver: UCB Press.

Straus, M.A. & Gelles, R. (1990). Measuring intrafamily conflict and violence. In M.A. Straux & R.J. Gelles (Eds.) Physical violence in American families. New Brunswick, NJ: Transaction publishers.

Straus, M.A., Gelles, R.J. & Steinmetz, S.K. (1980). *Behind closed doors: Violence in the American family.* New York: Anchor Books.

Straus, M.A., Hamby, S.L., Boney-McCoy, S. & Sugarman, D.B. (1996). The revised conflict tactics scales (CTS2): Development and preliminary psychometric data. *Journal of Family Issues, 17,* 283–316.

Sugarman, D.B. & Frankel, S.L. (1996). Patriarchal ideology and wife-assault: A meta-analytic review. *Journal of Family Violence, 11,* 13–40.

Westrup, D. (1998). Applying functional analysis to stalking behaviour. In J.R. Meloy (Ed.) *The psychology of stalking: Clinical and forensic perspectives* (pp.275–297). New York: Academic Press.

Westrup, D. & Fremouw, W. (1998). Stalking behaviour: A literature review and suggested functional analytic assessment technology, *Aggression and Violent Behavior, 3,* 255–274.

White, J., Kowalski, R.M., Lyndon, A. & Valentine, S. (2002). An integrative contextual developmental model of male stalking. *Violence and Victims, 15,* 373–388.

White, H.R. & Widom, C.S. (2003). Intimate partner violence among abused and neglected children in young adulthood: The mediating effects of early aggression, antisocial personality, hostility and alcohol problems. *Aggressive Behavior, 29,* 332–345.

Williams, K.R. & Houghton, A.B. (2004). Assessing the risk of domestic violence re-offending: A validation study. *Law and Human Behavior, 28,* 437–455.

Woodin, E.M. & O'Leary, K.D. (2009). Theoretical approaches to the etiology of partner violence. In D.J. Whittaker & J.R. Lutzker (Eds.) *Preventing partner violence: research and evidence-based intervention strategies* (pp 41–66). Washington, DC: American Psychological Association.

World Health Organization. (2005). *Summary Report: WHO multi-country study on women's health and domestic violence against women: Initial results on prevalence, health outcomes, and women's responses.* Geneva: World health organization Press.

Ylló, K.A. (2005). Through a feminist lens: Gender, diversity, and violence: Extending the feminist framework. In D.R. Loseke, R.J. Gelles & M.M. Cavanaugh (Eds.) *Current controversies on family violence* (pp 19–34) Thousand Oaks, Sage.

Zona, M.A., Palarea, R.E. & Lane, J.C.Jr. (1998). Psychiatric diagnosis and the offender-victim typology of stalking. In J.R. Meloy (Ed.) *The psychology of stalking: Clinical and forensic perspectives* (pp.70–83). San Diego, CA: Academic Press, Inc.

Zona, M.A., Sharma, K.K. & Lane, J. (1993). A comparative study of erotomanic and obsessional subjects in a forensic sample. *Journal of Forensic Science, 38,* 894–903.

ANNOTATED READING LIST

Archer, J. (2000). Sex differences in aggression between heterosexual partners: A meta-analytic review. *Psychological Bulletin, 126,* 651–680. *A meta-analytic review that examines sex differences in the perpetration of heterosexual IPV in studies that examined rates of physical violence by men and women.*

Davis, K., Ace, A. & Andra, M. (2000). Stalking perpetrators and psychological maltreatment of partners: Anger-jealousy, attachment insecurity, need for control and break-up context. *Violence and Victims, 15,* 407–425. *An empirical study that provides some support for an attachment-theory conceptualisation of stalking.*

Douglas, K.S. & Dutton, D.G. (2001). Assessing the link between stalking and domestic violence. *Aggression and Violent Behavior, 6,* 519–546. *A really useful overview of the issue of stalking and how conceptually it represents an extension of domestic violence behaviours for some individuals.*

Dutton, D.G. (2006). *Rethinking domestic violence.* Vancouver: UBC Press. *This book provides an overview of intimate partner violence from an evidence based perspective.*

Holtzworth-Munroe, A., Meehan, C., Herron, K., Rehman, U. & Stuart, G.L. (2000). Testing the Holtzworth-Munroe and Stuart (1994) batterer typology. *Journal of Consulting and Clinical Psychology, 68,* 1000–1019. *This empirical study tests the validity of the Holtzworth-Munroe and Stuart (1994) typology of male intimate partner violence perpetrators.*

Westrup, D. & Fremouw, W. (1998). Stalking behaviour: A literature review and suggested functional analytic assessment technology, *Aggression and Violent Behavior, 3,* 255–274. *A literature review that focuses on stalking as a unique phenomenon, providing a clear chronological account of the literature, as well as proposing the use of functional analysis in assessment, treatment and research to clarify the nature of stalking behaviour.*

11 Terrorism

Max Taylor

CHAPTER OUTLINE

This paper has drawn extensively on material produced by Dr John Horgan, and his contribution is acknowledged.

L'homme, l'homme, l'homme armé,
L'homme armé
L'homme armé doibt on doubter, doibt on doubter . . .

The man, the man, the armed man,
The armed man
The armed man should be feared, should be feared . . .

The study of terrorism is essentially a multidisciplinary endeavour, drawing on insights from a range of areas and perspectives, and in this respect, of course, it is no different from other forensic areas. In the following chapter, we will consider some of the central issues that might characterise our understanding of terrorism and the terrorist from a forensic psychological perspective. It will focus, in particular, on the idea of process as an organising concept.

WHAT IS TERRORISM?

To begin thinking about terrorism and forensic psychology, we must first of all consider what we mean by terrorism. Both *terrorism* and the *terrorist* (the individual who commits a terrorist offence) are contentious terms, which lack a universally agreed definition. In a sense this is like *crimes* and *criminals*, in that social and cultural contexts may affect what we might regard as a particular crime and, likewise, how we might understand the person who commits that crime. But in some senses the concept of terrorism is more complex than that of crime; although generally speaking we regard terrorism as a crime, its distinguishing quality is that it has a political context (as we will see) that, on the whole, crime does not; and furthermore, it is often loosely used as a pejorative rather than descriptive label.

Yet despite these uncertainties, terrorism (or something the contemporary viewer would recognise as such) has been with us for a very long time. The short quotation at the beginning of this chapter is the first three lines of a medieval French song that captures the sense of terror felt then and now when citizens are faced by armed men (Burk, 2005). The song is known to have existed in the 15th century, and contemporary scholarship suggests it may have had a dual meaning – beware the armed men (soldiers) of the state, or those claiming to represent the state, but also beware the reciprocal of that, armed citizens (Lockwood, 1973), which in medieval France might have been effectively the same thing.

Armed citizens, whether in the form of conscripted local militias or in the form of a more distributed sense of armed individuals acting collectively or individually to a purpose, captures an important sense of what we might recognise in the contemporary world as terrorism, and, as Burk notes, our modern day fears associated with terrorism echo those associated with the medieval 'l'homme armé'. The confused reciprocity between legitimate state activity (in exercising social control, for example), and illegitimate individual activity (as in armed men challenging a state, for example, which we might refer to as terrorism) implied by this song clearly hinges on what we mean by 'legitimate' and 'authority', and it is this relationship that continues to complicate our understanding of terrorism.

There is no universally agreed definition of terrorism (Carlile, 2007) but a widely accepted definition suggests the term means 'premeditated, politically motivated violence perpetrated against non-combatant targets by subnational groups, or clandestine agents' (US Law Code, Title 22, Ch.38, Para 2656f(d); Figure 11.1). If you think through what this might mean, you will see some of the complexity of understanding terrorism; but one thing that is quite clear is that terrorism is firmly grounded within essentially an instrumental and political context involving violence premised on the notion of state legitimacy. The use of violence to intimidate people (and terrorist violence is often directed towards people) in the absence of a political motive, although problematic and frequently illegal, is not in itself an example of terrorism (but might be thought of as a crime). It is political instrumentality focused against non-combatants that is the critical element in distinguishing between terrorism and criminal violence (in contrast, for example, to organised criminal activity with which it might be thought to share some common qualities).

FIGURE 11.1 *The CIA defines terrorism as 'premeditated, politically motivated violence perpetrated against non-combatant targets by subnational groups, or clandestine agents'.*

Source: © Dmitriy Shironosov. Used under licence from Shutterstock.

In the UK, and in Europe more broadly, the response to terrorism tends to be framed from within a civil and criminal law context, emphasising the role of civil society elements (the police, the judiciary and parliamentary control) in responding to terrorism. In contrast, the USA has tended to see the response to terrorism from a more military perspective (Oliverio, 2008). These very fundamentally different ways of approaching terrorism have profoundly shaped contemporary responses to terrorism.

THE PSYCHOLOGY OF TERRORISM

Contrary to popular media representation, to date forensic psychology has played a relatively small role in analyses of terrorism (Horgan, 2005; Silke, 2003). Indeed, unlike many other areas of forensic application, the study of terrorism generally lacks substantive evidence based research, and in particular has attracted relatively limited psychological analysis. Although the academic study of terrorism has massively expanded since 9/11, most of this expansion has been in social science disciplines such as political science. Four approaches to the study of terrorism can be identified (Horgan, 2005) that might guide our understanding. These are shown in Box 11.1.

9/11 attacks on US targets on 11 September 2001, in which al-Qaeda terrorists hijacked four airliners, crashing two into the World Trade Center, one into the Pentagon and one in Pennsylvania, killing nearly 4000 people.

It might be argued that separating the individual from his or her social context and, similarly, from the consequences of action, is inappropriate, and omits the significance of the totality of influences on behaviour. In the case of terrorism, and its focus on political influence, this may seem a very strong point. On the other hand, the starting point for forensic psychology analysis is presumably problematic and inappropriate behaviour;

and whatever long-term intentions of the perpetrator (or his organisation) might be, it is an *individual* who commits an act of terrorism and, as we have seen in other areas of criminality, it is by focusing on the factors that influence individual action that effective management provision can be made. In what follows, therefore, the focus taken is primarily from an individual perspective, exploring the role of the individual in the complex array of factors that are associated with terrorism.

Early psychologically focused studies of terrorism tended to focus on 'why' terrorists engage with violence. These explanations tended to be framed in terms of abnormality, psychopathology, or individual personality traits (Schmid & Jongman, 1988) and often either explicitly or implicitly drew on psychoanalytic perspectives. An extension of this approach, still current in some quarters, is sometimes expressed as psychological profiles (Russell & Miller, 1983). However, the consensus of contemporary views is that these approaches are unhelpful and generally do not contribute to our understanding of terrorism (Beck, 2002; Corrado, 1981; Crenshaw, 1992), and there is little evidence of mental illness or more generally psychopathology as a factor in either understanding or predicting terrorist behaviour (McCauley, 2002; Sageman, 2004).

More contemporary approaches have emphasised the significance of learning and the situational context to behaviour as factors in the development of terrorism. An early powerful theoretical model that has informed much of this approach is social learning theory (Akers, 1994; Bandura, 1990). This approach emphasises the role of observation in learning and, by extension, the social context in which learning might occur. Other contemporary approaches have drawn on *cognitive theories*, especially theories of aggression drawing on concepts such as social cognitions. Crenshaw (1988), for example, has suggested that principles of social cognition apply to both terrorist organisations and terrorists: 'the actions of terrorists are based on a subjective interpretation of the world rather than objective reality. Perceptions of the political and social environment are filtered through beliefs and attitudes that reflect experiences and memories' (Crenshaw, 1988, p.12).

BOX 11.1   FOUR FACTORS NECESSARY TO THE UNDERSTANDING OF TERRORISM

1. The individual, and the processes that might characterise involvement for the individual in terrorism.

2. The relationship between the individual and his or her political and social context.

3. The consequences of terrorism, in terms of how the individual and society might be affected by terrorism.

4. The methodological framework in which to study terrorism.

A difficulty with much of this early work is that it tended to focus on terrorism as something akin to a 'state of being', and in so doing asked questions related to *why* does terrorist behaviour occur, rather than asking questions about the behaviour itself. We noted earlier that the study of terrorism has been influenced by a range of disciplines, and it may well be that this emphasis is a reflection of a privileging of questions from largely theoretical driven disciplines such as political science, and a concern with assumptions about particular political qualities of social and individual motivation.

An implication of this approach is to tend to assume the terrorist makes a decisive 'choice' to become involved in terrorism (based on identifiable events, social disadvantage, life experiences or conditions). However, this does not seem to reflect what we know about how terrorists engage with terrorist activity. As Horgan and Taylor (in press) note: 'What we know of actual terrorists suggests that there is rarely a conscious decision made to become a terrorist. Most involvement in terrorism results from gradual exposure and socialisation towards extreme behaviour' (p.17). Furthermore, when we look at the characteristics of terrorists, we find little uniformity or commonality and no particular relationship with structural factors such as economic disadvantage, discrimination and so forth (Bakker, 2006; Travis, 2008; the report in Travis remains classified but is largely accepted – it suggests that most people convicted of terrorist offences in the UK are 'demographically unremarkable' and simply reflect the communities in which they live). Furthermore, and more importantly, when terrorists are asked why they became involved, they offer multiple accounts that vary over time, and may relate more to the context of questioning than 'reality'. This fundamental methodological problem should temper our understanding of the research in this area.

A common theme that does emerge from descriptive studies based on interview, however, is a sense of gradual socialisation into terrorism and an initial sense of involvement characterised by gradual increases in commitment. Given this, group factors may be centrally important in attempting to identify supportive qualities of initial and continuing engagement. Overall, we get a sense of the boundaries between apparent *degrees* of involvement, with a sense of premium attached not only to membership but also to certain, specific roles (Alonso, 2006).

We can conceptualise the process of terrorist involvement as reflecting three related but different elements; *becoming* involved in terrorism, *remaining* involved and *disengaging*. This has been termed the 'ARC' of terrorist involvement (i.e. drawing on the idea of an arch or curve embracing the elements of terrorist involvement: Horgan & Taylor, in press). The boundaries between these elements may be permeable and fuzzy, but as a

way of conceptualising the emergence of the 'terrorist' this approach has considerable merit. The existence of a complex set of dynamic, interacting factors, reflecting a process of assimilation and accommodation, and showing qualitatively distinct processes of incremental progression, has been apparent to researchers for some time (Taylor & Quayle, 1994), although there may well be different accounts that characterise different kinds of people at different stages of political and organisational development (Jamieson, 1989). Given this, it is worth noting that what we frequently fail to appreciate when considering contemporary terrorist movements such as the European and African **jihadi** affiliates of **Al Qaeda** is that even the same terrorist movement can attract and engage people in very different ways, whether they be home-grown or foreign activists, or the increasingly worrying 'local walk-ins' (McAllister, 2004; Veldhuis & Staun, 2009).

> **jihadi** someone who engages in the Muslim religious duty of jihad, meaning to 'struggle', sometimes interpreted as the struggle to maintain the faith or improve Muslim society. Can (inaccurately) refer to a supporter of radical Islamic terrorism.

> **Al Qaeda** a terrorist organisation/network that seeks to establish a radical form of Islam based on Sharia law. Until his death in 2011, it was led by Osama bin Laden.

Becoming, remaining, disengaging

Those who engage directly in terrorist violent activity are few in number relative to the overall movement; the actual perpetrator of a terrorist event is generally only one element or task within a much larger context. The **Provisional IRA** (Irish Republican Army), for example, had a complex organisational structure (Horgan & Taylor, 1997) that controlled logistics, financing and even research (into bomb-making techniques, for example; Figure 11.2). Terrorist movements can therefore be characterised by having a variety of roles, with many different kinds of involvement; the implication of this is that the visible terrorist is a tip of a larger supportive (both active and passive) iceberg. This diversity of function may be more difficult to appreciate in smaller groups, but it does exist.

> **Provisional IRA** an Irish paramilitary organisation that sought, through armed insurrection and terrorism, to produce a united Ireland. It has been responsible for the deaths of some 1800 people since 1969.

The multiplicity of organisational functional roles is relevant to thinking about the process of terrorism, and offers a way of understanding how an individual might move within an organisation, not only engaging in different activities and roles but by so doing strengthening and confirming involvement, and subsequently also reducing

FIGURE 11.2 *The visible terrorist is the tip of a larger supportive iceberg; for example, the* Provisional IRA *had a complex organisational structure that controlled logistics, financing and even research into bomb making techniques.*

Source: © arindambanerjee. Used under licence from Shutterstock.

FIGURE 11.3 *Since 9/11 we have seen a fundamental legal shift in the meaning of 'involvement in terrorism' to one of mere association, as opposed to a firm involvement in the planning, preparation or execution of a terrorist act.*

Source: © Ken Tannenbaum. Used under licence from Shutterstock.

and diminishing involvement. From this perspective, the reality of what 'becoming' a terrorist involves is a gradual progression into (and sometimes out of) certain roles. Involvement in terrorism is therefore best characterised as a dynamic process of incremental change based on initially supportive and attractive (to the recruit) qualities. From this perspective, it is not a state or condition that a person 'is in'; rather, terrorism (and the violence associated with it) is something that some members of an extremist movement do, amongst other things.

To move this forward, we therefore need to appreciate the kind of roles a terrorist might adopt. These have grown in complexity with the developments of new forms of terrorism (e.g. global Salafi jihad, single-issue terrorism, organised crime-related terrorism, and terrorist use of the internet). It is also important to note that not all of these roles are necessarily illegal, although since the events of 9/11 (Figure 11.3) we have seen a fundamental legal shift in the meaning of 'involvement in terrorism' to one of mere association as opposed to having a more firm involvement in the planning, preparation or execution of a terrorist act.

A further element to note is that increased engagement for the terrorist can often have positive qualities for that individual. These might include the rapid acquisition of some sort of skill or skills, an increased sense of empowerment, a sense of control, purpose and self-importance. Increased engagement, and changing roles,

> **Salafi** a form of Islam that is defined by its rejection of the 'taqlid' (imitation) of the four canonical Islamic madhahib, the traditional schools of Islamic jurisprudence, and suggests it is necessary to return to the original sources in order to make any judgment.

also act as a form of currency and give a tangible sense of acceptance within the group, and in combination with this the acquisition of status. We can identify these factors in groups such as the Provisional IRA, but the analysis is also consistent with Sageman's (2004) analysis of engagement with Al Qaeda.

Although recent examples of **lone wolf terrorism** might temper this, individuals tend to engage in terrorism in association with others in some sense, which suggests a potential role for group factors influencing behaviour (Kruglanski & Fishman, 2009). These may be evident in a potential both to attract members and to bind them together via sustained commitment and engagement. Extreme conformity and strict obedience, similarly, are organisational qualities that enhance the effective maintenance of a secret, and above all illegal, organisation. Illegality, therefore, is an important factor maintaining control and conformity, which, along with a shared purpose or sense of unity and direction and a clearly identifiable enemy, facilitates a sense of strong group cohesion. Other group influence factors, such as conformity to social norms and compliance, identification and internalisation, are all elements that might be expected to be of significance, as might processes such as

> **lone wolf terrorism** a lone wolf terrorist is someone who commits acts of terrorism in support of some political aspiration without being part of any formal terrorist group.

diffusion of responsibility and displacement of responsibility. Blaming victims, and dehumanisation of victims, are related processes that are generally explained by social psychological processes that also have clear relevance to understanding terrorist behaviour.

Social networks and social connections and relationships are also factors that influence individual behaviour, and might therefore be expected to be factors in understanding engagement with terrorist behaviour. Della Porta (1995) noted that what characterised early Italian terrorists' engagement was membership of a structured group that influenced its membership, and Sageman (2004) has extended this analysis to our understanding of what characterises mujahedeen involvement in jihadi organisations such as Al Qaeda. Enders and Jindapon (2010) have extended this analysis further to notions of terrorist readiness being a function of the 'shape' of the terrorist network to which they belong.

The theme of overall terrorist structure has been usefully explored by Post (1984; 1987; 1990), who identifies two major types of groups on the basis of the relationships they have with their environment (see Box 11.2). Post suggests that each type may exert psychological influences on those members in dissimilar ways and accordingly may differentially attract members on the basis of different kinds of expected rewards, and in turn differentially influence terrorist behaviour through membership.

The critical point that Post (1984; 1987; 1990) makes is that within *nationalist–separatist* groups the legitimisation of personal decision to engage in violent protest, as well as continuation of commitment in a more general way, can within the context of local circumstances (or communities) be seen as a rite of passage, a movement towards consolidation of identity within the broader community. These distinctions seem as relevant today as they were to the largely European groups of the 1970s and 1980s that Post focused on. There are obvious parallels with contemporary terrorist movements, particularly those based in the West Bank and Gaza Strip, where martyrs from **Hamas** and other movements are held in high esteem within the community. Hassan (2001), who interviewed many militants in the region, describes how in Palestinian neighbourhoods:

> **Hamas** the Palestinian political organisation that has governed the Gaza Strip since 2007. Its social welfare wing has a reputation for lack of corruption and effective service delivery. Its military wing is Izz ad-Din al-Qassam Brigades.

> . . . the suicide bombers' green birds appear on posters, and in graffiti – the language of the street. Calendars are illustrated with the 'martyr of the month'. Paintings glorify the dead bombers in Paradise, triumphant beneath a flock of green birds. This symbol is based on a saying of the Prophet Muhammad that the soul of a martyr is carried to Allah in the bosom of the green birds of Paradise.
>
> *(Hassan, 2001)*

Post *et al.* (2003) interviewed incarcerated members of various Palestinian-affiliated groups, in particular Hamas and its armed wing *Izz a-Din al Qassan*, **Hizbollah**, the *Islamic Jihad*, and others from secular movements. The researchers discovered similarities between the supportive qualities that shaped individual 'pathways' into terrorism, despite the wide variety in participants' backgrounds and histories:

> **Hizbollah** (or Hezbollah). A Shi'a political organisation and militant group known as 'the party of God', based in Lebanon. It receives political and financial support from Iran and Syria.

BOX 11.2   POST'S TWO MAJOR TERRORIST GROUPS

The anarchic–ideologue group

Italian Red Brigades an Italian Marxist-Leninist terrorist group active during the period from 1967 to the late 1980s.

Red Army Faction (also known as RAF, Rote Armee Fraktion, Baader-Meinhof Group). A left-wing terrorist group based in Germany from 1970 to the late 1990s. Its origins were in the student protests of the 1960s.

These are small, 'revolution-based' groups, committed to the overthrow of a current political or social regime, largely for ideological reasons. The old left-wing European terrorist movements, such as the **Italian Red Brigades** and Germany's most violent and prominent left-wing terror group the **Red Army Faction**, typified this type. Post (1984; 1987; 1990) describes 'alienation' from the member's families or immediate community as a characteristic of such groups.

The nationalist–separatist group

The *Provisional IRA*, with its long tradition of resistance against England and British rule in Ireland, is a good example of this type of group. In this type of terrorist group, members (at whatever level of peripheral or focused involvement) are not estranged from their families or communities whose interests they claim to represent. Lately our attention has been drawn to groups of this kind because of the threat of radical Islamic terrorism, but it may well be that in the future anarchic–ideologue groups will again become significant.

The boyhood heroes for the Islamist terrorists were religious figures, such as the radical **Wahabi** Islamist, *Abdullah Azzam*; for the secular terrorists, revolutionary heroes such as *Che Guevara* or *Fidel Castro* were identified. Most had some high school, and some had education beyond high school. The majority of the subjects reported that their families were respected in the community. The families were experienced as being uniformly supportive of their commitment to the 'cause'.

> **Wahabi** Wahabism is a radical branch of Islam developed by Muhammad ibn Abd al-Wahhab. It is the dominant form of Islam in Saudi Arabia and is characterised by an ultra-conservative interpretation of Islam

(Post et al., 2003, p.172)

This work serves not only to emphasise types of network and organisation, but also introduces the notion of role models that serve to offer a source of authoritative legitimacy as far as the justification of violent reaction is concerned. What the individual terrorist perceives to be the *authority* inherent in such roles is an important factor in sustaining the commitment of the individual, as well as facilitating commitment to the violent group more generally. In Post *et al.*'s (2003) analysis, the significance of social setting appears to be privileged (via implicit or explicit approval from peers and family), but other supportive qualities of involvement became clear via their interviews with imprisoned activists. The following suggests this:

> Perpetrators of armed attacks were seen as heroes, their families got a great deal of material assistance including the construction of new homes to replace those destroyed by the Israeli authorities as punishment for terrorist acts … the entire family did all it could for the Palestinian people, and won great respect for doing so. All my brothers are in jail. One is serving a life sentence for his activities in the Izz al-Din Al Qassam battalions.

(Post et al., 2003, p.177)

Post *et al.* (2003) suggest that joining a terrorist group increased 'social standing' among would-be recruits. Recruits were treated with great respect. A youngster who belonged was regarded more highly than one who did not belong to a group, and got better treatment than unaffiliated individuals. Similar themes can be seen in interviews with activists in Northern Ireland. Burgess *et al.* (2009), for example, interviewed one activist who pointed to his awareness of the importance associated with becoming involved in active resistance:

> The idols among our community shot up because they stood for something . . . As soon as your parents, and the priest at the altar, and your teacher are saying 'These men are good men. They are fighting a just thing here', it filters down quickly that these people are important and whatever they say must be right. So all of a sudden, you are bordering on supporting something that is against the government.

(Burgess et al., 2009, p.32)

Engagement in *nationalist–separatist* groups, therefore, carries status not only within an immediate circle of activists, but also within a relevant supportive community. Not only then is there acceptance within the group, but there is also an accompanying sense of status and excitement for the individual within the broader community. This can be a powerful factor not only for sustaining commitment, but also as an element in recruitment.

Some of these factors are illustrated in the case studies. Case Study 11.1 describes how both group and individual factors might operate in a real terrorist operation. It is an account of the events surrounding an attack related to the mooted publication of *The Jewel of Medina* in the UK, drawn from police and court records. Case Study 11.2 illustrates a much more personal focus on what is probably one of the most callous examples of a terrorist attack in modern times.

CASE STUDY 11.1   THE JEWEL OF MEDINA

This is an account of the events surrounding an attack related to the mooted publication of the novel *The Jewel of Medina* in the UK. The details of this incident give some insight into both its group and its individual context, and it is also an example of an intelligence-led counter terrorism operation that changed a potentially life-threatening attack into a relatively minor one. The book, by Sherry Jones, is a fictionalised version of the life of Aisha, one of the wives of the Prophet Mohammed. Although it is a fictionalised account, the book generated protests in many quarters.

(Continued)

In September 2008, three men drove through a square in London where Martin Rynja (the potential publisher of the book) lived. They drove through twice, before two of the men left the car and approached the front door with a fuel can in a white plastic bag. They poured diesel fuel through the letterbox and used a disposable lighter to set it on fire. They were arrested after being stopped by armed London Metropolitan Police officers as they attempted to flee the scene. Due to previous intelligence, police had warned the publisher and his partner to move out of their house. Prior to this incident, all three men were under close police surveillance. Two were seen carrying out reconnaissance 'drive-throughs' of the area in the weeks leading up to the attack. Hence, this was clearly a premeditated attack.

The proposal to publish the book had attracted a lot of adverse comments in some extremist quarters, and this attack gained wider meaning from this. Anjem Choudhary, one of the co-founders of *Al-Muhajiroun* (a radical Islamic group) said he was 'not surprised at all' by the attack and warned of possible further reprisals over the book:

> It is clearly stipulated in Muslim law that any kind of attack on his honour [i.e. the Prophet's honour] carries the death penalty . . . People should be aware of the consequences they might face when producing material like this. They should know the depth of feeling it might provoke.

> (Bingham, 2008)

Omar Bakri, the founder of Al-Muhajiroun, living in Lebanon having been excluded from the UK, said, '. . . if anybody attacks that man (Martin Rynja) I cannot myself condemn it' (Bingham, 2008).

(After Taylor, 2010)

CASE STUDY 11.2   AN ATTEMPTED BOMBING OF AN *EL AL* AIRCRAFT

This is probably one of the most callous acts of terrorism in recent times. Although no formal psychological assessments of the perpetrator, Nezar Hindawi, are available, interviews and other contact with him suggest he is someone who fully understands what he did and quite cynically used his pregnant girlfriend as a medium for carrying a bomb onboard an El Al flight. It also illustrates how states (in this case Syria) have used terrorism to further their own foreign policy objectives.

Hindawi was arrested in April 1986 at a hotel in west London. During interrogation, he admitted having handed his pregnant girlfriend (who was Irish) a bag containing an explosive device for her to take on a flight to Israel. This operation was planned and controlled by the Syrian government, through its intelligence service. Although Hindawi was a Jordanian passport holder, for this operation he held an official Syrian service passport, and members of Syrian Arab Airlines transported and aided him. Hindawi was offered $250,000 to undertake this mission.

Hindawi had an intermittent relationship with his girlfriend but appears to have left her after she became pregnant. On instructions from Damascus, he re-established contact with her and proposed marriage – and a honeymoon in Israel – which she accepted. (Hindawi was, in fact, already married to a Polish national.) On the day before the flight, Hindawi took the bag containing explosives to his girlfriend's flat where he filled it with some of her clothes. The following day he took her by taxi to Heathrow Airport. During the journey, he activated the detonator, then explained that he would follow on a later flight and left her to board the El Al aircraft.

Israeli security at the airport identified the bag, and Hindawi's girlfriend was arrested. Hindawi initially sought refuge with the Syrian authorities in London but, fearing for his life, he gave himself up to the UK police. Hindawi was convicted of attempting to place on an El Al aircraft at London (Heathrow) Airport a device likely to destroy or damage the aircraft contrary to section 1(1) of the Criminal Attempts Act 1981, and he was sentenced to 45 years' imprisonment. The judge commented that 'this was a well-planned, well-organised crime, which involved many others besides yourself, some of them people in high places. A more cruel and callous deception and a more horrendous massacre it is difficult to imagine' (Foreign and Commonwealth Office, 1986). Experts testified during the trial that had the device (which contained 1.5 kg of military explosive) been detonated, it would probably have caused the loss of the aircraft and the deaths of all 375 passengers and crew.

Radicalisation

A term frequently used in relation to the origins of terrorism, and which has gained currency over recent years, is 'radicalisation'. Radicalisation might be characterised as exposure to, and sympathy with, radical ideology. Although its usage has grown, particularly in the media, it is a very contentious term, particularly as few commentators make the critical distinction between holding radical views and engaging in the expression of those views through violence. The following summarises a range of potential factors that can be identified, which seem to relate to increased vulnerability to radicalisation. It is important to stress that these may or may not relate to *violent* radicalisation, and we lack adequate evidence at the moment to definitively resolve this issue.

Indeed, to elaborate on the caution expressed above; all of the following might be regarded as necessary conditions leading to violent radicalisation (in that in aggregate they may be evident) but none (in aggregate or individually) are a sufficient account of engagement in violence (Taylor, 2010). As we noted earlier, personal, organisational and situational factors are also important in an individual's engagement with violence, and this is further complicated by one of the few assertions we can make in this area: no one single socio-economic profile characterises potentially violent radicalised young people (Dalgard-Nielsen, 2010). However, in total, the following offers a global list of factors, explored in further

detail later, that have some measure of empirical verification. These factors relate to Islamic contexts, but there is evidence to suggest that in broad outline they address other forms of extremist narratives; for example, excluding the overt and obvious religious elements, the themes identified below would also characterise the terrorism of Western Europe in mid-20th century, and contemporary right-wing hate activity.

Major themes that characterise the justifications given for engagement with Islamic radicalisation (which it should be noted is only one form of radicalisation, but illustrates some of the pertinent points) are shown in Box 11.3.

Embedded in these themes are four separate narratives (Leuprecht *et al.*, 2010) that support and extend these themes, which are shown in Box 11.4.

We will now explore factors that are imbedded in these themes.

1. Factors related to ideology

Research on jihadi movements suggests that adherence to and influence by ideologies are significant that emphasise some or all of the following:

- structural exclusion (Buijs 2009);
- grievance, hostility of society lived in, disenfranchisement, lack of social justice, the significance of emblems as visual markers (for example, dress,

---

BOX 11.3   THEMES FOR ISLAMIC RADICALISATION

1. Islam is under attack (in the most recent iteration led by the USA as a form of crusade).

2. *Jihadis*, whom the West refers to as 'terrorists', are defending against this attack.

3. The actions they take in defence of Islam are proportional, just and religiously sanctified.

4. It is the duty of good Muslims to support these actions

(Betz, 2008)

BOX 11.4   NARRATIVES THAT SUPPORT RADICALISATION

A *political narrative* that focuses on the evils of the West, and includes neo-Marxist notions related to global inequities and distributive effects arising from Western hegemony and exploitation.

A *moral narrative* that focuses on the contradictory Western values that assert freedom as their core value, and equality and justice as their subsidiary values, although these values are unrealisable ideals and indeed (from a radical Islamic perspective) drivers of a society's moral decay.

A *religious narrative* that serves to legitimises violent struggle to defend Islam against the crusader West.

A *social-psychological narrative* that draws on classic in-group/out-group strategies to brand as 'infidels' those outside of the group, while promoting the brotherhood-of-arms as a means of countering social exclusion, and fulfilling a yearning for adventure and sacrifice that compels the 'true believer'.

(From Kessels, 2010)

such as wearing veil) (Change Institute, 2008b; Slootman & Tillie 2006);

- religious revival (Change Institute 2008b);
- focus on the plight of Muslims in various conflict zones around the world (Slootman & Tillie, 2006).

Given these factors, the core Islamic ideological elements that seem to be significant elements of radical views are (from the Change Institute, 2008b):

- an emphasis on *jihadism* (in Arabic this refers to a notion of a religious duty of 'struggle'; in the West, it is often used to imply a sense of *holy war*);
- the role of *takfir* (a declaration of apostasy, the result of someone knowingly abandoning Islam, the sentence for which may be interpreted as death);
- the world as *dar-al-harb* ('house of war') a reference to countries where Muslim law (*Shari'a*) is not in force);
- lack of discrimination between civilian and military targets;
- attack/confrontation with the enemy;
- an emphasis on the appropriateness and desirability of martyrdom;
- a looking forward to the return of the *Caliphate* (this refers to the first system of government that was established in Islam and that represented the political unity of the Muslim nation).

It is important to note that not all elements of these factors are necessarily equally held by everyone attracted to radicalised ideological narratives, and that one may not necessarily predict another. For example, Leuprecht *et al.* (2010) note that poll data from the 2007 Pew poll of US Muslims included items related to 'doubts about the war on terror', and 'justification of suicide bombing' showed low correlations. They suggest that this means that 'knowing who believes one aspect seems to say little about who believes the other aspect' (p.61). In psychological terms, probably the most significant consequences of ideological involvement of the form described here, as noted earlier, are dehumanisation of the opponent, enhanced group identification and, in the context of radical Islam ideology, a focus on martyrdom. The particular strength of these narratives is that they are enhanced by action and commitment.

2. Factors related to social context
In terms of social context, what seems to be most significant is engagement with a strong real or virtual peer group (Nesser, 2004), where needs to seek meaning are met, where participants can achieve a sense of belonging (Slootman & Tillie, 2006) and where reactions to perceived injustices elsewhere can be expressed (Slootman & Tillie, 2006). This might be expressed through engagement in protest activities (*actual*) or media, through the internet (*virtual*) (Change Institute, 2008a). Of particular significance, identification with a group perceived as victims can radicalise an individual who has not personally experienced any grievance. Quite clearly, many radicalised young people in the West have no direct experience of life in, say, Palestine, but can be drawn into a process of identification and social influence in this way. As noted earlier, a significant factor in facilitating membership is the presence of friends and/or family. Factors such as group polarisation, group competition and enhanced group cohesion under threat have been identified as significant *process* factors in the group dynamics of radicalisation.

3. Factors related to leadership/charismatic figures
The involvement of significant and charismatic leaders as part of broader peer group and social involvement (Change Institute 2008a; Slootman & Tillie, 2006) are of significance. Research suggests that returning jihadis from Afghanistan, Pakistan, the Balkans and Somalia may play particularly important roles as inspirational peer group figures (Change Institute, 2008a) in mosques or places of community gathering, as may family. The role of 'spiritual sanctioners' and 'operational leaders' can be identified from examining radicalised groups (NYPD, 2007), which have particular significance when expressed through returned jihadis. A sense of personal and social isolation may be an important element in understanding engagement with both ideology and peer group.

4. Factors related to situational and personal context
Recent research also suggests a strong transformative event may be of significance as part of the individual's pathway towards radicalisation (Change Institute, 2008a) although not necessarily to violence, which may be of either personal or collective significance. Related to this is the notion that an individual is angry because of the kind of events noted above, and seeks revenge for government action that harms that person or their loved ones. However, it is important to stress that personal grievance usually does not lead to action unless interpreted as part of some larger group grievance (McCauley & Moskalenko, 2008).

What is missing from this analysis is an extension of the argument into the factors that do not simply precipitate expression through engagement with radical ideas, but that precipitate expression of those ideas through violence. As we have noted earlier, the critical point to make here is that, individually, these factors have little predictive value – they do not explain why people 'become' terrorists. Taken in combination, however, they do provide us with a complex and powerful framework that may enable us to contextualise an 'openness' to involvement with terrorism or radicalisation.

Progression into terrorist activities: Autobiographical and biographical accounts

We have noted that a social and psychological quality of increased involvement in a terrorist movement is a sense of *gradual progression*. This might be characterised by a slow marginalisation away from broader, 'conventional' society towards a much narrower society where extremism becomes all embracing. Capturing knowledge of this in any systematic way is extremely difficult, however, given the clandestine and covert nature of terrorist organisations. Perhaps the most effective way of doing this is to use autobiographical accounts, which at least give a glimpse of long-term processes. Such accounts can be problematic, in that they are generally partial, written after the event, and may serve as justification by the author rather than an account of what actually happened. However, such accounts are probably all that is available to us to address this issue.

Both Kellen (1982), who examined the histories of German terrorists, and Taylor and Quayle (1994), who interviewed loyalist terrorists in Northern Ireland, identified as an emergent theme that involvement in terrorism featured not only a gradual socialisation into increasingly commitment, but a parallel sense of increasing disillusionment with alternatives. In a sense, the culmination of this was that the individual grew into an active terrorist, through the focusing of social and personal opportunities that limited the capacity to engage with alternatives. It is tempting to speculate that this may reflect a process similar to that identified by Hundeide (2003) as a 'community of practice'. Communities of practice are informal but potentially very powerful learning environments, where the individual learns from peers by example, and by exposure to common and shared experience. A byproduct of this may also be that increased commitment and ever greater and ever more focused involvement will carry with it for the individual the realisation that in difficult or challenging times, the need to 'stick it out' is paramount (Sherman, 2005).

We can supplement these accounts from what we know about terrorist organisations, which at least can act as a validity check. In the case of the Provisional IRA, for example, we know that when an individual expressed an intention to join the group, in some cases it might take weeks before the would-be recruit was actually accepted into the organisation (Horgan & Taylor, 1997). When the recruit was finally accepted, they did not necessarily embark upon the activities of *active service* for some time. There are a number of roles to be filled within terrorist organisations and active service is but one of these; it entails some degree of discipline and training, involving weapons use and explosives training (Taylor & Horgan, 2006). While expectations to occupy such a role may play a part in influencing a potential recruit to seek out opportunities for increased engagement, the recruit may find him- or herself having to occupy peripheral roles that might initially seem less attractive. A rare insight into a sense of 'role allocation' in Irish terrorist movements comes from documentation produced by the **Official IRA**, *The Reporter's Guide to Ireland*, a sophisticated intelligence manual written by the Official IRA Director of Intelligence for distribution to his regional intelligence officers, and subsequently used by the Provisional IRA (Horgan & Taylor, 1999).

> **Official IRA** in 1969 the Irish Republican Army split into two factions: the Official IRA, which sought to achieve unification of Ireland through largely political means; and the Provisional IRA, which advocated violent confrontation.

Autobiographical accounts of terrorists' lives (e.g. Collins with McGovern, 1997; McGartland, 1997; O'Callaghan, 1998) do reveal characteristics such as those described above; and particularly the sense of the process of movement into and out of different roles even within what may seem a very narrow community (Alonso, 2003). McCauley and Segal (1989) illustrate that before they became the Red Army Faction leaders, Ulrike Meinhof and Horst Mahler were involved in community activism opposing nuclear proliferation and the moderate *Socialist German Student Society*, respectively. A number of IRA members in Northern Ireland came from the ranks of *Sinn Fein* (the Irish Republican Party) and some later moved back into Sinn Fein roles. Clark (1983), in his study of **ETA (Euskadi Ta Askatasuna)**, an armed Basque nationalist and separatist organisation in Spain, notes that a picture of gradual socialisation towards increased involvement exists. However, what revealed this were ambiguities associated with attempting to define what being an *etarra* (ETA member) means:

> **ETA (Euskadi Ta Askatasuna)** a separatist Basque nationalist organisation, responsible for many terrorist attacks in Spain.

> ... the process by which new members are recruited is usually a slow and gradual one, and it is difficult to say exactly when a young man crosses the threshold of ETA

membership ... the process by which a Basque youth is transformed into a member of ETA is a long one full of detours and the exploration of competing alternatives. Even the actual recruiting process is a gradual one which may yield many potential etarras who resist for months or even years before yielding to the call to join.

(Clark, 1983, p.435)

In Italy, Jamieson (1989) interviewed the former Red Brigades (RB) member, Adriana Faranda. This is exceptionally revealing, providing an unusually lucid and reflective account of increased engagement. Jamieson notes that Faranda became engaged in politics around 1968 as a student in Rome. To her observation that she once heard Faranda describe her involvement as almost 'necessary', Faranda replied:

Things are never quite as clear as that. Countless others lived in Rome at the same time as me: kids of my age who weren't as involved as me, either in the political struggles or in the choices of the successive years. I suppose really it was the way I experienced the events of that time, my own personal standpoint on the problems, the crises, the hopes and the expectation that we had as well as what was happening outside which determined that particular path ... there were lots of little steps which led to where I ended up ... it wasn't a major leap in the true sense of the word. It was just another stage ... it was a choice.

(Jamieson, 1989, p.36)

Faranda's comment is especially important in that it reveals why, at one level, questions about motivation in terms of understanding involvement in terrorism are essentially unanswerable (e.g. 'I suppose really it was the way I experienced the events of that time' in the quote above) but it also epitomises the way in which any such career path is shaped by what she describes as 'lots of little steps'. She also added later in the interview that although she characterised her involvement as taking 'lots of little steps', she acknowledged that she saw herself as later having reached a 'point of no return'. In the sense in which Faranda uses it, reaching a point of 'no return', or achieving 'membership' does not appear to be clear-cut in any specific way, but might be characterised ritually, perhaps through engagement in a specific operation, where the previously virtual line between supportive activity and 'direct action' is no longer unambiguous. Naturally, this dynamic will differ depending on the kind of group in question and, for example, whether increased commitment necessitates a complete and total break from family and society (as raised in the analysis by Post mentioned earlier).

White and Falkenberg White (1991) interviewed an IRA veteran who pointed to a process of 'nurturing' upon his initial progression into the movement:

'... well it – there's progression, you know? When you would go in you wouldn't be, you would be given less difficult tasks initially. And then just as you become more experienced you would move along and somebody would come in behind you. And you know, and then somebody – people were probably getting arrested or interned or whatever, so there was that kind of progression along with military training until you were actively involved in operations ... I suppose it took maybe six or seven months.'

(White and Falkenberg White, 1991, p.120)

Other authors have noted similar qualities; Billig (1984), for example, describes the case of Red Army Faction (RAF) member 'Rolfe', who marked his involvement in the RAF initially as a courier, but some years later had progressed to active duty within the RAF and was involved in the kidnap and murder of German businessman Hans Martin Schleyer. Jamieson (1990) identified a similar (though more formalised) process within the Red Brigades. That movement's attempts to infiltrate and provoke left-wing factory-based movements in the early 1970s culminated in a process whereby a gradual move into illegality was fostered. Jamieson describes the situation in the Milan factories:

... a sympathiser would be given the task of distributing RB propaganda documents around his factory department, or store material, money, or even weapons in his home. Later he might be asked to spray graffiti on the factory walls, leave intimidatory messages in offices or at homes of factory management. These were known as 'individual illegal actions'. The 'real qualitative leap' came with the individual's participation in armed action ... with the individual member having been monitored through a series of prior *prove* or tests.

(Jamieson, 1990, p.2)

From these accounts, we get a sense of constant change and varying levels of activity, commitment and overall 'involvement'. At any one time, as McCauley and Segal (1989) note, some members are 'beginning to find out ... others are becoming committed, others are firmly committed, others becoming less committed, and still others are in the process of leaving entirely'. We can also see how profiling of terrorists, based on assumed invariant qualities are likely to be at best a snapshot of the current situation, and at worst misleading and limited.

A final feature of increased involvement to note for the individual is the sense that levels of engagement can have different values attached to them, which vary over time. These 'role values' are available to the leadership to direct and control members. For example, within the Provisional IRA, engagement with active service roles may be limited, but there is a sense of organisational and psychological value in keeping access to these roles available. A similar analysis might be made of the role of martyr in Hamas. Extensive interviews conducted with members of *al Qassam* by Hassan (2001) revealed that by limiting those accepted for martyrdom operations, 'others are disappointed. They must learn patience and wait until Allah calls them'.

As we can see from the above, increased engagement with a terrorist organisation is as much a developmental process as that which characterises initial involvement. In practical terms, however, there is a further point that can be made. The kinds of process we have identified that contribute to initial engagement, whilst overlapping with those that sustain engagement, are of a qualitatively different character. This might suggest that in terms of the practicalities of managing terrorism, different strategies need to be adopted to address different phases of development.

Disengagement

Of all the areas of study, the phase of disengagement with terrorism is least understood. It has not until recently attracted much interest, and research in this area remains limited. Bjørgo and Horgan (2009) suggest that disengaging from terrorism may be potentially as complex a process as that which helps us understand initial involvement in the first place, but the evidence we have to judge this is limited in the extreme.

Over recent times there have been a number of initiatives designed to diminish the presumed risk of incarcerated terrorists further engaging with terrorism on their release. Saudi Arabia, Singapore and Yemen are countries that have initiated well publicised formal programmes to 'deradicalise' convicted offenders, and many Western countries with convicted terrorists in some sense have less formal prison-based initiatives to address the risk of reoffending (Ashour, 2009). However, there is little clarity in the precise techniques or strategies used, and no consistency in the criteria to identify success or failure.

The issue of how to identify success or failure is particularly important. We know that not every radical will become involved in terrorism, and we also know (from arrested terrorists) that not every terrorist is necessarily radical, in the sense of holding extreme political views. Yet much of the literature on deradicalisation assumes a causal relationship between possession of radical views, and dangerousness. This raises a central question – is success to be measured in terms of changing radical attitudes and beliefs, or is it to be measured in terms of probability of subsequent offending (what we might term terrorist recidivism)? This dilemma reflects directly on the concept of risk, and how it might be measured and assessed in a terrorist context; and as we noted earlier, we lack validated and effective risk assessment tools.

What we do know about success in this area is limited, but not necessarily particularly positive. As Horgan and Taylor (in press) note, on 7 December 2010, the Director of National Intelligence (DNI) released a summary report on the re-engagement of detainees formerly held at **Guantanamo Bay** (GTMO) in Cuba. By October 2010, almost 600 detainees had been released from GTMO. The DNI reported that approximately 13.5 per cent of those released were confirmed as having re-engaged in terrorist or insurgent activities, compared to the 6 per cent reported by a detailed investigation published by Bergen *et al.* (2011). A further 11.5 per cent were deemed 'suspected' of re-engaging in terrorism after release (also see Bumiller, 2009). The adequacy of these assessments is unclear, and appears to be based on intelligence and threat information. The DNI report suggested that the first reporting of confirmed or suspected re engagement with terrorism emerged 'about 2.5 years between leaving GTMO and the first identified reengagement reports' (Horgan & Taylor, in press, p.1).

> **Guantanamo Bay** (also known as G-Bay, GITMO, GTMO). A detention camp established at the US naval base in Cuba to hold detainees from the wars in Afghanistan and Iraq.

SUICIDE TERRORISM AND POLITICAL SUICIDE

It may seem rather ghoulish to introduce a discussion of suicide terrorism following from the discussion of ending terrorism, but in a sense suicide terrorism is a very final and clear way, for the individual concerned, of ending terrorism. Of course, whilst the individual is deliberately killed by the act of suicide, the social consequences of the act itself often reverberate across time (as is very evident for the 9/11 bombers, or the UK **7/7** bombers), which, from the perspective of the terrorist, makes it a highly effective technique (Figure 11.4). Studying the individuals who commit suicide terrorist acts is of course extremely difficult, for they are no longer alive, and the

> **7/7** the coordinated suicide attacks conducted by four UK citizens on the London transport system on 7 July 2005. Some 52 people were killed, along with the suicide bombers, and about 700 injured.

FIGURE 11.4 *Whilst the individual is deliberately killed by the act of suicide, the social consequences of the act itself often reverberate across time, which, from the perspective of the terrorist, makes it a highly effective technique.*

Source: © Monika Wisniewska. Used under licence from Shutterstock.

researcher is dependent on whatever secondary material might be available.

Merari (2010) has published what is probably the most comprehensive and sophisticated analysis of suicide terrorism. He has had access to failed suicide bombers, and also their recruiters and dispatchers, incarcerated in Israeli prisons, and was able to conduct extensive interviews and administer a range of psychological tests. Unusually for this area, he adopted a quasi control procedure (using people convicted for non-suicide terrorist offences) and therefore has some systematic basis for comparative statements. Overall he found that failed suicide bombers tended to be more likely to have completed high school than the controls, were less likely to come from lower socio-economic backgrounds, tended to have higher levels of religiosity, and were less likely to have engaged in previous violent activities. Their recruiters tended to be older than the suicide bombers, or the control group. Merari suggests that the time between initial recruitment to dispatch was around 40 days, with limited and brief direct mission preparation; video statements (sometimes referred to as 'wills') tended to be made less than 24 hours before the attack.

Formal psychological assessments of suicide bombers revealed what initially are rather controversial findings, suggesting diagnoses of *avoidant–dependent personality disorder* (using the *Diagnostic and Statistical Manual of Mental Disorders* (DSM-IV-TR; American Psychiatric Association, 2000) description of personality disorders), and also higher symptoms of depression than controls. However, these findings have been criticised as being unreliable; McCauley and Moskalenko (2011) question the appropriateness of the diagnostic

categories used. There is also a more fundamental problem of any work involving incarcerated offenders, in that the process of apprehension and incarceration itself presumably affects how individuals reflect on their activities. For people who are failed suicide bombers, incarcerated in an Israeli prison, this might be assumed to be a significance issue.

Media representations of suicide terrorism often frame it as having a religious base, and particularly within an Islamic context emphasise the role of martyrdom. However, it is important to note that until recently, the most numerous examples of suicide terrorist attacks were undertaken by the **Tamil Tigers (Liberation Tigers of Tamil Eelam)**, an avowedly secular organisation.

> **Tamil Tigers (Liberation Tigers of Tamil Eelam)** a separatist organisation founded in 1976 in Northern Sri Lanka, seeking to create a separate state for the Tamil people. In 2009, it was defeated by the Sri Lankan Army.

It may be helpful to distinguish between political suicide and suicide terrorism (Taylor, 1991). Whatever the personal context may be, suicide terrorism, like all forms of terrorism, victimises non-combatant targets. Political suicide, in contrast, is suicide undertaken for a political purpose that does not victimise others. Suicide as protest is well known, and occurs with surprising regularity; it can be estimated from news reports that there are between one or two protest suicides per week (author's personal research), sometimes for political reasons, sometimes for personal reasons. **Self-immolation** suicide tends to occur in Eastern rather than Western cultural contexts

> **self-immolation** voluntarily setting oneself on fire as a form of protest and suicide.

but, as we will note below, there are notable Western examples of self-immolation.

Perhaps the most recent example was the self-immolation of Mohamed Barazizi in Tunisia on 17 December 2010. This suicide took place within a political context, but seems to be best understood as a personal statement rather than a collective initiative. That it became the emblem and perhaps precipitating event for a mass movement in Tunisia does not appear to have been Barazizi's intention, although it is of course impossible to know. There are a number of other similar examples of suicide for a political purpose, the most notable perhaps being Jan Palack's self-immolation in Wenceslas Square, Prague, on 16 January 1968 in protest against the Soviet invasion of Czechoslovakia, which similarly had profound political consequences. The Irish hunger strikes of 1981 were also in some ways a similar example of politically purposeful suicide, in that they did not involve the victimisation of third parties; but in contrast to Barazizi or Palack, these were undertaken within a very clear exploitative external political context.

ASSESSMENT OF DANGEROUSNESS

It is appropriate here at the end of this chapter to raise briefly the issue of assessment of dangerousness for terrorists. Assessments of this kind frequently constitute a substantial element of the forensic psychologist's workload when dealing with other forms of problematic behaviour (such as sexual offending, for example) and it might be thought this would also be the case with respect to terrorism. However, little progress has been made on the development of systematic assessment tools to assess risk in cases involving terrorism (Roberts & Horgan, 2008), either in terms of risk of engagement with violent terrorism, or risk after conviction of further engagement.

At first sight, assessment tools such as the HCR-20 (Webster et al., 1997) may have potential for use in terrorist cases (see Chapter 17 for a fuller description of this instrument). The HCR-20 is a widely used general violence risk assessment instrument, with well established validity, but its development was primarily focused on violent criminals who had a history of violence, and its use should be 'restricted mainly to settings where there is a high proportion of persons with a history of violence and a strong suggestion of mental illness or personality disorder' (Webster et al, 1997, p.5). Drawing on work using the HCR-20, Pressman (2009) has explored the development of the *Structured Professional Judgment Protocol for Risk Assessment of Violent Extremists* (VERA) and offers some evidence to support the logical use of such a tool. This approach depends upon an evaluator's judgment, informed by guidelines that reflect best practice. Because of this, assessors require training in the use of the tool to ensure standardisation of the judgements made, in terms of the meaning of the various items included, and their coding. The items included in VERA are: *attitude*; *contextual* (such as website activity, support or contact with violent extremists); *historical*; and *protective* (such as change in vision of enemy, shifts in ideology and rejection of violence to achieve goals), along with *demographic* items. These items are rated rather than scored, and the tool provides a guide, therefore, rather than a prescriptive list of qualities. However, for the moment, it remains an interesting development, but lacks empirical development and validation.

SUMMARY

- The study of terrorism and the terrorist is not something belonging to any particular discipline. In this chapter, there has been an emphasis on process as it might affect the individual, in terms of what is described as the 'ARC' of terrorist involvement: *becoming engaged*; *engagement*; and *disengagement*.

- Forensic psychology has a particular research role to play in understanding and exploring all of these processes, but multidisciplinary areas of study present particular challenges, and our understanding will require the difficult task of integrating the forensic perspective with others.

- It can be argued that the study of terrorism has suffered because it has not been sufficiently multidisciplinary in its approach, and has tended to privilege individual discipline-based accounts as opposed to accounts focused on the area of study or concern drawn from a range of disciplines.

- The central dilemma for anyone concerned with this area is that while lots of contributing factors can be identified as necessary elements in the terrorism story, none offers a sufficient account (Taylor, 2010).

- From the perspective of *forensic psychology*, addressing this central dilemma is a major priority. Yet study in this area is fraught with practical and methodological problems, for the following reasons:

  - The subject matter is generally illegal and engagement with it may be dangerous.

  - It is also an area where clandestine operations are as much the preserve of the state countering terrorism as of the terrorist engaged in violent acts.

- The clandestine qualities on both sides of this equation make access to reliable information difficult, which, when added to the political context to terrorism and counter terrorism, makes reliable assessment of the process involved very difficult.

- Perhaps these issues are no different in other areas of criminal study, but the extreme practical and political sensitivities around terrorism and its potential to damage should it occur places added constraints on the investigator's freedom to engage.

- What this chapter has sought to achieve from the perspective of forensic psychology is a broader and more grounded understanding of terrorism as a process. *L'homme armé* referred to at the beginning of the chapter is unlikely to go away, nor be controlled; we can, however, perhaps through sound psychological enquiry, at least gain a better understanding of terrorism.

Notes

Information on a country's specific counter terrorist strategy is usually available on their governmental website or in published reports. Britain's counter terrorist strategy can be found at www.homeoffice.gov.uk/counter-terrorism/uk-counter-terrorism-strat and the US counter terrorist strategy at www.state.gov/s/ct

ESSAY/DISCUSSION QUESTIONS

1. Assess the evidence that suggests terrorists are like other members of society.

2. How useful are terrorists' biographical accounts? What are the limitations to their use?

3. What is the 'ARC' of terrorist involvement? Is this a useful way to think about terrorism?

4. One of the great challenges in understanding terrorism is why so few people actually engage in it, given the extensive pool of political dissident activity (Taylor, 2010). Why do you think this might be the case?

REFERENCES

Akers, R.L. (1994). A social learning theory of crime. In F.T. Cullen & R. Agnew (Eds.) *Criminological theory: Past to present*. Los Angeles, CA: Roxbury Publishing Company.

Alonso, R. (2003). *The IRA and armed struggle*. London: Routledge.

Alonso, R. (2006). Individual motivations for joining terrorist organizations: A comparative qualitative study on members of ETA and IRA. In J. Victoroff (Ed.) *Social and psychological factors in the genesis of terrorism* (pp. 187–202). Amsterdam: IOS Press.

American Psychiatric Association. (2000). *Diagnostic and Statistical Manual of Mental Disorders, Fourth Edition, Text Revision (DSM-IV-TR)*. Washington, DC: American Psychiatric Association.

Ashour, O. (2009). *The deradicalization of jihadists: Transforming armed Islamist movements*. London: Routledge.

Bakker, E. (2006). Jihadi terrorists in Europe: Their characteristics and the circumstances in which they join the jihad: An exploratory study. Den Haag: Netherlands Institute of International Relations Clingendael. Retrieved 22 August 2011 from www.clingendael.nl/publications/2006/20061200_cscp_csp_bakker.pdf

Bandura, A. (1990). Mechanisms of moral disengagement. In W. Reich (Ed.) *Origins of terrorism: Psychologies, ideologies, theologies, states of mind* (pp. 161–191). Cambridge: Cambridge University Press.

Beck, A.T. (2002). Prisoners of hate. *Behavior Research and Therapy, 40*, 209–216.

Bergen, P., Tiedemann, K. & Lebovich, A. (2011, 11 January). How many gitmo alumni take up arms? *Foreign Policy*. Retrieved 22 August 2011 from www.foreignpolicy.com/articles/2011/01/11/how_many_gitmo_alumni_take_up_arms?page=full

Betz, D. (2008). The virtual dimension of contemporary insurgency and counterinsurgency. *Small Wars and Insurgencies, 19*, 520.

Billig, O. (1984). The case history of a German terrorist. *Studies in Conflict and Terrorism, 7*, 1–10.

Bingham, J. (2008, 28 September). Radical Islamic clerics warn of further attacks after publisher is firebombed. *The Telegraph*. Retrieved 5 October 2011 from www.telegraph.co.uk/news/uknews/3097350/Radical-Islamic-clerics-warn-of-further-attacks-after-publisher-is-firebombed.html

Bjørgo, T. & Horgan, J. (Eds.) (2009). *Leaving terrorism behind: Individual and collective perspectives*. London: Routledge.

Buijs, F.J. (2009). Muslims in the Netherlands: Social and political developments after 9/11. *Journal of Ethnic and Migration Studies, 35*, 421–438.

Bumiller, E. (2009, 20 May). Late terror link cited for 1 in 7 freed detainees. *New York Times* . Retrieved 5 October 2011 from www.nytimes.com/2009/05/21/us/politics/21gitmo.html

Burgess, M., Ferguson, N. & Hollywood, I. (2009). From individual discontent to collective armed struggle: personal accounts of the impetus for membership or non-membership in paramilitary groups. In W. Myers (Ed.) *The range of evil: Multidisciplinary studies of human wickedness* (pp.29–39). Oxford: Interdisciplinary Press.

Burk, K. (2005, 9 February). *At war with the French: The Hundred Years' War 1337–1453*. Lecture presented at Gresham College, London. Retrieved 24 September 2011 from www.gresham.ac.uk/lectures-and-events/at-war-with-the-french-the-hundred-years

Carlile, Lord (2007) *The definition of terrorism. A report by Lord Carlile of Berriew Q.C. Independent Reviewer of Terrorism Legislation*. London: TSO.

Change Institute (2008a). *Study on the best practices in cooperation between authorities and civil society with a view to the prevention and response to violent radicalisation*. London: The Change Institute.

Change Institute (2008b). *Studies into violent radicalisation: The beliefs, ideologies and narratives*. London: The Change Institute.

Clark, R.P. (1983). Patterns in the lives of ETA members. *Terrorism, 6*, 423–454.

Collins, E. with McGovern, M. (1997). *Killing rage*. London: Granta.

Corrado, R. (1981) A critique of the mental disorder perspective of political terrorism. *International Journal of Law and Psychiatry, 4*, 293–309.

Crenshaw, M. (1988). The subjective reality of the terrorist: Ideological and psychological factors in terrorism. In R.O. Slater & M. Stohl (Eds.) *Current perspectives in international terrorism* (pp.12–46). Basingstoke, Hampshire: Macmillan.

Crenshaw, M. (1992). How terrorists think: Psychological contributions to understanding terrorism. In L. Howard, (Ed.) *Terrorism: Roots, impact, responses* (pp.71–80). London: Praeger.

Dalgard-Nielsen, A. (2010). Violent radicalization in Europe: What we know and what we do not know. *Studies in Conflict and Terrorism, 33*, 797–814.

Della Porta, D. (1995). *Social movements, political violence and the state*. Cambridge: Cambridge University Press.

Enders, W. & Jindapon, P. (2010). Network externalities and the structure of terror networks. *Journal of Conflict Resolution, 54*, 262–280.

Foreign and Commonwealth Office (1986, November). *Background brief: The Hindawi Case: Syrian connexions*. Retrieved 5 October 2011 from http://212.150.54.123/articles/hindawi.htm

Hassan, N. (2001, 19 November). Letter from Gaza: An arsenal of believers – Talking to the human bombs. *The New Yorker*. Retrieved 22 August 2011 from www.newyorker.com/archive/2001/11/19/011119fa_FACT1?currentPage=all

Horgan, J. (2005). *The psychology of terrorism*. London: Routledge.

Horgan, J. & Taylor, M. (1997). The Provisional Irish Republican Army: Command and functional structure. *Terrorism and Political Violence, 9*, 1–32.

Horgan, J. & Taylor, M. (1999). Playing the green card – Financing the Provisional IRA – Part 1. *Terrorism and Political Violence, 11*, 1–38.

Horgan, J. & Taylor, M. (in press). Disengagement, de-radicalization and the arc of terrorism: Future directions for research. In R. Coolsaet (Ed.) *Jihadi terrorism and the radicalisation challenge in Europe* (2nd edn). Aldershot, Hampshire: Ashgate.

Hundeide, K. (2003). Becoming a committed insider. *Culture and Psychology, 9*, 107–127.

Jamieson, A. (1989). *The heart attacked: Terrorism and conflict in the Italian state*. London: Marian Boyars.

Jamieson, A. (1990). Entry, discipline and exit in the Italian Red Brigades. *Terrorism and Political Violence, 2*, 1–20.

Kellen, K. (1982). *On terrorism and terrorists: A Rand Note N-1942-RC*. Santa Monica, CA: Rand Corporation.

Kessels, E. (2010, January). Introduction. In National Coordinator for Counterterrorism (NCTb) *Countering violent extremist narratives*. Netherlands: National Coordinator for Counterterrorism (NCTb).

Kruglanski, A.W. & Fishman, S. (2009) Psychological factors in terrorism and counterterrorism: Individual, group and organisational levels of analysis. *Social Issues and Policy Review, 3*, 1–44.

Leuprecht, C., Hataley, T., Moskalenko, S. & McCauley, C. (2010). Narratives and counter-narratives for global jihad: Opinion versus action. In National Coordinator for Counterterrorism (NCTb) *Countering violent extremist narratives* (pp.58–71). Netherlands: National Coordinator for Counterterrorism (NCTb).

Lockwood, L. (1973). Aspects of the 'L'Homme Arme' Tradition. *Proceedings of the Royal Musical Society* 100, 1, 97–122.

McAllister, B. (2004). Al Qaeda and the innovative firm: Demythologising the network. *Studies in Conflict and Terrorism, 27*, 297–319.

McCauley, C. (2002). Psychological issues in understanding terrorism and the response to terrorism. In C.E. Stout (Ed.) *The psychology of terrorism: Theoretical understandings and perspectives* (pp.3–30). Westport, CT: Praeger Publishers.

McCauley, C. & Moskalenko, S. (2008). Mechanisms of political radicalization: Pathways towards terrorism. *Terrorism and Political Violence, 20*, 415–433.

McCauley, C. & Moskalenko, S. (2011). Do suicide terrorists have personality problems? A review of Ariel Merari, 'Driven to death: Psychological and social aspects of suicide terrorism'. *Terrorism and Political Violence, 23,* 108–111.

McCauley, C. & Segal, M.E. (1989). Terrorist individuals and terrorist groups: The normal psychology of extreme behavior. In J. Groebel & J.H. Goldstein (Eds.) *Terrorism* (pp.41–64). Seville: Publicaciones de la Universidad de Sevilla.

McGartland, M. (1997). *Fifty dead men walking.* London: Blake.

Merari, A. (2010). *Driven to death: Psychological and social aspects of suicide terrorism.* Oxford: Oxford University Press.

Nesser, P. (2004) *Jihad in Europe: A survey of the motivations for Sunni Islamist terrorism in post-millennium Europe.* Kjeller: FFI Norwegian Defence Academy.

NYPD. (2007). *Radicalization in the West: The homegrown threat.* New York: NYPD Intelligence Division, New York City Police Department.

O'Callaghan, S. (1998). *The Informer.* London: Bantam.

Oliverio, A. (2008) US versus European approaches to terrorism: Size really does matter. *Policing 2,* 452–464.

Post, J.M. (1984). Notes on a psychodynamic theory of terrorist behaviour. *Terrorism, 7,* 241–256.

Post, J.M. (1987). Rewarding fire with fire: The effects of retaliation on terrorist group dynamics. *Terrorism, 10,* 23–35.

Post, J.M. (1990). Terrorist psycho-logic: Terrorist behavior as a product of psychological forces. In W. Reich (Ed.) *Origins of terrorism: Psychologies, ideologies, theologies, states of mind* (pp.25–40). New York: Cambridge University Press.

Post, J.M. Sprinzak, E. & Denny, L.M. (2003). The terrorists in their own words: Interviews with 35 incarcerated Middle Eastern terrorists. *Terrorism and Political Violence, 15,* 171–184.

Pressman, D.E. (2009). *Risk assessment decisions for violent political extremism.* Ottawa: Public Safety Canada. Retrieved 22 August 2011 from www.publicsafety.gc.ca/res/cor/rep/2009-02-rdv-eng.aspx

Roberts, K. & Horgan, J. (2008). Risk assessment and the terrorist. *Perspectives on Terrorism, 2,* 3–9.

Russell, C.A. & Miller, B.H. (1983). Profile of a terrorist. In L.Z. Freedman & Y. Alexander (Eds.) *Perspectives on terrorism* (pp.33–41). Wilmington, DE: Scholarly Resources.

Sageman, M. (2004). *Understanding terror networks.* Philadelphia, PN: University of Pennsylvania Press.

Schmid, A.P. & Jongman, A.J. (1988). *Political terrorism: A new guide to actors, authors, concepts, data bases, theories, and literature.* New Brunswick, NJ: Transaction Books.

Sherman, N. (2005). *Stoic warriors. The ancient philosophy behind the military mind.* New York: Oxford University Press

Silke, A. (Ed.) (2003). *Terrorists, victims, society: Psychological perspectives on terrorism and its consequences.* Chichester: John Wiley & Sons, Inc.

Slootman, M. & Tillie, J. (2006). *Processes of radicalisation. Why some Amsterdam Muslims become radicals.* Amsterdam: Institute for Migrations and Ethnic Studies, University of Amsterdam.

Taylor, M. (1991). *The fanatics: A behavioural approach to political violence.* London: Brassey's Defence Publishers.

Taylor, M. (2010). Is terrorism a group phenomenon? *Aggression and Violent Behavior, 15,* 121–129.

Taylor, M. & Horgan, J. (2006). A conceptual model for addressing psychological process in the development of the terrorist. *Terrorism and Political Violence 18,* 585–601.

Taylor, M. & Quayle, E. (1994). *Terrorist lives.* London: Brassey's.

Travis, A. (2008, 20 August). MI5 report challenges views on terrorism in Britain. *The Guardian.* Retrieved 24 September 2011 from www.guardian.co.uk/uk/2008/aug/20/uksecurity.terrorism1

Veldhuis, T. & Staun, J. (2009) *Islamist radicalisation: A root cause model.* Den Haag: Clingendael Institute.

Webster, C., Douglas, K., Eaves, D. & Hart, S. (1997). *HCR-20 assessing risk for violence: Version II.* Burnaby, British Columbia: Mental Health, Law and Policy Institute, Simon Fraser University.

White, R.W. & Falkenberg White, T. (1991). Revolution in the city: On the resources of urban guerrillas. *Terrorism and Political Violence, 3,* 100–132.

ANNOTATED READING LIST

Alonso, R. (2003). *The IRA and armed struggle.* London: Routledge. *Based on extensive fieldwork, Alonso describes the key dynamics that occur in relation to recruitment to the Provisional IRA, and how its members justify their violent activity. It places the analysis within the broader framework of terrorist activity in Ireland.*

Cronin, A.K. (2009). *How terrorism ends: Understanding the decline and demise of terrorist campaigns.* Princeton, NJ: Princeton University Press. *Taking primarily a group focus, Cronin explores how terrorist organisations cease terrorist activity. She explores the role of decapitation and leadership removal, negotiation, success, clear failure, repression and reorientation across a wide range of terrorist organisations from Irish organisations to Al Qaeda.*

Leuprecht, C., Hataley, T., Moskalenko, S. & McCauley, C. (2010, January). Narratives and counter-narratives for global jihad: Opinion versus action. In National Coordinator for Counterterrorism (NCTb) *Countering violent extremist narratives*. Netherlands: National Coordinator for Counterterrorism (NCTb; http://english.nctb.nl). *This paper argues that different audiences accept different parts of the 'global jihad' narrative; that many agree with the narrative that will never engage in radical action or terrorism; and that counter terrorism initiatives should not target the narrative as if targeting terrorists. The analysis identifies likely targets for intervention, and suggests that different counter-narratives are required to combat each part of the 'global jihad' narrative and the subset of Muslims who believe it.*

Merari, A. (2010). *Driven to death: Psychological and social aspects of suicide terrorism*. Oxford: Oxford University Press. *Merari explores the sociodemographic and psychological qualities of failed Islamic suicide bombers, their recruiters, and a control group of non-suicide terrorists. He describes differences between them, and also suggests there is evidence for mental health differences between failed suicide bombers and the others.*

Sageman, M. (2004). *Understanding terror networks*. Philadelphia, PA: University of Pennsylvania Press. *Using social network analysis and case studies, Sageman illustrates how membership of jihadi terrorist groups originates through friendship and kinship networks. He argues that factors such as poverty and religious devotion are not the principal causes of membership.*

Taylor, M. & Horgan, J. (2006). A Conceptual Model for Addressing Psychological Process in the Development of the Terrorist *Terrorism and Political Violence*, 18, 585–660. *This paper describes how a process model might inform our understanding of engagement with terrorism, and its subsequent development. It takes a behavioural perspective, using examples from both Irish and Islamic terrorism.*

Part III
The Trial Process

12 Judicial Processes

Jacqueline M. Wheatcroft

To many psychologists, the criminal justice system often seems remote and complex, even mystifying. Even its main aim – is it to uncover 'the truth' or construct a case against the guilty? – may seem confusing. This chapter examines the interface between psychology and law and the courts. It aims to provide an overview and understanding of the two principal legal systems that operate in different parts of the world and to examine the psychological processes that could influence decision-making in the courtroom. Issues explored include the impact of different styles of questioning by advocates, pre-trial publicity and judicial pronouncements. In the UK and the USA, among other countries, judges and juries are central to the judicial process and the decisions taken. Research has explored how the composition, legal understanding and group dynamics of juries influence the verdicts they reach and, in systems that rely on judges and magistrates alone to pronounce on guilt, how they decide between the rival narratives of events offered by the prosecution and defence.

UNDERSTANDING THE JUSTICE SYSTEM

Adversarial versus inquisitorial systems of justice

The two principal systems of justice in the Western world are the adversarial and inquisitorial systems. The **adversarial court system** is based on the principles of common law, originating in England and now widely applied, both in the USA and most Commonwealth countries. A trial under the adversarial system has been described by Damaska (1973) as structured proceedings involving a dispute between two sides that are in position of theoretical equality, and where the court – whether judge, magistrate or jury – decides the outcome. In the UK, judges tend to be impartial umpires of procedure and are not involved in the investigation or preparation of cases or the evidence, although judges do sometimes decide *what* can be presented as evidence. Judges' main interests therefore lie in the fairness of the conduct of the trial rather than the outcome. According to the pure adversarial model, the judge plays a passive and disinterested role, merely ruling on legal technicalities when one or other side raises these. However, totally non-interventionist judges are somewhat mythical, particularly in civil or

adversarial court system frequently referred to as *accusatorial*. Each side presents a case (prosecution and defence) before a court. The judge gives no help to either side and does not participate in the discovering of the truth.

magistrates' courts where the judge may also become the trier of fact. More serious criminal matters are decided by juries, in the main consisting of laypersons without legal training but whose role and sworn duty is to faithfully try the defendant and give a true verdict according to that evidence.

Conversely, in **inquisitorial court systems** practiced in much of the European continent, judges are expected to arrive at the truth through their own investigations. Prior to trial, a full judicial investigation is conducted, including interviewing witnesses and examining the defence case (Figure 12.1). In France, for example, this is done by the *juge d'instruction*, who is half magistrate, half police detective. Whether a case proceeds or not is decided by the judge and the trial itself is seen as a disinterested investigation rather than a dispute.

inquisitorial court systems type of court proceeding frequently found in mainland Europe. The judges play an active role in assembling the case material and questioning witnesses. Typically, the judges determine whether the accused is guilty.

The major differences between the two systems (see Table 12.1 for a summary) include when and how evidence is presented, and the role of the judge: theoretically passive in the adversarial system, but playing a leadership role both in terms of process and decision-making in the inquisitorial system. However, in reality, neither system is wholly adversarial or totally inquisitorial. Several continental countries have introduced juries into inquisitorial processes, while in England and Wales, recent law reform, such as the right to silence and the need for magistrates to explain and justify their decisions, has led to inquisitorial elements being incorporated into the adversarial tradition.

Criminal versus civil cases

Both adversarial and inquisitorial systems distinguish between proceedings for **civil cases** and **criminal cases**. The two processes typically differ in terms of *standards of proof* and rules of evidence. In England and Wales, in civil cases the general standard for a finding of guilty is on the *balance of probability:* 'if the evidence is such that

civil cases cases that are concerned with private wrongs, as between one person and another.

criminal cases cases that are concerned with offences deemed to be against the public interest.

the tribunal can say that we think it more probable than not the burden is discharged, but if the evidence is equal it is not' (Eggleston, 1978, p.129). This suggests an even balance, although would a probability of 0.501 suffice? In reality, this would not be sufficient when the overall impact of a guilty verdict upon the parties involved is taken into account. For example, in civil cases involving the custody

FIGURE 12.1 *Prior to trial, a full judicial investigation is conducted, including interviewing witnesses and examining the defence case.*

Source: © Marcin Balcerzak. Used under licence from Shutterstock.

of children, the courts have taken the view that any decisions should be taken with a burden of proof akin to that in criminal cases.

The criminal standard of proof requires proof beyond *reasonable doubt* (*Woolmington v. DPP* (HL) [1935] AC 462). It represents a much higher standard than its civil counterpart, yet still falls well short of scientific certainty. Definitions of the standard have been attempted and have often realised greater confusion than the standard itself. Lord Denning set the standard as follows:

> Proof beyond reasonable doubt does not mean proof beyond the shadow of a doubt ... If the evidence against an individual is so strong that there is only a remote possibility in his favour ... the case is proved beyond reasonable doubt, but nothing short of that will suffice.
>
> (*Miller v. Minister of Pensions [1947] 2 All ER 372 at 3731947*).

More recently, so long as the judge conveys the high degree of certainty required to the jury then that is thought to be satisfactory.

Associated with civil and criminal cases is the regulation of the process of proof through *rules of evidence*, which are designed to ensure a fair trial in either system.

In civil cases the issues to be decided are typically those of liability and damages and since the introduction of the new Civil Procedure Rules in 1998 there has been a renewed emphasis on reducing cost, delay and complexity. Evidential issues may include issues of law and witness competence, and the weight to be attached to *expert evidence* (see Chapter 15). In criminal cases, the issue is one of guilt or innocence. The rules here cover styles of questioning, issues around hearsay and procedural rights, what the jury may hear and what use they can make of information in reaching their decision.

Magistrates' versus Crown Court

In England and Wales the great majority of criminal cases – some 95 per cent – are heard in *magistrates' courts*. The least serious, known as *summary offences*, are tried by magistrates themselves and even those charged with more serious criminal offences, such as murder, manslaughter, rape and robbery, first appear in the magistrates' court before passing to the *Crown Court* to be dealt with. Summary offences, such as common assault, must be tried in the magistrates' court, but 'either way' offences, such as theft, can be tried either by magistrates or by jury in the Crown Court, dependent on the circumstances of each case and the wishes of the defendant.

The dynamics of being tried in magistrates' court are different to those of the Crown Court. Legal perception is that defendants are more likely to be acquitted in Crown Court, perhaps partly due to the fact that 90 per cent of defendants in magistrates' court plead guilty compared with 70 per cent in Crown Court (Ashworth, 1994). Faith placed upon juror decision-making, however, could well be misplaced according to research reviewed later in this chapter. In magistrates' court there is no separation between interpretation of law and finding of fact. Thus, magistrates may need to decide whether some evidence is admissible, but regardless of their decision, those sitting the case will have already heard the evidence. In Crown Court the judge decides upon law and the jury decides facts, suggesting perhaps less room for bias in Crown Court procedures. Conversely, some lawyers have argued it is precisely because juries are not allowed access to important evidence that they reach perverse decisions (see Taylor, 2004). Whether in the

TABLE 12.1 *Key aspects of adversarial and inquisitorial systems of justice.*

System	Mode	Evidence	Judicial role	Judicial interest
Adversarial	Dispute	At trial	Passive	Fairness of process
Inquisitorial	Investigation	Prior to trial	Leadership	Case worthiness

Crown Court or magistrates' court, decisions need to be reached on reliable evidence and it is on the reliability of such evidence that much psychological research has been conducted.

EVIDENCE IN COURT

The impact of appearance and demeanour of witness and defendant on decision-making processes

Experimental research has shown that the attractiveness of a plaintiff is more likely to result in a favourable outcome for that complainant and accordingly, such individuals would receive greater compensatory damages (Stephan & Corder-Tully, 1977). Even attractive defendants found guilty attract demonstrably less severe punishment, regardless of case type, than unattractive ones (Zebrowitz & McDonald, 1991). This influence upon what represents goodness is known as the 'halo effect' (Cooper, 1981) and suggests that judgements of attractive people may be more positive on a variety of dimensions. Feild (1979) conducted an analysis of the effects of victim and defendant case characteristics in relation to rape cases. An overall impact of attractiveness of the victim on trial outcome was found but factors such as race, victim's sexual experience, evidence strength and type of rape committed, all moderated the effects of attractiveness, suggesting that the impact of attractiveness on jurors' decisions is far more complex than previously thought (see Memon et al., 2003 for review).

Other characteristics, such as tearful remorse, attract fewer guilty verdicts and those defendants with an evident

disability are more likely to receive the benefit of doubt with regard to guilt, responsibility and sentence leniency. However, those who have a lower moral character (Hans & Vidmar, 1986) or previous convictions, recent or old (unless both recent and dissimilar to the current charge – Lloyd-Bostock, 2006) are more likely to be convicted. Demeanour, whilst not evidence, seemingly influences both outcome and sentencing (Levenson, 2008).

Witness credibility

The kind of questioning styles used during cross-examination may influence the ways in which jurors perceive credibility. Wheatcroft et al. (2004) studied the effects of what they termed 'lawyerese' (i.e. the use of complex question forms) on the inferences made by those hearing the questioning, with regard to the accuracy and confidence of the witness. Mock jurors were most affected by observing the lawyerese with *negative feedback* style; judging the witness overall to be less accurate. Thus, implying the witness might be wrong through negative feedback may make observers doubt the accuracy of the witness's testimony (see Wheatcroft et al., 2001). Research has also demonstrated that when mock jurors hear inconsistent recall testimony they perceive the eyewitness to be less accurate and credible (Berman et al., 1995; Brewer et al., 1999).

Research also suggests jurors believe confidence is a valid predictor of accuracy. Hence, many studies have demonstrated that jurors and jurists rely heavily upon the demeanor of the witness; if the witness appears to be confident, she or he will be considered more accurate (Cutler et al., 1990; Kassin et al., 1991; Leippe et al., 1992; Lindsay, 1994; Sporer, 1993). However, in general, research outcomes with respect to accuracy and the relationship between confidence and accuracy (i.e. whether we can say that a confident witness is more likely to be correct in what s/he is stating than a witness showing a lack of confidence in his or her statements) remain quite poor and pose major difficulties for justice (Kebbell et al., 1996; Kebbell & Giles, 2000; Wheatcroft et al., 2004; Wheatcroft & Wagstaff, 2003). Furthermore, Wheatcroft et al. (2004) found that, regardless of questioning style, presenting the testimony of the least confident witness first appeared to spuriously boost confidence, and thereby perceived accuracy, in that witness's testimony. In this case, observers were possibly reliant upon their initial judgements and subsequently were unable to make sufficient adjustment upon hearing further witnesses (see Tversky & Kahneman, 1974 for details of anchoring effects). Therefore, presentation *order* could have significant implications for demeanor judgements.

CASE STUDY 12.1   CONVICTED FOR A SPEECH IMPEDIMENT?

Garry Coombe's downfall was his stutter. Charged with assaulting his wife, his speech impediment in court was mistaken for dishonesty. He was convicted after the magistrate did not believe his evidence because there was a noticeable tremor in his voice (Dick, 2006). Regardless of the legal facts or evidence presented at trial, Gary Coombe's case illustrates that there are effects of appearance and demeanor that may influence judicial assessments and impact upon the decision-making process.

Overall, it seems that confident and likeable witnesses may be more likely to be believed than timid, unattractive or unsavoury ones. Thus, appropriate credit may not be given where it is due. Correspondingly, the drawing of false inferences from appearance and demeanor remains worryingly high. Moreover, commentators have previously overlooked the potential role of immediate situational factors, such as examination styles, within the courtroom process itself.

Styles of examination and cross-examination by lawyers

In court, every witness is subject to examination both by the party who has called the person as a witness and all the other parties who are legally represented at the trial. Examinations consist of *examination-in-chief, cross-examination, re-examination*, and possible *examination by judge and/or magistrates* (Murphy, 1994). Examination-in-chief is a procedure that rests upon the notion of gaining the court's and jury's trust in the witness; a witness's own counsel will encourage the provision of a free narrative account of events, where leading and suggestive questions are disallowed. Cross-examination, however, has a different purpose: to establish witness creditworthiness. Thus, DuCann (1964) cites Lord Hanworth's statement: 'Cross-examination is a powerful and valuable weapon for the purpose of testing the veracity of a witness and the accuracy and completeness of his story' (p.95). Accordingly, a witness's knowledge of facts, impartiality, truthfulness, character, bias, unreliability, respect for oath and general demeanour may be challenged at this point. Unsurprisingly, therefore, cross-examination strategies are built around the development of the most effective way to discredit a witness's account and afford an examiner the opportunity to construct a competing interpretation or reanalysis of evidence, reflecting the adversarial nature of trials and focus on oppositional evidence (Ellison, 2007; Ellison & Wheatcroft, 2010). This constructive function of cross-examination is associated with heavy reliance on suppositional forms of questioning (Hickey, 1993; Hobbs, 2003; Wheatcroft & Wagstaff, 2003; Wheatcroft et al., 2004; see also Chapter 6) where distinctions are drawn between closed, specific and open question types. Propositional statements are embedded within questions that are then deliberately framed to elicit a simple confirmation or denial in the hope that the witness will adopt the cross-examiner's formulations as his or her own (Drew, 1992; Matoesian, 1993).

On the whole, however, cross-examination procedures have long been thought by the legal profession to be crucial for probing the accuracy of evidence obtained in examination-in-chief, and to expose unreliable or dishonest witnesses (Stone, 1988). Hence, a firm rationale has developed in legal culture whereby **leading questions** are permitted during cross-examination. Moreover, it is generally contended that asking questions containing false presupposition is a normal, useful and effective procedure for verifying doubtful information and introducing new information (Hickey, 1993). Arguably then, the admissibility of leading questions is based upon the notion that they serve to calibrate or assess the memories of witnesses. However, leading questions are usually suggestive to a degree (e.g. 'The car was black, wasn't it?'). Thus, such questioning aims to limit responses made to a two-alternative forced choice (i.e. yes/no) and elicit a preferred answer in the context of 'yeah-saying' (Harris, 1984; Kebbell et al., 2001). Of course, if one assumes that cross-examination of this kind tests the credibility of the witness to the full (i.e. a witness who rejects all attempts to be led, must be accurate in what he or she says), then, from the cross-examiner's point of view, there may be a downside if the witness refuses to be led or comply with the presupposition. Accordingly, some legal advisors have openly asserted that asking leading questions in cross-examination can be unwise (Evans, 1995). Consequently, serious concerns have been raised with regard to basic paradigms of justice and fairness in that lawyerese questions can suggest or compel responses (Brennan, 1995).

> **leading questions** questions worded in such a way as to suggest or imply the answer that is being sought.

Psychological research has raised serious doubts as to the impact of leading, presuppositional and complex questions on witness accuracy. Indeed, a number of studies have shown lawyerese questions to impede witness accuracy (Kebbell et al., 2010; Kebbell & Giles, 2000; Loftus, 1975; Wheatcroft et al., 2004; see also Chapter 13) and unwittingly provide obstructions to the truth (Loftus, 1975; Perry et al., 1995). Furthermore, Perry et al. (1995) found that confusing lawyerese questions reduced accuracy for younger children and that negatives, double negatives and multi-part questions posed the greatest problems for all age groups. Young or otherwise, vulnerable witnesses are demonstrably exposed to greater influence from such questions (see also Chapter 13). Rapid speech rate and antagonistic tone can confuse and intimidate witnesses (Ellison, 2001) and make victims feel re-traumatised by the process (Kebbell et al., 2003; Wheatcroft et al., 2009). The prospect that witnesses may benefit from *familiarisation* to courtroom processes has recently received some prominence in England and Wales in light of a judgement of the Court of Appeal endorsing the practice (Wheatcroft & Ellison, 2010).

Exponents argue (see Cooper, 2005) pre-trial preparation equips witnesses with essential courtroom skills and helps witnesses negotiate the peculiar demands of

CASE STUDY 12.2　THE CASES OF *R V. MOMODOU* (2005) AND *R V. SALISBURY* (2005)

In *Momodou*, the court held that pre-trial arrangements to familiarise witnesses with the general process of testifying were permissible and could improve the manner in which a witness gives evidence by, for example, reducing the tension arising from inexperience. Lord Justice Judge noted that sensible pre-trial preparation was to be welcomed, as witnesses should not be disadvantaged by ignorance of the criminal trial process and, when they come to give evidence, should not be taken by surprise at the way it works (for discussions see Ellison, 2007; Ellison & Wheatcroft, 2010; Wheatcroft, 2008). The Court of Appeal acknowledged the heavy demands placed on witnesses within adversarial systems and endorsed the practice of witness familiarisation in a criminal context. There was a dramatic distinction, the court held, between witness coaching that is prohibited and sensible preparation for the experience of giving evidence that could assist a witness to give of his or her best at a forthcoming trial. The professional standards committee of the Bar Council (2005) subsequently issued more detailed guidelines, which clarify that it is appropriate, as part of a witness familiarisation process, for barristers to advise witnesses as to the basic requirements for giving evidence, such as the need to listen to and answer the question put, to speak clearly and slowly in order to ensure that the court hears what the witness is saying, and to avoid irrelevant comments. Engaging a witness in a mock examination-in-chief, cross-examination or re-examination is also permissible, the guidelines state, provided that its purpose is simply to give the witness greater familiarity with and confidence in the process of giving oral evidence.

The criminal courts had a further opportunity to consider the propriety of witness preparation in *Salisbury*. In this case, a nurse was found guilty of attempting to murder two patients in her care. Professionals who worked with Salisbury were called as witnesses and, owing to concerns that the trial was causing undue stress and anxiety, the NHS trust concerned arranged for staff to receive advice on courtroom procedure and techniques of cross-examination. On receipt of this information, the defence applied to have the evidence of the witnesses excluded or, alternatively, for the proceedings to be stayed on the grounds of abuse of process. The Court of Appeal was satisfied, however, that what had taken place was no more than preparation for the exercise of giving evidence with witnesses undergoing instruction on the pitfalls of testifying. In the view of Lord Phillip (the judge in the case), this was an exercise that any witness would be entitled to enjoy were it available, noting: '. . . there is, in my view, a difference of substance between the process of familiarisation with the task of giving evidence coherently and the orchestration of evidence to be given. The second is objectionable and the first is not' (*R v. Salisbury* [2005] p.3103).

R v. Momodou (2005) W.L.R., 1, 3442
R v. Salisbury (2005) EWCA Crim 3107

cross-examination (Bond & Solon, 1999; Carson, 1990). While these claims have intuitive appeal, a review of the literature reveals a general lack of empirical research on witness preparation involving adult witnesses (Boccaccini *et al.*, 2005), with studies to date focusing overwhelmingly upon the pre-trial preparation of children (Dezwirek-Sas, 1992; Lipovsky & Stern, 1997; Murray, 1997). As early redress, Wheatcroft and Woods (2010) investigated the potential of simple witness preparation statements as counteractants to the effects of leading question styles as used with adult witnesses in criminal courts. Findings showed that familiarisation with directive leading questions allowed for significantly greater positive within-subjects (w-s) confidence-accuracy (c-a) relationships, compared with a non-directive equivalent condition; seemingly helping witnesses to apply the appropriate level of confidence to answers given. Nevertheless, the statements used were basic in character and arguably somewhat removed from techniques used in existing familiarisation programmes. Accordingly, Ellison and Wheatcroft (2010) considered the impact of more detailed preparation on witness accuracy and, broadly speaking, study outcomes found: (a) increased accuracy and reduced errors to complex questions; and (b) increased witness ability to seek clarifications from the examiner.

The impact of pre-trial publicity and judicial pronouncements upon outcome

In high profile cases, where there are no legal prohibitions on reporting, the public may gather information through media reports. Importantly, recent concern has been raised around juror access to the internet during trials, to assess material (e.g. a defendant's past history). Lord Chief Justice, Lord Judge was reported to have noted that 'the jury system may not survive if it is undermined by social networking sites' (BBC News, 2010). At this stage, of course, jurors cannot know whether the information is accurate or reliable. Yet, predictably, research demonstrates that those who hear media reports about a case are more likely to believe a suspect is guilty (Kerr, 1995; Steblay et al., 1999). In today's 24-hour news agenda, potential jurors can be repeatedly exposed to vivid and sometimes horrific images of crime. Ogloff and Vidmar (1994) examined the effects of print and television media in relation to prejudicial bias. The results again indicated that all media exposure had a prejudicial impact, but that the effects of television and print were particularly strong. Similarly, research has demonstrated an increase in guilty verdicts when mock jurors were exposed to negative pre-trial publicity (Hope et al., 2004). Negative pre-trial publicity then has a strong impact on trial outcome, at least for the accused (see Studebaker & Penrod, 1997 for review).

One reason for this is the biasing effects of *informational social* influence – the need to conform to sources of information other than our own because we believe others' interpretations are more accurate (Cialdini, 1993). Material that arouses emotions can exercise a particularly powerful influence. Kramer, Kerr and Carroll (1990) asked three groups of jurors to watch a trial of a man accused of robbery. Prior to watching, one group was exposed to emotional publicity (i.e. a car matching the one used in the robbery struck and killed a 7-year-old girl), one group was exposed to factual publicity (i.e. extensive criminal record) and a third group was exposed to no publicity. Jurors who were given emotional publicity were subsequently biased to return significantly more guilty verdicts than those who received the adverse factual information. Furthermore, neither instruction nor deliberation strategies reduced the impact of either publicity type – indeed, deliberation was shown to strengthen publicity biases, and illustrates the potential impact of social influence upon persuasibility. While judges can direct juries to disregard information, such directions might not necessarily be effective. In fact, they could even enhance jurors' attention by making such pronouncements (Fein et al., 1997). British judges, at the end of the trial, will sum up the case and give the jury instructions regarding law to consider during deliberation. The requirement for legal instruction stems from the fact that the jury is asked to decide whether a defendant is guilty according to the law rather than the truth of the evidence. However, jurors find instructions difficult to interpret, understand and apply, as they are written with the law rather than the layperson in mind (Steele & Thornburg, 1988) and a number of studies have shown that standard legal instructions can have adverse consequences for juror comprehension (Alfini et al., 1982; Severance & Loftus, 1982).

A comprehensive study conducted by Thomas (2010) for the Ministry of Justice in the UK reported judges' directions to be 'easily understood', though variations existed across jurisdictions and the three courts assessed. Arguably, complex issues are disguised, as, when understandings were assessed according to oral instructions (related to 'self-defence' law), greater understanding was shown for younger jurors (18–29 years of age) than those aged 30 years and above. Such an age decline questions the usefulness of some legal instructions with older jurors. Moreover, juror comprehension was compromised when both oral and written instructions were examined (related to 'actual bodily harm' and 'self-defence') with specific reference to the tests required for those offences (i.e. 'was force necessary' and 'was it reasonable'). Importantly, 36 per cent of jurors identified neither of the two legal questions. Thus, despite exposing juror difficulties since the 1970s, Dumas (2000) notes that standard instructions still tend to be written in dense, legal language.

Interestingly, Shaffer and Wheatman (2000) found that those with a dogmatic personality were more likely to apply instructions properly. The prospect of misunderstandings led lay jurors to tend to rely upon their own common sense and personal experiences as a guide, rather than assessments of the law. One commonly misunderstood direction is the proof required to satisfy the 'beyond reasonable doubt' criterion outlined above. Research suggests jurors have a tendency to apply the most stringent test – that of 100 per cent certainty – which is unrealistic (Montgomery, 1998; Zander, 2000). Moreover, judges themselves have problems in identifying a percentage that would satisfy 'beyond reasonable doubt' (Kagehiro, 1990). On the basis of research findings to date, pre-trial publicity should be kept to a minimum and judges should adopt jury-friendly versions of judicial directions, in order that jurors are better able to comprehend and accurately apply the information they receive.

JUDGES AS DECISION-MAKERS

Decision-making by judges in the European courts

In the civil courts in Britain and in the inquisitorial system of mainland Europe, judges rather than juries make decisions (Figure 12.2). Judges try to be impartial and derive their decisions purely from the law and the evidence, though research on judicial decision-making suggests this may not be so. According to Wagenaar et al. (1993),

FIGURE 12.2 *In the civil courts in Britain and in the inquisitorial system of mainland Europe, judges rather than juries make decisions.*

Source: © Minerva Studio. Used under licence from Shutterstock.

judges can be influenced by *anchored narratives*. According to Wagenaar *et al.*, 'anchors' are common-sense rules generally expected to be true: unquestioned assumptions concerning people, behaviour and ideas. These assumptions may be stereotypes that anchor any narrative to commonly held perceptions, such as 'once a thief always a thief' or 'drug abusers are always thieves' (Wagenaar, 1995). Such anchors, often embedded within legal decisions, are implicit rather than explicit. According to Wagenaar *et al.* (1993), legal fact-finding is predominantly a psychological process and often lacks logic. Anchors support propositions or facts and are derived from general impressions of the world but are not necessarily correct. From this standpoint, proof in criminal cases may lack rigorous justification of the anchors upon which it is based.

The availability of anchors through 'commonsense' understandings demonstrates lack of insight into the roots of our own decision-making. Furthermore, a consensus need not be achieved, as all involved tend to share

the common understanding in question. An example anchored in Dutch law is 'police officers in the line of duty never lie'. This anchor presupposes that the statement of a single police officer is proof enough. In a case cited by Wagenaar *et al.* (1993), a man was charged with illegally receiving unemployment benefits while he worked on an asparagus farm; the prosecutor successfully relied solely upon the statements of two police officers.

Spanish studies of past sentences also support the view that decisions are determined largely through systematic judgement biases (Fariña *et al.*, 2002). Fariña *et al.* considered 555 penal judgements from High Court and criminal courts in north-west Spain and estimated that anchoring drove 63.6 per cent of those judgements. Therefore, cultural anchors can impact upon decision-making and illuminate the reasons for inconsistent decisions.

An important component of a narrative is plausibility, which suggests 'an internal coherence' (Jackson, 1988, p.171). It is significant therefore that the aim of both parties in court is to put forward a plausible and credible account resembling what the judge and jury (i.e. in law, 'reasonable persons') *could* believe. Plausibility may be sensitive to external anchors that activate relevant *schemata* – those integrated networks of knowledge, beliefs and expectations related to a particular subject (Canter *et al.*, 2003). Interestingly, Canter *et al.* found that plausibility levels were lower when statements did not follow a temporal sequence of events: 'These processes relate both to "internal" structural constituents of narratives, especially the order in which they are presented, and to "external" stereotypes and belief systems on which an individual may draw to conceptualize and interpret particular components of the narrative' (Canter *et al.*, 2003. p.261).

Anchored narratives are potential biasing factors in judicial decision-making. Consequentially, in court, if decision-makers have to choose between two narratives they are likely to choose the most plausible one (Baudet *et al.*, 1994). Moreover, should a witness fail to articulate a coherent series of events that is both plausible and anchored in the appropriate narrative for the listener, then that witness's story may carry little weight, irrespective of its truth-value. However, for critical reason to occur, judges' awareness requires raising (Perkins, 1989) and training provided, perhaps in awareness of the need for multiple anchor points (Plous, 1993) and source biasing. But do such biases apply to judicial decision-making when groups of magistrates or judges are involved?

Decision-making by groups of magistrates or judges: Group dynamics

Research has demonstrated that magistrates' decision-making is inconsistent and sometimes uninformed.

For example, in bail use, limited information may be provided by the police that does not give the full picture to the courts (Dhami, 2004; Doherty & East, 1985). One implication is that defendants may be unnecessarily remanded in custody and may be subsequently acquitted or given a non-custodial sentence. For the penal system, unnecessary detentions before trial add to pressure on precious prison resources and force the penal authorities to release prisoners prematurely.

The gravest penalty available is the decision to impose an immediate custodial sentence, the average length of which has risen in the UK in recent years. In 1995 the average sentence for a man over 21 was 2.8 months compared to 2.6 months in 1990, while the corresponding figures for women were 2.3 and 2.4 months over the same period (Flood-Page & Mackie, 1998). It is unclear whether this increase reflected judgements derived from the facts of the cases, and that such increased punishment was warranted (Rumgay, 1995). Relatively little formal guidance exists to help judges and magistrates assess whether an offence is so serious that only a custodial sentence can be justified. In *Cox* (1993), however, Lord Justice Taylor affirmed that a *right-thinking persons* test was the correct approach. However, the seriousness of an offence is a subjective judgement, which can differ between individuals and/or over time (Ashworth & Hough, 1996). Worryingly, past research has repeatedly revealed inconsistency in sentencing decisions concerning similar cases between different courts (Parker *et al.*, 1981), within the same court (Parker *et al.*, 1989), and by the same individuals (Ashworth *et al.*, 1984). Indeed, Flood-Page and Mackie (1998) examined current UK sentencing practice in magistrates' courts and concluded that, whilst past research had shown considerable differences in sentences applied, 'since 1993 it is sentencing practice, not the legal framework that has changed' (p.139). Moreover, magistrates have been found to impose more severe sentences on the basis of video evidence than equivalent text accounts (Chenery *et al.*, 2001), potentially communicating incidents graphically and directly in ways that produce greater impact than a written statement (Davies, 2003). Therefore, the evolution and perpetuation of 'court cultures' that routinise interactions and decision-making could be invoked as an explanation for differences in magistrates' sentencing patterns. Some influences on group decision-making can be drawn from the literature on *conformity* to group pressure, where conformity increases significantly up to group sizes of three to four, but then plateaus and may even decline (Stang, 1976). Furthermore, *social impact theory* specifies that we conform when the group is one we care about, when members are unanimous in thoughts or behaviour, and when the group size is three or more (Latané, 1981). Other significant psychological research into group processes suggests that *groupthink* (i.e. maintenance of group cohesiveness; Janis, 1982), *polarisation* (i.e. making extreme decisions; Isenberg, 1986) and *social loafing* (Latané *et al.*, 1979) can all influence decision-making. A bench of magistrates or judges is a small group, commonly consisting of three people who interact with each other and are interdependent, in the sense that to fulfil their needs and goals, they must rely on each other (see Aronson *et al.*, 2005 for details). Thus groups of judges or magistrates are not immune to bias; indeed, they may be subject to additional pressures not experienced by judges sitting on their own.

JURIES AS DECISION-MAKERS

The impact of selection and profiling on outcome

There are numerous aspects that pertain to both process and individual that might impact upon the outcome of jury decision-making (Figure 12.3). However, with the jury room closed to scrutiny in the UK (see the Contempt of Court Act, 1981), the extent of impact remains the subject of constant attention by academics, psychologists and practitioners. In the absence of direct observation of juries, a rigorous debate rages in respect of the validity of jury research. Bornstein (1999), who conducted an analysis of jury simulation studies published in the first 20 years of *Law and Human Behavior*, identified a number of perceived weaknesses in simulation studies and asserted: 'these concerns are justified not only by fundamental principles governing the sound conduct of scientific research, but also by the desire to apply findings from simulation studies to understanding, and ultimately improving, the legal system' (p.2).

The principal concerns include the samples used in mock jury studies (i.e. undergraduates vs. community adults), the research setting (i.e. laboratory vs. courtroom), the trial medium (i.e. written summaries vs. listening to an actual trial), the trial elements included (e.g. presence or absence of deliberation), the dependent variables used (e.g. dichotomous verdicts vs. probability-of-guilt judgements), and the consequentiality of the task (i.e. hypothetical vs. real decision) (Diamond, 1997; Konecni & Ebbesen, 1979). One obvious drawback with the use of mock juries, for example, is that the defendant's future is not at risk and so gravity and importance may well be lost (Darbyshire *et al.*, 2002). The call for allowable juror research is subject to ongoing debate in the UK, although Zander (2005) has cautioned that such

FIGURE 12.3 *There are numerous aspects that pertain to both process and individual that might impact upon the outcome of jury decision-making.*

Source: © Junial Enterprises. Used under licence from Shutterstock.

research might show 'an intolerably high degree of irrationality, prejudice, stupidity and other forms of undesirable conduct in the jury retiring room' (p.2) that might lead to calls for the abolition of juries.

Regardless, studies of selection and composition have shown that males are over-represented and non-whites underrepresented (Zander & Henderson, 1993) and that women and ethnic minorities are still minimised on juries (Lloyd-Bostock & Thomas, 1999). The system by which potential jurors are summoned and excused can impact upon *representativeness*. For example, Airs and Shaw (1999) found that, in England and Wales, 38 per cent of potential jurors were excused for a variety of reasons and that only 34 per cent were available for service. Additionally, non-registration was found to be highest for ethnic minorities, people aged between 20 and 24 and those living in rented accommodation. Thus, random electoral roll samples do not necessarily lead to representative population samples.

One of the main factors expected to influence a jury is the *evidence* (Kalven & Zeisel, 1966) and to a large extent this is probably still the case. However, Ellsworth (1993) comments that individual jurors draw different conclusions about the right verdict on the basis of exactly the same evidence; thus evidence alone is likely to be insufficient to produce a uniform verdict. Studies examining the sex and age of jurors have also been found to influence decision-making. For example, women are significantly more likely to convict on circumstantial evidence (Sealy & Cornish, 1973). In this study, females also gave 78 per cent initial guilty verdicts in cases of rape and 71 per cent for murder cases, whilst the corresponding rates for males were 53 per cent and 50 per cent, respectively. More recently, Thomas (2010) found that first and final guilty verdicts remained stable for males whilst female guilty verdicts dropped from 41 per cent (first) to 33 per cent (final), illustrating that females might be more open to persuasion or reconsideration of facts. The same report argues no apparent gender bias in cases of rape. However, 52 per cent of verdicts found in the 'female 16 or over' category were classified not guilty, whilst 77 per cent of verdicts shown in the 'male 16 or over' category were classified as guilty, which perhaps suggests otherwise (see Wheatcroft *et al.*, 2009 for discussion). Upon further examination of the Sealy and Cornish data it was found that the difference in verdicts lay between black males and black females, rather than white males and white females, where no significant difference was observed. Indeed, between 2006–2008, white jurors have also been found to convict a larger percentage of black defendants (67 per cent) than white or Asian defendants (63 per cent and 63 per cent, respectively), though it is not clear whether these figures differed significantly. Kemmelmeier (2005) maintains race is a critical factor in white jurors' decision-making.

On the other hand, in a mock trial, male jurors alone are more likely to impose harsher punishments, such as longer sentences on criminal defendants who have committed rape, particularly when the female victim is attractive (Villemar & Hyde, 1983). Yet, increased levels of education have been shown to lead to a higher rate of acquittals by males (Mills & Bohannon, 1980). Such impact factors could be mediated by cognitive resource. For example, Hastie *et al.* (1983) found that only 48 per cent of case facts presented in testimonies were recalled by jurors with low education levels compared with 70 per cent for those jurors with high levels of educational attainment. Case Study 12.3 highlights some jury selection difficulties, although the interested reader is directed to Darbyshire *et al.* (2002) for a review of jury research and Hale-Starr and McCormick (2001) for jury selection discussions.

What one can conclude is that jury selection is far from an exact science. The voir dire process of juror questioning might eliminate jurors whose opinions differ with either side but, in addition, and in accordance with much academic opinion outlined in this chapter, juries can be influenced by a range of factors.

Visher (1987) has argued that personal characteristics are insignificant in predicting trial outcome compared to the wider factors of witness credibility and other evidence. Yet, there is a body of research that counters such an assertion and suggests that it is inappropriate to expect jurors to negotiate the justice process in an unbiased manner. This includes less obvious aspects of judicial processes, such as the use of specialist language and complexity, which also impact in particular ways.

CASE STUDY 12.3   THE TRIALS OF SCOTT DYLESKI AND O. J. SIMPSON

'Never forget, almost every case has been won or lost when the jury is sworn'

(Clarence Darrow, defence lawyer, 1936)

Juries decide thousands of cases each year. It is not surprising, therefore, that the jury system, where it operates throughout the world, is of central importance. Given this, jury selection services have become available, in the USA for example, to those willing to pay the associated fees. These services tend to be based on social-psychological and behavioural principles in order to apply the most sympathetic jurors to particular cases.

One such case was that of Scott Dyleski, who in August 2006 at the age of 17 was sentenced to life in prison without parole for the murder on 15 October 2005 of Pamela Vitale, the wife of prominent Californian defence lawyer Daniel Horowitz. Dyleski was convicted after the victim was found bludgeoned to death with a piece of crown moulding on the site of the couple's planned dream home. In such high profile cases, finding jurors with little knowledge of or opinion on the case can be more difficult than usual and the courts may call hundreds of potential jurors in an attempt to find those who have not yet formed opinions. In Dyleski's case, Judge Barbara Zuniga called 200 jurors to the Contra Costa County Superior Court, but many more may have been called if so required. In similar fashion, more than 1000 jurors were summoned

to Redwood City in the Scott Peterson trial during the same year.

In theory, large jury pools attempt to find people who are representative of the general population and exclude people with extreme views. However, 'in practice what you end up with is a jury that looks like the middle of a bell curve – it's not jury selection, it's a de-selection' (M. Rice, quoted in Krupnick, 2006).

The 1995 O.J. Simpson trial famously publicised jury selection techniques and, whether classified as selection or de-selection, such methods were demonstrable through the *voir dire* process. Oral voir dire consists of follow-up questions to questionnaires completed by prospective jurors and questions the lawyer specifically wants to ask orally in order to observe juror responses. In the O.J. Simpson case, an advisor to the prosecution, Don Vinson, compiled the jury profile to include one African American male, one Hispanic male, eight African American females and two Caucasian females. The emphasis on African American females came from voir dire questioning that showed that these women were more tolerant of physical force within marriage, and the belief that every relationship has its troubles; as one of the women said, 'people do get slapped around – it just happens'. Nevertheless, contrary to this view, Marcia Clark, the lead prosecutor in the case, believed that these women would be more likely to have experienced domestic violence in the past and would judge O.J. more harshly than males would.

Jurors' comprehension of complex material and legal terminology

Law would not exist without its specialist use of language and were it not for the close relationship between legal language and the legal system (Danet, 1984). As such, terminology embraced by the law has two main characteristics: first, it is technical because it uses a specialised vocabulary and second, it is culturally bound because law is above all a social science (Terral, 2004). It is not surprising, therefore, that legal terminology can lead to collective misunderstandings by juries. For example, a study conducted by Bornstein *et al.* (2005) demonstrated that the two most important negative juror perceptions of the court system were trial complexity and making the decision. According to Horowitz *et al.* (1996), jurors' perceptions of complexity fail to recognise that several evidential factors, such as volume to be processed, clarity and comprehensibility, are relevant to the term and may further add to misconceptions.

Trials often involve complex material presented to juries in a haphazard and disorganised manner, which hampers juries in reaching an appropriate verdict (Bennett & Feldman, 1981). Instead, juries synthesise the information into an organised narrative that makes sense to them but this may be at variance with the perceptions of the court (Wiener *et al.*, 2002). Indeed, cognitive research would suggest that complex cases require greater amounts of cognitive work by jurors without previous experience of such tasks, which could lead to overload. For example, Heuer and Penrod (1995) questioned real jurors who reported that they became progressively less confident in their verdict as the quantity of information increased, without additional instruction or other support. Thus, a positive correlation might be expected between cognitive overload and the employment of inappropriate *heuristics* (Gilovich *et al.*, 2001); excessive information might lead jurors to become confused and disengaged, and seek the most available commonsense outcome. The testimony of expert witnesses might assist or, conversely, skew comprehension. Cooper *et al.* (1996) found that mock jurors in the USA were more persuaded by high-level expert witnesses than less expert witnesses, but only when the testimony was highly complex. These effects, observed in mock juror studies, may be even greater in real trials, where the pressures on jurors are that much greater (Honess *et al.*, 1998; Jackson, 1996).

Decision-making processes in juries

The task of decision-making for a jury is unenviable and compounded by the gravity of its importance. Nevertheless, it is necessary for the jury to evaluate the strength of evidence presented and make a decision (Vidmar, 2005). Psychological research into decision-making processes and juror ability suggest that social-cognitive factors may be influential, though there is the same concern about the applicability of analogue studies to the courts.

Jury members are more likely to be influenced by group processes activated during the deliberations that follow a trial than by a single judge. Many studies have explored the impact on juror discussions of a range of factors including individual differences of jury members and the layout of the courtroom (see Hastie *et al.*, 1983 for a review). Group discussion tends to reinforce majority opinion: Meyers *et al.* (2001) observed that the position the majority of mock jurors favoured prior to group discussion became the final verdict in approximately 90 per cent of occasions. In such circumstances, there is a danger of group polarisation: groups make more extreme decisions in the direction of people's initial judgements. Views tend to polarise less, however, if the case for the prosecution is strong; those in favour of acquittal initially can be persuaded to convict (Arce *et al.*, 1996). More recent research in the USA has looked at the quality of deliberation (Gastil *et al.*, 2007). A study of 267 real jurors found that on all measures of deliberative quality (i.e. examination of the facts and judicial instructions; listening and debating opinions) jurors deliberated at a high level of competence. Such work suggests that we need to learn more about the *actual* processes involved in jurors' decision-making in groups.

Pennington and Hastie (1991) proposed an influential model of how individual jurors arrive at a decision: the *story model*. The model refers to an active, constructive comprehension process in which information is moulded into a coherent mental representation: the story (Pennington & Hastie, 1992). This process is hypothesised to occur for even the simplest discourse (Kintsch, 1988). However, research on discourse comprehension suggests that story chains have a higher order structure both when considering the discourse itself and when considering the listener's or reader's mental representations of the discourse. Therefore, these representations are as important for the interpreter of information as for the conveyer. Stories are organised into units called episodes (Trabasso & van den Broek, 1985) that represent attempts to apply meaning and thus plausibility to a series of statements or ideas. The resultant cognitive processing is central to decision-making and includes a range of relevant cognitions made up of scripts, schemas and heuristics (**social schema and scripts**). Schemata, for example, have been identified to explain

> **social schema and scripts** cognitive frameworks that guide an individual's behaviour by providing organisational structures for new experiences or social cues.

how people comprehend and remember a spoken or written story. For juries in particular, it has been argued that sense is made of the evidence by constructing 'their own stories of the case' (Wiener *et al.*, 2002, p.120), with obvious opportunities for bias and misunderstanding. The notion that humans instinctively need to make sense of information is central to the argument, as this hypothesised process can account for jurors making critical and devastating mistakes of interpretation guiding judgement. Understanding juror comprehension is at an early stage, but Pennington and Hastie's ideas continue to lead much research.

CONCLUSION

This chapter has highlighted psychological research on a number of important factors relevant to judicial processes. However, research into many issues is at an early stage and the translation into good practice must be cautious as a consequence. There are many issues, from the impact of inconsistency in testimony to the quality and quantity of group discussion, where further exploration is warranted.

In some areas, however, results are much more clear-cut. It is clear that pre-trial publicity should be kept to a minimum, and recent concern has focused on juror access to the internet during trials. Nevertheless, given that information exists and influences both judges and jurists, there is a vital need to explore further theoretical bases and why biasing effects occur. The most jury-friendly legal directions also require further clarification in order that jurors can more accurately apply and comprehend information. Further, one might assume that decision-making for judges would be notably less difficult to achieve than for juries. However, anchored narrative work suggests that judges may need to develop critical reasoning and awareness skills, perhaps with the assistance of psychologists. Magistrate bias in decision-making is also evident, signifying that research into influential court-culture is sorely needed. Small-group research points towards the requirement to learn more about the actual processes involved in jurors' decision-making in groups with a focus on real-life studies.

Finally, the whole process of hearing evidence, processing information and making judgements in legal contexts is under-researched, but enough has emerged to suggest that judicial decision-making can be prone to bias in some circumstances. Effective research on these topics will require input from and the cooperation of magistrates and judges in order to ask informed questions and, where necessary, engineer change – witness familiarisation research is evidence of such collaborations.

SUMMARY

- Psychologists have identified a number of important factors relevant to judicial processes. Many issues are at an early stage of research or are based on unrealistic legal assumptions and, as a consequence, the application of research findings to actual court practice must be cautious.

- Further exploration is warranted in particular on the impact of inconsistency in testimony, the quality and quantity of group discussion, and the theoretical bases of informational influence and biasing effects upon judges and jurists. More jury-friendly legal directions are also required in order that jurors can more accurately apply and comprehend information and instructions.

- The theory of anchored narratives suggests judges may need to develop critical reasoning and awareness skills, perhaps with help from psychologists.

- Magistrate decision-making appears also to be influenced by extra-evidential factors, signifying the need for further research into court culture. Small-group research points towards the requirement to learn more about the *actual* processes involved in jurors' decision-making in groups with a focus on real-life studies.

- The process of hearing evidence, processing information and making judgements in legal contexts is under-researched. Effective research on these topics will require input from and the cooperation of magistrates and judges in order to ask informed questions and where necessary, assist in developing fairer and more effective procedures.

ESSAY/DISCUSSION QUESTIONS

1. Discuss what psychological factors might influence evidence given in court.

2. Critically discuss the view that cross-examination is necessary to test witness accuracy and completeness.

3. Critically evaluate the effectiveness of judge and jury decision-making.

4. Evaluate how jury composition and legal understandings of jurors might influence the verdicts they reach.

REFERENCES

Airs, J. & Shaw, A. (1999). *Jury excusal and deferral. Home Office Research Development and Statistics Directorate Report No. 102.* London: Home Office.

Alfini, J., Sales, B. & Elwork, A. (1982). *Making jury instructions understandable.* Charlottesville, VA: Michie.

Arce, R., Fariña, F. & Sobral, J. (1996). From jurors to jury decision-making: A non-model approach. In G. Davies, M. McMurran, C. Wilson. & S. Lloyd-Bostock (Eds.) *Psychology, law and criminal justice. International developments in research and practice* (pp.435–439). Berlin: Walter de Gruyter.

Aronson, E., Wilson, T.D. & Akert, R.M. (2005). *Social psychology.* Upper Saddle River, NJ: Prentice-Hall.

Ashworth, A. (1994). *The criminal process: An evaluative study.* Oxford: Clarendon Press.

Ashworth, A., Genders, E., Mansfield, G., Peay, J. & Player, E. (1984). *Sentencing in the Crown Court: Report of an exploratory study.* Oxford: Centre for Criminological Research.

Ashworth, A. & Hough, M. (1996). Sentencing and the climate of opinion. *Criminal Law Review, November,* 776–786.

BBC News (2010, 19 November). *Top judge says internet 'could kill jury system'.* Retrieved 23 August 2011 from www.bbc.co.uk/news/uk-11796648

Bar Council. (2005). *Guidance on witness preparation.* London: Bar Council.

Baudet, S., Jhean-Larose, S. & Legros, D. (1994). Coherence and truth: A cognitive model of propositional truth attribution. *International Journal of Psychology, 29,* 219–350.

Bennett, W.L. & Feldman, M. (1981). *Reconstructing reality in the courtroom.* London: Tavistock.

Berman, G.L., Narby, D.J. & Cutler, B.L. (1995). Effects of inconsistent statements on mock jurors' evaluations of the eyewitness, perceptions of defendant culpability and verdicts. *Law and Human Behavior, 19,* 79–88.

Boccaccini, M., Gordon, T. & Brodsky, S. (2005). Witness preparation training with real and simulated criminal defendants. *Behavioral Sciences and the Law, 23,* 659–687.

Bond, C. & Solon, M. (1999). *The expert witness in court: A practical guide.* London: Shaw & Sons.

Bornstein, B.H. (1999). The ecological validity of jury simulations: Is the jury still out? *Law and Human Behavior, 23,* 75–91.

Bornstein, B.H., Miller, M.K., Nemeth, R.J., Page, G.L. & Musil, S. (2005). Jurors' reactions to jury duty: Perceptions of the system and potential stressors. *Behavioral Sciences and the Law 23,* 321–346.

Brennan, M. (1995). The discourse of denial: Cross-examining child victim witnesses. *Journal of Pragmatics, 23,* 71–91. Special issue: Laying down the law: Discourse analysis of legal institutions.

Brewer, N., Potter, R., Fisher, R.P., Bond, N. & Luszcz, M.A. (1999). Beliefs and data on the relationship between consistency and accuracy of eyewitness testimony. *Applied Cognitive Psychology, 13,* 297–313.

Canter, D.V., Grieve, N., Nicol, C. & Benneworth, K. (2003). Narrative plausibility: The impact of sequence and anchoring. *Behavioral Sciences and the Law 21,* 251–267.

Carson, D. (1990). *Professionals and the courts: Handbook for expert witnesses.* Sussex: Venture Press.

Chenery, S., Henshaw, C., Parton, P. & Pease, K. (2001). Does CCTV Evidence Increase Sentence Severity? *Scottish Journal of Criminal Justice Studies, 7,* 87–99.

Cialdini, R.B. (1993). *Influence: Science and practice* (3rd edn). New York: Harper Collins.

Civil Procedure Rules (1998). Retrieved 5 October 2011 from www.justice.gov.uk/guidance/courts-and-tribunals/courts/procedure-rules/index.htm

Cooper, J., Bennett, E.A. & Sukel, H.L. (1996). Complex scientific testimony: How do jurors make decisions? *Law and Human Behavior, 20,* 379–394.

Cooper, P. (2005). Witness preparation. *New Law Journal, 1753,* 155.

Cooper, W.H. (1981). Ubiquitous halo. *Psychological Bulletin, 90,* 218–244.

Cox (1993) 14 Cr App (S) 470.

Cutler, B.L., Penrod, S.D. & Dexter, H.R. (1990). Juror sensitivity to eyewitness identification evidence. *Law and Human Behavior, 14,* 185–191.

Damaska, M. (1973). Evidentiary boundaries to conviction and two models of criminal procedure: A comparative study. *University of Pennsylvania Law Review, 121,* 506.

Danet, B. (1984). Legal discourse. In T.A. van Dijk (Ed.) *Handbook of discourse analysis. Vol. 1: The disciplines of discourse analysis* (pp.273–291). London: Academic Press.

Darbyshire, P., Maughan, A. & Stewart, A. (2002). *What can the English legal system learn from jury research published up to 2001?* Occasional Paper Series 49. Kingston upon Thames, Surrey: Kingston Business School/Kingston Law School, Kingston University.

Davies, G.M. (2003). CCTV identification in court and in the laboratory. *Forensic Update, 72,* 7–10.

Dezwirek-Sas, L. (1992). Empowering child witnesses for sexual abuse prosecution. In H. Dent & R. Flin (Eds.) *Children as witnesses* (pp.181–200). Chichester: John Wiley & Sons, Inc.

Dhami, M.K. (2004). Conditional bail decision making in the magistrates court. *Howard Journal of Criminal Justice, 43,* 27–46.

Diamond, S.S. (1997). Illuminations and shadows from jury simulations. *Law and Human Behavior, 21,* 561–571.

Dick, T. (2006, August 3). Court out: How slip of tongue meant justice wasn't done. *Sydney Morning Herald.*

Doherty, M.J. & East, R. (1985). Bail decisions in magistrates' courts. *British Journal of Criminology, 25,* 251–266.

Drew, P. (1992). Contested evidence in courtroom cross-examination: The case of a trial for rape. In P. Drew & J. Heritage (Eds.) *Talk at work: Social interaction in institutional settings* (pp.470–520). Cambridge: Cambridge University Press.

DuCann, R. (1964). *The art of the advocate.* Harmondsworth: Penguin.

Dumas, B.K. (2000). Jury trials: Lay jurors, pattern jury instructions and comprehension issues. *Tennessee Law Review, 3,* 701–742.

Eggleston, R. (1978). *Evidence, proof and probability (Law in context)* (2nd edn). London: Butterworths Law.

Ellison, L. (2001). The mosaic art? Cross-examination and the vulnerable witness. *Legal Studies, 21,* 353–375.

Ellison, L. (2007). Witness preparation and the prosecution of rape. *Legal Studies, 27,* 171–187.

Ellison, L.E. & Wheatcroft, J.M. (2010). 'Could you ask me that in a different way please?' Exploring the impact of courtroom questioning and witness familiarisation on adult witness accuracy. *Criminal Law Review, 11,* 823–839.

Ellsworth, P.C. (1993). Some steps between attitudes and verdicts. In R. Hastie (Ed.) *Inside the juror: The psychology of juror decision making* (pp.42–64). Cambridge: Cambridge University Press.

Evans, K. (1995). *Advocacy in court: A beginner's guide* (2nd edn). London: Blackstone.

Fariña, F., Novo, M. & Arce, R. (2002). Heuristics of anchorage in judicial decisions. *Psicothema, 14,* 39–46.

Feild, H.S. (1979). Rape trials and jurors' decisions: A psycholegal analysis of the effects of victim, defendant case characteristics. *Law and Human Behavior, 3,* 261–284.

Fein, S., McCloskey, A.L. & Tomlinson, T.M. (1997). Can the jury disregard that information? The use of suspicion to reduce the prejudicial effects of pre-trial publicity and inadmissible testimony. *Personality and Social Psychology Bulletin, 23,* 1215–1226.

Flood-Page, C. & Mackie, A. (1998). *Sentencing practice: An examination of decisions in magistrates' courts and the Crown Court in the mid-1990s. Home Office Research Study No. 180.* London: HMSO.

Gastil, J., Burkhalter, S. & Black, L.W. (2007). Do juries deliberate? A study of deliberation, individual difference, and group member satisfaction at a municipal courthouse. *Small Group Research 38,* 337–359.

Gilovich, T., Griffin, D.W. & Kahneman, D. (Eds.) (2001). *The psychology of judgement: Heuristics and biases.* New York: Cambridge University Press.

Hale-Starr, V. & McCormick, M. (2001). *Jury selection.* New York: Aspenlaw.

Hans, V.P. & Vidmar, N. (1986). *Judging the jury.* New York: Plenum Press.

Harris, S. (1984). Questions as a mode of control in magistrates' courts. *International Journal of Society and Language, 49,* 5–27.

Hastie, R., Penrod, S. & Pennington, N. (1983). *Inside the jury.* Cambridge, MA: Harvard University Press.

Heuer, L. & Penrod, S.D. (1995). Jury decision-making in complex trials. In R. Bull & D. Carson (Eds.) *Handbook of psychology in legal contexts* (pp.527–541). Chichester: John Wiley & Sons, Inc.

Hickey, L. (1993). Presupposition under cross-examination. *International Journal for the Semiotics of Law, 1,* 89–109.

Hobbs, P. (2003). 'You must say it for him': Reformulating a witness testimony on cross-examination at trial. *Text, 23,* 477–511.

Honess, T.M., Levi, M. & Charman, E.A. (1998). Juror competence in processing complex information: Implications from a simulation of the Maxwell trial. *Criminal Law Review, November,* 763–773.

Hope, L., Memon, A. & McGeorge, P. (2004). Understanding pre-trial publicity: Predicisional distortion of evidence by mock jurors. *Journal of Experimental Psychology: Applied, 10,* 111–119.

Horowitz, I.A., ForsterLee, L. & Brolly, I. (1996). Effects of trial complexity on decision-making. *Journal of Applied Psychology, 81,* 757–768.

Isenberg, D.J. (1986). Group polarization: A critical review and meta-analysis. *Journal of Personality and Social Psychology, 50,* 1141–1151.

Jackson, B. (1988). *Law, fact, and narrative coherence.* Merseyside, UK: Deborah Charles Publications.

Jackson, J. (1996). Juror decision-making in the trial process. In G. Davies, M. McMurran, C. Wilson. & S. Lloyd-Bostock (Eds.) *Psychology, law and criminal justice. International developments in research and practice* (pp.327–336). Berlin: Walter de Gruyter.

Janis, I. (1982). *Groupthink: Psychological studies of policy decisions and fiascos* (2nd edn). Boston: Houghlin Mifflin.

Kagehiro, D.K. (1990). Defining the standard to proof in jury instructions. *Psychological Science, 1*, 187–193.

Kalven, H. & Zeisel, H. (1966). *The American jury*. Boston: Little Brown and Co.

Kassin, S.M., Rigby, S. & Castillo, S.R. (1991). The accuracy-confidence correlation in eyewitness testimony: limits and extension of the retrospective self-awareness effect. *Journal of Personality and Social Psychology, 61*, 698–707.

Kebbell, M., Deprez, S. & Wagstaff, G. (2003). The direct and cross-examination of complainants and defendants in rape trials: A quantitative analysis of question type. *Psychology, Crime and Law, 9*, 49–59.

Kebbell, M.R., Evans, L. & Johnson, S.D. (2010). The influence of lawyers' questions on witness accuracy, confidence and reaction times and on mock jurors' interpretation of witness accuracy. *Journal of Investigative Psychology and Offender Profiling, 7*, 262–272.

Kebbell, M.R. & Giles, D.C. (2000). Lawyers' questions and witness confidence: Some experimental influences of complicated lawyers' questions on witness confidence and accuracy. *The Journal of Psychology, 134*, 129–13.

Kebbell, M.R., Hatton, C., Johnson, S.D. & O'Kelly, C.M.E. (2001). People with learning disabilities as witnesses in court: How questions influence answers. *British Journal of Learning Disabilities, 29*, 1–5.

Kebbell, M.R., Wagstaff, G.F. & Covey, A.C. (1996). The influence of item difficulty on the relationship between eyewitness confidence and accuracy. *British Journal of Psychology, 87*, 653–662.

Kemmelmeier, M. (2005). The effects of race and social dominance orientation in simulated juror decision-making. *Journal of Applied Social Psychology, 35*, 1030–1045.

Kerr, N.L. (1995). Social psychology in court: The case of prejudicial pre-trial publicity. In G.G. Brannigan & M.R. Merrens (Eds.) *The social psychologists: Research adventures* (pp.247–262). New York: McGraw-Hill.

Kintsch, W. (1988). The role of knowledge in discourse comprehension: A construction-integration model. *Psychological Review, 95*, 163–182.

Konecni, V.J. & Ebbesen, E.B. (1979). External validity of research in legal psychology. *Law and Human Behavior, 3*, 39–70.

Kramer, G.P., Kerr, N.L. & Carroll, J.S. (1990). Pre-trial publicity, judicial remedies, and jury bias. *Law and Human Behavior, 14*, 409–438.

Krupnick, M. (2006, 18 July). Dyleski trial highlights jury selection difficulties. *Contra Costa Times*.

Latané, B. (1981). The psychology of social impact. *American Psychologist 36*, 343–356.

Latané, B., Williams, K. & Harkins, S. (1979). Social loafing. *Psychology Today, 110*, 104–106.

Leippe, M.R., Manion, A.P. & Romanczyk, A. (1992). Eyewitness persuasion: How and how well do fact finders judge the accuracy of adults' and children's memory reports? *Journal of Personality and Social Psychology, 63*, 181–197.

Levenson, L.L. (2008). Courtroom demeanour: The theater of the courtroom. *Minnesota Law Review, 573*, 92.

Lindsay, R.C.L. (1994). Expectations of eyewitness performance: Jurors verdicts do not follow from their beliefs. In D.F. Ross, J.D. Read & M.P. Toglia (Eds.) *Adult eyewitness testimony: Current trends and developments* (pp.362–382). New York: Cambridge University Press.

Lipovsky, J. & Stern, P. (1997). Preparing children for court: An interdisciplinary view. *Child Maltreatment, 2*, 150–163.

Lloyd-Bostock, S. (2006). The effects on lay magistrates of hearing that the defendant is of 'good character', being left to speculate, or hearing that he has a previous conviction. *Criminal Law Review*, 189–212.

Lloyd-Bostock, S. & Thomas, C. (1999). Decline of the Little Parliament: Juries and jury reform in England and Wales. *Law and Contemporary Problems, 7*, 21.

Loftus, E. (1975). Leading questions and the eyewitness report. *Cognitive Psychology, 7*, 560–572.

Matoesian, G. (1993). *Reproducing rape*. Cambridge: Polity Press.

Memon, A., Vrij, A. & Bull, R. (2003). *Psychology and law: Truthfulness, accuracy and credibility*. Chichester: John Wiley & Sons, Inc.

Meyers, R.A., Brashers, D.E. & Hanner, J. (2001). Majority/minority influence: Identifying argumentative patterns and predicting argument-outcome links. *Journal of Communication, 50*, 3–30.

Mills, C.J. & Bohannon, W.E. (1980). Juror characteristics: To what extent are they related to jury verdicts? *Judicature, 1*, 64.

Montgomery, J.W. (1998). The criminal standard of proof. *National Law Journal, 148*, 582.

Murphy, P. (1994). *Evidence & advocacy* (4th edn). London: Blackstone.

Murray, K. (1997). *Preparing child witnesses for court: A review of literature and research*. Edinburgh: Scottish Office.

Ogloff, J.R.P. & Vidmar, N. (1994). The impact of pre-trial publicity on jurors: A study to compare the relative effects of television and print media in a child sex abuse case. *Law and Human Behavior, 18*, 507–525.

Parker, H., Casburn, M. & Turnbull, D. (1981). *Receiving juvenile justice: Adolescents and state care and control*. Oxford: Blackwell.

Parker, H., Sumner, M. & Jarvis, G. (1989). *Unmasking the magistrates: The 'Custody or not' decision in sentencing young offenders*. Milton Keynes: Open University Press.

Pennington, N. & Hastie, R. (1991). A cognitive theory of juror decision-making: The story model. *Cardoza Law Review, 13*, 497.

Pennington, N. & Hastie, R. (1992). Explaining the evidence: Tests of the story model for juror decision making. *Journal of Personality and Social Psychology, 62*, 189–206.

Perkins, D.N. (1989). Reasoning as it and would be: An empirical perspective. In D.M. Topping, D.C. Crowell & V.N. Kobayaski (Eds.) *Thinking across cultures: The third international conference on thinking* (pp.175–194). Hillsdale, NJ: Erlbaum.

Perry, N., McAuliff, B., Tam, P., Claycomb, L., Dostal, C. & Flanagan, C. (1995). When lawyers question children: Is justice served? *Law and Human Behavior, 19*, 609–629.

Plous, S. (1993). *The psychology of judgment and decision-making*. New York: McGraw-Hill.

Rumgay, J. (1995). Custodial decision making in a magistrates' court. *British Journal of Criminology, 35*, 201–217.

Sealy, A.P. & Cornish, W.R. (1973). Jurors and their verdicts. *Modern Law Review, 36*, 496.

Severance, L.J. & Loftus, E.F. (1982). Improving the ability of jurors to comprehend and apply criminal jury instructions. *Law and Society Review, 17*, 153–198.

Shaffer, D. & Wheatman, S. (2000). Does personality influence reactions to judicial instructions? *Psychology, Public Policy and Law, 6*, 655–676.

Sporer, S.L. (1993). Eyewitness identification accuracy, confidence, and decision times in simultaneous and sequential lineups. *Journal of Applied Psychology, 78*, 22–33.

Stang, D.J. (1976). Group size effects on conformity. *Journal of Social Psychology, 98*, 175–181.

Steblay, N.M., Besirevic, J., Fulero, S.M. & Jimenez-Lorente, B. (1999). The effects of pre-trial publicity on juror verdicts: A meta-analytic review. *Law and Human Behavior, 21*, 283–297.

Steele, W.W. & Thornburg, E.G. (1988). Jury instructions: a persistent failure to communicate. *North Carolina Law Review, 67*, 77.

Stephan, C. & Corder-Tully, J. (1977). The influence of physical attractiveness of a plaintiff on the decisions of simulated jurors. *Journal of Social Psychology, 101*, 149–150.

Stone, M. (1988). *Cross-examination in criminal trials*. London: Butterworths.

Studebaker, C.A. & Penrod, S.D. (1997). Pretrial publicity: The media, the law, and common sense. *Psychology, Public Policy, and Law, 3*, 428–460.

Taylor, S.C. (2004). *Court licensed abuse: Patriarchal lore and the legal response to intra-familial sexual abuse of children*. New York: Peter Lang Publishing.

Terral, F. (2004). Cultural imprint of legal terms. *Meta, 49*, 876–890.

Thomas, C. (2010). *Are juries fair? Ministry of Justice Research Series 1/10*. London: Crown.

Trabasso, T. & van den Broek, P. (1985). Causal thinking and the representation of narrative events. *Journal of Memory and Language, 24*, 612–630.

Tversky, A. & Kahneman, D. (1974). Judgment under uncertainty: Heuristics and biases. *Science, 185*, 1124–1131.

Vidmar, N. (2005). Expert evidence, the adversary system, and the jury. *American Journal of Public Health, 95*, 137–143.

Villemar, N. & Hyde, J. (1983). Effects of sex of defence attorney, sex of juror and attractiveness of the victim on mock juror decision-making in a rape case. *Sex Roles, 9*, 879–889.

Visher, C.A. (1987). Juror decision making. The importance of evidence. *Law and Human Behavior, 11*, 1–17.

Wagenaar, W.A. (1995). Anchored narratives: A theory of judicial reasoning and its consequences. In G. Davies, M. McMurran, C. Wilson. & S. Lloyd-Bostock (Eds.) *Psychology, law and criminal justice. International developments in research and practice* (pp.267–285). Berlin: Walter de Gruyter.

Wagenaar, W.A., van Koppen, P.J. & Crombag, H.F.M. (1993). *Anchored narratives. The psychology of criminal evidence*. Hemel Hempstead: Harvester Wheatsheaf.

Wiener, R.L., Richmond, T.L., Seib, H.M., Rauch, S.M. & Hackney, A.A. (2002). The psychology of telling murder stories: Do we think in scripts, exemplars, or prototypes? *Behavioral Sciences and the Law, 20*, 119–139.

Wheatcroft, J.M. (2008). The trial process: Judicial processes. In G. Davies, C. Hollin & R. Bull (Eds.) *Forensic psychology* (pp.161–184). Chichester: John Wiley & Sons, Inc.

Wheatcroft, J.M. & Ellison, L.E. (2010). Courtroom questioning, pre-trial preparation and witness accuracy. *Forensic Update, 101*, 41–44.

Wheatcroft, J., Kebbell, M. & Wagstaff, G. (2001). The influence of courtroom questioning style on eyewitness accuracy and confidence. *Forensic Update, 65*, 20–25.

Wheatcroft, J.M. & Wagstaff, G.F. (2003). The interface between psychology and law in the courtroom: Cross-examination. *Forensic Update, 75*, 8–18.

Wheatcroft, J.M., Wagstaff, G.F. & Kebbell, M.R. (2004). The influence of courtroom questioning style on actual and perceived eyewitness confidence and accuracy. *Legal & Criminological Psychology, 9*, 83–101.

Wheatcroft, J.M., Wagstaff, G.F. & Moran, A. (2009). Re-victimising the victim? How rape victims experience the UK legal system. *Victims and Offenders, 4*, 265–284.

Wheatcroft, J.M. & Woods, S. (2010). Effectiveness of witness preparation and cross-examination non-directive and directive question styles on witness accuracy and confidence. *International Journal of Evidence & Proof, 14*, 189–209.

Zander, M. (2000). The criminal standard of proof–how sure is sure? *National Law Journal, 150*, 1517.

Zander, M. (2005). *Jury research and impropriety: A response to the Department of Constitutional Affairs' consultation paper (CP 04/05)*. Retrieved 23 August 2011 from www.lse.ac.uk/collections/law/staff%20publications%20full%20text/zander/Jury%20Research%20and%20Impropriety.pdf

Zander, M. & Henderson, P. (1993). *Crown Court study. Royal Commission on Criminal Justice, Research Study No 19* (pp.131–136). London: HMSO.

Zebrowitz, L.A. & McDonald, S. (1991). The impact of litigants' babyfacedness and attractiveness on adjudications in small claims courts. *Law and Human Behavior, 15*, 603–623.

ANNOTATED READING LIST

Ashworth, A. (1992). *Sentencing and criminal justice*. London: Weidenfeld and Nicholson. *The aim of this book is to examine English sentencing law in its context, drawing not only upon legislation and the decisions of the courts but also upon the findings of research and on theoretical justifications for punishment.*

Ellison, L.E. & Wheatcroft, J.M. (2010). 'Could you ask me that in a different way please?' Exploring the impact of courtroom questioning and witness familiarisation on adult witness accuracy. *Criminal Law Review, 11*, 823–839. *This paper reports on the effects of preparing adult witnesses (see also Wheatcroft & Woods, 2010).*

Fariña, F., Novo, M. & Arce, R. (2002). Heuristics of anchorage in judicial decisions. *Psicothema, 14*, 39–46. *This study reviews judicial judgements to assess impact of bias. Findings are discussed in terms of recommendations designed to mitigate bias.*

Hannibal, M. & Mountford, L. (2002). *The law of criminal and civil evidence: Principles and practice*. Harlow: Pearson. *This major introduction to the law of both criminal and civil evidence develops understanding of contemporary law in a practical and academic way.*

Hastie, R. (Ed.) (1993). *Inside the juror: The psychology of juror decision making*. Cambridge: Cambridge University Press. *Presents interesting aspects of juror decision-making that include facets drawn from social, cognitive and behavioural psychology, and considers the validity of existing research.*

Kaplan, M.F. & Martin, A.M. (2006). *Understanding world jury systems through psychological research*. New York: Psychology Press. *Examines diverse jury systems in nations around the world and considers impact features upon jury selection, composition, functioning, processes and trial outcomes.*

Wrightsman, L.S. (1999). *Judicial decision-making. Is psychology relevant?* New York: Kluwer Academic/Plenum Publishers. *This book examines decision-making by judges using contemporary concepts derived from a psychological viewpoint.*

13 Safeguarding Witnesses

Helen L. Westcott and Graham Davies

CHAPTER OUTLINE

Helen L. Westcott was formerly at the International Centre for Comparative Criminological Research, The Open University, United Kingdom.

Imagine being six years old and suddenly being taken from your bath, in your own home, by a complete stranger. You are then driven around the city where you live for 20 minutes, subjected to two serious assaults, and abandoned in a lane before the stranger drives off. It is January and you are naked and freezing.

This is probably not the most comfortable scenario you would like to imagine, and perhaps you are feeling unhappy or even angry that you have been asked to put yourself in this position. However, the needs of children and vulnerable adults who *have* endured similar experiences – or other difficult personal circumstances – and later come to court to talk about them, are the concern of this chapter. How can *their* emotions, needs and welfare be accommodated? Specifically, we will examine here what steps can be taken to safeguard witnesses' well-being, without compromising the rights of the accused.

> **safeguarding** the process of protecting individuals from abuse or neglect, preventing impairment of their health and development, and promoting their welfare and life chances.

What do we mean by **safeguarding**? The term has become increasingly important in child protection, in the UK at least. According to official guidance, 'safeguarding and promoting the welfare of children' refers to the 'process of protecting children from abuse or neglect, preventing impairment of their health and development, and ensuring they are growing up in circumstances consistent with the provision of safe and effective care which is undertaken so as to enable children to have optimum life chances and enter adulthood successfully' (Department of Education, 2011).

A witness may be vulnerable due to their 'youth, incapacity or circumstances' (Youth Justice and Criminal Evidence (YJCE) Act 1999; see Chapter 5). Members of any of the following groups may therefore be considered vulnerable: children, elderly people (Figure 13.1), individuals with learning difficulties, physically impaired witnesses, victims of sexual assault, intimidated witnesses and those with mental health problems. Burton *et al.* (2006) 'conservatively' estimate that 24 per cent of witnesses in their evaluation of the implementation of **special measures** (defined by the Home Office (2002, p.134, Appendix A) as 'the measures specified in the Youth Justice and Criminal Evidence Act 1999 which may be ordered in respect of some or all categories of eligible witness by means of a special measures direction'; see

> **special measures** the measures specified in the Youth Justice and Criminal Evidence Act 1999 that may be ordered for eligible witnesses by means of a special measures direction. They include screens, live link, video-recorded evidence-in-chief, intermediaries and aids to communication.

FIGURE 13.1 *Elderly people and children are two of the groups who may be considered vulnerable.*

Source: Left image: © Dean Mitchell; right image: © Gladskikh Tatiana. Both images used under licence from Shutterstock.

later discussion) were vulnerable or intimidated – two to three times the official estimate.

vulnerable witnesses a witness may be vulnerable due to their youth, incapacity or circumstances (e.g. children, elderly people, individuals with learning difficulties, physically impaired witnesses, victims of sexual offences, individuals with mental health problems).

What, then, might *safeguarding* mean for **vulnerable witnesses** in the courtroom? First, safeguarding requires that the *stress of testifying is minimised* as much as possible. Second, the circumstance (or process) of giving evidence in court needs to be made as *effective* as possible for vulnerable witnesses. Finally, the *implications of the court experience* for witnesses as they move on to the rest of their lives need to be considered. In this chapter, we are going to address these issues through consideration of

- witnesses' fears and perceptions about going to court;
- preparing witnesses for court;
- protecting witnesses at court; and
- challenging conventions.

If we reconsider our six-year-old child, what could we do to help them give an account of being abducted in court, in a way that is least stressful and most helpful?

WITNESSES' FEARS AND PERCEPTIONS ABOUT GOING TO COURT

It is important that witnesses' fears and perceptions about going to court are acknowledged, since they can contribute directly as well as indirectly to the success or otherwise of a prosecution. If a witness has extreme fears, for example that she will not be believed or will not be treated fairly, then she may decide to withdraw her complaint. Kelly *et al.* (2005) found that 14 per cent of rape complainants declined to complete the initial process, another 14 per cent withdrew at the investigative stage and a further 2 per cent withdrew at the prosecution and trial stages. Attrition figures in cases involving vulnerable witnesses portray a rather bleak picture (see Davies & Westcott, 2006 for a review). Most cases – about 70 per cent – drop out at the initial stages of an investigation and prosecution. These witnesses have therefore *not* been able to provide their evidence to the court. If individuals have a poor experience of involvement with the criminal justice system, then it is legitimate to question how far they will be willing to become involved

> **BOX 13.1 VICTIMS' AND WITNESSES' FEARS ABOUT PARTICIPATING IN A PROSECUTION AND/OR TRIAL**
>
> - Fear of harm by the abuser
> - Fear of rejection by the family
> - Fear of disbelief
> - Fear of others' reactions (e.g. carers being upset, professionals being insensitive)
> - Fear of family break-up, including their own removal from the family
> - Fear of embarrassment

again in the future (e.g. Esam, 2002; Hamlyn *et al.*, 2004; Plotnikoff & Woolfson, 2004).

Studies of victims and witnesses have reported a range of fears about participating in the investigative and prosecution process, and going to court (summarised in Box 13.1; see, for example, Harris & Grace, 1999; Kelly *et al.*, 2005; Sas *et al.*, 1991; 1995).

Additionally, the victim or witness may be feeling guilty, responsible, ashamed or intimidated (see Case Study 13.1). Family members may knowingly or unknowingly exert pressure on the witness to retract their statement (Sas *et al.*, 1991), or associates of the accused may actively seek to intimidate the witness to withdraw. Intimidation seems to be a particular problem facing vulnerable witnesses. Hamlyn *et al.* (2004) reported that 53 per cent experienced some form of intimidation in the period leading to trial, coming primarily from the accused (36 per cent), or from the accused's family (21 per cent).

WITNESSES' EXPERIENCES IN COURT

Although many victims and witnesses report such fears and apprehensions, they are not always borne out in practice (e.g. Gallagher & Pease, 2000; Kelly *et al.*, 2005; Sanders *et al.*, 1997; Westcott & Davies, 1996). However, many vulnerable witnesses *have* found the court experience to be extremely difficult, illustrated particularly in research with children (e.g. Plotnikoff & Woolfson, 2004; Wade, 2002; Wade & Westcott, 1997). Consider Case Study 13.1, which presents an extract from Mary's account.

Mary's experience highlights a number of concerns about the treatment of vulnerable witnesses in the

CASE STUDY 13.1   MARY

I am 12 years old. The man next door, Uncle Bob, he and his wife were good friends of our family, he did sex things to me for about three years. All our family liked him and I did too. He was always very kind to me and used to babysit for us ... I can't remember when it all began but he started doing things to me that I didn't like. At first I didn't understand what was happening and kept thinking I must be imagining things. I couldn't get him to stop although I asked him to. He made me feel like it was my fault and he told me nobody would believe me if I did say anything ... one day when the teacher at school asked me what was the matter, it just all came out. She said she would tell my mum and then everything would be alright. My mum was really upset but she believed me ... I tried not to think about going to court but one day my mum told me it was going to be next week.

We waited and then somebody came to tell me that I couldn't go into the television link room because it was being used by somebody else. They said I could give my evidence behind a screen but that meant I had to go into the courtroom. They said that if I wanted to wait for the television link we'd have to come back another day ... I felt I had to go ahead with it that day. I don't think I would have ever gone through with it if I hadn't done it then.

The first barrister was okay but he didn't ask me much and I didn't always understand what he was saying ... it was really embarrassing to say the details. I didn't tell them everything. I just couldn't. When the next barrister questioned me, she had a smiley face and made jokes with me. I began to think it wasn't going to be so bad. Then she seemed to change. She kept asking me about dates and times and I couldn't remember them exactly. I told her I could remember what had happened to me but not when. I didn't understand some of the long words she used ... She called me a liar. I still don't understand half of what went on. I felt dirty. They made me feel like I didn't exist. If I had known how it was going to be like at court, I never would have gone through with it.

(Le Roy, undated, quoted in Esam, 2002, pp. 309–310).

criminal courts, which we will return to throughout this chapter. As noted in the introduction, these concerns include the welfare of the witness, the effectiveness (or not) of their testimony and the implications of the experience for all involved. In particular, vulnerable witnesses are likely to raise issues in relation to cognitive, developmental and socio-emotional factors that have previously been considered in the interviewing of such witnesses (see Chapter 5). Some examples of these factors as they may apply to vulnerable witnesses are summarised in Box 13.2, but the extent of their influence on any particular witness (e.g. an elderly woman, a young man with learning difficulties, a traumatised rape victim) would need to be considered on an individual basis. Further reading giving more detail pertaining to these factors, their implications for safeguarding vulnerable witnesses, as well as case examples, is provided at the end of this chapter.

BOX 13.2   COGNITIVE, DEVELOPMENTAL AND SOCIO-EMOTIONAL FACTORS IN RELATION TO VULNERABLE WITNESSES

legalese refers to lexically and syntactically complicated language that has developed to meet the needs of the legal profession.

Memory factors: marked, negative, effect of delay on memory; problems with source-monitoring in relation to memories; susceptibility to misinformation effects on memory (e.g. through the influence of questioning); limited free recall; problems associated with script memory. (See, for example, Baker-Ward & Ornstein, 2002; Powell & Thomson, 2002; Saywitz, 2002; and Chapter 6.)

Language factors: less developed vocabulary and understanding of complex grammatical structures; limited vocabulary for sexual offences; unfamiliarity with, and confusion caused by, the use of **legalese**; use of non-verbal communication systems. (See, for example, Brennan & Brennan, 1988; Kennedy, 1992; Walker, 1993; 1994.)

Authority effects: particular sensitivity to the need to give socially desirable responses; heightened susceptibility to leading questions; acquiescence and naysaying; reluctance to talk; fear and anxiety. (See, for example, Ceci *et al.*, 1987; Meyer & Jesilow, 1993; Moston, 1992; Moston & Engelberg; 1992 Sanders *et al.*, 1997; and Chapter 6.)

STRESS FACTORS AND SPECIAL MEASURES FOR VULNERABLE WITNESSES

Spencer and Flin (1993) presented a model that pulled together the particular stressors that can affect child witnesses, together with mediating factors and likely effects. This model predates the broader conception of a vulnerable witness, but remains a helpful summary of issues that have been discussed so far in this chapter. It is reproduced in Figure 13.2.

What can be done to address the issues highlighted in this model? In fact, a number of interventions are possible, and have been implemented since this model was conceptualised. In England and Wales, the Youth Justice and Criminal Evidence Act 1999 introduced a raft of special measures in order to facilitate the testimony of vulnerable witnesses. These stemmed from a government review entitled *Speaking Up For Justice* (Home Office, 1998), which argued that the rights of victims and witnesses were not being met within the criminal justice system as it currently operated. A number of

these special measures, in fact, were already available to certain categories of witnesses (e.g. children), in certain categories of cases (e.g. sexual offences; Home Office, 1992). However, the 1999 Act extended such measures to a broader range of 'vulnerable' witnesses (Home Office, 2002). Box 13.3 summarises the special measures contained in the 1999 Act, which required legislative change (rather than new practice development or administrative action).

In addition, restrictions on evidence and questions about the complainant's sexual behaviour were introduced, as well as the prohibition of cross-examination by the accused in person in certain offences (e.g. rape and sexual offences). Further, the value of professional support to witnesses, both pre-trial and at court, was more formally recognised than had previously been the case. Existing guidance on interviewing witnesses for the purposes of criminal proceedings – The **Memorandum of Good Practice** (Home Office, 1992) – was revised and expanded and published as **Achieving Best Evidence** (Home Office, 2002; see Chapter 5). This new guidance was in turn revised, with increased coverage of how best to cope with witnesses who feared intimidation (Office for Criminal Justice Reform, 2007a) before being revised again in 2011 (Ministry of Justice, 2011).

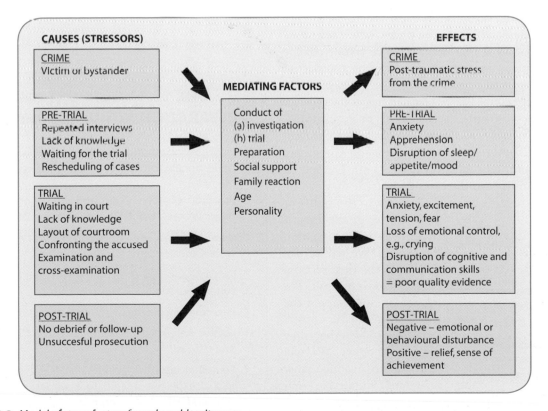

FIGURE 13.2 *Model of stress factors for vulnerable witnesses.*

Source: Reproduced from Spencer & Flin, 1993, p.364, with permission of Oxford University Press.

BOX 13.3   SUMMARY OF SPECIAL MEASURES IN THE YOUTH JUSTICE AND CRIMINAL EVIDENCE ACT 1999

- Use of *screens* so that the witness is protected from being confronted by the defendant
- Giving of *evidence by live link* (CCTV) from outside the courtroom
- Giving of *evidence in private* – the press and public may be excluded (except for one named person to represent the press) in cases involving sexual offences or intimidation
- *Removal of wigs and gowns* by barristers and the judge
- Showing of *pre-recorded evidence-in-chief*, cross-examination and re-examination
- Questioning through the use of *intermediaries* and *aids to communication*

The special measures listed in Box 13.3 differ in the extent to which they have required changes to law, procedure or practice in order to be implemented (Burton *et al.*, 2006). For example, removing the witness from the courtroom deviates from the assumed right of confrontation in person (Spencer, in press), whereas removing wigs and gowns represents a more minor change to legal practice. Internationally, different approaches have been taken to implementing such measures for witnesses, depending upon whether the country's justice system is adversarial (accusatorial) or inquisitorial, and how vulnerable witnesses are already accommodated (see Chapter 12, also Bottoms & Goodman, 1996; Cashmore, 2002; Spencer *et al.*, 1990). The special measures also differ in the extent to which they can be viewed as controversial, or challenging to the rights of the defendant, as in the use of pre-recorded cross-examination or **intermediaries**. We will return to this debate in the final section, 'Challenging Conventions'. For the purposes of this chapter, the special measures can be considered according to whether they apply *pre-* or *at* court. We will now move on to examine how they safeguard vulnerable witnesses in more detail, starting first with those measures that apply pre-court.

intermediaries one of the special measures permitted by the Youth Justice and Criminal Evidence Act 1999. An approved intermediary communicates the questions to the witness, then communicaties their response to the questioner.

PREPARING WITNESSES FOR COURT

Preparation and social support in practice

Preparation, and the provision of social support, are mediating factors in the model presented in Figure 13.2. That is, these can ameliorate the effects of pre-trial stressors if they are provided to vulnerable witnesses in the period before a court appearance – and hence safeguard the witness by reducing anxiety and promoting effective testimony. *Achieving Best Evidence* (Home Office, 2002; Office for Criminal Justice Reform, 2007a) in fact argues that witnesses should be properly prepared and supported from the very beginning of their involvement with the criminal justice system (e.g. preparation for the initial investigative interview; see Chapter 5). Research further suggests that perceiving such support to be available might serve to reduce attrition in cases involving vulnerable witnesses (e.g. Kelly *et al.*, 2005).

preparation activities concerned with assessing the needs of the witness, providing support, liaising and communicating on the witness's behalf, and preparing the witness for the trial (e.g. providing information, court visit).

What activities are incorporated into witness support and preparation? Box 13.4 summarises some different

BOX 13.4   SUPPORT AND PREPARATION ACTIVITIES PRE-TRIAL

- Provision of emotional support and liaison with professionals providing therapy or counselling before trial
- Provision of information and education (e.g. the *Young Witness Pack*; NSPCC & ChildLine, 1998)
- Understanding and conveying the witness's views, wishes and concerns about testifying
- Familiarisation of the witness with the court and court procedures
- Provision of a pre-trial visit to court
- Liaison between the witness, family, friends and professionals
- Communication with professionals who may have special expertise related to a witness's particular vulnerabilities (e.g. interpreters)

dimensions. *Which* support and preparation activities are actually provided, *by* whom and *to* whom, depends on local arrangements and the availability of resources (Murray, 1997; Plotnikoff & Woolfson, 1996). In brief, support and preparation activities are concerned with assessing the needs of the witness, providing support, liaising and communicating, and preparing for the trial (Home Office, 2002).

The development of support and preparation activities outlined in Box 13.4 has stemmed mostly from work with child witnesses, and has not been without controversy. Opponents have been concerned that supporters may coach the child (even to the point of making a false allegation) or rehearse their testimony, a concern that has been fiercely denied. (A similar complaint has been levelled at those who engage with the child in therapy or counselling pre-trial.) It is nonetheless vitally important that supporters are aware of 'evidential boundaries' (Home Office, 2002, p.88). They must not be a witness in the case and must not be given details of the case or of the witness's evidence. Further, they must not discuss the case or the witness's evidence as part of their activities. Should any indiscretions occur then it is likely that the witness's evidence will subsequently be compromised (see Chapter 6).

Once a supporter has been identified for a vulnerable witness, their role pre-trial is to 'seek the witness's views about giving their evidence and being at court; provide information about the criminal process and their role within it; support and general assistance [*sic*] to the witness to enable them to give their best evidence; liaise with others, as appropriate' (Home Office, 2002, p.92). A great deal of the supporter's work may be 'behind the scenes', such as liaising and communicating with different agencies or authorities involved in the case about the witness's needs and preferences. The supporter may also accompany the witness when they view a copy of their statement (which may involve seeing a recording of the witness's investigative interview), and if they meet the prosecution counsel before the proceedings. A recent survey of the pattern of witness support in different parts of England and Wales confirmed widespread variation in the amount of support offered (Plotnikoff & Woolfson, 2007a). A projected national scheme was abandoned in favour of official encouragement of local initiatives (Office for Criminal Justice Reform, 2009), which will inevitably lead to variations in level and quality of support in different areas of the country.

An increasing range of education and information materials is available for (mainly child) witnesses and their carers (Figure 13.3; see Home Office, 2002,

FIGURE 13.3 *An increasing range of education and information materials is available for child witnesses.*

Source: © Noam Armonn. Used under licence from Shutterstock.

BOX 13.5   *THE YOUNG WITNESS PACK* MATERIALS

- *Let's Get Ready for Court*: activity booklet for children aged 5–9 years

- *Tell Me More About Court*: booklet for young witnesses aged 10–15 years

- *Inside a Courtroom*: cardboard model of a courtroom with slot-in characters

- *Going to Court*: information for Crown Court witnesses aged 13–17 years

- *Young Witnesses at the Magistrates' Court and the Youth Court*: information for witnesses aged 9–17 years

- *Screens in Court*: information for witnesses aged 9–17 years

- *Giving Evidence: What's it Really Like?* DVD for young witnesses

- *Your Child is a Witness*: Information for parents and carers

- *Preparing Young Witnesses for Court*: booklet for child witness supporters

Appendix Q). This includes written materials, models of courtrooms and DVD recordings concerning what it is like to give evidence (e.g. NSPCC, 2000). Materials for witnesses who have learning difficulties are also available, including the development of a 'virtual' courtroom (Cooke, 2001). *The Young Witness Pack* (NSPCC & ChildLine, 1998) is perhaps the most widely known preparation material in the UK; its contents are outlined in Box 13.5 and give a glimpse of the range of people who may be involved in efforts to prepare a child for different types of court appearance.

Early evaluations of child witness support schemes were positive (Aldridge & Freshwater, 1993; Plotnikoff & Woolfson, 1995a; 1996), although a number of issues remain outstanding (especially regarding responsibility and resources for providing preparation, and witness access to such support; Plotnikoff & Woolfson, 2004). Young witnesses have themselves reported favourably on the materials and their supporters. For example:

> The supporter came to my home and went through the books with me so that I knew what the TV link was all about. Then we had the court visit. We also talked about what would happen if I got upset or tired. I knew that I could ask if I wanted a break when I gave my evidence. (Fiona, 10)

> I had a witness adviser just to help me out. He tells you everything, I had a tour of the court, he tells you who is going to be sitting where and obviously I felt a bit more at ease about what was going to happen. I got this support in both the magistrates' court and the Crown Court. (Colin, 16)
>
> (Plotnikoff & Woolfson, 2004, p.26).

Experimental approaches to preparing child witnesses

In essence, support and preparation activities are addressing the lack of knowledge (stressor), anxiety, and disruption of cognitive and communication skills (effects) experienced by vulnerable witnesses, as depicted in Figure 13.2. Although preparation activities are widely used, in fact empirical evaluation of the success of different components has not really been addressed (Murray, 1997). Developmental psychologists have also developed preparation programmes in experimental studies aimed at addressing the particular cognitive, developmental and socio-emotional factors that exist for vulnerable witnesses outlined in Box 13.2 (e.g. Saywitz *et al.*, 1993). These have included narrative elaboration, comprehension monitoring and resistance training. *Narrative elaboration* was a successful technique for increasing the amount of detail recalled by children, by prompting them to talk about information relating to participants, setting, action, conversations and consequences, through the use of 'cue cards'. *Comprehension-monitoring training* helped children to identify questions they did not understand, and to ask adult interviewers for rephrasing. Finally, *resistance training* enabled children to identify and respond appropriately to (i.e. resist) misleading questions put to them by interviewers. Evaluation of these techniques highlighted some unintended consequences (e.g. children becoming more reluctant to provide details) and they have yet to be considered in a genuine forensic context. Hence, although these experimental approaches have been found promising in empirical evaluations, their practical utility remains untested.

PROTECTING WITNESSES AT COURT

Before moving on to consider safeguarding witnesses in the courtroom, read Case Study 13.2, which introduces the use of information technology in the investigative and judicial process. This case study also highlights some of the other problematic issues that can arise when vulnerable witnesses testify in court.

CASE STUDY 13.2 SALLY

Sally described herself as having been sexually abused by her stepfather from the age of 7. She eventually confided in her school teacher when she was 12. An interview was immediately arranged and conducted with Sally's mother sitting behind a one-way mirror, where she could see and hear the interview . . . During the interview Sally was pre-occupied with the possible effects of her disclosure on her family, and gave only a disjointed account of a single incident of abuse. However, a medical examination found physical signs consistent with her allegation, and a prosecution followed. Sally's stepfather pleaded not guilty and at his trial the recording of Sally's interview was used as her evidence-in-chief. She was then cross-examined and, questioned about there having been only one incident of abuse, related another incident. In his final summing up, defence counsel cast doubt on the initial allegation and the subsequent allegation in court, as follows.

THE PRE-RECORDED INTERVIEW:

All she said in the video interview, if it is true, is that there was one incident when her stepfather [attempted intercourse]. Now, if this man is perverted, you would have expected some course of conduct wouldn't you? But according to her account there was only one occasion when he behaved indecently towards her.

THE ALLEGATION MADE IN COURT:

Out of the blue today came another allegation – that only weeks before the interview was recorded he [indecently assaulted her] in front of her mother, who was also on the sofa. This is nonsense. It took us all by surprise, the prosecution included . . . She says now she didn't want to distress her mother. But she had already spoken of intercourse. It surely wouldn't have slipped her mind, especially if it happened only a few weeks before the video was made. Either it emphasises the fragility of a child's mind, or the murky waters we are getting into.

Sally's father was subsequently acquitted by the jury after a short deliberation.

Source: (Wade & Westcott, 1997, pp.58–59)

The case studies of Sally and Mary both make reference to the use of video and later digital technology to assist witness in giving their evidence: the **live link** and pre-recorded interviews. Their cases pinpoint some of the problems as well as some of the advantages that have accompanied implementation of these particular special measures. Sally's experience further highlights some of the other challenges that surround the appearance of vulnerable witnesses in formal courtroom settings, in particular, cross-examination and the culture of the courtroom. These 'murky waters' will be discussed later in the chapter. First, however, we will briefly revisit the topic of social support.

> **live link** one of the special measures permitted by the Youth Justice and Criminal Evidence Act 1999.

Social support at court

Previously, we considered how preparation and social support could be provided pre-trial. At court, more 'behind the scenes' work will be carried out by supporters, such as providing information for the plea and directions hearing about the witness's requirements and preferred way of giving evidence. In addition, *Achieving Best Evidence* explicitly outlines the role of judges and magistrates in actively managing cases involving vulnerable witnesses, and in minimising distress as far as possible (see also Scottish Executive, 2003a). That is to say, they must protect (we might say, safeguard) the interests of vulnerable and intimidated witnesses. In some cases (e.g. with young witnesses), the judge may be prepared to meet the witness beforehand to help 'demystify' the court process, although this does not appear to happen for a sizeable minority of vulnerable witnesses (Hamlyn *et al.*, 2004). Lawyers and the judge may also remove their wigs and gowns, if the witness would prefer: this practice almost doubled from 8 to 15 per cent following the introduction of the special measures scheme (Hamlyn *et al.*, 2004).

> They asked me if I wanted them to take their wigs off and that, and I said 'yes'. And they took them off, so they looked okay. (16-year-old male with mild learning disability)
>
> (Sanders et al., 1997, p.65)

Finally, a court witness supporter may accompany the witness when they testify, to reduce the witness's anxiety and stress, and enable the witness to give their best evidence. For example, someone from the witness service may sit in the 'live link' room while a child provides their evidence. The live link was the first special measure exploiting technology to have been introduced in England and Wales (via the Criminal Justice Act 1988), and we will now examine its use in more detail.

Screens and the live link

The principal aim of the live link, or closed-circuit television, in court is to remove the vulnerable witness from the intimidating and unfamiliar environment of the courtroom, and to spare the witness from facing the defendant in court (Davies & Noon, 1991).

screens one of the special measures permitted by the Youth Justice and Criminal Evidence Act 1999.

Previously, some courts had used **screens** to ensure that the witness was 'shielded' from the defendant, but remained in view of other people in the courtroom. These are widely available today as one of the special measures for vulnerable witnesses who would prefer to give their testimony 'live' in the actual courtroom, but with a degree of protection (Figure 13.4). Screens have the benefit (unlike the live link) of physically shielding the witness from the defendant's view, and appear to be popular with those witnesses who use them (Burton et al., 2006). However, Hamlyn et al.'s survey (2004) suggests screens were used by just 8 per cent of vulnerable or intimidated witnesses. Screens can have particular appeal to witnesses who value their 'day in court' and the opportunity to speak publicly of their experiences and 'tell the world' what the defendant has done (Cashmore & De Haas, 1992).

FIGURE 13.4 *Screens* *are widely available as one of the special measures for vulnerable witnesses.*

Source: © plastique. Used under licence from Shutterstock.

It was my mother or the police who said ... I didn't want to go at the start. But then I was happy about going [to court]. When I knew it was to put him behind bars. (15-year-old autistic boy)

They asked me if I wanted to go to court and I said Yes. He had gone too far this time ... I just wanted him to go down. (20-year-old woman with mild learning disability)

(Sanders et al., 1997, pp.37–38)

Screens are one intervention that can promote effective testimony while reducing stress for the witness (and are also used in some cases involving 'non vulnerable' witnesses, where the identity of the witness needs to be concealed), but the witness may still be anxious about entering the courtroom. If a witness uses the live link, they are actually removed from the courtroom, whilst remaining in the court building. Two-way closed circuit television connects the courtroom with another small room in which the witness sits (with a supporter if agreed). Using the live link, the witness can see who is speaking to them, whilst the witness's picture is relayed to the court. Again, the live link is attempting to reduce the witness's anxiety and promote their effective testimony by addressing socio-emotional factors.

Initial evaluations of use of the live link in the UK and Australia with child witnesses (Cashmore & De Haas, 1992; Davies & Noon, 1991; Murray, 1995) reflected a generally positive reception for the technology, especially on the part of those concerned to safeguard children's welfare (see Chapter 5 for a full review of the research literature). Many supporters felt the live link enabled witnesses who otherwise would not have been able to testify, to provide their evidence to the court. Witnesses themselves have reported as much (Hamlyn et al., 2004):

If I was standing in a [witness] box, knowing me, if I saw [the defendant] I'd probably feel faint. I'd probably do summat. Or tell a lie. (Susie, 11 years)

'I wanted to give [my evidence] that way. I couldn't face him. I couldn't see him. If I'd have had to see him, that would have been that. I wouldn't have been able to go in. [But] I felt safe, not having to see him.' (Caitlin, 16 years)

(Wade, 2002, p.224)

Researchers evaluating the live link noted that children using the system were rated as self-confident and speaking fluently, and that audibility was rarely a problem (Davies & Noon, 1991). However, there were the inevitable teething problems, as well as a more fundamental opposition to the technology amongst some members of the legal profession (e.g. Davies & Noon, 1991; Hall & Sales, 2008; Murray, 1995).

Teething problems centred around the success of the technology itself – for example, early versions were oversensitive to background noise (e.g. Plotnikoff & Woolfson, 2004; Sanders *et al.*, 1997) – as well as some misuse of the technology. These included an incident when the whole screen in front of the child was filled with the eye of the defence barrister, and defence barristers standing in such a way that defendants were in full view behind them (Davies & Noon, 1991). One of the principal advantages of the live link is that it should enable witnesses to testify without seeing the defendant, as this is reported as one of the biggest concerns of vulnerable witnesses anticipating their court appearance (e.g. Hamlyn *et al.*, 2004; Plotnikoff & Woolfson, 2004; Sanders *et al.*, 1997). A continuing practical problem remains the availability of the live link, as illustrated in Mary's account (Case Study 13.1). This is not an atypical experience, and a sudden change of plan can be particularly alarming for vulnerable witnesses, especially if their preparation for court has been based around them testifying via live link (e.g. Plotnikoff & Woolfson, 2004).

More fundamental problems concerning 'resistance' to the technology have been reported by researchers. Davies and Noon (1991) noted that prosecution barristers were concerned that witnesses testifying via live link appeared more remote and that their testimony had less emotional impact on the jury. Perversely, witnesses *not* breaking down when testifying were seen as less likely to convince the jury of their account. Subsequent experimental research has supported the view that live evidence may be viewed more positively by observers than pre-recorded evidence, but not that the medium of giving evidence has an impact on the outcome of trials (Davies, 1999; Landstrom, 2008).

Finally, it is important not to overlook the witnesses' experience of live link itself. Although it works well for many witnesses, some children have reported difficulties with the technology, in ways perhaps unanticipated at its introduction, for example feeling like they were shut in a 'cupboard' (Plotnikoff & Woolfson, 2004) or struggling to adjust to the technology:

> It were a bit funny … it weren't as if … people were talking to me straight face to face. It were … really funny. I couldn't hear them right … It were loud enough. It's just that they had to keep repeating it over and over again because I couldn't understand. I couldn't hear them right. (Lucy, 13 years)
>
> *(Wade, 2002, p.225)*

Awareness of such perceptions can be addressed through preparation, especially if the witness has a court visit and can practise using the technology. Another important issue for preparation includes making witnesses aware that the defendant will be able to see them via the live link (and watch their recorded interview; see later in this chapter). Discovering this on the day has been reported as very disconcerting for witnesses, and as negatively influencing their ability to testify.

> It just felt horrible knowing he was watching that TV screen when I was saying [what he'd done to me]. He could be gloating over it and everything. (Ivy, 14 years)
>
> When he saw me on the television it was really frightening thinking about [him seeing me] and I'm not seeing him. (Gemma, 9 years)
>
> *(Wade, 2002, p.224)*

Perhaps one of the most significant lessons from the introduction of the live link has been that the *element of choice* about how to give their testimony is most important to witnesses (Cashmore & De Haas, 1992). Being able to decide whether or not to use the technology may be as important as the technology itself (Figure 13.5), which is why understanding witnesses' apprehensions and concerns, and their preferences for testifying, is such an important part of the supporter's role. The Youth Justice and Criminal Evidence 1999 included a presumption that all child witnesses would use the live link, so ensuring uniformity of practice across the courts. However, it did prevent children who wished to do so giving their evidence in the courtroom. An official report (Office for Criminal Justice Reform, 2005) recommended giving the courts greater flexibility to accommodate children's wishes, and legal changes are in train to provide this flexibility.

FIGURE 13.5 *The element of choice about how to give their testimony is important to witnesses; being able to decide whether to use the technology may be as important as the technology itself.*
Source: © kRie. Used under licence from Shutterstock.

Pre-recorded evidence-in-chief

As we have seen, the live link addresses mainly socio-emotional factors associated with testifying, although these may themselves impact on other cognitive factors outlined in Box 13.2. For example, stress at testifying may negatively affect a witness's recall of information (memory; Baker-Ward & Ornstein, 2002) and/or may exacerbate language factors (both comprehension and production: see Mary's comments in Case Study 13.1). In 1989, Judge Pigot chaired a government committee that evaluated the possibility for video technology to address other cognitive factors affecting child witnesses too (refer back to Box 13.2). The committee argued in its report (Pigot, 1989) that if children's initial interviews with police officers or social workers were recorded – at the early stages of a criminal investigation and/or child protection enquiry – then, this video-recording of a child's account could act as **video-recorded evidence-in-chief**, replacing the child's live evidence-in-chief at court. The Pigot Committee went on to argue that a subsequent cross-examination, conducted after the defence had viewed the child's account, could also be video-recorded, thus replacing the need for cross-examination at court (see Spencer, in press, for a review). This would help the child in the following ways:

> **video-recorded evidence-in-chief**
> usually an early investigative interview with a vulnerable witness by a trained practitioner. First introduced by the Criminal Justice Act 1991, and one of the special measures permitted by the YJCE Act 1999.

- *Memory:* both interview and cross-examination could be recorded soon after the child had made an allegation, or the investigating authority had received a referral, thus overcoming problems associated with the effect of delay on children's memory.
- *Language:* the interviewers would be trained to use developmentally appropriate language so that the child could understand the questions put to them (contrast case studies quoted above).
- *Authority effects:* the interviews would be conducted by specially trained non-uniformed police or social work personnel, in purpose-built interviewing suites with comfortable furnishings, located away from police stations to reduce stress.

According to the Pigot scheme, once the video interview(s) were completed, the child would be free to receive therapy, and would not need to attend trial at all (thus additionally addressing socio-emotional factors). At the time, the full Pigot proposals were considered too radical by the Home Office (Spencer &

Flin, 1993); however, video-recorded examination-in-chief for child witnesses of certain ages in specified sexual abuse offences was introduced in the Criminal Justice Act 1991 (Home Office, 1992): the 'half-Pigot' solution. Following the publication of *Speaking Up for Justice* (Home Office, 1998; see above), the full Pigot proposals for the range of vulnerable witnesses was included in the Youth Justice and Criminal Evidence Act 1999. As we shall see in the last section of this chapter, however, pre-recorded cross-examination appears to remain a 'bridge too far' for successive governments and judiciary.

Chapters 5 and 6 have reviewed the literature on practice in pre-recorded interviews with vulnerable witnesses, and the guidance governing such interviews in *The Memorandum of Good Practice* (Home Office, 1992) and *Achieving Best Evidence* (Home Office, 2002; Office for Criminal Justice Reform, 2007a; Scottish Executive, 1993b). In brief, this literature shows that interviewers generally do include all the four proposed phases of interview but struggle to ask sufficient open questions, asking too many specific and closed questions instead. Typically, the free narrative phase of the interview – when the child has the opportunity to recall events in their own words – is brief and sometimes omitted (e.g. Davies *et al.*, 1995; Sternberg *et al.*, 2001; Westcott *et al.*, 2006; Westcott & Kynan, 2006). The closure phase is also often poor or omitted.

As with live links, there were the inevitable technological teething problems following introduction of pre-recorded evidence-in-chief, especially problems with hearing child witnesses, and with compatibility of recording equipment pre- and at court (Davies *et al.*, 1995). However, the Home Office evaluation of such interviews with children reported that, generally, the reforms had been welcomed by members of the judiciary, police and social services (Davies *et al.*, 1995), principally as a means of reducing stress for witnesses. Witnesses giving their evidence via pre-recorded interview were perceived to be half as stressed as those who gave their evidence live at court (19 per cent vs. 37 per cent) and the trained interviewers were seen as more supportive than the barristers at court (37 per cent vs. 19 per cent), but both groups were anxious during live cross-examination. Again, there was some resistance amongst barristers, with prosecution barristers concerned (as with live link) that use of video-recorded evidence had a reduced impact on the jury, and defence barristers believing that witnesses would find it easier to lie and deceive if they were not physically present in the courtroom. Statistical analyses on prosecution and conviction rates conducted for the evaluation did not support either position (see also Burton *et al.*, 2006).

The presumption of the Youth Justice and Criminal Evidence Act 1999 that pre-recorded interviews will routinely be used in cases involving vulnerable witnesses has gone some way to 'overriding' such resistance. As with live links, it is important to pause to consider witnesses' experiences of such interviews, especially at the point of trial. Legal practice with child witnesses has varied, so that some witnesses are permitted to see their pre-recorded interview ahead of trial to 'refresh the witness's memory' in the same way as a written statement, while others have not (Hamlyn et al., 2004; Plotnikoff & Woolfson, 2004). Although most children have found it helpful to be reminded of what they said, many have found it distracting and distressing to see themselves on the recording.

> It was weird to see the video ahead of time – it didn't really seem like me. It helped refresh my memory about the things I couldn't remember clearly. I didn't like seeing the video again . . . it was weird . . . like when I had to describe everything that happened. It made me feel like I wanted to cry inside when I watched the video again. (Davina, 15)
>
> It is distressing to relive it. You are looking at how I felt the day after the offence. (Paul, 15)
>
> *(Plotnikoff & Woolfson, 2004, p.30)*

Where children see their recorded interview for the first time at trial, these feelings can be magnified.

> Watching the video reminded me too much about what it was like before the trial. I only saw it once on the day of the trial. I felt sad listening to what happened to me. I thought my voice was very strange. It would've been a help to see it before. (Sheila, 9)
>
> I didn't see my video before it was played to court. It was months before that I had been interviewed on the video. It felt very strange to watch the video. I have never had that feeling before. I thought that they'd all be laughing at me. It was difficult to concentrate on the video. (Hattie, 14)
>
> *(Plotnikoff & Woolfson, 2004, p.31)*

Vulnerable witnesses should be permitted to view their pre-recorded interview prior to trial, but their supporters should anticipate some of the emotions that may accompany its viewing.

Case Study 13.2 highlights one of the ways pre-recorded evidence has been used by defence lawyers to cast doubt on children's testimony; practitioners involved at the early stage of investigations have been frustrated by the lengths to which some courtroom counsel will go to have pre-recorded evidence wholly or partially excluded (e.g. Department of Health, 1994; Davies et al., 1995). In the final part of this chapter we examine some of these frustrations in more detail.

CHALLENGING CONVENTIONS

Why would powerful, experienced authority figures – as defence barristers undoubtedly are – find the possibility of pre-recorded evidence from vulnerable witnesses so troublesome? One might suggest that the reforms discussed in this chapter have been resisted because they challenge conventions: they aim to wrest some of the control away from the lawyers, and the legal setting, and they necessitate change to traditional ways of working that have operated largely unopposed for hundreds of years. Law is a self-referential system, ill-suited to consider the agendas of other systems such as psychology or welfare (e.g. Henderson, 2002; King & Piper, 1995; King & Trowell, 1992). Opening up such a system to outside scrutiny is therefore challenging for all involved, and many have found that the prevailing legal culture often works to override the spirit of the reforms intended to assist vulnerable witnesses (e.g. Davies & Noon, 1991; Davies et al., 1995; Plotnikoff & Woolfson, 1995b). This is not to deny that progress has been made – as illustrated by the reforms discussed in this chapter. Hamlyn et al. (2004) found that witnesses using special measures were more likely to be satisfied with their experience, less likely to experience anxiety and more prepared to give evidence again. However, the inertia and resistance offered by the prevailing legal culture can be overwhelming (Westcott, 2006). Four examples of this inertia and resistance come easily to mind.

Delay

Despite a number of targeted reforms and practice directions, delays in the processing of cases involving vulnerable witnesses appear endemic (e.g. Plotnikoff & Woolfson, 1995b, 2004). Typically, a child will wait approximately 10–12 months for their case to come to courts. Such delays have a negative impact on the child's memory (for the event and for their video-recorded evidence), as well as influencing socio-emotional development as their lives move on in the pre-trial period. The problem is also acute for witnesses with learning difficulties. *The Witness Charter* (Office for Criminal Justice Reform, 2007b) includes a pledge to 'ensure that cases involving vulnerable witnesses, including child witnesses, are brought to trial as quickly as possible' (Standard 13). However, it is unclear how these good intentions will survive the current budgetary reductions in personnel and resources within the criminal justice system in the UK.

Pre-recorded cross-examination

Despite the inclusion of relevant legislation in the Youth Justice and Criminal Evidence Act 1999 to permit video-recorded cross-examination, it is apparent that the judiciary continues to resist its introduction to the extent that plans for implementation have been abandoned. Pre-recorded cross-examination following on from pre-recorded evidence-in-chief as envisaged by the Pigot Report would have addressed all three categories of factors outlined in Box 13.2 – memory, language and authority – to the benefit of vulnerable witnesses. However, the 1999 Act proposed that pre-recorded cross-examination should take place immediately prior to trial, which would have robbed the innovation of many of its advantages. It is possible that the current arrangements may be ruled as in breach of the European Convention on Human Rights, thus putting additional pressure on the government to look again at Pigot's original proposals (Spencer, in press).

Intermediaries

Practitioners have reported successes using skilled interpreters in investigative interviews with children who have multiple impairments, including no verbal communication (e.g. Marchant & Page, 1992). The use of intermediaries as interlocutors between witness and barrister/judge is perhaps the *most* witness-centred of all the reforms introduced in the 1999 Act. It was also probably the most unpalatable to the legal profession, who have long regarded their right to *personally* question witnesses as fundamental (e.g. Spencer & Flin, 1993), despite numerous examples of poor practice with vulnerable witnesses (Henderson, 2002; Walker, 1993; 1994).

The *intermediary special measure* was the subject of a two-year pilot project (Plotnikoff & Woolfson, 2007b). During this period there were over 200 requests for assistance of which the largest group (57 per cent) concerned witnesses with impaired intelligence or social functioning. Some 61 per cent of clients were adults and the remainder children, of which only 14 per cent were referred on the basis of their age alone. Intermediaries were generally employed during the investigative and pre-trial phases and few had appeared at court by the end of the pilot. Almost all users reported finding the intermediaries of value. Plotnikoff and Woolfson (2007b) quote one judge as saying that the intermediary was 'strong and intervened when questions became too complex. Her interventions did not come too often but they were invaluable'. As a result of the success of the pilot, the intermediary scheme was rolled out throughout England and Wales in 2008 and a similar scheme has been mooted in Scotland (Criminal Justice Directorate, 2007).

Cross-examination

Commentators on the cross-examination of child witnesses have produced extensive analyses documenting their concerns about the implications of cross-examination practice for witnesses' welfare (e.g. Westcott & Page, 2002). For example:

> People with Down's syndrome in particular tend to be particularly sensitive to negative emotion. They therefore sometimes respond to what they perceive as aggression (e.g. 'tough' questioning) by attempting to appease the questioner, which can lead to suggestibility and contradictory testimony. Thus in [particular case] the result of two days questioning was a mass of contradictions with which the defence barrister regaled the victim. As a result of this one of the jurors burst into tears.
>
> *(Sanders et al., 1997, pp.76–77)*

British lawyers seem to be extremely concerned with the dangers of leading questions being posed by social workers, doctors or police officers during the early stages of a criminal investigation. Paradoxically, they do not seem to be the least bit concerned about their own use of leading questions in cross-examination and the effects this may have on the quality of a child's evidence. The characteristics of a typical interview conducted during cross-examination appear to violate all the principles of best practice, with the predicted outcome of maximising the risk of contaminating the evidence (Spencer & Flin, 1993, p.307).

As in Case Study 13.2, manipulative, unkind, or offensive cross-examination can have devastating consequences on the witness's self-esteem, and on the effectiveness of their testimony. Cross-examination has been repeatedly reported as one of most distressing aspects of the legal process for vulnerable witnesses (e.g. Hamlyn et al., 2004; Plotnikoff & Woolfson, 2004; Sanders et al., 1997; Sas et al., 1991).

Guidance from both the Home Office (2002) and the Scottish Executive (2003b) clearly states that the court has a duty to have regard for the welfare of witnesses, and that inappropriate questioning can be harmful. The *Prosecutor's Pledge* promoted by the Crown Prosecution Service (2005) states that prosecutors will 'protect victims from unwarranted or irrelevant attacks on their character and may seek the court's intervention where cross-examination is considered to be inappropriate or oppressive'. And of course, a skilled barrister does not have to demean a witness in order to make their point. Cross-examination was famously described as 'the greatest legal engine ever invented for the discovery of truth' (Wigmore, cited in Spencer & Flin, 1993, p.270) but research suggests that at least for children, it can have a detrimental effect on both accuracy and credibility. (Readers may be interested to know that Wigmore previously compared the role of cross-examination to that of torture in society, before extolling its virtues!) In an experimental study by Zajac and Hayne (2003), 5- to 6-year-old children observed an incident about which they gave a recorded interview and were later cross-examined, using question forms taken from actual child witness trials. In cross-examination, children changed 85 per cent of their original statements, the changes being as likely to be from truth to error as from error to truth. A later study with 10- to 11-year-old children produced fewer changes but the same disturbing pattern (Zakac & Hayne, 2006).

Protecting witnesses and testing their evidence

The use of pre-recorded cross-examination and intermediaries, and the practice of cross-examination, highlight clearly the tension between testing witnesses' evidence in court, and prioritising their needs and welfare. Of course, the defendant has a right to a fair trial, and the duty of the court is to ensure that this occurs. However, difficulties arise when we confuse *substantive* and *formal* equality between defendant and witness:

> [It] is necessary to put learning disabled victims, like other victims, on as equal a footing with the defendant as possible. This requires adopting a stance of 'substantive' as distinct from 'formal' equality … To subject an intelligent defendant and a learning disabled victim to identical complex questioning is not to treat them equally, except in the most artificial 'formal' sense. Truly equal treatment would ensure that the victim is as able to understand the proceedings as the defendant. The same applies to coping with the intimidating

nature of the court and its personnel. Thus it is on the basis of this substantive equality criterion that thought needs to be given to the conduct of trials, intervention in questioning by the judge, and the use of screens, video-recorded interviews, closed circuit TV, and so forth.

> *(Sanders et al., 1997, pp.81–82)*

In this chapter, we have seen how reforms have tried to progress *substantive* equality for vulnerable witnesses through special measures; however, experiences such as delays, cross-examination and the associated stress can moderate the success of special measures in practice so that, from the witness's perspective, *formal* equality is what results. Further, some of this poor practice can be most detrimental to witnesses' perceptions of the criminal justice process and to their welfare post-court, and can have lasting implications for certain witnesses (e.g. Goodman *et al.*, 1992; Hamlyn *et al.*, 2004; Sas *et al.*, 1991; 1995).

Hamlyn *et al.* (2004) found that vulnerable and intimidated witnesses remain less satisfied than all witnesses with their overall experience, and Burton *et al.* (2006) report a very patchy picture of implementation of the special measures. Vulnerable witnesses are being identified too late in the process to benefit from special measures, with the Crown Prosecution Service often applying for special measures on the day of trial itself (too late, and not part of the witness's preparation). Video-recorded interviews are being used for only a minority of the appropriate vulnerable witnesses, and preparation (e.g. pre-trial visits) is often not offered. Burton *et al.* (2006) describe the situation as one of 'significant unmet need' (p.vii), and highlight problems with the investigative and pre-trial processes as well as court. If we are truly to safeguard vulnerable individuals, then we have to aim to achieve substantive equality between defendant and witness – and be prepared to challenge conventional priorities, policies and practices in order to achieve this goal.

SUMMARY

- **Most witnesses find testifying at court a stressful experience, particularly where the witness is vulnerable by reason of age or mental or physical disability and/or a victim of crime.**

- **Among the fears of child witnesses going to court are suffering harm from defendants or their associates, rejection and the break-up of the family, and being disbelieved or embarrassed when giving evidence.**

- **In recent years, the courts in England and Wales have introduced a variety of special measures to assist witnesses in giving their best evidence while still preserving the adversarial nature of the trial process.**

- Special measures include the provision of pre-recorded evidence-in-chief, the use of a CCTV link to enable the witness to testify from outside the courtroom, social support within the courtroom, and the use of an intermediary to assist the witness with communication difficulties.

- Action on these issues needs to be matched by measures to tackle delays and postponements in hearing cases at court and a more proactive approach to overly aggressive cross-examination.

- Recognition of the needs of vulnerable witnesses is widespread within countries that share our common law tradition and there have been many experiments involving procedural change. However, the essentially adversarial nature of this legal process makes substantive equality for the vulnerable victim an elusive goal.

ESSAY/DISCUSSION QUESTIONS

1. What makes victims and witnesses vulnerable? How have special measures addressed the needs of vulnerable witnesses?
2. Discuss the concept of 'safeguarding' in relation to the reception of testimony from vulnerable witnesses.
3. Have recent attempts to safeguard witnesses in criminal courts in England and Wales gone far enough to meet their needs?
4. Discuss the statement that 'normal procedures which create formal equality between defendant and victim often create substantive inequality when the victim is vulnerable' (Sanders *et al.*, 1997, p.87).
5. To what extent can the needs of vulnerable witnesses and the rights of defendants be reconciled at court?

REFERENCES

Aldridge, J. & Freshwater, K. (1993). The preparation of the child witnesses. *Tolley's Journal of Child Law*, 5, 25–28.

Baker-Ward, L. & Ornstein, P.A. (2002). Cognitive underpinnings of children's testimony. In H.L. Westcott, G.M. Davies & R.H.C. Bull (Eds.) *Children's testimony: A handbook of psychological research and forensic practice*. Chichester: John Wiley & Sons, Inc.

Bottoms, B. & Goodman, G.S. (1996). *International perspectives on child abuse and children's testimony: Psychological research and law*. Thousand Oaks, CA: SAGE Publications.

Brennan, M. & Brennan, R.E. (1988). *Strange language: Child victims under cross-examination*. Wagga Wagga, NSW: Riverina Murray Institute of Higher Education.

Burton, M., Evans, R. & Sanders, A. (2006). Are special measures for vulnerable and intimidated witnesses working? Evidence from the criminal justice agencies. (Home Office Online Report 01/06). London: Home Office. Retrieved 23 August 2011 from http://webarchive.nationalarchives.gov.uk/20110220105210/rds.homeoffice.gov.uk/rds/pdfs06/rdsolr0106.pdf

Cashmore, J. (2002). Innovative procedures for child witnesses. In H.L. Westcott, G.M. Davies & R.H.C. Bull (Eds.). *Children's testimony: A handbook of psychological research and forensic practice*. Chichester: John Wiley & Sons, Inc.

Cashmore, J. & De Haas, N. (1992). *The use of closed-circuit television for child witnesses in the ACT*. A report for the Australian Law Reform Commission and the Australian Capital Territory Magistrates Court.

Ceci, S.J., Ross, D.F. & Toglia, M.P. (1987). Suggestibility of children's memory: Psycholegal implications. *Journal of Experimental Psychology: General*, 116, 38–49.

Cooke, P. (2001). The virtual courtroom: A view of justice. *Ann Craft Trust Bulletin*, 35, 2–5.

Criminal Justice Directorate. (2007). *The use of intermediaries for vulnerable witnesses in Scotland*. Edinburgh: Criminal Justice Directorate.

Crown Prosecution Service. (2005). The prosecutor's pledge. Retrieved 23 August 2011 from www.cps.gov.uk/publications/prosecution/prosecutor_pledge.html

Davies, G.M. (1999). The impact of television on the presentation and reception of children's evidence. *International Journal of Law and Psychiatry*, 22, 241–256

Davies, G.M. & Noon, E. (1991). *An evaluation of the Live Link for child witnesses*. London: Home Office.

Davies, G.M. & Westcott, H.L. (2006). Preventing withdrawal of complaints and psychological support for victims. In M.R. Kebbell & G.M. Davies (Eds.) *Practical psychology for forensic investigations and prosecutions*. Chichester: John Wiley & Sons, Inc.

Davies, G.M., Wilson, C., Mitchell, R. & Milsom, J. (1995). *Videotaping children's evidence: An evaluation*. London: Home Office.

Department of Education (2011) Every child matters: Children and young people. London: Department of Education. Retrieved 5 October 2011 from www.education.gov.uk/childrenandyoungpeople/safeguarding/safeguardingchildren

Department of Health. (1994). *The child, the court and the video: A study of the implementation of the 'Memorandum of Good Practice on video interviewing of child witnesses'*. London: Department of Health Social Services Inspectorate.

Esam, B. (2002). Young witnesses: Still no justice. In H.L. Westcott, G.M. Davies & R.H.C. Bull (Eds.) *Children's testimony: A handbook of psychological research and forensic practice*. Chichester: John Wiley & Sons, Inc.

Gallagher, B. & Pease, K. (2000). *Understanding the attrition of child abuse and neglect cases in the criminal justice system*. Unpublished Report to the ESRC (R000236891).

Goodman, G.S., Taub, E.P., Jones, D.P.H., England, P., Port, L.K. & Rudy, L. (1992). Testifying in criminal court: emotional effects on child sexual assault victims. *Monographs of the Society for Research in Child Development, 57* (Serial no. 229).

Hall, S.R. & Sales, B.D. (2008). *Courtroom modifications for child witnesses*. Washington, DC: American Psychological Association.

Hamlyn, B., Phelps, A., Turtle, J. & Sattar, G. (2004). *Are Special Measures working? Evidence from surveys of vulnerable and intimidated witnesses. (Home Office Research Study 283)*. London: Home Office.

Harris, J. & Grace, S. (1999). *A question of evidence? Investigating and prosecuting rape in the 1990s. (Home Office Research Study 196)*. London: Home Office.

Henderson, E. (2002). Persuading and controlling: The theory of cross-examination in relation to children. In H.L. Westcott, G.M. Davies & R.H.C. Bull (Eds.) *Children's testimony: A handbook of psychological research and forensic practice*. Chichester: John Wiley & Sons, Inc.

Home Office. (1992). *The Memorandum of Good Practice on video recorded interviews with child witnesses for criminal proceedings*. London: Home Office.

Home Office. (1998). *Speaking up for justice: Report of the interdepartmental Working group on the treatment of vulnerable and intimidated witnesses in the criminal justice system*. London: Home Office.

Home Office. (2002). *Achieving best evidence in criminal proceedings: Guidance for vulnerable or intimidated witnesses, including children*. London: Home Office Communication Directorate.

Kelly, L., Lovett, J. & Regan, L. (2005). *A gap or a chasm? Attrition in reported rape cases. (Home Office Research Study 293)*. London: Home Office RDS.

Kennedy, M. (1992). Not the only way to communicate: A challenge to voice in child protection work. *Child Abuse Review, 1*, 169–177.

King, M. & Piper, C. (1995). *How the law thinks about children* (2nd edn). Aldershot: Arena.

King, M. & Trowell, J. (1992). *Children's welfare and the law: The limits of legal intervention*. London: SAGE Publications.

Landstrom, S. (2008). *CCTV, live and videotapes: How presentation mode affects the evaluation of witnesses*. Gothenburg, Sweden: University of Gothenburg.

Marchant, R. & Page, M. (1992). *Bridging the gap: Child protection work with children with multiple disabilities*. London: NSPCC.

Meyer, J. & Jesilow, P. (1993). Obedience to authority: Possible effects on children's testimony. *Psychology Crime and Law, 3*, 81–95.

Ministry of Justice. (2011). *Achieving best evidence in criminal proceedings: Guidance on interviewing victims and witnesses, and guidance on using special measures*. London: Ministry of Justice.

Moston, S. (1992). Social support and children's eyewitness testimony. In H. Dent & R. Flin (Eds.) *Children as witnesses*. Chichester: John Wiley & Sons, Inc.

Moston, S. & Engelberg, T. (1992). The effects of social support on children's eyewitness testimony. *Applied Cognitive Psychology, 6*, 61–76.

Murray, K. (1995). *Live television link: An evaluation of its use by child witnesses in Scottish criminal trials*. Edinburgh: HMSO.

Murray, K. (1997). *Preparing child witnesses for court*. Edinburgh: The Stationery Office.

NSPCC. (2000). *Giving evidence – What's it really like?* London: NSPCC.

NSPCC & ChildLine. (1998). *The young witness pack*. London: NSPCC.

Office for Criminal Justice Reform. (2005). *Improving the criminal trial process for young witnesses*. London: Office for Criminal Justice Reform.

Office for Criminal Justice Reform. (2007a). *Achieving best evidence in criminal proceedings: Guidance on interviewing victims and witnesses, and using special measures*. London: Office for Criminal Justice Reform.

Office for Criminal Justice Reform. (2007b). *The witness charter: Standards of care for witnesses in the criminal justice system*. London: Office for Criminal Justice Reform.

Office for Criminal Justice Reform. (2009). *Young witness support: It's in your hands*. London: Office for Criminal Justice Reform.

Pigot, T. (1989). *Report of the advisory group on video evidence*. London: Home Office.

Plotnikoff, J. & Woolfson, R. (1995a). *The child witness pack – An evaluation. (Research Findings No.29)*. London: Home Office Research and Planning Unit.

Plotnikoff, J. & Woolfson, R. (1995b). *Prosecuting child abuse: An evaluation of the government's speedy progress policy*. London: Blackstone Press.

Plotnikoff, J. & Woolfson, R. (1996). Evaluation of witness service support for child witnesses. In Victim Support (Ed.) *Children in court*. London: Victim Support.

Plotnikoff, J. & Woolfson, R. (2004). *In their own words: The experiences of 50 young witnesses in criminal proceedings*. London: NSPCC.

Plotnikoff, J. & Woolfson, R. (2007a). *Evaluation of young witness support: Examining the impact on witnesses and the criminal justice system.* London: Home Office.

Plotnikoff, J. & Woolfson, R. (2007b). *The 'go between': Evaluation of intermediary pathfinder projects.* London: Home Office.

Powell, M. & Thomson, D. (2002). Children's memories for repeated events. In H.L. Westcott, G.M. Davies & R.H.C. Bull (Eds.) *Children's testimony: A handbook of psychological research and forensic practice.* Chichester: John Wiley & Sons, Inc.

Sanders, A. Creaton, J., Bird, S. & Weber, L. (1997). *Victims with learning disabilities: Negotiating the criminal justice system.* Oxford: University of Oxford Centre for Criminological Research.

Sas, L.D., Cunningham, A.H., Hurley, P., Dick, T. & Farnsworth, A. (1995). *Tipping the balance to tell the secret: Public discovery of child sexual abuse.* London, Ontario: London Family Court Clinic, Child Witness Project.

Sas, L.D., Hurley, P., Hatch, A., Malla, S. & Dick, T. (1991). *Three years after the verdict: A longitudinal study of the social and psychological adjustment of child witnesses referred to the child witness project.* London, Ontario: London Family Court Clinic, Child Witness Project.

Saywitz, K.J. (2002). Developmental underpinnings of children's testimony. In H.L. Westcott, G.M. Davies & R.H.C. Bull (Eds.) *Children's testimony: A handbook of psychological research and forensic practice.* Chichester: John Wiley & Sons, Inc.

Saywitz, K.J., Nathanson, R., Snyder, L. & Lamphear, V. (1993). *Preparing children for the investigative and judicial process: Improving communication, memory and emotional resiliency.* Final Report to the National Center on Child Abuse and Neglect (Grant No. 90CA1179).

Scottish Executive. (2003a). *Lord Justice General's Memorandum on child witnesses. Appendix to guidance on the questioning of children in court.* Edinburgh: The Stationery Office.

Scottish Executive. (2003b). *Guidance on the questioning of children in court.* Edinburgh: The Stationery Office.

Spencer, J.R. (in press). Evidence and cross examination. In M.E. Lamb, D.J. La Rooy, L.C. Malloy & C. Katz (eds.) *Children's testimony: A handbook of psychological research and forensic practice.* Chichester: John Wiley & Sons, Inc.

Spencer, J.R. & Flin, R.H. (1993). *The evidence of children: The law and the psychology* (2nd edn). London: Blackstone Press.

Spencer, J.R., Nicholson, G., Flin, R. & Bull, R. (1990). *Children's evidence in legal proceedings: An international perspective.* Cambridge: Cambridge University Faculty of Law.

Sternberg, K.J., Lamb, M.E., Davies, G.M. & Westcott, H.L. (2001). The Memorandum of Good Practice: Theory versus application. *Child Abuse & Neglect, 25,* 669–681.

Wade, A. (2002). New measures and new challenges: Children's experiences of the court process. In H.L. Westcott, G.M. Davies & R.H.C. Bull (Eds.) *Children's testimony: A handbook of psychological research and forensic practice.* Chichester: John Wiley & Sons, Inc.

Wade, A. & Westcott, H.L. (1997). No easy answers: Children's perspectives on investigative interviews. In H.L. Westcott & J. Jones (Eds.) *Perspectives on the Memorandum: Policy, practice and research in investigative interviewing.* Aldershot: Arena.

Walker, A.G. (1993). Questioning young children in court: A linguistic case study. *Law and Human Behavior, 17,* 59–81.

Walker, A.G. (1994). *Handbook on questioning children: A linguistic perspective.* Washington: ABA Center on Children and the Law.

Westcott, H.L. (2006). Child witness testimony: What do we know and where are we going? *Child and Family Law Quarterly, 18,* 175–190.

Westcott, H.L. & Davies, G.M. (1996). Sexually abused children's and young people's perspectives on investigative interviews. *British Journal of Social Work, 26,* 451–474.

Westcott, H.L. & Kynan, S. (2006). Interviewer practice in investigative interviews for suspected child sexual abuse. *Psychology, Crime & Law, 12,* 367–382.

Westcott, H.L., Kynan, S. & Few, C. (2006). Improving the quality of investigative interviews for suspected child abuse: A case study. *Psychology, Crime & Law, 12,* 77–96.

Westcott, H.L. & Page, M. (2002). Cross-examination, sexual abuse and child witness identity. *Child Abuse Review, 11,* 137–152.

Zajac, R. & Hayne, H. (2003). The effect of cross-examination on the accuracy ofw children's reports. *Journal of Experimental Psychology: Applied, 9,* 187–195.

Zajac, R. & Hayne, H. (2006). The negative effect of cross-examination style questioning on children's accuracy: Older children are not immune. *Applied Cognitive Psychology, 20,* 3–16.

ANNOTATED READING LIST

Burton, M., Evans, R. & Sanders, A. (2006). *Are Special Measures for vulnerable and intimidated witnesses working? Evidence from the criminal justice agencies. (Home Office Online Report 01/06).* London: Home Office. *Report of a multi-method research project carried out both before and after implementation of special measures. Reports on the extent to which the measures were working in practice, contains observations on 'cultural changes' required, and makes recommendations for future attention.*

Hamlyn, B., Phelps, A., Turtle, J. & Sattar, G. (2004). *Are Special Measures working? Evidence from surveys of vulnerable and intimidated witnesses. (Home Office Research Study 283).* London: Home Office. *Report of a research project that surveyed vulnerable witnesses' experiences of special measures before and after implementation of the new provisions.*

Kelly, L., Lovett, J. & Regan, L. (2005). *A gap or a chasm? Attrition in reported rape cases. (Home Office Research Study 293)*. London: Home Office RDS. *Report of a research project that examined over 2000 rape cases and explored victims' perceptions and experiences of the criminal justice system. Provides a breakdown of attrition rates in these cases, and makes detailed recommendations.*

Lamb, M.E., La Rooy D.J., Malloy L.C. & Katz, C. (Eds.) (2011). *Children's testimony: A handbook of psychological research and forensic practice.* Chichester: John Wiley & Sons, Inc. *A new edition of the handbook originally edited by Westcott et al. (2002). Comprehensive coverage of a range of issues pertaining to child witnesses, with a special emphasis on the use of the NICHD Protocol in interviewing children. Includes reviews and a glossary of relevant terminology featured in the book.*

Plotnikoff, J. & Woolfson, R. (2004). *In their own words: The experiences of 50 young witnesses in criminal proceedings.* London: NSPCC. *Report of a research project that interviewed 50 young witnesses about all aspects of their pre-trial and court experience. Includes detailed discussion of special measures, especially video-recorded interviews, live link, and pre-trial preparation and support.*

Sanders, A., Creaton, J., Bird, S. & Weber, L. (1997). *Victims with learning disabilities: Negotiating the criminal justice system.* Oxford: University of Oxford Centre for Criminological Research. *Report of a research project that examined 76 cases involving learning disabled victims. A step-by-step analysis of particular problems that these victims encountered at each stage of the investigative and prosecution process.*

Westcott, H.L., Davies, G.M. & Bull, R.H.C. (Eds.) (2002). *Children's testimony: A handbook of psychological research and forensic practice.* Chichester: John Wiley & Sons, Inc. *A comprehensive collection of papers covering a range of issues: cognitive and developmental underpinnings; memory and interviewing; court issues; and alternative perspectives on children's testimony.*

14   Identification Evidence

Tim Valentine

This chapter examines the psychology of memory, and explores reasons for the fallibility of eyewitness identification. Evidence is drawn both from laboratory experiments and analysis of identifications made by real witnesses or victims of crime. Methods used to obtain identification evidence are outlined, factors that affect eyewitness memory are described, and the influence of identification procedures on the reliability of eyewitness identification is discussed. The instructions given to witnesses, the selection of people in a **line-up**, and the effect of previous identification attempts are all considered. Procedures that may change the confidence of an eyewitness are discussed. Official guidance on identification procedures is critically evaluated in the light of the research literature. Widespread availability of CCTV increasingly provides an appealing opportunity to avoid the frailty of witness memory and use video imagery to identify a perpetrator. However, psychological science shows that identifying unfamiliar people from CCTV-type images can itself be error-prone.

> **line-up** a test of identification in which a suspect is placed amongst foils, who are not suspects. A line-up may be an array of photographs or a live line-up of people.

THE PROBLEM OF MISTAKEN IDENTIFICATION

Identification of a perpetrator is often disputed in criminal cases. In the absence of forensic evidence, for example DNA or fingerprints, the central issue for a court is to evaluate the accuracy of eyewitness identification. Evidence from the USA has shown that mistaken identification is a factor in 75 per cent of wrongful convictions. More than 275 people wrongly convicted have been exonerated by new DNA evidence. Case histories show that mistaken eyewitnesses may be confident in their identification and more than one eyewitness may make the same mistaken identification (Innocence Project, 2010).

The evidence provided by DNA exonerations in the USA that mistaken identification plays a major role in wrongful conviction, has again focused attention on the methods used to collect eyewitness identification. Previously the British Government commissioned an enquiry into eyewitness identification following a number of wrongful convictions due to mistaken eyewitness identification (Devlin, 1976). The considerable challenge in developing policy for eyewitness identification procedures is to minimise the possibility of mistaken identification, whilst making it as easy as possible for a reliable witness to identify a guilty suspect, thereby enhancing the probative value of eyewitness identification evidence. A further challenge for the criminal justice system is to ensure that eyewitness identification evidence is appropriately interpreted in the courts and the limitations of eyewitness identification evidence are properly recognised.

EYEWITNESS IDENTIFICATION AND HUMAN MEMORY

To be remembered, information must first be *encoded* by the eyewitness at the crime scene. An eyewitness may be unable to remember some aspect of an event because they did not attend to the relevant detail and therefore it was not encoded in memory. The information must be stored for the intervening period without being lost or corrupted. Finally it must be retrieved at the appropriate time; either by *recall* or *recognition* (see Chapter 5 for further details).

Human memory is an active process of reconstructing an account of an event from incomplete information encoded in memory. It is a mistake to think of memory as being like a video recording, which allows the viewer to freeze a frame and examine in close detail some aspect not previously noticed. When remembering, available information is used to actively reconstruct the event. This information may include the witness's own prior knowledge, expectations and assumptions. We tend to fill gaps in our memory with expectations of what 'must have happened'. The person remembering is usually unaware of this process, and so is unable to distinguish genuinely remembered information from new information included in the memory. Expectations are derived from memory of typical everyday events (*scripts*), such as buying goods in a shop or going out for a drink (Schank & Abelson, 1977) or stereotypes (e.g. that the driver of a van was a man). For example, a witness recalling a man getting into a car and driving away may assume that he got into the driver's seat. When remembering, we may also use information acquired since the event (**post-event information**), which may be derived from an investigator's questions or another witness's account. For example, a witness may be asked, 'Another witness mentioned that the man had a knife. Did you see a knife?' In summary, human memory is an active process that involves a creative component. This is why it is vulnerable to suggestion (from post-event information) and bias (from prior knowledge or assumptions).

> **post-event information** information that a witness may acquire after the relevant incident has occurred. Post-event information may affect a witness's testimony. Misleading post-event information may result in memory distortion.

Eyewitnesses are asked to perform a feat of *episodic memory*. They are required to remember what they saw at a specified place and time (i.e. an episode). When recalling an event a witness may misattribute a detail from a different event to the one being recalled. For example, a car seen earlier in the day may erroneously be remembered as being at the crime scene. This is known as a **source attribution** error.

source attribution the attribution of a memory to a specific source or episode. A source attribution error refers to a situation when a memory is mistakenly attributed to the incorrect source or episode.

Encoding may be affected by the extent to which attention is paid to the relevant item and the extent of cognitive processing of the item (*level of processing*). For example, consider two witnesses who notice that a car was parked near a crime scene at the relevant time. One witness may have noticed that it was a maroon car. This witness has engaged in a relatively shallow level of processing, which may make the item relatively vulnerable to retrieval failure when the witness is questioned about the event. The other witness may notice that it is a maroon Jaguar Mk II, similar to one driven by the television detective Inspector Morse. This witness has processed the item to a greater depth, relating its characteristics to their existing knowledge. The details of the car may be more resistant to retrieval failure for this witness.

The extent to which one can recall an event may be strongly dependent on the cues available when retrieval is attempted. The success of retrieval is related to the overlap of cues available at the time of retrieval and the cues stored in memory (the encoding specificity principle). For example, consider these two questions: 'Can you remember what you were doing on 31 August 1997?' and 'Can you remember what you were doing when you first heard that Princess Diana had died?' Providing the date (in the first question) is a poor cue to elicit a memory; but the death of Princess Diana was a shocking event that is likely to be relatively distinctive in memory. The point to note is that Diana died on 31 August 1997, so these two questions provide different retrieval cues for the same information. One is much more effective than the other.

Every time one attempts to remember, a new memory of the retrieval attempt is created, which can interfere with recall of the original event. Laboratory research has found that material recalled previously is more likely to be recalled subsequently, but related material not recalled previously is less likely to be recalled subsequently, an effect known as *retrieval-induced forgetting* (e.g. Bauml *et al.*, 2005). However, Odinot *et al.* (2009) found that partial repeated retrieval of an event watched on video enhanced recall of the rehearsed material but did not impair subsequent recall of the unpractised material. However, repeated recall increased confidence of both correct and incorrect answers, thereby inducing inappropriate high confidence of errors.

Psychologists distinguish *explicit* memory, such as giving a free recall of an event, from *implicit* memory. When memory has an effect of which one is not aware, it is said to be implicit memory. An example may be the influence of a script in memory used to fill in details of an everyday event.

The principles of memory described up to this point apply to eyewitness testimony in general. When asked to identify the face of a perpetrator, visual memory is involved. The general principles of memory described apply equally to visual memory. However, recall of visual memory, especially memory for faces, is very difficult partly because we do not have adequate language to describe each face uniquely (Figure 14.1). Therefore, when attempting to identify the face of a perpetrator we rely on recognition. Recognition yields superior memory performance to recall. The purpose of organising an identification procedure (such as a line-up) is to test whether a witness recognises the face of the suspect. A witness may recognise a face because they can recollect seeing that person on a specific occasion (episodic memory). However, they may recognise the face merely because it seems familiar. The influence of implicit memory may make a face seem familiar, in absence of any recollection of when the face was seen previously. Recognition memory for a face exceeds the ability to recall the context of encounter. Familiarity may then be misattributed to presence at a crime scene and potentially may lead to a mistaken identification.

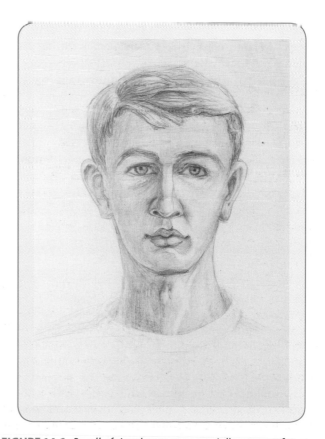

FIGURE 14.1 *Recall of visual memory, especially memory for faces, is very difficult, partly because we do not have adequate language to describe each face uniquely.*

Source: © Babich Alexander. Used under licence from Shutterstock.

DESIGN REQUIREMENTS FOR IDENTIFICATION PROCEDURES

Equipped with some understanding of human memory, and recognition memory in particular, the design of eyewitness identification procedures can be evaluated. It is useful to consider an identification procedure as a scientific experiment (Wells, 1993). The police have a hypothesis that the suspect is the perpetrator. The purpose of an identification procedure is to test the hypothesis, by establishing whether the witness can identify the suspect as the perpetrator. Such an experiment should enable a compliant but unreliable witness to be distinguished from a witness who makes a reliable identification of the perpetrator.

The simplest identification procedure is to allow the witness to see the suspect or their photograph and ask if this person is the perpetrator. This procedure is known as a *show-up* in the USA and as a *confrontation* in the UK. It is most commonly used at or near the scene shortly after a crime has been reported when there is insufficient justification to arrest a suspect. In these circumstances the procedure would be referred to as a *street identification* in the UK. Essentially the same procedure is also used as a *dock identification* during a trial under Scots Law, when a witness is asked whether they see the perpetrator present in the courtroom (see Case Study 14.1). The problem with these procedures is that there is no means of establishing whether a witness who makes an identification is mistaken. There are only two possible outcomes: a witness may decline to identify the person or they identify the suspect. The procedure may lead the witness to believe that the person concerned is the police suspect, or in the case of dock identification is the person who has been charged with the offence. The procedure may be highly suggestive. The information implied by seeking the identification may bias the witness's response.

A much better procedure is to ask the witness whether the perpetrator is present in a line-up of people, which includes one suspect. The **foils** in the line-up are not suspects. This procedure has three possible outcomes. The witness may identify the suspect, providing evidence that the suspect is the perpetrator. The witness may make no identification. Or the witness may identify a foil, making a known mistaken identification. Line-ups are widely used, especially in the UK and USA. In the USA, line-ups may consist of a live line of people or an array of photographs (a *photo-spread*). In the UK, official guidance states that photographs should not be used to obtain formal identification evidence of an arrested suspect. Historically, identification has been made by use of live line-ups, known as an *identity parade*. Recently, use of live line-ups in the UK has been replaced by **video identification** procedures, described in more detail below.

> **foils** volunteers who are not suspects but appear in a live, video or photographic line-up. Also known as distracters, fillers or line-up members; and as volunteers in England and stand-ins in Scotland.

> **video identification** a line-up in which the witness views successive video clips of the line-up members. It is used for the overwhelming majority of formal identification procedures in England and Wales, and has replaced the use of live line-ups.

CASE STUDY 14.1   THE MURDER OF JUSTIN MCALROY

Justin McAlroy was said to owe £50,000 in connection with a drugs deal. After visiting serious criminals in Perth Prison on 7 March 2002 he returned to his home shortly before 10pm, where a gunman was waiting for him. His wife was in the house. She heard three or four loud bangs and ran to the front door. Looking out of the window in the door, she saw a man in her driveway. She described him as wearing a blue-green hooded bomber jacket with the hood up and a similar coloured scarf or snood covering his nose and mouth. In her first statement, made about 40 minutes after the shooting, she said she would not be able to identify him.

Other witnesses provided similar descriptions of a padded jacket. One witness, Mr Madden, reported seeing a man in similar clothing get into a white car and remove a ski mask. At about 10.30pm a white Saab car was found abandoned some miles away. An attempt had been made to set it on fire. Inside was clothing including a hooded jacket and a drinks bottle, on which was William Gage's DNA. His DNA was also on gloves and a snood, with traces of the DNA of at least two other individuals. Firearms discharge was found on the jacket and the snood.

William Gage was arrested and charged with murder. The prosecution case depended on establishing that the white Saab was the getaway car and on identification evidence. The defence contended that the white Saab was not connected to the offence, and that William Gage had spent the evening with a girlfriend.

In the course of the investigation, the police showed Mrs McAlroy a tailor's mannequin dressed in the clothing recovered from the Saab. She identified the clothing as similar to that worn by the gunman, although it differed from her earlier description. For example, the jacket was a thin waterproof cagoule rather than a padded jacket. An identification parade had been arranged, but abandoned because Gage objected to the selection of foils. Neither Mrs McAlroy nor Mr Madden attended the parade but, instead, the prosecution sought to rely on dock identifications.

At trial, Mrs McAlroy identified Gage by his eyes: she said that the man running away had 'scary eyes' which she would never forget, but she had never mentioned his eyes in her statements. Mr Madden did not identify Gage at trial.

The jury convicted Gage of murder and he was sentenced to life imprisonment.

The case went to appeal in 2006 but was dismissed. The court noted that in a case involving circumstantial evidence, it was necessary to look at the evidence as a whole. Each piece of evidence might not be incriminating in itself, but the concurrence of testimony was critical. It was for the jury to decide how to interpret this evidence and they were entitled to reject inconsistent evidence if they so chose. In June 2009 the Scottish Criminal Cases Review Commission referred William Gage's conviction back to the Court of Appeal on the ground that the absence of a specific direction to the jury in relation to the dock identification may have given rise to a miscarriage of justice. The second appeal has yet to be heard.

Gage v. Her Majesty's Advocate [2006] Scot HCJ AC 7 (retrieved 27 September 2011 from www.bailii.org/scot/cases/ScotHC/2006/HCJAC_7.html)

---

system variables
factors that may affect the reliability of eye-witness memory, that are under the control of the criminal justice system. The selection of foils for a line-up is an example of a system variable (cf. *estimator variables*).

There is extensive research on the factors that affect the ability of eyewitnesses to identify a perpetrator from a line-up. It is useful to distinguish between factors that are under the control of the criminal justice system (known as **system variables**) and those that are not (known as **estimator variables**: see Wells, 1993; Box 14.1). Understanding the influence of estimator variables is important to evaluate the likely performance of eyewitnesses under various conditions. However, understanding the effects of system variables enables recommendations about best practice to be made.

estimator variables
factors that may affect the reliability of eyewitness memory that are not under the control of the criminal justice system (e.g the amount of time a witness was able to view the perpetrator) (cf. *system variables*).

BOX 14.1 ESTIMATOR AND SYSTEM VARIABLES

Estimator variables, which concern the circumstances of the witness's opportunity to view the culprit and are not under the control of the criminal justice system, include

* the time to view the perpetrator, the distance of the witness, the lighting and other circumstances of the incident;
* the distinctiveness of the appearance of the perpetrator;
* whether the perpetrator is known to the witness;
* the presence of a weapon;
* the number of perpetrators;
* the stress induced in the witness;
* differences in ethnicity between the witness and perpetrator; and
* the age of the witness.

System variables, which generally are under the control of the criminal justice system, include

* the selection of identification method (e.g. street identification, line-up procedure, dock identification);
* the mode of presentation (e.g. photographs, live, video);
* instructions given to the witness;
* 'blind' vs. 'non-blind' administration of a line-up;
* use of prior identification procedures (e.g. showing photographs prior to a line-up procedure);
* method used to select foils for a line-up;
* method of line-up administration (e.g. simultaneous vs. sequential presentation of line-up members); and
* feedback given to witnesses.

ESTIMATOR VARIABLES

Is it possible to judge from the circumstances of an eye-witness's view of the culprit whether their identification is likely to be accurate? In this section the effects of some estimator variables will be briefly reviewed. To begin, estimator variables that have a special status in English law will be considered from a psychological rather than a legal perspective. The section concludes by examining the effect of estimator variables in archival studies of real criminal cases.

The Turnbull guidelines

English case law is based on the premise that a distinction between good and poor eyewitness identification evidence is possible. Following a landmark ruling in the Appeal Court (*R v. Turnbull* (1976)), when identity is disputed a trial judge must advise the jury to consider carefully the circumstances of an identification (see Box 14.2).

The judgement in Turnbull arose from the Devlin enquiry (Devlin, 1976). Subsequent laboratory research has confirmed that most of the factors mentioned in the judgement do affect the accuracy of eyewitness identification. For example, witnesses who had 45 seconds to view a culprit were more likely to identify him from a line-up than witness who had only 12 seconds to view (Memon *et al.*, 2003). The ability to identify faces viewed under different levels of lighting and at a range

of distances has been investigated (Wagenaar & Van der Schrier, 1996). Faces of people known to the viewer are remembered in an episodic memory task with much greater accuracy than are unfamiliar faces, when a different view of the face is presented in the study and test phase of the experiment (Bruce, 1982). Fewer correct identifications are made after a long delay. For example, Shepherd (1983) reported that 65 per cent of faces were recognised after one week, 55 per cent after a month, 50 per cent after three months and 10 per cent after 11 months. In contrast, there was no effect of delay on mistaken identifications. Shapiro and Penrod (1986) found an effect of delay in a *meta-analysis* of 18 face recognition and eyewitness identification studies on both correct identifications (effect size = 0.43) and mistaken identifications (effect size = 0.33). The delay in the studies analysed had a mean of 4.5 days with a standard deviation of 21 days. The only factor mentioned in the Turnbull warning that seems difficult to justify from laboratory research is the issue of any material error of description. The research suggests that the quality of a verbal description is not strongly associated with the accuracy of a subsequent identification (e.g. Pozzulo & Warren, 2003).

Laboratory studies of estimator variables

In this section the effect of several factors on the accuracy of eyewitness identification will be reviewed. The issues that have attracted research attention in recent years will be highlighted.

BOX 14.2   THE TURNBULL GUIDELINES

In a case that relies substantially on disputed eyewitness identification evidence, the trial judge must warn the jury about the special need for caution before relying on the accuracy of eyewitness identification evidence to convict the defendant. The judge should make some reference to the possibility that a convincing witness may be mistaken and that a number of witnesses who make the same identification may all be mistaken. The judge should direct the jury to consider carefully the circumstances of each witness's identification. The relevant factors are often summarised by the acronym ADVOKATE.

1. **A**mount of time for which the perpetrator was in view.

2. **D**istance of the witness from the perpetrator.

3. **V**isibility of the perpetrator. How good was the lighting?

4. **O**bstruction to the witness's view?

5. **K**nown to the witness? Has the witness seen the suspect before? How often?

6. **A**ny reason to remember? If only seen occasionally before, did the witness have any reason to remember the suspect?

7. **T**ime delay between the incident and the formal Identification procedure.

8. **E**rror. Is there any material discrepancy between the description given to the police at the time of the incident and the appearance of the suspect?

R v. Turnbull (1976) 3 All ER 549

Weapon focus

When confronted by a perpetrator wielding a knife or a gun, the witness's attention is captured by the weapon (**weapon focus**; Figure 14.2). Under these circumstances there is believed to be a narrowing of attention, meaning that less attention is paid to other aspects of the scene. Therefore eyewitnesses are very capable of describing the detail of the knife or gun, but may be less able to recognise the face of the perpetrator. Steblay (1992) conducted a systematic analysis of 19 tests of the hypothesis and found a reliable but small effect (effect size = 0.13) on identification. Witnesses were less accurate in identifying a perpetrator when a weapon was present.

> **weapon focus**
> a victim threatened with a weapon tends to focus attention on the weapon and therefore does not attend to other aspects of the scene or the appearance of the perpetrator.

Stress

> **stress** emotional arousal induced in a victim or witness. High stress increases physiological arousal indicated by increased heart rate, faster respiration and increased muscle tone.

The presence of a weapon may exert its influence through inducing fear or **stress** in a witness, rather than directly by the capture of attention *per se*. Are witnesses who experience a very frightening or stressful event less reliable than witnesses who experience less stress? Morgan *et al.* (2004) examined the ability of solders to recall a person present at an interrogation. The solders had been detained for 12 hours in a mock prisoner of war camp. Each solder then underwent a high stress interrogation involving physical confrontation and a low stress interrogation. Twenty-four hours later the soldiers took part in an identification procedure. Identification was more accurate for the target person seen during a low stress interrogation (67 per cent) than for the person seen during a high stress interrogation (29 per cent).

Valentine and Mesout (2009) tested the ability of visitors to the London Dungeon to identify an actor they had met in the Horror Labyrinth. Only 18 per cent of visitors who reported feeling most anxious in the dark, disorienting environment of the labyrinth identified the actor from a nine-person photograph line-up. In contrast, 75 per cent of visitors who reported experiencing less anxiety in the labyrinth were able to identify the actor.

Deffenbacher *et al.* (2004) reported a meta-analytic review of studies that successfully manipulated stress, demonstrated by measures taken as soon as possible after encoding the target person. They found that heightened stress had a moderate negative effect on identification and on recall of a target person. The effect of stress on identification was restricted to the number of correct identifications made when the target person was included in the line-up; there was no effect of stress on the rate of correctly rejecting the line-up when the target person was not present.

Ethnicity

Witnesses tend to be less accurate in recognising a perpetrator of an ethnic origin different from their own. The effect size is moderate and may depend upon the experience of the witness. Chiroro and Valentine (1995) found that experience of people of a different ethnic origin in daily life may reduce or eliminate any effect of ethnicity, but does not necessarily do so. The quality of the social contact may be an important mediating factor. The effect of ethnicity on face recognition can be interpreted within a framework in which individual faces are recognised by their distinctive qualities in relation to the population of faces experienced in one's lifetime (Valentine, 1991; Valentine & Endo, 1992). For a review of the effect of ethnicity on face recognition see Meissner and Brigham (2001).

Witness age

Laboratory studies have found that older people make fewer correct responses in tests of face recognition (e.g. Bartlett & Fulton, 1991; O'Rourke *et al.*, 1989). O'Rourke *et al.* (1989) found that identification accuracy declined sharply at around age 50. The effect of witness age has been found in terms of older witnesses making both

FIGURE 14.2 *When confronted by a perpetrator wielding a knife or a gun, the witness's attention is captured by the weapon.*

Source: © corepics. Used under licence from Shutterstock.

fewer correct identifications and more mistaken identifications. (Searcy *et al.*, 1999; 2000; 2001).

Confidence

A confident eyewitness may provide compelling evidence and be highly influential on a jury or judge. It has been appreciated for a long time that a confident witness may be mistaken. Many studies of eyewitness identification have suggested that the relationship between confidence and accuracy is low or negligible, leading psychologists to conclude that witness confidence is an unreliable means to assess accuracy. In recent years our understanding of the confidence–accuracy relationship has become more sophisticated. The relationship is stronger when a wide range of viewing conditions is considered (Lindsay *et al.*, 1998). One factor that may have restricted the relationship in experimental studies is that participants usually view a live or video mock crime under identical conditions. Furthermore, the correlation is stronger (typically in the region of $r = 0.5$) if we only consider witnesses who identify somebody from a line-up; it is lower amongst witnesses who reject the line-up (Sporer *et al.*, 1995). However, a correlation of this order will still mean that confident but mistaken eyewitness will be encountered fairly frequently. See Brewer (2006) for a review.

Archival studies of estimator variables

At live line-ups conducted in England to investigate real criminal cases, approximately 40 per cent of witnesses identified the suspect, approximately 40 per cent of witnesses did not make any identification, and 20 per cent of witnesses made a mistaken identification of an innocent foil (Slater, 1994; Valentine, Pickering *et al.*, 2003; Wright & McDaid, 1996). Note that in archival studies it is not known how many line-ups contained the actual perpetrator. The known mistaken identifications were made despite the witness having been cautioned that the person they saw may or may not be present in the line-up. Archival data collected by the police from 1776 identity parades showed that the suspect was identified in 48 per cent of cases, but these data did not distinguish non-identifications from identification of a foil (Pike *et al.*, 2002). An archival analysis of 58 live line-ups conducted in US criminal cases found that the suspect was identified in 50 per cent of cases, a foil was identified in 24 per cent of cases and the witness was unable to make an identification or rejected the line-up in 26 per cent of cases (Behrman & Davey, 2001).

Valentine, Pickering *et al.* (2003) examined the effect of estimator variables on the outcome of identification attempts made by approximately 600 witnesses who viewed over 300 live line-ups organised by the London Metropolitan Police. The suspect was more likely to be identified if the witness was younger than 30, the suspect was a white European (rather than African-Caribbean), the witness gave a detailed description, viewed the culprit at the scene for over a minute and made a fast decision at the line-up. Sixty-five per cent of witnesses identified the suspect from line-ups held up to seven days later, while only 38 per cent of witnesses identified the suspect in line-ups held eight days or more after the incident. There were no independent, statistically reliable effects of the use of a weapon during the incident, or a suspect of a different ethnicity from the witness. Pike *et al.* (2002) also reported an effect of witness age, no effect of the use of a weapon during a crime, and no effect of a difference in ethnicity of the witness and suspect on the outcome of live line-ups conducted by British police.

Behrman and Davey's (2001) archival analysis of eyewitness identification in American criminal cases included an analysis of the outcome of 289 photographic line-ups. The typical format is to present the witness with six photographs simultaneously arranged in two rows of three images. They found that 48 per cent of witnesses identified the suspect. In common with the British studies cited above, there was no effect of the presence of a weapon in the crime on the likelihood of the suspect being identified. Line-ups held within seven days of the incident produced a higher rate of identifications of the suspect (64 per cent) than line-ups held after eight days or more (33 per cent). However, in contrast to the British data, Behrman and Davey did find an effect of ethnicity. Sixty per cent of witnesses of the same ethnicity as the suspect identified the suspect, compared to 45 per cent of witnesses of different ethnicity.

SYSTEM VARIABLES

The criminal justice system can exert influence over some aspects of identification procedures (system variables). For example, a line-up may be presented in photographs, video or live; the method of selecting the 'foils' for a line-up and the instructions given to witnesses are specified in official guidance.

Presentation mode

The effect of presenting line-ups in different media (photographs, video, live) and manipulating the richness of cues available (e.g. stills, moving images, people walking) is surprisingly small. A possible reason is that faces can be sufficiently well perceived from a good quality still photograph. Therefore, relying on cues such as gait, build or colour images adds little extra benefit. Reviewing the

BOX 14.3   THE BENEFITS OF VIDEO IDENTIFICATION PROCEDURES

- Video can dramatically reduce the delay before an identification can be organised. Live line-ups have been subject to long delays to enable a selection of appropriate foils to be available to stand on a line-up (typically of one to three months; see Valentine, Pickering *et al.*, 2003). In contrast, a video line-up can be produced within two hours of request.

- Approximately 50 per cent of live line-ups were cancelled, for example because a bailed suspect failed to attend. With video identification the cancellation rate has fallen to around 5 per cent (Pike *et al.*, 2000).

- A large database of video clips (approximately 23,000) is available, providing more foils for selection. This helps to make line-ups fairer (see text for further details).

- Video is less threatening to victims, who no longer have to attend an identification suite where, for example, their attacker may be physically present. Intimidation can result in a witness feeling too threatened to make a positive identification of a police suspect at a line-up. Use of video does not prevent witness intimidation but any means of reducing the perceived level of threat at an identification procedure is beneficial.

- Video equipment can be taken to a witness who is unable to attend the police station. In 2005, Abigail Witchalls, a victim of an attack who was left paralysed, was able to view a video line-up from her hospital bed. As a result, a suspect was eliminated from the enquiry.

literature, Cutler *et al.* (1994) concluded, 'With respect to current practices, the conservative conclusion is that, based on available research, there is no reason to believe that live line-ups, videotaped line-ups or photo arrays produce substantial differences in identification performance.' (p.181).

Fairness of video identification

Since 2003, video technology has replaced live identity parades in England and Wales. The video line-ups consist of 15-second clips of a head-and-shoulders shot of each line-up member. First they are looking at the camera and then they rotate their head to show both profiles before looking back at the camera. The images are captured under standardised conditions. Each line-up member is shown sequentially one at a time, with a digit in the top left corner of the screen that can be used to identify each individual. The benefits of video identification compared to live line-ups are listed in Box 14.3.

Research has shown that video line-ups from real criminal cases were fairer to the suspects than live line-ups (Valentine, Harris *et al.*, 2003; Valentine & Heaton, 1999). In these studies, participants (known as *mock witnesses*) were given the first description of the offender provided by the original witness and required to guess which line-up member was the suspect. The 'mock witness' had not seen the perpetrator, so the suspect should not have stood out in any way. In a perfectly fair line-up the suspect should not be chosen more often than any other line-up member. If the line-up contains a suspect and eight foils, the suspect should not be chosen by

more than one in nine (11 per cent) of mock witnesses. Valentine and Heaton (1999) found that the mock witnesses identified the suspect in live line-ups more frequently (25 per cent) than by chance but were not able to select the suspect from video line-ups (15 per cent) significantly more often than chance. Valentine, Harris *et al.* (2003) found video line-ups of African–Caribbeans and of white Europeans were equally fair, using equal numbers of mock witness from both ethnic backgrounds.

Instructions given to witnesses

A witness may assume that they would not have been invited to attempt an identification if the police did not have good reason to believe that their suspect was guilty, and that it will help the police if the witness identifies the suspect. It is important that the instructions to the witness should emphasise the possibility that making no identification may be the right thing to do because the suspect may not be guilty. Most commonly, this point is made by including an instruction that the person the witness saw 'may or may not be present'. Instructions that do not point out that the culprit may not be in the line-up are regarded as 'biased' instructions (e.g. 'Look at these photographs. Can you identify the man who assaulted you?'). A meta-analysis of 18 studies showed that when biased instructions are given, witnesses are more likely to make an identification, whether it is correct or incorrect. Biased instructions increase the likelihood of an innocent suspect being identified from culprit-absent line-ups (Steblay, 1997).

Blind administration of line-ups

blind administration
a method of administering a line-up in which neither the line-up administrator nor the witness know which line-up member is the suspect. Also known as 'double-blind administration'.

Blind administration is used in the sense of meaning that the person who administers the line-up procedure to the witness does not know (i.e. is blind to) the identity of the suspect in a line-up. The procedure is often referred to as 'double-blind', meaning that both the witness and the line-up administrator are blind to the identity of the suspect. The expectations of the experimenter can influence the outcome of behavioural research (Harris & Rosenthal, 1985). The line-up administrator should be blind to the identity of the suspect in order to prevent any inadvertent influence on the witness. Such influence can be very subtle and entirely unconscious. For example, the administrator may look at the witness when the suspect's image is being viewed, or be more likely to accept a tentative identification if it is of the suspect. Phillips *et al.* (1999) found that double-blind line-up administration led to a reduced rate of mistaken identification under some circumstances. Double-blind administration of identification procedures removes all possibility of leading the witness. Therefore, the integrity of identification evidence is enhanced and any potential claim of bias can be rebutted.

Prior exposure to photographs

If the police have not identified a suspect they may show the witness photographs (mugshots) of people previously convicted of a similar offence, in the expectation that the witness may be able to identify the perpetrator. In this procedure all of the people are suspects, therefore any identification will lead to that person being investigated. Later in the investigation the police may want to collect formal identification evidence from a line-up. Would a subsequent line-up be biased against the suspect if the witness has previously seen their photograph in a mugshot album?

Deffenbacher *et al.* (2006) provide a systematic review of the effects of mugshot exposure. They found that prior viewing of a photograph of somebody who subsequently appears in a line-up increases the probability of a mistaken identification from the line-up. The effect is due to transference of familiarity from the photograph, which is mistakenly attributed to having being seen at the crime scene. The effect is stronger when few mugshots were viewed (8–15 or less) than when more mugshots were viewed. The effect is particularly strong if the person was mistakenly identified as the perpetrator from the mugshot photographs. This is known as an effect of **commitment** to the earlier identification. There was no ill effect of showing photographs if none of the people seen appeared in the subsequent line-up. Deffenbacher *et al.* (2006) point out that transference of familiarity can occur for a bystander in the original mock crime who is included in the line-up. Experiments using this bystander design showed a significant effect of increased mistaken identification but the effect was stronger when the face had been seen in a mugshot rather than as a bystander. The increased risk of a mistaken identification when a bystander but not the perpetrator is included in a line-up is very relevant to cases in which the suspect admits presence at the scene but denies involvement in the offence (for example, a bystander at a fight).

commitment an effect whereby once a face has been identified by a witness, they become committed to the identification and are likely to identify the same face again, even when the initial judgement is mistaken.

Selection of foils

The code of practice in England and Wales specifies that the foils for line-ups must be selected to 'resemble the suspect'. This is known as a *suspect-resemblance* strategy. Luus and Wells (1991) argued that a better strategy is to select foils who match the witness's description of the culprit. It is reasonable to assume that the witness can remember the description that he or she gave to the police, and may expect to identify somebody who matches their description. Therefore, the witness may be inclined to disregard any foils that do not match their description, or conversely pay special attention to anybody who is a better match to their description than the rest. To be fair, all line-up members should match the witness's description of the culprit.

Luus and Wells (1991) suggested it does not introduce a bias against the suspect if line-up members differ on some feature that was not mentioned in the original description. Diversity amongst features not mentioned in the description will help a witness with a reliable memory to distinguish the culprit from the foils. If the suspect is not the culprit, he or she is no more likely to be mistakenly identified by some feature not mentioned in the description, because the witness has not seen the suspect before. A line-up that consists of a number of people chosen because they closely resemble the suspect in all aspects of their appearance will make it difficult even for a reliable witness to identify the culprit, if present.

When constructing a culprit-description line-up it may be necessary to take account of default values in descriptions. Sometimes people may not describe the sex or ethnicity of the person, or may neglect to say that somebody did not have a beard or was not wearing glasses. This may occur because the witness assumes a default value (Lindsay *et al.*, 1994).

In an immediate test after seeing a live staged theft, witnesses made significantly more correct identifications from culprit-description line-ups (67 per cent) than from suspect-resemblance line-ups (22 per cent) when the culprit was in the line-up, but the number of mistaken identifications from culprit-absent line-ups did not differ reliably (Wells *et al.*, 1993). Juslin *et al.* (1996) found a similar result. Forty-four per cent of participants correctly identified the perpetrator from a suspect-resemblance line-up and 52 per cent identified the culprit in a culprit-description line-up. When the perpetrator was not in the line-up, 9 per cent of participants identified the innocent suspect from both line-ups. Lindsay *et al.* (1994), Tunnicliffe and Clark (2000) and Darling *et al.* (2008) did not find a statistically significant difference in the rate of correct or mistaken identification between culprit-description and suspect-resemblance line-ups. At present the empirical evidence is too ambiguous to recommend that a suspect-resemblance strategy should be changed to a match-to-description strategy. However, it is clearly good practice to consider whether the suspect stands out in comparison to the witness's description.

Relative and absolute judgements: Sequential and simultaneous presentation

A persistent problem in understanding eyewitness identification is to explain why a sizable minority of witnesses (about one in five) make mistaken identifications, despite appropriate warnings that the perpetrator may not be present in the line-up. Wells (1993) demonstrated that at least part of the problem may be attributable to witnesses who make a *relative judgement* rather than an *absolute judgement*. When confronted with a line-up a witness may only identify a person if their resemblance to the culprit exceeds some criterion of similarity (an absolute judgement). Alternatively a witness may examine all the members of a line-up and identify the person who most closely resembles the perpetrator (a relative judgement). The influence of relative judgements was demonstrated using a method of removal without replacement (Table 14.1). The top line of Table 14.1 shows the distribution of selections made by 100 witnesses to a mock crime, who saw a six-person line-up in which the perpetrator was present. Fifty-four per cent identified the perpetrator and 21 per cent rejected the line-up. Other participants were presented with a five-person line-up from which the perpetrator was removed. One might expect that the witnesses who would correctly identify the perpetrator if he had been present, would reject the line-up. Instead the number of mistaken identifications increased dramatically. In the absence of the culprit, many witnesses appear to identify the foil who most closely resembles their memory of the perpetrator. Clark and Davey (2005) replicated this shift of choices from the perpetrator to

TABLE 14.1 *The distribution of identifications across members of a photograph line-up with the perpetrator present and with the perpetrator removed.*

| | Line-up member | | | | | | |
	1	2	3(p)	4	5	6	No choice
Perpetrator present	3%	13%	54%	3%	3%	3%	21%
Perpetrator removed	6%	38%	-	12%	7%	5%	32%

Source: Data from Wells (1993). Reproduced with permission of APA.

the foils. These data suggest that relative identification decisions may be a cause of mistaken identifications.

The method of sequential line-up presentation was developed to prevent witnesses from making a relative judgement. In a **sequential presentation**, photographs of faces are presented one at a time (Lindsay & Wells, 1985). The line-up administrator should be blind to the identity of the suspect. The witness is not told how many faces will be presented, but when each face is presented must decide whether or not it is the culprit before the next face is presented (Lindsay *et al.*, 1991). Furthermore, witnesses must not be allowed a second choice or to see again a face previously presented.

> **sequential presentation** a method in which a line-up is presented one person at a time. The witness decides whether each person is the perpetrator before they see the next person.

Steblay *et al.* (2011) carried out a meta-analytic comparison of the accuracy rates in sequential and simultaneous line-ups. The most relevant analysis was of 27 published tests that compared sequential and simultaneous presentation of both culprit-present and culprit-absent line-ups. When present in the line-up, more witnesses identified the culprit from simultaneous line-ups than from sequential line-ups (52 per cent vs. 44 per cent respectively). When the culprit was not in the line-up, there were more mistaken identifications of the designated innocent suspect from simultaneous than from sequential line-ups (28 per cent vs. 15 per cent). In summary, sequential presentation reduces the rate of choosing from both culprit-present and culprit-absent line-ups. Meissner *et al.* (2005) found that sequential line-ups induce a more conservative response criterion but do not affect discrimination accuracy. The effect of sequential presentation is to provide some protection against mistaken identification from culprit-absent line-ups, but at a cost to the sensitivity of the identification procedure when the culprit is in the line-up. Steblay *et al.* (2011) argue that an identification of the suspect from a sequential line-up has higher probative value (i.e. provides more reliable evidence of guilt), because sequential presentation reduces the rate of mistaken identification when the culprit is absent more than it reduces the rate of correct identification when the culprit is present.

Some police departments in the USA adopted a sequential presentation procedure for line-ups on the recommendation of eyewitness researchers. In Illinois the police ran a trial to compare double-blind sequential line-ups with the current procedure of (non-blind) simultaneous line-ups (Mecklenburg, 2006). The pilot included both photo-spreads and live line-ups. These are real cases, so the culprit may not be in the line-up. The results showed that the suspect was less likely to be identified from a sequential line-up than from a simultaneous line-up. This is consistent with laboratory research. However, contrary to the research findings, there were fewer mistaken identifications of fillers from simultaneous line-ups (Table 14.2). Unfortunately, the experimental design confounded the method of line-up presentation (simultaneous vs. sequential) with use of blind administration. It has been suggested that the police did not adequately record filler identifications from the non-blind simultaneous line-ups (Wells, 2008). However, subsequent laboratory research suggests that the superiority of sequential line-ups is not always observed, and that further research is required to establish the limits of the effect (Gronlund et al., 2009). The Illinois project has illustrated the difficulties of applying psychological science in the real world, and shows that further careful work is required if psychological science is to substantially improve the quality of identification evidence.

Video identification used in the UK naturally yields a sequential presentation, but mandatory procedure requires that the witness must watch the entire line-up twice before making any identification. Valentine et al. (2007) asked whether the effectiveness of video line-ups may be improved by changing the instruction to require a yes/no response to each face as it is presented (Lindsay et al., 1991). Participants had witnessed a staged live incident about a week prior to viewing a video line-up constructed by the police using a national police database to select line-up members. The existing (view twice) procedure was compared to the strict sequential instructions described by Lindsay et al. (1991). When the perpetrator was present in the line-up he was more likely to be identified using the current 'view twice' procedure (65 per cent compared to 36 per cent). When an innocent suspect was in the line-up 23 per cent of witnesses mistakenly identified a foil following the 'view twice' instruction compared to 10 per cent under the strict sequential instruction, but this difference was not statistically reliable. In conclusion, the strict sequential instruction significantly reduced the sensitivity of video line-ups but the reduction in foil identifications was not statistically significant. In this experiment, based closely on the operational context in the UK, the line-up instruction used was not confounded with blind administration – all witnesses were run double blind. Furthermore, the ground truth was known. These features make it easier to interpret the results of an ecologically-valid laboratory experiment with confidence, compared to the field trials conducted in Illinois.

MALLEABILITY OF WITNESS CONFIDENCE

An important research finding is that witness confidence is changeable and is influenced by information that the witness acquires after attending an identification procedure. Receiving feedback that the witness identified the suspect, or that somebody else made the same identification, will increase the witness's confidence in their identification (see Case Study 14.2). Not only does confirming feedback tend to make the witness subsequently more confident in their identification, but it also tends to inflate estimates of a range of subsequent testimony, including how long the culprit was seen for, how close they were and how much attention the witness paid (Wells & Bradfield, 1998). Furthermore, confirming post-identification feedback tends to make eyewitnesses overconfident; that is, they now express more confidence in their identification than is warranted (Semmler et al., 2004). Wright and Skagerberg (2007) showed that feedback affected the confidence of witnesses and victims of real crimes. By the time a witness gives evidence in court they are likely to have received confirming feedback or this has been inferred, if only by virtue of the fact that they have been called upon to give evidence. The witness is less likely to be asked to attend court if they had identified the 'wrong' person.

TABLE 14.2 *The outcome of the Illinois field trial of sequential and simultaneous line-ups.*

N = 548	Simultaneous (non-blind, n = 319)	Sequential (blind, n = 229)
Suspect ID	60%	45%
Filler ID	3%	9%
No ID	38%	47%

CASE STUDY 14.2   THE MURDER OF JILL DANDO

Jill Dando was a famous British TV presenter. On 26 April 1999 she returned to her home at about 11.30am. She was killed on her doorstep by a single shot from a hand-gun. Nobody saw the murder; two neighbours who heard a muffled cry looked out of their window and saw a man walking away from the house but neither realised at the time that there was anything wrong. It was accepted that the man seen by these two witnesses was undoubtedly the murderer. Initially, the police suggested that the murder had been carried out by an assassin but, a year later, Barry George, a local unemployed man, was charged with the murder.

Identification evidence was central to the case. Sixteen people who saw a man in Gowan Avenue either on the morning of the murder or the previous day attended an identification procedure. The first five witnesses saw a live parade and the remainder saw a video parade after George was advised by his solicitor not to attend any further live parades. Barry George had been clean-shaven at the time of the murder but now had a beard. Therefore, all of the men in the line-up had beards. Neither of Jill Dando's neighbours identified George. He was positively identified by only one witness. This witness had seen the face of a man for five to six seconds some hours before the murder and made her identification 17 months later.

After making her identification, the identifying witness was given a lift home in a police car with two other witnesses. During the journey the other witnesses discovered the positive identification she had made and, apparently influenced by this knowledge, both subsequently made statements that they too would have identified George but were hindered by not being able to see his build and height in the video.

The case set a legal precedent because identification evidence was admitted from four witnesses who did not make a positive identification at the line-up. In addition to the two retrospective identifications, a postman stated that the man he saw was not in the line-up, but he recognised a man he had had a conversation with about the Dando case in the days after the murder, a fact confirmed by Barry George. The prosecution argued that there is an underlying unity of the description of the man these witnesses saw that pointed to George as the murderer.

Barry George was convicted of murder in July 2001 by a majority verdict and was sentenced to life imprisonment. In July 2002 the Court of Appeal upheld the principle that a witness who did not identify the suspect can still give evidence in court (R v. George (2002)). However, in May 2007 the Criminal Cases Review Commission referred Barry George's conviction back to the Court of Appeal on the single ground that new evidence called into question the significance attached to the firearms discharge evidence at trial. His conviction was quashed in November 2007.

R v. George (2002) EWCA Crim 1923 (retrieved 27 September 2011 from www.bailii.org/ew/cases/EWCA/Crim/2002/1923.html)

R v. George (2007) EWCA Crim 2722 (retrieved 27 September 2011 from www.bailii.org/ew/cases/EWCA/Civ/2007/2722.html)

OFFICIAL GUIDANCE

The conduct of identification procedures in England and Wales is governed by Code D of the *Police and Criminal Evidence Act (1984) Codes of Practice*. The current code, which came into force in 2011, can be downloaded from the Home Office website (Home Office, 2011). The major provisions of the code are as follows. If identification is disputed, a video identification procedure containing moving images must be offered unless it is not practicable or a 'live' identity parade is more suitable. All line-ups should consist of a minimum of eight foils and one suspect. The foils should 'resemble the suspect in age, general appearance and position in life'. Witnesses must be advised that the person they saw may not be present and must view the entire line-up at least twice. The person who runs the procedure should not be involved in the investigation of the case. The suspect has the right for his or her legal representative to be present. The suspect and the legal representative may object to the procedure (e.g. the selection of foils) and their reason for objection must be recorded. If the witness has previously been shown photographs, details of the photographs shown should be recorded. Anything the witness says should be written down before he or she leaves the identification room.

In the USA, identification procedures are regulated at state level or below, so there is no one federal code of practice. Identification from photographs is commonplace. Procedures are often conducted by an investigating police officer. The US Department of Justice has issued a guide on identification procedures, but it does not have the force of law (Technical Working Group for Eyewitness Evidence, 1999). The guide makes recommendations for sequential and simultaneous line-ups of photographs or 'live' volunteers, but does not endorse one method over another. A minimum of five foils is required. Advice is provided on: selecting foils so that the suspect does not unfairly stand out; giving unbiased instructions; and carefully recording all identifications or non-identifications.

IDENTIFICATION FROM CCTV

In view of the fallibility of eyewitnesses it may be a comforting thought that in many cases we can rely on CCTV images to identify perpetrators, thus cutting out the human error involved in eyewitness testimony (Figure 14.3). In the UK, in particular, this idea has proved highly attractive to politicians and the public alike. The UK is believed to have the highest density of CCTV surveillance in the world (see Norris et al., 2004 for a review). CCTV does have many benefits, including its use in the investigation of crime. However, identification of perpetrators from CCTV has proved to be surprisingly susceptible to human error.

FIGURE 14.3 *In many cases the courts rely on CCTV images to identify perpetrators.*

Source: © Monkey Business Images. Used under licence from Shutterstock.

People are extremely good at recognising highly familiar individuals (e.g. work colleagues, friends and family) even from low quality images. Familiar people can be recognised from poor quality CCTV images with over 90 per cent accuracy (Bruce *et al.*, 2001; Burton *et al.*, 1999). However, we are surprisingly poor at matching images, taken by different cameras, of an otherwise unfamiliar person. For example, Bruce *et al.* (1999) asked participants to choose the face from an array of 10 high quality photographs that they thought matched a target face. The photograph of the target was taken from a studio video recording made on the same day on which the still photographs in the array were taken. The set of faces consisted of 120 young, male, clean-shaven Caucasian police trainees, and was supplied by the Home Office. The arrays consisted of faces judged to resemble each other so that selections could not be based on substantial differences in hairstyle, weight or age. When the viewpoint and facial expression of the target and the images in the array matched (i.e. a comparison is made under ideal conditions), participants only made the correct selection in 79 per cent of the arrays. Bruce *et al.* (1999) concluded, 'The implication of these findings is that courts must be aware that caution should be used when the impressions of resemblance are used to establish the identity of unfamiliar people, *even when the quality of video tape is high*'. (Emphasis as in the original. See Box 14.4.)

The forensic implications of a separate study of recognition of faces from a poor-quality video, typical of that recorded by a commercial security CCTV system, was summarised as follows: '. . . identification of these types of video sequences is very unreliable, unless the viewer happens to know the target person' (Burton *et al.*, 1999). Furthermore, Burton *et al's* study showed that police officers, with experience in forensic identification and an average of over 13 years service, perform as poorly as other participants unfamiliar with the targets. A police officer is no more likely to correctly identify somebody from video than anybody else who has a similar level of familiarity with the target.

Davis and Valentine (2009) examined people's ability to match a person filmed in a 40-second high quality video to somebody physically present in the room. This comparison was intended to simulate the task facing a member of the jury who watches a video sequence in a court in the presence of the defendant. The video displayed views of each actor's face and body from a number of different angles and was played up to three times. In half of the trials the defendant was not the person in the video. The overall error rate was approximately 20 per cent (22 per cent target present; 17 per cent target absent). That is, one in five 'witnesses' was mistaken under ideal conditions when there was no requirement to remember the culprit's face, and there was no time

BOX 14.4   FORENSIC IMPLICATIONS OF USING CCTV IMAGES FOR IDENTIFICATION

- Photographs of different people can look remarkably similar to each other.
- Two images of the same person can look very different, when taken with different cameras.
- Faces of familiar people (e.g. colleagues, friends or family) can be recognised accurately even from low quality images, such as those obtained from CCTV.
- Matching the identity of unfamiliar people in images taken by different cameras is error-prone, even if the images are high quality.
- Both inclusion errors (judging two different people to be the same person) and exclusion errors (judging images of the same person to be different people) are common.
- Matching facial identity is error-prone even when there is no requirement to remember a face.
- CCTV is a powerful investigative tool, which can help identify potential suspects worthy of further investigation. Evidential use of CCTV as a means of establishing disputed identification in court should be treated with great caution.

pressure. In the case of one particular actor, 44 per cent of participants incorrectly judged an 'innocent defendant' to be the actor in the video sequence.

Studies by Henderson, Bruce and Burton (2001) and by Davies and Thasen (2000) have found similarly high error rates in identifying previously unfamiliar persons from CCTV. Davies and Thasen report identification accuracy of 15–30 per cent, with false alarm rates of 60–65 per cent, showing that people are particularly prone to making a mistaken identification when the person they expect to identify is not present.

Why is recognition of familiar faces so robust but recognition of previously unfamiliar faces so vulnerable? It is known that familiar faces are relatively better recognised from their internal features (eyes, nose, mouth) than are unfamiliar faces (Ellis *et al*, 1979). When looking at unfamiliar faces, more reliance is placed on the external features (hair, face shape). The configuration of the internal features is a more reliable cue to identity across different views and lighting conditions. When recognising unfamiliar faces, we are more likely to rely on superficial similarities that are changeable (e.g. hairstyles, hairline).

Stills from CCTV are circulated to police officers in an attempt to obtain an identification from an officer who may have previously arrested or interviewed the offender. Recognition by police officers from CCTV is often used as identification evidence in court. The experimental evidence discussed above suggests that the degree of familiarity of the perpetrator to the police officer is a critical variable in assessing the reliability of the identification. This type of identification evidence raises the question: How familiar does one have to be with a face to recognise it reliably from video?

At present the scientific evidence on this point is rather sparse. Bruce *et al.* (2001) looked at matching

performance for faces that had been familiarised by 30 seconds' or one minute's exposure of a wide range of different views of the face immediately before performing the matching task. The task required matching of a target photograph to an array of 8–10 photographs. In half of the trials the target was not present in the array. There was little benefit of prior familiarisation, except when two participants viewed the faces together and were encouraged to discuss the faces during familiarisation. In these circumstances, when matching *good quality images in the same view*, participants who had received the prior 'social' familiarisation identified 98 per cent of targets and correctly rejected 68 per cent of 'target absent' arrays. This compares to 81 per cent and 39 per cent respectively for participants who received no prior familiarisation. In conclusion, prior brief social familiarisation can enhance matching under ideal conditions with no memory load. However, even under these ideal conditions (good-quality video images in the same view) there is a substantial false alarm rate when the 'target' is not present in the array (32 per cent of responses).

CONCLUSIONS

Our ability to judge that a face has been seen before can exceed our ability to recall the circumstances in which it was encountered. Reliance on a feeling of familiarity at a formal identification procedure can be especially prone to mistaken identification. There is ample evidence that mistakes by eyewitnesses occur frequently, and are the leading cause of wrongful convictions. Therefore, the procedures to obtain formal identification evidence should be designed and used with care.

Procedures that do not require selection amongst alternatives (e.g. dock identification, a show-up or street identification) do not provide a test that can expose an error by a witness, and the context can be highly suggestive. A witness should not participate in repeated identification procedures. In selection methods, which should be run blind, careful consideration must be given to the design of the procedure, including the choice of plausible foils and the instructions given to the witness. Two methods have been advocated to improve the probative value of line-up procedures: selection of foils who match the witness's description of the culprit (rather than on the basis of their similarity to the suspect) and sequential rather than simultaneous presentation of images. However recent evidence, especially in the operational context in the UK, shows at best mixed results. Recommendations to change existing practice in these respects would be inappropriate.

Increasing surveillance by CCTV has had a marked impact on criminal investigations. Identification of unfamiliar faces from CCTV images can be surprisingly error-prone. Images of different people can look very similar, whilst images of the same person, especially when taken with different cameras, can look very different. Although CCTV may appear to give an opportunity to overcome the frailties of human eyewitness memory, CCTV itself poses significant issues of human misidentification.

We are familiar with the image of crime scene investigators dressed in paper suits and latex gloves, taking care not to contaminate the crime scene by introducing rogue samples or destroying evidence, whilst endeavouring to detect every last minute trace that might link the offender to the scene. It is useful to extend this approach, by thinking of the memory of an eyewitness as part of a crime scene. The investigators need to use sensitive, unbiased procedures to obtain reliable eyewitness identification. Equally, the investigators must take great care to avoid contaminating the witness's memory by using multiple identification procedures, biased line-ups, or providing feedback to witnesses.

SUMMARY

- **Mistaken identification by eyewitnesses is the leading cause of wrongful convictions.**

- **Reliance on a feeling of familiarity can be especially error-prone.**

- **Factors that affect the accuracy of eyewitness identification include the length of time the witness was able to view the culprit, high stress experienced by a witness, and the age of the witness.**

- **A witness should not participate in repeated identification procedures, to avoid a potential misattribution of familiarity.**

- **Witnesses who make an accurate identification tend to express higher confidence than witnesses who make a mistaken identification; however, it is common for confident witnesses to be mistaken.**

- **The confidence of an eyewitness is affected by information acquired afterwards, for example, being told whether the person identified is the police suspect.**

- **Identification of unfamiliar faces from CCTV images can be surprisingly error-prone. Images of different people can look very similar, whilst images of the same person can look very different.**

- **The memory of an eyewitness should be regarded as part of a crime scene. Therefore, procedures must be designed to avoid distorting the witness's memory.**

ESSAY/DISCUSSION QUESTIONS

1. What insights does psychological science provide into our understanding of mistaken eyewitness identification?

2. Compare the strengths and weaknesses of laboratory studies of eyewitness identification with those of archival studies.

3. What practical advice, based on psychological research, would you offer to the police authorities regarding the fair and effective conduct of identification parades?

4. Discuss the strengths and limitations of CCTV evidence as an aid to identifying offenders.

REFERENCES

Bartlett, J.C. & Fulton, A. (1991). Familiarity and recognition of faces in old age. *Memory & Cognition, 19*, 229–238.

Bauml, K-H, Zellner, M. & Vilimek, R. (2005). When remembering causes forgetting: Retrieval-induced forgetting as recovery failure. *Journal of Experimental Psychology: Learning, Memory & Cognition, 31*, 1221–1234.

Behrman, B.W. & Davey, S.L. (2001). Eyewitness identification in actual criminal cases: An archival analysis. *Law and Human Behavior, 25*, 475–491.

Brewer, N. (2006). Uses and abuses of eyewitness identification confidence. *Legal and Criminological Psychology, 11*, 3–23.

Bruce, V. (1982). Changing faces: Visual and non-visual coding processes in face recognition. *British Journal of Psychology, 73*, 105–116.

Bruce, V., Henderson, Z., Greenwood, K., Hancock, P., Burton, A.M. & Miller, P. (1999). Verification of face identities from images captured on video. *Journal of Experimental Psychology: Applied, 5*, 339–360.

Bruce, V., Henderson, Z., Newman, C. & Burton, A.M. (2001). Matching identities of familiar and unfamiliar faces caught on CCTV images. *Journal of Experimental Psychology: Applied, 7*, 207–218.

Burton, A.M., Wilson, S., Cowan, M. & Bruce, V. (1999). Face recognition in poor quality video: evidence from security surveillance. *Psychological Science, 10*, 243–248.

Chiroro, P. & Valentine, T. (1995). An investigation of the contact hypothesis of the own-race bias in face recognition. *Quarterly Journal of Experimental Psychology, 48A*, 879–894.

Clark, S.E. & Davey, S.L. (2005). The targets-to-foils shift in simultaneous and sequential lineups. *Law and Human Behavior, 29*, 151–172.

Cutler, B.L., Berman, G.L., Penrod, S. & Fisher, R.P. (1994). Conceptual, practical and empirical issues associated with eyewitness identification test media. In D.F. Ross, J.D. Read & M.P. Toglia (Eds.) *Adult eyewitness testimony: Current trends and developments* (pp.163–181). Cambridge: Cambridge University Press.

Darling, S., Valentine, T. & Memon, A. (2008). Selection of lineup foils in operational contexts. *Applied Cognitive Psychology, 22*, 159–169.

Davies, G. & Thasen, S. (2000). Closed-circuit television: How effective an identification aid? *British Journal of Psychology, 91*, 411–426.

Davis, J.P. & Valentine, T. (2009). CCTV on trial: Matching video images with the defendant in the dock. *Applied Cognitive Psychology, 23*, 482–505.

Deffenbacher, K.A., Bornstein, B.H. & Penrod, S.D. (2006). Mugshot exposure effects: Retroactive interference, mugshot commitment, source confusion and unconscious transference. *Law and Human Behavior, 30*, 287–307.

Deffenbacher, K.A., Bornstein, B.H., Penrod, S.D. & McGorty, K. (2004). A meta-analytic review of the effects of high stress on eyewitness memory. *Law and Human Behavior, 28*, 687–706.

Devlin, P. (1976). *Report to the Secretary of State for the Home Department on the departmental committee on evidence of identification in criminal cases*. London: HMSO.

Ellis, H.D., Shepherd, J.W. & Davies, G.M. (1979). Identification of familiar and unfamiliar faces from internal and external features: Some implications for theories of face recognition. *Perception, 8*, 431–439.

Gronlund, S.D., Carlson, C.A., Dailey, S.B. & Goodsell, C.A. (2009). Robustness of the sequential lineup advantage. *Journal of Experimental Psychology: Applied, 15*, 140–152.

Harris, M.J. & Rosenthal, R. (1985). Mediation of interpersonal expectancy effects: 31 meta-analyses. *Psychological Bulletin, 97*, 363–386.

Henderson, Z., Bruce, V. & Burton, A.M. (2001). Matching the faces of robbers captured on video. *Applied Cognitive Psychology, 15*, 445–464.

Home Office (2011) *Police and Criminal Evidence Act 1984 code D of practice for the identification of persons by police officers*. Retrieved 24 November 2011 from http://www.homeoffice.gov.uk/publications/police/operational-policing/pace-codes/pace-code-d-2011

Innocence Project. (2010). *Eyewitness misidentification*. Retrieved 24 August 2011 from www.innocerceproject.org/understand/Eyewitness-Misidentification.php

Juslin, P., Olsson, N. & Winman, A. (1996). Calibration and diagnosticity of confidence in eyewitness identification: Comments on what can be inferred from the low confidence-accuracy correlation. *Journal of Experimental Psychology: Learning, Memory and Cognition, 22*, 1304–1316.

Lindsay, D.S., Read, J.D. & Sharma, K. (1998). Accuracy and confidence in person identification: The relationship is strong when witnessing conditions vary widely. *Psychological Science, 9*, 215–218.

Lindsay, R.C.L., Lea, J.A. & Fulford, J.A. (1991). Sequential lineup presentation: Technique matters. *Journal of Applied Psychology, 76*, 741–745.

Lindsay, R.C.L., Martin, R. & Webber, L. (1994). Default values in eyewitness descriptions: A problem for the match-to-description lineup foil selection strategy. *Law and Human Behavior, 18*, 527–541.

Lindsay, R.C.L. & Wells, G.L. (1985). Improving eyewitness identification from lineups: Simultaneous versus sequential presentation. *Journal of Applied Psychology, 66*, 343–350.

Luus, C.A.E. & Wells, G.L. (1991). Eyewitness identification and the selection of distracters for lineups. *Law and Human Behavior, 15*, 43–57.

Mecklenburg, S.H. (2006). *Report to the legislature of the State of Illinois: The Illinois pilot program on sequential double-blind identification procedures*. Retrieved 24 August 2011 from https://portal.chicagopolice.org/portal/page/portal/ClearPath/News/Statistical Reports/Legal Reports/Illinois Pilot Report on Eyewitness identification Methods

Meissner, C.A. & Brigham, J.C. (2001). Thirty years of investigating the own-race bias in memory for faces. *Psychology, Public Policy and Law, 7*, 3–35.

Meissner, C.A., Tredoux, C.G., Parker, J.F. & MacLin, O. (2005). Eyewitness decisions in simultaneous and sequential lineups: A dual-process signal detection theory analysis. *Memory & Cognition, 33*, 783–792.

Memon, A., Hope, L. & Bull, R. (2003). Exposure duration: Effects on eyewitness accuracy and confidence. *British Journal of Psychology, 94*, 339–354.

Morgan, C.A., Hazlett, G., Doran, A., Garrett, S., Hoyt, G., Thomas, P., Baranoski, M. & Southwick, S.M. (2004). Accuracy of eyewitness memory for persons encountered during exposure to highly intense stress. *International Journal of Law and Psychiatry. 27*, 265–279.

Norris, C., McCahill, M. & Woods, D. (2004). The growth of CCTV: A global perspective on the international diffusion of video surveillance in publicly accessible space. *Surveillance and Society, 2*, 110–135. Retrieved 24 August 2011 from www.surveillance-and-society.org/cctv.htm

Odinot, G., Wolters, G. & Lavender, T. (2009). Repeated partial eyewitness questioning causes confidence inflation but not retrieval induced forgetting. *Applied Cognitive Psychology, 23*, 90–96.

O'Rourke, T.E., Penrod, S.D. & Cutler, B.L. (1989). The external validity of eyewitness identification research: Generalizing across subject populations. *Law and Human Behavior, 13*, 385–397.

Phillips, M.R., McAuliff, B.D., Kovera, M.B. & Cutler, B.L. (1999). Double-blind photoarray administration as a safeguard against investigator bias. *Journal of Applied Psychology, 84*, 940–951.

Pike, G., Brace, N. & Kyman, S. (2002). *The visual identification of suspects: Procedures and practice. Briefing note 2/02.* London: Policing and Reducing Crime Unit, Home Office Research Development and Statistics Directorate. Retrieved 24 August 2011 from www.homeoffice.gov.uk/rds/prgbriefpubs1.html

Pike, G., Kemp, R., Brace, N., Allen, J. & Rowlands, G. (2000). The effectiveness of video identification parades. *Proceedings of the British Psychological Society, 8*, 44.

Pozzulo, J. & Warren, K.L. (2003). Descriptions and identifications of strangers by youth and adult eyewitnesses. *Journal of Applied Psychology, 88*, 315–323.

Schank, R.C. & Abelson, R.P. (1977). *Scripts, plans, goals and understanding.* Hillsdale NJ: Lawrence Erlbaum Associates Inc.

Searcy, J.H., Bartlett, J.C. & Memon, A. (1999). Age differences in accuracy and choosing in eyewitness identification and face recognition. *Memory & Cognition, 27*, 538–552.

Searcy, J.H., Bartlett, J.C. & Memon, A. (2000). Relationships of availability, lineup conditions, and individual differences to false identification by young and older eyewitnesses. *Legal and Criminological Psychology, 5*, 219–236.

Searcy, J.H., Bartlett, J.C., Memon, A. & Swanson, K. (2001). Ageing and lineup performance at long retention intervals. Effects of metamemory and context reinstatement. *Journal of Applied Psychology, 86*, 207–214.

Semmler, C, Brewer, N. & Wells, G.L. (2004). Effects of postidentification feedback on eyewitness identification and nonidentification confidence. *Journal of Applied Psychology, 89*, 334–346.

Shapiro, P.N. & Penrod, S.D. (1986). Meta-analysis of facial identification studies. *Psychological Bulletin, 100*, 139–156.

Shepherd, J.W. (1983). identification after long delays. In S.M.A. Lloyd-Bostock & B.R. Clifford (Eds.) *Evaluating eyewitness evidence* (pp.173–187). Chichester: John Wiley & Sons, Inc.

Slater, A. (1994). *Identification parades: A scientific evaluation.* London: Police Research Group (Police Research Award Scheme), Home Office.

Sporer, S., Penrod, S., Read, D. & Cutler, B.L. (1995). Choosing, confidence and accuracy: A meta-analysis of the confidence-accuracy relations in eyewitness identification studies, *Psychological Bulletin, 118*, 315–327.

Steblay, N.K. (1992). A meta-analytic review of the weapon focus effect. *Law and Human Behavior, 16*, 413–423.

Steblay, N.K. (1997). Social influence in eyewitness recall: A meta-analytic review of lineup instruction effects. *Law and Human Behavior, 21*, 283–297.

Steblay, N.K., Dysart, J.E. & Wells, G.L. (2011). Seventy-two tests of the sequential lineup superiority effect: A meta-analysis and policy discussion. *Psychology, Pubic Policy & Law, 17*, 99–139.

Technical Working Group for Eyewitness Evidence. (1999). *Eyewitness evidence: A guide for law enforcement.* Washington: US Department of Justice. Retrieved 24 August 2011 from www.ojp.usdoj.gov/nij/pubs-sum/178240.htm

Tunnicliff, J.L. & Clark, S.E. (2000). Selecting foils for identification lineups: Matching suspects or descriptions? *Law and Human Behavior, 24*, 231–258.

Valentine, T. (1991). A unified account of the effects of distinctiveness, inversion and race in face recognition. *Quarterly Journal of Experimental Psychology, 43A*, 161–204.

Valentine, T., Darling, S. & Memon, A. (2007). Do strict rules and moving images increase the reliability of sequential identification procedures? *Applied Cognitive Psychology, 21*, 933–949.

Valentine, T. & Endo, M. (1992). Towards an exemplar model of face processing: The effects of race and distinctiveness. *Quarterly Journal of Experimental Psychology, 44A*, 671–703.

Valentine, T., Harris, N., Colom Piera, A. & Darling, S. (2003). Are police video identifications fair to African-Caribbean suspects? *Applied Cognitive Psychology, 17*, 459–476.

Valentine, T. & Heaton, P. (1999). An evaluation of the fairness of police line-ups and video identifications. *Applied Cognitive Psychology, 13*, S59–S72.

Valentine, T. & Mesout, J. (2009). Eyewitness identification under stress in the London Dungeon. *Applied Cognitive Psychology, 23*, 151–161.

Valentine, T., Pickering, A. & Darling, S. (2003). Characteristics of eyewitness identification that predict the outcome of real lineups. *Applied Cognitive Psychology, 17*, 969–993.

Wagenaar, W.A. & Van der Schrier, J. (1996). Face recognition as a function of distance and illumination: A practical tool for use in the courtroom. *Psychology, Crime & Law, 2*, 321–332.

Wells, G.L. (1993). What do we know about eyewitness identification? *American Psychologist, 48*, 553–571.

Wells, G.L. (2008). Field experiments on eyewitness identification: Towards a better understanding of pitfalls and prospects. *Law and Human Behavior, 32*, 6–10.

Wells G.L. & Bradfield, A.L. (1998). 'Good you identified the suspect': Feedback to eyewitnesses distort their reports of the witnessing experience' *Journal of Applied Psychology, 66*, 688–696.

Wells, G.L., Rydell, S.M. & Seelau, E. (1993). The selection of distractors for eyewitness lineups. *Journal of Applied Psychology, 78*, 835–844.

Wright, D.B. & McDaid, A.T. (1996). Comparing system and estimator variables using data from real lineups. *Applied Cognitive Psychology, 10*, 75–84.

Wright, D.B. & Skagerberg, E.M. (2007). Postidentification feedback affects real eyewitnesses. *Psychological Science, 18*, 172–178.

ANNOTATED READING LIST

Bogan, P. & Roberts, A. (2011). *Identification: Investigation, trial and scientific evidence* (2nd edn). London: Jordans. *A comprehensive source on English law applied to identification evidence.*

Schachter, D.L. (1999). The seven sins of memory. Insights from psychology and cognitive neuroscience. *American Psychologist, 54*, 183–203. *An authoritative review of the evidence of the fallibility of human memory including memory distortions such as misattribution, suggestibility and bias. It is argued that these flaws of human memory are the byproduct of otherwise adaptive features of memory.*

Thompson, J. (2000, 18 June). I was certain but I was wrong, *New York Times*. Retrieved 24 August 2011 from http://truthinjustice. org/positive id.htm. *A compelling statement by Jennifer Thompson, who confidently identified Ronald Cotton as the man who raped her. Ronald Cotton was subsequently exonerated by DNA evidence after serving 11 years of a life sentence.*

Valentine, T. (2006). Forensic facial identification. In A. Heaton-Armstrong, E. Shepherd, G. Gudjonsson & D. Wolchover (Eds.) *Witness testimony; Psychological, investigative and evidential perspectives* (pp. 281–309). Oxford: Oxford University Press. *A literature review of eyewitness identification and identification from CCTV, which integrates the psychological literature with the procedures and cases in English law.*

Wells, G.L., Memon, A. & Penrod. S. (2006). Eyewitness evidence. Improving its probative value. *Psychological Science in the Public Interest, 7*, 45–75. *Review of eyewitness identification evidence principally from an American perspective; features a substantial review of interviewing witnesses and the cognitive interview.*

Wilcock, R., Bull, R. & Milne, R. (2009). *Witness identification in criminal cases: Psychology and practice*. Oxford: Oxford University Press. *Comprehensive review of research on eyewitness identification; includes material on person descriptions, vulnerable witnesses and identification by voice and gait.*

15 Role of the Expert Witness

BRIAN R. CLIFFORD

CHAPTER OUTLINE

expert witnesses the law of evidence recognises two types of witness: the *common witness to fact* and the *expert witness*. Expert witnesses are those qualified to express a professional opinion, by their training, knowledge and experience.

The use of **expert witnesses** by the court is not a modern phenomenon. Such witnesses have been employed since at least the 14th century (Wigmore, 1978) and experts have been appearing for the rival parties to a dispute since about the 18th century (Miller & Allen, 1998). While the legal purpose of engaging such witnesses has always been the same – to provide expertise that the triers of fact do not possess – the ground rules for their admissibility has undergone constant revision (R v. Turner [1975]; Clifford, 2003; Mackay et al., 1999).

In this chapter we will focus on three controversial forensic psychology areas – mistaken visual and voice identification; child witnesses, with specific reference to sexual abuse cases; and recovered memories – and explore the possible roles that expert witnesses can play in their resolution. We will see how the role of the expert witness has expanded, and note that there are differences in the acceptance of expert testimony in different countries and in different legal systems. At base, however, it will be argued that it is the quality of the science that experts rely upon in giving testimony that is at issue. It will be concluded that expert witnesses have the potential to aid the trial process but that realising this potential is not a simple or settled matter within the psychological community.

THE EVOLUTION OF THE EXPERT WITNESS

Historically, it can be seen that courts initially preferred experts who testified about non-human factors rather than human factors; then, later, experts who testified about human physical states rather than mental states. When experts concerning mental states were accepted, the courts preferred experts who testified about abnormal mental states rather than normal mental states. Within this, courts preferred psychiatric experts over clinical psychology experts because the former were grounded in medical science. Only lately have the courts come to accept experts whose expertise lies in experimental investigations of normal states of mind, who study memory, perception and language. Until fairly recently, such normal human processes were held to be within the knowledge and experience of the jury, the triers of fact, thus requiring no expert opinion to clarify or inform their rational decision-making roles (see Clifford, 2003; Mackay et al., 1999).

This evolution of the type of expert acceptable to the court can be traced in both the adversarial and inquisitorial court systems, although, historically, the inquisitorial system has employed experts for longer than the adversarial system (Spencer, 1998).

While the USA, UK, Australia, New Zealand and Canada all employ the adversarial method of trial, the use of normal-mental-state experts varies quite markedly among these countries (see Kapardis, 1997 for an excellent account of the admissibility of expert testimony in each of these jurisdictions). As an example, such expert testimony has been much more prevalent in the USA than the UK. Yet the use of experts in the USA is much more formalised and codified than in the UK. In the former the admissibility of experts is governed by landmark cases such as *Frye* (1923) (the **Frye test**; *Frye v. United States* 293 F.1013 [D.C.Cir.1023]) and later *Daubert* (1993) (the **Daubert test**; *Daubert v. Merrell Dow Pharmaceuticals Inc.* 509 U.S., 113 S.Ct. 2786 1993), which specify the conditions that must be met to allow an expert to testify. The judge in all jurisdictions, however, is the ultimate 'gatekeeper' of whether or not expert testimony is allowable.

Frye test US legal test to decide whether to admit or exclude expert testimony. Stipulated that scientific testimony was admissible only if it was based on a generally accepted theory or research findings in the field.

Daubert test a ruling on the admissibility of expert testimony, following *Daubert v. Merrell Dow Pharmaceuticals, Inc.* (1993), which stressed the testimony offered should be based on information on sound scientific methods.

If deemed admissible, whatever form the experts' opinion takes, on whatever subject matter, while the aim of that testimony is to aid the triers of fact in coming to a reasoned and reasonable decision, the expert must not trespass upon the 'ultimate issue'. This stipulation prohibits any witness from giving his or her opinion about a matter if it is the very question on which the court is called to determine (i.e. the fact at issue – for example, was *this specific child* sexually abused? Is *this specific witness* reliable?). This fine line, between addressing the ultimate issue but not opining upon it, lies at the heart of much of the controversy concerning the role of the expert witness.

WHO IS AN EXPERT?

An expert witness is so designated by the court system, not by one's profession. The British Psychological Society (BPS) publication, *Psychologists as Expert Witnesses: Guidelines and Procedures for England and Wales* (2007) defines an expert witness as 'a person who through special training, study or experience, is able to furnish the Court, tribunal, or oral hearing with scientific or technical information which is likely to be outside the experience and knowledge of a judge, magistrate, convenor or jury' (p.2). These guidelines stress that the expert's role is to assist the court and not the parties instructing them. It goes on to point out that the main difference between an expert witness and an ordinary witness (i.e. a witness to fact) is that the expert witness is able to give an opinion whereas the ordinary witness can only give factual statements or evidence. Thus, to give best evidence the expert must be qualified by education, training, experience, skill and knowledge. Their area of expertise must fit with the issue at trial. The database to which they make recourse must be sufficiently valid and reliable to allow definitive statements, opinions, conclusions and assertions under both direct and cross-examination, or in the face of counter experts. Lastly, the expert must be prepared to get involved in the adversarial process in which their scientific credentials, objectivity and expertise can be attacked by counsel less concerned with either truth or justice than with asserting his or her client's position and using any and all means — fair or foul – to have it prevail. The courtroom is the arena of choice of the barrister, not the expert. The barrister knows the rules of the game, what the game is and how best to play that game; the expert does not. The BPS guidelines (British Psychological Society, 2007) offer some useful suggestions on how to manage several of the practical, ethical and legal issues that can arise while serving as an expert witness.

An expert witness can give testimony in open court (Figure 15.1), or they may provide expert reports or opinions to be presented in court or after trial, but before sentencing, but not actually appear as a witness. Experts may also act as advisor to counsel faced with the other side's expert. Clearly, then, there are gradations of 'being an expert'. The nature, scope and practices of experts in the UK have been surveyed in three separate questionnaires by Gudjonsson (1985; 1996; 2007/8). More written reports were prepared than oral testimony was given. The ratio varied between civil and criminal proceedings, with oral testimony being much more prevalent in criminal cases. However, even in criminal courts most expert testimony is in the form of written reports, with oral testimony being the exception rather than the rule.

Some 45 per cent of all respondents who had given oral evidence said they were extensively cross-examined. In the 1995 survey (Gudjonsson, 1996), 44 per cent said they had faced an opposing expert, compared to the earliest, 1985, report (Gudjonsson, 1985), in which only 22 per cent experienced an opposing expert. Pleasingly, between 95 per cent and 97 per cent of those experts proffering expert testimony reported that they found the court positively disposed towards their testimony.

Irrespective of the type of case, an expert psychologist may be called upon either (a) to talk *directly to a fact or consideration at issue*, such as competence to stand trial,

FIGURE 15.1 *An expert witness can give testimony in open court, or provide expert reports or opinions to be presented in court or after trial.*
Source: © Stephen Coburn. Used under licence from Shutterstock.

hyper-suggestibility, being 'of sound mind' or (b) to *perform an educative function* such as discussing factors that could cause a witness to be unreliable, a victim to succumb to suggestion, or explain why an abused child could be asymptomatic (i.e. show no signs of abuse), had delayed disclosing the abuse, or recanted on one or more occasions. If the experts are asked to perform the first type of role they almost certainly will have examined the defendant and, as such, the expertise will be that of a psychologist, clinician or therapist. If asked to perform the latter role, the expert will not have interacted with the defendant, victim or witness, and the expertise will be that of a researcher or experimental psychologist. An example of this approach can be seen in one of my cases (Case Study 15.1). As we will see, the epistemological, or knowledge base, of these two types of testimony are held to be quite conflicting and antithetical.

Irrespective of the expert's area of expertise, clinical or scientific, a critical consideration is the reliability and validity of the database that the expert will rely upon to underpin his or her testimony. As we consider the role of the expert in certain controversial areas, we will note the centrality of database integrity and how issues such as **ecological validity**, generalisability, internal and external validity and replicability keep appearing.

ecological validity the degree to which experimental conditions reproduce real-life situations accurately. Ecological validity is closely related to external validity.

To ensure 'fitness for purpose', any expert witness must be an active researcher, that is, a person who publishes peer-reviewed papers, who reads the relevant literature carefully, critically and comprehensively, and has a reasoned grasp of the issues that could be raised by the parties to the dispute to which they have been summoned. In this regard, the *Guidelines on Memory and the Law: Recommendations from the Scientific Study of Memory* (British Psychological Society, 2008, revised 2010) is interesting. These guidelines urged the courts to rely exclusively upon expert testimony from what they termed 'memory experts', defined as those with 'relevant outputs' such as peer-reviewed publications. However, while peer-reviewed publications in the field of memory may be a necessary condition for presenting yourself as an expert witness, it may not be a sufficient condition. The highly published 'expert' who fails to appreciate the conceptual distinction between a child's testimony and an adult's recording of that testimony, or an adult's currently-expressed recollection of their childhood experience, will be exposed by the court as less than an expert. Such awareness may, in fact, be critical for a **de facto** as opposed to a **de jure** expert testimony that is helpful to the courts. Several recent appeal cases have served to make this point (for example, *R v. E* [2009] EWCA Crim 1370).

de facto literally, 'in actual fact'. What is in fact or in practice the case, irrespective of what legally or should in theory be the case.

de jure literally 'according to law; by right'. The legal or theoretical position, which may not correspond with reality.

CASE STUDY 15.1   APPEAL COURT, HIGH COURT OF JUDICIARY, EDINBURGH, 2004

Case: Murder
Expert witness: Professor Brian R. Clifford
Expert role: Experimentalist

In 2001 I received a call from the Scottish Criminal Cases Review Commission enquiring if I would be interested in acting as an expert witness in the third appeal of Campbell, Steele and Gray who were convicted on murder charges in what were known as the 'Ice Cream Wars' in Glasgow in 1984. The appeal aspect I was approached about concerned putative independent, verbatim-identical, recall by several policemen of a number of supra-span (i.e. exceeding short-term memory capacity) utterances allegedly made by the appellants, under various time delays and verbal interference conditions. At base this was a psycholinguistic issue that, by publication, training, experience and education (PhD in Psycholinguistics; MSc in Artificial Intelligence and Natural Language Processing), I was qualified to offer an expert opinion.

I decided that while extant psycholinguistic theory and data could talk to the issue of the possibility of verbatim recall under specific conditions of the case, novel, case-relevant data would be more compelling. I thus ran four experiments in which I manipulated mental set, various delay intervals and verbal interference conditions to ascertain if the degree of memory exhibited by the various police personnel in the case under appeal was probable. In the event, not one of my 224 participants was able to recall what all four police officers averred they did. Given that these new data replicated known limits of short-term verbatim memory, and meshed with accepted theory in psycholinguistics, the appeal judges concluded: 'In our view, the new evidence is of such significance that the verdicts of the jury, having been returned in ignorance of it, must be regarded as miscarriages of justice'.

H.M.A. v. Campbell, Steele & Gray. Appeal Court, High Court of Justiciary Opinion of the Court, 17 March 2004.

CONTROVERSY: MISTAKEN IDENTIFICATION

Known cases of mistaken identification (Scheck et al., 2000) imply the need for expert witnesses. Many exonerations, pardons or setting aside of previous convictions clearly indicate that something is amiss with this class of evidence (see Chapter 14).

The experimental psychologist would contend that a great many factors (see Clifford, 1979) and estimator and system variables (see Chapter 14; also Wells, 1978) are unknown to the lay person (jurors) and should be brought to their attention to ensure that justice is done.

There is another line of reasoning, however, that would drive an alternative conclusion. This line would concede that (a) we can agree that memory comprises encoding, storage and retrieval components, and (b) various system and estimator variables can impinge on one or more of these stages to reduce the veracity of memory. However, just what phases, and to what degree, we can never know, and certainly not in the case of a particular witness/victim in a particular case that is being tried. By offering expert testimony against this background of uncertainty, such testimony may unjustifiably increase scepticism on the part of jurors where it is not merited.

In addition, to what extent do controlled laboratory studies generalise to real-life crimes? How often should a finding replicate before it is regarded as a 'fact'? What if a finding replicates but in one case the variable's effect size (magnitude) is large (.8 or above), in another medium (.6) and in a third only small (.2)? And how do we weigh all the known (and possibly larger unknown) studies that have not replicated the effect?

Over and above factors that may or may not have been operational, and effects that may or may not be present in a particular case, there is another consideration. Experimental psychology is largely predicated upon group means, with overlap between the distributions. What this means in practice is that while an experimental group as a whole may perform 'better' than a control group, any one member of the experimental group may, in fact, perform more poorly than any one member of the 'poorer' group. More concretely, if we find that 70 per cent of an experimental group give an incorrect identification under condition x, how do we know that the particular witness in the particular case currently being tried, that involves condition x, falls into the 70 per cent category and not the 30 per cent category? We just cannot possibly know. How, then, can we possibly seek to educate the jury when what we may be doing is rendering them more sceptical than they need to be in the particular case

at hand? If this line of reasoning is adopted then expert testimony may be more prejudicial than probative (see Ebbesen & Konecni, 1996).

And yet, as concerned citizens, we must be disquieted by the findings of the Innocence Project (www.innocenceproject.org) that post-conviction DNA testing to prove innocence has, to date (February, 2011), served to exonerate 266 wrongfully convicted persons. In the majority of these cases eyewitness evidence is asserted to have been a leading cause of the convictions (see Valentine, this volume).

Expert testimony may be the mandated solution. However, because of the constantly shifting, refining and nuancing database that would underpin such testimony, testifying experts must be very circumspect as to what they will be prepared to testify about, and to what extent they will be prepared to present conditional, probabilistic, contextualised statements, rather than definitive, singular and certain opinions. The expert's true role is education, not advocacy or partisanship (e.g. Miller & Allen, 1998). Relevant testimony will explain the general principles relevant to the case, data relied upon in coming to a conclusion, and why these data were relied upon, and finally the lines of reasoning used to get from these data to the conclusion being offered. As an example, both the USA (see Yarmey, 2003) and the UK (PACE, 1984; 2005) have implemented guidelines for identification evidence and, as such, any deviations from these guidelines or protocols can and perhaps should be raised in court and would be a legitimate area of expert testimony.

As indicated above, one of the major concerns with using expert testimony in cases involving identification evidence is the possibility that such testimony will increase the general level of scepticism concerning all such evidence, where in fact such scepticism may not be justified in a particular case. Several studies have looked at this scepticism issue and, additionally, the possibility that such testimony can increase juror sensitivity to factors causing bias and thus unreliability in identification.

In a study by Devenport et al. (2002), 800 mock jurors viewed a videotaped trial that included information about a line-up identification procedure. Suggestiveness of the identification procedure varied in terms of foil selection bias, instruction bias (being told that the perpetrator may or may not be present, or not being told this) and presentation bias (simultaneous line-ups being categorised as biased, sequential line-ups as unbiased). The researchers were interested in the degree to which expert testimony would sensitise mock jurors to these three separate factors affecting line-up suggestiveness. They found that initially jurors were sensitive to foil-selection bias but not to instruction bias or presentation bias. Expert testimony served to enhance sensitivity to instruction but not presentation bias. Importantly, there was little evidence for expert testimony creating an overall sceptical attitude to identification evidence.

The second study was conducted by Leippe *et al.* (2004). In two experiments, 453 mock jurors read a murder trial transcript that either included or did not include general expert testimony about eyewitness memory. The expert testimony was given either before the evidence in the case, or after the evidence was presented. The judge's final instructions to the jury either did or did not remind the jury of the expert's testimony. Leippe *et al.* found that expert testimony decreased perception of guilt and eyewitness believability *if* it followed the evidence *and* was mentioned by the judge but not if it preceded the evidence and was not mentioned by the judge. This was the case whether the prosecution case was moderately weak or moderately strong. The fact that the timing of the expert testimony was critical, and that it needed to be supported by the judge's reminding, serves to rule out the fear that presentation of expert eyewitness testimony would have the effect of increasing scepticism about eyewitness evidence *per se*, whether justified or not in the specific case at hand.

These two studies taken together indicate that the introduction of expert testimony does not 'colour' the jurors' verdicts in a gross way by increasing global scepticism of all eyewitness testimony and identification. Rather they indicate that both general (Leippe *et al.*, 2004) and more specific expert testimony (Devenport *et al.*, 2002) can be beneficial in enhancing sensitivity to critical aspects of bias depending on its timing and support within the overall trial.

All that has been said above concerning visual identification also applies, only more so, to voice identification (Clifford, 1980; 1983; Yarmey, 2007). Voice identification has played a central role in several recent cases (see *HMA v. Thomas Sheridan* [2010] High Court, Glasgow, October–December; *R v. Doheny & Adams* [1997] (1) Cr App. R.369; *R v. Flynn & St John* EWCA Crim 970 [02 May 2008]; *R v. Khan & Bains* [2003] Central Criminal Court; *R v. O'Doherty* NICA B 51 [19 April 2002]; *R v. Robb* [1991] 93 Cr App. R.161). Cases involving voice identification, while exhibiting all the difficulties and conflicts inherent in visual identification, have an additional level of complexity. In voice identification cases three different sets of experts are likely to be involved: (a) experts concerned with the lay person's ability to recognise or identify either a familiar or a once, or infrequently, heard voice; (b) experts associated with aural-perceptual identification of voice similarity; and (c) those concerned with problems of **acoustic analysis** of speech

acoustic analysis (of speech samples). Methods of analysis used by phoneticians, which focus upon the use of computer-assisted analysis of the physical (not perceptual) properties of an utterance, such as fundamental frequency.

output from a reference source and a questioned source. These three sets of experts frequently differ both among themselves and with the other types of expert.

Experts on lay listener's voice memory ability are confronted with experimental evidence that shows that, for example, with familiar voices, recognition/identification accuracy can range from 100 per cent accuracy (e.g. Hollien *et al.*, 1983) through 80 per cent+ accuracy (e.g. Blatchford & Foulkes, 2006), 60 per cent accuracy (e.g. Goldstein & Chance, 1985) and 50 per cent accuracy (e.g. Barsics & Bredart, 2010), to only 30 per cent (e.g. Read & Craik, 1995). Aural-perceptual experts (phoneticians; **aural-perceptual analysis**) have to confront the fact of both intra- and inter-speaker differences, and the fact that the human listener cannot distinguish perceptually certain acoustic features of a speech signal. The acoustic expert has to accept the crucial issue of the comparability and compatibility of the reference and questioned sample, and the omnipresent issue of the lack of population statistics against which acoustic analysis can be tested.

aural-perceptual analysis (of *speech utterances*). Methods of analyses, used by phoneticians, which focus on discernable heard speech characteristics such as rate, pitch, 'breathiness' and particular types of articulation of vowels and consonants.

CONTROVERSY: RELIABILITY OF CHILDREN'S TESTIMONY

Children have always been a problem for the law (Spencer & Flin, 1990). Originally, in England and Wales, **corroboration** and demonstrable understanding of truthfulness were required. With the increase in crime levels and the veritable explosion of **child sexual abuse (CSA)** cases worldwide, the law's perception, in some countries, of the child witness/victim has changed. Increasingly children have begun to have their voices both heard and believed.

corroboration confirmation by other or additional sources.

child sexual abuse (CSA). Forcing or enticing a child or young person to take part in sexual activities, including prostitution, whether or not the child is aware of what is happening.

Just as this right was being recognised, however, research was appearing that children could be shown to be especially suggestible and that they could be made to assert things that were deliberately instilled in, or subtly suggested to, them via strategic questioning protocols and tactical questions of a leading and closed nature (e.g. Ceci & Bruck, 1993; 1995).

Experts in the child witnessing domain, just as in the other domains discussed in this chapter, are, therefore, confronted with an apparently less than cohesive and consensual date base of research findings (see, for example, Davies & Malloy, 2011).

The resolution of this conflicting database of child studies can be achieved by looking at the nature of the questioning rather than focusing on the nature of the respondent. Children are no different in many respects from adults; both can be shown to be suggestible, **malleable**, susceptible to misleading information, and persuaded by verbal feedback.

malleable capable of being shaped by extraneous forces, such as other witnesses, questioners or self-reflection.

A key insight then in forensic testimony involving children is that it is not so much the child's memory that is at issue but rather the questioning strategy and tactics that have led up to the testimony (Figure 15.2; see Chapters 5 and 6). Where guidelines representing a distillate of best practice in interviewing, designed to ensure

FIGURE 15.2 *In forensic testimony involving children, it is not so much the child's memory that is at issue but rather the questioning strategy and tactics that have led up to the testimony.*

Source: © Tomasz Trojanowski. Used under licence from Shutterstock.

reliable testimony from children or vulnerable adults, have been ignored or flouted, this becomes a legitimate area of expert witness comment.

While the reliability of children's testimony can be considered problematical in 'everyday' witnessing situations, it is much more problematical when the child alleges sexual abuse. In CSA cases there are frequently different types of expert, different sets of data and different epistemological starting points.

Berliner (1998) argues that expert testimony is necessary in such cases because fact finders have little knowledge of the nature of CSA situations (e.g. Morison & Greene, 1992) and are sceptical about abuse. In other words, the prevailing norm is negativity concerning the credibility of children's testimony in such matters (e.g. Goodman, 1984; Raitt & Zeedyk, 2003). When a psychological expert testifies for the prosecution and provides statements that support or confirm abuse, the likelihood of conviction of the defendant is higher compared to when no expert is used (Bottoms *et al.*, 2007).

To offset this negative bias, American researchers have suggested that one of two types of expert testimony can be given. One is what Walker and Monahan (1987) call social framework testimony. This type of testimony provides a framework or background context based upon conclusions from psychological research designed to inform jurors of something they did not already know, or disabuse them of common but erroneous misconceptions concerning the nature of sexual abuse, reaction of victims, and the ways trauma can affect memory. A second type of testimony, often referred to as substantive testimony, is where the expert specifically opines that the child in the case has been abused or exhibits the characteristics commonly found in sexually abused children.

Legally, in the USA, social framework testimony is frequently allowed; substantive testimony is frequently disallowed, because it is a direct comment upon credibility (e.g. *United States v. Whitted* [1993] 994 F.2d. 444 [8th Cir.]).

Scientifically, substantive testimony causes concerns for experimental psychologists because many researchers assert that the data that underpin such testimony are unscientific, psychometrically weak (i.e. lacking either validity or reliability, or both) and are based on subjective opinion rather than objective fact. As Berliner (1998) notes, there is no empirical evidence that clinicians reliably arrive at the same conclusions from identical data sets. Indeed, McAnulty (1993) goes further and asserts that the scientific bases for expert opinion of a substantive nature about sexual abuse may not be sufficiently valid and reliable for admission in court.

Scientific support for the notion of a unique or universal response symptomology in CSA is lacking (Berliner, 1998). As an example, Kendall-Tackett *et al.* (1993) found no one symptom was present in more than half of sexually abused children. In addition, symptoms frequently found in abused children (anxiety, depression, low self-esteem) are also found in non-abused children, and thus can have aetiologies other than CSA. This would also be predicted from base-rate considerations (i.e. the naturally occurring frequency of anxiety, depression, and so on in the general population; Melton, 1994).

Because CSA is multifaceted, varying in nature, intensity, duration and frequency, it is not surprising that several models and associated checklists have been developed. One is the child sexual abuse accommodation syndrome (CSAAS; Summit, 1983) but CSAAS is deemed not to be a medically accepted scientific concept in *Bussey J v. Commonwealth* (Appellee Supreme Court. Sept 6 697 S.W. 2d 139 [Ky. 1985]). Others are the child sexual abuse syndrome (CSAS; Sgroi, 1982); post-traumatic stress disorder (PTSD; Walker, 1990) and the traumagenic model (Finkelhor & Browne, 1985). However, as Fisher (1995; Fisher & Whiting, 1998) points out, these are all symptom-based models derived from therapeutic contexts that have not been tested scientifically to form the basis of diagnosing whether CSA has occurred. As Fisher and Whiting (1998) state, few if any empirical studies testing the validity of checklists based on these theoretical models have been reported. Summit (1992) specifically asserts that the CSAAS is a clinical opinion not a scientific instrument, and the cause and effect relationship between factors themselves and with actual abuse is generally obscure.

In the light of the ultimate issue question, the most the expert can say, following the mapping of the child's behaviour to the various syndrome checklists, is that the evidence is 'consistent with' or 'indicative of' CSA having taken place. This may satisfy the law, but it does not satisfy the scientist, because as Lawlor (1998) points out, such phrases attempt to do by connotation (implication) what cannot be done by denotation (demonstration). While such phraseology apparently avoids talking directly to the ultimate issue, it is designed to leave the impression that CSA has been detected, which is unwarranted by the facts. 'Consistent with' and 'indicative of' ignore the issue of equifinality (the fact that the same set of symptoms can have different causes) and equicausality (the fact that the same cause – abuse – can have a multitude of different effects) (Baker, 1969). Put another way, an event that is consistent with another event only raises the possibility of the second event, not its probability.

In the USA, symptomological-based, substantive testimony appears more allowable when it is used for 'rehabilitative' purposes (Myers, 1993). Thus, where a defence is mounted that (1) the allegedly abused child does not exhibit behaviours and emotions commonly thought to be associated with an abused child, therefore (2) the child was not abused, thus (3) the defendant is innocent, substantive testimony can be offered to rehabilitate the allegation of abuse. Known symptomology of CSA can be presented to explain that asymptomatic behaviour, non-spontaneity, delay in reporting, gradual disclosure, refusal to report, and even recantation are all recognised symptoms of CSA. From the scientists' point of view, however, such evidence in rehabilitation is still unacceptable – bad science is always bad science, irrespective of its intent.

While symptomological checklists are the most prevalent form of evidence given by experts in substantive testimony, other techniques have also been deployed but are equally questionable scientifically. For example, **anatomically correct dolls (ACDs)** suffer from what Fisher and Whiting (1998) call the problem of definitive differentiation: both abused and non-abused children demonstrate sexuality in doll play (e.g. Dawson *et al.*, 1991). Statement validity analysis (SVA) and the criterion-based content analysis (CBCA) part specifically appear to be equally unscientific. Vrij (2005), after conducting a qualitative review of the first 37 studies in CBCA, concluded, 'It is argued that SVA evaluations are not accurate enough to be admitted as expert scientific evidence in criminal courts' (p.3). In a later, quantitative, study, the same author failed to uncover the underlying theoretical principles of CBCA scores, and concluded, 'a lack of theoretical foundation . . . makes it unclear what the possibilities and restrictions of the instrument are' (Vrij & Mann, 2006, p.347).

It would appear then that most substantive testimony lacks empirically based psychometric foundations. Fisher and Whiting (1998) stress that the expert witness must avoid the employment of clinically relevant but diagnostically unsubstantiated techniques for assessing symptoms of CSA. An expert must not confuse clinical judgement with scientific fact, thereby potentially slipping from educator to advocate. An example of this slippage can be seen in Case Study 15.2.

> **anatomically correct dolls (ACDs)** (also known as *anatomically-detailed dolls*). Dolls that have human-like genitalia. Sometimes used for interviewing children suspected of having been sexually assaulted.

How effective is expert testimony in CSA cases?

Crowley *et al.* (1994) looked at the impact of social framework testimony. They presented a videotaped simulation of a trial in which an expert testified about delayed disclosure, memory, suggestibility and reality monitoring. The mock jurors who heard the expert testifying rated the child witness as higher on memory ability, reality monitoring and resistance to suggestion. However, there was no relation to the verdict.

Klettke *et al.* (2010) looked at the potential effects of the prosecution expert's credentials, evidence strength and coherence on jury decisions in eight CSA cases. They found that the expert's evidence strength and coherence had significant effects on jury verdicts concerning the defendant's guilt.

Kovera and Borgida (1998) presented participants with a three-and-a-half-hour video of a simulated child sexual abuse trial, in which the alleged abused child was played by either an 8-year-old or a 14-year-old actress. They compared the effects of (1) social framework testimony, (2) substantive testimony and (3) a no-expert testimony condition. The substance of the expert testimony concerned the typical set of victim reactions to sexual abuse, and, in young children, their frequent lack of knowledge to communicate effectively about their abusive experiences due to their age. They found that the no-expert testimony condition resulted in a higher conviction rate of the defendant when the witness was 14, than when the child was 8. However, the child witness's age did not influence conviction rate when jurors were presented with either type of expert testimony. The researchers concluded that both general and specific expert-testimony served to correct jurors' perception of counterintuitive behavioural reactions to abuse exhibited by the younger child compared to the no-expert testimony condition.

From these studies it can be concluded that expert testimony of both the social framework and substantive kind can effect an educative function, by correcting misperceptions that jurors may have about such things as anxiety, hesitation, and clarity of description in a sexually abused child.

However, other studies are less positive concerning the involvement of experts. McAuliff and Duckworth (2010) investigated whether 223 jury-eligible persons were able to detect internally invalid psychological testimony presented at a CSA trial. The defence expert presented a study he had conducted on witness memory and suggestibility. The testimony was either valid, lacked a control group, had a confound, or harboured an experimental bias. Only a missing control group was clearly detected, with confounding and experimental bias being missed. Thus, potential jurors exhibited limited detection of internal validity threats in an expert's evidence. However, this study only presented expert evidence for one side of the dispute. Could an opposing expert for the opposing party sensitise jurors to invalid science proffered by an expert?

Levett and Kovera (2008) presented jurors with a written summary of a CSA case in which they manipulated the defence expert's testimony such that it was valid, lacked control groups or lacked required counterbalancing of questions. An opposing expert's testimony either addressed these methodological shortcomings, or offered only generalised rebuttal critiques of the research. A third condition involved no opposing expert testimony. Levett and Kovera (2008) found strong scepticism effects. When an opposing expert was present, verdicts and ratings were affected, irrespective of the nature of the opposing expert's testimony. There was little evidence of sensitisation effects concerning the flawed methodology of the defence expert's testimony. Thus there was no evidence that opposing expert testimony helped jurors distinguish between flawed and valid scientific testimony. These researchers concluded that it is unlikely that opposing experts will prevent junk science entering the court.

CASE STUDY 15.2 *STATE V. MICHAELS* (1988); STATE V. J.Q. (1993)

Case: Sexual abuse of children, Wee Care Day Nursery, New Jersey
Expert: Eileen Treacy
Expert role: Substantive testimony

In 1988 Treacy gave testimony consisting of both background information (social context testimony) and child-specific statements (substantive testimony). Based on analysis of pre-trial interviews and behaviour described by relatives of the children, together with the children's court testimony, Treacy testified that the children's testimony and conduct were consistent with child sexual abuse. She went on to define 'consistent with' as 'having a high degree of correlation, over .6 in numerical terms, and a probability' (*State v. Michaels* (1993), p.501). The jury convicted Michaels of abusing 19 children and sentenced her to 47 years.

In 1993 an appeal court overturned the decision on the grounds that Treacy's 'testimony constituted nothing less than substantive evidence of defendant's guilt' (p.501). This was based on *State v. J.Q.* (1993) where it was decided that while an expert witness could describe symptoms found in victims of CSA to aid jurors in evaluating specific defences (*State v. J.Q.* (1993), p.1197) they could not offer the opinion that abuse had, in fact, occurred.

A question you may like to ask yourself is, where did Treacy get the figure .6 from?

State v. Michaels (1993). 625 A.2d 489 (N.J. Superior Ct. App. Div.) 1993; 136 N.J. 299, 642, A.2d. 1372 1994; 642 A.2d. 1372 (N.J.) 1994.

State v. J.Q. (1993). 617 A.2d 1196 (N.J. 1993).

CONTROVERSY: RECOVERED MEMORIES

As Schacter *et al.* (1997) point out, the recovered memory debate is the most passionately contested battle that has ever been waged about the nature of human memory, and has involved a clash of paradigms between clinicians and experimentalists. However, the debate is far from being parochial: it has touched the lives of thousands of families across the globe and the emotional stakes for all involved are huge.

Consequently, the false/recovered memory debate has been frequently acrimonious and emotional, generating more heat than light (e.g. Lindsay & Read, 1994; 1997). And yet at base the fundamental issue or issues *seem* simple: the veridicality – truthfulness – of human memory (Conway, 1997); memory, trauma and suggestibility (Yapko, 1997); and forgetting, distortion and accuracy (Schacter *et al.*, 1997). In reality each of the named issues is the tip of a very large iceberg adrift in an ocean of ignorance. The recovered/false memory debate is beautifully captured by Donald Rumsfeld's (2002) homily, '. . . there are known knowns . . . there are known unknowns . . . but there are also unknown unknowns'.

We know that child sexual abuse happens too frequently – 5 per cent to 33 per cent in girls, and 3 per cent to 30 per cent in boys (e.g. Ghate & Spencer, 1995) – and estimates of suppressed memories range between 20 per cent and 40 per cent in a sample of adults who report CSA (e.g. Epstein & Bottoms, 2002). We know that traumatic memories are formed in some ways that are different from normal memories (e.g. Cahill *et al.*, 1994). We know that **dissociation** can be used defensively, giving rise to **amnesia** that can dissipate at a later date (e.g. Hornstein, 1992). But we also know that memory can be both highly reliable and unreliable, and can be influenced by suggestion, discussion and misinformation (e.g. Ceci & Bruck, 1993; 1995).

When we move from the known knowns to the troublesome known unknowns, we tend to move from objective fact to subjective inference. As an example we know that traumatic experiences can be encoded somewhat differently from non-traumatic experiences (e.g. Horowitz & Reidbord, 1992), being more vivid and integrated than more routine memories. However, while there has been

dissociation (also disassociation). A defensive disruption in the normally occurring connections between feelings, thoughts, behaviours and memories, consciously or unconsciously invoked, to reduce psychological distress during or after traumatic episodes.

amnesia loss of memory. Such loss can be selective or global.

an attempt to subsume CSA under the PTSD umbrella, PTSD is characterised by flashbacks, while recovered memories of sexual abuse are characterised by no recollection until recovery. Why do these two types of traumatic memory operate so differently? We must admit we know we don't know.

Given there is no valid way to distinguish between a genuine memory and a confabulated or illusory memory, without external corroboration, and that the existence of a true memory and its accuracy are conceptually distinct, we must again conclude that we don't know how to verify a memory account in the absence of external verification.

Specifically within the recovered memory arena, we must accept that the combination of a vulnerable client and a theoretically driven therapist is a potentially lethal concoction, pregnant with possibilities for 'recovered' or 'false' memory (Figure 15.3). But can people be led to believe that they have been abused when in reality they have not? Case examples of virtually impossible forms of abuse, such as alien abduction, that are vividly remembered make it clear that the answer is yes (e.g. French, 2003).

Demonstration of true recovered memories requires evidence of the abuse having taken place, intermittent forgetting of the event, and eventual recovery of the event in the absence of any other way of gaining knowledge of the abuse (Schooler *et al.*, 1997; Wright *et al.*, 2006). As Wright *et al.* (2006) indicate, a less stringent set of criteria underlies the supposed 101 corroborated cases compiled by Cheit (2005). To ensure inclusion in the Cheit archive the case must have 'strong corroboration', such as confession, guilty pleas or self-incriminating statements; testimony from other witnesses; or 'significant' circumstantial evidence. A guilty verdict can also ensure inclusion, but, of course, other factors could play a role in achieving such a verdict.

Against the wall of claim and counter-claim concerning recovered memories, some experimental psychologists have been trying to chip away at both logical and practical aspects of the recovery debate. Logically for a case of recovered memory to have credence there must have been an original memory that was then lost, and then subsequently recovered. One line of attack by sceptical cognitive psychologists is to question the reality of the actual forgetting of memories that are later recovered. A study by Merckelbach *et al.* (2006) is informative. They began by asking participants to recall any childhood memories that they could remember. In the next phase, just one hour or two days after this explicit remembering phase, the participants were asked if they had thought about certain specific events recently. These specific events included both events they had recalled in phase one and other, previously unrecalled, events. Many participants reported not having thought about previously recalled

FIGURE 15.3 *Within the recovered memory arena, the combination of a vulnerable client and a theoretically driven therapist is a potentially lethal concoction, pregnant with possibilities for 'recovered' or 'false' memory.*
Source: © Phase4Photography. Used under licence from Shutterstock.

events for years – despite having just recalled them one hour or two days before. Interestingly, Merckelbach *et al.* went on to run the same experiment with participants who had either 'continuous' or 'recovered' memories of CSA. They found that those who had 'recovered' memories of CSA were more likely to forget remembering the recent events recalled than 'continuous' memory participants. If it is simply the case that people who testify to recovered memory simply forget what they have remembered more frequently than those who remember CSA episodes continuously, then the 'recovered' memory debate drops away – or at least part of it does.

Therapeutic **iatrogenic** issues, whereby therapy produces the breeding ground for suggestion, remain, but 'recovered' memory falls back into the study of memory *per se*.

> **iatrogenic** the impact of the treatment process itself on a patient's symptoms. The term originated in medicine but is now applied in psychology, particularly to the impact of therapy on patient reports.

However, Raitt and Zeedyk (2003) argue that to approach the recovered memory debate from a purely scientific memory perspective is flawed. Such an approach, focused as it is only on memory processes, tends to treat abuse (the thing recovered) as a background societal context rather than as one of the components central to understanding the syndrome and its symptoms. This immediately contrasts experimentalists with clinicians (researchers with therapists). Therapists argue that the use of decontextualising methods (experiments) to investigate decontextualised processes (memory) cannot provide the kinds of insights that are necessary to understand the more complex aspects of (recovered) memory.

We have met this confrontation before in the controversy over the reliability and credibility of children's testimony – between those who treat the problem (clinicians) and those who study the problem (experimental researchers). At base there is a difference in epistemological orientation. Therapists do not seek a simple objective truth: researchers do. Therapists are not concerned with the veracity of the precipitating memory: researchers are. Therapists take the memory as a given and ask what impact that memory has: researchers ask, is the memory real? The law, and justice, require to know what the reality is in this domain. Did abuse take place? Does the victim have a veridical memory of actual abuse that can act as strong evidence of its occurrence? Can that memory be forgotten and then later be recovered? Because a defendant's liberty or reputation is at stake, the law requires answers to these questions. A case in point is how the concept of infantile amnesia (expanded to childhood amnesia in the BPS

Guidelines; British Psychological Society, 2008/2010) has been deployed by memory experts in court cases. While most memory researchers would accept the concept of infantile amnesia – lack of recallable memories encoded before the age of 3 years – far fewer would agree with the expansion of this lack of recallable memories to the age of 7, as the guidelines aver when they state, 'In general the accuracy of memories dating to below the age of 7 years cannot be established in the absence of independent corroborating evidence' (British Psychological Society, 2008/2010, p.13). When this type of expert testimony has been proffered it has been rejected by the court as both weakly supported by available evidence, and as going against common sense, which the jury are held to have as a result of collective experience.

What role then exists for the expert witness who appears in such cases? Clearly the role will be a complex one. A clinician may be asked to offer an opinion on the probability of the recovered memory actually being true, probably by a hypothetical, but close-to-case, line of argument. They may be drawn into statements such as 'consistent with' but we have already seen that such statements try to do by connotation what cannot be done by denotation. If the expert is an experimentalist, she or he could be asked to educate the jury as to possible mechanisms of lost but later recovered memory. For many researchers, to offer more than this is to slip into advocacy and partisanship.

On the basis of their review of the existing research literature, Wright et al. (2006) argue, firstly, that newly remembered recovered memories of past trauma are sometimes accurate, sometimes inaccurate or a mixture of both; secondly, much of what is recalled cannot be confirmed or disconfirmed; and thirdly, because of the two previous points, reports of trauma based on recovered memories are not reliable enough to be the sole basis for legal decisions.

The way forward in this most controversial area of expert testimony may be that suggested by Brewin and Andrews (1997) in their discussion of repression – the assumed mechanism of recovered memories. They argue there must be a dialogue between clinicians and experimentalists. Both parties must accept that causal and intentional explanations have equal value in understanding human behaviour. They must accept that while their respective data may be very different, nonetheless, both can be regarded as equally valuable in explaining mental states. If this dialogue takes place, then an overly narrow view of what is 'scientific' may be broadened and the phenomenon of recovered memory more quickly understood. The expert witness would then have a more solid base upon which to offer testimony.

WHAT CAN THE EXPERT WITNESS TELL THE COURT?

To date I have indicated that expert witnesses have increasingly aided the court in reaching decisions. However, the willingness and openness to experts testifying about normal human processes has been hard won, and is more prevalent in some jurisdictions, for example, the USA, than in others, such as the UK. Today, experts who offer testimony in areas of abnormality such as brain damage and mental impairment are generally welcome in civil and criminal courts, as it is recognised that such testimony can educate and sensitise the jury or the court as to the likely outcomes of such conditions and thus guide their decision-making.

However, the latest acceptance of expert evidence in such areas as have been discussed in this chapter, have traditionally been regarded as falling within the purview of the jury, particularly in the UK. Expert testimony in what has been called here normal-mental-state cases is designed to sensitise jurors to matters they may not have considered, to disabuse them of long-held but perhaps erroneous assumptions, preconceptions and lay theories, thus allowing them to reach better decisions and thus serve justice better. These are the true roles of the expert witness in such cases.

Several studies have shown that the knowledge eyewitness experts agree upon differs markedly from the views held by legal personnel and jury-eligible respondents. This has been demonstrated in, for example, Canada (Yarmey & Jones, 1983; but see Read & Desmarais, 2009), the USA (Benton et al., 2006; Kassin et al., 1989; 2001; Wise et al., 2009), Australia (McConkey & Roche, 1989), Norway (Magnussen et al., 2010) and the UK (Noon & Hollin, 1987). Thus there is a prima facie case that the knowledge experts in this field would bring to the court differs from the knowledge (beliefs) that they would find there, although Alonzo and Lane (2010) make the point that one needs to distinguish between 'saying' and 'judging' in assessing knowledge of eyewitness memory. However, there are a number of strident and dissenting voices to this conclusion. Ebbesen and Konecni (1996) make the point that most findings are inconsistent, inapplicable or invalid because either experimental procedures or measures used to study various relationships are not well tied to legal procedures, or particular findings are not well substantiated. In addition, they argue that knowledge about, for example, memory is so complex that any honest presentation of this knowledge to a court would only serve to confuse rather than improve the jury decision-making

> **prima facie** on the first view; at first glance/sight; on the face of it.

process. While Clifford (1997) broadly agreed with the basic tenets of this view, but argued that they over-stated their case, Yarmey (1997; 2001) disagreed with their assertions, pointing out that a great number of findings upon which experts would be prepared to offer testimony are reliable and consistent.

Only slowly is the law coming to realise that the lay person's beliefs and understandings in many fields may be misguided, biased, unexamined and, frankly, wrong. To the extent that they are so, then, for justice to prevail, these misconceptions and misapprehensions have to be addressed at trial and experts may be best placed to address them.

But are judges not better placed to educate the jury as to the misconceptions that lay people may have about basic human processes? The 1993 Daubert ruling clearly places the judge as 'gatekeeper' of the admissibility of scientific and non-scientific testimony. But is the judge capable of this level of discrimination?

Dahir et al. (2005), in a survey of USA judges, found that they neither understood nor applied the more technical Daubert guidelines. Gatowski et al. (2001) surveyed 400 state trial court judges about their understanding of the basic scientific criteria outlined in Daubert. Only 4 per cent of judges could give clear explanation of 'falsifiability' and 35 per cent gave answers that were unequivocally wrong. Only 4 per cent could explain 'error rate' and 86 per cent gave answers that were unequivocally wrong. The British Psychological Society's (2009) response to the Law Commission consultation on the admissibility of expert evidence in criminal proceedings in England and Wales, *A New Approach to the Determination of Evidentiary Reliability*, concluded that the Law Commission's preferred option of placing a greater gatekeeping role upon judges, while commendable in principle, may be difficult to achieve in practice, underestimating as it did the necessary time and learning involved to acquire sufficient knowledge to make informed judgements on the evidential value of the diverse range of reports and oral testimony provided by experts today.

What about during the trial? In both the USA and the UK, stress has been placed on the judge's instruction to the jury concerning key aspects of the case being tried. Thus, for example, it is argued that judges' instructions to juries about the dangers of identification evidence, or more precisely, the indicants of reliable identification, are held to be sufficient to sensitise the jury as to the issues concerning this most venerable but vulnerable form of evidence. Yet we know from research in the USA that jurors often fail to understand judges' instructions (e.g. Cutler et al., 1990); that they fail to apply them when they do understand them; and the supposed indicants of reliable identification are far from infallible (e.g. Brigham et al., 1999; Wells & Murray, 1983).

In the light of these qualifications, and the increased pace of knowledge production, there can be little doubt that expert witnessing will continue to grow in all areas of jurisprudence and in all systems of adjudication (see Faigman & Monahan, 2005; Huff, 2002).

CONCLUSION

Unreliable expert evidence can put justice in jeopardy. In 2006, American scientists announced that they had found strong evidence that sudden infant death syndrome (cot death) was caused by a genetic disorder. This contrasts strongly with the assertion made in court by a highly respected and distinguished expert witness, Professor Sir Roy Meadow, that one cot death is a tragedy, two suspicious and three murder, and that there is only a 1:73 million chance that two children in the same family would die of cot death (*R v. Cannings* EWCA Crim 1 [19 January, 2004]).

Expert evidence is admitted to provide expertise that fact finders do not have. The aim of such admittance is to assist them to reach the right decision. Only the expert who is asked to act as such can decide if he or she is sufficiently schooled, skilled and knowledgeable enough to fulfil that role. It is a judgement call – but a call of such magnitude that it should not be made lightly or without a great deal of thought and consideration. Ceci and Hembrooke (1998) may well be right when they assert that the quality of justice may be diminished without expert witnesses but, conversely, such witnessing must be ethical, moral, reliable, relevant and admissible if it is to serve such lofty ideals.

SUMMARY

- Expert witnesses have been employed by the courts for several centuries, but over time the areas in which they have been asked to testify has broadened. However, the acceptance of normal mental state experts shows wide national variability and general resistance.

- The role played by the expert witness can be that of clinician, experimentalist, actuary or advisor. Whatever the role, the expert must be qualified by education, training, experience, skill and knowledge.

- The major debate over the acceptance of expert witnesses is the nature and quality of the research that the expert would draw upon to offer testimony. In the case of normal mental state issues, the law believes the jury is sufficiently competent while international studies suggest they may not be. Within the psychological community generally, debate concerns the relative probative value of clinical judgement versus scientific fact. Within the experimental psychology community specifically, the concern is the reliability, validity, generalisability and hence applicability of laboratory-based findings to real-life forensic concerns.

- These debates were highlighted in the domains of face and voice identification, child witnesses and CSA cases, and false/recovered memory. In each area, differing roles for the expert witness were explored. Cutting across these three areas, however, was the stress on the expert witness role being one of education and information provision, rather than advocacy or partisanship.

- Cited studies in these three areas demonstrated that expert testimony could: enlighten juries as to problems in identification procedures while not creating an unjustified scepticism in overall witness testimony; dispel misconceptions about child sexual abuse, and its behavioural sequelae; and, in the case of recovered memories, give due consideration to both causal and intentional explanations of human behaviour, the respective roles of clinical and scientific knowledge, and the dangers of decontextualising the study of memory.

- Overall, it is considered that sound, research-based, expert witnessing has the power to enhance the quality of justice, while unsound, opinion-based, testimony can only diminish it.

ESSAY/DISCUSSION QUESTIONS

1. Select one area of potential legal dispute and identify the database that would be addressed by an expert called to give evidence in the case. How reliable and valid is that database?

2. How should psychology best address the transparency doctrine formulated by *R v. Turner* (1975) that non-disordered behaviour is fully transparent and therefore not in need of explanation or clarification by experts?

3. Are researchers and clinicians inevitably and irredeemably confrontational and conflicting?

4. Should experimental psychologists ever act as expert witnesses? Give reasons for your answer.

5. What, in your view, constitutes expertise in an expert witness?

REFERENCES

Alonzo, J.D. & Lane, S.M. (2010). Saying versus judging: Assessing knowledge of eyewitness memory. *Applied Cognitive Psychology, 24,* 1245–1264.

Baker, F. (1969). Review of general systems concepts and their relevance for medical care. *Systematics, 7,* 209–229.

Barsics, C. & Bredart, S. (2010). Recalling episodic information about personally known faces and voices. *Consciousness and Cognition, 2,* 303–308.

Benton, T.R., Ross, D.F., Bradshaw, E., Thomas, W.N. & Bradshaw, G.S. (2006). Eyewitness memory is still not common sense: Comparing jurors, judges and law enforcement to eyewitness experts. *Applied Cognitive Psychology, 20,* 115–129.

Berliner, L. (1998). The use of expert testimony in child sexual abuse cases: In S.J. Ceci & H. Hembrooke (Eds.) *Expert witnesses in child abuse* (pp.11–27). Washington, D.C.: American Psychological Association.

Blatchford, H. & Foulkes, P. (2006). Identification of voices in shouting. *Journal of Speech, Language and the Law. 13,* 241–254.

Bottoms, B.L., Golding, J.M., Stevenson, M.C., Wiley, T.R.A. & Yozwiak, J.A. (2007). A review of factors affecting jurors' decisions in child sexual abuse cases. In M.P. Toglia, J.D. Read, D.F. Ross & R.C.L. Lindsay (Eds.) *Handbook of eyewitness psychology* (pp.509–543). Mahwah, NJ; Lawrence Erlbaum.

Brewin, C.R. & Andrews, B. (1997). Reasoning about repression: Inferences from clinical and experimental data. In M.A. Conway (Ed.) *Recovered memories and false memories* (pp.192–205). Oxford: Oxford University Press.

Brigham, J.C., Wasserman, A.W. & Meissner, C.A. (1999). Disputed eyewitness identification evidence: Important legal and scientific issues. *Court Review, 36,* 12–25.

British Psychological Society. (2007). *Psychologists as expert witnesses: Guidelines and procedures for England and Wales.* Leicester: British Psychological Society.

British Psychological Society. (2008/2010). *Guidelines on memory and the law: Recommendations from the scientific study of human memory.* Leicester: British Psychological Society.

British Psychological Society. (2009, July). *Admissibility of expert evidence: British Psychological Society response to the Law Commission consultation: The admissibility of expert evidence in criminal proceedings in England and Wales (A new approach to the determination of evidentiary reliability).* Retrieved 23 August 2011 from www.justice.gov.uk/lawcommission/docs/cp190_Expert_Evidence_Consultation.pdf

Cahill, L., Prins, B., Weber, M. & McGaugh, J. (1994). B-adrenergic activation and memory for emotional events. *Nature, 371,* 702–704.

Ceci, S.J. & Bruck, M. (1993). The suggestibility of children's recollections: An historical review and synthesis. *Psychological Bulletin, 113,* 403–439.

Ceci, S.J. & Bruck, M. (1995). *Jeopardy in the courtroom: A scientific analysis of children's testimony.* Washington, D.C.: American Psychological Association Press.

Ceci, S.J. & Hembrooke, H. (1998). Introduction. In S.J. Ceci & H. Hembrooke (Eds.) *Expert witnesses in child abuse cases.* (pp.1–8). Washington D.C.: American Psychological Association.

Cheit, R.E. (2005). *The archive: 101 corroborated cases of recovered memory.* Recovered Memory Project. Retrieved 23 August 2011 from www.brown.edu/Departments/Taubman_Center/Recovmem/archive.html

Clifford, B.R. (1979). The relevance of psychological investigation to legal issues in testimony and identification. *Criminal Law Review, March,* 153–163.

Clifford, B.R. (1997). A commentary on Ebbesen and Konecni's eyewitness memory research: Probative v. prejudicial value. *Expert Evidence, 6,* 140–143.

Clifford, B.R. (1980). Voice identification by human listeners: On earwitness reliability. *Law and Human Behavior, 4,* 373–394.

Clifford, B.R. (1983). Memory for voices: The feasibility and quality of earwitness evidence. In S. Lloyd-Bostock & B.R. Clifford (Eds.) *Evaluating witness evidence* (pp.189–218). Chichester: John Wiley & Sons, Inc.

Clifford, B.R. (2003). Forensic psychology. In R.Bayne & I. Horton (Eds.) *Applied psychology* (pp.67–78). London: Sage.

Conway, M.A. (1997). Introduction: What are memories? In M.A. Conway (Ed.) *Recovered memories and false memories* (pp.1–22). Oxford: Oxford University Press.

Crowley, M.J., O'Callaghan, M.G. & Ball, P.G. (1994). The judicial impact of psychological expert testimony in a simulated child sexual abuse trial. *Law and Human Behaviour, 18,* 89–105.

Cutler, B.L., Dexter, H.R. & Penrod, S.D. (1990). Non adversarial methods for sensitising jurors to eyewitness evidence. *Journal of Applied Social Psychology, 20,* 1197–1207.

Dahir, V.B., Richardson, J.T., Ginsburg, G.P., Gatowski, S.J., Dobbin, S.A. & Merlino, M.L. (2005). Judicial application of Daubert to psychological syndrome and profile evidence. *Psychology, Public Policy and Law, 14,* 62–82.

Davies, G. & Malloy, L.C. (2011). Relationship between research and practice. In M. Lamb, D. La Rooy, L. Malloy & C. Katz (Eds.) *Children's testimony: A handbook of psychological research and forensic practice* (2nd edn.) Chichester: John Wiley & Sons, Inc.

Dawson, B., Vaughan, A.R. & Wagner, W.G. (1991). Normal responses to sexually anatomically detailed dolls. *Journal of Family Violence, 7,* 135–152.

Devenport, J.L., Stinson, V., Cutler, B.L. & Kravitz, D.A. (2002). How effective are the cross examination and expert testimony safeguards? Juror's perceptions of the suggestiveness and fairness of biased lineup procedures. *Journal of Applied Psychology, 87,* 1042–1054.

Ebbesen, E.B. & Konecni, V.J. (1996). Eyewitness memory research: Probative v. prejudicial value. *Expert Evidence, 5,* 1–2, 2–28.

Epstein, M.A. & Bottoms, B.L. (2002). Explaining the forgetting and recovery of abuse and trauma memories: Possible mechanisms. *Child Maltreatment, 7,* 210–225.

Faigman, D. L. & Monahan, J. (2005). Psychological evidence at the dawn of the law's scientific age. *Annual Review of Psychology, 56,* 631–659.

Finkelhor, D. & Browne, A. (1985). The traumatic impact of child sexual abuse: A conceptualisation. *American Journal of Orthopsychiatry, 55,* 530–541.

Fisher, C.B. (1995). The American Psychological Association's ethics code and the validation of sexual abuse in day-care settings. *Psychology, Public Policy and Law, 1,* 461–468.

Fisher, C.B. & Whiting, K.A. (1998). How valid are child sexual abuse validations? In S.J. Ceci & H. Hembrooke (Eds.) *Expert witnessing in child abuse cases* (pp.159–184). Washington D.C.: American Psychological Association.

French, C.C. (2003). Fantastic memories. *Journal of Consciousness Studies, 10,* 153–174.

Gatowski, S., Dobbins, S., Richardson, J., Ginsburg, G., Merlino, M. & Dahir, V. (2001). Asking the gatekeepers: A national survey of judges in judging expert evidence in a post-Daubert world. *Law and Human Behavior, 25,* 433–458.

Ghate, D. & Spencer, L. (1995). *The prevalence of child sexual abuse in Britain: A feasibility study for a large-scale national survey of the general population.* London: HMSO.

Goldstein, A.G. & Chance, J.E. (1985, May). *Voice recognition: The effects of faces, temporal distribution of 'practice' and social distance.* Paper presented at the annual meeting of the Mid-western Psychology Association, Chicago, IL.

Goodman, G.S. (1984). Children's testimony in historical perspective. *Journal of Social Issues, 40,* 9–31.

Gudjonsson, G.H. (1985). Psychological evidence in court: Results from the BPS survey. *Bulletin of the British Psychological Society, 38,* 327–330.

Gudjonsson, G.H. (1996). Psychological evidence in court: Results from the 1995 survey. *The Psychologist, May,* 213–217.

Gudjonsson, G.H. (2007/8). Psychologists as expert witnesses: The 2007 BPS survey. *Forensic Update, 92,* 23–29.

H.M.A. v. Campbell, Steele & Gray. Appeal Court, High Court of Justiciary Opinion of the Court, 17 March 2004.

Hollien, H., Bennett, G. & Gelfer, M.P. (1983). Criminal identification comparison: Aural versus visual identification resulting from simulated crime. *Journal of Forensic Sciences, 28,* 208–221.

Hornstein, G. (1992). The return of the repressed. *American Psychologist, 47,* 254–263.

Horowitz, M. & Reidbord, S. (1992). Memory, emotion and response to trauma. In S. Christianson (Ed.) *The handbook of emotion and memory: Research and theory* (pp.343–358). Hillsdale, N.J.: Erlbaum.

Huff, C.R. (2002). Wrongful conviction and public policy: The American Society of Criminology 2001 presidential address. *Criminology, 40,* 1–18.

Kapardis, A. (1997). *Psychology and law: A critical introduction.* Cambridge: Cambridge University Press.

Kassin, S.M., Ellsworth, P.C. & Smith, V.L. (1989). The general acceptance of psychological research on eyewitness testimony: A survey of the experts. *American Psychologist, 44,* 1089–1098.

Kassin, S.M., Tubb, V.A., Hosch, H.M. & Memon, A. (2001). On the general acceptance of eyewitness testimony research: A new survey of the experts. *American Psychologist, 56, 5,* 405–416.

Kendall-Tackett, K.A., Williams, L.M. & Finkelhor, D. (1993). Impact of sexual abuse on children: A review and synthesis of recent empirical studies. *Psychological Bulletin, 113,* 164–180.

Klettke, B., Graesser, A.C. & Powell, M.B. (2010). Expert testimony in child sexual abuse cases: The effects of evidence, coherence and credentials on jury decision-making. *Applied Cognitive Psychology, 24,* 481–494.

Kovera, M.B. & Borgida, E. (1998). Expert scientific testimony on child witnesses in the age of Daubert. In S.J. Ceci & H. Hembrooke (Eds.) *Expert witnessing in child abuse cases* (pp.185–215). Washington D.C.: American Psychological Association.

Lawlor, R.J. (1998). The expert witness in child sexual abuse cases: A clinician's view. In S.J. Ceci & H. Hembrooke (Eds.) *Expert witnessing in child abuse cases* (pp.105–122). Washington D. C.: American Psychological Association.

Leippe, M.R., Eisenstadt, D., Rauch, S.M. & Seib H.M. (2004). Timing of eyewitness expert testimony, jurors' need for cognition and case strength as determinants of trial verdicts. *Journal of Applied Psychology, 89,* 524–541.

Levett, L.M. & Kovera, M.B. (2008). The effectiveness of opposing expert witnesses for educating jurors about unreliable expert evidence. *Law and human Behavior, 32,* 363–374.

Lindsay, D.S. & Read, D.J. (1994). Psychotherapy and memories of child sexual abuse: A cognitive perspective, *Applied Cognitive Psychology, 8,* 281–338.

Lindsay, D.S. & Read, D.J. (1997). 'Memory work' and recovered memories of childhood sexual abuse: Scientific evidence and public, professional and personal issues. *Psychology, Public Policy and Law, 1,* 845–908.

Mackay, R.D., Colman, A.M. & Thornton, P. (1999). The admissibility of expert psychological and psychiatric testimony. In A. Heaton-Armstrong, E. Shepherd & D. Wolchover (Eds.) *Analysing witness testimony: A guide for legal practitioners and other professionals.* London: Blackstone Press.

Magnussen, S., Melinder, A., Stridbeck, U. & Raja, A.Q. (2010). Beliefs about factors affecting the reliability of eyewitness testimony: A comparison of judges, jurors and the general public. *Applied Cognitive Psychology, 24,* 122–133.

McAnulty, R.D. (1993). Expert psychological testimony in cases of alleged child sexual abuse. *Archives of Sexual Behaviour, 22,* 311–324.

McAuliff, B.D. & Duckworth, T.D. (2010). I spy with my little eye: Jurors' detection of internal validity threats in expert evidence. *Law and Human Behavior, 34,* 489–499.

McConkey, K.M. & Roche, S.M. (1989). Knowledge of eyewitness testimony. *Australian Psychologist, 24,* 337–384.

Melton, G.B. (1994). Doing justice and doing good: Conflicts for mental health professionals. *The Future of Children, 4,* 102–118.

Merckelbach H., Smeets, T., Geraerts, E., Jelicic, M., Bouwen, A. & Smeets, E. (2006). I haven't thought about this for years! Dating recent recalls of vivid memories. *Applied Cognitive Psychology, 20,* 33–42.

Miller, J.S. & Allen, R.J. (1998). The expert as an educator. In S.J. Ceci & H. Hembrooke (Eds). *Expert witnesses in child abuse cases* (pp.137–155). Washington D.C.: American Psychological Association.

Morison, S. & Greene, E. (1992). Juror and expert knowledge of child sexual abuse. *Child Abuse & Neglect, 16,* 595–613.

Myers, J.E.B. (1993). Expert testimony regarding child sexual abuse. *Child Abuse & Neglect, 17,* 175–185.

Noon, E. & Hollin, C.R. (1987). Lay knowledge of eyewitness behaviour: A British survey. *Applied Cognitive Psychology, 1,* 143–153.

PACE (1984, 2005). *Police and Criminal Evidence Act 1984, updated codes of practice 2005.* British Home Office. London: HMSO.

Raitt, F.E. & Zeedyk, M.S. (2003). False memory syndrome: Undermining the credibility of complainants in sexual offences. *International Journal of Law and Psychiatry, 26,* 453–471.

Read, J.D. & Craik, F.I.M. (1995). Earwitness identification: Some influences on voice recognition. *Journal of Experimental Psychology: Applied, 1,* 6–18.

Read, J.D. & Desmarais, S.L. (2009). Lay knowledge of eyewitness issues: A Canadian evaluation. *Applied Cognitive Psychology, 23*, 301–326.

Rumsfeld, D. (2002). *DoD News Briefing – Secretary Rumsfeld and Gen. Myers.* Retrieved 23 August 2011 from www.defenselink.mil/ Transcripts/Transcript.aspx?TranscriptID=2636

Schacter, D.L., Norman, K.A. & Koutstaal, W. (1997). The recovered memories debate: A cognitive neuroscience perspective. In M.A. Conway (Ed.) *Recovered memories and false memories* (pp.63–99). Oxford: Oxford University Press.

Scheck, B., Neufeld, P. & Dwyer, J. (2000). *Actual innocence.* New York: Doubleday.

Schooler, J.W., Ambada, A. & Bendiksen, M. (1997). A cognitive corroborative case study approach for investigating discovered memories of sexual abuse. In J.D. Read & D.S. Lindsay (Eds.) *Recollections of trauma: Scientific research and clinical practices* (pp.379–388). New York: Plenum.

Sgroi, S.M. (1982). *Handbook of clinical intervention in child sexual abuse.* Lexington, MA.: Lexington Books.

Spencer, J.R. (1998). The role of experts in the common law and the civil law: A comparison. In S.J. Ceci & H. Hembrooke (Eds.) *Expert witnesses in child abuse cases* (pp.29–59). Washington D.C.: American Psychological Association.

Spencer, J.R. & Flin, R. (1990). *The evidence of children: The law and the psychology.* London: Blackstone Press.

State v. Michaels (1993). 625 A.2d 489 (N.J. Superior Ct. App. Div.) 1993; 136 N.J. 299, 642, A.2d. 1372 1994; 642 A.2d. 1372 (N.J.) 1994.

Summit, R. (1983). The child sexual abuse accommodation syndrome. *Child Abuse & Neglect, 7*, 177–192.

Summit, R. (1992). Abuse of the child sexual abuse accommodation syndrome. *Journal of Child Sexual Abuse, 1*, 153–161.

Vrij, A. (2005). Criteria-based content analysis: A qualitative review of the first 37 studies. *Psychology, Public Policy and Law, 11*, 3–41.

Vrij, A. & Mann, S. (2006). Criteria-based content analysis: An empirical test of its underlying processes. *Psychology, Crime and Law, 12*, 337–349.

Walker, L.E. (1990). Psychological assessment of sexually abused children for legal evaluation and expert witness testimony. *Professional Psychology: Research and Practice, 21*, 344–353.

Walker, L.E. & Monahan, J. (1987). Social frameworks: A new use of social science in law. *Virginia Law Review, 73*, 559–598.

Wells, G.L. (1978). Applied eyewitness testimony research: system variables and estimator variables. *Journal of Personality and Social Psychology, 36*, 1546–1557.

Wells, G.L. & Murray, D.M. (1983). What can psychology say about the Neil v. Biggers criteria for judging eyewitness accuracy? *Journal of Applied Psychology, 68*, 347–362.

Wigmore, J. H. (1978). *Evidence in trials at common law.* Boston: Little Brown.

Wise, R.A., Pawlenko, N.B., Safer, M.A. & Meyer, D. (2009). What US prosecutors and defence attorneys know and believe about eyewitness testimony. *Applied Cognitive Psychology, 23*, 1266–1281.

Wright, D.B., Ost, J. & French, C.C. (2006). Recovered and false memories. *The Psychologist, 19*, 352–355.

Yapko, M. (1997). The troublesome unknowns about trauma and recovered memories. In M.A. Conway (Ed.) *Recovered memories and false memories* (pp.23–33). Oxford: Oxford University Press.

Yarmey, A.D. (1997). Probative v. prejudicial value of eyewitness memory research. *Expert Evidence, 5*, 89–97.

Yarmey, A.D. (2001). Expert testimony: Does eyewitness memory research have probative value for the courts? *Canadian Psychology. 42*, 92–100.

Yarmey, A.D. (2003). Eyewitness identification guidelines and recommendations for identification procedures in the United States and Canada. *Canadian Psychology, 44*, 181–189.

Yarmey, A.D. (2007). The psychology of speaker identification and earwitness memory. In R.C.L. Lindsay, D.F. Ross, J.D. Read & M.P. Toglia (Eds.) *The handbook of eyewitness psychology: Vol. 2. Memory for people* (pp.101–136). N. J.: Lawrence Erlbaum Associates.

Yarmey, A.D. & Jones, H.P.T. (1983). Is the psychology of eyewitness identification a matter of common sense? In S. Lloyd-Bostock & B.R. Clifford (Eds.) *Evaluating witness evidence* (pp.18–40). Chichester, UK: John Wiley & Sons, Inc.

ANNOTATED READING LIST

Ceci, S.J. & Hembrooke, H. (Eds.) (1998). *Expert witnesses in child abuse cases.* Washington D.C.: American Psychological Association. *An excellent text that focuses on child sexual abuse and the possible roles of experts. It also touches on certain aspects of false/ recovered memories.*

Conway, M.A. (Ed.) (1997). *Recovered memories and false memories.* Oxford: Oxford University Press. *A scholarly approach to the debates surrounding false/recovered memories.*

Costanzo, M., Krauss, D. & Pezdek, K. (Eds.) (2007). *Expert psychological testimony for the courts.* Mahwah NJ.: Lawrence Erlbaum Associates. *A wide-ranging book that looks at such areas as identification, interrogation, sexual harassment, battered women, risk assessment and dangerousness, always from an expert witness point of view.*

Cutler, B.L. (Ed.) (2009). *Expert testimony on the psychology of eyewitness identification*. Oxford: Oxford University Press. *A text that takes an in-depth look at the promises and pitfalls of expert evidence in cases of disputed identification from an experimentalist and legal perspective.*

McQuiston-Surrett, D. & Saks, M.J. (2009). The testimony of forensic identification science: What expert witnesses say and what fact finders hear. *Law and Human Behavior, 33,* 436–453. *An important paper that indicates that **how** an expert expresses a view can have markedly different effects on jury decision-making. The testimony concerns hair samples and unique identification.*

Martire, K.A. & Kemp, R.I. (2009). The impact of eyewitness expert evidence and judicial instruction on juror ability to evaluate eyewitness testimony. *Law and Human Behavior, 33,* 225–236. *This paper draws a contrast between 'real' and 'fictional' eyewitness paradigms in assessing the value or otherwise of expert testimony as opposed to judicial warning in sensitising fact finders to the accuracy of an eyewitness.*

Part IV
Dealing with Offenders

16 Crime and Punishment: 'What Works'?

James McGuire

KEY TERMS

celerity • certainty • covert sensitisation • criminogenic needs • deterrence • deterrence theory • directed masturbation • effect size • incapacitation • integrity • meta-analysis • multimodal programmes • olfactory aversive conditioning • penology • programmes • rehabilitation • restoration • retribution • risk factors • risk–need–responsivity (RNR) model • self-management • sentence • severity • tertiary prevention

CHAPTER OUTLINE

This chapter approaches the nature and the outcomes of sentencing from a psychological perspective, and outlines the roles that psychologists may play in the different stages of sentencing decisions; though generally with reference to what happens *after* those decisions have been made. Other chapters have addressed earlier stages of the legal process, such as police investigation and the presentation of evidence in court, while Chapters 17 and 18 examine treatment for offenders in more detail.

The opening section of this chapter takes us into the field of **penology** – the study of legal punishments. It outlines what are generally considered to be the main objectives of sentencing, and the rationale underpinning them in each case. These objectives include **retribution**, **incapacitation**, **deterrence**, **rehabilitation**, and **restoration**.

To the extent that sentencing is intended to achieve certain socially desirable effects, mainly in terms of its impact on those made subject to it, the second section of the chapter reviews research findings relevant to this, examining whether it is possible to reduce rates of recidivism (a pattern of repeated criminality) amongst persistent offenders. Research clearly shows that the nature of a **sentence** is much less important in this respect than what happens during the course of it. Alongside other professions, psychologists have made significant contributions to this area in a number of ways, for example: in terms of identifying **risk factors** for recurrent involvement in crime; in designing and implementing methods of working with frequently convicted offenders; and in evaluating the outcomes of psychosocial interventions.

The final section of the chapter considers the somewhat paradoxical situation in which psychology finds itself in relation to the practice of criminal justice.

Note that there is no universally agreed definition of the word 'crime' and present space does not permit discussion of the complexities within this. As used here the term refers simply to the breaking of the criminal law, however that is formulated in a given jurisdiction at a given time. See McGuire (2004) for more extended discussion.

Glossary margin

penology the study of legal punishment and how it is administered.

retribution one of the objectives of sentencing, and an influential theory of the sentencing process, based on the proposal that the harm done by offenders requires society to rectify the imbalance by punishing them appropriately.

incapacitation an objective of sentencing; the use of criminal justice intervention to reduce criminality by removing offenders from crime opportunities.

deterrence one of the objectives of sentencing, based on the premise that adverse consequences (punishment) will make recurrence of offending (criminal recidivism) less likely.

rehabilitation an objective of sentencing and allied criminal justice initiatives, concerned with constructive efforts to provide education, training or other services to enable offenders to become reintegrated in society, and reduce recidivism.

restoration (also *restorative justice*) a relatively recent departure, entailing services through which offenders make reparations to their victims for the harm they have done, sometimes through a carefully managed negotiation and reconciliation process.

sentence the penalty imposed on an individual found guilty of an offence in a court of law; sentencing is the process through which this is decided.

risk factors individual or environmental variables that have been shown through empirical research to be associated with greater likelihood of involvement in criminal activity. Can be *static* (set by past events) or *dynamic* (more immediate).

SENTENCING

Individuals found guilty of committing a crime can expect to be sentenced by the courts. This has been standard practice in many countries for several hundred years. Broadly speaking, there is a rough correspondence between the seriousness of crimes committed and the severity of sentences imposed. Where there are marked departures from this – mainly when sentences are deemed too lenient – controversy often erupts. Centuries of accumulated experience notwithstanding, many aspects of the process remain poorly understood. Until recently some of them had not been very searchingly examined. For the criminal courts, at least at present, the culmination of the legal process is the finding of guilt or innocence and the passing of sentence.

The word 'sentence' derives (via Middle English and Old French) from the Latin word *sententia*, meaning a feeling or opinion communicated by someone to others. This captures something crucial about it: other than in highly exceptional circumstances, sentencing is a public process. Magistrates, judges and others engaged in it are reflecting and embodying the community's distaste, perhaps revulsion, regarding something someone has done. Hence, sentencing is often considered to serve a primarily *expressive* function: it conveys to the offender the public's reaction to his or her conduct in the criminal offence.

Penology

This is the study of sentencing and of how it is administered. This occurs within that segment of criminal justice usually referred to as the *penal system*, a term loosely denoting the arrangement of courts, prisons, probation, youth justice and allied agencies within society. Since these arrangements have developed in stepwise fashion over very many years, to call the end-product a 'system' may be, as Ashworth (2005) has remarked, 'merely a convenience and an aspiration' (p.67), rather than an accurate description.

Potentially, psychology has a significant contribution to make at numerous places within this system, and although the number of psychologists directly employed within it is still low relative to other professions, it has been steadily expanding in recent years. Since the process of sentencing should entail an understanding of why someone acted as he, or she, did; and that process is also intended to reduce the chances of similar actions recurring, psychology should perhaps be playing a far more influential role than has been the case so far. For arguably, if this does not sound too grandiose, the operation of law is in one sense a form of *applied psychology*.

The objectives of sentencing

Within the criminal law and specifically within penology, sentencing has been conceptualised as serving a number of distinct but interconnected and overlapping purposes. The core of these is the idea of punishment, the signalling of society's displeasure concerning what the offender has done, by the imposition of a penalty. But this apparently straightforward idea conceals a number of underlying complexities. The following outline borrows from several texts addressing this issue (Ashworth, 2005; Duff & Garland, 1994; Easton & Piper, 2005; Miethe & Lu, 2005). Although there is no definitive consensus on these matters, sentencing is currently thought to perform five main kinds of function.

Retribution and (just) deserts

From one perspective, society responds to offenders by punishing them purely and simply because it has to. While there are various nuances within this, the reasoning that underpins the concept of retribution is as follows. There is a fundamental principle at stake when an individual acts against society by breaking its laws. The harm caused by such actions gives society an automatic right, indeed an obligation, to inflict pain on the offender in response. Conversely, so the argument continues, the offender also has a right to be punished. Retributive action corrects an imbalance created by the offences, by rectifying the wrong the offender has done; a concept that informs the familiar notion of *just deserts*.

The origins of this idea can be traced back to ancient Judeo-Christian texts enunciating the 'law of retaliation' or *lex talionis*, where punishment corresponds to the crime both in its severity and its type ('an eye for an eye'). Such a viewpoint underpins practices that are still applied in some countries where pain is inflicted on the lawbreaker commensurate with that inflicted on the original victims. But the modern conceptual framework for this is usually attributed to the 18th century German philosopher Immanuel Kant (1724–1804), who argued that in committing a crime, an offender gains an unfair advantage over those who have adhered to the law. Under the general political obligation that binds individuals to each other and to the state, there is a necessary reciprocity: punishment then restores a proper balance between the offender and the rest of society (Figure 16.1), in that the offender owes and must repay a debt to law-abiding members of the community (Murphy, 1994).

A more recent reformulation of this is contained in the idea of *censure*, or expression and attribution of blame. Sentencing serves a reprobative function, and to be just it should be based on the principle of proportionality between the amount of harm done and the amount of punishment dispensed (von Hirsch, 1994).

Overall, the philosophy of retribution is not concerned with instrumental effects or outcomes. Punishment is viewed as '. . . intrinsically appropriate' (Garland & Duff, 1994, p.7) and the cycle of crime and official response is, as it were, a closed loop. But as we will see below, the idea of retribution can also be combined with other elements whereby sentences can be designed to accomplish a number of goals simultaneously.

FIGURE 16.1 *Under the general political obligation that binds individuals to each other and to the state, there is a necessary reciprocity: punishment then restores a proper balance.*

Source: © interlight. Used under licence from Shutterstock.

Sentencing as incapacitation

In almost complete contrast, incapacitation refers to the possibility of crime control by removing offenders from circumstances where they are likely to commit crimes: by restricting their freedom to act. The most palpable means of doing this in contemporary societies is through imprisonment, or detention in other locked-up residential settings (ranging from children's homes to high security hospitals). Thereby, offenders are removed from society and from situations in which they have opportunities to take vehicles, break into houses, sell drugs or get into fights (though unfortunately as we know, some of these activities continue in prison). Apart from physical incarceration, liberty can also be restricted to varying degrees by community penalties. This is achieved, for example, by: night curfews or electronically monitored home confinement; exclusion from a neighbourhood where previous crimes were committed; or a requirement to attend for supervision at specified times. There is wide civic endorsement of the principle that persons who have inflicted serious or repeated harm upon others (or in some instances upon themselves) should be restrained in some way, encapsulated in frequently heard phrases such as 'public protection' and 'community safety'.

But the idea of incapacitation has a similarly ancient history to that of retribution. In the distant past, individuals might have been exiled or banished from their communities. Not so long ago, a parallel of this was practised in the transportation of many thousands of offenders from the UK to Australia (see the National Archives page on the transportation of convicts at: www .nationalarchives.gov.uk/records/research-guides/trans portation-australia.htm). In medieval Europe, the use of bodily restraints such as stocks and pillories, and that most durable symbol of penal confinement, the ball and chain, was designed to incapacitate as well as to punish in other ways. While modern methods of doing this are less overtly physical, the net effect is similar in seeking to control the offender's scope for antisocial action.

Sentencing as deterrence

A third declared intention that drives the sentencing process is that it should alter criminal behaviour by attaching negative consequences to it. This is the paradigmatic example of what is entitled the *utilitarian* or *consequentialist* rationale for punishment as a response to crime (Walker, 1991). It is founded on the idea that legal sanctions will have an impact on individuals made subject to them. This set of expectations is sometimes referred to as **deterrence theory** (Gibbs, 1986) (or occasionally deterrence doctrine)

deterrence theory in penology, the doctrine that the costs of committing crimes suppress criminal activity. *General deterrence* refers to the effect on the population, *specific deterrence* to the effect on convicted individuals.

and it is probably the most widely taken-for-granted purpose of sentencing.

Deterrent effects can be subdivided with respect to different scales of intended outcomes. One basic, conventional distinction is that between *specific* and *general* deterrence (Stafford & Warr, 1993). The former refers to the impact of punishment on the individual made subject to it: theoretically, when someone is punished for committing a crime, he or she should be less likely to do it again. The latter refers to the wider effect this is expected to have on others, and on the community as a whole. If committing crimes is known to be punished, the public-at-large should be less likely to do it, as they have observed that it will result in unpleasantness for them. These are useful conceptual distinctions, but in everyday reality there is likely to be a complex interplay between specific and general deterrent effects (Stafford & Warr, 1993).

Penologists have recognised that the objective features of sentencing are probably less important to prospective offenders than its subjective or perceptual features (Gibbs, 1986). *Objective* properties are those that might be recorded by the police, or by a government statistician, showing for example rates of detection, arrest, or subsequent imprisonment for different types of crime. *Subjective* or perceptual properties are those that are meaningful to an individual offender, who may be wholly uninformed concerning criminal statistics but is probably conscious of peers who have escaped arrest, or who have been arrested, for specific misdemeanours. The real operative factors in everyday decision-making by anyone considering an offence are likely to be immediate personal knowledge rather than official databases.

There are several features of sentences that may be considered from either objective or subjective standpoints: certainty, celerity, and severity. **Certainty** refers to the likelihood of legal punishment as a result of committing a crime. Defined objectively, certainty refers to the proportion of crimes of a specific type that result in formal punishment; subjectively, however, it reflects individual offenders' estimates of the chances of being caught. **Celerity** refers to the amount of time that lapses between an offence being committed and an official sanction being imposed. **Severity** refers to the magnitude of a punishment or the estimated amount of pain or discomfort a convicted offender would endure.

certainty in penology, the likelihood of legal punishment as a result of committing a crime. May be assessed objectively (using official statistics) or subjectively (from the experience of individual offenders).

celerity in penology, the amount of time that elapses between an offence being committed and an official sanction being imposed.

severity in penology, the magnitude of a punishment or the estimated amount of pain or discomfort a convicted offender would be likely to endure.

To draw an everyday parallel, just as most people preparing to drive off in their cars think an accident is unlikely to happen to them (though they may be distantly aware of statistics concerning such a risk), so most individuals contemplating a crime tend to discount measured probabilities and focus on the details of their own actions and circumstances. Penologists have discovered that it is changes in the perceived features of sanctions that are more likely to influence the behaviour of individuals who are inclined to break the law (von Hirsch et al., 1999).

Sentencing as rehabilitation

Retribution, incapacitation and deterrence are often in themselves believed to promote a further effect, that of *rehabilitating* the offender. The individual's recognition of how society perceives his or her actions, conjoined with the unpleasantness of losing liberty or enduring other effects of punishment, will encourage him or her to become reformed and to desist from criminal acts. Thus some penologists consider that rehabilitation is integrally achieved through retributive and deterrent effects.

Others, however, take the view that the sentence of the court should incorporate procedures explicitly designed to support rehabilitation. The latter might include, for example: remedial education; employment training; various types of psychotherapy where indicated; developing awareness of victims; or participation in specially designed programmes for the reduction of offending behaviour. Each of these will (potentially) reduce both the alienation that many offenders already experience and the additional stigmatisation induced by the sentencing process, while also enhancing the individual's prospects of becoming a more fully-fledged citizen and a law-abiding member of the community.

It is with reference to this that psychology has perhaps had its farthest-reaching influence on practices in the criminal justice system in recent years. The model that informs such work begins with the observation that some kinds of individual differences are reliably associated with risks of repeated involvement in crime.

These risk factors (see Chapter 17 for more details of risk factors and measures to assess these) derive not from variations in personality traits, as was hypothesised at an earlier stage, but in a range of other variables. They include patterns of criminal associates, antisocial attitudes, a tendency towards impulsiveness, poor emotional self-regulation, and deficits in a number of social, cognitive, and problem-solving skills (Andrews & Bonta, 2010; McGuire, 2004). Identification of these risk factors led to the proposal that if they could be successfully remedied by psychosocial interventions, individuals might be less likely to commit further offences as a result. There is now substantial evidence to support such proposals and some of the key findings in this area will be described later in this chapter.

Sentencing as restoration and reparation

A fifth and relatively novel perspective on punishment has emerged over approximately the last 25 years, influenced in part by a steadily growing recognition of the rights and needs of crime victims. One application of this in some countries has been the provision to victims of opportunities to make *impact statements* in court that might influence the deliberations of those delivering sentences (Ashworth, 2005).

But the more innovative development has been influenced by approaches to crime taken in some non-Western societies. This has introduced the concept of *restorative justice* (Johnstone & Van Ness, 2006), of attempted reconciliation between offenders and victims, with the former making direct reparations to the latter where possible, as traditionally occurred amongst some indigenous communities in various parts of the world. The fundamental principle here is the repair of the damage done to the victim and community by the commission of the offence. But it takes a quite different direction from the punitive sanctions customary in a retributive approach. It may entail a variety of elements, including the acknowledgement by the offender or his or her responsibility for the offence, the offering of an apology, or making of direct restitution in some manner settled jointly between victims, offenders and other interested parties.

In several jurisdictions an extensive application of restorative models has occurred in which special arrangements have been made to include all relevant parties – the victim, the offender, their families and community representatives – in collective decision-making to agree a response to the offender's actions. From early initiatives in New Zealand and Australia these procedures have been piloted in many other countries, although to date they have remained on the margins of other longer-established sentencing procedures (Leibmann, 2007). Evaluations of such projects have typically shown that they produce higher levels of satisfaction for victims than the more impersonal proceedings of formal court hearings (Graef, 2001).

The various philosophies of punishment just outlined can be combined, so that a single sentence might represent an attempt to achieve several objectives at once. In some circumstances judges may enunciate this, indicating how they arrived at a given sentence by designating portions of it intended to serve different penal purposes (Ashworth, 2005).

The prevailing sentencing framework for England and Wales, the Criminal Justice Act 2003, specifies the purposes of sentencing in a way that makes explicit the possibility of integrating different judicial purposes in a single sentencing decision (Taylor *et al.*, 2004), in a manner characterised by Ashworth (2005, p.74) as a 'pick-and-mix' approach. Details of the types and severity of sentences that can be applied to different offences are set out in a series of documents produced by the Sentencing Guidelines Council (2008, with respect to magistrates' courts), which also provides advice on clarifying the objectives of sentences (available on the Sentencing Guidelines Council's website at http://sentencingcouncil.judiciary.gov.uk). For magistrates' courts, the decision itself, at the final stage of sentencing, should be accompanied by a statement of the reasons why the bench has arrived at the sentence to be imposed.

The legal framework of courts, their sentencing powers, the sentencing options available to them, and many other features of criminal justice, vary considerably between different countries and are subject to change over time. It is advisable for any psychologist working in the penal system to become familiar with the principal features of the context in which he or she is working. Numerous textbooks, websites and other information sources exist to facilitate this in virtually every country and there are also integrative volumes summarising key attributes of criminal justice taking a comparative, international approach (e.g. Newman *et al.*, 2001).

The impact of sentencing

Is it possible to answer the question posed in the title of this chapter, and draw any firm conclusions about the usefulness of sentencing, about whether it 'works'? As suggested earlier, to the extent that sentencing might have a solely retributive or 'non-consequentialist' purpose, its application does not involve an appeal to direct empirical testing, since there is no primary concern with outcome effects. If its purpose is meant to be expressive and symbolic, then as Garland (1990) has argued, those who seek to evaluate its effectiveness have somehow missed the point.

Other declared objectives of sentencing are potentially testable in principle, but there are variations in the extent to which doing so would be feasible in practice. To evaluate general deterrence, for example, societies are scarcely likely to embark on large-scale experiments in which they temporarily suspend their laws for hypothesis-testing purposes. This reluctance may lead us to conclude that it is the existence of criminal sanctions that holds society together; that it is only the general deterrent effect of the portfolio of state punishments that restrains citizens from more or less constantly violating each other's interests.

However, a partial test of general deterrence might be adduced from other sources. One is observation of what occurs when there is a breakdown of law and order in society, for example, during episodes of civil unrest. History is replete with relevant examples, and indeed rates of many crimes often do rise sharply during such episodes. When social order disintegrates, however, so many changes are happening in parallel that it is problematic to attribute the resultant lawlessness to any one of them. In less extreme situations, it can be difficult to discern the role of criminal justice agencies as a component of the observed changes, and their impact appears to be marginal. For example, following the downfall of communism in the then Soviet Union in the early 1990s and the social liberalisation that ensued, there was a 50 per cent rise in crime rates in a period of just two years (Gilinskiy, 2006). (Recorded crimes per 100,000 population rose from 1242 in 1990 to 1856 in 1992.) But this was almost certainly a function of many influences, involving simultaneous economic, political and social change. The network of police and courts continued to operate in the same manner through this period, but had no observable restraining effect on a trend that was driven by other factors.

Perhaps more surprisingly, even when the police are not available to arrest wrongdoers – because they are on strike, for example – there is no convincing evidence of upward surges in crime (Figure 16.2). There was a 'rash of crimes' following a one-day police strike in Montreal in 1969 (Clark, 1977), but apart from this instance other studies of industrial action by police do not support what has been called the 'thin blue line' hypothesis. There were public riots during a longer strike in Boston in 1919, but analysis suggests these events were about to happen in any case, and would have done so whether or not the police had gone on strike (White, 1988). Pfuhl (1983) analysed crime-rate data for police strikes in 11 US cities during the 1970s. Strikes ranged in duration from three to 30 days. While there were increases in rates of some crimes in some locations, in the majority there were no changes at all. Similarly, following a police strike in Finland in 1976 no upsurge in crime nor other social upheaval occurred (Makinen & Takala, 1980). Thus, our predilections notwithstanding, there is no overall pattern supportive of police presence as a major deterrent against crime.

There are other sound reasons for suggesting that the presence of criminal sanctions is not necessarily the fundamental force that holds back a tide of lawbreaking on a daily basis. There are clear 'normative' factors influencing individuals' self-regulation of their own conduct in society. Tyler (2006) has strong evidence to suggest that the everyday law-abiding behaviour of most people is a function of their endorsement of the law and perception

FIGURE 16.2 *Even when the police are not available to arrest wrong-doers, there is no convincing evidence of upward surges in crime.*
Source: © r.naqy. Used under licence from Shutterstock.

of its operation as legitimate, rather than their fear of detection and punishment. Tyler conducted a series of structured interviews with a random sample of 1575 respondents in Chicago, 804 of whom were re inter viewed one year later. Participants were asked about their experience and perceptions of the law, the extent of any contacts with the police or courts, and various factors potentially linked to their behaviour. The key influence underpinning most individuals' adherence to lawful behaviour was their commitment to doing so, arising partly from personal morality and partly from beliefs in the appropriateness of laws. Thus, where the law is perceived to have legitimacy, that is, where its rationale is considered sound and its operation perceived as fair, most citizens regularly and willingly act in accordance with it. Where individuals disagree with laws or experience their enactment as unjust, their compliance is weakened; some laws may then be difficult, even impossible to enforce, *despite* the availability of punitive sanctions.

The effects of criminal sanctions/ sentencing

Crime and punishment are inextricably linked in our culture and within everyday discourse and public expectations. Notwithstanding the range of penal philosophies reviewed above, the presumed individual deterrent function of the sentence is arguably pivotal in perceptions of the process as a whole. 'Whichever sentencing principles are used to decide the exact form and amount of punishment, there is a widespread assumption that the resulting punishment *will* deter the convicted offender from re-offending, or potential offenders from offending' (Easton & Piper, 2005, p.101, italics in original). Given the central place allotted to punitive sanctions in the legal systems of the world, does the available evidence justify these ubiquitously held expectations that individuals will be deterred from future offending by the experience of official punishment? Several types of evidence indicate that these expectations are very badly misplaced.

If punitive sanctions reliably achieved individual or specific deterrence, it would be not unreasonable to expect the following. We might expect that there would be a relationship between the experience of punishment and what individuals say in relation to their behaviour as a result. We might expect there to be an association between the severity of sentences and recidivism outcomes, when other variables are held equal, with heavier penalties leading to larger effects. We might anticipate that in specially designed studies where some offenders are dealt with more severely, they would go on to commit fewer crimes. In a pattern that might at first appear counterintuitive, none of these expectations is supported by the evidence that has been collected to date.

The first type of evidence is derived from what individuals say has had an impact on them and has influenced them to change their behaviour (where that occurred) after being arrested for offences such as theft or substance abuse. Klemke (1982) interviewed young people some time after their first arrest to explore levels of subsequent involvement in offending. Individuals who had desisted from offending were very unlikely to attribute this to any deterrent effect of their contacts with the criminal justice system. Of course, some researchers would regard self-report data of this kind as a rather weak form of evidence, given variables such as impression management, fear of arrest, and other factors potentially at work.

A second type of evidence is likely to be regarded as more robust, being based on officially recorded statistics: patterns of re-conviction following different types of sentences, usually involving very large samples. These data are of particular interest as they allow comparisons to be made between *actual* offence rates and those that would be *expected*, based on predictions made by using a specially designed scale to assess risk of reoffending, derived from information on individuals' previous criminal histories.

The Offender Group Reconviction Scale (now in Version 3: Howard *et al.*, 2009; see Chapter 17 for further details of this measure) was developed for this purpose, but when Lloyd *et al.* (1994), and later Kershaw (1999), used it to compare the impact of different types of sentences (e.g. imprisonment versus community penalties), they found that rates of recidivism two years later were virtually identical. Patterns of subsequent criminality appeared wholly unaffected by the type of punishment imposed (see McGuire, 2002). There was no evidence that the more severe sanction had any suppressant or punitive effect. Similarly, in a large-scale review for the Solicitor General of Canada, integrating data from 23 studies, and with an aggregate sample of 68,248, Gendreau *et al.* (1999) found no clear relationship between the lengths of prison sentences and rates of subsequent recidivism, once other differences between samples were taken into account.

But perhaps the strongest kind of test of the deterrence hypothesis comes from specially designed experiments in which the intervention consists of *enhanced* (i.e. harsher) punishments whilst the comparison sample received typical punishments. There have been numerous studies of this type, and they more or less uniformly show that the net effects of dealing with offenders in this way are either absent (the effect size is zero) or actually negative; that is, people got worse and committed more crimes (Gendreau *et al.*, 2001; McGuire, 2004). A particularly stark illustration of this comes from evaluation of the 'three strikes and you're out' policy implemented in some US states since 1994. In California, a recent comparison found effects that were the reverse of what had been predicted. Those jurisdictions that used the law the *least* experienced larger declines in violent crimes than those counties that used it most (Center on Juvenile and Criminal Justice, 2008).

If we accept this evidence, and conclude that deterrent effects are very weak, simply non-existent or actually harmful, we may be left with what looks like a paradox. Most people probably assume that the unpleasantness of being punished for doing something is likely to decrease our chances of doing it. Behavioural psychology has demonstrated the power of reinforcement and punishment in shaping patterns of human behaviour (see Chapter 18, for descriptions of behavioural programmes).

But research in that field has also shown that for punishment to work efficiently, certain conditions have to be met. For example, in order to be effective, it should be virtually certain to happen, and should follow swiftly on the problem behaviour to be reduced. These circumstances are rarely if ever met in the criminal justice system, and other evidence suggests that individuals on the verge of committing crimes are unlikely to be thinking in any detailed way about the possible negative consequences of their actions (McGuire, 2004).

REDUCING OFFENDING BEHAVIOUR

Fortunately there are other approaches to addressing the problem of offender recidivism at the individual level that have emerged as more effective than official sanctions. This field of activity is sometimes denoted as **tertiary prevention** (Gendreau & Andrews, 1990) as it focuses on adjudicated offenders – those who have been convicted of crimes and duly sentenced. More colloquially, drawing on the title of a journal paper by Martinson (1974), which famously drew negative conclusions regarding early evidence on offender rehabilitation, it is often referred to simply as 'what works'.

> **tertiary prevention** systematic attempt to reduce further offence recidivism by work with convicted offenders within the criminal justice system. (Primary prevention has a long-term focus; secondary prevention works with those at risk of delinquency.)

(This is sometimes contrasted with *primary prevention*, which is focused on long-term developmental family- and community-based initiatives (see, for example, Farrington & Welsh, 2007) and *secondary prevention*, which focuses on work with groups considered to be already 'at risk' of involvement in delinquency (see, for example, Goldstein, 2002).)

Research in this field took a sizeable stride forward some years ago when several review studies were published based on the application of statistical integration or **meta-analysis** of research findings (see Chapter 18 for evidence of meta-analyses of treatment for dangerous violent and sexual offenders). Since its initial use in the field of criminal justice in 1985, this approach has been employed in a number of reviews of treatment-outcome studies with offenders (Wilson, 2001). The pace of development was such that by mid-2008, a total of 75 meta-analyses of tertiary-level offender treatment had been published (McGuire, 2008; 2009). While much research remains to be done, the cumulative findings of this work provide some firm indications concerning which approaches to working with offenders are most likely to yield intended outcomes in terms of lowering criminal recidivism.

The evidence base

The majority of the reviews conducted in this field, and the bulk of the primary research on which they are based, originate from North America, although data from many countries are encompassed within them. Several have been conducted in Europe, and these have been reviewed separately, as a validation or generalisability test of the American results (Redondo et al., 2002). Most are published in the English language, but in the largest review so far conducted (Pearson et al., 1997), contacts were made with 14 non-English speaking countries and more than 300 reports were obtained in languages other than English.

The overwhelming majority of the primary studies deals with male offenders, which is unsurprising given that most crimes were committed by men. In one of the largest meta-analyses, carried out by Lipsey (1992; 1995), only 3 per cent of published studies focused exclusively on samples of female offenders. With regard to age, roughly two-thirds of the reviews focus on interventions with adolescent or young adult offenders in the age range 14 to 21 years. This covers the peak age for delinquency in most countries (Farrington & Welsh, 2007). The remaining studies are either concerned exclusively with adults, or include offenders across a wide range of ages. Concerning ethnicity, while many studies provide data on the proportions of offenders from different ethnic groups, the pattern of this is variable and it is not consistently recorded. However, given the over-representation of minority communities under criminal justice jurisdiction in many countries, these findings are based on populations containing a broad mixture in terms of ethnicity.

Findings of the reviews

While some reviews have addressed specific types of offending behaviour (e.g. violence, driving while intoxicated, sexual assault), the focus in most has been on the relative impact of different intervention methods. Reviews have dealt with educational and vocational programmes; with the impact of specially designed socio-therapeutic prison regimes in Germany; and with the effects of therapeutic communities defined in broader terms. There is a meta-analysis on the importance of addressing cognition as a mediating variable in behavioural change, several on the effectiveness of structured cognitive-behavioural programmes, and others of family-based interventions and school-based interventions respectively. Meta-analysis has also been used to synthesise findings from evaluations of restorative justice and victim-offender mediation. Moderator variables, including (as we saw earlier) the impact of age, gender and ethnicity, and the importance of staff skills and other aspects of organisational practices, have also been reviewed in this way.

In meta-analysis, the principal outcome of interest is known as the **effect size**. This can be represented in various ways, but the function in each case is the same: to provide a measure of the extent of any difference between 'experimental' and 'control' conditions in an intervention study. There are different methods of calculating effect sizes, and given the complexities of meta-analysis, some researchers have been critical of it. McGuire (2004) provides an overview of these issues, and of how effect sizes can be interpreted and compared. Figure 16.3 displays some selected effect sizes for different types of psychosocial interventions compared to no-intervention controls.

> **effect size** a statistic used to compare the magnitude of the effect of an independent variable across different studies expressed in standard deviation units. Two commonly reported effect sizes are *Cohen's d* and *Pearson's correlation (r)*.

The overall finding from these meta-analyses of offender treatment sharply contradicts the once commonly repeated assertion that 'nothing works' with offenders (Hollin, 2001; McGuire, 2004). The impact of psychosocial interventions on criminal recidivism is on average positive, that is, it is associated with a net reduction in reoffending rates in experimental relative to comparison samples. However, the average effect taken across a broad spectrum of different types of treatment or intervention is relatively modest. Expressed as a correlation coefficient, it is estimated on average to be approximately 0.10. This average finding obtained from the meta-analyses corresponds to recidivism rates of 45 per cent for experimental groups and 55 per cent for control groups. Though this figure is low, it is

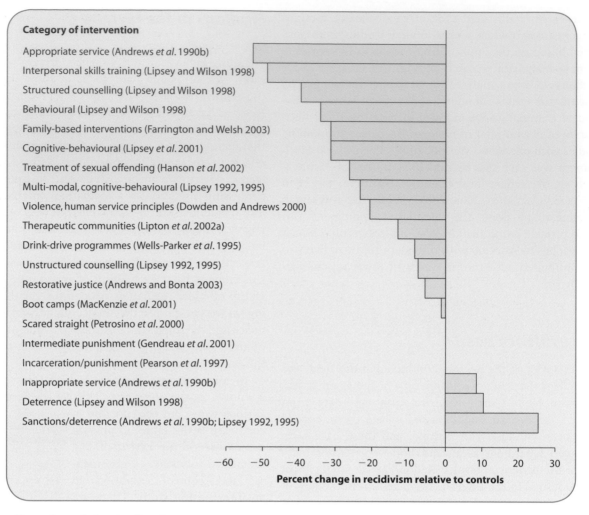

Category of intervention

- Appropriate service (Andrews *et al.* 1990b)
- Interpersonal skills training (Lipsey and Wilson 1998)
- Structured counselling (Lipsey and Wilson 1998)
- Behavioural (Lipsey and Wilson 1998)
- Family-based interventions (Farrington and Welsh 2003)
- Cognitive-behavioural (Lipsey *et al.* 2001)
- Treatment of sexual offending (Hanson *et al.* 2002)
- Multi-modal, cognitive-behavioural (Lipsey 1992, 1995)
- Violence, human service principles (Dowden and Andrews 2000)
- Therapeutic communities (Lipton *et al.* 2002a)
- Drink-drive programmes (Wells-Parker *et al.* 1995)
- Unstructured counselling (Lipsey 1992, 1995)
- Restorative justice (Andrews and Bonta 2003)
- Boot camps (MacKenzie *et al.* 2001)
- Scared straight (Petrosino *et al.* 2000)
- Intermediate punishment (Gendreau *et al.* 2001)
- Incarceration/punishment (Pearson *et al.* 1997)
- Inappropriate service (Andrews *et al.* 1990b)
- Deterrence (Lipsey and Wilson 1998)
- Sanctions/deterrence (Andrews *et al.* 1990b; Lipsey 1992, 1995)

−60 −50 −40 −30 −20 −10 0 10 20 30

Percent change in recidivism relative to controls

FIGURE 16.3 *Illustrative variations in effect sizes.*

Source: McGuire, 2004. Reproduced with the kind permission of Open University Press. All rights reserved.

statistically significant, and it compares reasonably well with effects found in many other fields. Some healthcare interventions that are generally regarded as producing worthwhile benefits have lower mean treatment effects. But crucially, when different subgroups of studies are compared, the variations between them show some consistent patterns that prove to be much more informative in illuminating aspects of intervention associated with higher rates of success.

A key discovery here, with reference to methods of intervention, is that there are some markedly divergent outcomes. As discussed in the earlier part of this chapter, deterrent sanctions overall have no, or even negative, effects. Hence, counter to what might widely be expected, they are associated with net increases in recidivism. Some interventions have positive but rather weak effects, whereas others have effects that are both statistically and practically meaningful in terms of reductions in rates of reoffending.

There is now a widespread consensus that it is possible to maximise effect sizes by combining a number of elements in offender programmes (Andrews, 2001; Gendreau, 1996; Hollin, 1999). Effective interventions are thought to possess certain common features that Andrews *et al.* (1990), in an early but highly influential review, called 'principles of human service', subsequently formulated as the **risk–need–responsivity (RNR) model** (Andrews *et al.*, 2006). When Andrews and his associates (1990) pinpointed those features that contributed separately to enhancing effect size, they found that the combination of them produced an additive effect. Interventions that possessed these features yielded an average reduction in recidivism rates of 53 per cent. So although the mean effect size across all

> **risk–need–
> responsivity (RNR)
> model** a risk manage-
> ment rehabilitation
> model that seeks to
> reduce offenders' predis-
> position to reoffend by
> strengthening, reducing
> or controlling personal-
> ity and/or situational
> variables as appropriate.

studies is not especially large, that is partly as a result of the negative effects of punishment. When interventions are appropriately designed and delivered it is possible to secure positive and much larger effects.

Probably the most widely disseminated innovation flowing from the above findings has been the synthesis of methods and materials into a number of specially prepared formats known as **programmes**. This word

> **programmes** structured sequences of learning opportunities, with objectives and contents planned in advance, designed to support and encourage change; usually accompanied by a manual or other materials.

sounds sinister to some people as it conjures up images of a rigid and insensitive method of working. But strictly defined, a programme consists simply of a planned sequence of learning opportunities (McGuire, 2001). Used in criminal justice settings, its general objective is to reduce

participants' subsequent criminal recidivism. Within that context, the typical programme is a pre-arranged set of activities, with clearly stated objectives, entailing a number of elements interconnected according to a planned design, which can be reproduced on successive occasions.

The largest single part played by psychologists in translating research findings into practice has been in designing structured programmes for use in this way (see, for example, Hanson *et al.*, 2009 and Hollin & Palmer, 2006). Most such programmes currently employed in the UK and Canadian criminal justice systems use methods derived from cognitive social learning theory and are known as *cognitive-behavioural* interventions. While this is far from being the only theoretical option available, to date it has been most consistent in yielding positive outcomes. Programmes of this type are usually supported by a specially prepared manual and other supporting materials (see Chapters 17 and 18 for more details about offender programmes).

Implications for effective practice

Expert reviewers agree that there are certain features of criminal justice interventions that maximise the likelihood of securing a practical, meaningful impact in terms of reduced reoffending. The major findings that arise from this are shown in Box 16.1.

BOX 16.1   MAJOR FINDINGS REGARDING EFFECTIVE PRACTICE

A clear theory and evidence base

Intervention efforts are more likely to succeed if they are based on a theory of criminal behaviour that is conceptually sound and has good empirical support. This provides a rationale for the methods that are used and it should identify the 'vehicle of change' considered to be at work when an individual participates in and benefits from the programme. This might be accomplished, for example, by learning new skills, changing attitudes, improving ability to communicate, increasing self-knowledge, solving problems, or overcoming bad feelings.

Assessment of risk level

It is generally regarded as good practice to assess risk levels and allocate individuals to different levels of services accordingly. Risk assessment is usually based on information about an individual's criminal history, such as the age at which he or she was first convicted of a crime, and the total number of convictions to date. The most intensive types of intervention should be reserved for those offenders assessed as posing the highest risk of reoffending; individuals estimated as posing a low risk should not be exposed to such interventions. This has been called the **risk principle** (Andrews & Bonta, 2010) and it has acquired

substantial support from review of the relevant literature (Lowenkamp *et al.*, 2006).

Identifying risk–need factors as targets of change

Research on the emergence of delinquency suggests that certain patterns of social interaction, social or cognitive skills, antisocial attitudes, the influence of delinquent peer-groups and other factors are associated with its onset and maintenance. If working with offenders is to make a difference to their prospects of reoffending, those variables should be its targets of change; they are factors that need to be addressed to alter offending and are therefore entitled **criminogenic needs**. Given their susceptibility to change, they are sometimes called *dynamic risk factors* and there are strong reasons for prioritising them in rehabilitation services.

> **criminogenic needs** features of individuals associated with the risk of involvement in crime that change over time and are susceptible to change by direct effort, thereby reducing risks of criminal activity. Also known as *dynamic risk factors*.

Use of multiple targets

Given the multiple factors known to contribute to criminal activity, there is virtual unanimity amongst researchers

(Continued)

that more effective interventions will comprise a number of ingredients, addressed at a range of the aforementioned risks. Interventions that successfully do this are called **multimodal programmes**. For example, working with a group of persistent young offenders might involve training them in social skills, learning self-control of impulses, and providing support for these changes through a mentoring scheme.

> **multimodal programmes** a term used to describe intervention programmes that have more than one target of change (social skills, thinking, substance abuse and so on) or employ more than one method of achieving it.

Responsivity

There are certain methods or approaches that have a superior record in engaging, motivating and helping participants in criminal justice interventions to change (Andrews, 2001; Gendreau & Andrews, 1990; Harkins & Beech, 2007; McMurran, 2002). There are two aspects of this. First, rehabilitative efforts will work better if they have clear, concrete objectives, their contents are structured, and there is a focus on activity and the acquisition of skills. Personnel involved in providing this should possess high quality interpersonal skills and foster supportive, collaborative relationships within clearly explained boundaries (general responsivity). Second, it is vital to adapt intervention strategies to accommodate diversity amongst participants with respect to age, gender, ethnicity, language, and learning styles (specific responsivity).

(Programme) integrity

Lipsey (1995) and other, more recent, meta-analyses have found that intervention services appear to work better when they are being actively researched. Regular collection of data on how an intervention is delivered sustains its clarity of purpose, and its adherence to the methods it was intended to deploy. This feature is called the **integrity** or *fidelity* of an intervention (Bernfeld, 2001; Hollin, 1995), and in the best intervention services it is regularly monitored and checked.

> **integrity** the extent to which an intervention is delivered as planned and in accordance with the model of change on which it is based; sometimes called *fidelity*, *programme integrity* or *treatment integrity*.

To provide the most favourable conditions for the delivery of the above kinds of services, many other ingredients should be in place, for example to ensure the validity of the assessment methods used and the thoroughness of monitoring and evaluation procedures, alongside larger-scale strategies for managing the implementation of services within the provider agency (for fuller discussion, see Andrews, 2001).

Examples of effective interventions

(Note that these are descriptions of generic work. For ideas about more specific interventions for offenders see Chapters 17 & 18.)

There are some variations, but also important overlaps, between the kind of interventions shown to have the largest impact on adolescent, and adult, offenders. For young offenders who have committed more serious offences, applying results from his own meta-analyses Lipsey (1995; 2009) recommends that intervention programmes generally need to be provided for a duration of not less than six months, with a minimum of two contacts per week. On the basis of the large-scale reviews, several methods have emerged as more likely to be effective for working with this group (Dowden & Andrews, 1999; Lipsey & Wilson, 1998) as shown in Box 16.2.

BOX 16.2   EFFECTIVE INTERVENTIONS FOR WORKING WITH ADOLESCENT OFFENDERS

Interpersonal skills training

This consists of a series of exercises designed to improve participants' skills in interacting with others. Working in a small group, individuals identify situations in which they are not sure how to act, or which they sometimes mishandle, for example giving in to pressure applied by others.

Suitable ways of managing the situation are discussed, then tried out using role-play, plus practice and feedback.

Behavioural interventions

In work with offenders this has included contingency contracts, where individual offenders and their supervisors compose a list of problem behaviours and a system of rewards for progress in modifying them. Behavioural training procedures, such as modelling and graduated practice, form part of many other types of interventions.

Cognitive skills training

There are several programmes of this type. Most consist of a series of structured sessions, each containing exercises designed to help participants acquire or develop their abilities in the domain of thinking about and solving everyday (usually interpersonal) problems. Typical material includes work on putting an everyday problem into words, gathering information about it, generating possible solutions, linking means and ends, anticipating consequences, making decisions, and allied skills.

Structured individual counselling

In its most widely used format, counselling is a relatively unstructured activity, in which the counsellor acts in a person-centred, non-directive manner, allowing the client to take the lead. This can be valuable for a number of

purposes, but it has not emerged as an effective means of reducing offender recidivism. In order for it to work in that context, research suggests it needs to be more directive and structured, and based on a 'reality therapy' or 'problem-solving' framework.

Teaching family homes

These are residential units or group homes in which specially trained adults work in pairs as 'teaching parents'. Their role is to develop positive working alliances with residents, impart a range of social and self-management skills, clarify boundaries, and provide counselling and advocacy services. Young people can continue to attend school and return to their homes of origin at weekends. Some of the largest effect sizes published so far have been obtained from *functional family therapy*, *Parenting Wisely*, family empowerment and similar therapeutic approaches, which involve working with young offenders and their families (Gordon, 2002). The most elaborate approach is *multi-systemic therapy* (MST), which comprises work with the young person, his or her family, and school staff (Henggeler *et al.*, 1998).

For adult offenders, as mentioned earlier average effect sizes are generally lower than for those at the younger age range (indicating less strong results). Nevertheless, the results are meaningful in practice, and comparable patterns emerge in respect of the types of intervention most likely to work. With this age group, with the

exception of intimate partner violence programmes (see Chapter 10 for a discussion of the issues of working with this group), family-based work is uncommon and interventions are almost exclusively conducted with individuals themselves, though often employing a group format. Box 16.3 shows what works with adult offenders.

BOX 16.3 WHAT WORKS WITH ADULT OFFENDERS

'Manualised' cognitive-behavioural programmes focusing on risk factors for criminal recidivism

These are the best-validated and most widely disseminated approaches (Lipsey *et al.*, 2007; Lipton *et al.*, 2002a; Tong & Farrington, 2006; Wilson *et al.*, 2005). Variants of the approach have been well supported primarily for individuals with mixed patterns of offending that may include property, violent, and substance-related crimes (Hollin, 2001; McGuire, 2006; Motiuk & Serin, 2001). These types of programme have also yielded positive results when disseminated on a large scale in probation service settings (Hollin *et al.*, 2008; McGuire *et al.*, 2008; Palmer *et al.*, 2007). Despite initially high drop-out rates, after the delivery process had become better established the level of completion showed substantial improvement (National Offender Management Service, 2008). There is evidence that on two-year follow-up, the actual rate of reconviction

of those attending such programmes is significantly below the expected rate (Hollis, 2007).

Specially designed programmes with additional components

These have been developed for adults who have committed violent offences (Figure 16.4; see Chapter 18 for a fuller description of such programmes). This may include a focus on anger control, modulation of moods, and recognition and self-management of risk (Bush, 1995; Henning & Frueh, 1996). While there have been some very strong findings from anger management programmes, such as those of Dowden *et al.* (1999) who reported an 86 per cent reduction in violent reoffending over a three-year follow-up with high-risk prisoners in Canada, in other instances treatment gains have been very marginal and more research is needed on the appropriateness of allocation to

(Continued)

FIGURE 16.4 *Specially designed programmes with additional components have been developed for adults who have committed violent offences.*

Source: © Marcin Balcerzak. Used under licence from Shutterstock.

this type of programme and the related issue of 'readiness to change'. Treatment for sex offenders (see Chapter 18) would include specialised components.

Therapeutic communities

For offenders with lengthy histories of substance abuse, therapeutic communities have been shown to be beneficial. These may be located in institutions or in the wider community and there are several different models on which they can be based (Lipton *et al.*, 2002b). Other multi-modal, integrated programmes containing several ingredients have also demonstrated good effects for reducing substance misuse (Springer *et al.*, 2003).

The evidence base concerning the usefulness of programmes of some of the above types is sufficiently impressive to have led to their adoption and implementation on a sizeable scale in prison and probation services in England and Wales (Hollin & Palmer, 2006). This became a component of a major government initiative and policy, the *Crime Reduction Programme*, which became operational in 2000. As part of it, an independent panel of experts, the Correctional Services Accreditation Panel (CSAP), was created, as a means of ensuring quality control and monitoring the process of introduction and 'rollout' of the programmes. By 2008, there were no fewer than 27 separate programmes validated for use in custodial settings and 20 for use in probation settings (with some approved for both) (Correctional Services Accreditation Panel, 2009). Maguire *et al.* (2010) describe the history and work of the accreditation panel from an 'insider' perspective.

Many, probably the majority, of the programmes currently in most widespread use are delivered in a group format. This has potential advantages in terms of including larger numbers of participants, achieving greater cost-efficiency in services, and also in generating additional 'change factors' that can enhance the effects of some of the methods employed (Bieling *et al.*, 2006). However, a large proportion of the work done with many people who have broken the law takes place on an individual basis. Case Studies 16.1 and 16.2 illustrate applications of psychologically-based methods to the reduction of different types of offending behaviour.

CASE STUDY 16.1   TREATMENT FOR THEFT (SHOPLIFTING)

Aust (1987) described working alongside a psychologist in order to help Diane, a young woman given a suspended prison sentence and placed on probation after a series of shoplifting offences. Assessment indicated that she had committed numerous shop thefts and, despite having been arrested and sentenced on several previous occasions, felt unable to control her urges to steal, which had been a feature of her life since the age of 16. She described a cycle of elation and compulsion when in shops but at other times suffered from depressed moods. Diane had two children and was now expecting a third, and was highly distressed by the imminent prospect, should she reoffend, of giving birth to her child in prison.

covert sensitisation a method developed in behaviour therapy, which applies conditioning principles to induce individuals to associate socially or personally unacceptable feelings and behaviour with an experience of disgust, thereby reducing their potency.

Diane, her probation officer and the psychologist worked out an intervention plan to help her overcome her compulsive stealing. This had two main components. One was **covert sensitisation**, a behaviour therapy procedure that in Diane's case entailed recording an audiotape in which she told herself the story of being arrested, with all its dreaded consequences. The power of this was such that she simply had to look at it rather than listen to it in order for it to have its effects. The second was practice of several techniques of **self-management**, which included a range of actions such as drawing the attention of staff whenever she went shopping, for example by asking them to show her where an item was; keeping receipts as a record of purchases; avoiding wearing clothes in which she could conceal items; and using a large, transparent carrier bag. While she implemented these changes she also joined gym sessions, which helped raise her self-esteem and underlying moods, providing an alternative to the 'buzz' of shoplifting. At her subsequent appearance in court, the judge deferred sentence for six months to allow her to work on this plan; at the end of this period, she had successfully avoided shop theft, and gained a new equilibrium in having reduced her impulses and replaced them with new patterns of behaviour. It is interesting to place this study in the context of research carried out by Carroll and Weaver (1986) who found remarkably different patterns of cognitions amongst a group of 'expert' shoplifters as compared with a 'novice' group.

self-management a form of cognitive behavioural intervention designed to increase an individual's capacity for exercising internalised control over aspects of their thoughts, feelings or behaviour that are causing difficulty or distress.

Psychological contributions to offender assessment and management

Forensic psychologists working in prisons, probation or youth justice settings have progressively extended their roles from their previous 'niche', focused more or less exclusively on assessment and allocation, to a broader function in which they now contribute to risk assessment, delivery of interventions at the individual level, design and evaluation of programmes, report-writing, and research on all of these issues.

In recent years the risk–need–responsivity framework has been used to construct a number of more complex, in-depth assessment instruments for prediction of future involvement in crime. Several scales now exist for combined assessment of *static* and *dynamic* risk factors. The former refers to factors that are fixed at a given point in time (for example, an individual's age on first appearance in court). The latter refers to influences that fluctuate over time and are also potentially susceptible to change through intervention (for example, antisocial attitudes, level of self-control,

or problem-solving skills). Probably the best-known example of an assessment combining this spectrum of variables is the Level of Service/Case Management Inventory (LS/CMI; Andrews *et al.*, 2004) (see Chapter 17 for a more in-depth description of this measure). However, there are numerous specialised methods of carrying out this work for general case-management purposes (for an overview of basic concepts involved in this, see Hollin, 2002; for a recent review of predictive accuracy of some prominent tools, see Yang *et al.*, 2010).

This type of approach, based on amalgamation of variables, is widely perceived as having more practical value than any single theoretical model. In addition to yielding predictions of the likelihood of reoffending, these approaches also generate information that can be applied in risk management, identifying target areas on which psychologists and other criminal justice staff can focus their efforts with individual offenders.

Psychologically-based research and other approaches in criminology linked to it have made enormous strides

CASE STUDY 16.2   SEX OFFENDER TREATMENT

Marshall (2006) has described a treatment programme carried out with Bill, a 38-year-old lorry driver who had convictions for sexual offences against children. Over a period of 20 years he had molested eight girls aged between 6 and 10 years of age. He was given early release from prison on condition that he attended treatment at a community-based clinic. Bill's history showed a pattern of sexual fantasies concerning younger girls, and of failure in his relationships with females closer to his age, feeling he had been humiliated in these encounters. As an only child who had grown up in an isolated rural area, his development was characterised by very limited social contacts, and more extensive assessment showed negative attitudes towards women, some distortions in his views of children whom he saw as submissive but also as provocative, and an undervaluing of himself. Assessment by *phallometry* (using the *penile plethysmograph (PPG)*) showed a pattern of strongest arousal to children but some evidence of arousal to adult women.

Intervention with Bill involved a multifaceted programme that focused on a series of areas including reduction of his sexual interest in children. This was approached by means of a combination of **olfactory**

aversion therapy (or olfactory aversive conditioning), in which he learned to associate sexual arousal to children with a foul odour in a series of 40 conditioning trials over a four-week period; and **directed masturbation** associated with images of adult women. These interventions were accompanied by a separate series of sessions of cognitive restructuring, designed to address attitudes and beliefs he held that were supportive of offending. The treatment programme proved to be effective in altering both Bill's sexual preferences and his habitual thoughts and feelings, and a follow-up over two years indicated that the changes were sustained. By that point in time, he had developed a stable relationship with an adult female partner.

olfactory aversive conditioning a behaviour therapy technique, based on conditioning principles, employed with individuals who have committed sexual offences as a result of socially unacceptable patterns of sexual arousal and associated behaviour.

directed masturbation also called masturbatory reconditioning. A behaviour therapy technique, based on conditioning principles, to help individuals with inappropriate sexual urges or attractions to divert their interests in more socially acceptable or less harmful ways.

over approximately the last two decades, with respect to developing an understanding of the factors that contribute to criminal behaviour, the traditional and entrenched practices that have no impact on it, and methods that can genuinely help reduce the chances of its recurrence. None of this has achieved a state of perfection of course, but the advances made have been significant nonetheless.

Given this accumulated knowledge base, coupled with the level of public and governmental concern over crime, there remains a surprisingly large gap between

this acquired information and everyday practice in many criminal justice agencies. The widespread perception that seeking to understand individual factors in crime implies that psychologists believe those are the *only* operative factors takes a very long time to dissipate. Apart from further research and knowledge accumulation then, a sizeable challenge remains in translating available findings judiciously into practice, and convincing other concerned parties that psychology has something valuable to offer in this field.

SUMMARY

The main areas covered in this chapter are as follows:

- **the principal objectives of sentencing in courts of law (retribution/desert, incapacitation, deterrence, rehabilitation, and restoration/reparation) and the rationale given for each**

- **an overview of the effects of penal sentences on recidivism**

- **a more specific review of the evidence for sanctions and deterrence**

- an outline of the evidence concerning the impact of psychosocial interventions on criminal behaviour, including a summary of the findings of 75 meta-analytic reviews and trends amongst the findings within them

- a survey of implications for practice in criminal justice and allied agencies

- illustration of the types of interventions that have been shown to be effective in reducing offending behaviour, including group programmes and individual case studies

- a brief outline of some current psychological contributions to offender assessment and management.

ESSAY/DISCUSSION QUESTIONS

1. Summarise the main arguments for the use of punishment as the principal component of society's response to criminal offending. Explain whether, in your view, some approaches to this have a sounder basis than others.

2. Evaluate evidence concerning the extent to which those who have repeatedly broken the criminal law can be 'rehabilitated' using psychosocial interventions. Give your views on whether this evidence might be of interest to policy makers in criminal justice.

3. Psychological research on offending and how to reduce it has tended to focus on serious crimes such as violence and sexual assault, or on the links between crime and mental disorder. What in your view are the reasons for this and on whether such an emphasis is justifiable?

4. Briefly survey current applications of psychological knowledge in the penal system and roles psychologists play within it. Propose possible extensions to these applications and roles, and provide appropriate justifications for them.

REFERENCES

Andrews, D.A. (2001). Principles of effective correctional programs. In L.L. Motiuk & R.C. Serin (Eds.) *Compendium 2000 on effective correctional programming* (pp.9–17). Ottawa: Correctional Service Canada.

Andrews, D.A. (2011). The impact of nonprogrammatic factors on criminal-justice interventions. *Legal and Criminological Psychology, 16*, 1–23.

Andrews, D.A. & Bonta, J. (2010) *The psychology of criminal conduct* (5th edn). Newark, NJ: LexisNexis/Matthew Bender.

Andrews, D.A., Bonta, J. & Wormith, J.S. (2004). *Level of Service/Case Management Inventory (LS/CMI)*. Toronto: Multi-Health Systems.

Andrews, D.A., Bonta, J. & Wormith, J.S. (2006). The recent past and near future of risk and/or need assessment. *Crime & Delinquency, 52*, 7–27.

Andrews, D.A., Zinger, I., Hoge, R.D., Bonta, J., Gendreau, P. & Cullen, F.T. (1990). Does correctional treatment work? A clinically relevant and psychologically informed meta-analysis. *Criminology, 28*, 369–404.

Ashworth, A. (2005). *Sentencing and criminal justice* (4th edition). Cambridge: Cambridge University Press.

Aust, A. (1987). Gaining control of compulsive shop theft. *Probation Journal, 34*, 145–146.

Bernfeld, G.A. (2001). The struggle for treatment integrity in a 'dis-integrated' service delivery system. In G.A. Bernfeld, D.P. Farrington & A.W. Leschied (Eds.) *Offender rehabilitation in practice: Implementing and evaluating effective programmes* (pp. 184–204). Chichester: John Wiley & Sons, Inc.

Bieling, P.J., McCabe, R.E. & Antony, M.M. (2006). *Cognitive-behavioral therapy in groups*. New York: Guilford Press.

Blackburn, R. (2003). *The psychology of criminal conduct* (2nd edn). Chichester: John Wiley & Sons, Inc.

Bush, J. (1995). Teaching self-risk-management to violent offenders. In J. McGuire (Ed.) *What works: Reducing reoffending: guidelines from research and practice* (pp.139–154). Chichester: John Wiley & Sons, Inc.

Carroll, J. & Weaver, F. (1986). Shoplifters' perceptions of crime opportunities: A process-tracing study. In D.B. Cornish & R.V. Clarke (Eds.) *The reasoning criminal: Rational choice perspectives on offending* (pp.19–38). New York: Springer-Verlag.

Center on Juvenile and Criminal Justice. (2008). *Research update: Does more imprisonment lead to less crime?* San Francisco, CA.: Center on Juvenile and Criminal Justice.

Clark, G. (1977). What happens when the police strike? In R.M. Ayres & T.L. Wheelen (Eds.) *Collective bargaining in the public sector: Selected readings in law enforcement* (pp.440–449). Alexandria, VA: International Association of Chiefs of Police.

Correctional Services Accreditation Panel (CSAP). (2009). The Correctional Services Accreditation Panel Report 2008–2009. London: Ministry of Justice/Correctional Services Accreditation Panel Secretariat. Retrieved 24 August 2011 from www.justice.gov.uk/publications/docs/correctional-services-report-20080-09.pdf

Dowden, C. & Andrews, D.A. (1999). What works in young offender treatment: A meta-analysis. *Forum on Corrections Research, 11,* 21–24.

Dowden, C., Blanchette, K. & Serin, R.C. (1999). Anger management programming for federal male inmates: An effective intervention. *Research Report R-82.* Ottawa, ON: Correctional Service of Canada.

Duff, R.A. & Garland, D. (Eds.) (1994). *A reader on punishment.* Oxford: Oxford University Press.

Easton, S. & Piper, C. (2005). *Sentencing and punishment: The quest for justice.* Oxford: Oxford University Press.

Farrington, D.P. & Welsh, B.C. (2007). *Saving children from a life of crime: Early risk factors and effective interventions.* Oxford: Oxford University Press.

Garland, D. (1990). *Punishment and modern society: A study in social theory.* Oxford: Clarendon Press.

Garland, D. & Duff, R.A. (1994). Introduction: Thinking about punishment. In R.A. Duff & D. Garland (Eds.) *A reader on punishment.* (pp.1–43). Oxford: Oxford University Press.

Gendreau, P. (1996). Offender rehabilitation: What we know and what needs to be done. *Criminal Justice and Behavior, 23,* 144–161.

Gendreau, P. & Andrews, D.A. (1990). Tertiary prevention: What the meta-analyses of the offender treatment literature tell us about 'what works'. *Canadian Journal of Criminology, 32,* 173–184.

Gendreau, P., Goggin, C. & Cullen, F.T. (1999). The effects of prison sentences on recidivism. *Report to the Corrections Research and Development and Aboriginal Policy Branch.* Ottawa: Solicitor General of Canada.

Gendreau, P., Goggin, C., Cullen, F.T. & Andrews, D.A. (2001). The effects of community sanctions and incarceration on recidivism. In L.L. Motiuk & R.C. Serin (Eds.) *Compendium 2000 on effective correctional programming* (pp.18–21). Ottawa: Correctional Service Canada.

Gibbs, J.P. (1986). Deterrence theory and research. In G.B. Melton (Ed.) *The law as a behavioral Instrument: Nebraska Symposium on Motivation, 198* (pp.87–130). Lincoln and London: University of Nebraska Press.

Gilinskiy, Y. (2006). Crime in contemporary Russia. *European Journal of Criminology, 3,* 259–292.

Goldstein, A.P. (2002). Low-level aggression: Definition, escalation, intervention. In J. McGuire (Ed.) *Offender rehabilitation and treatment: Effective programmes and policies to reduce re-offending* (pp.169–192). Chichester: John Wiley & Sons, Inc.

Gordon, D.A. (2002). Intervening with families of troubled youth: Functional Family Therapy and Parenting Wisely. In J. McGuire (Ed.) *Offender Rehabilitation and Treatment: Effective Programmes and Policies to Reduce Re-Offending* (pp.193–219). Chichester: John Wiley & Sons, Inc.

Graef, R. (2001). *Why restorative justice? Repairing the harm caused by crime.* London: Calouste Gulbenkian Foundation.

Hanson, R.K., Bourgon, G., Helmus, L. & Hodgson, S. (2009). The principles of effective correctional treatment also apply to sexual offenders: A meta-analysis. *Criminal Justice and Behavior, 36,* 865–891.

Harkins, L. & Beech, A.R. (2007). A review of the factors that can influence the effectiveness of sexual offender treatment: Risk, need, responsivity, and process issues. *Aggression and Violent Behavior, 12,* 615–627.

Henggeler, S.W., Schoenwald, S.K., Borduin, C.M., Rowland, M.D. & Cunningham, P.B. (1998). *Multisystemic treatment of antisocial behavior in children and adolescents.* New York: Guilford Press.

Henning, K.R. & Frueh, B.C. (1996). Cognitive-behavioral treatment of incarcerated offenders: An evaluation of the Vermont Department of Corrections' cognitive self-change program. *Criminal Justice and Behavior, 23,* 523–542.

Hollin, C.R. (1995). The meaning and implications of program integrity. In J. McGuire (Ed.) *What works: Reducing reoffending: guidelines from research and practice* (pp.195–208). Chichester: John Wiley & Sons, Inc.

Hollin, C.R. (1999). Treatment programmes for offenders: Meta-analysis, 'what works', and beyond. *International Journal of Law and Psychiatry, 22,* 361–371.

Hollin, C.R. (2001). To treat or not to treat? An historical perspective. In C.R. Hollin (Ed.) *Handbook of offender assessment and treatment* (pp.3–15). Chichester: John Wiley & Sons, Inc.

Hollin, C.R. (2002). Risk-needs assessment and allocation to offender programmes. In J. McGuire (Ed.) *Offender rehabilitation and treatment: Effective programmes and policies to reduce re-offending* (pp.309–332). Chichester: John Wiley & Sons, Inc.

Hollin, C.R., McGuire, J., Hatcher, R.M., Bilby, C.A.L., Hounsome, J. & Palmer, E.J. (2008). Cognitive skills offending behavior programs in the community: A reconviction analysis. *Criminal Justice and Behavior, 34,* 269–283.

Hollin, C.R. & Palmer, E.J. (Eds.) (2006). *Offending behaviour programmes: Development, application, and controversies.* Chichester: John Wiley & Sons, Inc.

Hollis, V. (2007). *Reconviction analysis of interim accredited programmes software (IAPS) data.* London: Research Development Statistics, National Offender Management Service.

Howard, P., Francis, B., Soothill, K. & Humphreys, L. (2009). OGRS 3: The revised Offender Group Reconviction Scale. Research Summary 7/09. London: Ministry of Justice. Retrieved 24 August 2011 from www.justice.gov.uk/publications/docs/oasys-research-summary-07-09-ii.pdf

Johnstone, G. & Van Ness, D.W. (2006). *Handbook of restorative justice.* Cullompton, Devon: Willan.

Kershaw, C. (1999). Reconviction of offenders sentenced or released from prison in 1994. Research Findings, 90. London: Home Office Research, Development and Statistics Directorate. Retrieved 24 August 2011 from http://members.multimania.co.uk/lawnet/RECONVIC.PDF

Klemke, L.W. (1982). Reassessment of Cameron's apprehension-termination of shoplifting finding. *California Sociologist, 5*, 88–95.

Leibmann, M. (2007). *Restorative justice: How it works.* London: Jessica Kingsley Publishers.

Lipsey, M.W. (1992). Juvenile delinquency treatment: A meta-analytic inquiry into the variability of effects. In T. Cook, D. Cooper, H. Corday, H. Hartman, L. Hedges, R. Light, T. Louis & F. Mosteller (Eds.) *Meta-analysis for explanation: A casebook* (pp.83–127). New York: Russell Sage Foundation.

Lipsey, M.W. (1995). What do we learn from 400 studies on the effectiveness of treatment with juvenile delinquents? In J. McGuire (Ed.) *What works: Reducing re-offending: Guidelines from research and practice* (pp.63–78). Chichester: John Wiley & Sons, Inc.

Lipsey, M.W. (2009). The primary factors that characterize effective interventions with juvenile offenders: a meta-analytic overview. *Victims and Offenders, 4*, 124–147.

Lipsey, M.W., Landenberger N.A. & Wilson S.J. (2007). *Effects of cognitive-behavioral programs for criminal offenders.* Campbell Systematic Reviews. DOI: 10.4073/csr.2007.6

Lipsey, M.W. & Wilson, D.B. (1998). Effective intervention for serious juvenile offenders: A synthesis of research. In R. Loeber & D.P. Farrington (Eds.) *Serious and violent juvenile offenders: Risk factors and successful interventions* (pp.313–345). Thousand Oaks, CA: Sage Publications.

Lipton, D.S., Pearson, F.S., Cleland, C.M. & Yee, D. (2002a). The effects of therapeutic communities and milieu therapy on recidivism. In J. McGuire (Ed.) *Offender rehabilitation and treatment: Effective programmes and policies to reduce re-offending* (pp.39–77). Chichester: John Wiley & Sons, Inc.

Lipton, D.S., Pearson, F.S., Cleland, C.M. & Yee, D. (2002b). The effectiveness of cognitive-behavioural treatment methods on recidivism. In J. McGuire (Ed.) *Offender rehabilitation and treatment: effective programmes and policies to reduce re-offending* (pp.79–112) Chichester: John Wiley & Sons, Inc.

Lloyd, C., Mair, G. & Hough, M. (1994). *Explaining reconviction rates: A critical analysis. Home Office Research Study, 136.* London: HMSO.

Lowenkamp, C.T., Latessa, E.J. & Holsinger, A.M. (2006). The risk principle in action: What have we learned from 13,676 offenders and 97 correctional programs? *Crime and Delinquency, 52*, 77–93.

Maguire, M., Grubin, D., Lösel, F. & Raynor, P. (2010). 'What works' and the Correctional Services Accreditation Panel: Taking stock from an insider perspective. *Criminology and Criminal Justice, 10*, 37–58.

Makinen, T. & Takala, H. (1980). 1976 police strike in Finland. In R. Hauge (Ed.) *Policing Scandinavia.* Oslo: Universitetsforlaget.

Marshall, W.L. (2006). Olfactory aversion and directed masturbation in the modification of deviant sexual preferences: A case study of a child molester. *Clinical Case Studies, 5*, 3–14.

Martinson, R. (1974). What works? Questions and answers about prison reform. *The Public Interest, 10*, 22–54.

McGuire, J. (2001). Defining correctional programs. In L.L. Motiuk & R.C. Serin (Eds.) *Compendium 2000 on effective correctional programming* (pp.1–8). Ottawa: Correctional Service Canada.

McGuire, J. (2002). Criminal sanctions versus psychological interventions with offenders: A comparative empirical analysis. *Psychology, Crime and Law, 8*, 183–208.

McGuire, J. (2004). *Understanding psychology and crime: Perspectives on theory and action.* Maidenhead: Open University Press/McGraw-Hill Education.

McGuire, J. (2006). General offending behaviour programmes. In C.R. Hollin & E.J. Palmer (Eds.) *Offending behaviour programmes: Development, application, and controversies* (pp.69–111). Chichester: John Wiley & Sons, Inc.

McGuire, J. (2008). A review of effective interventions for reducing aggression and violence. *Philosophical Transactions of the Royal Society B, 363*, 2577–2597.

McGuire , J. (2009). Reducing personal violence: Risk factors and effective interventions. In S. Hodgins, E. Viding & A. Plodowski (Eds.) *The neurobiological basis of violence: Science and rehabilitation* (pp.287–327). Oxford: Oxford University Press.

McGuire, J., Bilby, C.A.L., Hatcher, R.M., Hollin, C.R., Hounsome, J.C. & Palmer, E.J. (2008). Evaluation of structured cognitive-behavioral programs in reducing criminal recidivism. *Journal of Experimental Criminology, 4*, 21–40.

McMurran, M. (Ed.) (2002). *Motivating offenders to change: A guide to enhancing engagement in therapy.* Chichester: John Wiley & Sons, Inc.

Miethe, T.D. & Lu, H. (2005). *Punishment: A comparative historical perspective.* Cambridge: Cambridge University Press.

Motiuk, L.L. & Serin, R.C. (Eds.) (2001). *Compendium 2000 on effective correctional programming.* Ottawa: Correctional Service Canada.

Murphy, J.G. (1994). Marxism and retribution. In R.A. Duff & D. Garland (Eds.) *A reader on punishment* (pp.44–70). Oxford: Oxford University Press.

National Offender Management Service (2008). *Annual report for accredited programmes 2006–2007.* London: National Probation Service.

Newman, G., Bouloukos, A.C. & Cohen, D. (Eds.) (2001). *World factbook of criminal justice systems.* Washington, DC: Department of Justice. Retrieved 24 August 2011 from http://bjs.ojp.usdoj.gov/content/pub/html/wfcj.cfm

Palmer, E.J., McGuire, J., Hounsome, J.C., Hatcher, R.M., Bilby, C.A.L. & Hollin, C.R. (2007). Offending behaviour programmes in the community: The effects on reconviction of three programmes with adult male offenders. *Legal and Criminological Psychology, 12*, 251–264.

Pearson, F.S., Lipton, D.S. & Cleland, C.M. (1997, November). *Rehabilitative programs in adult corrections: CDATE meta-analyses.* Paper presented at the Annual Meeting of the American Society of Criminology, San Diego, CA.

Pfuhl, E.H. (1983). Police strikes and conventional crime – A look at the data. *Criminology, 21*, 489–503.

Redondo, S., Sánchez-Meca, J. & Garrido, V. (2002). Crime treatment in Europe: A review of outcome studies. In J. McGuire (Ed.) *Offender rehabilitation and treatment: Effective programmes and policies to reduce re-offending* (pp.113–141). Chichester: John Wiley & Sons, Inc.

Sentencing Guidelines Council (2008). *Magistrates' court sentencing guidelines.* London: Sentencing Guidelines Council. Retrieved 24 August 2011 from www.sentencingcouncil.org.uk/docs/web_sgc_magistrates_guidelines_including_update_1__2__3_web.pdf

Springer, D.W., McNeece, C.A. & Arnold, E.M. (2002). *Substance abuse treatment for criminal offenders: An evidence-based guide for practitioners.* Washington, DC: American Psychological Association.

Stafford, M.C. & Warr, M. (1993). A reconceptualisation of general and specific deterrence. *Journal of Research on Crime and Delinquency, 30*, 123–135.

Taylor, R., Wasik, M. & Leng, R. (2004). *Blackstone's guide to the Criminal Justice Act 2003.* Oxford: Oxford University Press.

Tong, L.S.J. & Farrington, D.P. (2006). How effective is the 'Reasoning and Rehabilitation' programme in reducing re-offending? A meta-analysis of evaluations in three countries. *Psychology, Crime and Law, 12*, 3–24.

Tyler, T.R. (2006). *Why people obey the law.* Princeton, NJ: Princeton University Press.

von Hirsch, A. (1994). Censure and proportionality. In R.A. Duff & D. Garland (Eds.) *A reader on punishment* (pp.112–160). Oxford: Oxford University Press.

von Hirsch, A., Bottoms, A.E., Burney, E. & Wikström, P.O. (1999). *Criminal deterrence and sentencing severity: An analysis of recent research.* Oxford: Hart Publishing.

Walker, N. (1991). *Why punish? Theories of punishment reassessed.* Oxford: Oxford University Press.

White, J.R. (1988). Violence during the 1919 Boston police strike: An analysis of the crime control myth. *Criminal Justice Review, 13*, 61–68.

Wilson, D.B. (2001). Meta-analytic methods for criminology. *Annals of the American Academy of Political and Social Science, 578*, 71–89.

Wilson, D.B., Bouffard, L.A. & Mackenzie, D.L. (2005). A quantitative review of structured, group-oriented, cognitive-behavioral programs for offenders. *Criminal Justice and Behavior, 32*, 172–204.

Yang, M., Wong, S.C.P. & Coid, J. (2010). The efficacy of violence prediction: A meta-analytic comparison of nine risk assessment tools. *Psychological Bulletin, 136*, 740–767.

ANNOTATED READING LIST

Ashworth, A. (2005). *Sentencing and Criminal Justice.* Oxford: Oxford University Press. Easton, S. & Piper, C. (2005). *Sentencing and Punishment: The Quest for Justice.* Oxford: Oxford University Press. *Both of these books provide more detailed background on the law with particular reference to sentencing and punishment (though primarily focused on England and Wales).*

Andrews, D.A. & Bonta, J. (2010). *The psychology of criminal conduct* (5th edn). Cincinnati, OH: Andersen Publishing; Blackburn, R. (2003). *The psychology of criminal conduct.* Chichester: John Wiley & Sons, Inc.; McGuire, J. (2004). *Understanding psychology and crime: Perspectives on theory and action.* Maidenhead: Open University Press/McGraw-Hill Education; and Hollin, C.R. (2007). Criminological psychology. In Maguire, M., Morgan, R. & Reiner, R. (Eds.) *The Oxford handbook of criminology* (4th edn) (pp.43–77). Oxford: Oxford University Press. *These sources provide recent and more extensive introductions to the relationships between psychology and crime in general.*

MacKenzie, D.L. (2006). *What works in corrections: Reducing the criminal activities of offenders and delinquents.* Cambridge: Cambridge University Press. *Provides a wide-ranging review of the research on the main categories of criminal justice interventions.*

McGuire, J. (Ed.) (2002). *Offender rehabilitation and treatment: Effective practice and policies to reduce re-offending,* Chichester: John Wiley & Sons, Inc. *Provides a fuller description of research concerning psychosocial interventions to reduce offending behaviour.*

Miethe, T.D. & Lu, H. (2005). *Punishment: A comparative historical perspective.* Cambridge: Cambridge University Press. *Provides an in-depth discussion of the history, and numerous other aspects, of punishment.*

Tyler, T.R. (2006). *Why people obey the law.* Princeton: Princeton University Press. *Provides an overview of research on the relationship between punishment and other factors mediating law-abiding behaviour.*

17 Risk Assessment and Offender Programmes

RUTH HATCHER

CHAPTER OUTLINE

During the latter quarter of the 20th century, the *What Works* movement contributed a plethora of evidence regarding the effectiveness of different ways of working with offenders. Perhaps the most influential volume of evidence came from a number of collective reviews of a large number of studies, using the method for integrating research findings known as **meta-analysis**. These evaluations have advanced our knowledge concerning the components of interventions most effective in reducing recidivistic behaviour and have been particularly influential in shaping modern day correctional service provision. As a consequence, offending behaviour programmes, and the associated practice of **risk assessment**, are now commonplace within many correctional services of the world, including those within the UK, Europe, Australasia and North America.

> **risk assessment** a set of procedures and methods for estimating the likelihood of future offending by an individual or the level of harm that might be caused by it, and for identifying the factors associated with it.

Andrews *et al.*'s (1990) meta-analysis of intervention evaluation studies is perhaps one of the most prominent of the What Works papers to date. Within this and subsequent publications, Andrews and colleagues founded the evidence-based principles of risk, need, and responsivity of offender programming that have since influenced the design and implementation of offending behaviour programmes. These shall each be discussed in turn.

> **risk principle** states that the level of intervention received by an offender should match the level of risk that offender poses. Higher risk individuals should receive a higher level of intervention than lower risk individuals.

The **risk principle** dictates that to impact on offending behaviour, the level of intervention received by an offender should depend on the level of risk that s/he poses. Offenders assessed as high-risk cases should, therefore, receive a greater level of intervention than offenders who are low risk. Clearly, the accurate assessment of risk is necessary to allocate offenders to individually appropriate levels of intervention.

While the risk principle is concerned with the dosage of programming, the **need principle** determines the targets of treatment. Andrews and Bonta (2010) make the distinction between general problems or needs present within the offenders' lives, and those linked to their offending behaviour. The need principle proposes that to reduce recidivistic behaviour, interventions should target only those needs (or risk factors) that contribute to offending behaviour. Such factors have been termed **criminogenic needs**.

> **need principle** states that interventions should target only those needs (or risk factors) that contribute to offending behaviour.

The third principle, **responsivity**, is concerned with how the intervention is delivered to the offender. The **responsivity principle** states that those programmes that successfully match the style and method of delivery to the learning styles of the attendees will be more effective. The issue of responsivity will be discussed in more detail in the second half of this chapter. We will first look into the theory and practice of the assessment of risk and need before considering some examples of tools commonly used by correctional services in North America and the UK.

> **responsivity** a design feature that contributes to effectiveness of intervention programmes with offenders. Can be general (an overall approach) or specific (taking into account factors that reflect diversity amongst participants).

> **responsivity principle** proposes that the method of delivery of an intervention should match the learning styles of those to whom it is delivered.

RISK ASSESSMENT WITHIN OFFENDER MANAGEMENT

Risk assessment within offender management operates on much the same principles as risk assessment within other fields. When you apply for insurance, for example, your insurance company generally requests particular information about you and your personal circumstances. This information is used by the company to judge the likelihood of the outcome occurring that they are insuring against. In general, the higher the likelihood of the outcome or, to put it another way, the more risky it is for the company to insure you, the more expensive your premium will be. Consider the cost of a car insurance premium, for example. A 35-year-old driver with 15 years of driving experience, no motoring convictions, and no previous car insurance claims would be able to obtain a lower insurance quote than a 21-year-old with two years' driving experience, a conviction for driving over the speed limit and a previous insurance claim to cover repairs to the vehicle acquired in an accident involving the car and a lamp post! It is easy to see that the likelihood of a future claim is higher in the second scenario than the first: the driver has less experience of driving, has displayed risky driving behaviour and has a history of crashing the car. The insurance premium is thus adjusted to reflect the higher risk to the insurance company of having to finance a future claim.

In much the same manner, the risk assessment of offenders draws on information about the offender and their circumstances in order to reach judgements about their likely future behaviour. Such assessments may consider how likely an offender is to reoffend, be reconvicted or cause harm to others. The choice of which future behaviour is the subject of the prediction will depend on the purpose of the assessment.

The efficacy of risk assessment, then, rests on the ability to accurately predict future behaviour. Prediction, however, is not an exact science. If we recall our insurance illustration for a moment, a life insurance company will use information relating to our age, current health status, lifestyle, family medical history and, maybe at some point in the future, our genes, to determine the probability of future serious illness or death. The premium is then calculated on this perceived risk. It is perhaps obvious, however, that such information will not allow for the prediction of more idiosyncratic threats to health, such as being hit by a bus or struck by lightning. In much the same way, an assessment of offender risk of reconviction or harm is open to the same inaccuracies.

Figure 17.1 presents the four potential outcomes in relation to prediction. When an event is predicted to occur, it then can either occur (outcome one) or not (outcome two). Likewise when an event is predicted to not occur, it then can either occur (outcome three) or not (outcome four). The consequences of incorrect prediction (outcomes two and three) can be rather unpalatable. For example, in the case of offender recidivism prediction, an offender deemed by the risk assessment as unlikely to reoffend could, on the basis of that prediction, be given a non-custodial sentence or released from incarceration. If the prediction is incorrect and the offender recidivates (i.e. outcome two), the previous decisions, predicated on the incorrect risk assessment, will inevitably impact on society creating real and unwelcome consequences. At the individual level, the subsequent offending behaviour creates additional victims and the associated distress of victimisation, while society is also affected by the monetary costs of the administration of further investigation and justice.

| | | Prediction | |
		Reoffend	Not-reoffend
Actual Event	Reoffend	Outcome 1 Correct prediction (true positive)	Outcome 3 Incorrect prediction (false negative)
	Not-reoffend	Outcome 2 Incorrect prediction (true positive)	Outcome 4 Correct prediction (false negative)

FIGURE 17.1 *Possible outcomes in risk assessment.*

A false positive outcome is also undesirable: an offender's application for parole may be rejected on the basis of a risk assessment, which predicts future offending behaviour. If the risk assessment was incorrect, and the offender would not have reoffended on release (i.e. outcome three), it could be argued that the faulty assessment had contributed to an infringement of the detained individual's human rights and the squandering of public money spent on continued imprisonment. In all risk assessments, then, the overarching aim is to maximise the proportion of correct predictions whilst minimising the false positives and false negatives.

Methods of assessing risk

While there are a number of ways of determining an individual's level of risk, these tend to fall broadly into two categories: clinical and actuarial risk assessments. *Clinical risk assessment*, as the name implies, draws on the clinical skills of the assessor to evaluate the offender's risk level. Hence, clinical assessment involves the collection of background information and observation of the offender by professionals. The clinician utilises the information gleaned from such observations, alongside their experience and training, to guide the formulation of the risk prediction. Originating from the medical field (Monahan, 1981), this practice can be construed as a diagnostic assessment of risk (Howells & Hollin, 1989).

Actuarial prediction is really quite different. Actuarial methods typically employ statistical **algorithms**, or equations, to generate risk scores from specific items of information. These scores can be construed as estimated likelihoods of the occurrence of the event of interest (i.e. on a scale of 0 to 100, for example) or can be categorised into risk bands such as low, medium and high risk. The algorithms utilised within actuarial prediction are generally determined through large cohort longitudinal research projects assessing the factors associated with the outcome in question. The resultant assessments are hence derived through the comparison of the individual's risk predictors against the amassed knowledge of a similar sample's outcomes.

Both clinical and actuarial assessments draw on a range of data points. These data can be static (or historic factors), such as the offender's number of previous convictions, their age and their gender. Such factors are termed 'static' as they are not amenable to change through intervention or otherwise. Furthermore, both types of assessment can also utilise dynamic, or theoretically changeable, factors such as psychological (cognitive distortions, attitudes to crime), social (employment status, the nature of peer relationships) or behavioural

algorithm a mathematical procedure that must be followed in a set order and will derive an overall score.

FIGURE 17.2 *Should the prisoner be released? Keeping him in jail unnecessarily is an infringement of his human rights, but miscalculating the risk and letting him go could lead to others being harmed.*

Source: © CURA Photography. Used under licence from Shutterstock.

(levels of impulsivity, displayed aggression) measures. Hence the choice of information used by the two kinds of assessment can overlap partially or indeed fully; it is the employment of this information that differs between the clinical and actuarial prediction fields (Figure 17.2).

A longstanding debate within the field of psychology has centred on the comparative merits of these two methods of risk assessment. Advocates of the clinical method argue that the generalisation of information from a group to an individual is in itself problematic (Dingwall, 1989). Others have claimed that actuarial methods oversimplify the complexity of factors involved in an offender's decision to reoffend or cause harm (Grubin, 1997; Grubin & Wingate, 1996; Litwack, 2001) and fail to attend to idiosyncrasies that might be highly predictive. In contrast, Grove and Meehl (1996) have argued that actuarial risk assessment 'involves a formal, algorithmic, objective procedure (e.g. equation) to reach the decision' (p.293) whilst clinical prediction 'relies on an informal, "in the head", impressionistic, subjective conclusion, reached (somehow) by a human clinical judge' (p.294). This view was predicated on the findings of their meta-analysis, which compared the predictive accuracy of both methods and concluded in favour of actuarial assessments.

This view is now generally accepted (Howe, 1994; Milner & Campbell, 1995; Quinsey *et al.*, 1993). Moreover, some authors have gone so far as to propose the 'complete replacement' of clinical assessments with actuarial measures (Quinsey *et al.*, 1998). Others have proposed that such statements are too hasty. Douglas *et al.* (1999) argue that:

... the actuarial method, while useful, is not a panacea, and that it has limitations in the risk assessment field. The function of actuarial prediction methods is simply that – prediction. Risk assessment as conceived here is broader than prediction. Prediction is a necessary first step. Yet risk management and prevention are equally necessary steps. Once a person is defined as high risk, it is in everyone's best interest to suggest means by which such risk can be attenuated.

(Douglas et al., 1999, p.155)

The authors endorse a combination of clinical and actuarial methods into an 'empirically validated, structured clinical assessment' (Douglas *et al.*, 1999, p.157) of risk and need. Such tools draw on the expertise of professionals' decisions and allow them to highlight idiosyncrasies which may impact on risk, whilst also providing an empirically derived and validated risk score or banding. Indeed the combination of clinical assessment with actuarial methods, it has been argued, can play an important role in identifying the factors that contribute to the outcome of interest (Limandri & Sheridan, 1995). As such, the development of structured clinical judgement, sometimes referred to as third generation tools, allows for the objective assessment of risk whilst also supplying an empirically derived and individualised profile of criminogenic needs. In the next section of this chapter, we will examine some of the more commonly used assessment tools.

Risk and need instruments for offenders

Within England and Wales, the prison population has been growing over recent years and, despite a slowdown in growth since 2008, at the time of writing (February 2011) the population is approaching the 85,000 figure. An additional 240,000 convicted offenders are also serving their sentences in the community under the supervision of the probation service; this figure includes those sentenced to a *probation order* and those now on licence after serving part of their sentence in custody.

The crimes that these individuals have committed cover the full spectrum from benefit fraud and shoplifting to the more heinous crimes of sexual assault, manslaughter and murder, and hence, at the point of contact with prison and probation services, they will have varying levels of risk and need. Risk and need instruments can therefore be used to determine the risks that offenders pose to themselves, others, and society, and to decide how the risks and needs are best managed by the correctional services. Indeed, the key principle of offender management within the England and Wales **National Offender**

Management Service (NOMS) is that 'resources should follow risk' (National Offender Management Service, 2006a, p.22). This rule of offender management echoes the earlier message of Andrews and colleagues in their discussion of the risk principle, which, if you remember, stated that higher risk individuals should receive longer and more intensive interventions than those of lower risk. The operational consequence of these principles is that the levels of containment, supervision, and intervention imposed on an offender are determined by their risk of reoffending, risk of harm and level of need, all of which can be derived though the utilisation of risk and need assessment tools.

National Offender Management Service (NOMS) a directorate of the Ministry of Justice within England and Wales, tasked with reducing reoffending and protecting the public. Encompasses the prison and probation services.

In practice then, risk and need assessment tools are often administered prior to sentencing to inform decisions on the requirements placed on the offender as part of their sentence. For example, the court may decide that the potential risk of harm to others an offender poses, coupled with their high risk of reconviction, is too high to allow a community penalty and hence sentence them to a period of imprisonment, or, it may feel that a medium risk of reoffending can be mediated by attendance at a rehabilitative offending behaviour programme within the community. Furthermore, community agencies may use the outcomes of risk and need assessments to inform the detail of offenders' sentence plans, parole decisions and risk management plans within custody or on release into the community. Case Study 17.1 presents an example of how risk assessment information can be used to inform decisions within prison settings. It also highlights the need not only to ensure useful and accurate assessments but also to ensure that the outcomes of such assessments are taken seriously and used to inform decisions about the management of offenders.

The following three examples describe assessment tools used commonly within correctional services. These tools are general in nature and hence aim to predict, or derive treatment targets in relation to, recidivism or reconviction *per se* as opposed to any particular type or classification of reoffending behaviour.

The Offender Group Reconviction Scale (OGRS) (Copas & Marshall, 1998; OGRS2: Taylor, 1999; OGRS3: Howard et al., 2009)

The Offender Group Reconviction Scale (OGRS; Copas & Marshall, 1998) is an actuarial risk of reconviction instrument developed within England and Wales. The latest version OGRS3 (Howard *et al.*, 2009) calculates, from six pieces of criminal history and demographic information,

CASE STUDY 17.1　　THE DEATH OF ZAHID MUBAREK

Consider the potentially volatile setting of a prison. Risk assessment can be used to minimise the risk of harm posed by a prisoner to other prisoners or staff. For example, when an individual's risk assessment indicates that they pose a risk to staff, their management plan can be adapted to include provision to manage this risk – they might only be allowed out of their cell when two or more prison officers are there. Likewise, such assessments can identify whether an offender poses a risk to other prisoners, based, for example, on offence history or ethnicity. Such information can be used by prison staff to inform cell allocation, for example. The high profile and tragic case of Zahid Mubarek, murdered whilst sleeping in his own cell by his cellmate, Robert Stewart, is an example of the consequences of ignoring the outcome of, or, as in this case, failing to conduct, such assessments. The report of the inquiry into the death of Zahid Mubarek (House of Commons, 2006) states that Robert Stewart was known to have strong racist views, a history of violent behaviour and possible mental health problems. Since this tragic incident, the prison service has introduced and evaluated the 'cell-sharing risk assessment form'. This is now completed as part of the reception process into the prison in an attempt to reduce the possibility of such events in the future. At the time of the inquiry, however, the training provided for the completion of these assessments was lacking and the report questioned 'whether this initial assessment results in an accurate predictor of risk' (House of Commons, 2006, p.500). It seems then that, despite steps forward within this field of risk assessment, there is still some way to go.

the probabilities that an offender will be reconvicted within the following one and two years. The development of OGRS3 was based on a study of almost 80,000 offenders discharged from prison or sentenced to a community penalty in early 2002. The sample's subsequent reconviction history was elicited from the police national computer and was used to assess the predictive utility of a range of static data points. Those that proved to be efficient in predicting reconviction were incorporated into the OGRS3 algorithm, which produces a risk of reconviction score of between 0 and 100. The data used within OGRS3 to predict reconviction are presented in Table 17.1.

The OGRS instrument is widely used within correctional services within the UK; the ease and speed of the tool has ensured its practicality. The risk assessment tool has been criticised, however, for focusing solely on static and historic criminal history and demographic variables at the expense of more dynamic social and behavioural items. As such, the tool acts exclusively as a risk of reconviction estimator and hence does not provide any assessment of offender need. Despite this, the accuracy of the tool is good: the authors report Area Under the Curve statistics (AUC: a measure of predictive validity) as between 80 per cent and 84 per cent.

Level of Service Inventory–Revised (LSI–R) (Andrews & Bonta, 1995)

The LSI–R is a 54-item risk and need assessment instrument, originally designed utilising Canadian data (Andrews, 1982), and has been used extensively with a variety of offender samples within Europe and North America. This tool not only provides an assessment of the risk of reoffending but also information relating to the treatment needs of the assessed offender. The items

TABLE 17.1　*Variables used within OGRS3 to predict risk of reconviction.*

1.　Offender age at time of at risk period
2.　Gender
3.　Current offence
4.　The Copas rate: a function of the rate at which the offender has been convicted (i.e. number of sanctions combined with length of criminal career)
5.　Sanctioning history: whether or not the current sanction is a conviction and whether it is a first, second or other sanction.

Source: Based on data from Howard *et al.*, 2009.

of the LSI–R, which comprise both static and dynamic factors, produce scores relating to 10 subcomponents. These subcomponents provide information relating to the offender's needs within the domains of criminal history, education/employment, finances, family/marital, accommodation, leisure/recreation, companions, alcohol/drug problems, emotional/personal and attitude/orientations. These domain scores are also weighted according to how efficiently previous research has shown them to predict reconviction to produce a composite score. The composite score hence represents the likelihood of future offending. Lower scores represent a lower prevalence of criminogenic risk factors and hence a lower risk of future offending.

Hollin and Palmer (2003) have described the LSI-R as an effective and efficient assessment instrument for needs-risk assessment with offenders. Indeed, research findings attest to the validity and reliability of the assessment tool: with the general offender population (Raynor, 2007); in relation to females (Coulso et al., 1993); minority ethnic groups (Schlager & Simourd, 2007); violent offenders (Hollin & Palmer, 2003); sexual offenders (Simourd & Malcolm, 1998); and young offenders (Shields, 1993; Shields & Simourd, 1991).

The Offender Assessment System (OASys)

The turn of the 21st century saw the ambitious development and subsequent implementation of a new risk and needs assessment tool within the prison and probation services of England and Wales. Prior to the development of the Offender Assessment System (OASys), the prison and probation services within England and Wales used a range of risk prediction tools, including the assessment, case management and evaluation (ACE) instrument (Roberts et al., 1996), OGRS and LSI–R. The provision of a common tool that could be used across prison and probation environments, it was argued, would allow for continued assessment and evaluation throughout NOMS.

The data required to complete OASys, which comprise both static and dynamic risk factors, are collected through file review and offender interviews. As such, OASys is a structured clinical assessment tool – it relies on both actuarial methods and practitioner interpretation of the offender's circumstances in the formation of the final risk assessment. The main criticism of OASys, however, is the time required to complete the assessment. The Home Office (2003, cited in Raynor, 2007) has estimated that a full OASys assessment can take two and a half hours compared to the LSI–R, which can take as little as 10 minutes (Raynor, 1997, cited in Raynor, 2007).

The payback for this resource outlay, however, is the richness of data that OASys produces. These data are

TABLE 17.2 *The components of the OASys risk and need assessment tool.*

1. **Risk of reconviction and offending related factors**
   a) Offending information
   b) Analysis of offences
   c) Accommodation
   d) Education, training and employability
   e) Financial management and income
   f) Relationships
   g) Lifestyle and associates
   h) Drug misuse
   i) Alcohol misuse
   j) Emotional well-being, including anxiety and depression
   k) Thinking and behaviour
   l) Attitudes towards offending and supervision

2. **Risk of serious harm, risks to the individual and other risks**

3. **OASys summary sheet**

4. **Sentence planning**

5. **Self-assessment**

Source: Based on data from Moore, 2006.

contained within the five components of OASys, which are summarised in Table 17.2. The first of these components, which comprises the main section of OASys, consists of the assessment of 12 offending related factors (see Table 17.2). Similar to the LSI–R, the scores obtained for each section are weighted and summed to provide risk scores. The most recent version of OASys provides a general risk of reconviction score (OGP) and a risk of violent reconviction score (OVP) – an improvement on the previous version, which provided a general risk of reconviction score only. The OVP score predicts homicide and assaults, threats and harassment, possession of offensive weapons, public order offences, criminal damage and violent acquisitive crime, whereas OGP predicts other reoffending (not including sex offending).

As can be seen from Table 17.2, however, the OASys tool provides more than just a risk of reconviction score. The second section provides an analysis of risk of serious harm, defined as 'a risk which is life-threatening and/or traumatic, and from which recovery, whether physical or psychological, can be expected to be difficult or impossible' (OASys manual, cited in Howard et al., 2006, p.7), through the evaluation of actuarial, social and personal factors. The output from this section, therefore, is intended to inform the employment of risk management procedures. The summary sheet and sentence planning sections of OASys are also designed to inform the management and supervision of the offender. Finally, OASys has provision for a *self-assessment questionnaire*, which provides the opportunity for practitioners to gain an insight into the offenders' own views of their needs. A recent evaluation of the self-assessment questionnaires of over 100,000 offenders concluded that offenders tended to be more optimistic about their chances of desisting from crime than their OASys assessment would predict and less likely than practitioners to identify problem areas in their lives (Moore, 2007).

The development of OASys has received positive acclaim: 'OASys is a very comprehensive and strongly research-based assessment instrument, informed by detailed study of others including LSI–R and ACE' (Raynor, 2007, p.135). Indeed, OASys, which has been adopted for use outside England and Wales (Bunton & Morphew, 2007), has been subject to an extensive piloting and review process that has refined and improved the tool in line with the ongoing research. For example, research into the predictive utility of the previous version of OASys led to the introduction of OVP and the refinement of the prediction of general offending (OGP). This evidence-based amendment had improved the validity of the tool; both OGP and OVP outperform OGRS3 and the previous OASys risk score in the prediction of reoffending (Howard, 2009).

Risk and need instruments for violent offenders

According to the British Crime Survey, there were approximately two million violent offences against adults within England and Wales during the year 2009/10, representing approximately 20 per cent of all crime during this period (Flatley et al., 2010). When a violent offender is reprimanded it is helpful to be able to assess, first, how likely they are to reoffend in a violent manner and, second, their level of criminogenic need, in order to inform decisions relating to their sentencing and management. For example, an offender who has a history of violent offending and harbours strong negative views against a certain sector of society would be managed in a different way from an individual who, after consuming large amounts of alcohol, offended violently towards a partner. It is hence necessary to assess, for each individual, the presence of factors that indicate repeat violent behaviour, and the triggers of that potential behaviour. We have seen that the OASys tool incorporates an assessment of violent risk. Another such tool is the HCR–20.

Historical, Clinical, Risk Management–20 (HCR–20) (Webster et al., 1997)

The HCR–20 is a risk assessment instrument that incorporates structured clinical judgements to provide an assessment of future violent behaviour amongst civil psychiatric, forensic, and criminal justice populations. Cooke (2000) has stated that the HCR–20 is 'the best known, and best researched, empirically-based guide to risk assessment' (p.155). The tool consists of 20 items: 10 *historical*, five *clinical* and five *risk* management factors (see Table 17.3). Indeed the tool takes its name from the initial letter of each of these domains – HCR – and

TABLE 17.3 *The components of the HCR–20.*

Historical items	Clinical items
1. Previous violence	1. Lack of insight
2. Young age at first violent incident	2. Negative attitudes
3. Relationship instability	3. Active symptoms of major mental illness
4. Employment problems	4. Impulsivity
5. Substance use problems	5. Unresponsive to treatment
6. Major mental illness	**Risk management items**
7. Psychopathy	1. Plans lack feasibility
8. Early maladjustment	2. Exposure to destabilisers
9. Personality disorder	3. Lack of personal support
10. Prior supervision failure	4. Noncompliance with remediation attempts
	5. Stress

Source: Based on data from Webster *et al.,* 1997.

the number of items which comprise the tool. The HCR–20 currently in use is the second version, which was developed following careful consideration of the empirical literature on the original version, which was subsequently amended in the light of evidence from the clinical experience of early trials. The use of consultation with forensic clinicians in the development and refinement of the tool is seen positive: 'as such, the HCR–20 is an attempt to merge science and practice by offering an instrument that can be integrated into clinical practice but also is empirically based and testable' (Douglas *et al.*, 2006; p.4).

The HCR–20 tool has been shown to be predictive of inpatient violence by civil psychiatric clients (Klassen, 1999) as well as violent crime by the same population on release from hospital (Douglas & Webster, 1999). Research on forensic populations, both community and prison-based, also attests to its predictive ability in relation to violence (Douglas & Webster, 1999; Strand *et al.*, 1999; Wintrup, 1996). Indeed, the authors of the HCR–20 tool periodically maintain an annotated list of research papers that assess the utility of the HCR–20 with a range of populations both civil and criminal. The latest update contained in the region of 100 studies reporting on the usefulness of this violence risk and need tool (Douglas *et al.*, 2006).

Risk and need instruments for sex offenders

Sex offending represents a small but significant proportion of all crime. In England and Wales, in 2009/10, out of a total of 4.3 million crimes, approximately 54,500 crimes of a sexual nature were reported to the police (Flatley *et al.*, 2010). It is apt to remember, however, that official figures are considered to underestimate the true prevalence of sex offences – some individuals are reluctant, feel too ashamed or are unable to report such crimes. Indeed, the British Crime Survey indicates that only 11 per cent of victims of serious sexual assault tell the police about their victimisation (Povey *et al.*, 2009). Even allowing for this, however, it seems that sex offences represent a small fraction of all crimes committed. Nevertheless, correctional services still need to be equipped with the tools to assess the risk and need of the perpetrators of this type of offence.

> **grooming** attempting to befriend a child with the intention of gaining their trust in order to have sexual contact with them. Deemed a criminal offence in England and Wales by the Sexual Offences Act 2003.

The term 'sex offending' encompasses a wide variety of different behaviours with varying levels of severity – from stranger rape and child sexual assault, through the collection of child abuse images and **grooming** behaviour, to indecent exposure and **voyeurism**. As such, those individuals deemed by their behaviour to be 'sex offenders' are not homogenous in nature but will present to correctional agencies with very different risk and need profiles. Given the destructive effects of sex offending, the reduction and prevention of such violence should be the ultimate goal of risk and need assessment. The identification of dynamic risk factors, which inform targets for treatment and the content of management plans, and the assessment of sexual recidivism risk, are therefore the aims of sex offender risk and need tools. One such tool, the Structured Assessment of Risk and Need (SARN), was developed empirically using the sex offender literature and is used alongside the England and Wales Prison Service's Sex Offender Treatment Programme (SOTP) to inform the intervention work of those on the programme.

> **voyeurism** the derivation of sexual pleasure from observing other individuals involved in sexual acts. Non-consensual voyeurism is deemed to be an illegal act in England and Wales under section 67 of Sexual Offences Act 2003.

Structured Assessment of Risk and Need (SARN) (Thornton, 2002) and Risk Matrix 2000 (RM2000) (Thornton et al., 2003)

The SARN initially measures static risk through the use of the Risk Matrix 2000, a purely actuarial risk tool (Thornton *et al.*, 2003). Based on the earlier Structured Anchored Clinical Judgement (Thornton, 1997) and Static 99 (Hanson & Thornton, 1999) tools, the Risk Matrix 2000 uses a two-step process to determine the offender's judged risk banding (low, medium, high or very high). Step one provides an initial assessment of risk level through the evaluation of the number of sex offence sentences, the number of any criminal offence sentences, and the offender's age on release from prison. The second step considers the presence of aggravating factors and adjusts the initial assessed risk level, if needed. The presence of two or more factors results in the increase of the initial risk level by one unit. Level two risk factors are: a male victim in any previous sex offence; a stranger victim in any previous sex offence; any non-contact sex offence; having never been married.

Once the Risk Matrix 2000 banding has been determined, the second step of the SARN assesses the presence or absence of 16 dynamic risk factors that, through empirical research, have been linked to sex offender recidivism (Thornton, 2002). These risk factors are grouped across four domains: sexual interests, distorted attitudes, social and emotional functioning, and self-management. The 16 factors are scored twice, in relation to their relevance, first, to the offender's offence chain and, second, to the offender's life generally. Utilising psychometric data, personal history information, interview material and file review, each factor is rated as 0 (not present), 1 (present but not a central characteristic) or 2 (a central characteristic). Any factor that receives a score of 2, both for the offence chain and the offender's general life, is designated as a relevant treatment need for that particular offender. This tool, therefore, provides a risk score in conjunction with a needs profile that can be utilised within treatment planning.

Webster *et al.* (2006), mindful that the clinical scoring of the 16 risk factors may vary between assessors, have conducted an evaluation of the inter-rater reliability of the SARN. Using two pools of assessors, the authors found that experienced, or 'expert', raters showed greater levels of reliability than less experienced raters. The authors argue that in the field of sex offending, where the offenders often display denial and minimisation to confuse and manipulate assessors, very high levels of reliability are perhaps unattainable. The finding that reliability is further weakened when less experienced or poorly trained assessors are used brings the authors to conclude that:

> ...it is not appropriate to use the SARN framework to make quantitative predictions about risk of reoffending. It is our view, however, that the studies reported in this paper support the use of the SARN as an instrument for guiding clinical assessment of treatment need. Provisos for its use to this end are as follows: users of the SARN should have demonstrated reasonable inter-rater reliability before conducting assessments without supervision, the SARN should be applied wherever possible by experienced psychologists rather than trainee-level staff, and the use of the SARN should continue to be monitored and evaluated
>
> (Webster et al., 2006, p.451)

Mentally disordered offenders

Within England and Wales, there are 4,300 mentally disordered offenders currently detained within hospitals (Ministry of Justice, 2010a). In line with prison populations these numbers have increased, year on year, since 1999 (Ministry of Justice, 2010a). There is a common misconception (perhaps fuelled by certain sections of the media) that all mentally disordered people are dangerous individuals who consequently present a risk of harm to the general population. Furthermore, this viewpoint seems to place the cause of this assumed dangerousness at the door of the mental disorder itself. Such a position, however, fails to consider those members of the population who are diagnosed with a mental disorder but are law-abiding citizens and present no risk of harm to the public. At the same time, this stance assumes that the correlates of dangerousness in the non-disordered criminal population are inherently different to those in the disordered criminal population.

To some degree, the direction of research within this field has historically concurred with these assumptions, choosing to focus on clinical or psychopathological factors in their investigations of risk amongst the mentally disordered. Meta-analytical research in this field, however, has found that 'the major predictors of recidivism were the same for mentally disordered offenders as for non-disordered offenders...clinical variables showed the smallest effect sizes' (Bonta *et al.*, 1998, p.123). On the basis of such conclusions, there is a call for a shift away from clinical or psychopathological variables, to an investigation of the role social psychological and criminological factors play in the relationship between mental disorder and recidivism.

Having said this, there is one type of mental disorder that perhaps has a closer link with offending behaviour than others. Previously, psychopathy was legally defined by the Mental Health Act 1983 as 'a persistent disorder or disability of mind (whether or not including significant impairment of intelligence) which results in abnormally aggressive or seriously irresponsible conduct on the part of the person concerned' (p.2) and hence is, by definition, closely linked with offending behaviour.

Within England and Wales, the dangerous and severe personality disorder (DSPD) programme, which spans the Ministry of Justice, NOMS, probation and prison services and the Department of Health, aims to protect the public from people who present a high risk of committing serious offences as a result of a severe personality disorder, and provides support and treatment to improve the mental health outcomes of these individuals. A severe personality disorder is defined by the DSPD programme as one characterised by either a very high score (30+) on the Psychopathy Checklist – Revised (PCL–R), or a high score on the PCL–R (25+) plus at least one personality disorder (other than antisocial personality disorder), or two or more personality disorders.

At present, the DSPD programme provides a variety of specialised services for these individuals within high security prison units and two high security hospitals (Broadmoor and Rampton). At the time of writing, however, these services are under review by the coalition government and are subject to a consultation that proposes to move provision from high security hospitals and medium secure units to prisons and the community (see Chapter 20 for a detailed description of mentally disordered offenders).

Psychopathy Checklist–Revised (PCL–R) (Hare, 1991)

Designed to guide clinical assessment, the PCL–R provides a framework for diagnosis of psychopathic disorder. As such it is not strictly a risk assessment tool but has been found to predict violent recidivism among adult (Hart *et al.*, 1994; Serin, 1991; Serin *et al.*, 1990) and young (Forth *et al.*, 1990) male offenders. Based on the work of Cleckley (1964), Hare conducted an empirically based assessment of the clinical factors that comprise psychopathy (Hare, 1980). The resultant checklist, and its later revision (Hare, 1991), is now used widely within the forensic and clinical fields and has been described as the 'gold standard for the diagnosis of psychopathy worldwide' (Morana *et al.*, 2005, p.2).

The 20 items of the PCL–R cover demographic, criminological, social and psychological domains (see Table 17.4), and the presence or absence of these is determined through interview, file and case history review. Each item is scored 0 (not evident in the record of the offender), 1 (some but not complete evidence) or 2 (the characteristic is definitely present). The maximum possible score is hence 40. The cut-off score for a diagnosis of psychopathy has been the subject of debate within forensic psychology and psychiatry circles. Hare (1991) recommends that only those individuals who score at, or above, a score of 30 should be deemed to be psychopathic. This high number was set in order to reduce the number of false positives within the psychopathic group. Rice and Harris (1995), however, reported that the validity of the tool is maximised when the cut-off score of 25 is applied; furthermore, different cut-offs have been used depending on the population under review (Morana *et al.*, 2005).

Summary: Risk assessment

As has been described within this section, the method of assessing risk in relation to offender recidivism has been, and continues to be, the subject of much debate. Actuarial tools seem to be more reliable in predicting future outcomes than clinical judgement alone, but they are not sensitive to idiosyncratic evidence of risk in the way a clinician would be and also provide little detail about the needs of the assessed offender. In light of this, there has been a move in recent years to develop structured tools that combine actuarial and clinical methods of assessment. These 'third generation' assessment tools provide not only judgement as to the risk the individual poses, but also rich needs information that informs subsequent rehabilitative work with the offender. The remaining sections of this chapter will focus on the frameworks of rehabilitative work that is currently untaken with offenders.

TREATMENT DELIVERY

The number of offending behaviour programmes available to practitioners for use with offenders continues to grow apace. An illustration of this can be seen within the correctional services of England and Wales. Within this jurisdiction, the components of effective practice identified by meta-analytic reviews of programme evaluations have been formalised into a set of programme accreditation principles (see Table 17.5).

TABLE 17.4 *Items within the PCL–R.*

Superficial charm
Grandiose sense of self-worth
Need for stimulation/easily bored
Pathological lying
Manipulative
Lack of remorse or guilt
No emotional depth
Callous
Parasitic lifestyle
Poor behavioural control
Promiscuous sexual behaviour
Early behaviour problems
Lack of long term planning
Impulsive
Irresponsible
Failure to accept responsibility for own actions
Frequent marital failures
Delinquent as a juvenile
Poor record on probation or other conditional releases
Versatile as a criminal

Source: Adapted from Hare, 1991; 2003.

TABLE 17.5 *Correctional Services Accreditation Panel accreditation criteria.*

1. Programmes must be based within a clear model of change.
2. Programmes should have clear and justified selection criteria for selection of offenders.
3. Programmes should intervene on a range of dynamic risk factors.
4. Programmes should use effective methods of change.
5. Programmes should encompass skills orientated targets
6. The dosage (sequencing, intensity, and duration) of programmes should be outlined and based within research.
7. Programmes should be designed so as to attend to motivation and engagement issues.
8. There should be clear links between the programme and the management of the offender both within prison and in the community (i.e. continuity of programmes and services).
9. Programmes should attend to issues of programme integrity.
10. Programmes should be designed such as to allow for continued evaluation.

The latest report from the England and Wales Correctional Services Accreditation Panel (CSAP), the role of which is to assess programmes and provide accredited status to those which satisfy all criteria, describes 45 programmes that have provisional or full accreditation for use within either the prison or probation services (Correctional Services Accreditation Panel, 2011).

Manualised programmes have now been developed for a wide range of offenders, including violent offenders, sex offenders, drink impaired drivers, offenders whose crimes are committed to support drug use, psychopathic offenders, female offenders and acquisitive offenders. Additionally, there are a number of *general offending programmes*, developed not to address offence specific treatment needs, but for the needs of recidivistic offenders who have usually been convicted of a variety of offences. These programmes will now be examined in some detail. See Chapter 18 for details of specific programmes for dangerous violent and sexual offenders.

GENERAL OFFENDING BEHAVIOUR PROGRAMMES

General offending behaviour programmes draw on the theory of cognitive social learning (Bandura, 1977; 2001), which proposes that an individual does not require direct experience of an event in order to learn from it. Instead learning can occur indirectly through the observation of an event happening to some other person. Moreover, this observational learning, or **vicarious reinforcement**, is thought to explain how people acquire and maintain certain behavioural patterns. Bandura proposed that there are three classes of people from whom the individual may learn: *family members, peer groups* and *figurative models* (viewed, for example, through the media). General offending behaviour programmes, therefore, promote the reduction of offending behaviour, through the acquisition of new skills. Using reinforcement strategies, offenders are encouraged to improve their problem-solving skills to enable the selection of alternatives to criminal behaviour. Furthermore, general offending behaviour programmes promote the acquisition of self-management and social interaction skills.

There are a number of group-based general offending programmes accredited for use within prisons and probation in England and Wales. These are the *Enhanced Thinking Skills (ETS)* programme; *Think First*; *Reasoning and Rehabilitation (R&R)*; the *Cognitive Skills Booster* programme (designed to reinforce the learning of the general offending behaviour programmes); the *JETS Living Skills* programme (targeted at male juveniles); and the

recently developed *Thinking Skills Programme (TSP)*. Case Study 17.2 provides an example of how an offender would be referred to the TSP and how they may feel about the process.

The R&R programme

The R&R programme was the first of these programmes to appear on the correctional scene (Ross & Fabiano, 1985a). This programme was developed in Canada and has been implemented in at least 17 different countries (Antonowicz, 2005). However, delivery of the R&R programme within custodial and community settings in England and Wales was discontinued in 2004. Following this, the ETS programme was utilised by the prison service as its sole general offending behaviour programme, while the ETS programme and Think First were available to community-based offenders.

The ETS programme

The ETS programme was developed in the 1990s by the prison service of England and Wales to complement the R&R programme (a long programme that, in line with the risk principle, targeted high risk offenders), and to provide an intervention for medium risk offenders. The focus of the ETS programme is on the provision of interpersonal problem-solving and social and moral reasoning skills, through interactive programme delivery (Clark, 2000). The programme also heavily promotes the use of 'prosocial modelling' whereby the facilitators model positive behaviours and interaction. This curriculum is delivered using a combination of direct tutoring and more interactive learning, with the main focus being on the latter, more 'Socratic', method of provision. Within this programme, deliverers utilise role-plays, guided discussion, group exercises and small-group work.

The Think First programme

The Think First programme (McGuire, 2000) differs from ETS and R&R in that, in addition to the social cognitive components of problem-solving, self-management and social skills training, it is also offence-focused. As such, the programme provides for an analysis of the offender's own criminal behaviour with the intention of enabling behaviour modification. Through the use of the '5–WH' exercises, programme participants break down their offences and analyse in detail what happened, who was involved, when it happened, where it happened and why it occurred. The repetition of this exercise, focusing

CASE STUDY 17.2   JOHN

John is a 22-year-old man who has just been convicted by his local magistrates' court of burglary. John has a history of similar criminal behaviour and has also previously breached a community order. John was assessed prior to sentencing as having an OGRS2 score of 64 (medium to high risk of reoffending) and also as being deficient in cognitive skills such as self-control and problem recognition. John's pre-sentence report, therefore, recommended to the court that John be sentenced to a community penalty with the requirement of attending a general offending behaviour programme. This sentence was passed by the magistrate. John therefore has to report to his offender manager (a probation officer) once a fortnight, and attend the Thinking Skills Programme (TSP).

During John's supervision meetings with his offender manager, John has the opportunity to address those needs, identified by his OASys assessment, which are related to his offending behaviour. His OASys profile has indicated John has offending related needs in the fields of accommodation and employment. In his supervision meetings with his offender manager, John has the opportunity to discuss how his unemployment status results in a lack of money and hence he feels he has no option but to commit burglary in order to live. He is also able to discuss his accommodation problems and to receive advice on how these might be alleviated.

After a period of four weeks from sentence, John is asked to attend the next TSP programme. John is nervous about doing so as he had particularly bad experiences at school and consequently does not have very good literacy skills. Once he starts the programme, however, John quickly realises that the programme is quite different from school: although it is challenging in that it makes him think about how his own thoughts, feelings and behaviours interact with each other, it is more relaxed and the tutors are less authoritarian than his old school teachers. Despite this, there are clear and strict rules about attendance – if he misses two sessions he will be sent back to court.

Eleven weeks later, John and his programme colleagues complete the TSP programme. This process has not been easy but a total of six group members have got to the end of the programme. John has also arranged some permanent accommodation and has started to apply for jobs. In conversations with his offender manager, he states that the TSP programme has made him stop and think about his behaviour and what the consequences might be before acting. John is proud of himself for completing the programme (he has even received a certificate!) and is hopeful that with his new skills he can resist offending again in the future.

on the offender's series of crimes, allows for the emergence of patterns of behaviour and highlights contributory factors. Avoidance strategies are then developed to prevent the repetition of the problem behaviours

The Thinking Skills Programme

The Thinking Skills Programme (TSP) is a recent addition to the suite of available general offending behaviour programmes and has been designed for male and female offenders at medium to high risk of reconviction. TSP aims to reduce reoffending, first, through the development of thinking skills and, second, through the application of these skills to the management of personal risk factors and the development of protective factors. TSP also aids the offender in setting prosocial goals supportive of relapse prevention. As such, the TSP, like the Think First programme, is offence-focused and requires offenders to explore their patterns of offending to develop awareness of their risk and protective factors in relation to their offending behaviour.

The TSP is arranged into three modules of learning, each consisting of six sessions: five delivered within a group format and one as an individual session. These modules focus on self-control, problem-solving and positive relationships. The modules are supplemented with an individual introductory session, bringing the total number of sessions to 19 (15 group and 4 individual). In contrast to R&R, ETS and Think First, the programme can be delivered either in a fixed group format, whereby the group remains the same throughout the three modules, or in a rolling group format, whereby offenders can start and finish at any module and hence the group composition alters throughout the programme.

The Aggression Replacement Training programme

The Aggression Replacement Training (ART) programme (Goldstein et al., 1998; Goldstein & Glick, 1987) is perhaps the most widely available programme

FIGURE 17.3 *The aggression replacement training programme (ART), perhaps the most widely available programme for generally violent offenders, was developed for aggressive youths and is also available in a revised format for adult violent offenders.*

Source: © siamionau pavel. Used under licence from Shutterstock.

for generally violent offenders. Developed originally for aggressive youths, the programme is also available in a revised format for adult violent offenders (Figure 17.3). Goldstein *et al.* (1998) argue that an aggressive act derives from multiple causes. They propose that the internal influences on an individual's aggressive behaviour can be traced to three factors: first, to a general shortfall in personal, interpersonal and social-cognitive skills, the combination of which usually ensure prosocial behaviour; second, to the overuse of impulsive and aggressive behaviour coupled with a low level of anger control; third, to an immature, egocentric and concrete style of moral reasoning. The ART programme, therefore, aims to tackle these three factors through skillstreaming, anger control and moral reasoning training. The behavioural skillstreaming component draws on social learning theory in the identification, development and practice of social skills that form prosocial behaviour. These skills are developed further through role-play, discussion, and performance feedback. Anger control training draws on the early anger control work of Novaco (1975) and Miechenbaum (1977). This emotion-oriented component aims to equip the individual with the ability to manage their anger and aggression. These self-control sessions identify personal triggers and the likely consequences of anger and aggression. The increased self-awareness gained from such exercises

is then used to develop alternative prosocial coping strategies, such as negotiation, self-talk or even avoidance of the situations that trigger anger. The moral reasoning component addresses concrete and egocentric thinking typically seen in those who display aggressive behaviour (Antonowicz & Ross, 2005; Barriga & Gibbs, 1996; Liau *et al.*, 1998; Ross & Fabiano, 1985b). Thus, this component aims to enhance the offenders' moral reasoning which is associated with increased prosocial behaviour.

The ART programme has been evaluated across different client groups, settings and outcomes, resulting in a body of evidence that suggests that ART can be an effective intervention (for a review, see Goldstein, 2004). An evaluation of the community-based adult version of ART (Hatcher *et al.*, 2008) concluded that simply being allocated to the ART programme resulted in a 13.3 per cent reduction in reconviction compared to matched controls, whilst completers of the programme performed even better and demonstrated a 15.5 per cent reduction in reconviction.

Efficacy of interventions

General offending behaviour programmes have been subject to a steadily increasing number of evaluations of their effectiveness. A meta-analytic review of the R&R programme in Canada, the USA, the UK and Sweden concluded that programme attendees were 14 per cent less likely to reoffend than the control group participants (Tong & Farrington, 2006). Evaluations of the Think First programme have also concluded that the programme produces positive changes on psychometrics tests (McGuire & Hatcher, 2001; Steele, 2002a) and in relation to reconviction (Roberts, 2004; Steele, 2002b). Indeed a national evaluation of R&R, ETS, and Think First in community settings concluded that all three programmes produced significant reductions in reconviction amongst the programme completer group comparative to the controls (Hollin *et al.*, 2004; 2008; Palmer *et al.*, 2007). A comparison of the three programmes showed that, across the three programmes, Think First outperformed ETS and R&R in relation to attrition and reconviction rates (Palmer *et al.*, 2007). Given its recent development and implementation, TSP is yet to establish a solid evidence base; however, pilot studies undertaken with group facilitators and male and female programme participants (Barnett, in press; Turner, 2008) have influenced the design of the programme. An outcome evaluation, currently underway within prison and community settings, should be completed within the next two or three years.

ISSUES RELATED TO OFFENDING BEHAVIOUR PROGRAMMES

Engagement and programme non-completion

One of the biggest challenges to the delivery of offending behaviour programmes is that of offender engagement (or rather a lack of it!). Poor offender engagement can result in reduced understanding and skills acquisition, and consequently a reduction in treatment gains. Alternatively, low engagement can result in attrition (i.e. dropout) from the programme.

Programme attrition is far more prevalent within community, as opposed to custodial, settings. General offending behaviour programme non-completion rates within prison have been reported to be in the region of 11 per cent (Cann et al., 2003) to 16 per cent (Pelissier et al., 2003). Hollin et al. (2004) reported community-based attrition, however, to be as high as two-thirds of those sentenced to the programme. More recently, Hatcher (2009) reported a community-based ETS attrition rate of 57 per cent; 41.6 per cent failed to commence the programme to which they were sentenced (non-starters) and 15.4 per cent commenced but did not complete ETS (non-completers).

The main concern regarding low engagement is that those individuals who meet the criteria, and hence are identified as having a need for intervention, fail to benefit from the intervention. Hollis (2007) compared predicted OGRS2 reconviction rates against actual two-year reconviction rates. Programme completers were seen to fare well: a reduction of 17 per cent was observed between the predicted (64.3 per cent) and actual (47.3 per cent) rate of reconviction. Differences between predicted and actual rates were not observed, however, for non-starters and non-completers. As such, those who failed to complete the programme took no benefit from it.

Other research has indicated, however, that rather than merely failing to benefit, dropouts may actually have detrimental outcomes. McMurran and Theodosi (2007) conducted a meta-analysis that compared the recidivism rates of programme non-completers against untreated comparisons of comparable risk. Non-completion was found to be associated with *elevated* levels of reoffending ($d = -0.16$). Such a pattern appears to be emerging across the literature; Hollin et al. (2008), van Voorhis et al. (2004), Hatcher (2009) and Hatcher et al. (in press) have all reported the reconviction rates of programme dropouts to be higher than appropriate no-intervention comparison groups, indicating a detrimental 'non-completion' effect. Emerging research suggests it is early dropouts (those that complete less than 40 per cent of the programme) that are responsible for this effect (Hatcher et al., 2011); the reconviction rates of later dropouts do not differ significantly from the comparison group. The argument as to whether the non-completion effect is a function of methodological design, self-selection, some facet of the intervention or the organisational processes supporting it, or the process of dropout itself, continues to be debated within the literature. The challenge for services and practitioners, however, is to determine how to increase engagement and reduce attrition from offender interventions.

Targeting and selection

You may remember from earlier in this chapter that the accreditation criteria for offending behaviour programmes recommend the selection of offenders based on their risk and need. Despite this, there is clear evidence of the selection for offending behaviour programmes of offenders falling outside of the specified criteria. For example, Palmer et al. (2008; 2009) have demonstrated that the rate of 'appropriate' allocation within the community varied between probation areas from 37.1 per cent to 82.1 per cent, with almost half of all offenders falling outside the recommended banding. Likewise Turner (2006) reported that a quarter of ETS programme participants had risk scores below the targeting criteria and Gill (2004) found that half of the Think First programme non-completers had risk scores above the upper limit whilst only one of the programme completers fell above this range.

Within Hatcher's (2009) work assessing community-based offending behaviour programme attrition, 7 per cent of the sample had risk scores that fell below the targeting criteria and over 33 per cent were considered to be too high risk for the programme. With completion rates varying with risk, such that high risk offenders are the least likely group to complete programmes (30.2 per cent compared to 46.4 per cent from the appropriate risk category and 80.9 per cent of the too low risk category), the finding that over a third of those allocated were 'too high' risk lends weight to the argument that organisational factors perhaps contribute to attrition rates.

When considering this finding alongside subsequent reconviction rates, however, Palmer et al. (2008) found evidence of a large effect of completion on these individuals: 'too high' programme completers were 44.7 per cent less likely to be reconvicted than the comparison group. Given this, it would seem that correctional services have a conundrum to solve: the rate of programme completion amongst high risk offenders is low; however, those that do complete fare very well in terms of reconviction. The question for correctional services to consider is whether the reduction in reconviction amongst the minority of this group outweighs the effects of dropout and its subsequent consequences on reconviction. Of course, such rates are not necessarily static: further research on the correlates of dropout could inform practices that support larger proportions of high risk offenders through programmes.

In relation to the offenders who have risk scores below the targeting criteria, the completion rate of 80.9 per cent (Hatcher, 2009) might appear to justify allocation of these individuals to an intervention. However, Palmer *et al.* (2008) reported no differences in reconviction between the programme completers in the 'too low' category and their appropriate comparisons. As such, the programme had little to no effect on the reconviction rate of this group. As the risk principle would dictate, these offenders are of a level of risk of reconviction such that an intensive intervention is not required.

Manualised groupwork

While the objective of the rigorous programme accreditation process is to ensure quality evidence-based programmes, opponents have criticised manualised groupwork on the basis that it is not tailored to individual needs, is at odds with the theoretical principles of **cognitive behavioural therapy (CBT)**, and acts to deskill treatment deliverers by removing their ability to practice 'clinical artistry' (Wilson, 1996, p.295). Respondents to these criticisms have suggested the combination of one-to-one and groupwork interventions allowing more individualised approaches whilst retaining the practical and economic efficiencies of groupwork (Hollin & Palmer, 2006). Further, it has been proposed that a reduction in clinical artistry, whilst

> **cognitive behavioural therapy (CBT)** based on the notion that thoughts, attitudes and beliefs are interrelated and hence influence each other. It attempts to identify and alter thoughts, attitudes and beliefs that contribute to problem behaviour.

perhaps demoralising to staff, may not negatively impact on the programme or its efficacy (Hollin, 2006). Hollin has proposed that the limiting of this practice by manualisation might indeed protect against threats to the concept of programme integrity.

The term 'programme integrity' refers to the practice of delivering an intervention in line with the programme manual's instructions. If a well designed and evidence-based programme is not delivered as intended, it is likely that the effectiveness of this programme will be undermined. The importance of this concept is demonstrated in its adoption as one of the principles of effective practice (see Table 17.5). Hollin (1995) has described three potential threats to programme integrity: programme drift (the gradual alteration of the aims and method of delivery of the programme); programme reversal (the undermining of the programme and its delivery due to resistance and opposition to the aims and methods); and programme non-compliance (the programme facilitators tinker with the programme, altering the contents, aims or treatment targets). All three of these threats compromise the programme in some way and could hence render the work completed as, at best, worthless or, at worst, damaging to the overall aim of reducing recidivism.

A study of the implementation of programmes within community settings in England and Wales discovered that practitioners were often confused about the perceived conflict between maintaining programme integrity and the need to ensure the Andrews and Bonta (2010) principle of responsivity (Hollin *et al.*, 2002). As mentioned earlier in this chapter, responsivity refers to the matching of the style and methods of delivery to the learning styles of the programme participants to ensure offender engagement with the intervention. On the one hand, therefore, practitioners understand that their practice should not deviate from the programme manual but, on the other hand, often feel the need to do so to be responsive to the needs of the programme participants. As such, the success of the programme may lie, in part, in the programme facilitator's ability to do just this. The skills required to undertake this work successfully should not therefore be underestimated.

SUMMARY

- **Evidence-based offending behaviour programmes are now commonplace within correctional services throughout the western world.**

- **The number of offenders who completed a programme in the year 2009–2010 in England and Wales alone reached 26,500 (Ministry of Justice, 2010b).**

- Despite this prolific use, there is still a great deal to learn about how these programmes impact on the lives of those who are subject to them.

- We can be confident, from the results of meta-analytical research, that these programmes can reduce the recidivistic behaviour of offenders who complete them.

- We are still to gain answers to more specific questions, however, such as why people drop out from programmes, how offenders can be motivated to increase their engagement, and how organisational factors may impact on programme effectiveness.

- It is only through the conduct of good quality research that these questions can be answered and correctional provision further enhanced.

ESSAY/DISCUSSION QUESTIONS

1. Compare actuarial and clinical risk assessment methods. What are the limitations of these methods when they are used to assess the likelihood of an individual reoffending in the future?

2. Discuss the potential consequences of failing to conduct a comprehensive risk assessment on an offender. How might this impact on the offender, other individuals, and society?

3. How effective is the 'one size fits all' approach to offender rehabilitation? Has programme accreditation been successful in the aim of reducing recidivist behaviour?

4. What are the methodological problems with evaluating offending behaviour programmes? What methodology would you use to test whether such programmes reduce recidivism?

REFERENCES

Andrews, D.A. (1982). *The Level of Supervision Inventory (LSI): The first follow-up.* Toronto: Ontario Ministry of Correctional Services.

Andrews, D.A. & Bonta, J. (1995). *The Level of Service Inventory – Revised manual.* Toronto: Multi-Health Systems.

Andrews, D.A. & Bonta, J. (2010). *The psychology of criminal conduct* (5th edn). New Providence, NJ: LexisNexus.

Andrews, D.A., Zinger, I., Hoge, R.D., Bonta, J., Gendreau, P. & Cullen, F.T. (1990). Does correctional treatment work? A clinically relevant and psychologically informed meta-analysis. *Criminology, 28,* 369–404.

Antonowicz, D.H. (2005). The Reasoning and Rehabilitation program: outcome evaluations with offenders. In M. McMurran & J. McGuire (Eds.) *Social problem solving and offending* (pp.163–181). Chichester: John Wiley & Sons, Inc.

Antonowicz, D.H. & Ross, R.R. (2005). Social problem-solving deficits in offenders. In M. McMurran & J. McGuire (Eds.) *Social problem-solving and offending: Evidence, evaluation and evolution* (pp.91–102). Chichester: John Wiley & Sons, Inc.

Bandura, A. (1977). *Social learning theory.* New York: Prentice-Hall.

Bandura, A. (2001). Social cognitive theory: An agentic perspective. *Annual Review of Psychology, 52,* 1–26.

Barnett, G. (in press). Gender-responsive programming: A qualitative exploration of women's experiences of a gender-neutral cognitive skills programme. *Psychology, Crime and Law.*

Barriga, A.Q. & Gibbs, J.C. (1996). Measuring cognitive distortion in antisocial youth: Development and preliminary validation of the 'How I Think' questionnaire. *Aggressive Behavior, 22,* 333–343.

Bonta, J., Law, M. & Hansen, K. (1998). The prediction of criminal and violent recidivism among mentally disordered offenders: A meta-analysis. *Psychological Bulletin, 123,* 123–142.

Bunton, J. & Morphew, R. (2007). Continuing professional development: Lessons from a European Union twinning project. *Forensic Update, 89,* 25–28.

Cann, J., Falshaw, L., Nugent, F. & Friendship, C. (2003). Understanding what works: Accredited cognitive skills programmes for adult men and young offenders. *Home Office Research Findings, 226.* London: Home Office.

Clark, D.A. (2000). *Theory manual for enhanced thinking skills.* Prepared for Joint Prison-Probation Accreditation Panel. London: Home Office.

Cleckley, H. (1964). *The mask of sanity.* St. Louis, MI: CV Mosby.

Cooke, D. (2000). Annex 6: Current risk assessment instruments. In Scottish Executive, Report of the committee on serious and violent offenders. Edinburgh: Scottish Executive.

Copas, J.B. & Marshall, P. (1998). The Offender Group Reconviction Scale: The statistical reconviction score for use by probation officers. *Journal of the Royal Statistical Society, Series C47*, 159–171.

Correctional Services Accreditation Panel. (2011). *The Correctional Services Accreditation Panel report 2009–10*. London: Home Office.

Coulson, G., Nutbrown, V. & Giulekas, D. (1993). Using the Level of Supervision Inventory in placing female offenders in rehabilitation programmes or halfway houses. *IARCA Journal, 5*, 12–13.

Dingwall, R. (1989). Some problems about predicting child abuse and neglect. In O. Stevenson (Ed.) *Child abuse: Public policy and professional practice* (pp.28–53). Hemel Hempstead: Harvester Wheatsheaf.

Douglas, K.S., Cox, D.N. & Webster, C.D. (1999). Violence risk assessment: Science and practice. *Legal and Criminological Psychology, 4*, 149–184.

Douglas, K.S., Guy, L.S. & Weir, J. (2006). *HCR-20 violence risk assessment scheme: Overview and annotated bibliography*. Burnaby, Canada: Department of Psychology, Simon Fraser University.

Douglas, K.S. & Webster, C.D. (1999). The HCR-20 violence risk assessment scheme: Concurrent validity in a sample of incarcerated offenders. *Criminal Justice and Behavior, 26*, 3–19.

Flatley, J., Kershaw, C., Smith, K., Chaplin, R. & Moon, D. (2010). *Crime in England and Wales 2009/10. Home Office Statistical Bulletin 12/10*. London: Home Office.

Forth, A.E. Hart, S.D. & Hare, R.D. (1990). Assessment of psychopathy in male young offenders. *Psychological assessment, 2*, 342–344.

Gill, E.J. (2004). *Attrition or completion on the Think First programme: Offender perspectives*. Unpublished thesis (MSc Forensic Psychology). Manchester: Manchester Metropolitan University.

Goldstein, A.P. (2004). Evaluations of effectiveness. In A.P. Goldstein, R. Nensen, B. Daleflod & M. Kalt (Eds.) *New perspectives on aggression replacement training* (pp.230–244). Chichester: John Wiley & Sons, Inc.

Goldstein, A.P. & Glick, B. (1987). *Aggression replacement training: A comprehensive intervention for adolescent youth*. Champaign, IL: Research Press.

Goldstein, A.P., Glick, B. & Gibbs, J.C. (1998). *Aggression replacement training* (Revised edn). Champaign, IL: Research Press.

Grove, W.M. & Meehl, P.E. (1996). Comparative efficiency of informal (subjective, impressionistic) and formal (mechanical, algorithmic) prediction procedures: The clinical–statistical controversy. *Psychology, Public Policy, and Law, 2*, 293–323.

Grubin, D. (1997). Predictors of risk in serious sex offenders. *British Journal of Psychiatry, 170*, s17–s21.

Grubin, D. & Wingate, S. (1996) Sexual offence recidivism: Prediction versus understanding. *Criminal Behaviour and Mental Health, 6*, 349–359.

Hanson, R.K. & Thornton, D. (1999). *Static 99: Improving the predictive accuracy of actuarial risk assessments for sex offenders*. Ottawa: Public Works and Government Services Canada.

Hare, R.D. (1980). A research scale for the assessment of psychopathy in criminal populations. *Personality and Individual Differences, 1*, 111–119.

Hare, R.D. (1991). *The Hare Psychopathy Checklist–Revised*. Toronto, Ontario: Multi-Health Systems

Hare, R.D. (2003). *The Hare Psychopathy Checklist–Revised (PCL–R)* (2nd edn). Toronto, Canada: Multi-Health Systems.

Hart, S.D., Hare, R.D. & Forth, A.E. (1994). Psychopathy as a risk marker for violence: Development and validation of a screening version of the Revised Psychopathy Checklist. In J. Monahan & J. Steadman (Eds.) *Violence and mental disorder: Developments in risk assessment* (pp.81–98). Chicago, IL: University of Chicago Press.

Hatcher, R.M. (2009). An investigation of attrition from community-based offending behaviour programmes (Doctoral dissertation). Retrieved 25 August 2011 from http://research-archive.liv.ac.uk/1220/1/HatcherRuth_Apr_2009_1220.pdf

Hatcher, R.M., McGuire, J., Bilby, C.A.L., Palmer, E.J. & Hollin, C.R. (in press). Methodological considerations in the evaluation of offender interventions: The problem of attrition. *International Journal of Offender Therapy and Comparative Criminology*.

Hatcher, R.M., McGuire, J., Palmer, E.J. & Hollin, C.R. (2011, March). *Dosage, appropriateness of selection, and reconviction amongst completers and non-completers of community based offender interventions in England and Wales*. Paper presented at the North American Correctional and Criminal Justice Psychology Conference, Sheraton Centre, Toronto.

Hatcher, R.M., Palmer, E.J., McGuire, J., Hounsome, J.C., Bilby, C.A.L. & Hollin, C.R. (2008). Aggression replacement training with adult male offenders within community settings: A reconviction analysis. *Forensic Psychiatry and Psychology, 19*, 517–532.

Hollin, C.R. (1995). The meaning and implications of 'programme integrity'. In J. McGuire (Ed.) *What works: Reducing reoffending-Guidelines from research and practice* (pp.195–208). Chichester: John Wiley & Sons, Inc.

Hollin, C.R. (2006). Offending behaviour programmes and contention: Evidence-based practice, manuals, and programme evaluation. In C.R. Hollin & E.J. Palmer (Eds.) *Offending behaviour programmes: Development, application, and controversies.* (pp.33–67). Chichester: John Wiley & Sons, Inc.

Hollin, C.R., McGuire, J., Palmer, E.J., Bilby, C., Hatcher, R. & Holmes, A. (2002). *Introducing Pathfinder programmes into the probation service: An interim report. Home Office Research Study, 247*. London: Home Office Research, Development and Statistics Directorate.

Hollin, C.R. & Palmer, E.J. (2003). Level of service inventory-revised profiles of violent and nonviolent prisoners. *Journal of Interpersonal Violence, 18,* 1075–1086.

Hollin, C.R. & Palmer, E.J. (2006). Offending behaviour programmes: Controversies and resolutions. In C.R. Hollin & E.J. Palmer (Eds.) *Offending behaviour programmes: Development, application, and controversies* (pp.247–278). Chichester: John Wiley & Sons, Inc.

Hollin, C.R., Palmer, E.J., McGuire, J. Hounsome, J., Hatcher, R. & Bilby, C. (2004). *An evaluation of Pathfinder Programmes in the Probation Service.* Unpublished research report to the Home Office Research, Development, and Statistics Directorate.

Hollin, C.R., Palmer, E.J., McGuire, J., Hounsome, J., Hatcher, R. & Bilby, C. (2008). Cognitive skills offending behaviour programmes in the community: A reconviction analysis. *Criminal Justice and Behavior, 35,* 269–283.

Hollis, V. (2007). *Reconviction analysis of programme data using Interim Accredited Programmes Software (IAPS).* London: National Offender Management Service.

House of Commons. (2006). *Report of the Zahid Mubarek Inquiry.* London: HMSO.

Howard, P. (2009). *Improving the prediction of re-offending using the Offender Assessment System. Ministry of Justice Research Summary 02/09.* London: Ministry of Justice.

Howard, P., Clark, D. & Garnham, N. (2006). *An evaluation of the Offender Assessment System in three pilots 1999–2001.* London: Home Office.

Howard, P., Francis, B., Soothill, K. & Humphreys, L. (2009). *OGRS3: The revised Offender Group Reconviction Scale. Ministry of Justice Research Summary 07/09.* London, Ministry of Justice.

Howe, E. (1994). Judged person dangerousness as weighted averaging. *Journal of Applied Social Psychology, 24,* 1270–1290.

Howells, K. & Hollin, C.R. (1989). *Clinical approaches to violence.* Chichester: John Wiley & Sons, Inc.

Klassen, C. (1999). *Predicting aggression in psychiatric inpatients using 10 historical factors: Validating the 'H' of the HCR-20.* Unpublished thesis. Vancouver: Simon Fraser University.

Liau, A.K., Barriga, A.Q. & Gibbs, J.C. (1998). Relations between self-serving cognitive distortions and overt versus covert antisocial behavior in adolescents. *Aggressive Behavior, 24,* 335–346.

Limandri, B. & Sheridan, D. (1995). Prediction of interpersonal violence; Fact or fiction. In J.C. Campbell (Ed.) *Assessing dangerousness: Violence by sexual offenders, batterers, and child abusers* (pp.1–19). Thousand Oaks, CA: Sage Publications.

Litwack, T.R. (2001). Actuarial versus clinical assessments of dangerousness. *Psychology, Public Policy and Law, 7,* 409–443.

McGuire, J. (2000). *Think First: Programme manual.* London: National Probation Service.

McGuire, J. & Hatcher, R. (2001). Offence focused problem solving: Preliminary evaluation of a cognitive skills program. *Criminal Justice and Behaviour, 28,* 564–587.

McMurran, M. & Theodosi, E. (2007). Is treatment non-completion associated with increased reconviction over no treatment? *Psychology, Crime and Law, 13,* 333–344.

Miechenbaum, D.M. (1977). *Cognitive behavior modification.* New York: Plenum Press.

Milner, J.S. & Campbell, J.C. (1995). Prediction issues for practitioners. In J. Campbell (Ed.) *Assessing dangerousness: Violence by sexual offenders, batterers, and child abusers* (pp.41–67). Thousand Oaks, CA: Sage Publications

Ministry of Justice. (2010a). *Offender management caseload statistics 2009. Ministry of Justice Statistics Bulletin.* London: Ministry of Justice.

Ministry of Justice. (2010b). *National Offender Management Service: Annual report and accounts 2009–2010.* London: Ministry of Justice.

Monahan, J. (1981). *The clinical prediction of violence.* Beverley Hills, CA. Sage.

Moore, R. (2006). The Offender Assessment System (OASys) in England and Wales. *Probation in Europe, 37,* 12–13.

Moore, R. (2007). *Adult offenders' perceptions of their underlying problems: Findings from the OASys self assessment questionnaire. Home Office Research Findings 284.* London: Home Office.

Morana, H.C.P., Arboleda-Flórez, J. & Câmara, F.P. (2005). Identifying the cut-off score for the PCL–R scale (Psychopathy Checklist–Revised) in a Brazilian forensic population. *Forensic Science International, 147,* 1–8.

National Offender Management Service. (2006a). *The NOMS offender management model.* London: Home Office.

Novaco, R.W. (1975). *Anger control: The development and evaluation of an experimental treatment.* Lexington, MA: D.C. Heath.

Palmer, E.J., McGuire, J., Hatcher, R.M., Hounsome, J., Bilby, C.A.L. & Hollin, C.R. (2008). The importance of appropriate allocation to offending behaviour programmes. *International Journal of Offender Therapy and Comparative Criminology, 52,* 206–221.

Palmer, E.J., McGuire, J., Hatcher, R.M., Hounsome, J., Bilby, C.A.L. & Hollin, C.R. (2009). Allocation to offending behavior programmes in the English and Welsh Probation Service. *Criminal Justice and Behavior, 36,* 909–922.

Palmer, E.J., McGuire, J., Hounsome, J.C., Hatcher, R.M., Bilby, C.A.L. & Hollin, C.R. (2007). Offending behaviour programmes within the community: The effects on reconviction of three programmes with adult male offenders. *Legal and Criminological Psychology, 12,* 251–264.

Pelissier, B., Camp, S.D. & Motivans, M. (2003). Staying in treatment: How much difference is there from prison to prison? *Psychology of Additive Behaviours, 17,* 134–141.

Povey, D., Coleman, K., Kaiza, P. & Roe, S. (2009). *Homicides, firearm offences and intimate violence 2007/08 (Supplementary Volume 2 to Crime in England and Wales 2007/08). Home Office Statistical Bulletin 02/09.* London: Home Office.

Quinsey, V.L., Harris, G.T., Rice, M.E. & Cormier, C.A. (1998). *Violent offenders: Appraising and managing the risk.* Washington D.C: American Psychological Association.

Quinsey, V.L., Harris, G.T., Rice, M.E. & Lalumière, M.L. (1993). Assessing treatment efficacy in outcome studies of sex offenders. *Journal of Interpersonal Violence, 8*, 512–523.

Raynor, P. (2007). Risk and need assessment in British probation: The contribution of LSI–R. *Psychology, Crime and Law, 13*, 125–138.

Rice, M.E. & Harris, G.T. (1995). Violent recidivism: Assessing predictive validity. *Journal of Consulting and Clinical Psychology, 63*, 737–748.

Roberts, C. (2004). An early evaluation of a cognitive offending behaviour programme (Think First) in probation areas. *Vista: Perspectives on Probation, 8*, 130–136.

Roberts, C., Burnett, R., Kirby, A. & Hamill, H. (1996). *A system for evaluating probation practice. Probation Studies Unit Report 1*. Oxford: University of Oxford Centre for Criminological Research.

Ross, R.R. & Fabiano, E.A. (1985a). *Reasoning and Rehabilitation: Manual*. Ottawa: AIR Training & Associates.

Ross, R.R. & Fabiano, E.A. (1985b). *Time to think: A cognitive model of delinquency prevention and offender rehabilitation*. Johnson City, TN: Institute of Social Sciences and Arts.

Schlager, M.D. & Simourd, D.J. (2007). Validity of the Level of Service Inventory–Revised among African American and Hispanic male offenders. *Criminal Justice and Behavior, 34*, 545–554.

Serin, R.C. (1991). Psychopathy and violence in criminals. *Journal of Interpersonal Violence, 6*, 423–431.

Serin, R.C., Peters, R. & Barbaree, H. (1990). Predictors of psychopathy and release outcomes in a criminal population. *Psychological Assessment, 2*, 419–422.

Shields, I.W. (1993). The use of the Young Offender Level of Service Inventory (YO-LSI) with adolescents. *IARCA Journal, 5*, 10–26.

Shields, I.W. & Simourd, D.J. (1991). Predicting predatory behaviour in a population of incarcerated young offenders. *Criminal Justice and Behavior, 18*, 180–194.

Simourd, D.J. & Malcolm, P.B. (1998). Reliability and validity of the Level of Service Inventory–Revised among federally incarcerated sex offenders. *Journal of Interpersonal Violence, 13*, 261–274.

Steele, R. (2002a). *Psychometric features of Think First participants' pre and post programme*. Liverpool: Research and Information Section, National Probation Service, Merseyside.

Steele, R. (2002b). *Reconviction of offenders on Think First*. Liverpool: Research and Information Section, National Probation Service, Merseyside.

Strand, S., Belfrage, H., Fransson, G. & Levander, S. (1999) Clinical and risk management factors in risk prediction of mentally disordered offenders – more important than historical data. *Legal and Criminological Psychology, 4*, 67–76.

Taylor, R. (1999). *Predicting reconvictions for sexual and violent offences using the revised Offender Group Reconviction Scale. Home Office Research Findings 104*. London: Home Office.

Thornton, D. (1997). *Structured anchored clinical judgement*. Paper presented at the NOTA Annual conference, Southampton.

Thornton, D. (2002). Constructing and testing a framework for dynamic risk assessment. Sexual Abuse: A Journal of Research and Treatment, 14, 139–153.

Thornton, D., Mann, R., Webster, S., Blud, L., Travers, R., Friendship, C. & Erikson, M. (2003). Distinguishing and combining risks for sexual and violent recidivism. In R.A. Prentky, E.S. Janus & M.C. Seto (Eds.) Sexually coercive behavior: Understanding and management. *Annals of the New York Academy of Sciences, 989*, 225–235. New York: New York Academy of Sciences.

Tong, L.S.J. & Farrington, D.P. (2006). How effective is the 'Reasoning and Rehabilitation' programme in reducing reoffending? A meta-analysis of evaluations in four countries. *Psychology, Crime and Law, 12*, 3–24.

Turner, R. (2006). *Developing understanding of accredited programmes completions: The role of case-management and barriers to completion*. Unpublished report, West Yorkshire Probation Area.

Turner, R. (2008). *A qualitative evaluation of the new cognitive skills programme pilots (second phase)*. Unpublished research report: RDT Consultancy.

van Voorhis, P., Spruance, L.M., Ritchey, P.N., Listwan, S.J. & Seabrook, R. (2004). The Georgia cognitive skills experiment: A replication of Reasoning and Rehabilitation. *Criminal Justice and Behavior, 31*, 282–305.

Webster, C.D., Douglas, K.S., Eaves, D. & Hart, S.D. (1997). *HCR-20: Assessing risk for violence, version 2*. Burnaby, British Columbia: Mental Health, Law, & Policy Institute, Simon Fraser University.

Webster, S.D., Mann, R.E., Carter, A.J., Long, J., Milner, R.J., O'Briern, M., Wakeling, H.C. & Ray, N.L. (2006). Inter-rater reliability of dynamic risk assessment with sexual offenders. *Psychology, Crime and Law, 12*, 439–452.

Wilson, G.T. (1996). Manual-based treatments: The clinical application of research findings. *Behaviour, Research and Therapy, 34*, 295–314.

Wintrup, A. (1996). *Assessing risk of violence in mentally disordered offenders with the HCR-20*. Vancouver: Simon Fraser University.

ANNOTATED READING LIST

Beech, A.R., Craig, L.A. & Browne, K.D. (2009). *Assessment and treatment of sex offenders: A handbook.* Chichester: John Wiley & Sons, Inc. *An edited book that not only discusses theoretical and practical issues in the treatment of sex offenders but also tackles issues such as diagnostic problems with sex offenders, and risk assessment of sex offenders.*

Hollin, C.R. (Ed.) (2001). *Handbook of offender assessment and treatment.* Chichester: John Wiley & Sons, Inc. *A comprehensive guide to offender assessment and treatment, covering issues such as risk assessment, the discussion of theoretical approaches to treatment, and the assessment and treatment of different types of offenders. All chapters are written by experts within each field. Also available as a shorter 'essential' handbook.*

Hollin, C.R. & Palmer, E.J. (Eds.) (2006). *Offending behaviour programmes: Development, application, and controversies.* Chichester: John Wiley & Sons, Inc. *A perfectly readable edited book, which introduces offending behaviour programmes for general and offence specific offenders. Provides a detailed view of the current situation relating to offending behaviour programmes, the evaluative evidence for and against them, and the issues and controversies that surround them.*

McGuire, J. (Ed.) (1995). *What works: Reducing reoffending: Guidelines from research and practice.* Chichester: John Wiley & Sons, Inc. *A classic text that stimulated the debate concerning 'What Works' in offender rehabilitation during the mid-1990s and onwards. Covers a discussion of the 'What Works' debate, as well as issues in practice, delivery and implementation or offending behaviour programmes.*

Palmer, E.J., McGuire, J., Hounsome, J.C., Hatcher, R.M., Bilby, C.A.L. & Hollin, C.R. (2007). Offending behaviour programmes within the community: The effects on reconviction of three programmes with adult male offenders. *Legal and Criminological Psychology, 12,* 251–264. *A fairly recently published national evaluation of three general offending behaviour programmes within community settings in England and Wales.*

18 Interventions with Dangerous Offenders

Leigh Harkins, Jayson Ware and Ruth Mann

CHAPTER OUTLINE

The effective treatment of dangerous offenders has important implications for society in general and for the offenders themselves. By definition, dangerous offenders pose a risk of serious harm to other people. The rates of reoffending for violent offenders tend to be higher, when compared to other non-violent offenders (Motuik & Belcourt, 1997). Canadian research published in 1999 showed that approximately 40 per cent of offenders incarcerated for violent offences were returned to custody for a similar offence within two years (Dowden *et al.*, 1999). While sexual recidivism rates are roughly in the range of 11 per cent (Hanson & Morton-Bourgon, 2009) to 14 per cent (Hanson & Morton-Bourgon, 2005), it is acknowledged that this is likely an underestimate of the true rates of sexual reoffending (Ahlmeyer *et al.*, 2000).

Effective treatment hopefully means the prevention or reduction of future harm, but also that the offenders can move past their offending and on to more positive lives that are incompatible with offending. The aim of this chapter is to describe briefly

- the types of serious violent/sex offenders who can receive treatment;
- the types of treatment typically undertaken with these offenders;
- the evidence base for the effectiveness of such treatments; and
- the factors that need to be considered when working with such dangerous offenders.

TYPES OF DANGEROUS OFFENDERS TYPICALLY TREATED IN CRIMINAL JUSTICE SETTINGS

Violent offenders

Individuals convicted of violent offences tend to make up a significant proportion of prison populations. From a psychological (treatment) perspective, violence has been described as the intentional and malevolent physical injury of another (Blackburn, 1993). Violence can take many forms and there is a great deal of variability between offenders in terms of what may have caused and maintained their violent behaviours.

Violent offenders may include those who have assaulted their partner or children, been involved in a serious fight or fights, committed violence within a gang context or committed violence in the course of a robbery, as well those who have killed someone.

There is a relatively small group of violent offenders that can be characterised as persistent, or repeat, offenders. These offenders have been termed 'life-course-persistent offenders' (Moffit, 1993). These men tend to have more frequent, and more violent, offending than other offenders, as well as diverse and frequent non-violent offences (Polaschek *et al.*, 2004). It is these serious violent offenders who are likely to commit further serious violent crimes unless appropriate treatment and management is provided. These offenders are most usually assessed on risk assessment measures as being at *high risk* of violent reoffending. It is these offenders we attempt to target into the treatment, irrespective of their offence type. We will now briefly describe different forms of violence.

Instrumental versus expressive violence

Violence is often referred to as either *instrumental* or *expressive* (Berkowitz, 1993). Instrumental violence is usually characterised as goal-oriented or purposeful, controlled, and unemotional. It is often used as a means to an end. For example, an individual may use violence in the course of a robbery, to ensure that he or she is successful. Expressive violence may also be labelled *reactive, angry, emotional* or *impulsive* (McGuire, 2008). Expressive violence often occurs when an individual is attempting to decrease an unpleasant internal state – such as their anger or physiological arousal. For example, someone may commit a violent act purely because they are angry. However, aggressive acts commonly serve more than one function and may be planned, yet still involve high levels of anger (Daffern *et al.*, 2007).

Intimate partner violence

Intimate partner violence (IPV) or domestic violence (see Chapter 10 for a more in-depth discussion of IPV) involves the use of aggression between partners in intimate relationships. Terms such as *battering, spousal abuse* and *marital violence* are often used interchangeably to describe it (Graham-Kevan & Wigman, 2009). IPV is considered not only to include physical aggression, but also to extend to acts of verbal and emotional abuse (including yelling, swearing, threats and name calling) and sexual abuse, in addition to destruction of pets and property and other coercive behaviours.

Murder

Dearden and Jones (2008) report that around 40 per cent of murder victims are killed by a family member, and nearly 25 per cent by an intimate partner. Contrary to popular opinion, convicted murderers are extremely unlikely to be convicted of a second homicide, even without treatment. They are also comparatively unlikely to be convicted of a further offence of any kind. Data from New South Wales published in 1995 showed that 13 per cent of offenders convicted for homicide were reconvicted for lesser offences within two years of release (Thompson, 1995). (This figure was only 8 per cent for those for whom it was a first imprisonment.) Only 2 per cent of individuals in this sample were returned for a violent offence and none were reconvicted for another homicide.

Sexual offenders

A sexual offence occurs when an individual forces another to engage in sexual behaviour, exposes their genitals or sexually touches someone against their will, or if they engage in sexual behaviour with someone who is not of a sufficient age or does not otherwise have the ability to consent. This includes exposing sexual material to others against their will, production of sexual material depicting individuals who are not old enough to consent to sexual activity, and possession of such images. It also includes observing unsuspecting people who are naked or engaged in sexual activity (i.e. voyeurism).

Child sexual offenders

Individuals who sexually abuse children are a wide-ranging group from those who are completely *paedophilic* (attracted to prepubescent children) to those who are attracted to pubescent children (*hebephilic*), through to those who are aroused to both children (typically teenagers) and adults, to those who are aroused to adults but who abuse children for a variety of reasons to do with power, control or sense of entitlement (i.e. incestuous offenders). It is common practice in both research and reviews (Bourget & Bradford, 2008; Laws & O'Donohue, 2008) to describe

sexual offenders in relation to the type of offence they committed. The term *child sexual abuse* is used to describe sexual activity with a child, including both familial (incestuous) and extra-familial victims. The term *child abuser* is commonly used in the UK and the equivalent term *child molester* is commonly used in North America. These terms broadly cover all those who have committed offences against children (regardless of gender and relationship to the victim). Individuals who abuse children are most commonly classified according to their relationship with the victim (i.e. related/unrelated), the gender of victim they target (male/female/both), and age group (pre/post-pubescent).

Rapists

Rape is defined as a sexual assault upon an adult, usually involving, or with the intent to commit, penetrative sexual acts without the victim's permission. Marshall (2000) has pointed out that offenders who commit rapes are typically not that different from other more general offenders, or for that matter from non-offenders. Early research evidence for this can be found in work by Malamuth (1981) who found in a survey of US college males that 35 per cent of the sample reported that they would be willing to rape if they were assured of not being punished.

Rapist typologies exist that highlight the underlying motivations for rape. Generally, the overarching themes of rapist typologies focus on whether the rape was motivated by sexual or non-sexual needs (Beech *et al.*, 2005; Robertiello & Terry, 2007). See Box 18.1 for a classification of types of rapist as outlined by Knight and Prentky (1990).

Sexual murderers

Estimates would suggest that there are around 200 men within the prison system in the UK who have committed a murder with an apparent, or admitted, sexual motivation (A. Carter, Lifer Unit, HM Prison Service, personal communication, May 2003). For the most part, until only recently, such individuals have been managed within the prison system in the same way as other, non-sexual violent offenders because of their status as a murderer rather than a sex offender (given that currently no offence of sexual murder exists in the UK). It is only in the last 10–15 years that the sexual element of their crime has been formally recognised in terms of treatment provision, with men who have killed their victims (where it is suspected or known that there was a sexual component to the killing) now accounting for approximately 5 per cent of all men going through sex offender treatment (Beech *et al.*, 2005). See Box 18.2 for a classification of sexual murderers suggested by Beech *et al.* (2005).

BOX 18.1   CLASSIFICATION OF RAPISTS (ACCORDING TO KNIGHT & PRENTKY, 1990)

Here, rapists are grouped around three motivational types: sexual motivation, anger motivation and sadistic motivation. There are two types of *sexually motivated rapist* identified in the system:

- *The opportunistic rapist*, where the offender has a number of pro-offending attitudes, including the belief that there is nothing wrong with having coercive sex. The sexual assault committed by this type of rapist is an impulsive, predatory act, controlled more by situational circumstances than by explicit sexual fantasy or anger.
- *The non-sadistic sexual rapist*, where there will be a high level of sexual fantasy that precedes the offence(s). These fantasies will reflect sexual arousal and distorted attitudes about women and sex. Typically, there may be comparatively low levels of interpersonal aggression in this type of offender, with the offender using instrumental force to ensure compliance from the victim.

There are two types of *anger-motivated rapist* identified in the Knight and Prentky system:

- *The vindictive rapist*. Women are the central and exclusive focus of these men's anger. The sexual assault is marked by behaviours that are physically damaging and intended to degrade and humiliate the victim(s). There is no evidence that anger is eroticised or that the rapist is preoccupied with sexual fantasies. The system notes that the violence of the vindictive rapist may be so severe that it results in murder.
- *The pervasively angry rapist*. This type of offender is motivated by undifferentiated anger in all aspects of his life. Such offenders are equally likely to express their unmanageable aggression towards men and women. These men will have long histories of antisocial behaviour, where rape is another expression of their anger and hostility.

There is one further type in this system, referred to as the *sadistic sexual rapist*, where there is a fusion of sex and aggression. Knight and Prentky note that here there is a frequent occurrence of erotic and destructive thoughts and fantasies, and that anger is eroticised.

BOX 18.2   CLASSIFICATION OF SEXUAL MURDERERS

- *Sadistically motivated*. Here, the offender is under extreme internal compulsion to kill. The murder arises because the offender carries out his deviant/sadistic fantasies related to sex murder. This type of sexual murderer could be seen as a more extreme version of the sadistic rapist described in Box 18.1.
- *Sexually motivated*. Here, the murder is motivated by the offender's need to keep his victim quiet or to prevent detection during, or after, the commission of a sexual assault. The primary motivation in this type of offender is to sexually offend. In this way, the perpetrator either impulsively kills or has planned to kill his victim to avoid

detection. Hence, this type of offender could be seen as an extreme version of either the sexually motivated opportunistic rapist (sexual assault plus impulsive murderer) or the non-sadistic sexual rapist (sexual assault plus planned murder) described above.

- *Grievance-motivated*. Here, the murder and associated sexual attack arise out of a strong build-up of violence. This tension arises from protracted conflict with another person(s) or circumstances usually unrelated to the murder victim. This type of sexual murderer could be seen as a more extreme version of the anger-driven rapist (especially the vindictive type) described in Box 18.1.

TREATMENT FRAMEWORKS

Treatment frameworks for violent offenders

Within their review of the rehabilitation efforts with violent offenders, Polaschek and Collie (2004) usefully distinguished violent offender treatment on the basis of

their theoretical approaches. They classified treatment programmes as being based on *anger management, cognitive skills, interpersonal violence programmes* or *multimodal approaches*. Anger management and cognitive skills treatment programmes tend to be shorter and less intense (typically less than 150 hours). They are both based on the assumption that one factor (anger or antisocial thinking) is the cause of violent behaviours. Multimodal programmes tend to be far more intensive (typically 300+ hours) than other approaches. They assume that many factors are involved in the causation and maintenance of violent behaviour, targeting a large number of psychological and behaviours factors (such as social skills, thinking, substance abuse, and so on). We will now briefly describe each of these approaches in more detail.

Anger management

Some of the most common types of programme used with violent offenders are **anger management programmes**

> **anger management programmes** typically focus on increasing the offender's awareness of anger and its triggers, then providing a range of skills to assist the offender to decrease anger arousal and strengthen anger control.

(Novaco, 1975). Anger management programmes tend to be facilitated in groups and are brief in duration (i.e. 10–20 two-hour sessions). They typically focus on increasing the offender's awareness of anger and its triggers (Figure 18.1) and then providing a range of skills, including social skills and relaxation training, to assist the offender to decrease anger arousal and strengthen anger control.

This approach assumes that the violence was caused by, or as a consequence of, the individual's anger. Howells (2004), for example, notes that violent acts have been labelled as 'angry behaviours' (p.190). However, there are studies (e.g. Mills & Kroner, 2003) that do not find support for a link between anger and violent criminal behaviours. Given that many proponents of anger management programmes also note that anger should be considered a contributing factor to violence, 'particularly when occurring with a number of other conditions' (Howells, 2004, p.189), or that anger is not even necessary for violence to occur (such as when violence

is instrumental or even sadistic), then it seems necessary also to target the other conditions; hence the need for multifaceted treatment (Polaschek, 2006).

Cognitive skills programmes

Cognitive skills programmes have also been used explicitly in the treatment of violent offenders (Bush, 1995; Robinson, 1995). Examples of cognitive skills programmes include *Reasoning and Rehabilitation* (Antonowicz, 2005), *Think First* (McGuire, 2005), and the *cognitive self-change model* (Bush, 1995).

These programmes are based on the notion that violent offending is caused by antisocial cognitions, and are focused towards helping offenders recognise their thought patterns that are conducive to crime and to acquire new ways of thinking about and solving their problems. They are facilitated in groups and tend to be brief, although comparatively longer than anger management programmes. Robinson (1995) reported on a cognitive skills programme in Canada that consisted of 36 two-hour sessions. Bush's (1995) cognitive self-change model, however, has been reported to last up to three years with two sessions per week. Henning and Frueh (1996) reported a mean length of 10 months' attendance in a sample of 55 offenders.

Ward and Nee (2009) have argued that cognitive skills programmes are unlikely to meet the needs of serious high risk violent offenders, who have well-rehearsed and entrenched beliefs and attitudes about aggression and violence. They argue that these programmes are based upon a relatively narrow approach to changing cognitions that may not be adequate on their own for such violent offenders.

Intimate partner violence (IPV) programmes

IPV programmes have historically been educational and developed around feminist theories of why IPV occurs (see Chapter 10 for more details of this). Consequently they tend to focus on issues such as power and control, abusive/coercive behaviours within intimate relationships, and communication and stress management techniques (Graham-Kevan & Wigman, 2009), and hence IPV programmes have developed quite separately from those for generally violent men (Polaschek, 2006). This has been the result of an assumption that men who physically assault their partners are different from generally violent men. However, although Hanson and Wallace-Capretta (2000) report that IPV offenders are more likely to possess attitudes tolerant of partner assault, including attitudes related to sex roles and relationships with women, they also found that IPV offenders shared many characteristics of the generally violent offenders, such as high levels of antisocial attitudes.

FIGURE 18.1 *Anger management programmes typically focus on increasing the offender's awareness of anger and its triggers, then provide a range of skills to assist the offender to decrease anger arousal and strengthen anger control.*

Source: © FuzzBones. Used under licence from Shutterstock.

More recently, many researchers/clinicians in the field of IPV research take a gender inclusive approach (i.e. women also perpetrate violence towards men). Thus it has been argued (e.g. Dixon *et al.*, submitted; Dutton, 2006) that feminist oriented approaches are not adequate to address violence perpetrated by women, while Mederos (1999) has argued that the focus of IPV programmes is too narrow and that they do not currently take into account the heterogeneity of IPV offenders; and Norlander and Eckhardt (2005) note that the relevance of alcohol abuse is often overlooked by IPV programmes.

Multimodal programmes

McGuire (2008) has noted (on the basis of a review of effective aggression and violence treatment) that 'it is almost certainly necessary to increase the duration and intensity of treatment ('dosage') above presently inadequate levels' (p.2591). The more recently developed multimodal treatment programmes for high-risk violent offenders tend to be of greater intensity and target a larger and broader range of issues than do anger management or cognitive skills programmes.

Multimodal programmes such as the *New Zealand Violence Prevention Unit* (Polaschek *et al.*, 2005) typically are reserved for men with a history of serious violent behaviour who have been assessed as having a higher risk of recidivism. They are usually staffed by multidisciplinary teams consisting of psychologists, custodial staff and other educational and programme staff. The duration of such programmes is usually at least 12 months, with treatment being delivered primarily in a group therapy setting with additional individual treatment as is necessary.

These programmes, at least in theory, allow for a greater level of individualisation of therapeutic targets within the treatment programme and a longer period of time in which to achieve these. These programmes also operate on the assumption that violence may have been caused by multiple issues and therefore all of these issues need to be targeted in treatment (Polaschek, 2006). In this sense they are of far greater intensity than anger management or cognitive skills programmes and target a greater range of issues.

TREATMENT CONTENT OF PROGRAMMES FOR VIOLENT OFFENDERS

A longstanding question regarding the treatment of violent offenders is whether they require specialised treatment or can simply attend and benefit from more general offending programmes (Polaschek & Collie, 2004). The ultimate question is whether serious violent offenders have treatment needs that are different from those of non-violent offenders. This is complicated by the fact that non-violent high risk offenders tend to have histories of at least one violent offence (Bourgon & Armstrong, 2005) and that risk factors or **criminogenic needs** for violence appear to be better predictors of non-violent reoffending (see for example, Wong & Gordon, 2006).

When planning for treatment, the most important factor to consider is the heterogeneity among violent offenders. Specifically, it is critical that the function of the violence for the offender and the causative and maintaining factors are well understood (Howells & Day, 2002). Given the wide range of violent behaviours, it is entirely plausible that two individuals who have committed what appear to be very similar violent crimes, may have offended for very different reasons.

It is equally important when planning treatment to consider how to prepare and motivate the violent offender. Howells and Day (2002) discussed this in terms of the offender's readiness for treatment (see the later section in this chapter on this subject). Violent offenders are typically ambivalent at best regarding the need for treatment, or are simply not ready to benefit from this. Violent offender treatment is further complicated by the difficulties therapists may face in working with violent offenders.

As described in Chapter 16, Andrews and Bonta (2006) initially coined the term *criminogenic needs* to describe the attributes of offenders that are directly linked to criminal behaviour and that should therefore be the focus of treatment. Polaschek (2006) reviewed the evidence base for criminogenic needs for violent offender treatment. She noted that there was 'a need for more research on serious violent offenders' as there were 'still few studies for example that have investigated their criminogenic needs' (p.145). However, most multimodal treatment violent offender programmes target a number of issues, many of which appear to have at least some relationship to risk of recidivism and are therefore likely to be criminogenic needs (Polaschek, 2006). As an example, negative/antisocial attitudes may reflect generally antisocial attitudes, or they may reflect attitudes specifically condoning the use of violence.

Polaschek *et al.* (2004) have demonstrated that both a general criminal attitude measure and a measure of violent attitudes predicted recidivism risk. A number of studies have shown impulsivity to be higher in violent than non-violent offenders (e.g. Nussbaum *et al.*, 2002). We have listed a number of criminogenic needs identified as being relevant to violent offenders in Box 18.3. See Case Study 18.1 for an example of treatment approaches with a violent offender.

BOX 18.3 TREATMENT NEEDS OF VIOLENT OFFENDERS

- Anger
- Negative/antisocial attitudes
- Hostility
- Substance abuse
- Impulsivity
- Active symptoms of major mental illness
- Interpersonal and problem-solving skill deficits
- Antisocial personality
- Social information-processing deficits
- Relationship instability
- Empathy deficits
- Education/employment
- Antisocial companions

Frameworks for treating sexual offenders

Although sex offenders are commonly studied and discussed according to offence type, treatment for sexual offenders in general is primarily targeted to address the treatment needs of child molesters. Rapists are generally treated alongside child molesters, although there is little evidence to support this practice (Gannon *et al.*, 2008). It would also appear that of the men who attend treatment, only 15 per cent are rapists, despite rapists making up roughly 50 per cent of all of the incarcerated sexual offenders in the UK (Beech *et al.*, 2005). See Case Study 18.2 for an example of how these treatment approaches can be implemented. We will now examine current treatment approaches for sexual offenders.

Cognitive-behavioural treatment

The most common method of treatment of sexual offenders is cognitive-behavioural therapy (CBT). The cognitive component addresses the pro-offending beliefs

CASE STUDY 18.1 TREATING A VIOLENT OFFENDER

Ron was 28 years old when he was incarcerated for the third time. All of his prison sentences were for violent and drug-related crimes but he also had a long list of theft, fraud and driving convictions. He had been unemployed for most of his life. His most recent violent offences all occurred on the same evening. The initial offence involved a serious assault on an unknown 18-year-old male, which happened outside a busy pub. Police witnesses described it as a totally unprovoked attack. The second offence occurred within two hours of the first. It involved an assault on a 55-year-old petrol station attendant during the commission of an armed robbery. Ron and two friends were armed with meat cleavers. Both the victims suffered injuries that required hospitalisation.

When asked about the offences during an assessment, Ron described the night in question as 'a little fun with me mates'. He was not concerned over either victim's injuries and stated that the 18-year-old pushed him when he was buying a drink (insulting him) and that the robbery was simply a way of 'getting more money for their drugs'. He also stated that 'everyone needs a little bashing now and again – it toughens you up'. Ron reported consuming a large quantity of alcohol and drugs over a 24-hour period prior to being in the pub. He reported being 'a little bit' angry at his girlfriend whilst at

the pub and then also added that he thought that the victim was a 'good looking little jerk'. Later, Ron acknowledged that he had seen the victim talk to his girlfriend. Ron's description of the robbery indicated that it was not very well planned. Ron and his friends simply needed more money to pay for drugs and had previously discussed maybe 'doing over' the petrol station.

MAIN TREATMENT TARGETS/CRIMINOGENIC NEEDS

- Offence supportive attitudes towards the use of violence ('It was a little fun' and 'everyone needs a bashing')
- Probable antisocial personality (three previous violent offences and other convictions)
- Antisocial companions (would he have committed these offences if not with his friends?)
- Substance abuse (violence appears to be used as a means to get money for alcohol and drugs)
- Anger (the treatment question was whether the important emotional state to target was anger or jealousy/fear of rejection)
- Relationship instability

(Continued)

- Interpersonal and problem-solving skill deficits
- Impulsivity (Ron's decision to assault the victim was impulsive, without planning)
- Employment/education

TREATMENT APPROACH

Given the multiple treatment targets, Ron is unlikely to benefit from only a cognitive skills or anger management programme. In fact, he had completed an anger management programme whilst incarcerated previously. In his case the violence appears to have been caused by multiple issues and therefore all of these should be targeted within a multimodal treatment programme (or through

the use of a number of specific programmes such as alcohol and drug programmes, cognitive skills programmes).

A multimodal treatment approach would involve the development of an overarching **relapse prevention/self-management** plan, which would determine the multiple situations in which Ron was likely to use violence and plan strategies to assist Ron in resisting the impulse. Treatment would also need to target all of the criminogenic needs, particularly given that Ron's use of violence was both reactive and instrumental.

relapse prevention a self-control programme designed to help people from relapsing into episodes of problem behaviour, often used in the treatment of sex offenders. Originally conceptualised for the treatment of addictive behaviours such as alcoholism.

that individuals have, as well as cognitions that affect mood state and behaviours in ways that increase the likelihood of offending. Cognitive therapy therefore aims to encourage an individual to think differently about events, specifically enabling insight into how cognitions influence their sexual behaviours; trains them to identify their own thinking patterns related to sexual offending;

and uses various tools to help individuals re-evaluate these thinking patterns.

The behavioural aspect of CBT addresses the overt and covert behaviour of an individual. Originally this was confined to the use of procedures to alter behaviour, based on the principles of learning theory (i.e. rewarding desired behaviours and punishing unwanted behaviours),

CASE STUDY 18.2   TREATMENT FOR A SEXUAL OFFENDER

Joe is a 23-year-old offender who has been convicted of sexual activity with a female child under 16. He has no previous offences. When asked about the offence during an assessment, Joe describes having a three-week 'relationship' with the victim, who was 12 at the time of the offence. He claims he was in love with the victim and believes his sexual activity with the victim was not an offence because she enjoyed it. He describes the relationship as 'just a little fun' and mentions three others with age-appropriate females, each lasting no more than a few days.

Joe is very close to his parents and will move back in with them when released. He worries that he will struggle to find a job because his previous experience has involved working with young people and he will be prevented from doing this. He spends most of his spare time with people generally aged between 13–21 years as he shares similar interests such as skateboarding and video games. He reports that he feels people of his own age are intimidating. Joe's older sister is supportive of him. She believes Joe is innocent and occasionally asks him to babysit her two children.

Treatment targets/criminogenic needs: Offence supportive attitudes (e.g. 'It was not an offence because she

enjoyed it'); emotional congruence with children (e.g. having 'relationships' with kids, having interests similar to children and finding adults intimidating); and lack of emotionally mature relationships with adults.

Relapse prevention approach: Treatment would involve developing a relapse prevention plan, which would include determining potential risky situations Joe might encounter and how to avoid these. For instance, Joe would likely identify that socialising with children would put him at an increased risk of reoffending and therefore needs to develop techniques for avoiding such situations, such as leaving a gathering if someone underage joins them. He would also develop a number of potential responses to cope with his sister asking him to babysit, even if she is desperate for help.

Good lives model (GLM) approach: Treatment would involve identifying which 'goods' Joe was trying to meet through his offending. It is likely that Joe was attempting to meet the good of (intimate and romantic) friendship. A GLM approach would assist Joe to develop the skills needed to increase his confidence to pursue intimate relationships with age-appropriate partners.

but has since broadened out to include modelling (demonstrating a desired behaviour) and skills training (teaching specific skills through behavioural rehearsal). CBT, therefore, provides a comprehensive approach to treating sex offenders, which now has research evidence to support its efficacy (see the section on treatment efficacy later in this chapter).

Relapse prevention approaches

A significant addition to the CBT approach was the adaptation of the relapse prevention (RP) approach from the addictions field (Marshall & Laws, 2003; Pithers *et al.*, 1983). RP is a self-management approach designed to teach individuals who are trying to change their behaviour, how to anticipate and cope with the problem of relapse. As applied to sex offenders, a relapse is a return to sexually deviant fantasies or reoffence. RP is intended to help clients maintain control of their sexual deviance over time and across various high-risk situations they may encounter in the community. However, more recently issues regarding the overall usefulness of RP as a one-size-fits-all approach has been questioned, in that

- it presumes that all offenders follow the same pathway to offending (Laws & Ward, 2006). However, evidence suggests that there are multiple potential pathways that sex offenders may take in the lead-up to an offence (Bickley & Beech, 2002; Ward & Hudson, 1998; Ward & Siegert, 2002); and

- it also has a rather negative focus in treatment, in that it presumes offenders must avoid multiple situations to minimise their risk of reoffending, which makes it less appealing to the offenders than approaches that have a more positive focus. There is clearly evidence that using *approach* rather than *avoidance* goals in treatment results in greater engagement (Mann *et al.*, 2004).

However, in spite of the issues that have been raised with RP, it is still a component in many current CBT programmes.

Treatment targeting risk/need/responsivity

The principles of risk, need and responsivity (RNR) have been described in Chapter 16 as key elements of effective rehabilitation of offenders. But to briefly summarise here, this means prioritising *high-risk* cases, treating their identified *psychological problems* (their *criminogenic needs*) in a way that is appropriate to the person in question (**responsivity** issues). In relation to sex offenders in particular, risk level would most appropriately be determined using a specific sex offender risk assessment measure (see Chapter 16). Criminogenic need variables specific to

sex offenders can be encompassed under four overarching domains proposed by Thornton (2002), that is, their level of: (1) [deviant] *sexual interests* (i.e. are they sexually aroused to children, or coercive sex with adult victims?); (2) *distorted attitude* (do they have thoughts that give them permission to have sex with children or coercive sex with adults?); (3) [low levels of] *socio-affective functioning* (i.e. intimacy or hostility issues towards others); and (4) [problems in] *self-management* (i.e. poor control of their behaviours/emotions).

Problems in these four key areas have been shown to be related to recidivism (e.g. Craig *et al.*, 2007; Hanson *et al.*, 2007; Thornton, 2002). When assessments of criminogenic needs are made before and after treatment, typically they are seen to improve as a result of treatment (e.g. Marques *et al.*, 2005; Olver *et al.*, 2007). Therefore, criminogenic needs are the most important variables to consider as treatment targets within sexual offender treatment (Mann *et al.*, 2010).

In terms of responsivity, some make the distinction between *internal and external responsivity* factors (Looman *et al.*, 2005). Internal responsivity factors include motivation. External responsivity factors are those that exist outside the individual but influence their ability to benefit from treatment, such as therapist characteristics and therapeutic climate (Looman *et al.*, 2005). These will be discussed in more detail in the final section of this chapter.

In terms of evidence for the utility of the RNR principles, Hanson *et al.* (2009) identified 23 studies (n = 6746) that met the basic criteria for quality of design. All studies were rated on the extent to which they adhered to the RNR principles. Hanson *et al.* found that the sexual recidivism rate in untreated samples was 19 per cent, compared to 11 per cent in treated samples. Studies that adhered to all three RNR principles were found to produce recidivism rates that were less than half of the recidivism rates of comparison groups. Studies that followed none of the RNR principles had little effect in reducing recidivism levels.

In spite of the evidence for the effectiveness of the RNR approach, a number of criticisms have been levelled at it. In particular it has been argued that the focus on criminogenic need in treatment means that other problems the individual has are neglected; the person is not treated as a whole, but as a collection of criminogenic needs. It is noted that if the focus is only on targeting criminogenic need, without also illustrating how this will improve the person's life, this will likely hold little appeal to the client (Willis *et al.*, 2011). As RNR is primarily focused on risk management, it does not maximise client engagement as much as approaches that consider the client's values and priorities in life.

The 'good lives' model

Newer approaches have been suggested that address the criticisms of the RNR framework. In particular, the movement towards more positively oriented (as opposed to just risk management oriented) theoretical frameworks of offender rehabilitation have been received very positively by practitioners. The **good lives model**

good lives model (GLM) a strength-based offender rehabilitation theory that seeks to reduce or manage *dynamic risk factors* by providing offenders with the internal and external resources to achieve important personal goals.

(GLM) (Ward & Stewart, 2003) is such a framework that is increasingly being used with sex offenders. Such positive rehabilitation theories recognise the utility of offering treatment in a manner that will likely hold more appeal to the individual and thus increase their likelihood of benefiting from treatment. According to

this theory, all human beings, including sex offenders seek a set of 11 primary 'goods' (see Chapter 21; also Ward *et al.*, 2006; Ward & Stewart, 2003). Sexual offending, according to this framework (e.g. Ward *et al.*, 2006; Ward & Stewart, 2003) arises as a result of an attempt to obtain these goods in inappropriate ways (Figure 18.2). Treatment aims to instil in the individual the knowledge, skills and competence in order to lead successful lives,

FIGURE 18.2 *According to positive rehabilitation theories, all human beings seek primary 'goods' and sexual offending arises as a result of an attempt to obtain these goods in inappropriate ways.*
Source: © Felix Mizioznikov. Used under licence from Shutterstock.

incompatible with offending, in the context to which they will be released (Ward *et al.*, 2006).

The main criticism of the GLM to date is the lack of empirical evidence for its effectiveness. However, evidence is beginning to accumulate to support the use of this approach (e.g. Harkins *et al.*, in press). In spite of the criticism of this framework, many are beginning to recognise the potential in combining the positive, motivational framework of the GLM approach with the empirically supported framework of RNR (Ward *et al.*, 2007; Willis *et al.*, 2011).

Integrated frameworks

Modern theories of sexual offending integrate biological, social and psychological causes (e.g. Marshall & Barbaree, 1990; Ward & Beech, 2006; Ward *et al.*, 2006). It could be argued that treatment frameworks have not yet quite caught up with this integrated approach, being mainly psychological, and focusing on issues such as offence-supportive attitudes, relationships, and self-regulation.

The majority of North American programmes described themselves as cognitive-behavioural in a recent survey (McGrath *et al.*, 2010), with about half describing themselves as following the RP model (respondents were able to select more than one option to describe their theoretical approach). Less than one third of programmes described themselves as adhering to the RNR model, despite the superiority of the evidence backing this approach (e.g. see Andrews, 2011). Even fewer programmes described themselves as following a sexual trauma model, or as multi-systemic therapy – an empirically supported approach for juvenile sexual offenders. Despite the evidence base for augmenting psychological treatment with medical treatment for those offenders who suffer from sexual preoccupation or compulsive sexual fantasies, less than 20 per cent of North American programmes reported the availability of a physician to prescribe anti-libidinal medication or selective serotonin reuptake inhibitors (SSRIs).

Obviously, some lead-in time is required for programme content to catch up with changes in the evidence base, particularly for large or multi-site manualised programmes such as the prison and probation programmes in England and Wales. The process of changing the design of a programme can take several years, especially if the changes have to be approved by an external body, as is the case in jurisdictions that operate a system of programme accreditation (McGuire *et al.*, 2010).

The first decade of this millennium has seen some important developments in our knowledge about the causes of sexual offending as well as in evidence about effective treatment components, but there are still numerous unanswered questions about sexual offending and how it should be treated. For example, as Hanson

(2010) concluded, the causes of paedophilia are still not known. Although some (e.g. Caimilleri & Quinsey, 2008; Seto, 2008) have explicitly stated their support for neurodevelopmental explanations of paedophilia, this evidence base is still in its early days, and the translation of this knowledge into a treatment paradigm is yet to come.

At present, the best integrated treatment frameworks would aim to strengthen biological, social and psychological resources, would operate in line with the RNR principles, and would recognise that programme goals must be viewed as attractive and achievable by treatment participants. There are arguments for and against manualised treatments (e.g. Mann, 2009a; Marshall, 2009), although most people would agree that some pre-defined structure for a programme is necessary to maintain treatment fidelity and to permit evaluation studies. Most treatment programmes are group programmes, which are generally preferred not just for their efficiency but also because they offer the opportunity for participants to develop interpersonal skills in a way that would not occur in individual therapy; but there is no evidence to speak of that supports one modality over the other (Ware *et al.*, 2009).

Treatment content of sex offender programmes

A survey of 1379 sexual offender treatment programmes across North America (McGrath *et al.*, 2010) revealed, somewhat surprisingly, that the majority of programmes focus on issues that have not been shown to have a strong relationship with recidivism, such as *taking responsibility* for *offending* and *victim empathy*.

It is likely that the focus on these matters stems from influential earlier texts on sexual offender treatment (e.g. Salter, 1988), written before criminogenic need research became so well established. Mann *et al.* (2010) have attempted to encourage a change in treatment programme design by reviewing the risk factor literature to create lists of those risk factors (and hence those areas that should be targeted in treatment) with the greatest empirical support. Table 18.1 summarises the outcome of this review – further description of each risk factor can be found in the source paper.

Mann *et al.* (2010) concluded that these empirically supported risk factors should be the main focus of treatment programmes. However, as McGrath *et al.* (2010) revealed, this is not always the case in practice. For example, deviant sexual interest is the risk factor with the strongest relationship with recidivism, yet only about two thirds of programmes in the USA reported addressing this issue. McGrath *et al.* (2010) concluded that treatment targets of many sexual offending programmes 'are often at odds with' the research into the factors that predict sexual recidivism.

The discrepancy between practice and the evidence base probably exists because it takes some time for treatment programmes to change – for instance, manuals may have to be rewritten, staff may have to be retrained, and so on. In some cases, where research contradicts strongly held beliefs (such as the very widespread belief that offenders must take responsibility for their offending in order to reduce their risk), staff may actively resist change. Programme designers may therefore be likely to wait for some time after publication of research findings before introducing major changes to treatment programmes.

TABLE 18.1 *Empirically-based risk factors for sexual recidivism.*

Empirically supported risk factors	Promising risk factors	Unsupported but with interesting exceptions/worth exploring	Not risk factors
• Sexual preoccupation • Sexual preference for children • Sexualised violence • Multiple paraphilias • Offence supportive attitudes • Emotional congruence with children • Lack of emotionally intimate relationships with adults • Lifestyle impulsivity • Self-regulation problems • Poor problem-solving • Resistance to rules • Grievance thinking • Negative social influences	• Hostility towards women • Machiavellianism • Callousness • Sexualised coping • Externalising	• Denial • View of self as inadequate • Major mental illness • Loneliness • Adversarial sexual attitudes • Fragile narcissism • Sexual entitlement	• Depression • Poor victim empathy • Lack of motivation for treatment at treatment intake • Poor social skills

THE EVIDENCE BASE FOR THE TREATMENT OF DANGEROUS OFFENDERS

Violent offenders

There is a surprising lack of empirical evidence from which to draw conclusions as to the effectiveness of violent offender treatment. This probably reflects the fact that most jurisdictions have focused their resources on the treatment of other offenders – most notably sexual offenders (Howells et al., 1997; Polaschek, 2006). That said, most criminal justice systems recognise the importance of providing treatment to these serious violent offenders. Therefore, they either provide general criminogenic programmes (as outlined above) or have developed specific intensive treatment programmes for this group (Serin et al., 2009). This explains why there have been comparatively few attempts to thoroughly evaluate specific violent offender treatment programmes.

In the first extensive review of violent offender treatment, Polaschek and Collie (2004) summarised the outcomes of nine studies that they considered to be of sufficient methodological rigour to warrant inclusion. Two of these were cognitive skills programmes, three were anger management programmes, and the remaining three were classed as multimodal programmes. Each of these studies reported promising outcomes. However, Polaschek and Collie (2004) considered all of these studies to have methodological weaknesses, or a lack of information, which prevented any firm conclusions as to the effectiveness of violent offender treatment being drawn. More recently, Jolliffe and Farrington (2007) systematically reviewed the effectiveness of violent offender programmes and could find only 11 outcome studies that met their methodological criteria for the identification of good treatment programmes.

Since the initial Polaschek and Collie (2004) review, there have been a number of evaluations of multimodal (intensive) violent offender programmes. These have also produced inconsistent results. Polaschek et al. (2005) reported on the New Zealand prison-based intensive violence prevention unit programme. This intensive group-based programme ran for four sessions per week over a 28-week period. Polaschek et al. (2005) compared the first 22 completers of the programme with a matched control group for a minimum two-year follow-up period. Thirty-two per cent of the treated sample had reoffended compared to 63 per cent of the control group, and the treated

offenders who reoffended took twice as long to commit a further offence as the matched controls.

Cortoni et al. (2006) compared 500 violent offenders who completed the 94-session prison-based violence prevention programme (VPP) in Canada with 466 matched untreated controls. They found that offenders who completed the VPP had significantly fewer major institutional misconduct charges in the six-month and one-year periods following completion of the programme. More importantly, untreated offenders were more than twice as likely to be reconvicted for a violent offence over a 12-month period.

Serin, Gobeil, and Preston (2009) evaluated the Canadian persistently violent offender programme with less positive results. They found that violent offenders who had completed this 144-hour programme were as likely to reoffend as offenders who completed an anger management programme or no programme at all. Similarly, there was little difference between offenders with respect to institutional misconducts or measures of treatment change.

Results regarding the efficacy of anger management programmes have produced mixed results. Dowden et al. (1999) reported an 86 per cent reduction in violent reoffending for 110 anger management programme participants over a three-year follow-up. In contrast, anger management programmes evaluated in Australia appear to have produced only small effects (Howells et al., 2002). It is of note that these programmes appear to have been shorter, and less intense, than those reported by Dowden et al. (1999).

Evaluations of cognitive skills programmes have also produced mixed results. In a large scale Canadian study, Robinson (1995) reported reductions in recidivism of up to 36 per cent. Offenders with a variety of convictions completed these 36-session prison-based reasoning and rehabilitation cognitive skills programmes; here, violent offenders were more likely to benefit from the programme compared to offenders convicted of theft offences. A similarly large evaluation in England and Wales (Falshaw et al., 2004) found no differences between the two-year recidivism rates of offenders who completed cognitive skills programmes and a matched control group.

Babcock et al. (2004) conducted a large meta-analysis of IPV programmes based on 22 studies. They concluded that IPV programmes had, at best, a small positive impact on reoffending, but for the most part these programmes were not effective. Polaschek (2006) contended that some optimism should be maintained regarding the impact of these programmes and provided a blueprint for how to increase their effectiveness.

Treatment effectiveness of sex offender therapy

The effectiveness of sex offender treatment has been studied and reviewed extensively (Gallagher *et al.* 1999; Hall, 1995; Hanson *et al.*, 2002; Kenworthy *et al.*, 2004; Rice & Harris, 2003). Numerous factors should be considered when determining the effectiveness of treatment (see Harkins & Beech, 2007 for a review). These include the type of treatment (e.g. insight oriented, CBT), the study methodology (e.g. incidental cohort, randomised control trial (RCT); see Marshall and Marshall (2007) for a discussion of the problems with using RCT with sex offenders, and Seto *et al.* (2008) for a rebuttal) and how effectiveness is measured (e.g. recidivism, change within treatment).

A useful method for evaluating various treatment approaches has been through the use of meta-analysis. This combines results from a number of studies to determine if there is an overall effect. It allows for small effect sizes to be detected in the large sample sizes that typically result from amalgamating studies.

Hanson *et al.* (2002) conducted a meta-analysis examining treatment evaluation studies identified prior to May 2000. The studies analysed all had a comparison group, including those who had received no treatment, as well as those who attended programmes that were determined to be inadequate or inappropriate. This search yielded 43 studies ($N = 9534$) from 23 published and 20 unpublished community and institutional treatment programmes, with an average length of follow-up time being 46 months. Hanson *et al.* reported a significant effect of treatment (12.3 per cent for treated vs. 16.8 per cent for untreated samples). Averaged across all types of treatment there was a significant effect of treatment. Breaking down treatment by type of approach, Hanson *et al.* found that 'older treatment' options (i.e. non-behavioural/non-CBT) appeared to have little effect in reducing and CBT had a positive treatment effect.

Lösel and Schmucker (2005) reported similar results, analysing 69 studies ($N = 22,181$) that were completed prior to June 2003. This meta-analysis also identified a positive effect of treatment with treated sexual offenders. They found that physical treatments (i.e. surgical castration and hormone treatments) had larger effects than psychosocial approaches. Both CBT and classical behaviour therapy were also shown to have a significant impact on sexual recidivism. In contrast, more psychotherapeutic approaches (i.e. insight oriented, therapeutic community, and other unclear psychosocial approaches) did not significantly influence recidivism.

In the most recent meta-analysis, Beech *et al.* (in preparation) examined 54 treatment studies ($N = 14,694$), which included a range of different designs all using a control group. Results indicated a positive effect of treatment for both sexual and general recidivism, with an advantage of systemic and CBT approaches, in reducing both sexual and general recidivism. Beech *et al.* (in preparation) suggest that these results lend support for the efficacy of sexual offender treatment, particularly when the strongest treatment designs (i.e. randomised control trials and incident cohort combined) are used, with systemic therapy and CBT appearing to hold the most promise for effective interventions.

CONSIDERATIONS IN WORKING WITH DANGEROUS OFFENDERS

There are a number of considerations when working with dangerous offenders; we will now briefly consider some of these.

The psychopathic offender

Psychopathy is a condition marked by: (1) self-serving interpersonal traits (e.g. grandiosity), pathological lying, manipulativeness, shallow affect (e.g. lack of emotional depth), lack of empathy, guilt or remorse; and (2) a set of broadly antisocial traits (e.g. impulsivity, persistent violation of social norms) (see Chapter 1 and Hare, 2003). There are a number of studies and reviews discussing the commonly stated position that men who score high in psychopathy tend to respond poorly, as a group, to traditional treatment programmes (Hare *et al.*, 2000; Hare & Neumann, 2009; Hobson *et al.*, 2000). (A score of 30 on the PCL–R is used as a cut-off to indicate psychopathy; Hare, 2003.) Some studies have even seemed to indicate that treatment may make highly psychopathic men worse (i.e. more likely to recidivate; Hare *et al.*, 2000; Looman *et al.*, 2005; Rice *et al.*, 1992; Seto & Barbaree, 1999). However, there are some problems with studies indicating negative treatment outcome for psychopaths, and more current work suggests that psychopaths do not invariably have high recidivism rates (Abracen *et al.*, in press; Barbaree, 2005; Langton *et al.*, 2006).

Reviews of the available literature on the treatment of psychopaths have generally concluded that there is not enough evidence to support the view that men who score high on the PCL–R have a negative response to treatment (Abracen *et al.*, 2008; Doren & Yates, 2008;

D'Silva *et al.*, 2004; Loving, 2002; Olver & Wong, 2009; Thornton & Blud, 2007). It is possible that psychopathy presents an obstacle to therapy because psychopaths are more of a challenge to treat than non-psychopaths, but they may be treatable nonetheless. In particular, it is possible that psychopaths do not respond well to traditional treatment programmes, but may be more responsive to programmes designed specifically to meet their needs (Harkins, Beech & Thornton, in press; Thornton & Blud, 2007; Wong & Hare, 2005).

Treatment readiness

Some suggest these responsivity issues should be considered under the broader term of 'treatment readiness' (Serin, 1998; Ward *et al.*, 2004). This concept incorporates a variety of personal factors (e.g. beliefs, emotions, skills) and context factors (e.g. treatment setting and availability, external supports, availability of qualified therapists) that promote engagement and enhance change (Ward *et al.*, 2004). According to this theory, a person will be ready to change based on the extent to which they possess certain internal qualities in the context of external factors that promote the changes the person is trying to make (Ward *et al.*, 2004; 2006).

Ward *et al.* (2004) suggest that treatment outcome can be improved by addressing issues surrounding treatment readiness. Such issues might include learning difficulties, a lack of verbal skills and literacy deficits, cultural factors whereby the therapist is of a different culture, a genuine lack of motivation to change and denial of the violent offences, all of which have been highlighted as important issues to address before an individual commences treatment (Howells *et al.*, 1997; Serin & Preston, 2001). Any or all of these issues may result in an offender being 'resistant' to therapeutic efforts. This is a critically important issue given that dangerous offenders who drop out of treatment are almost always found to have higher recidivism rates than offenders who did not receive any treatment (e.g. for violent offending, this was 40 per cent vs. 17 per cent respectively; Dowden & Serin, 2001).

Therapeutic climate

The therapeutic climate of a group refers to the context in which treatment occurs. It encompasses factors such as therapist characteristics and the interrelationships between individuals in a group. Therefore, in addition to characteristics of the offender being important, the characteristics of the therapist and the group itself should not be undervalued. From a review of the literature,

Marshall, Fernandez *et al.* (2003) suggest aggressively confrontational approaches should be avoided and a more empathic, respectful type of supportive but firmly challenging style should be employed. Marshall and colleagues (Marshall *et al.*, 2002; Marshall, Serran *et al.*, 2003) found that a number of therapist features, including empathy, warmth, a rewarding style and being directive, were related to positive change within treatment. Harsh confrontation was adversely related to treatment change. This 'motivational' approach is also supported by a number of other researchers, both for sex offenders (e.g. Drapeau, 2005; Fernandez, 2006; Garland & Dougher, 1991; Kear-Colwell & Pollock, 1997; Preston, 2000) and for the general criminal population (e.g. Andrews & Bonta, 2003; Ginsberg *et al.*, 2002; Mann *et al.*, 2002). A motivational approach has also been related to positive group environment among sex offenders (Beech & Fordham, 1997).

In terms of the group environment, Beech and Fordham (1997) examined the characteristics of successful sex offender treatment groups, demonstrating that effective groups instil a sense of hope in members, are cohesive, well-organised, have desirable group norms, and are well-led. Beech and Hamilton-Giachritsis (2005) examined whether the therapeutic environment of sexual offender groups was related to changes in pro-offending attitudes within treatment (Beech & Hamilton-Giachritsis, 2005). They found that significant treatment change on measures of criminogenic need (i.e. victim empathy, cognitive distortions, and emotional identification with children) was associated with level of cohesiveness in the group and the extent that group members felt able and encouraged to express themselves within the group.

Treatment context

Treatment programmes are often seen as the main route by which risk can be reduced, but the truth is that even the best designed programme will only be effective if it is delivered in a context that reinforces the messages of treatment and where the treatment participant feels safe and supported. Treatment programmes in correctional settings therefore pose a considerable challenge, perhaps particularly for sexual offenders, who are viewed as 'the lowest of the low' by both their fellow offenders and many criminal justice personnel. As Glaser (2010) has pointed out, where programmes are required activities of a criminal justice system, they take on the features of punishment rather than rehabilitation: that is, they do not have the best interests of the participant as their first priority but rather they exist to support the social goal of public protection; they tend not to offer the same standards of confidentiality as non-forensic mental health treatments; and attendance at treatment is often enforced by the courts and hence does not respect the offender's autonomy or right to choice. Treatment programmes in prison face additional challenges, in that prison rules and codes often respect different principles than those promoted by treatment programmes. For instance, treatment programmes, as we have seen, often place considerable store on taking responsibility for offending, whereas survival in prison often depends on the offender providing acceptable excuses for his sexual crimes.

Mann (2009b) has outlined some of the key contextual issues for prison programmes in particular. These include: the mistrust that prisoners often feel for prison staff, which extends to programme staff; the expectation of hostile reactions from others; and the fear of stigma.

Mann suggested that some simple alterations to the way in which sex offenders are managed in prison could increase treatment take-up, including: taking more time to listen to and understand the sex offender's experience of prison; taking more action to counter popular prison myths about treatment; communicating the strength-based aims of treatment; making referrals quickly and sensitively; educating non-treatment staff about the purpose, principles and effectiveness of treatment; and ensuring that prison leaders encourage pro-social modelling and a supportive environment.

While programmes for violent offenders, and programmes in community settings, are probably less vulnerable than sex offender programmes in prison, they also share the feature that 'treatment' is inextricably intertwined with punishment, and hence the context of treatment inevitably works against rather than with the personal aims and priorities of the offender.

SUMMARY

- This chapter has highlighted the importance of providing effective treatment for dangerous offenders.

- In spite of criticisms for all treatment approaches, it would appear that the best approaches to treatment are those that take an integrated or multimodal approach, use an overall risk–need–responsivity (RNR) framework for delivering treatment, and have programme goals that are appealing and attainable by those attending treatment.

- The best current evidence suggests that some of the best treatment targets (i.e. criminogenic needs) for sexual offenders include sexual preoccupation, a sexual preference for children or sexualised violence, emotional congruence with children, lack of emotionally intimate relationships, and lifestyle impulsivity.

- Evidence from the various approaches to treating violent offenders is limited and inconsistent, but does suggest some of the approaches (anger management, cognitive skills, and multimodal approaches) are promising.

- The most promising treatment targets for violent offenders include anger, hostility, impulsivity, substance abuse and relationship instability, amongst others.

- Meta-analyses provide support for the effectiveness of RNR, cognitive-behavioural therapy (CBT), physical, behavioural and systemic approaches to treating sex offenders.

- For all treatment approaches aimed at dangerous offenders, it is useful to consider the potential influence of psychopathy and the offender's level of treatment readiness.

- It is also important to attend to the therapeutic climate of a group, including the characteristics of the therapist and the context in which treatment is provided. Attention to these factors should take us some of the way towards preventing or reducing future harm, alongside improving the future prospects of individuals who have committed dangerous offences.

ESSAY/DISCUSSION QUESTIONS

1. Critically discuss treatment approaches for violent offenders.
2. What are important considerations in delivering effective sex offender treatment?
3. What is the evidence for the effectiveness of treatment approaches for dangerous offenders?
4. What is the evidence for the effectiveness of treatment approaches for sexual offenders?
5. What are the main considerations when working with dangerous offenders?

REFERENCES

Abracen, J., Looman, J., Ferguson, M., Harkins, L. & Mailloux, D. (in press). Recidivism among treated sexual offenders and comparison subjects: Recent outcome data from the Regional Treatment Centre (Ontario) high intensity Sex Offender Treatment Progamme. *Journal of Sexual Aggression.*

Abracen, J., Looman, J. & Langton, C.M. (2008). Treatment of sexual offenders with psychopathic traits: Recent developments and clinical implications. *Trauma, Violence, and Abuse, 9,* 144–166.

Ahlmeyer, S., Heil, P., McKee, B. & English, K. (2000). The impact of polygraphy on admissions of victims and offences in adult sexual offenders. *Sexual Abuse: A Journal of Research and Treatment, 12,* 123–138.

Andrews, D.A. (2011). The impact of nonprogrammatic factors on criminal-justice interventions. *Legal and Criminological Psychology, 16,* 1–23.

Andrews, D.A. & Bonta, J. (2003). *The psychology of criminal conduct* (3rd edn). Cincinnati, OH: Anderson.

Andrews, D.A. & Bonta, J. (2006). *The psychology of criminal conduct* (4th edn). Cincinnati, OH: Anderson.

Antonowicz, D.H. (2005). The Reasoning and Rehabilitation programme: outcome evaluations with offenders. In M. McMurran & J. McGuire (Eds.) *Social problem solving and offending: Evidence, evaluation and evolution* (pp.163–181). Chichester: John Wiley & Sons, Inc.

Babcock, J.C., Green, C.E. & Robie, C. (2004). Does batterers' treatment work? A meta-analytic review of domestic violence treatment. *Clinical Psychology Review, 23,* 1023–1053.

Barbaree, H.E. (2005). Psychopathy, treatment behavior, and recidivism: An extended follow-up of Seto and Barbaree (1999). *Journal of Interpersonal Violence, 20,* 1115–1131.

Beech, A.R. & Fordham, A.S. (1997). Therapeutic climate of sexual offender treatment programs. *Sexual Abuse: A Journal of Research and Treatment, 9,* 219–237.

Beech, A.R. & Hamilton-Giachritsis, C.E. (2005). Relationship between therapeutic climate and treatment outcome in a group-based sexual offender program. *Sexual Abuse: A Journal of Research and Treatment, 17,* 127–140.

Beech, A.R., Oliver, C., Fisher, D. & Beckett, R.C. (2005). *STEP 4: The sex offender treatment programme in prison: Addressing the needs of rapists and sexual murderers.* Retrieved 25 August 2011 from www.hmprisonservice.gov.uk/assets/documents/100013DBStep_4_SOTP_report_2005.pdf

Beech, A.R., Robertson, C. & Freemantle, N. (in preparation). *A meta-analysis of treatment outcome studies: Comparisons of treatment designs and treatment delivery.* Unpublished manuscript.

Berkowitz, L. (1993). *Aggression: Its causes, consequences, and control.* New York: McGraw-Hill.

Bickley, J.A. & Beech, A.R. (2002). An investigation of the Ward and Hudson pathways model of the sexual offence process with child abusers. *Journal of Interpersonal Violence, 17,* 371–393.

Blackburn, R. (1993). *The psychology of criminal conduct: Theory, research and practice.* Chichester: John Wiley & Sons, Inc.

Bourget, D. & Bradford, J.M.W. (2008). Evidential basis for the assessment and treatment of sex offenders. *Brief Treatment and Crisis Intervention, 8,* 130–146.

Bourgon, G. & Armstrong, B. (2005). Transferring the principles of effective treatment into a 'real world' setting. *Criminal Justice and Behavior, 32,* 3–25.

Bush, J. (1995). Teaching self-risk management to violent offenders. In J. McGuire (Ed.) *What works: Reducing re-offending: Guidelines from research and practice* (pp. 139–154). Chichester: John Wiley & Sons, Inc.

Camilleri, J.A. & Quinsey, V.L. (2008). Pedophilia: Assessment and treatment. In D.R. Laws & W.T. O'Donohue (Eds.) *Sexual deviance: Theory, assessment and treatment, second edition* (pp.183–212). New York: Guilford.

Cortoni, F., Nunes, K. & Latendresse, M. (2006). *An examination of the effectiveness of the violence prevention program. Research Report R–178.* Ottawa, Canada: Correctional Service Canada.

Craig, L.A., Thornton, D., Beech, A.R. & Browne, K.D. (2007). The relationship between statistical and psychological risk markers to sexual recidivism. *Criminal Justice and Behavior, 34,* 314–329.

Daffern, M., Howells, K. & Ogloff, J. (2007). What's the point? Towards a methodology for assessing the function of psychiatric inpatient aggression. *Behaviour Research and Therapy, 45*, 101–111.

Dearden, W. & Jones, W. (2008). *Homicide in Australia: 2006–2007 National Homicide Monitoring Program Annual Report.* Canberra, Australia: Australian Institute of Criminology, Canberra.

Dixon, L., Archer, J. & Graham-Kevan, N. (submitted). *Perpetrator programmes for partner violence: Are they based on ideology or evidence?* Manuscript submitted for publication.

Doren, D.M. & Yates, P.M. (2008). Effectiveness of sex offender treatment for psychopathic sexual offenders. *International Journal of Offender Therapy and Comparative Criminology, 52*, 234–245.

Dowden, C., Blanchette, K. & Serin, R.C. (1999). *Anger management programming for federal male inmates: An effective intervention. Research report R–82.* Ottawa, Canada: Correctional Service Canada.

Dowden, C. & Serin, R. (2001). *Anger management programming for offenders: The impact of programme performance measures. Research Report No. R–106.* Ottawa, Canada: Correctional Service of Canada.

Drapeau, M. (2005). Research on the processes involved in treating sexual offenders. *Sexual Abuse: A Journal of Research and Treatment, 17*, 117–125.

D'Silva, K., Duggan, C. & McCarthy, L. (2004). Does treatment really make psychopaths worse? A review of the evidence. *Journal of Personality Disorders, 18*, 163–177.

Dutton, D.G. (2006). *Rethinking domestic violence.* Vancouver-Toronto: UBC Press.

Falshaw, L., Friendship, C., Travers, R. & Nugent, F. (2004). Searching for 'What Works': HM Prison Service accredited cognitive skills programmes. *The British Journal of Forensic Practice, 6*, 3–13.

Fernandez, Y.M. (2006). Focusing on the positive and avoiding negativity in sexual offender treatment. In W.L. Marshall, Y.M. Fernandez, L.E. Marshall & G.E. Serran (Eds.) *Sexual offender treatment: Controversial issues*, pp.187–197. Chichester: John Wiley & Sons, Inc.

Gallagher, C.A., Wilson, D.B., Hirschfield, P., Coggeshall, M.B. & McKenzie, D.L. (1999). A quantitative review of the effects of sex offender treatment on sexual offending. *Corrections Management Quarterly, 3*, 19–29.

Gannon, T.A., Collie, R.M., Ward, T. & Thakker, J. (2008). Rape: Psychopathology, theory, and treatment. *Clinical Psychology Review, 28*, 981–1008.

Garland, R.J. & Dougher, M.J. (1991). Motivation intervention in the treatment of sex offenders. In W. Miller & S. Rollnick (Eds.) *Motivational interviewing: Preparing people to change addictive behavior* (pp.303–313). New York: Guilford.

Ginsberg, J.I.D., Mann, R.E., Rotgers, F. & Weekes, J.R. (2002). Motivational interviewing with criminal justice populations. In W. Miller & S. Rollnick (Eds.) *Motivational interviewing: Preparing people to change addictive behavior* (pp.333–346). New York: Guilford.

Glaser, B. (2010). Sex offender programmes: New technology coping with old ethics. *Journal of Sexual Aggression, 16*, 261–274.

Graham-Kevan, N. & Wigman, S.J.A. (2009). Treatment approaches for interpersonal violence: Domestic violence and stalking. In J.L. Ireland, C.A. Ireland & P. Birch (Eds.) *Violent and sexual offenders: Assessment, treatment and management* (pp.198–232). Cullompton, Devon: Willan Publishing.

Hall, G.C.N. (1995). Sexual offender recidivism revisited: A meta analysis of recent treatment studies. *Journal of Consulting and Clinical Psychology, 63*, 802–809.

Hanson, R.K. (2010). Dimensional measurement of sexual deviance. *Archives of Sexual Behavior, 39*, 401–404.

Hanson, R.K., Bourgon, G., Helmus, L. & Hodgson, S. (2009). The principles of effective correctional treatment also apply to sexual offenders: A meta-analysis. *Criminal Justice and Behavior, 36*, 865–891.

Hanson, R.K., Gordon, A., Harris, A.J.R., Marques, J.K., Murphy, W., Quinsey, V.L. & Seto, M.C. (2002). First report of the collaborative outcome data project on the effectiveness of psychological treatment for sex offenders. *Sexual Abuse: A Journal of Research and Treatment, 14*, 169–194.

Hanson, R.K. Harris, A.J.R., Scott, T. & Helmus, L. (2007). *Assessing the risk for sexual offenders on community supervision: The Dynamic Supervision Project.* Ottawa, Canada: Corrections Research, Public Safety and Emergency Preparedness Canada. Retrieved 25 August 2011 from www.publicsafety.gc.ca/res/cor/rep/_fl/crp2007-05-en.pdf

Hanson, R.K. & Morton-Bourgon, K.E. (2005). The characteristics of persistent sex offenders: A meta-analysis of recidivism studies. *Journal of Consulting and Clinical Psychology, 73*, 1154–1163.

Hanson, R.K. & Morton-Bourgon, K.E. (2009). The accuracy of recidivism risk assessments for sex offenders: A meta-analysis of 118 prediction studies. *Psychological Assessment, 21*, 1–21.

Hanson, R.K. & Wallace-Capretta, S. (2000). *Predicting recidivism among male batterers. Research Report 2000–06.* Ottawa, Canada: Department of the Solicitor General Canada.

Hare, R.D. (2003). *The Hare Psychopathy Checklist–Revised (PCL–R)* (2nd edn). Toronto, Canada: Multi-Health Systems.

Hare, R.D., Clarke, D., Grann, M. & Thornton, D. (2000). Psychopathy and the predictive validity of the PCL–R: An international perspective. *Behavioral Sciences and the Law, 18*, 623–645.

Hare, R.D. & Neumann, C.S. (2009). Psychopathy: Assessment and forensic implications. *The Canadian Journal of Psychiatry, 54*, 791–802.

Harkins, L. & Beech, A.R. (2007). Measurement of the effectiveness of sex offender treatment. *Aggression and Violent Behavior, 12*, 36–44.

Harkins, L., Beech, A.R. & Thornton, D. (in press). The influence of risk and psychopathy on the therapeutic climate in sex offender treatment. *Sexual Abuse: A Journal of Research and Treatment.*

Harkins, L., Flak, V.E. & Beech, A.R. (in press). Evaluation of a community-based sex offender treatment program using a Good Lives Model approach. *Sexual Abuse: A Journal of Research and Treatment.*

Henning, K.R. & Frueh, B.C. (1996). Cognitive-behavioral treatment of incarcerated offenders: An evaluation of the Vermont department of corrections' cognitive self-change program. *Criminal Justice Behavior, 23,* 523–542.

Hobson, J., Shine, J. & Roberts, R. (2000). How do psychopaths behave in a prison therapeutic community? *Psychology, Crime and the Law, 6,* 139–154.

Howells, K. (2004). Anger and its links to violent offending. *Psychiatry, Psychology and Law, 11,* 189–196.

Howells, K. & Day, A. (2002). Grasping the nettle: Treating and rehabilitating the violent offender. *Australian Psychologist, 37,* 222–228.

Howells, K., Day, A., Bubner, S., Jauncey, S., Williamson, P., Parker, A. & Heseltine, K. (2002). Anger management and violence prevention: Improving effectiveness. *Trends and Issues in Crime and Criminal Justice, 227,* 1–6.

Howells, K., Watt, B., Hall, G. & Baldwin, S. (1997). Developing programs for violent offenders. *Legal and Criminological Psychology, 2,* 117–128.

Jolliffe, D. & Farrington, D.P. (2007). A systematic review of the national and international evidence on the effectiveness of interventions with violent offenders. *Ministry of Justice Research Series, 16/07.* London: Ministry of Justice.

Kear-Colwell, J. & Pollock, P. (1997). Motivation or confrontation: Which approach to the child sex offender? *Criminal Justice and Behavior, 24,* 20–33.

Kenworthy, T., Adams, C.E., Bilby, C., Brooks-Gordon, B. & Fenton, M. (2004). Psychological interventions for those who have sexually offended or are at risk of offending. *Cochrane Database of Systematic Reviews. Issue 4.*

Knight, R.A. & Prentky, R.A. (1990). Classifying sexual offenders: The development and corroboration of taxonomic models. In W.L. Marshall, D.R. Laws & H.E. Barbaree (Eds.) *Handbook of sexual assault: Issues, theories, and treatment of the offender* (pp.23–52). New York: Plenum.

Langton, C.M., Barbaree, H.E., Harkins, L. & Peacock, E.J. (2006). Sexual offenders' response to treatment and its association with recidivism as a function of psychopathy. *Sexual Abuse: A Journal of Research and Treatment, 18,* 99–120.

Laws, D.R. & O'Donohue, W.T. (Eds.) (2008). *Sexual deviance: Theory, assessment, and treatment.* New York: Guilford.

Laws, D.R. & Ward, T. (2006). When one size doesn't fit all: The reformulation of relapse prevention. In W.L. Marshall, Y.M. Fernandez, L.E. Marshall & G.A. Serran (Eds.) *Sexual offender treatment: Controversial issues.* (pp.241–254). Chichester: John Wiley & Sons, Inc.

Looman, J., Abracen, J., Serin, R. & Marquis, P. (2005). Psychopathy, treatment change, and recidivism in high-risk, high-need sex offenders. *Journal of Interpersonal Violence, 20,* 549–568.

Looman, J., Dickie, I. & Abracen, J. (2005). Responsivity in the treatment of sexual offenders. *Trauma, Violence, and Abuse, 6,* 330–353.

Lösel, F. & Schmucker, M. (2005). The effectiveness of treatment for sexual offenders: A comprehensive meta-analysis. *Journal of Experimental Criminology, 1,* 117–146.

Loving, J.L. (2002). Treatment planning with the Psychopathy Checklist–Revised (PCL–R). *International Journal of Offender Therapy and Comparative Criminology, 46,* 281–293.

Maguire, M. Grubin, D., Lösel, F. & Raynor, P. (2010). What works and the correction services accreditation panel: An insider perspective. *Criminology and Criminal Justice, 10,* 37–58.

Malamuth, N.M. (1981). Rape proclivity among males. *Journal of Social Issues, 37,* 138–157.

Mann, R.E. (2009a). Sexual offender treatment: The case for manualisation. *Journal of Sexual Aggression, 15,* 121–132.

Mann, R.E. (2009b). Getting the context right for sex offender treatment. In D. Prescott (Ed.) *Building motivation for change in sexual offenders.* Brandon, VT: Safer Society Press.

Mann, R.E., Ginsberg, J.I.D. & Weekes, J.R. (2002). Motivational interviewing with offenders. In M. McMurran (Ed.) *Motivating offenders to change: A guide to enhancing engagement in therapy* (pp. 87–102). Chichester: John Wiley & Sons, Inc.

Mann, R.E., Webster, S.D., Schofield, C. & Marshall, W.L. (2004). Approach versus avoidance goals with sexual offenders. *Sexual Abuse: A Journal of Research and Treatment, 16,* 65–75.

Mann, R.E., Hanson, R.K. & Thornton, D. (2010). Assessing risk for sexual recidivism: some proposals on the nature of psychologically meaningful risk factors. Sexual Abuse: A Journal of Research and Treatment, 22, 191–217.

Marques, J.K., Wiederanders, M., Day, D.M., Nelson, C. & van Ommeren, A. (2005). Effects of a relapse prevention program on sexual recidivism: Final results from California's Sex Offender Treatment and Evaluation Program (SOTEP). *Sexual Abuse: A Journal of Research and Treatment, 17,* 79–107.

Marshall, W.L. (2000). Adult sexual offenders against women. In C.R. Hollin (Ed.) *Handbook of offender assessment and treatment* (pp.333–348). Chichester: John Wiley & Sons, Inc.

Marshall, W.L. (2009). Manualisation: A blessing or a curse? *Journal of Sexual Aggression, 15,* 109–120.

Marshall, W.L. & Barbaree, H.E. (1990). An integrated theory of the etiology of sexual offending. In W.L. Marshall, D.R. Laws & H.E. Barbaree (Eds.) Handbook of sexual assault: Issues, theory and treatment of offenders. New York: Plenum Press.

Marshall, W.L., Fernandez, Y.M., Serran, G.A., Mulloy, R., Thornton, D., Mann, R.E. & Anderson, D. (2003). Process variables in the treatment of sexual offenders: A review of the relevant literature. *Aggression and Violent Behavior, 8,* 205–234.

Marshall, W.L. & Laws, D.R. (2003). A brief history of behavioural and cognitive approaches to sexual offenders: Part 2, the modern era. *Sexual Abuse: A Journal of Research and Treatment, 15,* 93–120.

Marshall, W.L. & Marshall, L.E. (2007). The utility of the random controlled trial for evaluating sexual offender treatment: The gold standard or an inappropriate strategy? *Sexual Abuse: A Journal of Research and Treatment, 19*, 175–191.

Marshall, W.L., Serran, G.A., Fernandez, Y.M., Mulloy, R., Mann, R. & Thornton, D. (2003). Therapists' characteristics in the treatment of sexual offenders: Tentative data on their relationship with indices of behaviour change. *Journal of Sexual Aggression, 9*, 25–30.

Marshall, W.L., Serran, G.A., Moulden, H., Mulloy, R., Fernandez, Y.M., Mann, R. & Thornton, D. (2002). Therapist features in sexual offender treatment: Their reliable identification and influence on behaviour change. *Clinical Psychology and Psychotherapy, 9*, 395–405.

McGrath, R.J., Cumming, G. F., Burchard, B.L., Zeoli, S. & Ellerby, L. (2010). *Current practices and emerging trends in sexual abuser management: The Safer Society 2009 North American Survey.* Brandon, VT: Safer Society Press.

McGuire, J. (2005). Social problem solving: Basic concepts, research and applications. In M. McMurran & J. McGuire (Eds.) *Social problem-solving and offending: Evidence, evaluation and evolution* (pp. 3–29). Chichester: John Wiley & Sons, Inc.

McGuire, J. (2008). A review of effective interventions for reducing aggression and violence. *Philosophical Transactions of the Royal Society B, 363*, 2577–2597.

Mederos, F. (1999). Batterer intervention programs: The past, and future prospects. In M. F. Shepard & E. L. Pence (Eds.) *Co-ordinating community responses to domestic violence: Lessons from Duluth and beyond* (pp.127–150). Thousand Oaks, CA: Sage.

Mills, J.F. & Kroner, D.G. (2003). Anger as a predictor of institutional misconduct and recidivism. *Journal of Interpersonal Violence, 18*, 282–294.

Moffitt, T. (1993). Adolescent limited and life-course persistent antisocial behavior: A developmental taxonomy. *Psychological Review, 100*, 674–701.

Motiuk, L. & Belcourt, R. (1997). Profiling federal offenders with violent offences. *Forum on Corrections Research, 9*, 8–13.

Norlander, B. & Eckhardt, C.I. (2005). Anger, hostility, and male perpetrators of intimate partner violence: A meta-analytic review. *Clinical Psychology Review, 25*, 119–152.

Novaco, R.W. (1975). *Anger control: The development and evaluation of an experimental treatment.* Lexington, MA: Lexington Books.

Nussbaum, D., Collins, M., Cutler, J., Zimmerman, W., Farguson, B. & Jacques, I. (2002). Crime type and specific personality indicia: Cloninger's TCI impulsivity, empathy and attachment subscales in non-violent, violent and sexual offenders. *American Journal of Forensic Psychology, 20*, 23–56.

Olver, M.E. & Wong, S.C. (2009). Therapeutic responses of psychopathic sexual offenders: Treatment attrition, therapeutic change, and long-term recidivism. *Journal of Consulting and Clinical Psychology, 77*, 328–336.

Olver, M.E., Wong, S., Nicholaichuk, T. & Gordon, A. (2007). The validity and reliability of the Violence Risk Assessment Scale – Sex Offender version: Assessing sex offender risk and evaluating therapeutic change. *Psychological Assessment, 19*, 318–329.

Pithers, W.D., Marques, J.K., Gibat, C.C. & Marlatt, G.A. (1983). Relapse prevention with sexual aggressors: A self-control model of treatment and maintenance of change. In J.G. Greer & I.R. Stuart (Eds.) *The sexual aggressor: Current perspectives on treatment* (pp.214–239). New York: Van Nostrand Reinhold.

Polaschek, D.L.L. (2006). Violent offender programmes: concept, theory and practice. In C.R. Hollin & E.J. Palmer (Eds.) *Offending behaviour programmes: Development, application, and controversies* (pp.113–154). Chichester: John Wiley & Sons, Inc.

Polaschek, D.L.L. & Collie, R.M. (2004). Rehabilitating serious violent adult offenders: An empirical and theoretical stocktake. *Psychology, Crime and Law, 10*, 321–334.

Polaschek, D.L.L., Collie, R.M. & Walkey, F.H. (2004). Criminal attitudes to violence: Development and preliminary validation of a scale for male prisoners. *Aggressive Behavior, 30*, 484–503.

Polaschek, D.L.L., Wilson, N.J., Townsend, M.R. & Daly, L.R. (2005). Cognitive-behavioural rehabilitation for violent offenders: An outcome evaluation of the violence prevention unit. *Journal of Interpersonal Violence, 20*, 1611–1627.

Preston, D.L.L. (2000). Treatment resistance in corrections. *Forum on Corrections Research, 12*, 24–28.

Rice, M.E. & Harris, G.T. (2003). The size and sign of treatment effects in sex offender therapy. In R.A. Prentky, E.S. Janus & M.C. Seto (Eds.) *Sexually coercive behavior: Understanding and management. Annals of the New York Academy of Sciences, 989*, 428–440.

Rice, M.E., Harris, G.T. & Cormier, C.A. (1992). An evaluation of a maximum security therapeutic community for psychopaths and other mentally disordered offenders. *Law and Human Behavior, 16*, 399–412.

Robertiello, G. & Terry, K.J. (2007). Can we profile sex offenders? A review of sex offender typologies. *Aggression and Violent Behavior, 12*, 508–518.

Robinson, D. (1995). *The impact of cognitive skills reasoning on post-release recidivism among Canadian federal offenders. No. R–41.* Ottawa, Canada: Research Branch, The Correctional Services.

Salter, A.C. (1988). *Treating child sex offenders and victims: A practical guide.* Thousand Oaks, CA: Sage.

Serin, R.C. (1998). Treatment responsivity, intervention, and reintegration: A conceptual model. Forum on Corrections Research, 10, 29–32.

Serin, R.C., Gobeil, R. & Preston, D.L. (2009). Evaluation of the Persistently Violent Offender Treatment Program. *International Journal of Offender Therapy and Comparative Criminology, 53*, 57–73.

Serin, R.C. & Preston, D.L. (2001). Programming for violent offenders. *Forum on Corrections Research, 5*, 3–5.

Seto, M. (2008). Pedophilia: Psychopathology and theory. In D.R. Laws & W.T. O'Donohue (Eds.) *Sexual deviance: Theory, assessment and treatment* (2nd edn) (pp.164–182). New York: Guilford.

Seto, M.C. & Barbaree, H.E. (1999). Psychopathy, treatment behavior, and sex offender recidivism. *Journal of Interpersonal Violence, 14*, 1235–1248.

Seto, M.C., Marques, J., Harris, G.T., Chaffin, M., Lalumière, M.L., Miner, M.H., *et al.* (2008). Good science and progress in sex offender treatment are intertwined: A response to Marshall and Marshall (2007). *Sexual Abuse: A Journal of Research and Treatment, 20*, 247–255.

Thompson, B. (1995). *Recidivism in NSW: General study. Research publication, No. 31*. Sydney, Australia: NSW Department of Corrective Services.

Thornton, D. (2002). Constructing and testing a framework for dynamic risk assessment. *Sexual Abuse: A Journal of Research and Treatment, 141*, 139–153.

Thornton, D. & Blud, L. (2007). The influence of psychopathic traits on response to treatment. In H. Hervé & J.C. Yuille (Eds.) *The psychopath: Theory, research, and practice* (pp.505–539). New York: Routledge.

Ward, T. & Beech, A.R. (2006). An integrated theory of sex offending. *Aggression and Violent Behavior, 11*, 44–63.

Ward, T. & Hudson, S.M. (1998). A model of the relapse process in sexual offenders. *Journal of Interpersonal Violence, 13*, 700–725.

Ward, T., Mann, R. & Gannon, T.A. (2007). The good lives model of rehabilitation: Clinical implications. *Aggression and Violent Behavior, 12*, 87–107.

Ward, T. & Nee, C. (2009). Surfaces and depths: Evaluating the theoretical assumptions of cognitive skills programmes. *Psychology, Crime and Law, 15*, 165–182.

Ward, T., Polachek, D.L.L. & Beech, A.R. (2006). *Theories of sexual offending*. Chichester: John Wiley & Sons, Inc.

Ward, T. & Siegert, R.J. (2002). Toward a comprehensive theory of child sexual abuse: A theory knitting perspective. *Psychology, Crime, and Law, 8*, 319–351.

Ward, T. & Stewart, C.A. (2003). The treatment of sex offenders: Risk management and the good lives model. *Professional Psychology: Research and Practice, 34*, 353–360.

Ward, T., Vess, J., Collie, R.M. & Gannon, T.A. (2006). Risk management or good promotion: The relationship between approach and avoidance goals in treatment for sex offenders. *Aggression and Violent Behavior, 11*, 378–393.

Ware, J., Mann, R.E. & Wakeling, H.C. (2009). Group versus individual treatment: What is the best modality for treating sexual offenders? *Sexual Abuse in Australia and New Zealand, 2*, 2–13.

Willis, G., Gannon, T., Yates, P., Collie, R. & Ward, T. (2011, Winter). 'In style' or evolving through research? Misperceptions about the Good Lives Model. *The ATSA Forum, XXIII* (1).

Wong, S.C.P. & Gordon, A. (2006) The validity and reliability of the Violence Risk Scale: A treatment friendly violence risk assessment tool. *Psychology, Public Policy and Law, 12*, 279 –309.

Wong, S.C.P. & Hare, R.D. (2005). *Guidelines for a psychopathy treatment program*. Toronto: Multi-Health Systems.

ANNOTATED READING LIST

Beech, A.R., Craig, L.A. & Browne, K.D. (Eds.) (2009). *Assessment and treatment of sex offenders: A handbook.* Chichester: John Wiley & Sons, Inc. ISBN 978-0470019009. *An up-to-date review of assessment and treatment of a number of different groups of offenders (including male, female adult, adolescent, women, and people with mental disorders, personality disorders and intellectual disabilities).*

Marshall, W.L. & Laws, D.R. (2003). A brief history of behavioural and cognitive approaches to sexual offenders: Part 2, the modern era. *Sexual Abuse: A Journal of Research and Treatment, 15*, 93–120. *This paper provides a historical perspective on the development and implementation of many treatment approaches that are currently in use with sex offenders.*

McGrath, R.J., Cumming, G.F., Burchard, B.L., Zeoli, S. & Ellerby, L. (2010). *Current practices and emerging trends in sexual abuser management: The Safer Society 2009 North American Survey.* Brandon, VT: Safer Society Press. *This paper outlines a number of the sex offender treatment approaches that are currently used, and provides evidence for their use in practice in the USA and Canada.*

McGuire, J. (2008). A review of effective interventions for reducing aggression and violence. *Philosophical Transactions of the Royal Society B, 363*, 2577–2597. *A useful review of the effectiveness of aggression and violence treatments.*

Polaschek, D.L.L. & Collie, R.M. (2004). Rehabilitating serious violent adult offenders: An empirical and theoretical stocktake. *Psychology, Crime and Law, 10*, 321–334. *This paper usefully distinguishes violent offender treatments on the basis of their theoretical approaches and provides summaries of studies the authors deem to be of the highest methodological rigour.*

Ward, T., Day, A., Howells, K. & Birgden, A. (2004). A multifactor offender readiness model. *Aggression and Violent Behavior, 9*, 645–673.

Ward, T., Polachek, D.L.L. & Beech, A.R. (2006). Theories of sexual offending. Chichester: John Wiley & Sons, Inc. *Outlines and critiques all the historical and current theories of relevance in treating sexual offenders.*

19 Interventions for Offenders with Intellectual Disabilities

WILLIAM R. LINDSAY, JOHN L. TAYLOR AND AMANDA M. MICHIE

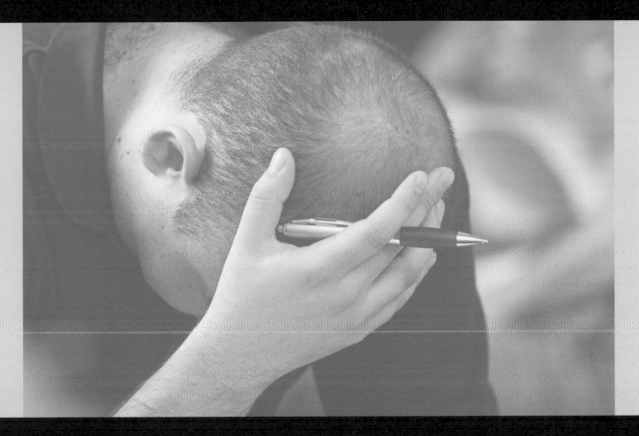

The fact that a subgroup of offenders is known to have significant intellectual limitations has, for many years, presented difficulties for the development of assessment, management and treatment services in the criminal justice system (CJS). Therefore, researchers and service planners have been interested in prevalence, characteristics of offenders with intellectual limitations, types of crimes and so on. Once characteristics and special needs have been established, procedures must be adapted so that individuals can engage meaningfully with the CJS and other agencies. Finally, an important question is the extent to which services can reduce reoffending and enable individuals to return to community living. In a worst-case scenario, it may be that any particular subgroup of offenders is impervious to intervention aimed at rehabilitation and the prevention of reoffending.

It will not be possible to review research on all these issues in this chapter and we will restrict ourselves to the effectiveness of assessment and treatment for offenders with **intellectual disability (ID)**. We will evaluate the evidence on the psychometric properties of assessments for psychological variables related to offending. We will also evaluate the effectiveness of treatment of some main criminal behaviours, such as violence and sexual offending.

> **intellectual disability (ID)** internationally recognised term for people who have an IQ less than 70 and have deficits in at least two areas of adaptive behaviour, with the onset of these deficits having occurred before adulthood.

THE PREVALENCE OF ID IN OFFENDER POPULATIONS

Lindsay, Hastings *et al.* (2011) have noted three major methodological difficulties in studying the prevalence of offenders with ID in criminal populations. Firstly, studies have been conducted in a variety of settings, including prisons (MacEachron, 1979), probation services (Mason & Murphy, 2002) and appearances at court (Vanny *et al.*, 2009). Vanny *et al.* (2009) studied 250 individuals appearing in magistrates' courts in New South Wales, Australia and, using an intellectual screening test, found that 10 per cent fell into the category of ID while a further 20 per cent fell into the category of borderline intelligence. On the other hand, MacEachron (1979) found prevalence rates of 0.6–2.3 per cent in state prisons in Maine and Massachusetts, USA. She concluded that the method used in the assessment made a significant difference to the rates found.

Screening tools tend to find higher prevalence rates than full psychometric assessment since screening assessments are designed to be over-inclusive, identifying people for further more exhaustive assessment. A third source of variation is the inclusion criteria used, particularly if those considered to be functioning in the borderline intelligence range (IQ 70–80) are included. It can be seen in the Vanny *et al.* (2009) study that prevalence would triple from 10 per cent to 30 per cent, if people with borderline intelligence were included in those offenders with ID. Indeed, when low intelligence is considered in studies on offenders (e.g. Farrington, 2005), IQ under 85 is sometimes the criterion.

A number of recent reports have arrived at similar findings. In a study on prisons in the UK, Hayes *et al.* (2007) used a full psychometric assessment and also assessed **adaptive behaviour** in 140 prisoners, and found that 2.9 per cent of their sample fell in the range of ID (Figure 19.1). Herrington (2009) used a screening assessment to re-evaluate 185 young adult male prisoners in a young offender's institution. He reported 10 per cent of prisoners fell into the ID range. A study in Norway (Søndenaa *et al.*, 2008), on 143 inmates randomly chosen from the prison population, used a screening instrument to assess for intellectual disability. They reported that 10.8 per cent of their sample fell into the category of ID. It is important to remember that screening tools are designed to be over-inclusive.

> **adaptive behaviour** assessed using a recognised, standardised assessment such as the Vineland Adaptive Behaviour Scale (VABS) or the American Association of Intellectual and Developmental Disabilities Adaptive Behaviour Scale – Residential and Community 2nd Edition (ABS:RC2).

FIGURE 19.1 *One study on prisons in the UK used a full psychometric assessment and assessed adaptive behaviour in 140 prisoners and found that 2.9% of their sample fell in the range of ID.*

Source: © Eric Von Seggern. Used under licence from Shutterstock.

The methodological differences between studies continue. Crocker *et al.* (2007) attempted to assess 749 offenders in a pre-trial holding centre in Montreal. For a number of reasons, including refusal to participate, administrative difficulties and technical problems, they were only able to assess 281 participants with three subscales of a locally standardised mental ability scale (equivalent to a screening test). They reported that 18.9 per cent were in the probable ID range and a further 29.9 per cent in the borderline range. This is an unusually high prevalence. On the other hand, Holland and Persson (2011) investigated all sentenced male prisoners released from prisons in Victoria, Australia, from July 2003 until June 2006 (9481 prisoners). Using the Wechsler Adult Intelligence Test, 3rd edition (WAIS III) to assess IQ and using a criterion of IQ less than 70, they found a prevalence rate of 1.3 per cent, which is consistent with the general population.

Clearly, there are huge methodological differences between these two studies, one assessing a proportion of those presenting in a pre-trial holding centre and the other assessing all prisoners in a state, one using an intelligence screening and the other using a full **cognitive assessment**. The method of assessment, the location of the sample and the extent of the sample are likely to be the source of the differences in findings between studies. In a systematic review of studies of prevalence in prison, Fazel *et al.* (2008) concluded that in studies that fulfilled their criteria for scientific integrity, typically, 0.5–1.5 per cent of prisoners were diagnosed with ID. This figure falls at the lower end of the prevalence estimates but, Fazel *et al.* concluded, still represents a highly significant number of individuals with ID in prisons and has implications for policy and practice.

> **cognitive assessment** completed using a recognised test such as one of the Wechsler group of tests. The Wechsler Adult Intelligence Test 4th edition UK is the most commonly employed assessment.

These methodological differences also are likely to be the source of differences found between studies in characteristics of offenders with ID. Walker and McCabe (1973) reported a high prevalence of sexual offences and arson in this client group. Lunsky *et al.* (2011) also found a higher rate of firesetting and property destruction in offenders with ID held in psychiatric institutions when compared to those without ID. Hogue *et al.* (2006) reviewed a number of characteristics of offenders with ID across community, medium/secure and high secure settings. They found that the rates of arson as an index offence depended on the setting, with low rates in the community sample (2.9 per cent) and higher rates in the medium secure sample (21.4 per cent). This suggested that while rates of arson in offenders with ID are consistent with mainstream offenders, there may be a tendency to refer arsonists with ID to medium secure

psychiatric settings, such as that found in the Lunsky *et al.* (2011) study, raising the prevalence in this setting.

ASSESSMENT OF OFFENDERS WITH ID

While it is so obvious that it hardly needs to be said, it is a basic requirement that the process of assessment must be understood by the clients completing it. Since people with ID are typified by significant deficits in literacy and comprehension skills, *all* assessments must be suitably adapted to simplify the language and concepts employed. Unfortunately, there are examples where this obvious tenet has been ignored. For example, it is fairly common practice in a research study on assessment in prisons to distribute a number of assessment schedules for prisoners to complete on their own in their cells. However, given the difficulties with reading and writing, this procedure excludes those offenders who have ID. Therefore assessments have to be altered to cater for the linguistic limitations of the client group (Lindsay & Skene, 2007).

A second important consideration in the context of lengthy forensic assessments is that because of literacy deficits, all material will have to be read and explained to respondents. Therefore both the item and the response categories require explanation. These issues have been dealt with extensively elsewhere (e.g. Lindsay, 2009; Taylor & Novaco, 2005) and it is not our intention to review them in detail here. However, this has two consequences. Assessment will take much longer and it is impossible to give the respondent a series of questionnaires and receive them back the following week. Secondly, because the assessor has to read the item and explain their responses, all such assessments take the form of a structured interview. The client's reactions to questions, and emotional responses, will all be available to the assessor as part of the process. This is a significant amount of additional information and can add to the richness of any assessment process and report.

Because both the assessment instrument and the process require a different approach, the adaptations for assessment of offenders with ID are extensive. Following from this, it is important that the psychometric properties of the assessment remain intact and that the integrity of the process is not undermined or reduced by these adaptations. Several authors have now reviewed the psychometric properties of adapted assessments that can be used with offenders with ID.

Keeling *et al.* (2007a) investigated the psychometric properties of adapted versions of a number of assessments. One of the difficulties of their study was that it was a convenience sample drawn from the population of *special needs* offenders of the Australian correctional system. This population was more diverse than offenders with ID and included participants with acquired brain injury, significant literacy deficits and communication deficits. Although the population was predominantly individuals with ID, it also included men with borderline intelligence and even with average IQ (with acquired brain injury). In order to assess the validity and integrity of the adaptations, they compared these individuals with 53 mainstream sexual offenders. They found that the *Social Intimacy Scale*, the *Criminal Sentiment Scale* and the *Victim Empathy Distortions Scale* broadly retained their psychometric properties after adaptation and simplification. The least successful adaptation was in the *Relationship Scale Questionnaire*, which had a low internal consistency. Test-retest reliability was high and there were good correlations between the original and adapted versions, especially for the Social Intimacy Scale and the Victim Empathy Scale.

Williams *et al.* (2007) assessed the psychometric properties of six self-report measures with sex offenders with ID. These instruments were: the *Sex Offender Self-Appraisal Scale* (Bray, 1996); the *Sex Offender Opinion Test* (Bray, 1996); the *Victim Empathy Consequence Test* (Offending Behaviour Programmes Unit, HM Prison Service, 1996); the *Self-Esteem Questionnaire* (Webster *et al.*, 2007); the *Emotional Loneliness Scale* (from Russell *et al.*, 1980); and the adapted *Relapse Prevention Interview* (from Beckett *et al.*, 1997).

Their population was 211 men who had undertaken an HM prison service adapted sex offender treatment programme. The average IQ was 71.9 and the accepted participants had an IQ up to 80, well outside the range of ID. However, the literacy skills seemed similar, in that all the assessments and questionnaires were read to participants who were then helped to complete the answers. The assessments had good internal consistency with alpha coefficients in excess of 0.75. These two examples (i.e. Keeling *et al.*, 2007a; Williams *et al.*, 2007) demonstrate the way in which existing assessments can be adapted to suit offenders with ID. The following sections will describe specific assessments for specific problems.

Assessment of anger-motivated offenders

The clinical and research literature on offenders with ID has demonstrated that anger and aggression are the most common problems (Didden *et al.*, 1997; Lindsay, Michie *et al.*, 2006; Lindsay *et al.*, 2010; O'Brien *et al.*, 2010). Several authors have developed assessments for this

frequent problem. Oliver *et al.* (2005) reported that the *Modified Overt Aggression Scale*, an informant-rated measure of the frequency and severity of aggression, had high levels of inter-rater reliability when administered to a small number of people with ID as part of treatment outcome research study. Willner *et al.* (2005) developed the *Profile of Anger Coping Skills* to assess the extent to which people with ID use specific skills in managing anger situations. Informants were asked to rate clients' use of eight anger management strategies in specific anger coping situations. The strategy included relaxation skills, counting to 10, walking away calmly, requesting help, using distraction activities, cognitive reframing and being assertive. Willner *et al.* found that the assessment had acceptable psychometric properties and was sensitive to change associated with anger intervention. One of the most important aspects of the study was that it directly assessed the use of anger management strategies, illustrating that participants employed the skills taught. It may be thought that counting to 10, and relaxing, were the most common pieces of advice given during anger management; however, these two skills were the least frequently used in the assessed range.

Novaco and Taylor (2004) evaluated the reliability and validity of several modified anger assessment measures with ID detained offenders: the *Novaco Anger Scale* (NAS: Novaco, 2003), the *Spielberger State-Trait Anger Expression Inventory* (STAXI: Spielberger, 1996) and the *Provocation Inventory* (a self-report anger reactivity scale; Novaco, 2003), along with the *Ward Anger Rating Scale* (WARS: Novaco & Taylor, 2004). The modified anger self-report measures were found to have high internal consistency and reasonable test-retest reliability. There were substantial inter-correlations between the NAS and STAXI, providing evidence for concurrent validity. The WARS staff ratings of patient anger correlated significantly with the self-report measures and these self-reports were significantly correlated with records of assault behaviour. The NAS significantly predicted whether the patient had physically assaulted others following admission to hospital and the total number of assaults carried out. Therefore there was evidence of significant concurrent validity for the anger measures.

In a further development, Taylor, Novaco, Guinan *et al.* (2004) developed the *Imaginal Provocation Test* (IPT) as an additional ideographic anger assessment procedure with people with ID. This samples key elements of the experience and expression of anger and was sensitive to change associated with anger treatment. The IPT produced four indices relevant to the individual clients' experience of anger: *anger reaction; behavioural reaction; a composite of anger and behavioural reaction;* and *anger regulation.* The IPT had good internal reliability and correlated positively with the NAS and the STAXI. Alder and Lindsay (2007) also produced a provocation inventory – the *Dundee Provocation Inventory* (DPI) – which is easily accessible and easy to use. It is based on Novaco's (1975; 1994) analysis and construction of anger as an emotional problem. One of the facets of Novaco's analysis is that the individual may misconstrue internal and external stimuli and respond to a perception of theft rather than a more appropriate, less aggressive response. The DPI was administered to 114 participants with ID, and Alder and Lindsay (2007) found that it had good reliability and convergent validity. The DPI correlated significantly with the NAS (r = .57) and with the PI (r = .75), indicating that the DPI and PI have good convergence. They also found a five-factor structure consisting of threat to self-esteem, external locus of control, disappointment, frustration and resentment. The strongest factor was threat to self-esteem and this certainly accords with Novaco's analysis of anger and its relationship with threat. Therefore, the DPI may provide a quick assessment of provocation in relation to a range of relevant factors in offenders with ID.

Assessment of sexual offenders

Keeling *et al.* (2007a) and Williams *et al.* (2007) have developed or adapted assessments that can be used with sex offenders with ID with some confidence (as outlined above). Griffiths and Lunsky (2003) have developed the *Social Sexual Knowledge and Attitudes Tool* (SSKAT) revised, which is designed to assess knowledge and attitudes in a range of areas related to social and sexual relationships. These include parts of the body, adolescent development, romantic relationships, sexual relationships, procreation, birth control, sexually transmitted diseases, use of alcohol and illegal substance use, and maintenance of sexual health. The SSKAT was used by Michie *et al.* (2006) in an assessment of sexual knowledge in sex offenders with ID. They tested a hypothesis of *counterfeit deviance*, first proposed by Hingsburger *et al.* (1991) referring to behaviour that is undoubtedly deviant, but may be precipitated by factors such as lack of sexual knowledge, poor social and heterosexual skills, limited opportunities to establish sexual relationships, and social naïveté, rather than a preference or sexual drive towards inappropriate individuals or behaviours. If this is the case, remediation should focus on educational issues and developmental maturation rather than inappropriate sexuality. Griffiths *et al.* (1989) give a number of examples illustrating the concept of counterfeit deviance.

Michie *et al.* (2006) compared sex offenders with controls and found that sexual offenders with ID had higher levels of sexual knowledge than ID controls. In a second comparison, 16 sex offenders were compared with 15 controls. Michie *et al.* (2006) found a significant positive correlation between IQ and the SSKAT total score for the control group but no significant relationship between IQ and the SSKAT for the sex offender cohorts. Michie *et al.* suggested two possibilities for the first finding:

- By definition, all of the sex offender cohorts have some experience of sexual interaction. It is unlikely that these experiences of sexual interaction are random and one might therefore conclude that these sex offenders have given some thought and attention to sexuality, at least in the period prior to the perpetration of inappropriate sexual behaviour and sexual abuse. Therefore, we can be sure that they have at least some experience of sexual activity, which is not the case for the control participants.

- The second possible explanation was that these individuals might have a developmental history of increased sexual arousal. This may have led to selective attention and interest in sexual information gained from informal sources. Such persistence of attention would lead to greater retention of information through rehearsal and perhaps to a higher level of associated appropriate sexual activity such as masturbation. These behavioural and informal educational experiences would lead to a higher level of sexual knowledge. In this latter hypothesis, sexual arousal and sexual preference might be considered to interact with knowledge acquisition and, perhaps, attitudes and beliefs.

In a second test of counterfeit deviance, again using the SSKAT, Lunsky *et al.* (2007) compared two categories of sexual offenders and control participants. They divided the offenders into deviant persistent offenders (those who committed contact sexual offences and offences against children) and naïve offenders (public masturbation, indecent exposure). They found that the naïve offenders did indeed have lower levels of sexual knowledge than the deviant offenders, although the naïve offenders did not have poorer knowledge than the control group as might be expected from the counterfeit deviance hypothesis. However, the fact that they found differences between the two groups of sexual offenders suggested the importance of the assessments of sexual knowledge.

Cognitive distortions (distorted attitudes that legitimise offending) have, for some time, been considered important in the pathways leading to a sexual offence and, consequently, in the assessment of important factors for sexual offenders. A number of assessments have been developed for mainstream offenders (such as Bumby's (2006) RAPE and MOLEST scales) but the language is overly complex for people with ID (Kolton *et al.*, 2001).

The most widely used assessment of cognitive distortions for sex offenders with ID is the *Questionnaire on Attitudes Consistent with Sexual Offending* (QACSO), which has been designed for and standardised on offenders with ID (Lindsay *et al.*, 2007). The QACSO contains a series of scales that evaluate attitudes across rape and attitudes to women, voyeurism, exhibitionism, dating abuse, homosexual assault, the offences against children and stalking. They found that six of the seven scales in the QACSO were valid and reliable measures of cognitive distortions held by sex offenders with ID (the exception was homosexual assault). Lindsay, Michie *et al.* (2006) also found that the rape and offences against children scales in particular discriminated between offenders against adults and offenders against children. The former had higher scores on the rape scale and lower scores on the offenders against children scale while the latter had significantly higher scores on the offenders against children scale. Therefore, it would appear that cognitive distortions in sex offenders with ID can be assessed with some reliability and validity.

Lindsay and colleagues were cautious when considering the relationship of cognitive distortions to risk. They wrote that changes in attitudes may reflect a number of processes such as suppression, the influence of social desirability and even lying. They recommended that the results from the QACSO should be considered in relation to a range of risk assessment variables, including actuarial risk, socio-affective functioning and self-regulation abilities.

Assessment of arsonists (firesetters)

Despite the importance of this issue for individuals, communities and the courts, there are relatively few published studies regarding the assessment and treatment of firesetters with ID. Very few measures specific to firesetting behaviour have been developed and evaluated in terms of reliability and validity.

As in any forensic clinical context, it is important to collect and collate information systematically from a range of sources (self- and informant reports, behavioural observations, file reviews, clinical assessments) in order to formulate risk, needs and intervention plans. Taylor, Thorne *et al.* (2004) reported on the use of a newly designed *Pathological Fire-Setters Interview* (PFSI). This is a structured interview, augmented with collateral information from patients' records, staff observations and patient and informant-completed clinical assessments, that gathers information in a functional analytic framework (cf. Jackson, 1994) concerning: (a) demographic, personal, family and offending history details; (b) personal setting conditions; (c) situational setting conditions;

(d) antecedents to firesetting; (e) motives for setting fires; and (f) consequences (thoughts, feelings and actual) of setting fires.

Murphy and Clare (1996) have developed the *Fire Setting Assessment Schedule* (FSAS) for use with adult firesetters with ID. The construction of the FSAS was guided by the functional analytical approach to firesetting proposed by Jackson *et al.* (1987) in which firesetting is hypothesised to be associated with a number of psychological functions including the need for peer approval, need for excitement, a need to alleviate or express sadness, mental illness, a wish for retribution and a need to reduce anxiety. The FSAS is comprised of 16 items concerning cognitions and feelings *prior* to setting fires (for example, 'I started fires to make people pay attention and listen to me'; 'I started fires to get out of going somewhere or doing something'; 'I started fires because I felt angry with people') and a further 16 items pertaining to the individual's thoughts and feelings *after* setting fires (for example, 'After the fires began I felt calmer'; 'After the fires people took more notice of me'; 'I felt happier after the fires'). All items are rated as true or false.

Murphy and Clare (1996) interviewed 10 adult firesetters with ID using the FSAS. They found that the participants in their study identified antecedents to firesetting with more reliability than consequences. The most frequently endorsed antecedents were anger, followed by being ignored and then feelings of depression. This assessment has proven to be clinically useful since its inception, but there has been little further research on its reliability and validity until Taylor, Thorne *et al.* (2002) used the FSAS in the assessment and treatment of a group of 14 people with mild–borderline ID to review the effectiveness of a firesetting programme for this client group. Consistent with the results of Murphy and Clare (1996), Taylor, Thorne *et al.* (2002) found that anger, being ignored and depression (in rank order) were the most frequently endorsed items on the FSAS in terms of antecedents to and consequences of participants' firesetting behaviour. In a further study of six women with mild ID who had set fires, Taylor, Robertson *et al.* (2006) also found that anger and depression were the most frequently endorsed items in participants prior to fire-raising incidents.

Murphy and Clare (1996) also developed the *Fire Interest Rating Scale* (FIRS) for use with clients with ID and histories of firesetting. The FIRS consists of 14 descriptions of fire-related situations (for example, 'Watching a bonfire outdoors, like on bonfire night'; 'Watching a fire engine come down the road'; 'Striking a match to set fire to a building'). Respondents are asked to rate how they would feel in each situation using a seven-point scale from 'most upsetting/absolutely horrible' to 'very exciting, lovely, nice'.

Taylor, Thorne *et al.* (2002) developed a series of *Goal Attainment Scales* (GAS; Kiresuk & Sherman, 1968) to support the clinical evaluation of the responses of firesetters with mild–borderline ID to a group therapy intervention. Based on their answers in a semi-structured interview, a group therapist and an independent rater used the GAS to score clients in relation to six offence-related treatment targets: (i) acceptance of guilt; (ii) acknowledgement of responsibility; (iii) understanding of victim issues; (iv) understanding of high risk elements of the offence cycle; (v) appropriate expression of emotion; and (vi) ability to form and maintain relationships. Assessors used a five-point scale from 0 'much worse than expected', through to 4 'much better than expected' for each GAS using operationalised scoring criteria.

Assessment of risk for any future incidents

There have now been several important developments in the assessment of risk of future incidents in the field of forensic ID. Fitzgerald *et al.* (2011) assessed the predictive validity of a number of criminal history variables with 145 offenders with ID. In a follow-up over two years, they found that the number of previous offences, the number of previous drug offences and the number of previous acquisitive offences were all significantly related to future of offending. A history of alcohol abuse and a history of drug abuse was also related to reoffending. Fitzgerald *et al.* then used risk assessment developed for use on probation settings containing six variables: gender, current offence, age at first conviction, age at current conviction, number of previous custodial sentences and total number of previous convictions. This risk assessment, based on previous assessments, was highly predictive of future reoffending for these offenders with ID.

Lindsay, Elliot *et al.* (2004) conducted a study to review the predictive value of a range of previously identified variables in relation to recidivism for 52 male sex offenders with ID. Significant variables to emerge from the regression models were generally similar to those variables identified in mainstream studies. However, certain items such as employment history or deviant victim choice, which had been highly associated with recidivism in studies of mainstream offenders, did not emerge as predictor variables. On the other hand, dynamic variables and those related to start behaviour and attitudes did emerge as strong predictors. The authors considered that this may be an indication of the way in which professionals making up assessments in this field should adjust their perceptions. For example, while fewer individuals with ID have an employment history, they are likely to have alternative regimes of special educational placement, occupational placement and the like, which make up a weekly routine of engagement with society. Noncompliance with this regime did emerge as a significant variable, suggesting that individuals with ID should be judged in relation to their peers.

Quinsey *et al.* (2004) conducted an assessment of the *Violence Risk Appraisal Guide* (VRAG) in a 16-month follow-up of 58 participants with ID. They found significant predictive value for violent incidents with a medium effect size and that staff ratings of client behaviour significantly predicted antisocial incidents. They also assessed the value of dynamic/proximal risk indicators (see Chapter 17). They found that in the month prior to the violent/sexual incident, dynamic indicators of antisociality were significantly higher than for those recorded six months prior to the incident. This, they concluded, provided persuasive evidence of the value of dynamic assessment; the increase in dynamic risk factors one month prior to the offence could not be attributed to any bias in the light of offence occurring. Once again, the study highlighted the importance of dynamic risk factors for this client group.

In a more extensive investigation into the VRAG, the HCR–20 (Historical, Clinical, Risk Management–20, see Chapter 17 for details; Webster *et al.*, 1995) and the *Psychopathy Checklist – Revised* (see Chapter 17 for details; Hare, 1991, 2003), Gray *et al.* (2007) compared 145 forensic patients with ID and 996 mainstream forensic patients, all discharged from hospital. They found that all of the assessments predicted reconviction rates in the ID sample with the effect sizes as large as or larger than the mainstream sample. In a further risk assessment comparison study, Lindsay *et al.* (2008) employed a mixed group of 212 violent and sexual offenders with ID. They followed participants for one year and found that the VRAG was a significant predictor of future violent incidents, and the *Static 99* (Hanson & Thornton, 2000; see Chapter 17 for a description of static risk assessment measures for sexual offenders) was a significant predictor of future sexual incidents. Camilleri and Quinsey (2011) reviewed risk assessment for this client group and also conducted a small study on the VRAG. In a total sample of over 700 participants, they found that the VRAG produced equivalent predictive values for those falling in the ranges of borderline intelligence and mild ID ranges when compared to the rest of the sample. Taylor *et al.* (2007) have reviewed the psychometric properties of predictive validity of the HCR–20. They found that inter-rater reliability was acceptable at over 80 per cent agreement for all scales and Cronbach's alpha was acceptable for the H scale (0.75) but low for the C and R scales (0.59 and 0.39 respectively). They also found that the R scale had the highest predictive value in relation to recorded incidents over a period of one year. Based on these studies, we can

BOX 19.1   THE ARMIDILO (ASSESSMENT OF RISK AND MANAGEABILITY OF INTELLECTUALLY DISABLED INDIVIDUALS WHO OFFEND; BOER *ET AL.*, 2004)

The ARMIDILO contains 30 items in four broad categories:

* the first section, on stable dynamic environmental and staff factors, contains items such as communication amongst staff and attitudes towards sex offenders with ID;
* the second section relates to stable dynamic factors in the offender being rated, with items such as compliance with supervision and self-management of sexuality;

* the third section, on acute dynamic environmental factors, includes items on new supervisory staff and any changes in monitoring; and
* the final section relates to offender acute dynamic factors and contains items such as changes in social support, changes in substance abuse or changes in sexual preoccupation.

conclude that the VRAG, the HCR–20 and the Static 99 have utility in forensic ID services.

Employing a similar design to that of Quinsey *et al.* (2004), Lindsay, Allan *et al.* (2004) tested the *Dynamic Risk Assessment and Management System* (DRAMS) on which staff made daily ratings of clients' mood, antisocial behaviour, aberrant thoughts, psychotic symptoms, self-regulation, therapeutic alliance, compliance with routine, and renewal of relationships. Ratings were compared between those taken on the day of the incident, the day prior to the incident and for a control day at least seven days distant from an incident. There were significant increases in ratings for the day prior to the incident for mood, antisocial behaviour, aberrant thoughts and DRAMS total score. Steptoe *et al.* (2008) conducted a larger study on the predictive utility of the DRAMS using the same design. There were highly significant differences, with large effect sizes, between assessments taken one or two days prior to an incident and control assessments conducted at least seven days from an incident. Therefore, dynamic risk assessment seemed to perform well in both concurrent and predictive validity in relation to offenders with ID.

In a new approach to risk assessment for sex offenders with ID, Boer *et al.* (2004) developed the ARMIDILO (see Box 19.1).

Blacker *et al.* (2011) assessed the predictive value of the subscales on the ARMIDILO and found that the combined acute sections predicted future incidents with a medium effect size. Lofthouse *et al.* (submitted) also evaluated the predictive utility of the ARMADILO with 64 sex offenders with ID who were followed up for six years. They found that the ARMADILO total score was highly predictive of future offences. These results would suggest that dynamic variables have significant utility in the prediction of future sexual and violent incidents in offenders with ID. Quinsey *et al.* (2004), Lindsay, Allan *et al.* (2004), Blacker *et al.* (2011), and Lofthouse *et al.* (submitted) all found that dynamic variables predicted future incidents as well as, or better than, static variables.

INTERVENTIONS WITH OFFENDERS WITH ID

One of the main developments in the expansion of offender rehabilitation programmes in prisons and probation services has been in the improvement of social problem solving and cognitive skills (see Chapters 16 and 18). The purpose of cognitive skills programmes is to equip offenders with thinking skills that will promote alternative, prosocial means of approaching situations in which the person is at risk of offending. These alternative thinking styles will allow the individual to move out of the habits of offending lifestyles that may be reinforced by criminal thinking styles. Wilson *et al.* (2005) evaluated the range of cognitive behavioural programmes for offenders. They found that in general, programmes that concentrated on appropriate problem-solving skills produced a significant reduction in reoffending (7–33 per cent). They also concluded that high quality studies with greater programme integrity produced the highest reductions in reoffending. Subsequent reviews (Joy Tong & Farrington, 2006; Pearson *et al.*, 2002) also concluded that such programmes reduce reoffending by 14–21 per cent.

Given that offenders with ID are likely to have deficits in social problem solving due to lower intellectual functioning, these developments have only been extended to this field recently. Lindsay, Hamilton *et al.* (2011) have developed a *Social Problem Solving and Offence Related Thinking* (SPORT) programme designed for offenders with ID. They described 10 case studies treated in two groups of five who participated in the programme. Following treatment, participants reported feeling more positive about interpersonal problems, and also were assessed as being less impulsive and less avoidant in social situations. These improvements maintained at three-month follow-up. Despite these positive results, these results can only be considered to be of a preliminary nature. We will now examine interventions for specific groups of ID offenders in more detail.

Treatment for anger and violence

Within this field, the most common treatment approach for offenders has been behavioural interventions (Carr et al., 2000). One difficulty in employing behavioural approaches with offenders is that they generally require contingencies to be organised in a consistent and reliable fashion, in a controlled institutional environment with a reasonable staff ratio. Such conditions contrast with those in services for offenders with ID who may be relatively high functioning (in relation to other services for people with ID), display infrequent yet very serious aggression and live in relatively uncontrolled community settings. In response to the need for more 'self-actualising' treatments that promote generalised self-regulation of anger and aggression, several authors employed cognitive behavioural treatments based on the approach developed by Novaco (1975; 1994). This approach employs cognitive restructuring, arousal reduction and behavioural skills training, as well as stress inoculation techniques.

Taylor (2002) and Taylor and Novaco (2005) have reviewed a number of case studies and uncontrolled group anger treatment studies involving individual and group therapy formats, incorporating combinations of cognitive behavioural techniques including arousal reduction, skills training and self-monitoring. Generally, these case studies have produced good outcomes in reducing anger and aggression, and improvements have been maintained for assessment. Many of these case studies (e.g. Black & Novaco, 1993; Murphy & Clare, 1991; Rose & West, 1999) have been conducted in hospital and community settings with individuals who have been assessed as having histories of aggressive behaviour.

There have also been a small number of case studies of cognitive behavioural anger treatment involving offenders with ID that have yielded positive outcomes. Lindsay et al. (2003) reported on six men with mild ID, all of whom had been involved with the CJS for reasons of aggression and violence. Anger treatment involved group therapy that included psycho-education, arousal reduction, role-play, problem-solving, and stress inoculation through imagination of anger-provoking situations. Treatment was assessed using self-report measures, reports of aggressive incidents and an anger diary. All measures improved significantly and these improvements were maintained at 15-month follow-up. None of the participants had been violent at four-year follow-up.

In another single case study, Novaco and Taylor (2004) described individual anger management training for a man who was referred for violent behaviour in a medium secure setting. Self-report for anger and response to provocation was significantly reduced (by 3.3 and 2.8 standard deviations respectively). Care staff observations of reductions in violence were convergent with these findings and improvements were maintained to four-month follow-up. Allen et al. (2001) report treatment for five women with mild to borderline ID, all of whom had been involved with the CJS for reasons of violence. Treatment was similar to that described by Lindsay et al. (2003), with significant improvements following intervention and at 15-month follow-up. Only one of the women had a further incident of violence, and improved scores on the self-reported inventories were maintained. While these case evaluations have generally demonstrated a positive outcome, they have all been uncontrolled demonstrations of effectiveness.

Controlled studies of anger management training (AMT)

There have now been a number of controlled trials of AMT. In a randomised controlled trial of anger management, Willner et al. (2002) invited community support teams to refer individuals who would benefit from attendance at an anger management group. They then allocated 14 individuals randomly to the treatment and control conditions. Treatment consisted of nine two-hour sessions but not all individuals attended every group session. The intervention was evaluated using two inventories of anger provoking situations completed independently by clients and their carers. Clients in the treated group improved on both self- and carer-ratings relative to their own pre-treatment scores and to the control post-treatment scores. Clients in the treated group showed further improvement at three-month follow-up. Although this study did not recruit individuals through the CJS, it did use a randomised control procedure and as a result has strengths not evident in waiting list controlled comparisons.

Using a research design in which the control participants were placed on a waiting list, Taylor, Novaco et al. (2002) evaluated the effectiveness of cognitive behavioural treatment for anger. Twenty adult men with mild ID were employed as participants. All had been detained under sections of the England and Wales Mental Health Act 1983 for reasons of violence and aggression. Ten were allocated to the AMT condition while 10 were placed on the waiting list. The programme involved a preparatory phase of six sessions designed to present information on the nature and purpose of anger treatment, encourage more division to change and develop basic skills including self-disclosure, emotional awareness and self-monitoring. Participants then proceeded to the 12-session treatment phase that included core components of cognitive restructuring, arousal reduction and behavioural

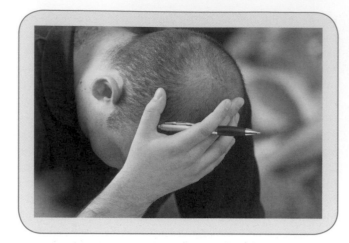

FIGURE 19.2 *Participants reported anger intensity was significantly lower following cognitive behavioural treatment for anger.*

Source: ene. Used under licence from Shutterstock.

skills training. All participants were evaluated using a version of the Novaco Provocation Inventory (Novaco, 1986) and the WARS. Participants reported anger intensity was significantly lower following the anger treatment (Figure 19.2) compared to the routine care waiting list control condition. Key nurse ratings were taken following the completion of treatment and at one-month follow-up. The means for the post-treatment ratings suggested modest improvement and these improvements were maintained to the follow-up assessment. None of the participants in the AMT condition became worse on any of the dimensions after treatment, whereas the self-report ratings for the control group participants were slightly poorer at the post-treatment assessment point.

In a study employing participants referred to a community forensic ID service, Lindsay, Allan *et al.* (2004) compared 33 court-referred participants who received AMT with 14 who made up a waiting list control condition. Treatment lasted for 40 sessions and control participants were on the waiting list for around six months. For the AMT group, there were significant within-group improvements on all measures. In post-treatment comparisons between the two groups, there were no differences on the Provocation Inventory while the self-report diaries and the anger provocation role-plays showed significant differences between groups. These improvements were maintained at the 15-month follow-up. The study also reported on the number of aggressive incidents and reoffences recorded for both groups. At the post-waiting-list assessment point (six months follow-up), 45 per cent of the control group had committed a further assault, while at the post-treatment assessment point (nine months), 14 per cent of the treatment group had committed further incidents of assault. Therefore, although the follow-up period was relatively short, there was some evidence that

AMT had a significant impact on the number of aggressive incidents recorded in these participants.

In an extension of the Taylor, Novaco *et al.* (2002) study, Taylor, Novaco *et al.* (2005) reported on a larger study with 40 men who had mild to borderline ID and histories of offending. All participants were detained in a specialist forensic ID service under sections of the Mental Health Act 1983. The intervention employed the same detailed protocol (Taylor & Novaco, 2005), with 20 participants allocated to the AMT condition and 20 allocated to routine care waiting list control condition. Scores on self-reported anger disposition and reactivity indices were significantly reduced following intervention in the treatment group compared with scores for the control group, and these differences were maintained to four-month follow-up. Staff ratings of study participants' anger disposition converged with self-report ratings but did not reach statistical significance. This study is the most extensive and well controlled piece of research in the field of AMT evaluation. It uses a treatment manual with a waiting list control condition and a four-month follow-up.

A number of treatment studies have now been conducted on the anger and violence in offenders with ID. The most extensive of these is the group of studies by Taylor and colleagues (Taylor, Novaco *et al.*, 2002; Taylor, Novaco, Guinan *et al.*, 2004; Taylor, Novaco, Gillmer *et al.*, 2005) evaluating AMT on detained and violent offenders in a secure setting. These studies have shown significant improvements on self-reported measures of anger and behavioural reaction indices with improvements maintained for up to four months following treatment. Supporting this body of work are a number of controlled research studies from different treatment centres. These not only demonstrate the superiority of anger treatment over control conditions but also suggest that treatment produces a reduction in the number of incidents perpetrated by participants. This body of evidence suggests that AMT interventions can be effective for offenders with ID.

Treatment of sexual offenders with ID

Early reports of treatment focused on skills training and sex education. Griffiths *et al.* (1989) described a series of 30 cases to illustrate their methods, and they also reported no reoffending after one-year follow-up. Haaven *et al.* (1990) described a wide-ranging series of treatments including social skills training, sex education and the promotion of self-control in a comprehensive programme that addressed sexual offending under a behavioural management regime. The report was related to a secure inpatient treatment unit and participants were supervised constantly throughout the follow-up period and had little opportunity to reoffend.

CASE STUDY 19.1   ANGER/VIOLENCE PROBLEMS

Bill is a 28-year-old man with an IQ of 71, referred from supported accommodation because of extreme violence. One evening he was playing on his computer when staff asked him to help prepare dinner. He complained he was being treated like a slave, the incident escalated and he attacked two members of staff then barricaded himself in his room. The police were called. Next day, Bill appeared in court for breach of the peace. Bill had been arrested on three previous occasions for altercations/assaults. After appearing in court, Bill began anger management treatment (AMT) as a condition of a probation order. Treatment followed the standard AMT procedures, introducing the concept of anger as an emotion, beginning some anxiety reduction exercises, and developing an understanding of how to record incidents daily and weekly. The next phase of treatment involved analysing the components and functions of anger. There was also an analysis of the way in which threat was perceived in a range of situations, both general and individual. For the final phase, a number of techniques were involved including the construction of a range of anger-provoking situations, including an analysis of the situations that are actually threatening, and stress inoculation in imagination and through role-play, so that Bill could develop coping strategies for individual situations.

The Novaco Anger Scale (NAS) was used throughout treatment to review Bill's feelings of anger and reaction provocation. The repeated measures can be seen in Table 19.1. The NAS contains three anger expression scales and three anger regulation scales: cognitive, behavioural and arousal respectively. The lowest possible score on any of the expression scales is 16 while the poorest score, indicating no anger regulation strategies, on each regulation scale is four. As can be seen

from Table 19.1, Bill reported extremely high levels of anger expression on all three scales at both baseline assessments (one taken prior to attending court and the second prior to commencement of treatment). As treatment progressed, and as his understanding of the emotion of anger developed, his anger expression scores reduced fairly regularly until they were at a relatively manageable level. It is interesting that his reports reflecting cognitions related to anger maintained at a higher level than the behavioural and arousal domains. Bill continued to maintain that he felt justified if he was going to be angry and that there were a number of people it would be impossible for him to trust. These cognitions contributed to this higher score on the cognitive expression domain. These improvements maintained to follow-up at one month and six months.

At first, Bill found it completely impossible to generate any regulations skills or coping skills that he might use when he was angry. As treatment developed he began to recognise and report a number of coping strategies and these are reflected in his course on the anger regulation domains. Once again, these improvements maintained until one- and six-month follow-up. During this period – nine months of treatment and six months follow-up – there were no reported aggressive incidents that required the intervention of the police. Indeed, staff reported that Bill maintained generally good relationships with those around him. There were periods when they observed that he was pent-up with rage and commented that he was able to control his anger without having an outburst of verbal or physical aggression. This was a huge improvement on his normal way of dealing with what they perceived as provocation and intimidation.

TABLE 19.1 *Bill's repeated measures on the Novaco Anger Scale.*

NAS scale	Baseline1	Baseline 2	3 months	6 months	Post-treatment	Follow-up 1	Follow-up 2
Anger expression							
Cognitive	42	44	35	32	30	34	33
Behavioural	40	45	38	25	23	24	25
Arousal	38	45	30	25	24	22	22
Anger regulation							
Cognitive	4	4	4	6	9	9	10
Behavioural	4	4	5	6	7	9	10
Arousal	4	4	5	7	7	9	8

However, the most significant development in the field of sex offender treatment has been based on problem-solving and cognitive behavioural therapy (CBT) techniques. The application of CBT to sexual offenders with ID came somewhat later than in mainstream sex offender research. One of the first studies was by O'Conner (1996), who developed a problem-solving intervention for 13 adult male sex offenders with ID. This involved the consideration of a range of risky situations in which offenders had to develop safe solutions for both themselves and potential victims. O'Conner reported positive results from the intervention, with most participants having achieved increased community access.

In a series of case studies, Lindsay and colleagues (Lindsay, Marshall et al., 1998; Lindsay, Neilson et al., 1998; Lindsay, Olley et al., 1998; Lindsay et al., 1999) reported the development of treatment based on cognitive principles in which various forms of denial and mitigation of the offence were challenged over treatment periods of up to three years. They noted several aspects of treatment that involved the adaptation of basic principles from mainstream work to that of offenders with ID, and these principles and adaptations remain to the present day (Lindsay, 2009; Rose et al., in press). In the case studies reported by Lindsay and colleagues, all participants showed reductions in aberrant cognitions, and when followed up for a minimum period of four years, they found that only one individual had reoffended and one individual was suspected of reoffending.

One of the difficulties in evaluating outcomes in several treatment studies is illustrated by the report on six sex offenders with ID by Craig et al. (2006). They conducted a seven-month treatment programme incorporating sex education, addressing cognitive distortions, reviewing the offence cycle and promoting relapse prevention. They found no significant improvement on any of the measures but in a follow-up period of 12 months, they reported no further sexual offending. However, they also noted that all participants received 24-hour supervision in which individuals were continually supervised in the community or elsewhere, so presumably they had little opportunity to engage in any inappropriate behaviour, including sexual behaviour. Therefore, the value of outcome data in these studies is limited.

The most important information to be reported in terms of social policy is the extent and seriousness of any further incidents following treatment (Lindsay & Beail, 2004). Ideally, the effects of treatment should be evaluated in the absence of other major variables such as supervision and escort. This criticism could be levelled at a number of reports (Haaven et al., 1990; O'Conner, 1996). By contrast, in the reports by Lindsay and colleagues (Lindsay, Marshall et al., 1998; Lindsay, Neilson et al., 1998; Lindsay, Olley et al., 1998; Lindsay et al., 1999) it is

noted that all individuals had free access to the community and lived in a range of community settings.

Rose et al. (2002) reported on a 16-week group treatment for five men with ID who had perpetrated sexual abuse. The group treatment included self-control procedures, consideration of the effects of offences on victims, emotional recognition and strategies for avoiding risky situations. Participants were assessed using the QACSO attitudes scale, a measure of locus of control, a sexual behaviour and the law measure and the victim empathy scale. Significant differences from pre- to post-treatment were found only on the locus of control scale. However, they reported that participants had not reoffended at a one-year follow-up. In an extension of their work, Rose et al. (in press) reported on a six-month treatment group for sex offenders living in the community. Basing part of their programme on the theoretical writing of Lindsay (2005; 2009), they made efforts to involve aspects of the offender's broader social life into treatment by inviting carers to accompany the participants. They found significant improvements on the QACSO scale, changes in the locus of control measure – unfortunately towards more external locus of control – and no reoffending at one-year follow-up.

Although there are a number of treatment comparison studies evaluating the effect of sex offender treatment, they all tend to fall well short of adequate experimental standards and it is important to consider any results in the light of the methodological shortcomings. The strongest comparison is by Lindsay and Smith (1998) when they compared seven individuals who had been in treatment for two or more years with another group of seven who had been in treatment for less than one year. There were no significant differences between the groups in terms of severity or type of offence. The group who had been in treatment for less than one year showed significantly poorer progress and those in this group were more likely to reoffend than those treated for at least two years. Therefore, it seemed that shorter treatment periods might be of limited value for this client group.

Keeling et al. (2007b) compared 11 sexual offenders with 'special needs' with 11 mainstream offenders, matched on level of risk, victim choice, offence type and age. The authors noted a number of limitations, including the fact that: special needs was not synonymous with ID and as a result they were unable to verify intellectual differences between the mainstream and special needs populations; the treatments were not directly comparable because of adaptations; and the assessments for the special needs populations had to be modified. At post-treatment, there were a few differences between groups but follow-up (post-release) data identified that none of the offenders in either group committed further sexual offences. Lindsay, Michie et al. (2011) compared the treatment progress of 15 offenders against women and 15 offenders against children. They found that both groups improved significantly over a three-year period of treatment and that progress was fairly even (linear trend) over the treatment period. There were no differences between groups in reoffending rates (around 23 per cent for both groups).

Outcome studies evaluating sex offender interventions

Three fairly large-scale studies have appeared recently, describing the characteristics of sex offenders living in the community, their treatment and the outcome of the treatment process. Following a programme of deinstitutionalisation in Vermont, USA, McGrath et al. (2007) reviewed the effects of the treatment and management regime on 403 adult sex offenders with ID. Treatment included procedures to promote social and living skills, and skills for managing risk. Over half of the offenders had a history of committing more than one type of sexual offence. In an 11-year follow-up, with an average of 5.8 years, they reported 11 per cent reoffending. McGrath et al. (2007) compared this cohort to other samples. First, they reported on 195 treated and untreated adult male sexual offenders with ID who had been imprisoned and then followed up for an average period of 5.72 years, 23 per cent of whom were charged

CASE STUDY 19.2   SEXUAL OFFENDING

Andrew is 36-year-old man with mild learning disabilities (measured IQ of 66). He was charged following an offence of lewd and libidinous behaviour with an eight-year-old girl. While babysitting, he had asked her to sit on his knee while they were watching television and had felt between her legs, outside her clothing, and rubbed against her to ejaculation. The girl had commented to her mother the next day on what she thought was unusual and strange behaviour. She also mentioned that it had happened before when Andrew had been babysitting. Andrew was arrested and admitted the behaviour of the previous evening during police interview. He denied that it had ever happened before and police charged him with the incident in question. He received a three-year probation order with court ordered treatment. Treatment followed the usual format, which is outlined in detail elsewhere (Lindsey, 2009 and Chapter 18). It covered modules on disclosure of the relevant incident, understanding pathways into offending, challenging cognitive

distortions related to offending, victim empathy, the use of pornography, developing relationships, relapse prevention, and developing a future positive quality of life using the 'good lives' model (see Chapters 18 and 21). Measures were taken using the QACSO on two occasions prior to the commencement of treatment and regularly thereafter until treatment finished. Data from the QACSO are shown in Table 19.2.

As can be seen from Table 19.2, Andrew endorsed an unusually high number of cognitive distortions prior to the onset treatment. As treatment progressed, the number of cognitions that he endorsed reduced from high to relatively low levels. A follow-up assessment at four years, one year after the cessation of formal treatment, indicated that the improvements had maintained. Andrew did not reoffend during the period of treatment or follow-up and there were no further indications that he showed any sexual interest in children.

TABLE 19.2 QACSO scores for Andrew.

QACSO scale	Pre 1	Pre 2	6 months	12 months	18 months	24 months	30 months	36 months	48 months
Rape	7	8	5	2	1	1	2	2	2
Voyeurism	5	5	5	2	0	0	1	0	1
Exhibitionism	6	5	5	2	0	0	1	0	0
Stalking	8	5	3	1	0	0	1	0	0
Dating abuse	4	5	4	5	0	0	0	0	2
Children	11	12	9	8	2	1	2	2	2
Social desirability	5	5	4	4	3	5	4	4	4

with a new sexual offence at some point in the follow-up period. In a second comparison, they reported on 122 treated and untreated male sexual offenders without ID who had received probation orders and follow-up of 5.24 years, 6.5 per cent of whom were charged with a new sexual offence. Therefore, their experimental sample had a reoffending rate of 11 per cent compared with 23 per cent for the imprisoned sex offenders with ID who had no community follow-up.

From a scientific point of view, as with other studies, one of the difficulties in the McGrath *et al.* (2007) ID cohort was that 62 per cent had received 24-hour supervision, which limited their access to potential victims. However, McGrath *et al.* also considered that this level of supervision resulted in a more comprehensive identification of future incidents when compared to the two other cohorts who had remained unsupervised. They also reported a considerable amount of harm reduction in that 83 per cent of participants were classified as contact offenders while only 45 per cent of the offences were contact offences.

Lindsay and colleagues (Lindsay, Smith *et al.*, 2004; Lindsay, Steele *et al.*, 2006; Lindsay, Haut *et al.*, 2011) have published a series of reports evaluating the effectiveness of a community forensic ID service. The most recent report tracked 309 offenders with ID, cumulated over a period of 20 years. Of those individuals, 156 men had committed a sexual offence or sexual abuse, 126 men had committed another type of offence, and 27 were female. Women made up 9 per cent of this cohort, indicating that the relative numbers of women and men amongst offenders with ID was consistent with that in the general population. Treatment in the service was comprehensive, including sex offender treatment, anger management treatment, individual psychiatric review, nursing interventions, occupational therapy, the establishment of work and educational placements and individual treatment as appropriate. The main outcome measure was reoffending over the 20-year period. As with the McGrath *et al.* (2007) study, all participants were monitored closely in the community by social work and community nursing staff, and so any incident of reoffending (whether or not it was reported to the police) was likely to be reported to the forensic ID service.

Unlike the McGrath *et al.* (2007) study, all participants had free access to the community and lived in some community setting such as the family home, an independent flat, a supported tenancy or a group home. Lindsay and colleagues reported a reoffending rate among sex offenders of 23.5 per cent, which is high compared to other studies. However, it must be remembered that all participants had open access to the community and it is likely that any incident would

be reported back to the service and be counted in the study. Since they had such comprehensive information on incidents, Lindsay and colleagues also calculated the amount of harm reduction over 20 years. They compared the number of incidents two years prior to referral with the number of incidents up to 20 years after referral and found that for reoffenders only, the sex offenders recorded a 70 per cent reduction in the number of incidents. Taking into account the full cohort of sex offenders, the reduction in recidivism was over 95 per cent. These were highly significant results with very large effect sizes.

Murphy *et al.* (2010) conducted a treatment study of 46 sex offenders with ID who were living in community settings. Treatment groups were conducted over a period of one year and assessments included several attitudinal measures. Murphy *et al.* found that sexual knowledge, victim empathy and cognitive distortions improved significantly following treatment but only improvements in sexual knowledge and reduced cognitive distortions were maintained to six-month follow-up. They also reported that 9 per cent of their sample reoffended after a one-year treatment programme. Two incidents were of sexual touching (outside clothing) and the rest were non-contact offences (public masturbation and stalking). Separately, Murphy and Sinclair (2006) reported that although the study was designed as a treatment controlled trial, it proved difficult to recruit and retain control participants.

Although these various studies are service evaluations and treatment trials without a no-treatment control, it is possible to conclude tentatively that in terms of treatment of sex offenders with ID, psychological treatment based on cognitive behavioural principles and structured interventions appears to yield reasonable outcomes. Longer periods of treatment result in better outcomes, these outcomes maintain over several years and organised forensic ID services seem to produce significant reductions in the amount of harm done to local communities.

Treatment of firesetters

There has been a historical association between firesetting and low intelligence in the literature (e.g. Walker & McCabe, 1973), although more recent research found that firesetting accounted for only a small proportion (4 per cent) of those referred to ID services due to offending and antisocial behaviour (O'Brien *et al.*, 2010). On the other hand, the proportion of people in secure ID services with histories of firesetting is significant. Hogue *et al.* (2006) found that just over 21 per cent of those detained in low/medium secure services in a UK study sample had an index offence of arson. Looking at the same population, Taylor, Thorne et al. (2004) found that 19 per cent of patients had arson convictions and a further 13 per cent had documented histories of firesetting.

Over the last 30 years, there have been a number of case studies, case series, and pre- and post-group studies showing that interest in fire and a propensity to set fires can be treated successfully, but there have been no systematic, controlled evaluations. Rice and Chaplin (1979) conducted a study that involved the delivery of a social skills training intervention to 10 firesetters (two groups of five) in a high security psychiatric facility in North America. One of the groups was reported to be functioning in the 'mild to borderline range of mental retardation' (p.105). Following treatment, both groups improved significantly on a reliable observational rating scale of role-played assertive behaviour. At the time of reporting, 8 out of the 10 patients treated in this study had been discharged for around 12 months and none had been convicted or suspected of setting fires.

Clare et al. (1992) reported a case study involving a man with mild ID admitted to a high secure hospital following convictions for two offences of arson. He had a prior history of arson and making hoax telephone calls to the emergency services. Following his transfer to a regional specialist inpatient unit, he received a comprehensive treatment package, including social skills and assertiveness training, development of coping strategies, covert sensitisation, and facial surgery (for a significant facial disfigurement). Significant clinical improvements were observed following treatment. The client was discharged to a community setting and had not engaged in any fire-related offending behaviour at 30-months follow-up.

More recently, cognitive behavioural approaches to working with firesetters have been developed. Hall et al. (2005) considered arson in relation to people with ID and described how cognitive analytical therapy (CAT), an integrative model of short-term psychotherapy (Ryle, 1990), can be applied to arsonists with ID to successfully reformulate the origins of the distress and maladaptive coping strategies that result in firesetting behaviour. The same authors also described the delivery of a 16-session group cognitive-behavioural approach to six male patients with ID and histories of firesetting detained in a UK specialist NHS medium secure unit. The intervention aimed to help patients identify personal risk factors associated with their firesetting and develop alternative coping strategies to reduce the risk of reoffending. The programme involved three sequential phases: (i) 'introduction to fires', which considers the dangers of fires and the views of society and the media concerning arson and firesetters; (ii) 'personal firesetting', which looks at individual patients' firesetting

behaviour and offending cycles within a behavioural framework; and (iii) 'alternative ways of coping', which includes work on identifying personal risk factors and strategies for managing these. To facilitate the programme aims, following completion of the initial 16 sessions, two group follow-up sessions were held; the first was held six weeks after the original group and the second after six months.

Although Hall et al. (2005) describe a pre-post intervention A–B design to evaluating the group intervention using fire-specific and clinical assessments, no post-treatment data were provided. However, most group participants were reported to have responded positively to the intervention in terms of their clinical presentations, and two patients were successfully transferred to less secure placements following completion of the programme.

Taylor, Thorne et al. (2002) reported a group study involving 14 men and women with ID and arson convictions who were assessed pre- and post-treatment on a number of fire-specific, anger, self-esteem and depression measures. The intervention is a cognitive behaviourally framed approach developed especially for this patient group. It is a multifaceted programme based on the approach outlined by Jackson (1994), which is underpinned by the 'functional analysis paradigm' (Jackson et al., 1987, p.175). It comprises seven modules delivered over approximately 40 sessions that involve work on offence cycles, education about the costs associated with setting fires, training of skills to enhance future coping with emotional problems associated with previous firesetting behaviour, and work on personalised plans to prevent relapse. Given the demonstrated importance of anger and/or revenge as an antecedent to firesetting in this population (Murphy & Clare, 1996; Taylor, Thorne et al., 2002), up to 10 sessions are dedicated to developing anger coping strategies using an evidence-based intervention developed by Taylor and Novaco (2005).

The intervention described by Taylor, Thorne et al. (2002) successfully engaged these patients, all of whom completed the programme delivered over a period of four months. Despite their intellectual and cognitive limitations, all participants showed high levels of motivation and commitment. Following treatment, significant improvements were obtained on the fire-specific and anger and self-esteem scales.

In an extension of this work, Taylor, Thorne et al. (2004) described a case series of four detained men with ID and convictions for arson offences who were evaluated before and after completion of the same treatment procedure. The patients engaged well in treatment, and all showed high levels of motivation and commitment that were reflected in generally improved attitudes with regard to personal responsibility, victim issues and awareness of risk factors associated with their firesetting behaviour.

Taylor, Robertson *et al.* (2005) used the same methods in a further case series of six women with ID and convictions for arson. Once again, the participants were reported to have engaged well and all completed the programme. Their scores on measures related to fire-specific treatment targets generally improved following the intervention. All but one of the participants had been discharged to community placements at two-year follow-up, and there had been no reports of participants setting any fires or engaging in fire risk-related behaviour.

SUMMARY

- There have been significant advances in methods for assessment of offenders with ID. This is especially true in the areas of anger and violence and sexual offending.

- Standard assessments for propensities towards anger have been adapted and standardised for populations of offenders with ID. This allows the clinician and researcher to assess the client and have a reasonable confidence in the result. It also allows clinicians to compare individual client assessments with results from larger cohorts of people with ID and compare the result with mainstream populations. This is a significant clinical advance enabling much clearer judgements about an individual client's violence.

- Assessments have also been developed for specific relevant issues related to sex offending. We can now understand more clearly the relationship between sexual knowledge and inappropriate sexual behaviour in clients with ID. There are comprehensive sexual knowledge assessments that have norms on both general populations with ID and offenders with ID. There have also been developments in the assessment of fire interest and social problem solving. There have also been significant advances in the assessment of risk for future violence and future sexual offences.

- Corresponding to the developments in the assessment techniques, treatment services and procedures are now fairly well established for both anger/violence and inappropriate sexual behaviour. Approaches such as anger management treatment and cognitive behaviour therapy for sex offenders have been adapted to be suitable for offenders with ID. Detailed descriptions of treatment are now available so that practitioners can implement their own programmes suitable to their own particular settings.

- Treatments have been evaluated in research and service settings. The best established treatment approach with a number of controlled evaluations is anger management treatment. There are a large number of evaluations regarding sex offender treatment but they do not reach a similar methodological standard as evaluations of anger treatment for this population at this time.

ESSAY/DISCUSSION QUESTIONS

1. What are the difficulties in the assessment of risk in offenders with intellectual disability?
2. Contrast the evidence on the effectiveness of treatment for violent offenders and sexual offenders.
3. Describe how you would conduct an assessment for criminogenic factors in offenders with a learning disability.
4. Low functioning offenders can be assessed and treated in much the same way as any other offender. Discuss this statement.

REFERENCES

Alder, L. & Lindsay, W.R. (2007). Exploratory factor analysis and convergent validity of the Dundee Provocation Inventory. *Journal of Intellectual and Developmental Disabilities, 32,* 179–188.

Allan, R., Lindsay, W.R., Macleod, F. & Smith, A.H.W. (2001). Treatment of women with intellectual disabilities who have been involved with the criminal justice system for reasons of aggression. *Journal of Applied Research in Intellectual Disabilities, 14,* 340–347.

Beckett, R.C., Fisher, D., Mann, R. & Thornton, D. (1997). The relapse prevention questionnaire and interview. In H. Eldridge (Ed.) *Therapists' guide for maintaining change: Relapse prevention manual for adult male perpetrators of child sexual abuse.* Thousand Oaks, California: Sage Publications.

Black, L. & Novaco, R.W. (1993). Treatment of anger with a developmentally disabled man. In R.A. Wells & V.J. Giannetti (Eds.) *Casebook of the brief psychotherapies.* New York: Plenum Press.

Blacker J., Beech A.R., Willcox D. & Boer D.P. (2011) The assessment of dynamic risk and recidivism in their sample of special-needs sexual offenders. *Psychology, Crime and Law, 17,* 75–92

Boer, D.P., Tough, S. & Haaven, J. (2004). Assessment of risk manageability of developmentally disabled sex offenders. *Journal of Applied Research in Intellectual Disabilities, 17,* 275–284.

Bray, D.G. (1996). *The Sex Offender Self-Appraisal Scale* (SOSAS). Unpublished manuscript. North Warwickshire, NHS Trust.

Bumby, K. (1996). Assessing the cognitive distortions of child molesters and rapists: Development and validation of the RAPE and MOLEST scales. *Sexual Abuse: A Journal of Research and Treatment, 8,* 37–54.

Camilleri, J.A. & Quinsey, V.L. (2011). Appraising the risk of sexual and violent recidivism among intellectually disabled offenders. *Psychology, Crime & Law, 17,* 59–74.

Carr, J.E., Coriaty, S., Wilder, D.A., Gaunt, B.T., Dozier, C.L., Britton, L.N., Avina, C. & Reed, C.L. (2000). A review of 'noncontingent' reinforcement as treatment for the aberrant behaviour of individuals with development disabilities. *Research in Developmental Disabilities, 21,* 377–391.

Clare, I.C.H., Murphy, G.H., Cox, D. & Chaplain, E.H. (1992). Assessment and treatment of fire setting: A single case investigation using a cognitive behavioural model. *Criminal Behaviour and Mental Health, 2,* 253–268.

Craig, L.A., Stringer, I. & Moss, T. (2006). Treating sexual offenders with learning disabilities in the community. *International Journal of Offender Therapy and Comparative Criminology, 50,* 111–122.

Crocker, A.J., Cote, G., Toupin, J. & St-Onge, B. (2007). Rate and characteristics of men with an intellectual disability in pre-trial detention. *Journal of Intellectual and Developmental Disability, 32,* 143–152.

Didden, R., Duker, P.C. & Corzilius, H. (1997). Meta-analytic study on treatment effectiveness for problem behaviours with individuals who have mental retardation. *American Journal of Mental Retardation, 101,* 387–399.

Farrington D.P. (2005). Childhood origin of antisocial behaviour. *Clinical Psychology and Psychotherapy, 12,* 177–189.

Fazel, S., Xenitidis, K. & Powell, J. (2008). The prevalence of intellectual disabilities among 12.000 prisoners: A systematic review. *International Journal of Law and Psychiatry, 31,* 369–373.

Fitzgerald S., Gray, N.S., Taylor, J. & Snowden, R.J. (2011). Risk factors for recidivism in offenders with intellectual disabilities. *Psychology, Crime and Law, 17,* 43–58.

Gray, N.S., Fitzgerald, S., Taylor, J., MacCulloch, M.J & Snowden, R.J. (2007). Predicting future reconviction in offenders with intellectual disabilities: The predictive efficacy of VRAG, PCL–SV and the HCR–20. *Psychological Assessment, 19,* 474–479.

Griffiths, D. & Lunsky, Y. (2003). Sociosexual Knowledge and Attitudes Assessment Tool (SSKAAT–R). Wood Dale, IL: Stoelting Company.

Griffiths, D.M., Quinsey, V.L. & Hingsburger, D. (1989). *Changing inappropriate sexual behaviour: A community based approach for persons with developmental disabilities.* Baltimore, MD: Paul Brooks Publishing.

Haaven, J., Little, R. & Petre-Miller, D. (1990). *Treating intellectually disabled sex offenders: A model residential programme.* Orwell, VT: Safer Society Press.

Hall, I., Clayton, P. & Johnson, P. (2005). Arson and learning disability. In T. Riding, C. Swann & B. Swann (Eds.) *The handbook of forensic learning disabilities* (pp.51–72). Oxford: Radcliffe Publishing.

Hanson, R.K. & Thornton, D. (2000). Improving risk assessments for sexual offenders: A comparison of three actuarial scales. *Law & Human Behaviour, 24,* 119–136.

Hare, R.D. (1991). *The Hare Psychopathy Checklist – Revised.* Toronto, Ontario: Multi-Health Systems.

Hare, R.D. (2003). *The Hare Psychopathy Checklist – Revised (PCL–R)* (2nd edn). Toronto, Canada: Multi-Health Systems.

Hayes, S., Shackell, P., Mottram, P. & Lancaster, S. (2007). The prevalence of learning disability in a major UK prison. *British Journal of Intellectual Disabilities, 35,* 162–167.

Herrington V. (2009) Assessing the prevalence of intellectual disability among young male prisoners. *Journal of Intellectual Disability Research, 53,* 397–410.

Hingsburger, D., Griffiths, D. & Quinsey, V. (1991). Detecting counterfeit deviance: Differentiating sexual deviance from sexual inappropriateness. *Habilitative Mental Health Care Newsletter, 10,* 51–54.

Hogue, T.E., Steptoe, L., Taylor, J.L., Lindsay, W.R., Mooney, P., Pinkney, L., Johnston, S., Smith, A.H.W. & O'Brien, G. (2006). A comparison of offenders with intellectual disability across three levels of security. *Criminal Behaviour and Mental Health, 16,* 13–28.

Holland, S. & Persson P. (2011). Intellectual disability n the Victorian prison system: Characteristics of prisoners with an intellectual disability released from prison in 2003–2006. *Psychology, Crime and Law, 17,* 25–42.

Jackson, H.F. (1994). Assessment of fire-setters. In M. McMurran & J. Hodge (Eds.) *The assessment of criminal behaviours in secure settings.* (pp.94–126). London: Jessica Kingsley.

Jackson, H.F., Glass, C. & Hope S. (1987). A functional analysis of recidivistic arson. *British Journal of Clinical Psychology, 26,* 175–185.

Joy Tong, L.S. & Farrington, D.P. (2006). How effective is the 'Reasoning and Rehabilitation' programme in reducing offending? A meta-analysis of evaluations in four countries. *Psychology, Crime and Law, 12,* 3–24.

Keeling, J.A., Rose, J.L. & Beech, A.R. (2007a). A preliminary evaluation of the adaptation of four assessments for offenders with special needs. *Journal of Intellectual and Developmental Disability, 32,* 62–73.

Keeling, J.A., Rose, J.L. & Beech, A.R. (2007b). Comparing sexual offender treatment efficacy: Mainstream sexual offenders and sexual offenders with special needs. *Journal of Intellectual and Developmental Disability, 32,* 117–124.

Kiresuk, T. & Sherman, R. (1968). Goal attainment scaling: a general method of evaluating comprehensive mental health programmes. *Community Mental Health Journal, 4,* 443–453.

Kolton, D.J.C., Boer, A. & Boer, D.P. (2001). A revision of the Abel and Becker Cognition Scale for intellectually disabled sexual offenders. *Sexual Abuse: A Journal of Research & Treatment, 13,* 217–219.

Lindsay, W.R. (2005). Model underpinning treatment for sex offenders with mild intellectual disability: Current theories of sex offending. *Mental Retardation, 43,* 428–441.

Lindsay, W.R. (2009). *The treatment of sex offenders with developmental disabilities: A practice workbook.* Chichester: Wiley-Blackwell.

Lindsay, W.R., Allan, R., Macleod, F., Smart, N. & Smith, A.H.W. (2003). Long term treatment and management of violent tendencies of men with intellectual disabilities convicted of assault. *Mental Retardation, 41,* 47–56.

Lindsay, W.R., Allan, R., Parry, C., Macleod, F., Cottrell, J., Overend, H. & Smith, A.H.W. (2004). Anger and aggression in people with intellectual disabilities: Treatment and follow-up of consecutive referrals and a waiting list comparison. *Clinical Psychology and Psychotherapy, 11,* 255–264.

Lindsay, W.R. & Beail, N. (2004). Risk assessment: Actuarial prediction and clinical judgement of offending incidents and behaviour for intellectual disability services. *Journal of Applied Research in Intellectual Disabilities, 17,* 229–234.

Lindsay, W.R., Elliot, S.F. & Astell, A. (2004). Predictors of sexual offence recidivism in offenders with intellectual disabilities. *Journal of Applied Research in Intellectual Disabilities, 17,* 299–305.

Lindsay, W.R., Hamilton, C., Moulton, S., Scott, S., Doyle, M. & McMurran, M. (2011). Assessment and treatment of social problem solving in offenders with intellectual disability. *Psychology, Crime and Law, 17,* 181–197.

Lindsay, W.R., Hastings, R.P. & Beech, A.R. (2011). Forensic research in offenders with intellectual and development of disabilities: Prevalence·and risk assessment. *Psychology, Crime and Law, 17,* 3–7.

Lindsay W.R., Haut F., Steptoe, L. & Brewster, E. (2011). An evaluation and twenty-year follow up of a community forensic intellectual disability service. *Submitted for publication.*

Lindsay, W.R., Hogue, T., Taylor, J.L., Steptoe, L., Mooney, P., Johnston, S., O'Brien, G. & Smith, A.H.W. (2008a). Risk assessment in offenders with intellectual disabilities: A comparison across three levels of security. *International Journal of Offender Therapy & Comparative Criminology, 52,* 90–111.

Lindsay, W.R., Marshall, I., Neilson, C.Q., Quinn, K. & Smith, A.H.W. (1998). The treatment of men with a learning disability convicted of exhibitionism. *Research on Developmental Disabilities, 19,* 295–316.

Lindsay, W.R., Michie, A.M., Haut, F., Steptoe, L. & Moore F. (2011). Comparing offenders against women and offenders against children on treatment outcome for offenders with intellectual disability. *Journal of Applied Research in Intellectual Disability, 24,* 361–369.

Lindsay, W.R., Michie, A.M., Whitefield, E., Martin, V., Grieve, A. & Carson, D. (2006). Response patterns on the Questionnaire on Attitudes Consistent with Sexual Offending in groups of sex offenders with intellectual disability. *Journal of Applied Research in Intellectual Disabilities, 19,* 47–54.

Lindsay, W.R., Murphy, L., Smith, G., Murphy, D., Edwards, Z., Grieve, A., Chettock, C. & Young, S.J. (2004). The Dynamic Risk Assessment and Management System: An assessment of immediate risk of violence for individuals with intellectual disabilities, and offending and challenging behaviour. *Journal of Applied Research in Intellectual Disabilities, 17,* 267–274.

Lindsay, W.R., Neilson, C.Q., Morrison, F. & Smith, A.H.W. (1998). The treatment of six men with a learning disability convicted of sex offences with children. *British Journal of Clinical Psychology, 37,* 83–98.

Lindsay, W.R., O'Brien G., Carson, D., Holland, A.J., Taylor, J.T., Wheeler, J.R., Middleton, C., Price, K., Steptoe, L. & Johnston, S. (2010). Pathways into services for offenders with intellectual disabilities. *Criminal Justice and Behavior, 37,* 678–694.

Lindsay, W.R., Olley, S., Baillie, N. & Smith, A.H.W. (1999). The treatment of adolescent sex offenders with intellectual disability. *Mental Retardation, 37,* 320–333.

Lindsay, W.R., Olley, S., Jack, C., Morrison, F. & Smith, A.H.W. (1998). The treatment of two stalkers with intellectual disabilities using a cognitive approach. *Journal of Applied Research in Intellectual Disabilities, 11,* 333–344.

Lindsay, W.R. & Skene, D.D. (2007). The Beck Depression Inventory II and The Beck Anxiety Inventory in people with intellectual disabilities: Factor analyses and group data. *Journal of Applied Research in Intellectual Disability, 20,* 401–408.

Lindsay, W.R. & Smith, A.H.W. (1998). Responses to treatment for sex offenders with intellectual disability: A comparison of men with 1 and 2 year probation sentences. *Journal of Intellectual Disability Research, 42,* 346–353.

Lindsay, W.R., Smith, A.H.W., Law, J., Quinn, K., Anderson, A., Smith, A. & Allan, R. (2004). Sexual and non-sexual offenders with intellectual and learning disabilities: A comparison of characteristics, referral patterns and outcome. *Journal of Interpersonal Violence, 19,* 875–890.

Lindsay, W.R., Steele, L., Smith, A.H.W., Quinn, K. & Allan, R. (2006). A community forensic intellectual disability service: Twelve year follow-up of referrals, analysis of referral patterns and assessment of harm reduction. *Legal and Criminological Psychology, 11,* 113–130.

Lindsay, W.R., Whitefield, E. & Carson, D. (2007). An assessment for attitudes consistent with sexual offending for use with offenders with intellectual disability. *Legal and Criminological Psychology, 12,* 55–68.

Lofthouse R., Lindsay W.R., Totsika, V., Hastings, R. Boer D. & Haaven J. (submitted) *Prospective dynamic assessment of risk of sexual reoffending in individuals with an intellectual disability and a history of sexual offending behaviour.*

Lunsky, Y., Frijters, J., Griffiths, D.M., Watson, S.L. & Williston, S. (2007). Sexual knowledge and attitudes of men with intellectual disabilities who sexually offend. *Journal of Intellectual and Developmental Disability, 32,* 74–81.

Lunsky, Y., Gracey, C., Koegl, C., Bradley, E., Durbin, J. & Raina, P. (2011). The clinical profile and service needs of psychiatric inpatients with intellectual disabilities and forensic involvement. *Psychology Crime and Law, 17,* 9–25.

MacEachron, A.E. (1979). Mentally retarded offenders prevalence and characteristics. *American Journal of Mental Deficiency, 84,* 165–176.

McGrath, R.J., Cumming, G., Livingston, J.A. & Hoke, S.E. (2003). Outcome of a treatment programme for adult sex offenders. *Journal of Interpersonal Violence, 18,* 3–17.

McGrath, R.J., Livingston, J.A. & Falk, G. (2007). Community management of sex offenders with intellectual disability: characteristics, services and outcome of a Statewide programme. *Intellectual and Developmental Disabilities, 15,* 391–398.

Mason, J. & Murphy, G. (2002). Intellectual disability amongst people on probation: Prevalence and outcome. *Journal of Intellectual Disability Research, 46,* 230–238.

Michie, A.M., Lindsay, W.R., Martin, V. & Grieve, A. (2006). A test of counterfeit deviance: A comparison of sexual knowledge in groups of sex offenders with intellectual disability and controls. *Sexual Abuse: A Journal of Research and Treatment, 18,* 271–279.

Murphy, G. & Clare, I. (1991). MIETS: A service option for people with mild mental handicaps and challenging behaviour or psychiatric problems. *Mental Handicap Research, 4,* 180–206.

Murphy, G.H. & Clare, I.C.H. (1996). Analysis of motivation in people with mild learning disabilities (mental handicap) who set fires. *Psychology, Crime and Law, 2,* 153–164.

Murphy, G. & Sinclair, N. (2006, December). *Group cognitive behaviour treatment for men with sexually abusive behaviour.* Paper presented to 6th Seattle Club Conference on Research and People with Intellectual Disabilities

Murphy, G.H., Sinclair N., Hays, S.J., et al. (SOTSEC–ID) (2010) Effectiveness of group cognitive behavioural treatment for men with intellectual disabilities at risk of sexual offending. *Journal of Applied Research in Intellectual Disabilities, 23,* 537–551.

Novaco, R.W. (1975). *Anger control: The development and evaluation of an experimental treatment.* Lexington, MA: Heath.

Novaco, R.W. (1986). Anger as a clinical and social problem. In R. Blanchard & C. Blanchard (Eds.) *Advances in the study of aggression (Volume 2)* (pp.131–169). New York: Academic Press.

Novaco, R.W. (1994). Anger as a risk factor for violence among the mentally disordered. In J. Monahan & H.J. Steadman (Eds.) *Violence in mental disorder: Developments in risk assessment.* Chicago, IL: University of Chicago Press.

Novaco, R.W. (2003). *The Novaco Anger Scale and Provocation Inventory Manual (NAS–PI).* Los Angeles, CA: Western Psychological Services.

Novaco, R.W. & Taylor, J.L. (2004). Assessment of anger and aggression in offenders with developmental disabilities. *Psychological Assessment, 16,* 42–50.

O'Brien G, Taylor J.L., Lindsay W.R., Holland, A.J., Carson, C., Steptoe, L., Price K., Middleton C. & Wheeler J. (2010). A multicentre study of adults with learning disabilities referred to services for antisocial offending behaviour: demographic, individual, offending and service characteristics. *Journal of Learning Disabilities and Offending Behaviour, 1,* 5–15.

O'Conner, W. (1996). A problem solving intervention for sex offenders with intellectual disability. *Journal of Intellectual & Developmental Disability, 21,* 219–235.

Offending Behaviour Programmes Unit, HM Prison Service. (1996). *The adapted victim empathy consequences task.* Unpublished manuscript.

Oliver P.C., Crawford, M., Rao, B., Reece, B. & Tyrer, P. (2005). Modified Overt Aggression Scale (MOAS) for people with intellectual disability and aggressive challenging behaviour: A reliability study. *Journal of Applied Research in Intellectual Disabilities, 20,* 368–372.

Pearson, F.S., Lipton, D.S., Cleland, C.M. & Yee, D.S. (2002). The effects of behavioural/cognitive behavioural programmes on recidivism. *Crime and Delinquency, 48,* 476–496.

Quinsey, V.L., Book, A. & Skilling, T.A. (2004). A follow-up of deinstitutionalised men with intellectual disabilities and histories of antisocial behaviour. *Journal of Applied Research in Intellectual Disabilities, 17,* 243–254.

Rice, M.E. & Chaplin, T.C. (1979). Social skills training for hospitalised male arsonists. *Journal of Behaviour Therapy and Experimental Psychiatry, 10,* 105–108.

Rose, J., Jenkins, R., O'Conner, C., Jones, C. & Felce, D. (2002). A group treatment for men with intellectual disabilities who sexually offend or abuse. *Journal of Applied Research in Intellectual Disabilities, 15*, 138–150.

Rose, J., Rose, D., Hawkins, C. & Anderson, C. (in press). Sex offender treatment group for men with intellectual disabilities in community settings. *Journal of Forensic Practice.*

Rose, J. & West, C. (1999). Assessment of anger in people with intellectual disabilities. *Journal of Applied Research in Intellectual Disabilities, 12*, 211–224.

Russell, D., Peplan, C.A. & Cutrona, C.A. (1980). The revised UCLA Loneliness Scale: Concurrent and discriminant validity evidence. *Journal of Personality and Social Psychology, 39*, 472–480.

Ryle A. (1990) *Cognitive analytic therapy: Active participation in change.* Chichester: John Wiley and Sons, Inc.

Søndenaa, E., Rasmussen, K., Palmstierna, T. & Nøttestad, J. (2008). The prevalence and nature of intellectual disability in Norwegian prisons. *Journal of Research in Intellectual Disabilities, 53*, 1129–1137.

Speilberger, C.D. (1996). State–Trait Anger Expression Inventory, research edition: Professional manual. Odessa, FL: Psychological Assessment Resources.

Steptoe, L., Lindsay, W.R., Murphy, L. & Young, S.J. (2008). Construct validity, reliability and predictive validity of the Dynamic Risk Assessment and Management System (DRAMS) in offenders with intellectual disability. *Legal and Criminological Psychology, 13*, 309–321.

Taylor, J.L. (2002). A review of the assessment and treatment of anger and aggression in offenders with intellectual disability. *Journal of Intellectual Disability Research, 46*, (Suppl. 1) 57–73.

Taylor, J.L., Lindsay, W.R., Hogue, T.E., Mooney, P., Steptoe, L., Johnston, S. & O'Brien, G. (2007). Use of the HCR-20 in offenders with intellectual disability. *Paper presented to the annual conference of the BPS forensic division, Edinburgh.*

Taylor, J.L., Lindsay, W.R., Hogue, T.E., Mooney, P., Steptoe, L., Johnston, S. & O'Brien, G. (2007, May). Use of the HCR–20 in offenders with intellectual disability. *Paper presented to the British Psychological Society Forensic Division Conference, Edinburgh.*

Taylor, J.L. & Novaco, R.W. (2005). *Anger treatment for people with developmental disabilities: A theory, evidence and manual based approach.* Chichester: John Wiley & Sons, Inc.

Taylor, J.L., Novaco, R.W., Gillmer, B. & Thorne, I. (2002). Cognitive behavioural treatment of anger intensity among offenders with intellectual disabilities. *Journal of Applied Research in Intellectual Disabilities, 15*, 151–165.

Taylor, J.L., Novaco, R.W., Gillmer, B.T. & Robertson, A. (2004). Treatment of anger and aggression. In W.R. Lindsay, J.L. Taylor & P. Sturmey (Eds.) *Offenders with developmental disability* (pp.201–220). Chichester: John Wiley & Sons, Inc.

Taylor, J.L., Novaco, R.W., Gillmer, B.T., Robertson, A. & Thorne, I. (2005). Individual cognitive behavioural anger treatment for people with mild–borderline intellectual disabilities and histories of aggression: A controlled trial. *British Journal of Clinical Psychology, 44*, 367–382.

Taylor, J.L., Novaco, R.W., Guinan, C. & Street, N. (2004). Development of an imaginal provocation test to evaluate treatment for anger problems in people with intellectual disabilities. *Clinical Psychology and Psychotherapy, 11*, 233–246.

Taylor, J.L., Robertson, A., Thorne, I., Belshaw, T. & Watson, A. (2005). Responses of female fire-setters with mild and borderline intellectual disabilities to a group based intervention. *Journal of Applied Research in Intellectual Disabilities, 19*, 179–190.

Taylor, J.L., Thorne, I., Robertson, A. & Avery, G. (2002). Evaluation of a group intervention for convicted arsonists with mild and borderline intellectual disabilities. *Criminal Behaviour and Mental Health, 12*, 282–293.

Taylor, J.L., Thorne, I. & Slavkin, M.L. (2004). Treatment of fire setting behaviour. In W.R. Lindsay, J.L. Taylor & P. Sturmey (Eds.) *Offenders with developmental disabilities* (pp.221–240). Chichester: John Wiley & Sons, Inc.

Vanny, K.A., Levy, M.H., Greenberg, D.M. & Hayes, S.C. (2009). Mental illness and intellectual disability in magistrates courts in New South Wales. *Journal of Intellectual Disability Research, 53*, 289–297.

Walker, N. & McCabe, S. (1973). *Crime and insanity in England. Volume 2 – New solutions and new problems.* Chicago, IL: Adeline Publishing Company.

Webster, C.D., Eaves, D., Douglas, K.S. & Wintrup, A. (1995). *The HCR–20: The assessment of dangerousness and risk.* Vancouver, Canada: Simon Fraser University and British Colombia Forensic Psychiatric Services Commission.

Webster, S.D., Mann, R.E., Thornton, D. & Wakeling, H.C. (2007). Further validation of the Short Self-esteem Scale with sexual offenders. *Legal and Criminological Psychology, 19*, 217–236.

Williams, F., Wakeling, H. & Webster S.D. (2007). A psychometric study of six self-report measures for use with sexual offenders with cognitive and social functioning deficits. *Psychology Crime and Law, 13*, 505–522.

Willner, P., Brace, N. & Phillips, J. (2005). Assessment of anger coping skills in individuals with intellectual disabilities. *Journal of Intellectual Disability Research, 49*, 329–339.

Willner, P., Jones, J., Tams, R. & Green, G. (2002). A randomised controlled trial of the efficacy of a cognitive behavioural anger management group for clients with learning disabilities. *Journal of Applied Research in Intellectual Disabilities, 15*, 224–253.

Wilson, D.B., Bouffard, L.A. & MacKenzie, D.L. (2005). A quantitative review of structured group orientated cognitive behavioural programmes for offenders. *Criminal Justice and Behavior, 32*, 172–204.

ANNOTATED READING LIST

Farrington D.P. (2005). Childhood origin of antisocial behaviour. *Clinical Psychology and Psychotherapy, 12*, 177–189. *Farrington and colleagues have conducted a long series of studies on developmental factors leading to criminal careers and pathways into offending. This paper is one of several summaries of this major research project. Farrington outlines risk factors from childhood including troublesome behaviour in childhood, poor housing in childhood, poor parental behaviour at eight years, having convicted parents and low IQ.*

Fazel, S., Xenitidis, K. & Powell, J. (2008). The prevalence of intellectual disabilities among 12.000 prisoners: A systematic review. *International Journal of Law and Psychiatry, 31*, 369–373. *This Cochrane review assesses the quality of evidence in studies on the prevalence of offenders with intellectual disability in prison populations. It concludes that in those studies with good quality experimental designs, the prevalence is between 1 per cent and 2 per cent.*

Lindsay, W.R., O'Brien G., Carson, D., Holland, A.J., Taylor, J.T., Wheeler, J.R., Middleton, C., Price, K., Steptoe, L. & Johnston, S. (2010). Pathways into services for offenders with intellectual disabilities. *Criminal Justice and Behavior, 37*, 678–694. *This article introduces a major research project reviewing the differences between referrals to community forensic services and secure services. It reviews offenders with ID referred to generic community services, specialist community forensic services, low/medium secure and maximum secure services.*

Lindsay, W.R., Steele, L., Smith, A.H.W., Quinn, K. & Allan, R. (2006). A community forensic intellectual disability service: Twelve year follow-up of referrals, analysis of referral patterns and assessment of harm reduction. *Legal and Criminological Psychology, 11*, 113–130. *This article provides a description of a mature community forensic learning disabilities service. Lindsay et al. found that sex offenders and other types of offender were quite separate in the offending history that reflected current offending. Sex offenders were generally older than other types of offender and were more frequently referred from the criminal justice system. Treatment outcome demonstrated significant amount of harm reduction quantified at around 70 per cent.*

Michie, A.M., Lindsay, W.R., Martin, V. & Grieve, A. (2006). A test of counterfeit deviance: A comparison of sexual knowledge in groups of sex offenders with intellectual disability and controls. *Sexual Abuse: A Journal of Research and Treatment, 18*, 271–279. *This study tests the hypothesis known as 'counterfeit deviance', which suggests that men with intellectual disabilities commit sexual offences through a misunderstanding of appropriate behaviour and a lack of sexual knowledge. In two linked studies, it was found that the opposite was the case and that sexual offenders had a higher level of sexual knowledge than non-offenders. Level of knowledge was significantly correlated with IQ in the non-offenders but showed no relationship with IQ in the sex offender group.*

Murphy, G.H., Sinclair N., Hays, S.J., et al. (SOTSEC–ID) (2010) Effectiveness of group cognitive behavioural treatment for men with intellectual disabilities at risk of sexual offending. *Journal of Applied Research in Intellectual Disabilities, 23*, 537–551. *In this large collaborative study, 46 sex offenders with ID were treated for one year using a manualised CBT programme. The men were from community and secure settings and were treated in small groups. As with the previous studies on sex offenders, participants showed improvements on measures of victim empathy, sexual knowledge and cognitive distortions, with changes maintaining to six-month follow-up. Only the presence of autism spectrum disorders was related to offending, although other studies (see above) have found ASD not to be over-represented in offender populations and not to feature in predictions of offender pathways.*

Taylor, J.L., Novaco, R.W., Gillmer, B.T., Robertson, A. & Thorne, I. (2005). Individual cognitive behavioural anger treatment for people with mild–borderline intellectual disabilities and histories of aggression: A controlled trial. *British Journal of Clinical Psychology, 44*, 367–382. *This research group has conducted a number of controlled treatment trials on anger management treatment. The study compares 40 men convicted for violence-related incidents, split equally between an experimental and a control group. The treated group showed superior progress over the control group on most measures, including the Novaco anger scale and staff ratings. Improvements were maintained to a four-month follow-up.*

Dawn Fisher, Michelle Ginty and Jagjit Sandhu

CHAPTER OUTLINE

The whole area surrounding services, legislation and specialised practice for mentally disordered offenders has come to be known as *forensic mental health*. The word 'forensic' simply means 'pertaining to or used in a court of law' and so has come to be associated with those who transgress the law. Forensic mental health combines the fields of mental health with the working of the *criminal justice system* (CJS). This presents a unique challenge for the professionals, who have to balance the needs of mentally disordered offenders with the demands of the CJS, and the potential risk to the public. This approach emphasises the need for effective multidisciplinary working, creativity, and external scrutiny.

Central to effective working in this area is good cooperation between criminal justice and health services. Ultimately this means that such offenders receive appropriate care and treatment for their mental disorders at various stages of them coming into contact with the CJS. This could be from the point of arrest, through to diversion to hospital, as part of the sentencing process via a hospital order, or post-sentence by way of a prison transfer. (In simple terms this latter group of patients typically develop mental illness subsequent to establishing their offending behaviour.) Parallel to the criminal justice route into forensic mental health services is the generic psychiatric route. In such instances the risky behaviours that require specialist forensic management and intervention develop after the onset of mental illness. Although these patients could be convicted of offences, such as violence, these prosecutions are not always supported by the CJS because of the debates about criminal responsibility in the context of severe mental illness.

Psychologists who work within forensic mental health services have historically tended to be clinical, or counselling, psychologists who have specialised in working with offenders. However, more recently, *forensic psychology* as a distinct specialism has increasingly been recognised. This is a broad field, however, and can include a number of areas that pertain to the legal system without necessarily incorporating mental illness. Therefore, forensic psychologists, who work with mentally disordered offenders, typically have had additional training in the field of mental health. This chapter will provide an overview of the area. It will describe

- the history of services to this population;
- the range of illnesses commonly seen in mental health settings;
- the mental health legislation associated with the duty of care for these patients;
- the role of psychology when working with this client group.

A final section of the chapter outlines the role of the psychology assistant, which is a typical first job for a psychology graduate wishing to embark on a career in forensic, and/or clinical psychology.

HISTORY OF FORENSIC MENTAL HEALTH SERVICES IN THE UK

Although specialised forensic services have expanded greatly in the last 30 to 40 years, legislation and provision pertaining to this population has been in existence for far longer. In the UK individuals with mental illness were typically 'looked after' in large asylums, later called

FIGURE 20.1 *Individuals with mental illness were once 'looked after' in large asylums, later called psychiatric hospitals; this print shows a corridor outside confinement cells in Sainte Anne Asylum in 1868.*

Source: © Antonio Ambrignani. Used under licence from Shutterstock.

psychiatric hospitals (Figure 20.1). Those who were considered dangerous to themselves or others would be restrained but there was no specific provision made for them.

Hospital provision for mentally disordered offenders (in special hospitals, medium and low secure units)

The first purpose-built hospital for mentally disordered offenders was Broadmoor Hospital in Berkshire, UK. It was completed in 1863, and was built under an act of Parliament to reform the inadequate conditions of psychiatric institutions such as the Bethlem Hospital in London. Broadmoor is one of four high security *special hospitals* in the UK; the others are Ashworth (previously Moss Side and Park Lane); Rampton; and Carstairs in Scotland. The role of the special hospitals has been to house and provide treatment for the most serious mentally disordered offenders who were assessed as needing a high level of security. As a result of there only being four special hospitals, mentally disordered offenders were typically a long distance from their home area, which posed difficulties for family visits and rehabilitation when they were ready to leave high security. A further problem was the huge difference between high security and returning to the community, which created difficulties in adjustment for the patients and difficulties for professionals in identifying whether individuals would be able to cope safely in the community.

In response to these difficulties, the Glancy Report (Department of Health and Social Security, 1974) and the Butler Report (Department of Health and Social

Security, 1975) outlined the need for more regionally based medium secure units, which would enable patients both to be nearer to home and to be treated in conditions of lesser security than special hospitals. The Butler Report was particularly concerned with the gradual rehabilitation of patients from high security. The Glancy Report focused on the needs of patients in general psychiatric hospitals who were behaving in a dangerous way that indicated that they required conditions of security, but were not sufficiently dangerous to warrant admission to a special hospital. It was envisaged that these initiatives would enable gradual rehabilitation into the community whilst offering the ability to observe the patient's behaviour and retain control over the individual's treatment in a secure environment.

As a result of the Butler and Glancy reports it was recommended that regional secure units offering a level of medium security should be opened throughout England and Wales. These units came to be known as *medium secure units* (MSUs). Following on from the opening of MSUs came the advent of low secure services to offer a more complete care pathway and a gradual reduction of levels of security for the individuals being rehabilitated. It was also recognised that patients should be managed in the least restrictive environment possible, and thus low security offered an alternative to medium security when this was not warranted. Over time psychiatric intensive care units have tended to cater for patients who present in an acute stage of their mental illness, while low secure units (LSUs) have tended to cater for patients with more long-standing illnesses who respond poorly to treatment. In addition to these specialised units (such as the special hospitals, MSUs and LSUs), there are also other settings in which mentally disordered offenders are catered for, in the community and in prison settings. The Centre for Mental Health reported in April 2011 that 'secure services cost the NHS about £1.2 billion and treat about 8,000 patients at a time, mostly in medium and low secure hospital units. Spending on secure services more than doubled between 2002 and 2010, taking up 30 percent of all new money for mental health services during that period.'

Community service provision

Community forensic services were set up following the recommendations of the Reed Report (Department of Health and Home Office, 1992), which recommended that for an individual patient the level of control and security should be the least restrictive possible, in order to best manage that individual's risk to themselves and others. Community forensic teams began to be set up and by 2006 there were 37 services across England and Wales. Their remit is to provide a service both to patients who have been discharged from secure units and to those who have never been sent to a secure unit in the first place. These tend to be offenders being managed by the probation service who have received a community order. Such offenders may be subject by the court to a mental health treatment requirement, which can last for up to three years and requires a named *responsible clinician* who will be responsible for overseeing the treatment of the offender.

Mentally disordered offenders in prison

There are a large number of offenders with mental health problems in the prison system. When mental health problems are suspected within a prison setting, assessments of mental health are undertaken by visiting forensic professionals such as psychiatrists and psychologists. Prisons have their own hospital wing and will look after the most disturbed patients until they can be assessed and transferred to an appropriate secure unit. Despite this, a significant number of individuals with mental health problems remain in the prison system.

Figures quoted by the Prison Reform Trust (2009) state that 72 per cent of male, and 70 per cent of female sentenced prisoners, suffer from two or more mental health disorders; and that one in five prisoners have four of the five major mental health disorders. Psychotic disorders were present in 7 per cent of males and 14 per cent of female sentenced prisoners. This represents 14 and 23 times the level found in the general population. It is also of note that the estimated rate for prisoners with disabilities and learning difficulties is said to be between 20 and 30 per cent. This represents a serious problem, which is yet to be fully addressed in prison settings.

TYPES OF MENTAL ILLNESS/ FORENSIC BEHAVIOURS SEEN IN FORENSIC MENTAL HEALTH SETTINGS

Forensic mental health services work with individuals who suffer from a range of mental illnesses and disorders. There are also high rates of comorbidity, that is to say, patients who fulfil diagnostic criteria for more than one disorder (*dual diagnosis*). Although the vast majority of mentally disordered offenders are male, there are also a small but significant number of females. Specialist services exist for them. There are also a small number of specialist services for adolescents.

There are two major nosological systems currently in use to classify mental illnesses and disorders. The *International Classification of Diseases and Causes of Death* (ICD–10; World Health Organization, 1992) is used in the UK; the *Diagnostic and Statistical Manual of Mental Disorders, Version Four, Text Revision* (DSM–IV–TR; American Psychiatric Association, 2000) is used in the USA. Release of DSM–V is in progress (see details from the American Psychiatric Association at www.dsm5 .org/Pages/Default.aspx) and a consultation process in respect of developing ICD–11 is underway in preparation for its release in 2014. We will examine the most common forms of mental illness found in the settings outlined above, based on ICD10/DSM–IV criteria.

Schizophrenia

Schizophrenia is the most common diagnosis within forensic mental health settings. It is a severe and chronic illness that is characterised by episodes of significant perceptual disturbance (the *positive symptoms* of hallucinations, delusions and thought disorder) that may or may not be accompanied by the *negative symptoms* (including flattened affect, avolition, anhedonia and so on). These result in major changes in an individual's thinking, emotions and behaviours. While none of these specific symptoms are exclusive to schizophrenia, or are essential to diagnosis, symptoms must have been present for at least a month and should not be accounted for by other conditions such as organic brain injury and substance misuse. For diagnosis there is also a need for evidence of social dysfunction that has persisted for at least six months.

The episodic nature of schizophrenia is often characterised by disturbances in people's hearing, sight, sense of touch, taste and smell and significant changes in their thinking and beliefs (positive symptoms). In this context the term 'positive' denotes psychotic experiences that can be viewed as having been 'added to' an individual's day-to-day experiences, which under normal circumstances would not be present. This could range from the person hearing voices that other people present cannot experience, to the unwavering conviction with which the person may hold fixed beliefs known as delusions, without reasonable evidence to support them.

During or following a psychotic episode, negative symptoms are also common (Figure 20.2). In this context, 'negative' is a term used to denote symptoms that represent something being taken away from them, such as their drive, energy and enthusiasm. Negative

FIGURE 20.2 *During or following a psychotic episode, negative symptoms are common.*

Source: © Andrew Lever. Used under licence from Shutterstock.

symptoms can mirror a depressive episode and indeed reactive depression can be triggered by the trauma and sense of loss often experienced after a psychotic episode and following an initial diagnosis. Generally schizophrenia is considered to have a poor prognosis in spite of advancements in antipsychotic medication and thus 80 per cent of patients will experience more than one psychotic episode after a formal diagnosis has been made. Nevertheless, there are extremely wide variations in individual outcomes. Relapse behaviours can be triggered by poor medication compliance, and/or psychosocial stressors.

Paranoid schizophrenia

Paranoid schizophrenia (see Case Study 20.1) is the most common form of schizophrenia found in forensic mental health settings. It is characterised by persecutory and sometimes grandiose delusions (positive symptoms). In some cases, an individual's offending behaviour can be directly linked to psychotic experience, for example

CASE STUDY 20.1   PARANOID SCHIZOPHRENIA

Mr B. is a 45-year-old man with a diagnosis of paranoid schizophrenia. He first became mentally ill in his late teens and has had repeated admissions to psychiatric hospital. In response to delusional beliefs, he had become increasingly aggressive towards others and could no longer be safely contained at his local psychiatric hospital. He was admitted to the low secure forensic service where he responded well to the stricter boundaries, and the frequency of his aggressive outbursts diminished. Psychological formulation suggested that his aggressive outbursts were in response to his fixed delusional beliefs.

Unfortunately, Mr B.'s mental illness has not responded well to medication and he falls within the 'treatment resistant' category. He is not amenable to psychological treatment due to his disturbed mental state and limited ability to engage, along with poor motivation. For him, quality of life is a key issue and the primary treatment aims are to prevent deterioration and to engage him in as many activities as possible to keep him occupied and provide him with some enjoyment and purpose in life. If he remains settled the plan is to move him to a locked rehabilitation unit with increased access to the community. If this is successful he may then be rehabilitated back to his local area.

in one case where a man stabbed his partner during a psychotic episode in which he believed that she was poisoning him and their children. In other cases, symptoms are best understood as being linked indirectly, by virtue of the way that they might interfere with an individual's capacity to think clearly and make rational decisions.

Major affective disorders

Major affective disorders are characterised by dramatic fluctuations in mood states, as is the case for bipolar disorder or persistent and extreme mood states, such as depression, which interfere with an individual's functioning. In extreme cases, psychotic symptoms can be present during episodes of illness, such as auditory and visual hallucinations and delusions. However, what assists clinicians in distinguishing these from a schizophrenic episode is that the psychotic experiences are always mood congruent, that is to say they reflect the mood being experienced. For example, an individual may believe that they own a property empire or that they are a music celebrity, in association with a manic episode.

Personality disorder

Personality theory suggests that individuals exhibit stable characteristics across a range of situations. These characteristics are shaped by a combination of temperamental and environmental factors (Millon, 1990). It is likely that a number of individuals are born with a biological propensity to develop personality disorders, whilst in others it appears to be due to adverse life events. Hence, when

an individual is considered to be 'personality disordered' the normal developmental process has been derailed in some way. This is because some individuals with personality disorders have had difficult life experiences that have prevented one or more fundamental emotional needs from being met. This results in the child developing quite extreme coping strategies necessary for psychological survival, and having attachment difficulties (see Chapter 10 for a brief description of these).

Individuals with personality disorders commonly experience a variety of mental health problems and psychological distress. The distinction between 'disorder' and 'illness' is important, though, because it conveys the stable nature of the condition in contrast to an episodic mental illness. For example, individuals with schizophrenia typically experience periods of being mentally well but can relapse into periods of being mentally unwell. Individuals with personality disorders may experience crises when their difficulties seem more pronounced but in general terms their emotional and behavioural problems are persistent. See Case Study 20.2 for a description of an individual with *borderline personality disorder* – a particularly intractable personality disorder.

Personality disorder is recognised when these coping strategies have failed to mature with the individual into adulthood and thus are no longer adaptive. For example, a young child who has been separated from their mother for significant intervals as a result of illness may grow up believing that they cannot cope independently and yet are likely to be abandoned by anyone they rely upon. As a child they may have learned to look to other adults when their mother is unavailable in order to have their needs met. They may also have learned that such adults were more likely to take on a caring role towards them

CASE STUDY 20.2 BORDERLINE PERSONALITY DISORDER

Ms A. is a 25-year-old woman who was sent to a medium secure unit for assessment prior to sentencing for arson. She had a previous history of self-harm and a diagnosis of borderline personality disorder. She disclosed a history of sexual abuse by her father and was estranged from her family as a result of this disclosure. Her father has never been prosecuted. Psychological assessment (see elsewhere in this chapter) and interview confirmed her diagnosis of borderline personality disorder. Furthermore, psychometric testing showed that she had very low self-esteem, was emotionally lonely, had an external locus of control, and was impulsive. A psychological formulation suggested that her arson and self-harm behaviours were associated with a need to feel in control and were triggered by negative life events, particularly problems in interpersonal relationships.

She was assessed as being suitable for treatment in a medium secure unit and was placed on a section 37 of the Mental Health Act 1983 (see Box 20.2). Treatment involved including her in a dialectical behaviour therapy (DBT) programme, which was made up of both group and individual sessions covering 'distress tolerance, skills training and mindfulness' (see Linehan, 1993). Following this, Ms A. underwent individual work to address her victimisation issues with a focus on developing self-compassion before more specific offence-focused work on her firesetting. As the work progressed, and she gained more control of her behaviour, she moved from medium security to low security before finally being discharged to supported accommodation in the community, under the care of her community team.

when they behaved well and made very few demands. As an adult this strategy for developing relationships may have become entrenched but ultimately counter-productive. Fearing abandonment has led to the adult prioritising the needs of the other person, thereby subjugating their own. Although this may maintain relationships, it is unfulfilling and can lead to significant distress, underpinned by deep-rooted resentment. This vicious circle would be typical for individuals who fulfil the criteria for a dependent personality disorder.

Assessment of personality disorder is a very important but nonetheless challenging area of forensic mental health. There is ongoing disagreement around diagnosis of various personality disorders, and in terms of how many forms exist, between DSM–IV–TR and ICD–10. Nevertheless, appropriate identification is crucial. Diagnosis can be made in adulthood, but it is good practice not to diagnose before the age of 25 years, because of the nature of personality development up until this point. Diagnosis can arise from clinical observations, self-report assessments (for example, the third version of the *Millon Clinical Multiaxial Inventory* (MCMI–III); Millon, 2009) and structured clinical interviews, (for example, the *International Personality Disorder Examination* (IPDE); Loranger *et al.*, 1994).

Sole reliance on self-report measures is not recommended for a number of reasons. They can be susceptible to problems of comprehension and poor insight. The results can also be unwittingly distorted by an individual's mood and mental state, and deliberately as a consequence of poor compliance. Within forensic mental

health settings, this last point is especially pertinent. It is important to maintain a healthy scepticism with regard to accepting a patient's self-report at face value because they will undoubtedly be aware that the results of assessments can have a profound impact upon their care pathway, treatment and judgments about risk. Assessment of personality disorder is further complicated by the fact that only 15 per cent of people with personality disorders fulfil criteria for a single disorder. Most satisfy criteria for two or three forms of the disorder. Personality disorder in forensic mental health populations is also common in individuals with diagnoses of mental illness like schizophrenia. **Comorbidity** (the presence of more than one diagnosis) makes diagnosis difficult.

Psychopathy

Psychopathy is a highly pertinent issue in forensic mental health, but is nevertheless a very contentious one (see Chapters 4 and 17 for more discussion of this topic). Diagnosis does not form any part of DMS–IV, or ICD–10, but it has been suggested that it might be included in DSM–V. The concept of psychopathy, as a clinical entity, has been further complicated by the legal term of *psychopathic disorder*. This was a category by which individuals could be detained under the Mental Health Act 1983 and pertained to the broad spectrum of personality disorders. Psychopathy as a clinical term, however, is a specific type of antisocial personality disorder characterised by a 'chronic disturbance in an individual's relations with self, others and their environment resulting in distress or failure to fulfil social roles and obligations' (American Psychiatric Association, 2000).

Some clinicians view psychopathy as an extreme form of antisocial, or dissocial, personality disorder and so it could be argued that this would lead to duplication or considerable overlap. Thus all those deemed to be psychopaths would satisfy criteria for *antisocial personality disorder* (APD) or *dissocial personality disorder* (DPD), but only a third of those who satisfy criteria for APD or DPD would meet the threshold for diagnosis of psychopathy. In order to be diagnosed as having psychopathy, an individual must be assessed by a specially trained clinician using the revised version of the *Psychopathy Checklist–Revised* (PCL–R; Hare, 1991; 2003) and must score above a set threshold (typically a score of 30 from a maximum score of 40).

The reason that psychopathy is so relevant to the work with mentally disordered offenders is because the PCL–R (Hare, 1991) has good predictive validity as an assessment tool for violence and recidivism (Webster *et al.*, 1997). Some critics argue that this is self-explanatory because in their view the concept of psychopathy simply medicalises criminality.

The traditional view is that psychopaths are dangerous, manipulative and untreatable. Therefore individuals who are given this label can expect to have their stay in prison or hospital significantly extended comparative to their non-psychopathic peers, because the outcome of the PCL–R appears to have a disproportionate level of influence on their care and treatment. Admissions also become protracted because potential community services are often reluctant to accept responsibility for their care. Indeed, a number of services do not accept psychopaths as they believe they require specialist services that they are unable to provide. As a response to the need to provide specialist services for psychopaths, four dangerous and severe personality disordered (DSPD) units were opened in 1999.

Intellectual disability and developmental disorders

Intellectual disability is typically defined as a global impairment in intelligence that has arisen during the developmental period that persists across the lifespan and results in impairment in global functioning. Individuals with moderate and severe intellectual disability are not typically seen in forensic mental health settings. The nature of their day-to-day needs and functioning necessitates high levels of support and supervision that would ordinarily prevent them from engaging in serious offending (see Chapter 19 for further discussion of this area).

Some individuals with mild intellectual disability who exhibit relatively minor offending behaviour may also escape prosecution because other people excuse their behaviour on account of their disability. This can lead to under-reporting. The danger with failing to identify or define some individuals' behaviour as offending is that they do not receive timely interventions that could prevent more frequent, or more serious, offending from occurring. However, it is also possible that individuals with a mild intellectual disability are over-represented in offender populations because they are more likely to be apprehended. Individuals with intellectual disabilities have been shown to be more susceptible to mental illness. This risk is dramatically increased with the level of intellectual disability, and if there are comorbid diagnoses such as **autistic spectrum disorders (ASDs)**.

> **autistic spectrum disorders (ASDs)** a spectrum of psychological conditions characterised by widespread abnormalities of social interaction and communication, as well as 'special interests' and repetitive behaviour.

Over recent years, increases in referrals of individuals with ASDs have been observed within forensic mental health services. This is likely to have come about by a combination of a greater awareness and identification of ASD. It is also likely that specific characteristics of the disorder may contribute to increased instances of risky behaviour comparative to the general population. For example, individuals with ASD can be prone to poor impulse control and have deficits with regard to interpersonal skills that undermine their ability to interpret social situations and to empathise with others. This has led to the development of specialist ASD forensic mental health units.

Acquired brain injury

Measuring the prevalence of *acquired brain injury* (ABI) in forensic populations and drawing conclusions about the links between acquired brain injury and offending is complex. This is because many incidences of head injury are not reported and the adverse impact can be underestimated. It is also apparent that the factors that make an individual susceptible to offending behaviour are similar to those that increase the risk of acquired brain injury, especially when individuals misuse substances.

ABI (Figure 20.3) can be associated with impulsive reactions and antisocial behaviour because of the significant impact upon cognitions, emotions and personality functioning. Common problems in cognitive functioning following acquired brain injury can be: impairments in concentration; memory; and executive functioning. These problems can lead to reduced information-processing, reduced processing speed and reduced ability to plan, organise, think flexibly and solve

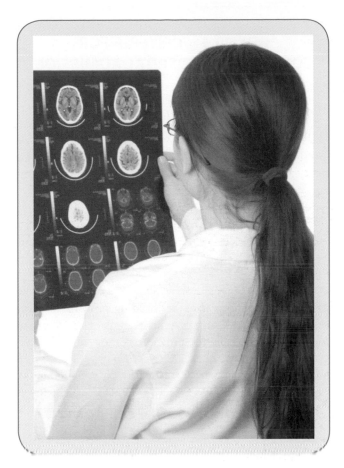

FIGURE 20.3 *Acquired brain injury can be associated with impulsive reactions and antisocial behaviour because of the significant impact upon cognitions, emotions and personality functioning.*

Source: © Lusoimages. Used under licence from Shutterstock.

problems. Corresponding changes in personality can include egocentricity, tactlessness, impulsivity, lack of concern, lack of insight and poor judgment.

Pertinent to the problem of mentally disordered offenders with ABI are reduced emotional regulation skills, and how these can manifest in terms of increased irritability, hostility and aggression. Specialist forensic mental health services exist for mentally disordered offenders with significant ABI. Nevertheless, professionals need to be mindful of the high incidence of less serious ABI within mentally disordered offender populations and the potential impact that this can have on their functioning.

substance misuse
an umbrella term to describe conditions such as intoxication, harmful use/abuse, dependence, withdrawal, and psychoses or amnesia associated with the use of the substance, typically associated with drugs and alcohol.

Substance misuse disorders

Substance misuse disorders are highly prevalent in this population for a number of reasons. As a diagnosis, substance misuse disorder is not used as a primary disorder with regard to justifying detention, but it is typically comorbid with other mental health conditions and has an enormous impact upon prognosis. According to the Department of Health, between one-third to one-half of all people with severe mental health problems have comorbid problematic substance misuse (Department of Health, 2002). There is a wealth of evidence that, among psychiatric populations, substance misuse is the most significant risk factor for relapse and associated violence. The association between substance misuse and offending more generally has been widely supported by research.

Poorly controlled anger (with resultant aggression and violence)

Poorly controlled anger with resultant aggression and violence is the most common 'risk' that necessitates a patient's transfer to forensic mental health services, irrespective of whether individuals come through the mental health or criminal justice care pathway and irrespective of the nature of the mental health problem. Management of violence is also viewed as a priority within the general public and as such the media is understandably quick to highlight when services have been inadequate in this regard. It should be noted that violence to the self in respect of serious self-harm and suicidal behaviour can also lead to admission to forensic services.

Management of violence within secure settings includes the threat of imminent violence and violence that is predicted within the medium- and long-term and within different contexts including the community. Therefore, services need to take account of immediate and distal factors that could have a bearing on an individual's risk. Other offending behaviours, such as sexual offending and firesetting, are also the focus of forensic mental health services and have started to feature more prominently within specialist intellectual disability, and women's services, in particular. We will now examine the legislation involved in governing work with mentally disordered offenders.

LEGISLATION PERTAINING TO MENTALLY DISORDERED OFFENDERS

Due to the fact that mentally disordered offenders present a threat to themselves or others, they frequently require supervision, monitoring and detention until it is deemed that they no longer present a risk. In order to enable authorities to have the power to supervise, monitor and detain individuals, appropriate legislation is required that outlines the range of powers the relevant authorities have and the circumstances under which these powers can be used. In addition to legislation providing powers to detain and treat individuals, there is also legislation to ensure the rights and humane treatment of those who are detained. We will now examine these legislative arrangements in more detail.

Mental health legislation/ arrangements

Mental health legislation has been in existence in one form or another for centuries and is continually being revised and updated to remain relevant to the demands of the current population. The Mental Health Act 1983 applies only to England and Wales, with Scotland and Northern Ireland having their own legislation. The Mental Health Act was amended in 2007 and significant changes were introduced. Mental disorder is defined very broadly under the 2007 amendment as 'any disorder or disability of the mind'. Mental health care is regulated by a body known as the *Care Quality Commission*, established in 2009, whose role is to inspect and regulate health and social care services in England and Wales.

The Mental Health Act covers every aspect pertaining to mentally disordered offenders and their care and detention. It lays out the criteria that enable an individual to be 'sectioned', and detained, in order to be assessed and treated against their will. It also empowers certain professional groups with the powers to enforce the Act. Under the (2007) amended Act, a range of professionals can become the *responsible clinician* who carries the ultimate responsibility for the decisions made about the care and detention of the individual. The criteria for compulsory hospital admission are shown in Box 20.1. It is of note that 'medical treatment' is broadly defined as being to alleviate, or to prevent a worsening of, the disorder or one or more of its symptoms or manifestations. This includes nursing care, psychological interventions and rehabilitation, alongside medical care and treatment.

In order to detain an individual against their wishes and enforce assessment and treatment, a range of sections is available that enable detention for differing periods of time. After this they have to be reviewed and the responsible clinician can renew the section in specific circumstances. It is beyond the scope of this chapter to describe all the sections, but Box 20.2 shows some examples of those most common sections used in forensic

---

BOX 20.1   CRITERIA FOR COMPULSORY HOSPITAL ADMISSION

1. The individual must have, or be suspected to have, a mental disorder.

2. The mental disorder must be of a nature or degree to warrant detention in or to receive medical treatment in hospital.

3. Detention must be in the interests of the patient's health and safety or for the protection of others.

4. Appropriate treatment must be available.

---

units. Other sections provide 'holding powers' to registered mental health nurses, enable transfers from prison to hospital and enable the police to remove an individual to a place of safety.

Legislation to safeguard the patient

In order to safeguard the rights of patients, and ensure their appropriate care, there is additional legislation specific to ensuring that individuals are not detained unnecessarily. As mentioned above, the Care Quality Commission regulates and inspects all forensic healthcare provision for mentally disordered offenders. In addition, individuals sectioned under the Mental Health Act are entitled to apply to a *mental health review tribunal*, an independent judicial body, which will review their case and can override the recommendations of both the clinical team and the Ministry of Justice and discharge the individual if it thinks continued detention in hospital is no longer warranted.

The mental health review tribunal is made up of a panel comprising a legal representative, a medical representative and a layperson. The panel hears the evidence presented by the clinical team and the individual's solicitor may also examine the evidence of the team. Detained patients in hospital are also entitled to a hospital manager's hearing where, again, they can be discharged. A more recent development for safeguarding patients is the mental health advocacy system, which has been endorsed by the Mental Health Act 2007. This ensures that all detained patients can have access to a mental health advocate who can sit in on meetings between the mental health professionals and the patient (such as ward rounds and Care Programme Approach reviews – see below) and speak on the patient's behalf if required.

BOX 20.2   COMMONLY USED MENTAL HEALTH ACT SECTIONS

Section 3: This is a six-month order that enables the individual to be detained for treatment. It can then be renewed for a further six months, and then annually. The application has to be made by at least two doctors, and another approved mental health professional.

Section 37: This is known as a 'hospital order' and only applies to those who have been convicted of an imprisonable offence. It is imposed by the court on the recommendation of at least two doctors. It enables detention for six months, renewal for six months, and then on an annual basis.

Section 41: This is known as a 'restriction order' and can only be imposed by the Crown Court. It is used where the individual is thought to pose a risk of serious harm to others. Decisions regarding leave from the hospital, transfer and discharge can only be made by the Ministry of Justice,

which limits the power of the responsible clinician to make such decisions. Individuals can also be subject to conditional discharges whereby certain conditions are imposed upon them, such as the requirement to continue taking medication and to maintain contact with their mental health team. If the individual does not comply or their mental health deteriorates, they can be compulsorily recalled to hospital.

Community Treatment Order: The 2007 Mental Health Act amendment introduced this order, which allows for individuals who have been subject to either sections 3, or 37, to be discharged into the community under certain conditions, similar to those imposed on section 41. Individuals who do not comply can then be recalled. The purpose of this order is to ensure compliance from those individuals who are not on restriction orders.

Capacity to consent

Capacity to consent to treatment is a complex issue and as such has legislation pertaining to it. Depending on the section under which they are detained, an individual can be forced to take medication against their will for a period of up to three months. After this, the responsible clinician has to either obtain the consent of the patient or seek a second opinion from a second opinion appointed doctor. Treatment can only be mandatorily applied in a hospital and does not apply to prisoners.

A further issue to be addressed is the individual in question's capacity to be able to give meaningful consent. The Mental Capacity Act 2005 was designed to ensure that the individual was assessed fully as to their capacity to understand, make decisions and communicate their wishes regarding a specific issue. With regard to consent to treatment, the Mental Health Act can override the Mental Capacity Act so that where an individual has capacity but chooses not to have treatment this can be enforced against their will.

Multi-Agency Public Protection Arrangements (MAPPA)

Due to the concern over the management of potentially risky individuals once they have been discharged into the community, and the need to ensure information-sharing, multi-agency panels were set up by the Criminal Justice and Court Services Act 2000. Although the police,

probation and prison services are the lead agencies, there is a duty upon healthcare services to cooperate with **Multi-Agency Public Protection Arrangements (MAPPA)**. Sexual and violent mentally disordered offenders, and those thought to pose a serious risk of harm, are included under MAPPA. They are allocated to one of three levels from level 1 (least risky) to level 3 (most risky). For mental health professionals the disclosure of information about the patient without the informed consent of that patient breaches confidentiality and leads to professionals having to make a decision about the benefits of disclosure versus the risks.

> **Multi-Agency Public Protection Arrangements (MAPPA)** MAPPA is now recognised as one of the most advanced frameworks of offender management currently available. The process structures the way the offender is assessed and managed through effective identification of risk and through information exchange.

Care Pathway Approach arrangements

From the point of contact with forensic health services, a *Care Pathway Approach* (CPA) is identified for the individual. The CPA is based on a *multi-disciplinary treatment* (MDT) model in order to provide holistic interventions to individuals with mental health problems. The MDT is typically made up of psychologists, psychiatrists, social workers, nurses and occupational therapists. In ASD services it is becoming usual also to have input from a speech and language therapist, and most MDTs now have additional input from a pharmacist.

THE ROLE OF THE PSYCHOLOGIST IN FORENSIC MENTAL HEALTH SETTINGS

Although psychologists are uncommon within community services, they are often central to the work within residential forensic mental health settings because of their specialist skills in assessing complex needs and developing sophisticated formulations that enable services to prioritise interventions accordingly. This includes being able to assess mental health and risk and to formulate how these can be linked. Within their training they also develop a good understanding of team working and can provide relevant consultation and support to inpatient staff. Psychologists also undertake a wide variety of duties as shown below.

Assessments

Psychologists are involved in undertaking core assessments with patients upon their reception into hospital, and to assess progress. These include cognitive functioning assessments (i.e. IQ assessments using the Weschler Adult Intelligence Scale, Version 4, WAIS–IV); neurological test batteries; personality assessments (such as the MCMI–111); specific offence-related assessments; and assessments of attitudes/schemas. Further assessments may be conducted dependent on individual risk and treatment need. Pre- and post-group assessments are routinely undertaken with both staff and patient groups, dependent on the intervention delivered at the time. In order to provide an evidence base for all work carried out, it is routine to use pre- and post-psychometric assessments alongside all interventions.

Risk assessment

Risk management is one of the key concerns of forensic mental health professionals, and creates a need for carefully considered risk management procedures to ensure the best quality of life for the individual whilst protecting the public. It is now a requirement from the Department of Health that all mentally disordered offenders have to undergo a risk assessment using a structured risk assessment measure known as the *HCR–20* (Historical, Clinical, Risk Management–20; Webster *et al.*, 1997). (See Chapter 17 for a description of this instrument.) The HCR–20 is used to assess the risk of future violent reconviction and the items included are those that have been shown by research to be associated with increased risk of violence. As part of the completion of these risk assessments, a risk management plan is drawn up. This highlights the circumstances under which risk may be increased and the likely consequences, and helps the MDT to devise an appropriate plan for the individual's safe future management. Risk assessments are regularly reviewed and updated and are shared with other professionals involved in the care of the patient.

Treatment

Forensic mental health services have a dual responsibility in treating mental illness and/or disorder and in managing and minimising risk. In some cases the risky behaviour is directly associated with the episode of illness, and so treating mentally disordered offenders' mental health problems is the first priority. If the factors that underpin an individual's risk of reoffending are complex, specific interventions to target these can only be effective if sufficient progress has been achieved in stabilising the individual's mental state first. Once an individual's mental state has been stabilised, mental health professionals play a considerable role in providing psycho-education to improve insight and understanding, in order that the patient is empowered to play a greater role in maintaining their mental health in the future (Figure 20.4).

It is beyond the scope of this chapter to describe the vast array of interventions that may be used with mentally disordered offenders. As with any mental health client, the intervention used is based on an assessment of the individual's needs and abilities to ensure engagement and motivation. Interventions can be individual or group based. Although generally based on a cognitive-behavioural treatment (CBT) approach, other approaches such as **dialectical behaviour therapy (DBT), mindfulness, cognitive analytic therapy (CAT), eye movement desensitisation and reprocessing (EMDR), acceptance and commitment therapy (ACT)** and **compassion-focused therapy (CFT)** may be used.

It is usual for programmes aimed at specific offence behaviours also to be available (i.e. sexual offending, anger management, substance misuse, firesetting) along with programmes aimed at improving problem-solving abilities, such as enhanced thinking skills, general social and relationship skills, and relapse prevention/preparation for discharge groups (see Chapter 18 for a review of these interventions

dialectical behaviour therapy (DBT) a system of therapy originally developed by Marsha Linehan to treat people with borderline personality disorder. Combines cognitive-behavioural techniques with concepts such as mindfulness, largely derived from Buddhist meditative practice.

mindfulness refers to a psychological quality that involves bringing one's complete attention to the present experience on a moment-to-moment basis, and non-judgmentally.

FIGURE 20.4 *Forensic mental health services have a dual responsibility in treating mental illness and/or disorder and in managing and minimising risk.*

Source: © Gina Sanders. Used under licence from Shutterstock.

guidelines (see http://guidance .nice.org.uk/Topic/PublicHealth). However, the complexity of the cases, including comorbidity and the chronic nature of some mentally disordered offenders' mental disorders, demonstrates that the evidence base is inadequate. Forensic mental health services also need to take account of competing agendas, when developing intervention plans for mentally disordered offenders, in terms of the rights of the individual and the protection of the public.

A further tier of intervention may include individual or group based sessions to promote self-awareness and impart psycho-education to patients. An example of this is assisting patients to understand the link between physical tension and mental activity via biofeedback sessions, or using mindfulness practice to reduce rumination and help them learn to cope with and tolerate distressing experiences. Patients are thus encouraged to utilise these skills in everyday life and/or stressful situations, enhancing their abilities to observe and monitor themselves to control their tension and anxiety-based arousal levels.

eye movement desensitisation and reprocessing (EMDR) developed to resolve trauma-related disorders resulting from exposure to traumatic or distressing events, such as rape or military combat.

acceptance and commitment therapy (ACT) an empirically-based psychological intervention that uses acceptance and mindfulness strategies mixed in different ways with commitment and behaviour-change strategies, to increase psychological flexibility.

compassion-focused therapy (CFT) a form of psychotherapy rooted in Mahayana Buddhist psychology, which emphasises the development of self-compassion in people who are prone to feelings of shame and self-criticism. Created by Paul Gilbert and colleagues.

cognitive analytic therapy (CAT) a form of psychological therapy developed in the UK by Anthony Ryle. It is distinctive due to its intensive use of reformulation, its integration of cognitive and analytic practice and its collaborative nature.

with mainstream offenders). Box 20.3 shows the types of problems in treating psychotic disorders (i.e. schizophrenia, major affective disorders), while Box 20.4 shows some indicative treatments for personality disorders.

Such interventions are underpinned by research from evidence-based practice, including the National Institute of Clinical Excellence (NICE)

The psychology assistant

In many secure mental health settings, it is also usual for qualified psychologists to have assistants working with them under their direct supervision. It is common for those intending to train as chartered clinical or forensic psychologists to work at assistant level and gain experience in a clinical setting prior to commencing their full training. The types of work often undertaken by psychology assistants are shown in Box 20.5.

BOX 20.3   THE DIFFICULTIES OF TREATING PSYCHOTIC OFFENDERS

Lack of insight, poor motivation, poor compliance with treatment and frequent additional problems such as substance misuse, present a challenge in effectively treating psychotic offenders.

The positive symptoms of *schizophrenia* (with the exception of delusions) generally respond well to the wide variety of antipsychotic medications that have been developed. Negative symptoms can be persistent by virtue of

(Continued)

the fact that they are less amenable to pharmacological treatments. Nevertheless, they are an important target of interventions because of the way in which they can lead to significant disability by impairing an individual's day-to-day functioning.

Major advancements have been made in the field of pharmacology that have enabled clinicians to stabilise *affective disorders*. Poor compliance with mood stabilisers is a common precursor to relapse in major affective disorders. This can present a particular challenge to mental health services, because the early stages of a manic episode, characterised by increased energy, hopefulness and positive self-belief, can be so enticing to the patient that they do not want to lose these features.

Patients with the dual diagnosis of both *schizophrenia* and *substance misuse* show poorer compliance with medication and other care, reduced stability of social functioning and increased hospitalisation rates, and increased reconviction rates following discharge from medium security. It is therefore a key area for intervention for individuals in secure settings in order to support recovery, improve functioning and reduce offending.

BOX 20.4   THE DIFFICULTIES OF TREATING PERSONALITY DISORDER

There is growing evidence for some pharmacological treatments having some efficacy for treating symptoms that stem from *personality disorder*, particularly emotional lability. However, the majority of targeted treatments for personality disorder are based on psychological models.

In a review of cognitive behavioural treatment (CBT) interventions by Rice and Harris (1997), a number of themes emerged regarding the efficacy of particular treatment strategies for particular categories of personality disorder, based on the clusters from DSM–IV:

- Social skills programmes targeted at individuals with Cluster A (i.e. the *dependent personality disorders*) were found to be most effective. Emotional management skills training was also found to be most effective with individuals with anxious and depressive/dependent personality disorders, as well as those with pronounced affective liability as is the case with *borderline personality disorder*.
- Individuals with Cluster B *independent personality disorders*, whose difficulties are often characterised by impulsivity and hostile reactions have been shown to respond best to life skills training.

Substance misuse often coexists with *personality disorders*. By virtue of the fact that the basis of personality disorder is characterised by pervasive and entrenched patterns of responding, progress in moderating the impact of this in forensic mental health settings can be slow. Thus, personality disorder *per se* can be a marker for a poorer prognosis. For this reason, there is a need for the application of sophisticated treatments, but these depend on the correct identification of the disorder in the first place.

BOX 20.5   PSYCHOLOGICAL ASSISTANT ROLES IN FORENSIC MENTAL HEALTH SETTINGS

In secure forensic mental health settings, assistant psychologists may be involved in differing levels of psychological therapeutic interventions with patients (subject to their level of motivation, responsivity and mental state) including

- assessing a patient's needs, abilities or behaviour using a variety of methods, including psychometric tests, interviews and direct observation of behaviour;
- assisting in the devising and monitoring of appropriate programmes of treatment;
- delivering therapy for difficulties relating to anxiety, depression, addictions, social and interpersonal problems and challenging behaviour;

- evaluating service provision;
- assisting in carrying out research.

Assistants have key involvement in setting up and delivering low-level interventions that aim to introduce appropriate communication and interaction skills in a group setting.

Assistants also collate information for completion of risk assessments, which are required to be used routinely with all forensic patients as part of risk assessment and risk management.

SUMMARY

- Psychologists working in forensic mental health settings are typically involved in the care pathway approach, risk assessment, general assessment and formulation of problem behaviours and treatment of patients.

- Psychologists work closely with staff members from other disciplines including psychiatry, occupational therapy and nursing within secure mental health settings. Together these professionals form the multidisciplinary team.

- Such work is to stabilise and maintain an individual's mental health and to manage and minimise the risk of reoffending behaviour in the least restrictive environment possible.

- This poses an interesting challenge to psychologists, and other mental health professionals, who work in forensic settings. Clearly they have a duty of care to treat and rehabilitate their patients. Nevertheless, they have the additional role of protecting the public from risks presented by their patients.

ESSAY/DISCUSSION QUESTIONS

1. Describe the primary considerations for a psychologist working in a forensic mental health setting.
2. Mental illness can be a key factor in leading to crime. Discuss.
3. How might the rehabilitation process differ in forensic settings compared to general mental health settings?
4. Describe the range of treatment approaches that might be specific to forensic settings.
5. What might be the advantages of multidisciplinary working in forensic mental health setting?

REFERENCES

American Psychiatric Association. (2000). *Diagnostic and statistical manual of mental disorders. Fourth edition. Text revision (DSM–IV–TR)*. Washington, DC: American Psychiatric Association.

Centre for Mental Health. (2011). *Pathways to unlocking secure mental health care*. London: Centre for Mental Health.

Department of Health. (2000). *Effective care co-ordination in mental health services: Modernising the care programme approach, A policy booklet*. London: Department of Health.

Department of Health (2002). *A study of the prevalence and management of co-morbidity amongst adult substance misuse and mental health treatment*. London: Department of Health.

Department of Health and Home Office. (1992). *Review of health and social services for mentally disordered offenders and others requiring similar services*. (The Reed report). London: HMSO.

Department of Health and Social Security. (1974). *Security in NHS hospitals for mentally ill and the mentally handicapped*. (Glancy report). London: DHSS.

Department of Health and Social Security. (1975). *Report of the Committee on Mentally Abnormal Offenders*. (Butler Report). London: HMSO.

Hare, R.D. (1991). *The Hare Psychopathy Checklist – Revised*. Toronto, Ontario: Multi-Health Systems.

Hare, R.D. (2003). *The Hare Psychopathy Checklist – Revised (PCL–R)* (2nd edn). Toronto, Canada: Multi-Health Systems.

Linehan, M.M. (1993). *Cognitive-behavioural treatment of borderline personality disorder*. New York: Academic Press.

Loranger, A.W., Sartorius, N., Andreoli, A., Berger, P., Buchheim, P., Channabasavanna, S.M., Coid, B., Dahl, A., Diekstra, R.F.W., Ferguson, B., Jacobsberg, L.B., Mombour, W., Pull, C., Ono, Y. & Regier, D.A. (1994). The International Personality Disorder Examination (IPDE). *Archives of General Psychiatry, 51*, 215–224.

Millon, T. (1990). *Towards a new personology: An evolutionary model.* New York: Wiley.

Millon, T., Millon, C., David, R. & Grossman, S. (2009). *Millon Clinical Multiaxial Inventory (MCMI–III) Manual* (4th edn). Minneapolis, MN: Pearson Assessments.

Prison Reform Trust. (2009). *Bromley Briefings Prison Factfile, November 2009.* London: Prison Reform Trust.

Rice, M.E. & Harris, G.T. (1997). The treatment of mentally disordered offenders. *Psychology, Public Policy and Law, 3,* 126–183.

Webster, C.D., Douglas, K.S., Eaves, D. & Hart, S.D. (1997). *HCR-20: Assessing risk for violence (Version 2).* Vancouver, Canada: Simon Fraser University.

World Health Organization. (1992). *Classifications of Mental and Behavioural Disorder: Clinical Descriptions and Diagnostic Guidelines (ICD–10).* Geneva: World Health Organization.

ANNOTATED READING LIST

Gibbon, S., McMurran, M. & Khalifa, N. (2009). *Forensic mental health.* Cullompton, Devon: Willan. *This book provides 'a clear overview of the key concepts in forensic mental health as well as the way the discipline operates in the broader context of criminal justice and mental health care systems'. It is an excellent starting point as an introduction to the main issues and describes the working of the multidisciplinary team, the legislation involved and the care pathway taken by the patient.*

Hodgins, S. (2008). Criminality among persons with severe mental illness. In K. Soothill, P. Rogers & M. Dolan, M. (Eds.) *Handbook of forensic mental health.* Cullompton, Devon: Willan. *This chapter provides an excellent overview of the association between crime and mental illness and considers the prevalence of crime among the severely mentally ill.*

Mental Health Act 1983 and Mental Health Act 2007. *It is worth looking at these in order to gain an understanding of the legislation covering forensic mental health patients and the duties and responsibilities of the mental health teams who care for them. An alternative reference that provides a guide to the Act is:* Jones, R. (2008). *The Mental Health Act Manual.* London: Sweet and Maxwell.

Soothill, K., Rogers, P. & Dolan, M. (Eds.) (2000). *Handbook of forensic mental health.* Cullompton, Devon: Willan Publishing. *This book provides an in-depth description of the field of forensic mental health. The first section considers the administrative and social framework, the second section covers the process and systems in place, the third section considers the key issues in forensic mental health and the final section covers the skills for forensic mental health practitioners.*

World Health Organization (2005). *International Statistical Classification of Diseases and Related Health Problems, 10th revision (ICD–10).* Geneva: World Health Organization. *This is the World Health Organization coding used in Europe by clinicians concerned with diagnosing and classifying all known diseases and disorders, including mental health problems. It contains the criteria for diagnosis for each disorder. It is worth looking at this to obtain an idea of the types of symptomatology for the various disorders classified under the Mental Health Act 1983.*

KEY TERMS

- criminogenic needs • desistance • good lives model (GLM) • need principle • rehabilitation • relapse prevention
- responsivity principle • risk–need–responsivity (RNR) model • risk principle

CHAPTER OUTLINE

The rehabilitation of offenders is a multifaceted process involving re-entry, and ultimately reintegration, into social networks and the broader society. While offenders need to work hard at modifying their offence-related personal characteristics, the community also has an obligation to buttress this individual work with social supports and resources. Once amends have been made through undergoing punishment, individuals are entitled to have a chance at redemption and reconciliation (Ward & Salmon, 2009). The presumption of human beings' equal value is a cornerstone of a decent and just society, and applies just as much to offenders as to the rest of us. Furthermore, the rehabilitation of offenders is a normative and capacity-building process and therefore, from a practice perspective, both science and ethical judgment are equally important. In our view, the only legitimate place to start a journey that has involved the infliction of significant harm upon others is one where all human beings are regarded as equal in dignity and moral standing (Laws & Ward, 2011).

Practitioners require rehabilitation theories, essentially conceptual maps, to help them traverse the various challenges and problems that emerge when working with offenders (Ward & Maruna, 2007). Ideally, these maps will provide guidance on pressing matters such as the overall aims of intervention, what constitutes risk, what the general causes of crime are, how best to manage and work with individuals, and how to best balance offender needs with the interests of the community. In recent years, *strengths-based* or 'restorative' approaches to working with offenders have been formulated as an alternative to the very popular **risk–need–responsivity (RNR) model** (Andrews & Bonta, 2006) of offender rehabilitation (see Ward & Maruna, 2007). But in a nutshell, the primary practice focus of risk management approaches lies in the detection and modification of *dynamic* risk factors (i.e. **criminogenic needs**), while strengths-based perspectives seek to create competencies in offenders and reduce risk more indirectly.

Offenders *are* people like us, and if we start relating to them in ways that reflect this attitude, correctional outcomes may well improve and reoffending rates drop. The desistance research is clear that offenders respond well to practitioners who demonstrate an interest in them and believe in their capacity to turn their lives around (Figure 21.1; McNeill *et al.*, 2005). What is more, treating offenders with respect and decency rather than as sources of contamination to be quarantined (not cured) is likely to make us better people and lessen the risk that we might acquire some of the vices we despise in those who commit crimes.

The purpose of this chapter is to (i) consider the nature of offender rehabilitation and the efficacy of interventions in reducing reoffending rates; (ii) briefly

FIGURE 21.1 *Offenders respond well to practitioners who demonstrate an interest in them and believe in their capacity to turn their lives around.*

Source: © Yan Lev. Used under licence from Shutterstock.

review desistance research; (iii) describe the RNR model and highlight its limitations, including its weak fit with desistance theory and research; and (iv) provide a detailed description of a recent strength-oriented theory of offender rehabilitation, the **good lives model (GLM)**. In the following discussion we often refer to the literature on sexual offending to reinforce our argument. This is merely for ease of exposition, however, and our comments are intended to apply, more generally, to all types of offenders.

WHAT IS THE NATURE OF OFFENDER REHABILITATION?

A bewildering number of terms have been used and different theoretical justifications given for rehabilitation practices. Terms such as **rehabilitation**, *reintegration*,

desistance the psychological and social process of ceasing to offend. It is characterised by a series of lapses, relapses and recoveries rather than by a definitive stopping point.

re-entry and **desistance**, among others, have been employed to refer to the social and psychological processes involved in assisting individuals to cease criminal activity and pursue productive, socially responsible lives (Ward & Maruna, 2007). Psychologists tend to prefer the term 'rehabilitation' while criminologists are understandably suspicious of its connotation that individuals are being returned to a previously acceptable functional state, opting for the less question-begging terms of *integration* or *desistance* (Laws & Ward, 2011; Ward & Laws, 2010). While appreciating the points being made in the above debate, we have decided to stick with the label of *rehabilitation,* as it captures the mainstream discourse in correctional and forensic practice settings.

But exactly what is a rehabilitation theory? Aside from the terminological disputes mentioned above, there has also been a reluctance to analyse the concept of a rehabilitation theory and to outline its core features. This is problematic because unless some kind of analysis is provided, it is almost impossible to critically compare or evaluate different rehabilitation theories. In brief, we view a rehabilitation theory as depicting the overarching aims, values, principles, justifications and aetiological assumptions used to guide forensic and correctional interventions and help practitioners translate these principles into day-to-day practice (Ward & Maruna, 2007).

Rehabilitation theories are essentially hybrid theories, containing a mixture of theoretical, ethical, scientific and practice elements. They can be distinguished from types of aetiological theory (e.g. cognitive-behavioural or psychodynamic) or treatment theories, which are more specific in nature and involve the application of principles and practical strategies to change an aspect of the behaviour of individuals. Based on this analysis, the questions posed in Box 21.1 should be asked when evaluating the adequacy of rehabilitation interventions in the forensic and correctional domains.

Values and rehabilitation

The task of engaging individuals in efforts to change their criminal attitudes and dispositions is a normative (i.e. value-laden) and capacity-building process that has as its primary focus the construction of personally meaningful and socially acceptable practical identities (Laws & Ward, 2011; Lösel, 2010; Ward & Laws, 2010). The 'normative' dimension of rehabilitation is illustrated in Box 21.2.

The capacity-building dimension of rehabilitation is intimately connected to the normative one by virtue of its stress on the provision of resources and opportunities. The aim is to provide offenders with the internal (i.e. skills, knowledge, attitudes, beliefs) and external (i.e. social supports, employment, education, intimate relationships, leisure activities) conditions to secure their personally endorsed goals and, in this process, result in better or good lives. Good lives can be described as ones that are characterised by individuals having a sense of purpose, higher levels of well-being, and adherence to socially proscribed norms (Ward & Maruna, 2007).

BOX 21.1   EVALUATING THE ADEQUACY OF INTERVENTION IN CRIMINAL JUSTICE SETTINGS

1. Is there a rehabilitation theory underpinning practitioners' actions?

2. Can this theory explain in general terms the origins of the relevant offending behaviour in the context of mental illness?

3. What are the broad aims of rehabilitation? How do they relate to the causes of offending?

4. What are the proposed change mechanisms at work in the rehabilitation process?

5. Does the rehabilitation theory specify the attitudinal, motivational and relational aspects of treatment?

   Is there guidance on the therapeutic alliance, including how to manage issues relating to the process of therapy? Is there an integration of content and process?

6. What are the ethical/philosophical values embedded in the rehabilitation theory? For example, how are offenders represented? Is punishment or treatment emphasised? What is the relative balance between individual and societal rights? How is the risk conceptualised?

BOX 21.2   CONCEPTS BEHIND REHABILITATION AS IT IS CURRENTLY PRACTICED

a) The concept of an *offender* is a moral one, where individuals have been judged to have acted wrongly (and illegally) and have been punished accordingly.

b) The successful pursuit of a meaningful life relies on individuals identifying what is truly valuable and constructing ways of living that can help them to achieve the outcomes, activities, and traits that reflect these values.

c) The notion of risk reduction, which is typically a major aim of all correctional programmes and intervention efforts, is a value-laden one in the sense that the aim is to reduce, manage and monitor the probability of harmful outcomes to the offender and the community.

d) Practical or narrative identities that have been demonstrated to be important components of successful desistance are constituted by a diverse range of values (e.g. *role standards* or *expectations, personal traits, activities, practices*).

WHAT ARE THE ESSENTIAL FEATURES OF EFFECTIVE OFFENDER REHABILITATION?

In his recent review of *What Works* in offender rehabilitation (see Chapter 16 for more details of this approach), Lösel (2010) systematically evaluated the theoretical and empirical literature in the correctional domain. His review of the research evidence indicates that a combination of effective rehabilitation programmes, a greater use of community measures, and adopting a developmental perspective on prevention are likely to culminate in lower levels of crime. Lösel (2010) and other correctional researchers, such as Bonta and Andrews (2010), have also identified the features that contribute to the effectiveness of certain types of correctional interventions, and the inadequacy of others.

In brief, the outcome literature on general, and violent, offenders reveals that programmes that are based on a *social learning model* of offending, that are structured, skills-oriented, delivered with manuals by qualified staff and that operate within supportive environments, can result in between 10 per cent and 30 per cent reductions in offending (Lösel, 2010). For example, there have been a number of recent methodologically sound evaluations of the effectiveness of sex offender treatment programmes, all reaching similar conclusions.

In their meta-analytic review of sex offender treatment, Lösel and Schmucker (2005) set out to improve on previous reviews by broadening the scope of studies included and increasing the size of the sample pool. They ultimately incorporated 69 studies ($n = 22,181$) up until 2003 into their meta-analysis, a third of which came from countries outside North America (USA and Canada).

The results supported the efficacy of treatment, with 'treated' sex offenders reoffending at a significantly lower rate (11.1 per cent) than the various comparison groups (17.5 per cent). Furthermore, similar results were evident for general offending and also suggested that cognitive behavioural therapy (a skills-oriented method) was more effective than other types of treatment. By way of contrast, there was no evidence for the efficacy of purely punitive or deterrent measures such as boot camps, or psychodynamic treatment for sex offenders or other types of offenders (Bonta & Andrews, 2010; Hanson *et al.*, 2009).

More recently, research has broadened the scope of evaluation and looked more critically at the content of standard intervention programmes. Porporino (2010) argues that the field may have reached a point where further refinement of so-called evidence-based programmes will not produce significant improvements because there is too much uncertainty about *how* such programmes exert their effect. In relation to the RNR model, he notes that:

'. . . unattended to in that paradigm is how exactly offenders go about constructing new pro-social identities for themselves, what might spark them to do this, what are the motivational pressures that might support the change, where these pressures come from, and how is a new identity (and the future pro-social self it implies) reconciled with the criminal past it is choosing to abandon.'

(Porporino, 2010, p.63).

Porporino highlights problems with our current knowledge base including that we do not know how evidence-based programmes influence life outcomes years after they were delivered (he cites Farral, 2004a; 2004b who found that when offenders were asked, they only gave passing credit to these programmes).

Porporino (2010) draws on the desistance literature to suggest different ways of working with offenders, including developing programmes that do not aim to change or fix offenders, but rather aim simply to help them '. . . look at their lives though some new lenses, sort out their needs and wants, refine their vague wishes and commit to some . . . goals' (p.78).

Porporino (2010) emphasises the importance of contexts – and highlights that teaching skills in isolation serves little purpose, noting that: 'We seem to believe that once they have the recipe, the meal they cook will be tasty automatically' (p.80).

Martin *et al.* (2010) used a quasi-experimental design to investigate whether inclusion of an intervention targeting social and employment integration was more efficacious than social cognitive training (a Spanish adaptation of the Reasoning and Rehabilitation programme) alone. The total sample consisted of 117 repeat offenders, including 87 males and 30 females, mostly convicted for property/drug offences, but also offences against the person. Social and employment integration was facilitated by a social worker and included contact with employers and work places to secure jobs (this group was small, $n = 12$). In a six-year follow-up, survival analyses indicated that the Reasoning and Rehabilitation (R&R) programme produced a statistically significant delay in time to reoffence, compared to the control group. Although not significant (perhaps due to low statistical power), participants receiving R&R *and* the social and employment integration intervention took a longer time to reoffend (and had a lower percentage of reoffences) than participants receiving R&R alone. Thus, social and employment integration appeared to strengthen the effects of the social cognitive training programme. These findings provide a positive view of R&R but suggest that the programme fails to take into account an individual's social and economic context.

Using a mixture of quantitative and qualitative methods, Bahr *et al.* (2010) explored factors associated with successful re-entry into the community (defined as successful completion of parole) in the three years following prison release, using a sample of 51 offenders who had committed felonies and spent at least one year in prison (drug offences were the most common offences). The authors drew upon Laub and Sampson's (2001; 2003) *life course theory* and hypothesised that drug treatment, peer associations, employment, age, marriage/cohabitation and parenthood would be associated with success. Parolees were interviewed shortly after release and again at one, three, and six months following the first interview. Attending a substance abuse programme in prison and spending more time in enjoyable activities with friends were both associated with success. Also, among the employed

parolees, working at least 40 hours per week w... ciated with success. Contrary to predictions, having a partner, being married, being a parent, being close to parents and education level were not associated with greater re-entry success. That said, qualitative data showed that successful parolees had more support from family and friends and more self-efficacy, both of which helped in participants' efforts to stay away from drugs.

In a Canadian study, Martin and Stermac (2010) sought to investigate whether hope was related to risk for recidivism and whether male (50) and female (50) inmates differed in their levels of hope. There was a significant negative correlation between total scores on the *Hope Scale* (Snyder *et al.*, 1991) and the *Level of Service Inventory–Revised* (LSI–R; Andrews & Bonta, 1995) (a measure of recidivism risk; see Chapter 17 for a description of this measure). This result suggests that higher levels of hope were related to a lower estimated risk of recidivism. However, looking at the subscales of the Hope Scale in isolation (*pursuing goals*; *agency*; and *pathways*), only the agency scale was related to risk of recidivism (i.e. higher agency = lower risk estimate). Martin and Stermac concluded that *hope* may be a protective factor, lessening the risk of involvement in future crime.

Most studies examining the relationship between employment and recidivism have simply considered whether employment decreases the likelihood of further offending, and few studies have investigated whether obtaining employment increases time to reoffend (Figure 21.2). Tripodi *et al.* (2010) investigated this relationship utilising a random sample ($n = 250$) of men on parole from Texas prisons. They found that when controlling for offence history variables (and other known predictors of recidivism), while obtaining employment on release from prison was not associated with a significant decrease in likelihood of reincarceration it was associated with a significantly greater time to reincarceration. The authors noted the consistency of their findings with conceptualisations of desistance (see below) from crime as a process rather than an outcome. These findings suggest that motivation to remain crime-free might lessen over time, and the authors encourage the use of motivational interviewing and other motivational enhancing techniques to assist offenders in remaining focused on long-term prosocial goals.

Bouman *et al.* (2009) examined the relationship between subjective well-being and (i) self-reported offending over a three-month period; and (ii) officially recorded recidivism at a three-year follow-up amongst patients with personality disorders ($n = 135$). They found that satisfaction with health and general life satisfaction buffered a high risk level for violent reconvictions over a three-year follow-up.

FIGURE 21.2 *Most studies have considered whether employment decreases the likelihood of further offending; few have investigated whether obtaining employment increases the amount of time before the individual reoffends.*
Source: © StockLite. Used under licence from Shutterstock.

A closer analysis of which programmes are effective indicates that, in addition to the above requirements, those that adhere to the principles of risk, need and responsivity (as outlined in the *risk–need–responsivity model of offender rehabilitation* section below) reliably result in greater reductions in reoffending rates (Andrews & Bonta, 2006). Furthermore, there are a number of resilience or desistance factors associated with successful crime reduction, including access to social models that promote a non-offending lifestyle, employment, a stable emotional relationship, good social support, cognitive competencies, development of an adequate self-concept and the acquisition of a sense of meaning in life (Laws & Ward, 2011; Lösel, 2010; Maruna, 2001).

There is a growing convergence between the findings of desistance, programme evaluations and resilience research traditions, which shows it is not enough to concentrate on the technical aspects of interventions. Indeed, the message is clear that practitioners and policy makers ought to take greater care to ensure programmes are responsive to offenders' personal goals and incorporate social and community groups in any intervention plans (Marshall *et al.*, 2006; Maruna & Roy, 2007; Sampson & Laub, 1993). In a nutshell, it is a mistake to continue looking exclusively inwards towards the person

and to ignore, or downplay, the important role of social relationships and community involvement in the rehabilitation process (Laws & Ward, 2011; McNeill, 2006).

The above brief review of what works in correctional programmes and interventions stresses the crucial role of social supports, self-transformation, acquiring a sense of meaning, and competency building. The default aetiological assumption appears to be that offending is a product of faulty social learning and individuals commit offences because they have a number of skill deficits that make it difficult for them to seek reinforcement in socially acceptable ways (Andrews & Bonta, 2006; Laws & Ward, 2011; Ward & Laws, 2010; Ward, Polaschek *et al.*, 2006). Thus, the primary mechanisms underpinning offending are thought to be social and psychological, although it is acknowledged that some individuals' antisocial actions are partly caused by dysfunctional biological mechanisms such as abnormal hormonal functioning (Andrews & Bonta, 2006; Mitchell & Beech, 2011; Ward, Polaschek *et al.*, 2006).

The major goal is to teach offenders skills to change the way they think, feel and act, and to use this knowledge to avoid or escape from future high-risk situations. There are usually discrete treatment modules devoted to the following problem areas: cognitive distortions, deviant sexual interests, social skill deficits, impaired problem-solving and cognitive skills, empathy deficits, intimacy deficits, emotional regulation difficulties, impulsivity, lifestyle imbalance, substance abuse, and post-offence adjustment or **relapse prevention** (Bonta & Andrews, 2010; Ward & Maruna, 2007).

Increasingly, there is greater attention paid to the utility of orientating treatment and interventions towards approach or positive goals, rather than being exclusively preoccupied with risk reduction (Laws & Ward, 2011). This has the advantage of capitalising on individuals' natural predispositions towards prudential outcomes and also makes it much easier to assist them in the construction of more adaptive self-schemas or narratives. These rehabilitation perspectives have been labelled 'strength-based approaches' because they provide the resources to enable offenders to implement ways of living that centre upon their preferences and, ultimately, core values.

DESISTANCE FROM CRIME

The shift in focus evident in recent correctional and forensic rehabilitation interventions indicates movement towards greater use of community resources and an appreciation of what have been called 'desistance factors' (Laws & Ward, 2011). In contrast to the forensic psychology literature's focus on factors implicated in offending and reoffending, the desistance literature seeks to understand the lifestyle change process associated with disengagement from crime (e.g. Laws & Ward, 2011; Serin & Lloyd, 2009). To suggest that a reduction in dynamic risk factors solely explains desistance, in our view, is unconvincing. Such an explanation is arguably somewhat simplistic and ignores the normative dimension of human action – the fact that human beings actively seek outcomes that are personally meaningful and valued (Ward & Maruna, 2007). The desistance literature unravels *how* offenders effect change to dynamic risk factors, and therefore provides a richness not captured by the forensic psychology literature (Laws & Ward, 2011; McNeill, 2006). Available evidence indicates that there are a number of social and psychological factors that facilitate the desistance process (Laws & Ward, 2011). These events are variously referred to, for example, as 'turning points' (Laub & Sampson, 2003; Sampson & Laub, 1993), 'hooks for change' (Giordano et al., 2007), a 'change in narrative identity' (McNeill et al., 2005), or 'making good' (Maruna, 2001).

Perhaps the most influential contributions to the desistance literature in recent years are those of Laub and Sampson (Laub & Sampson, 2001; Sampson & Laub, 1993) and Maruna (2001). Laub and Sampson conducted an extended and comprehensive follow-up of men from Sheldon and Eleanor Glueck's landmark research (Glueck & Glueck, 1950; 1968) on factors that differentiated serious and persistent delinquent boys from a matched group of non-delinquent boys. Laub and Sampson found that conventional adult social bonds such as marriage and employment explained variations in crime that could not be predicted by other variables such as childhood adversity. Specifically, they found that strong social bonds, strong marital attachment and job stability could facilitate the lifestyle change required for criminal desistance.

Laub and Sampson's findings have been echoed throughout the desistance literature (e.g. Graffam et al., 2004; Maruna, 2001; Petersilia, 2003; Uggen, 2000), and parallel findings have been reported in the forensic psychology literature (e.g. Hanson & Harris, 2000; Hanson & Morton-Bourgon, 2005). Laub and Sampson also replicated the longstanding finding in criminology that the frequency of offending decreases with age (e.g. see Gottfredson & Hirschi, 1990); and acknowledged the role of human agency, noting that men who desisted played an active role in the desistance process through making choices to disengage from crime. Maruna (2001) replicated Laub and Sampson's findings regarding the importance of social bonds, but also found that human agency or cognitive transformation (i.e. creation of a new, more adaptive narrative identity) was the key to desistance. In sum, both external factors (e.g. social support, access to employment opportunities) and internal factors (e.g. making a conscious decision to want a different life) are required to facilitate the lifestyle change process associated with desistance.

To recap our argument so far, the concept of offender rehabilitation is at its core a deeply normative one that manifests in individual lives in the construction of practical or narrative identities, and at the social level in terms of correctional policy directed at risk reduction and management. However, it is increasingly apparent that theories of offender rehabilitation need to cast their net widely and seek to equip offenders with the values and competencies to live more satisfying lives while also reducing their reoffending risk. The two most prominent correctional theories of rehabilitation, the RNR and the *good lives model* (GLM), prioritise different aspects of this equation: the RNR is focused primarily on risk management while the GLM has a primary interest in enhancing offender well-being, while not ignoring risk. We will now discuss each of these theories in turn.

THE RISK–NEED–RESPONSIVITY MODEL OF OFFENDER REHABILITATION

The risk management approach to offender rehabilitation emerged from Andrews and Bonta's seminal book, *The Psychology of Criminal Conduct* (2006). Andrews and Bonta sought to explain criminal behaviour through empirically derived predictors of recidivism using what the authors termed a general personality and social psychology perspective. The authors provide three empirically based principles aimed at reducing offenders' risk of recidivism: *risk*, *need* and *responsivity* (Andrews & Bonta, 2006; Andrews, Bonta *et al.*, 1990), commonly referred to in the forensic psychology literature as the RNR model of offender rehabilitation, a term synonymous with the risk management approach. Hence, an underlying assumption of the risk management approach is that offenders are bearers of risk for recidivism, and the primary aim of offender rehabilitation is to reduce this recidivism risk through adherence to following the RNR principles.

The **risk principle** states that the dosage or intensity of interventions should match an offender's risk level, such that intensive interventions are directed at high-risk offenders, and less intense (or no) interventions are aimed at lower risk offenders.

The **need principle** informs intervention targets, specifically that interventions should target criminogenic needs, also known as *dynamic risk factors*, which are those factors causally related to offending that, for a given individual, are changeable. Dynamic risk factors include antisocial attitudes and antisocial associates (Andrews & Bonta, 2006), and, in the case of sexual offending, deviant sexual interests and self-regulation difficulties (e.g. Hanson & Morton-Bourgon, 2005). The aim of treatment is to reduce dynamic risk factors and, according to the needs principle, directing intervention efforts at non-criminogenic needs such as low self-esteem and a history of victimisation will prove ineffective, given they have not been linked with recidivism (Andrews & Bonta, 2006; Hanson & Morton-Bourgon, 2005).

Finally, the **responsivity principle** informs the actual delivery of interventions in order to maximise their efficacy. General responsivity advocates structured cognitive behaviour therapy interventions, given its general acceptance as the best treatment currently available for groups such as sex offenders (e.g. Hanson *et al.*, 2002). *Relapse prevention* (RP; e.g. Laws, 1989) constitutes the predominant format for delivering cognitive-behavioural treatment with sex offenders (McGrath *et al.*, 2003), and was adapted for use with sex offenders from the addictions treatment literature. Enhancing specific responsivity requires considering cognitive ability, learning style, personality profile, culture, and other characteristics of individual offenders, and delivering treatment accordingly. The RNR has been hugely influential in offender rehabilitation initiatives internationally, forming the basis of correctional treatment since its inception in the early 1990s (Bonta & Andrews, 2010).

Limitations of the RNR model

As stated above, meta-analyses have found support for the efficacy of RNR-based treatment programmes in reducing recidivism amongst general and sexual offenders (e.g. Andrews & Dowden, 2005; Andrews, Zinger *et al.*, 1990; Bonta & Andrews, 2010; Hanson *et al.*, 2002; 2009; Lösel & Schmucker, 2005). However, some researchers argue that the available evidence is insufficient to conclude current treatment programmes are in fact efficacious (e.g. Marques *et al.*, 2005; Rice & Harris, 2003). Putting the question of treatment effectiveness to one side, the fact that anywhere between 12 per cent (e.g. Hanson *et al.*, 2002) and more than 50 per cent (e.g. Prentky *et al.*, 1997) of treated child molesters (and as many as 46 per cent of treated general offenders – Wilson *et al.*, 2005) go on to reoffend, underscores that considerable scope remains for improving offender rehabilitation and reintegration initiatives (Figure 21.3).

The most heavily cited criticism of the RNR model revolves around its failure to motivate and engage offenders in the rehabilitation process (e.g. Mann, 2000; Ward & Maruna, 2007). Jones *et al.* (2006) found that a judge's recommendation for treatment significantly predicted whether sex offenders volunteered for treatment, suggesting that external motivators such as parole eligibility influence decisions to enter treatment. Moreover, attrition from sex offender treatment programmes is particularly high, with reported rates as high as 30–50 per cent (e.g. Browne *et al.*, 1998; Moore *et al.*, 1999; Ware & Bright, 2008), which have been attributed to poor treatment engagement (e.g. Beyko & Wong, 2005). Consistent evidence shows that men who drop out of treatment are more likely to reoffend compared to treatment completers (e.g. Hanson *et al.*, 2002; Marques *et al.*, 2005) as well as untreated comparison groups (Hanson *et al.*, 2002). Without addressing the problem of treatment attrition, current treatment programmes fail to deliver to groups of sex offenders most requiring treatment (Beyko & Wong, 2005), and therefore fail to adhere to the RNR risk principle. Thus, although empirically derived, in reality the risk principle is one that is difficult to adhere to.

FIGURE 21.3 *Considerable scope remains for improving offender rehabilitation and reintegration initiatives; as many as 46% of treated general offenders go on to reoffend*

Source: © Victor Newman. Used under licence from Shutterstock.

What is behind the failure of the risk management approach to engage clients in rehabilitation? At the outset, the risk management approach differs substantially from therapeutic models used with other client populations (e.g. in the treatment of mental health problems) in the orientation of treatment goals, limited collaboration between client and therapist, and limited attention to problems not causally related to the problem behaviour (i.e. in the case of offending, non-criminogenic needs such as self-esteem or personal distress). Addressing the first issue, risk management interventions rely heavily on *avoidant* goals through encouraging hypervigilance to threats of relapse and the reduction of dynamic risk factors (Mann, 2000). By contrast, *approach* goals provide individuals with guidance on how best to achieve their goals (i.e. the stress is on achieving specific outcomes rather than simply avoiding negative consequences). It has been suggested that individuals driven by approach goals focus on positive outcomes and thus persevere longer than people driven by avoidance goals, who tend to focus on threats (e.g. Higgins, 1996). Reframing the overarching goal of treatment (i.e. reducing risk of reoffending) as an approach goal might be 'to become someone who lives a satisfying life that is always respectful of others' (Mann, 2000, p.194). Such a goal remains consistent with avoiding relapse, given that it is incongruent with offending, and can be separated into personally meaningful sub-goals that provide corrections clients with direction in life, for example, increasing confidence in socialising with adult women. Thus, by using approach goals, treatment can help offenders live a better life, not just a less harmful one, in ways that are personally meaningful and socially acceptable – and risk reducing (Mann, 2000; Ward & Maruna, 2007). Indeed, Mann *et al.* (2004) showed that an approach-goal focused intervention with sex offenders was associated with increased treatment engagement compared to a traditional avoidant-goal focused intervention.

Secondly, treatment goals in the risk management approach are enforced upon offenders rather than mutually agreed upon in therapy (Mann, 2000), thereby compromising the therapeutic relationship. Marshall and his colleagues (e.g. Marshall *et al.*, 2003; Serran *et al.*, 2003) demonstrated that confrontational therapeutic styles had a negative impact on attitude and behaviour changes, whereas displays of empathy, warmth and encouragement, and some degree of directiveness, facilitated treatment change, suggesting that careful attention to the therapeutic relationship might increase treatment engagement. The didactic nature of the risk management approach, however, allows limited scope for enhancing the therapeutic relationship. Third, some researchers have convincingly argued that a sole focus on criminogenic needs obstructs treatment engagement, and that attention to non-criminogenic needs, such as those relating to enhanced well-being and quality of life, might enhance treatment engagement (Ward & Maruna, 2007). More specifically, targeting non-criminogenic needs might be a necessary predecessor for targeting criminogenic needs through enhancing the therapeutic alliance (Ward & Stewart, 2003). For example, attempting to address criminogenic needs in the context of personal distress or financial crisis (both non-criminogenic needs) will likely prove fruitless if the more acute issues are not sufficiently addressed (Ward & Maruna, 2007).

Another general limitation of the risk management approach is its minimal consideration paid to re-entry and reintegration into the social environment (outside of identifying and then actively avoiding high-risk situations). The desistance literature emphasises the crucial role of environmental systems such as close, supportive relationships and employment in ceasing offending. Thus, building and strengthening environmental opportunities, resources and supports should be central to offender rehabilitation and reintegration endeavours. Moreover, in the case of treated offenders, environmental factors have the potential to facilitate or impede the maintenance of treatment-related changes to dynamic risk factors. In a recent paper Ward and Nee (2009) argued that effective treatment generalisation requires an environment that supports and reinforces newly learned concepts, such as the restructuring of offence-supportive beliefs. Associating with people endorsing such beliefs, for example, will likely not be conducive to maintaining treatment-induced restructured beliefs.

We argue that the failure of the risk management approach to engage criminal justice clients in the rehabilitation process is derived from its theoretical underpinnings (or lack thereof – for a detailed discussion see Ward & Maruna, 2007), which ignore the nature of human beings as value-laden, meaning-seeking, goal-directed beings. The risk management approach, we argue, is overly mechanistic and reductionist – that is, there is an implicit assumption that through fixing a malfunction, offenders are (hopefully) restored to their optimal functioning state. Humans, on the other hand, are arguably not simply clusters of mechanisms but also people with an array of values. We argue that it is not enough simply to rectify personal deficits, or reduce criminogenic needs, and expect individuals who have committed crimes in the pursuit of perceived valued outcomes to be rehabilitated. In other words, the theoretical grounding in managing risk, rather than improving the lives of offenders, compromises client engagement and their capacity for change (Ward & Maruna, 2007).

In summary, critics argue that the RNR approach commonly current in offender rehabilitation and reintegration endeavours constitutes a necessary, but not sufficient, foundation for effective interventions (Ellerby, Bedard & Chartrand, 2000; Maruna, 2001; Ward & Maruna, 2007; Ward & Stewart, 2003). We are committed to the idea of subjecting offenders to interventions that are empirically supported; however, it is our contention that there is still much to be done in the arena of correctional practice and that desistance theory and research can offer those working with offenders a plethora of good ideas and practices. It has been convincingly argued that offender rehabilitation endeavours require a dual focus: reducing risk, but also promoting human needs and values through approach goals, thereby engaging offenders in the treatment process (Ward & Brown, 2004).

The GLM was developed as an alternative approach to rehabilitation that accommodates this dual focus. In other words, the very nature of the GLM addresses limitations of the risk management approach, including motivating offenders to engage in treatment and desist from further offending, and consideration for offenders' environmental contexts (Ward *et al.*, 2007; Ward & Maruna, 2007; Ward & Stewart, 2003). Although developed independently, as will be shown the GLM is a natural ally of desistance theory because of the overlapping nature of the theoretical assumptions

of both perspectives and their common stress on the importance of both offender agency and social resources.

THE GOOD LIVES MODEL

The good lives model (GLM), first proposed by Ward and Stewart (2003) and further developed by Ward and colleagues (e.g. Ward & Gannon, 2006; Ward & Marshall, 2004), is a strengths-based approach to offender rehabilitation. It is a strengths-based rehabilitation theory because it is responsive to offenders' particular interests, abilities, and aspirations. It also directs practitioners to explicitly construct intervention plans that help offenders to acquire the capabilities to achieve the things that are personally meaningful to them. It assumes that all individuals have similar aspirations and needs, and that one of the primary responsibilities of parents, teachers and the broader community is to help each of us acquire the tools required to make our own way in the world.

Criminal behaviour results when individuals lack the internal and external resources necessary to satisfy their values using prosocial means. In other words, criminal behaviour represents a maladaptive attempt to meet life values (Ward & Stewart, 2003). Rehabilitation endeavours should therefore equip offenders with the knowledge, skills, opportunities and resources necessary to satisfy their life values in ways that do not harm others. Inherent in its focus on an offender's life values, the GLM places a strong emphasis on offender agency. That is, offenders, like the rest of us, actively seek to satisfy their life values through whatever means are available to them. The GLM's dual attention to an offender's internal values and life priorities and external factors such as resources and opportunities give it practical utility in desistance-oriented interventions. We argue that the GLM has the conceptual resources to incorporate desistance ideas by virtue of its stress on agency, interdependency and development. In other words, there is natural resonance between desistance theory and the GLM because of their overlapping theoretical ideas and broad way of conceptualising the relationship between human beings and their social world.

The GLM is a theory of offender rehabilitation that contains three hierarchical sets of assumptions: (1) general assumptions concerning the aims of rehabilitation; (2) aetiological assumptions that account for the onset and maintenance of offending; and (3) practical implications arising from the first and second sets of assumptions. Each set of assumptions will be detailed, followed by a summary of empirical research investigating the utility of the GLM.

General assumptions of the GLM

The GLM is grounded in the ethical concept of human dignity (see Ward & Syversen, 2009) and *universal human rights*, and as such it has a strong emphasis on human agency. That is, the GLM is concerned with individuals' ability to formulate and select goals, construct plans and act freely in the implementation of these plans. A closely related assumption is the basic premise that offenders, like all humans, value certain states of mind, personal characteristics and experiences, which are defined in the GLM as *primary goods*. Following an extensive review of psychological, social, biological and anthropological research, Ward and colleagues (e.g. Ward & Brown, 2004; Ward & Marshall, 2004) first proposed nine classes of primary goods. In more recent work (e.g. Ward & Gannon, 2006; Ward et al., 2007), they produced 11 classes of primary goods, as shown in Box 21.3 (see Figure 21.4).

While it is assumed that all humans seek out all of these primary goods to some degree, the weightings or priorities given to specific primary goods reflect an individual's values and life priorities. Moreover, the existence of a number of practical identities, based on, for example, family roles (e.g. being a parent), work (e.g. being a psychologist) and leisure (e.g. being a football/tennis player) mean that an individual might draw on different value sources in different contexts, depending on the normative values underpinning each practical identity.

Instrumental goods, or *secondary goods*, provide concrete means of securing primary goods and take the form

FIGURE 21.4 *Primary goods from the GLM model.*
Source: © Yeko Photo Studio. Used under licence from Shutterstock.

of approach goals (Ward, Vess et al., 2006). For example, completing an apprenticeship might satisfy the primary goods of *knowledge* and *excellence in work*, whereas joining an adult sports team or book club might satisfy the primary good of *friendship*. Such activities are incompatible with dynamic risk factors, meaning that avoidance goals are indirectly targeted through the GLM's focus on approach goals. Refer to Case Studies 21.1 and 22.2 to see an example of a good lives plan in action.

Aetiological assumptions of the GLM

According to the GLM there are two primary routes that lead to the onset of offending: direct and indirect (Ward & Gannon, 2006; Ward & Maruna, 2007). The direct pathway is implicated when an offender actively attempts (often implicitly) to satisfy primary goods through his or her offending behaviour. For example, an individual lacking the competencies to satisfy the good of intimacy with an adult might instead attempt to meet this good through sexual offending against a child. The indirect pathway is implicated when, through the pursuit of one or more goods, something goes awry, which creates a ripple or cascading effect leading to the commission of a criminal offence. For example, conflict between the goods of intimacy and autonomy might lead to the break-up of a relationship, and subsequent feelings of loneliness and distress. Maladaptive coping strategies such as the use of alcohol to alleviate distress might, in specific circumstances, lead to a loss of control and culminate in sexual offending (Ward et al., 2007). Four types of difficulties in offenders' attempts to secure primary goods have been proposed (see Box 21.4).

Empirically identified criminogenic needs are conceptualised in the GLM as *internal* or *external* obstacles that interfere with the acquisition of primary goods. Indeed, as outlined by Ward and Maruna (2007), each of the primary goods can be linked with one or more criminogenic needs.

BOX 21.3   PRIMARY GOODS FROM THE GLM MODEL

- Life (including healthy living and functioning)
- Knowledge acquisition
- Excellence in play (being good at something)
- Excellence in work (including mastery experiences)
- Excellence in agency (being in control and the ability to be able to get things accomplished)
- Inner peace (freedom from emotional turmoil and stress)
- Friendship (having intimate, romantic and family relationships)
- Community (being part of wider social networks)
- Spirituality (finding meaning and purpose in life)
- Happiness
- Creativity

BOX 21.4   INAPPROPRIATE ROUTES TO SECURING PRIMARY GOODS

1. The most common of these in the direct route to offending, is the use of *inappropriate strategies* (secondary goods) to achieve primary goods.

2. An individual's implicit good lives plan might suffer from a lack of scope, in that a number of goods are omitted from his or her life plan.

3. There may be *conflict* in the pursuit of goods that might result in acute psychological stress and unhappiness.

4. An individual might lack *internal and external capabilities* to satisfy primary goods in the environment in which he or she lives. Internal capabilities include relevant knowledge and skill sets, while external capabilities include environmental opportunities, resources, and supports (some of which are desistance factors – Laws & Ward, 2011).

Taking the primary good of agency as an example, *impulsivity* might obstruct good fulfilment. Similarly, poor *emotional regulation* might block attainment of inner peace.

Practical implications of the GLM

To reiterate, the aim of correctional intervention according to the GLM is the promotion of primary goods, or human needs that, once met, enhance psychological well-being (Ward & Brown, 2004). In applying the GLM, assessment begins with mapping out an offender's good lives conceptualisation by identifying the weightings given to the various primary goods. This is achieved through: (i) asking increasingly detailed questions about an offender's core commitments in life and his or her valued day-to-day activities and experience; and (ii) identifying the goals and underlying values that were evident in an offender's offence-related actions. Once an offender's conceptualisation of what constitutes a good life is understood, future-oriented secondary goods aimed at satisfying an offender's primary goods in socially acceptable ways are formulated collaboratively with the offender and translated into a good lives treatment plan. Treatment is individually tailored to assist an offender to implement his or her good lives intervention plan and simultaneously address criminogenic needs that might be blocking goods fulfilment. Accordingly, intervention might include building internal capacity and skills and maximising external resources and social supports to satisfy primary human goods in socially acceptable ways.

Ward *et al.* (2007) outlined a group-based application of the GLM based on seven modules typical of current best-practice sex offender treatment programmes: (i) establishing therapy norms; (ii) understanding offending and cognitive restructuring; (iii) dealing with deviant arousal; (iv) victim impact and empathy training; (v) affect regulation; (vi) social skills training; and (vii) relapse prevention. They highlighted that most modules were associated with an overarching primary good, consistent with the notion that dynamic risk factors can be considered

CASE STUDY 21.1   A GOOD LIVES PLAN

Sam is a 42-year-old member of a Native American gang. He has a long criminal history and in the past has had several periods of imprisonment for assault, rape and robbery. Sam's good lives plan (GLP) explicitly linked the goods of knowledge, community and relatedness to his practical identities (secondary goods and contexts) of being a university student and a member of the university and local Native American support and cultural groups. He learned how to manage his anger, alcohol and drug use, and to apply more adaptive norms and beliefs when dealing with people, during therapy he received from a correctional psychologist. This work built upon his past participation in RNR violence programmes but, because the strategies were recruited in the service of goals he was committed to, were more eagerly utilised by Sam. It was anticipated that he would cultivate social and even romantic relationships with the non-gang people he mixed with in the various support groups he attended, possibly taking up the numerous opportunities to join in recreational and sporting activities. The whole range of primary goods was built into Sam's GLP with an emphasis on the two primary practical identities of being a Native American history and culture student and being a member of a Native American community and tribe.

CASE STUDY 21.2   A GOOD LIVES PLAN

Peter is a 33-year-old single male who was convicted of sexually molesting two teenage girls while giving them tennis lessons. Peter's good lives plan is built around two primary goods and their respective practical identities, mastery and service to the community. Concerning mastery, it was decided that taking into account Peter's love of teaching and his demonstrated ability, he would train as a teacher of literacy at a local education institution. This identity was one that Peter endorsed and it would also meet his need to be of service to his community, given that he would be working with men who were struggling and down on their luck. In order to take full advantage of the training opportunity, Peter agreed to work on his mild anxiety and assertiveness problems and to develop the confidence and ability to communicate more effectively with adult men and woman. He required relatively little specialised psychological therapy for his sexual offences and most of the rehabilitation focus was on developing and strengthening his social and vocational relationships and opportunities.

maladaptive means of securing primary goods. For example, an overarching good in the understanding offending and cognitive restructuring module is that of knowledge, attained through providing offenders with an understanding of how their thoughts, feelings and actions led them to offend. The social skills training module is associated with the overarching goods of friendship, community and agency. Offenders' individual good lives plans (GLPs) should inform the nature of interventions provided in this module. Some offenders, for example, may value other primary goods such as excellence in play and work over the good of friendship; thus, basic social skills training will likely suffice. Other offenders, however, may highly value intimate relationships; thus, intensive therapeutic work on intimacy and relationships might be required.

Empirical research supporting the utility of the GLM

The most commonly cited criticism of the GLM is its lack of empirical support (Bonta & Andrews, 2003; Ogloff & Davis, 2004). However, the GLM is not a *treatment* theory but rather is a rehabilitation framework that is intended to supply practitioners with an overview of the aims and values underpinning practice. It functions as a broad *map* that needs to be supplemented by specific mini-theories concerning concrete interventions such as cognitive behavioural treatment techniques (Ward & Maruna, 2007). Thus, the criticism that the GLM has not been empirically supported entirely misses the point. Rather, it is intended to provide a more comprehensive framework for offender practice than currently exists. However, programmes can be/are constructed that reflect GLM assumptions and these can (and should) be evaluated. These are best construed as GLM-consistent programmes, however, and are not the GLM itself (Laws & Ward, 2011; Ward & Maruna, 2007).

Keeping this general point in mind, there is a growing body of research studies that have incorporated principles of the GLM into interventions for sexual offending with positive results (Gannon et al., in press; Harkins et al., 2008; in press; Lindsay et al., 2007; Marshall et al., 2011; Simons, McCullar & Tyler, 2008; Ware & Bright, 2008; Whitehead et al., 2007), while other research studies have offered support for the GLM's underlying assumptions (Barnett & Wood, 2008; Bouman et al., 2009; Willis & Grace, 2008; Willis & Ward, in press; Yates, 2009). Together, these studies suggest that adoption of the GLM enhances treatment engagement and positive therapeutic relationships, as well as the promotion of longer-term desistance from offending.

To sum up, the GLM has demonstrated preliminary effectiveness in addressing key limitations of the risk management approach to offender rehabilitation, more specifically through enhancing treatment engagement, fostering desistance, and paying increased attention to environmental contexts. Moreover, a growing body of research supports the GLM's underlying assumptions.

SUMMARY

- Individuals with a history of criminal offending are more than bearers of risk and, as such, rehabilitation and reintegration endeavours require more than managing risk.

- The risk management approach has been hugely influential and we do not wish to reject the primary RNR principles. Rather, we would like to integrate the principles of risk, need and responsivity within a broader, strengths-based rehabilitation theory, of the GLM. Through acknowledging that offenders are *people like us*, the GLM engages offenders in the process of desistance, thereby bettering their lives and the lives of people they come into contact with.

- A problem with risk management practice models is that they tend to be overly focused on individual offenders and lack sufficient theoretical and ethical resources to enlarge their vision to the broader social and cultural vista.

- Helping offenders to turn their lives around requires attending to their needs and value commitments, as well as their potential for behaving harmfully towards others.

- In fact, according to the GLM, assisting individuals to acquire the capabilities to pursue and achieve their personal goals is also likely to make them safer.

ESSAY/DISCUSSION QUESTIONS

1. What is a rehabilitation theory?

2. What role do values play in the process of offender rehabilitation?

3. Outline the concept of desistance and describe its role in offender reintegration.

4. Outline and critically evaluate the RNR model of offender rehabilitation.

5. Outline and critically evaluate the GLM model of offender rehabilitation.

6. Contrast and compare the RNR and GLM models of rehabilitation.

REFERENCES

Andrews, D.A. & Bonta, J. (1995). *The Level of Service Inventory – Revised manual*. Toronto: Multi-Health Systems.

Andrews, D.A. & Bonta, J. (2006). *The psychology of criminal conduct* (4th edn). Cincinnati, OH: Anderson Publishing.

Andrews, D.A., Bonta, J. & Hoge, R.D. (1990). Classification for effective rehabilitation: Rediscovering psychology. *Criminal Justice and Behavior, 17*, 19–52.

Andrews, D.A. & Dowden, C. (2005). Managing correctional treatment for reduced recidivism: A meta-analytic review of programme integrity. *Legal and Criminological Psychology, 10*, 173–187.

Andrews, D.A., Zinger, I., Hoge, R.D., Bonta, J., Gendreau, P. & Cullen, F.T. (1990). Does correctional treatment work? A clinically relevant and psychologically informed meta-analysis. *Criminology, 28*, 369–404.

Bahr, S.J., Harris, L., Fisher, J.K. & Armstrong, A.H. (2010). Successful reentry: What differentiates successful and unsuccessful parolees? *International Journal of Offender Therapy and Comparative Criminology, 54*, 667–692.

Barnett, G. & Wood, J.L. (2008). Agency, relatedness, inner peace, and problem solving in sexual offending: How sexual offenders prioritize and operationalize their good lives conceptions. *Sexual Abuse: Journal of Research and Treatment, 20*, 444–465.

Beyko, M.J. & Wong, S.C.P. (2005). Predictors of treatment attrition as indicators for program improvement not offender shortcomings: A study of sex offender treatment attrition. *Sexual Abuse: A Journal of Research and Treatment, 17*, 375–389.

Bonta, J. & Andrews, D. (2010). Viewing offender assessment and rehabilitation through the lens of the risk–need–responsivity model. In F. McNeill, P. Raynor & C. Trotter (Eds.) *Offender supervision: New directions in theory, research, and practice* (pp.19–40). Abingdon, UK: Willan Publishing.

Bonta, J. & Andrews, D.A. (2003). A commentary on Ward and Stewart's model of human needs. *Psychology, Crime & Law, 9*, 215–218.

Bouman, Y.H.A., Schene, A.H. & de Ruiter, C. (2009). Subjective well-being and recidivism in forensic psychiatric outpatients. *International Journal of Forensic Mental Health, 8*, 225–234.

Browne, K.D., Foreman, L. & Middleton, D. (1998). Predicting treatment drop-out in sex offenders. *Child Abuse Review. Special Issue: Working with sex offenders, 7*, 402–419.

Ellerby, L., Bedard, J. & Chartrand, S. (2000). Holism, wellness, and spirituality: Moving from relapse prevention to healing. In D.R. Laws, S.M. Hudson & T. Ward (Eds.) *Remaking relapse prevention with sex offenders: A sourcebook* (pp.427–452). Thousand Oaks, CA: Sage Publications.

Farrall, S. (2004a). Supervision, motivation and social context: Which matters most when probationers desist? In G. Mair. (Ed.) *What matters?* (pp.187–209). Cullompton, Devon: Willan Publishing.

Farrall, S. (2004b). What makes people stop offending? *Safer Society, 22* (Autumn), 23–25.

Gannon, T., King, T., Miles, H., Lockerbie, L. & Willis, G.M. (in press). Good lives sexual offender treatment for mentally disordered offenders. *British Journal of Forensic Practice.*

Giordano, P.C., Schroeder, R.D. & Cernkovich, S.A. (2007). Emotions and crime over the life course: A neo-Meadian perspective on criminal continuity and change. *American Journal of Sociology, 112*, 1603–1661.

Glueck, S. & Glueck, E. (1950). *Unraveling juvenile delinquency.* New York: The Commonwealth Fund.

Glueck, S. & Glueck, E. (1968). *Delinquents and nondelinquents in perspective.* Cambridge, MA: Harvard University Press.

Gottfredson, M.R. & Hirschi, T. (1990). *A general theory of crime.* Stanford, CA: Stanford University Press.

Graffam, J., Shinkfield, A., Lavelle, B. & McPherson, W. (2004). Variables affecting successful reintegration as perceived by offenders and professionals. *Journal of Offender Rehabilitation, 40*, 147–171.

Hanson, R.K., Bourgon, G., Helmus, L. & Hodgson, S. (2009). The principles of effective correctional treatment also apply to sexual offenders: A meta-analysis. *Criminal Justice and Behavior, 36*, 865–891.

Hanson, R.K., Gordon, A., Harris, A.J.R., Marques, J.K., Murphey, W., Quinsey, V.L., et al. (2002). First report of the collaborative outcome data project on the effectiveness of psychological treatment for sex offenders. *Sexual Abuse: A Journal of Research and Treatment, 14*, 169–194.

Hanson, R.K. & Harris, A.J.R. (2000). Where should we intervene?: Dynamic predictors of sexual assault recidivism. *Criminal Justice and Behavior, 27*, 6–35.

Hanson, R.K. & Morton-Bourgon, K.E. (2005). The characteristics of persistent sexual offenders: A meta-analysis of recidivism studies. *Journal of Consulting and Clinical Psychology, 73*, 1154–1163.

Harkins, L., Flak, V.E. & Beech, A.R. (2008). *Evaluation of the N–SGOP Better Lives Programme.* Report prepared for the Ministry of Justice.

Harkins, L., Flak, V.E. & Beech, A.R. (in press). *Evaluation of a community based sex offender treatment program using a Good Lives Model approach.*

Higgins, E.T. (1996). Ideals, oughts and regulatory focus: Affect and motivation from distinct pains and pleasures. In P.M. Gollwitzer & J.A. Bargh (Eds.) *The psychology of action: Linking cognition and motivation to behaviour* (pp.91–114). New York: Guilford.

Jones, N., Pelissier, B. & Klein-Saffran, J. (2006). Predicting sex offender treatment entry among individuals convicted of sexual offense crimes. *Sexual Abuse: A Journal of Research and Treatment, 18*, 83–98.

Laub, J.H. & Sampson, R.J. (2001). Understanding desistance from crime. *Crime and Justice, 28*, 1–69.

Laub, J.H. & Sampson, R.J. (2003). *Shared beginnings, divergent lives: Delinquent boys to age 70.* Cambridge, MA: Harvard University Press.

Laws, D.R. (1989). *Relapse prevention with sex offenders.* New York: Guilford Press.

Laws, D.R. & Ward, T. (2011). *Desistance and sexual offending: Alternatives to throwing away the keys.* New York: Guilford Press.

Lindsay, W.R., Ward, T., Morgan, T. & Wilson, I. (2007). Self-regulation of sex offending, future pathways and the Good Lives Model: Applications and problems. *Journal of Sexual Aggression, 13*, 37–50.

Lösel, F. (2010, 25 October). *What works in offender rehabilitation: A global perspective.* Keynote given at the 12th Annual Conference of the International Corrections and Prisons Association, Ghent, Belgium.

Lösel, F. & Schmucker, M. (2005). The effectiveness of treatment for sexual offenders: A comprehensive meta-analysis. *Journal of Experimental Criminology, 1*, 117–146.

Mann, R.E. (2000). Managing resistance and rebellion in relapse prevention intervention. In D.R. Laws, S.M. Hudson & T. Ward (Eds.) *Remaking relapse prevention with sex offenders: A sourcebook* (pp.187–200). Thousand Oaks, CA: Sage Publications.

Mann, R.E., Webster, S.D., Schofield, C. & Marshall, W.L. (2004). Approach versus avoidance goals in relapse prevention with sexual offenders. *Sexual Abuse: A Journal of Research and Treatment, 16*, 65–75.

Marques, J.K., Wiederanders, M., Day, D.M., Nelson, C. & van Ommeren, A. (2005). Effects of a relapse prevention program on sexual recidivism: Final results from California's Sex Offender Treatment and Evaluation Project (SOTEP). *Sexual Abuse: A Journal of Research and Treatment, 17*, 79–107.

Marshall, W.L., Marshall, L.E., Serran, G.A. & Fernandez, Y.M. (2006). *Treating sexual offenders: An integrated approach*. New York: Routledge.

Marshall, W.L., Marshall, L.E., Serran, G.A. & O'Brien, M.D. (2011). *Rehabilitating sex offenders: A strength-based approach*. Washington, DC: American Psychological Association.

Marshall, W.L., Serran, G.A., Fernandez, Y.M., Mulloy, R., Mann, R.E. & Thornton, D. (2003). Therapist characteristics in the treatment of sexual offenders: Tentative data on their relationship with indices of behaviour change. *Journal of Sexual Aggression, 9*, 25–30.

Martin, A.M., Hernandez, B., Hernandez-Fernaud, E., Arregui, J.L. & Hernandez, J.A. (2010). The enhancement effect of social and employment integration on the delay of recidivism of released offenders trained with the R&R programme. *Psychology, Crime and Law, 16*, 401–413.

Martin, K. & Stermac, L. (2010). Measuring hope: Is hope related to criminal behaviour in offenders? *International Journal of Offender Therapy and Comparative Criminology, 54*, 693–705.

Maruna, S. (2001). *Making good: How ex-convicts reform and rebuild their lives*. Washington, DC: American Psychological Association.

Maruna, S. & Roy, K. (2007). Amputation or reconstruction? Notes on the Concept of 'knifing off' and desistance from crime. *Journal of Contemporary Criminal Justice, 23*, 104–124.

McGrath, R.J., Cumming, G.F. & Burchard, B.L. (2003). *Current practices and trends in sexual abuser management: The Safer Society 2002 nationwide survey*. Brandon, VT: Safer Society Press.

McNeill, F. (2006). A desistance paradigm for offender management. *Criminology and Criminal Justice, 6*, 39–62

McNeill, F., Batchelor, S., Burnett, R. & Knox, J. (2005). *21st century social work. Reducing reoffending: Key practice skills*. Edinburgh: Scottish Executive.

Mitchell, I.J. & Beech, A.R. (2011). Towards an attachment related neurobiological model of offending. *Clinical Psychology Review, 31*, 872–882.

Moore, D.L., Bergman, B.A. & Knox, P.L. (1999). Predictors of sex offender treatment completion. *Journal of Child Sexual Abuse, 7*, 73–88.

Ogloff, J.R.P. & Davis, M.R. (2004). Advances in offender assessment and rehabilitation: Contributions of the risk–needs–responsivity approach. *Psychology, Crime and Law, 10*, 229–242.

Petersilia, J. (2003). *When prisoners come home: Parole and prisoner reentry*. New York: Oxford University Press.

Porporino, F.J. (2010). Bringing sense and sensitivity to corrections: From programmes to 'fix' offenders to services to support desistance. In J. Brayford, F. Cowe & J. Deering (Eds.) *What else works? Creative work with offenders* (pp. 61–85). Portland, OR: Willan Publishing.

Prentky, R.A., Lee, A.F.S., Knight, R.A. & Cerce, D. (1997). Recidivism rates among child molesters and rapists: A methodological analysis. *Law and Human Behavior, 21*, 635–659.

Rice, M.E. & Harris, G.T. (2003). The size and sign of treatment effects in sex offender therapy. In R. Prentky, E. Janus, M. Seto & A.. Burgess (Eds.) Understanding and managing sexually coercive behavior. *Annals of the New York Academy of Sciences, 989*, 428–440.

Tripodi, S.J., Kim, J.S. & Bender, K. (2010). Is employment associated with reduced recidivism? The complex relationship between employment and crime. International *Journal of Offender Therapy and Comparative Criminology, 54*, 706–720.

Sampson, R.J. & Laub, J.H. (1993). *Crime in the making: Pathways and turning points through life*. Cambridge, MA: Harvard University Press.

Serin, R.C. & Lloyd, C.D. (2009). Examining the process of offender change: The transition to crime desistance. *Psychology, Crime, & Law, 15*, 347–364.

Serran, G., Fernandez, Y., Marshall, W.L. & Mann, R.E. (2003). Process issues in treatment: Application to sexual offender programs. *Professional Psychology: Research and Practice, 34*, 368–374.

Simons, D.A., McCullar, B. & Tyler, C. (2008, October). The utility of the self-regulation model to re-integration planning. Paper presented at the 27th Annual Association for the Treatment of Sexual Abusers Research and Treatment Conference.

Snyder, C.R., Harris, C., Anderson, J.R., Holleran, S.A., Irving, L.M., Sigmon, S.T., *et al.* (1991). The will and the ways: Development and validation of an individual differences measure of hope. *Journal of Personality and Social Psychology, 60*, 570–585.

Uggen, C. (2000). Work as a turning point in the life course of criminals: A duration model of age, employment, and recidivism. *American Sociological Review, 65*, 529–546.

Ward, T. & Brown, M. (2004). The Good Lives Model and conceptual issues in offender rehabilitation. *Psychology, Crime and Law, 10*, 243–257.

Ward, T. & Gannon, T.A. (2006). Rehabilitation, aetiology, and self-regulation: The comprehensive good lives model of treatment for sexual offenders. *Aggression and Violent Behavior, 11*, 77–94.

Ward, T. & Laws, D.R. (2010). Desistance from Sexual Offending: Motivating change, enriching practice. *International Journal of Forensic Mental Health, 9*, 11–23.

Ward, T., Mann, R.E. & Gannon, T.A. (2007). The good lives model of offender rehabilitation: Clinical implications. *Aggression and Violent Behavior, 12*, 87–107.

Ward, T. & Marshall, W.L. (2004). Good lives, aetiology and the rehabilitation of sex offenders: A bridging theory. *Journal of Sexual Aggression. Special Issue: Treatment & Treatability, 10*, 153–169.

Ward, T. & Maruna, S. (2007). *Rehabilitation: Beyond the risk assessment paradigm*. London, UK: Routledge.

Ward, T. & Nee, C. (2009). Surfaces and depths: Evaluating the theoretical assumptions of cognitive skills programmes. *Psychology, Crime, & Law, 15*, 165–182.

Ward, T., Polaschek, D. & Beech, A. (2006). *Theories of sexual offending*. Chichester: John Wiley & Sons, Inc.

Ward, T. & Salmon, K. (2009). The ethics of punishment: Correctional practice implications. *Aggression and Violent Behavior, 13*, 239–247.

Ward, T. & Stewart, C.A. (2003). The treatment of sex offenders: Risk management and good lives. *Professional Psychology: Research and Practice, 34*, 353–360.

Ward, T. & Syversen, K. (2009). Human dignity and vulnerable agency: An ethical framework for forensic practice. *Aggression and Violent Behavior, 14*, 94–105.

Ward, T., Vess, J., Collie, R.M. & Gannon, T.A. (2006). Risk management or goods promotion: The relationship between approach and avoidance goals in treatment for sex offenders. *Aggression and Violent Behavior, 11*, 378–393.

Ware, J. & Bright, D.A. (2008). Evolution of a treatment programme for sex offenders: Changes to the NSW Custody-Based Intensive Treatment (CUBIT). *Psychiatry, Psychology and Law, 15*, 340–349.

Whitehead, P.R., Ward, T. & Collie, R.M. (2007). Time for a change: Applying the Good Lives Model of rehabilitation to a high-risk violent offender. *International Journal of Offender Therapy and Comparative Criminology, 51*, 578–598.

Willis, G.M. & Grace, R.C. (2008). The quality of community reintegration planning for child molesters: effects on sexual recidivism. *Sexual Abuse: A Journal of Research and Treatment, 20*, 218–240.

Willis, G.M. & Ward, T. (in press). *Striving for a good life: The Good Lives Model applied to released child molesters*. Manuscript submitted for publication.

Wilson, D.B., Bouffard, L.A. & Mackenzie, D.L. (2005). A quantitative review of structured, group-oriented, cognitive-behavioral programs for offenders. *Criminal Justice and Behavior, 32*, 172–204.

Yates, P.M. (2009). Using the Good Lives Model to motivate sexual offenders to participate in treatment. In D.S. Prescott (Ed.) *Building motivation to change in sexual offenders*. Portland, OR: Safer Society Press.

ANNOTATED READING LIST

Bonta, J. & Andrews, D. (2010). Viewing offender assessment and rehabilitation through the lens of the risk–need–responsivity model. In F. McNeill, P. Raynor & C. Trotter (Eds.) *Offender supervision: New directions in theory, research, and practice* (pp.19–40). Abingdon, UK: Willan Publishing. *In this chapter the two creators of the RNR, Bonta and Andrews, provide a comprehensive overview of its major principles. They draw from the extensive empirical literature in the correctional field and evaluate the utility of the RNR and its components.*

Laub, J.H. & Sampson, R.J. (2003). *Shared beginnings, divergent lives: Delinquent boys to age 70*. Cambridge, MA: Harvard University Press. *In this pioneering book, Laub and Sampson report on a study spanning well over 50 years, of a group of delinquent boys. They discuss the factors that are associated with successful desistance from offending and conclude that social bonds, self-transformation and community support are among the most important desistance variables.*

Maruna, S. (2001). Making good: *How ex-convicts reform and rebuild their lives.* Washington, DC: American Psychological Association. *In this seminal book, Maruna investigates the divergent lives and aspirations of offenders who desist from, or continue, offending. He argues that a crucial aspect of successful rehabilitation is the degree to which offenders' self-conceptions are redemptive in nature.*

Porporino, F.J. (2010). Bringing sense and sensitivity to corrections: From programmes to 'fix' offenders to services to support desistance. In J. Brayford, F. Cowe & J. Deering (Eds.) *What else works? Creative work with offenders* (pp.61–85). Portland, OR: Willan Publishing. *In this chapter, a father of correctional interventions and developer of an influential model cognitive skills training, reviews current theoretical and practice models in the correctional area. He concludes that, while progress has been made, there is still much to be learned. Furthermore, he suggests that the incorporation of desistance- and strength-based ideas may add value to intervention initiatives.*

Ward, T. & Laws, D.R. (2010). Desistance from Sexual Offending: Motivating change, enriching practice. *International Journal of Forensic Mental Health, 9*, 11–23. *In this book Laws and Ward review the criminological theoretical and empirical literature on desistance and draw out its implications for offender rehabilitation. More specifically they demonstrate how an enriched version of the good lives model of offender rehabilitation can be fruitfully integrated with desistance ideas.*

Ward, T. & Maruna, S. (2007). *Rehabilitation: Beyond the risk assessment paradigm.* London, UK: Routledge. *In this book Ward and Maruna carefully analyse the concept of a rehabilitation theory and argue for its importance in guiding practitioners and researchers working with offenders. They then go on to describe the two most comprehensive rehabilitation theories currently in use, RNR and GLM, and critically evaluate both models.*

Glossary

7/7 the coordinated suicide attacks conducted by four UK citizens on the London transport system on 7 July 2005. Some 52 people were killed, along with the suicide bombers, and about 700 injured.

9/11 attacks on US targets on 11 September 2001, in which Al-Qaeda terrorists hijacked four airliners, crashing two into the World Trade Center, one into the Pentagon and one in Pennsylvania, killing nearly 4000 people.

acceptance and commitment therapy (ACT) an empirically-based psychological intervention that uses acceptance and mindfulness strategies mixed in different ways with commitment and behaviour-change strategies, to increase psychological flexibility.

ACE model used to examine the relative contributions of genetics and environment. Heritability is represented by the letter 'A', the common or shared environment by 'C' and environmental conditions by 'E'. Also known as 'non-shared environmental influences'.

Achieving Best Evidence (ABE) from 2001, the official guidance in England and Wales for all parties (e.g. legal personnel; police officers; social workers) and covering all vulnerable witnesses, from the initial interview through to court appearance.

acoustic analysis (of speech samples). Methods of analysis used by phoneticians, which focus upon the use of computer-assisted analysis of the physical (not perceptual) properties of an utterance, such as fundamental frequency.

acquisitive crime types of crime that involve property being stolen or acquired fraudulently.

actus rea literally, a 'guilty act'; that a criminal act has occurred.

adaptive behaviour assessed using a recognised, standardised assessment such as the Vineland Adaptive Behaviour Scale (VABS) or the American Association of Intellectual and Developmental Disabilities Adaptive Behaviour Scale – Residential and Community 2nd Edition (ABS:RC2).

adolescent-limited offending describes delinquent/antisocial behaviour that occurs during an individual's teen years, but ceases when they become adults.

adversarial court system frequently referred to as *accusatorial*. Each side presents a case (prosecution and defence) before a court. The judge gives no help to either side and does not participate in the discovering of the truth.

algorithm a mathematical procedure that must be followed in a set order and will derive an overall score.

Al Qaeda a terrorist organisation/network that seeks to establish a radical form of Islam based on Sharia law. Until his death in 2011, it was led by Osama bin Laden.

amnesia loss of memory. Such loss can be selective or global.

anatomically correct dolls (ACDs) (also known as **anatomically-detailed dolls**). Dolls that have human-like genitalia. Sometimes used for interviewing children suspected of having been sexually assaulted.

anger management programmes such programmes typically focus on increasing the offender's awareness of anger and its triggers, and then providing a range of skills including social skills and relaxation training to assist the offender to decrease anger arousal and strengthen anger control.

attachment theory a well-developed theory of early development, which focuses on the formation of early relationships and the implications of how these relationships are formed for later childhood and adult functioning.

aural-perceptual analyses (of *speech utterances*) methods of analyses, used by phoneticians, which focus on discernable heard speech characteristics such as rate, pitch, 'breathiness' and particular types of articulation of vowels and consonants.

autistic spectrum disorders (ASDs) a spectrum of psychological conditions characterised by widespread abnormalities of social interaction and communication, as well as 'special interests' and repetitive behaviour.

behavioural distinctiveness the principle that offenders commit their crimes in different ways to one another.

behavioural investigative advisors experts who are employed by or consulted by the police, and who provide behavioural advice for police investigations.

blended memories a mix of initial and post-event memory details.

blind administration a method of administering a line-up in which neither the line-up administrator nor the witness know which line-up member is the suspect. Also known as 'double-blind administration'.

British Crime Survey an annual survey that measures the amount of crime in England and Wales by asking a sample of the population about their experiences of crime in the preceding year.

Cambridge Study in Delinquent Development a prospective longitudinal survey of 411 South London males first studied at age 8 in 1961, with the aim of advancing knowledge about conviction careers up to age 50 and life success up to age 48.

celerity in penology, the amount of time that elapses between an offence being committed and an official sanction being imposed.

certainty in penology, the likelihood of legal punishment as a result of committing a crime, which may be assessed objectively (with reference to official statistics) or subjectively (with reference to the experience of individual offenders).

change order cognitive interview prompt to recall the initial event in a different order (e.g. backwards).

change perspective cognitive interview prompt to recall the initial event from another perspective.

Child Protection Plan details areas of concern, planned action and monitoring for a child who is considered to be in need of protection from physical, sexual and/or emotional abuse and/or neglect.

child sexual abuse (CSA) forcing or enticing a child or young person to take part in sexual activities, including prostitution, whether or not the child is aware of what is happening.

civil cases cases that are concerned with private wrongs, as between one person and another.

coerced-compliant false confession a false confession given in the face of coercion by the investigator, but only to appease the investigator and not accepted by the suspect.

coerced-internalised false confession a false confession given in the face of coercion by the investigator, which becomes fully accepted as the truth by the suspect.

cognitive-affective personality system (CAPS) a model of personality devised by Mischel and Shoda (1995).

cognitive analytic therapy (CAT) a form of psychological therapy initially developed in the UK by Anthony Ryle. It is distinctive due to its intensive use of reformulation, its integration of cognitive and analytic practice and its collaborative nature, involving the patient very actively in their treatment.

cognitive assessment completed using a recognised test such as one of the Wechsler group of tests. The Wechsler Adult Intelligence Test 4th edition UK is the most commonly employed assessment.

cognitive behavioural therapy (CBT) based on the notion that thoughts, attitudes and beliefs are interrelated and hence influence each other. It attempts to identify and alter thoughts, attitudes and beliefs that contribute to problem behaviour.

cognitive processing therapy a form of therapy for post-traumatic stress disorder.

commitment an effect whereby once a face has been identified by a witness, they become committed to the identification and are likely to identify the same face again, even when the initial judgement is mistaken.

comorbidity the diagnosis of a second (or more) disorder in addition to the initial diagnosis of a disorder.

compassion-focused therapy (CFT) a form of psychotherapy rooted in Mahayana Buddhist psychology, which emphasises the development of self-compassion in people who are prone to feelings of shame and self-criticism. Created by Paul Gilbert and colleagues.

conduct disorder (CD) in childhood is a repetitive, and persistent, pattern of behaviour in which the basic rights of others, or societal conventions, are flouted. Many individuals with CD show little empathy and concern for others, and may frequently misperceive the intentions of others as being more hostile and threatening than is actually the case.

context reinstatement a cognitive interview prompt to reinstate mentally the surrounding context of the initial event.

control behaviours behaviours performed by the partner of an individual to restrain their freedom or control how that individual can act or behave, e.g. controlling how often they are allowed out of the family home.

control question test (CQT) a method of polygraph testing that compares reactions to control questions concerning past transgressions to questions relevant to the crime under investigation; a guilty person should react more strongly to the relevant questions.

conversation management (CM) an interview technique, proposed by Shepherd, that emphasises the police officer's awareness and management of the interview, both verbally and non-verbally.

corroboration confirmation by other or additional sources.

covert sensitisation a method developed in behaviour therapy, which applies conditioning principles to induce individuals to associate socially or personally unacceptable feelings and behaviour with an experience of disgust, thereby reducing their potency.

crime linkage an analytical technique whereby potential crime series are identified through the analysis of the offender's crime scene behaviour.

crime linkage practitioner a person employed by the police, or who is consulted by the police, who conducts crime linkage analysis.

criminal cases cases that are concerned with offences deemed to be against the public interest.

criminogenic needs features of individuals associated with the risk of involvement in crime that change over time and are susceptible to change by direct effort, thereby reducing risks of criminal activity. Also known as *dynamic risk factors*.

criteria-based content analysis (CBCA) method for analysing children's statements in terms of indices that are believed to reflect truthfulness. It comprises 19 criteria, broken down into 3 general characteristics, 10 specific content, 5 motivation-related content criteria and one offence-specific element criterion. Part of **statement validity analysis**.

Daubert test a ruling on the admissibility of expert testimony, following *Daubert v. Merrell Dow Pharmaceuticals, Inc.* (1993), which stressed the testimony offered should be based on information on sound scientific methods.

de facto literally 'in actual fact'. What is in fact or in practice the case, irrespective of what legally or in theory should be the case.

de jure literally 'according to law; by right'. The legal or theoretical position, which may not correspond with reality.

desistance the psychological and social process of ceasing to offend. It is characterised by a series of lapses, relapses and recoveries rather than by a definitive stopping point.

deterrence one of the objectives of sentencing, based on the premise that adverse consequences (punishment) will make recurrence of offending (criminal recidivism) less likely.

deterrence theory in penology, the doctrine that the costs of committing crimes suppress criminal activity. *General deterrence* refers to the effect on the population, *specific deterrence* to the effect on convicted individuals.

developmental propensity theory a theory that aims to explain the factors in development that lead certain individuals to develop an underlying propensity for conduct disorder and juvenile delinquency.

dialectical behaviour therapy (DBT) a system of therapy originally developed by Marsha Linehan to treat people with borderline personality disorder. DBT combines standard cognitive-behavioural techniques for emotion regulation and reality-testing with concepts of distress tolerance, acceptance and mindful awareness, largely derived from Buddhist meditative practice.

directed masturbation also called *masturbatory reconditioning*. A behaviour therapy technique, based on conditioning principles, employed to help individuals with inappropriate sexual urges or attractions to divert their interests in more socially acceptable or less harmful ways.

dissociation (also disassociation). A defensive disruption in the normally occurring connections between feelings, thoughts, behaviours and memories, consciously or unconsciously invoked, to reduce psychological distress during or after traumatic episodes.

dizygotic (DZ) twins *see* **monozygotic (MZ)/dizygotic (DZ) twins**.

dysregulation of the emotion and stress pathways relatively poor regulation of emotion and stress due to physiological responses.

ecological validity the degree to which experimental conditions reproduce real-life situations accurately. Ecological validity is closely related to external validity.

effect size a statistic used to compare the magnitude of the effect of an independent variable across different studies expressed in standard deviation units. Two commonly reported effect sizes are *Cohen's d* and *Pearson's correlation (r)*.

electroencephalogram (EEG) a procedure in which changes in the electrical potential of the brain are recorded.

encoding the process by which information is registered in human memory.

episodic relating to a specific episode or event.

estimator variables factors that may affect the reliability of eyewitness memory that are not under the control of the criminal justice system (e.g. the amount of time a witness was able to view the perpetrator) (*see also* **system variables**).

ETA (*Euskadi Ta Askatasuna*) a separatist Basque nationalist organisation, responsible for many terrorist attacks in Spain.

evidence-based practice psychological practice that is informed by the best theory and/or the best evidence available at that time.

executive functioning brain processes responsible for higher order cognitive tasks, such as planning, abstract reasoning and problem solving. *Executive dysfunction* involves impairments with, for example, impulse control, self-regulation, sustained attention, planning and problem-solving.

expert witnesses the law of evidence recognises two types of witness: the *common witness to fact* and the *expert witness*. Expert witnesses are those qualified to express a professional opinion, by their training, knowledge and experience.

externalising behaviours/symptoms these refer to problems that are manifested in outward behaviour and reflect a child's negative reactions to her/his environment, including aggression, delinquency and hyperactivity. Other terms used include *conduct problems* and *antisocial*.

eye movement desensitisation and reprocessing (EMDR) developed to resolve trauma-related disorders resulting from exposure to traumatic or distressing events, such as rape or military combat.

factual approach the disclosure by the interviewer of all available evidence to the suspect, sometimes even false information, with the presumption that this will to lead to a quick confession, as the suspect believes that further resistance is useless.

false confession any confession or any admission to a criminal act that the confessor did not commit.

familial trauma abuse or neglect perpetrated by a family member.

familiarity a feeling that a detail has previously been experienced in the absence of contextual details.

family bonding activities that keep parents and children in harmony, ensuring they share the same goals and attitudes within the family.

foetal alcohol syndrome (FAS) is not a uniform clinical picture, but a spectrum of disorders, varying in severity.

foils volunteers who are not suspects but appear in a live, video or photographic line-up. Also known as distracters, fillers or line-up members; and as volunteers in England and stand-ins in Scotland.

Frye test US legal test to decide whether to admit or exclude expert testimony. Stipulated that scientific testimony was admissible only if it was based on a generally accepted theory or research findings in the field.

functional analysis an approach to understanding behaviour that focuses on determining its function for the individual.

functional magnetic resonance imagery (fMRI) technique of imaging activity with widespread uses in psychology, including searching for neural correlates of deception.

fuzzy-trace theory dual-processes model of memory; verbatim and gist traces are encoded for each detail.

gender role the adoption of socially proscribed behaviours and norms that are appropriate for each gender.

geographical proximity the closeness of two (crime) locations in space.

good lives model (GLM) a strength-based offender rehabilitation theory that seeks to reduce or manage *dynamic risk factors* by providing offenders with the internal and external resources to achieve important personal goals.

grooming attempting to befriend a child with the intention of gaining their trust (and possibly that of the child's carers) with the intent of having sexual contact with the child. This behaviour was deemed a criminal offence in England and Wales by the Sexual Offences Act 2003.

ground truth the reality of what actually occurred in a given event. Sometimes impossible to establish in criminal investigations on the basis of witness statements alone.

Guantanamo Bay (also known as G-Bay, GITMO, GTMO). A detention camp established at the US naval base in Cuba to hold detainees from the wars in Afghanistan and Iraq.

guilt-presumptive process style of interviewing that assumes the guilt of the suspect.

guilty knowledge test (GKT) a method of polygraph testing. Suspects are given multiple-choice questions about the crime; a guilty suspect should experience more physiological arousal to a correct choice that only a guilty person would know.

Hamas the Palestinian political organisation that has governed the Gaza Strip since 2007. Its social welfare wing has a reputation for lack of corruption and effective service delivery. Its military wing is Izz ad-Din al-Qassam Brigades.

high-stake lies lies, the effectiveness of which are critical to the freedom of the liar; typically lies told by a suspect during a police interview.

Hizbollah (or Hezbollah). A Shi'a political organisation and militant group known as 'the party of God', based in Lebanon. It receives political and financial support from Iran and Syria.

homology assumption the assumption that, because there is a relationship between crime scene actions and offender characteristics, offenders with similar crime scene behaviour will share similar characteristics.

iatrogenic the impact of the treatment process itself on a patient's symptoms. The term originated in medicine but is now applied in psychology, particularly to the impact of therapy on patient reports.

incapacitation an objective of sentencing; the use of criminal justice intervention to reduce criminality by removing offenders from crime opportunities.

indicators of series membership features of a crime, which could be behavioural, spatial or temporal, which suggest that it belongs to a crime series.

indirect victimisation feeling victimised through witnessing someone else being victimised, such as watching another person being bullied or parent(s) being violent to each other.

inquisitorial court systems type of court proceeding frequently found in mainland Europe. The judges play an active role in assembling the case material and questioning witnesses. Typically, the judges determine whether the accused is guilty.

integrated cognitive antisocial potential (ICAP) theory a theory primarily designed to explain offending by lower-class males, and influenced by the results obtained in the Cambridge Study.

integrity the extent to which an intervention is delivered as planned and in accordance with the model of change on which it is based; sometimes called *fidelity*, *programme integrity* or *treatment integrity*.

intellectual disability (ID) internationally recognised term for people who have an IQ less than 70 and have deficits in at least two areas of adaptive behaviour, with the onset of these deficits having occurred before adulthood.

interactional theory a theory focusing on the factors that encourage antisocial behaviour at different ages and assume bidirectional effects (e.g. poor parental supervision causes antisocial behaviour and antisocial behaviour causes poor parental supervision).

intergenerational cycle of maltreatment maltreated children becoming familial abusers themselves.

intermediaries one of the special measures permitted by the Youth Justice and Criminal Evidence Act 1999. An approved intermediary communicates the questions to the witness, then communicates their response to the questioner.

internalising symptoms emotional and behavioural difficulties within an individual, such that the individual tries to over-control internal anxieties and worries (e.g. anxiety/depression).

interrogation manuals books, memoranda or other printed recommendations principally written by police officers, detectives or former staff members of scientific crime laboratories. The methods suggested are most often confession-seeking procedures based on an uncritical and subjective use of psychological knowledge.

interviewer bias where an interviewer shapes the course of the interview to maximise disclosures that are consistent with what they believe a child witnessed or experienced.

intimate partner violence physical, sexual, psychological aggression and/or controlling behaviours used against a current or past intimate partner of any sex.

investigative interviewing a broader term than interrogation, describing a fair, dualistic and open-minded communication to obtain accurate and reliable information conducted within the framework of national law and the UN agreements on human, civil and political rights.

Italian Red Brigades an Italian Marxist-Leninist terrorist group active during the period from 1967 to the late 1980s.

jihadi someone who engages in the Muslim religious duty of jihad, meaning to 'struggle', sometimes interpreted as the struggle to maintain the faith or improve Muslim society. Can (inaccurately) refer to a supporter of radical Islamic terrorism.

layered voice-stress analysis (LVA) a lie detection technique based on highly sophisticated technology. It uses a computer program to analyse a digitised raw signal (sound) to identify errors in speech. Such errors are very difficult for the human ear to detect, but it is argued that they can be measured by more refined methods.

leading questions questions worded in such a way as to suggest or imply the answer that is being sought.

legalese refers to lexically and syntactically complicated language that has developed to meet the needs of the legal profession.

life-course-persistent offending describes delinquent/antisocial behaviour that persists throughout an individual's lifetime, often starting in childhood.

lifestyle theory seeks to redress the problems created by psychology's dependence on theoretical mini-models by offering an overarching conceptual framework that combines the insights of yesterday's grand theories with the methodological rigour of today's mini-models. It assumes that delinquency is part of a characteristic lifestyle.

line-up a test of identification in which a suspect is placed amongst foils, who are not suspects. A line-up may be an array of photographs or a live line-up of people.

linguistic inquiry and word count (LIWC) a computer-based technique that creates linguistic profiles by categorising words into different classes.

live link one of the special measures permitted by the Youth Justice and Criminal Evidence Act 1999.

lone wolf terrorism a lone wolf terrorist is someone who commits acts of terrorism in support of some political aspiration without being part of any formal terrorist group.

longitudinal study a research design that involves repeated observations over a long period of time.

long-term memory stores personally significant information over time. Some of this information is fairly easy to recall, while other memories are much more difficult to access. Long-term memory is susceptible to forgetting, but some memories last a lifetime.

low-stake lies lies that have trivial consequences; typically, the lies told by participants in laboratory studies of deception.

maladaptive beliefs beliefs that demonstrate a pattern of thinking that does not show positive adaptation (e.g. self-blame is associated with poorer physical health)

malleable capable of being shaped by extraneous forces, such as other witnesses, questioners or self-reflection.

Memorandum of Good Practice (MOGP) original official guidance introduced in 1992 for police officers and social workers in England and Wales conducting video-recorded investigative interviews with child witnesses for possible criminal proceedings. Subsequently superseded by **Achieving Best Evidence**.

mens rea literally, 'guilty mind'; that the defendant is aware of criminal intent and responsible for their actions.

meta-analysis a statistical technique that allows the combination of the results of several quantitative studies in the attempt to answer a research question.

mindfulness refers to a psychological quality that involves bringing one's complete attention to the present experience on a moment-to-moment basis, and non-judgmentally.

misinformation effect social (acquiescence) and psychological (memory) factors that affect people's encoding, storage, retrieval and reporting of events.

misinformation paradigm a three-phased paradigm originated by Loftus for testing the misinformation effect.

mock crime a technique much used in forensic psychology in which unsuspecting observers are exposed to a realistic but contrived criminal act.

monozygotic (MZ)/dizygotic (DZ) twins MZ (identical) twins arise from a single ovum and have exactly the same genetic material. DZ (fraternal) twins arise from two separate ova, and like any siblings, share 50 per cent of the same genes.

Multi-Agency Public Protection Arrangements (MAPPA) MAPPA is now recognised as one of the most advanced frameworks of offender management currently available. The process structures the way the offender is assessed and managed through effective identification of risk and through information exchange.

multimodal programmes a term used to describe intervention programmes that have more than one target of change (social skills, thinking, substance abuse, and so on) or employ more than one method of achieving it.

National Offender Management Service (NOMS) a directorate of the Ministry of Justice within England and Wales, tasked with reducing reoffending and protecting the public. Encompasses the prison and probation services.

need principle states that interventions should target only those needs (or risk factors) that contribute to offending behaviour.

neuroimaging scanning techniques used to examine brain anatomy and activity.

offender consistency hypothesis the assumption that offenders will commit their crimes in a relatively consistent manner. This means that their crimes should be similar in terms of the behaviour they display.

offender profiling in its narrowest sense, refers to making predictions about offenders' characteristics from the way they behaved during a crime.

Official IRA in 1969 the Irish Republican Army split into two factions – the Provisional IRA and the Official IRA. The Official IRA sought to achieve unification of Ireland through largely political means, as opposed to the Provisional IRA, which advocated violent confrontation.

olfactory aversive conditioning a behaviour therapy technique, based on conditioning principles, employed with individuals who have committed sexual offences as a result of socially unacceptable patterns of sexual arousal and associated behaviour.

PEACE model of interviewing mnemonic denoting the phases of an interview: *Planning and preparation*; *Engage and explain*; *Account, clarification and challenge*; *Closure*; and *Evaluation*.

penology the study of legal punishment and how it is administered.

Police and Criminal Evidence Act 1984 known as PACE; Act introduced in England and Wales in 1984 governing the conduct of police investigations and interactions with suspects.

polygraph sometimes called a *lie detector*. A machine that measures, typically, galvanic skin response, cardiovascular activity and breathing patterns in suspects under questioning.

post-event information information that a witness may acquire after the relevant incident has occurred. Post-event information may affect a witness' testimony. Misleading post-event information may result in memory distortion.

preparation at court, this refers to activities concerned with assessing the needs of the witness, providing support, liaising and communicating on the witness's behalf, and preparing the witness for the trial (e.g. providing information, court visit).

prima facie on the first view; at first glance/sight; on the face of it.

programmes structured sequences of learning opportunities, with objectives and contents planned in advance, designed to support and encourage change; usually accompanied by a manual or other materials.

prolonged exposure therapy a cognitive-behavioural form of therapy for post-traumatic stress disorder.

prospective longitudinal surveys studies that follow a group of individuals (a cohort) over time, with repeated measures.

Provisional IRA an Irish paramilitary organisation that sought, through armed insurrection and terrorism, to produce a united Ireland. It has been responsible for the deaths of some 1800 people since 1969.

psychological stress evaluator (PSE) alternative name for **voice stress analysis**.

rapport preliminary interview phase during which the interviewer attempts to develop a friendly relationship with the interviewee.

reality monitoring (RM) the process by which people distinguish memories of real events from memories of imagined events. The distinction is based on such considerations as contextual information concerning time and place, and semantic information.

Red Army Faction (also known as RAF, Rote Armee Fraktion, Baader-Meinhof Group). A left-wing terrorist group based in Germany that existed from 1970 to the late 1990s. Its origins were in the student protests of the 1960s.

rehabilitation an objective of sentencing and allied criminal justice initiatives, concerned with constructive efforts to provide education, training or other services to enable offenders to become reintegrated in society, and reduce recidivism.

relapse prevention a self-control programme designed to help people from relapsing into episodes of problem behaviour, often used in the treatment of sex offenders. Originally conceptualised for the treatment of addictive behaviours such as alcoholism.

report all cognitive interview prompt to tell everything about the incident under investigation.

resilience no agreed definition, but usually taken to mean the absence of psychopathology and successful functioning over a number of domains.

responsivity a design feature that contributes to effectiveness of intervention programmes with offenders. Can be general (an overall approach) or specific (taking into account factors that reflect diversity amongst participants).

responsivity principle developed by Andrews and colleagues alongside the principles of risk and need, the responsivity principle proposes that the method of delivery of an intervention should match the learning styles of those to whom it is delivered.

restoration (also *restorative justice*) a relatively recent departure, entailing services through which offenders make reparations to their victims for the harm they have done, sometimes through a carefully managed negotiation and reconciliation process.

retribution one of the objectives of sentencing, and an influential theory of the sentencing process, based on the proposal that the harm done by offenders requires society to rectify the imbalance created by punishing them appropriately.

retrieval interference refers to the fact that more recently encoded or stronger information blocks access to the memory trace of an initially experienced event.

risk assessment a set of procedures and methods for estimating the likelihood of future offending by an individual or the level of harm that might be caused by it, and for identifying the factors associated with it.

risk principle states that the level of intervention received by an offender should match the level of risk that offender poses. Higher risk individuals should receive a higher level of intervention than lower risk individuals.

risk–need–responsivity (RNR) model a risk management rehabilitation model that seeks to reduce offenders' predisposition to reoffend by strengthening, reducing or controlling personality and/or situational variables as appropriate.

safeguarding the process of protecting individuals from abuse or neglect, preventing impairment of their health and development, and promoting their welfare and life chances.

Salafi a form of Islam that is defined by its rejection of the 'taqlid' (imitation) of the four canonical Islamic madhahib, the traditional schools of Islamic jurisprudence, and suggests it is necessary to return to the original sources in order to make any judgment.

scientific content analysis (SCAN) a technique originally developed by Sapir, based on the assumption that a statement based on a memory of an actual experience differs in content from a statement based on invention.

screens one of the special measures permitted by the Youth Justice and Criminal Evidence Act 1999.

self-immolation voluntarily setting oneself on fire as a form of protest and suicide.

self-management a form of cognitive behavioural intervention designed to increase an individual's capacity for exercising internalised control over aspects of their thoughts, feelings or behaviour that are causing difficulty or distress.

self-manipulations hand/finger and leg/foot movements popularly believed to be associated with deception.

sentence the penalty imposed on an individual found guilty of an offence in a court of law; sentencing is the process through which this is decided.

sequential presentation a method in which a line-up is presented one person at a time. The witness decides whether each person is the perpetrator before they see the next person.

serial murder refers to a series of murders that may have been committed by the same individual(s).

serial offenders offenders who have committed more than one offence against different victims. This term can be applied to specific crime types (e.g. *serial rape, serial murder,* or *serial burglary*).

severity in penology, the magnitude of a punishment or the estimated amount of pain or discomfort a convicted offender would be likely to endure.

shoemark evidence   physical forensic evidence left at a crime scene, consisting of an impression of the shoe/footwear worn by the offender.

situational factors   factors within an individual's environment that influence his/her behaviour.

social control theory   a theory proposing that people are inhibited from offending according to the strength of their bonding to society.

social learning theory   suggests that people learn from one another, via observation, imitation, and reinforcement. The theory has been described as a bridge between behaviourist and cognitive learning theories because it encompasses attention, memory, and motivation.

social schema and scripts   cognitive frameworks that guide an individual's behaviour by providing organisational structures for new experiences or social cues.

sociocultural factors   factors within both society and cultures that guide the thoughts and behaviour of people.

source attribution   the attribution of a memory to a specific source or episode. A source attribution error refers to a situation when a memory is mistakenly attributed to the incorrect source or episode.

source monitoring error   incorrect attribution of the source of a memory (e.g. confusing internal thoughts with physical reality).

special measures   measures, specified in the Youth Justice and Criminal Evidence Act 1999, that may be ordered by the judge for eligible witnesses by means of a special measures direction. They include screens, live links, video-recorded evidence-in-chief, intermediaries and aids to communication.

stalking   a range of unwanted and repeated actions directed towards a specific individual that induce fear or concern for safety, or that induce feelings of harassment.

statement validity analysis (SVA)   a technique, widely used in Germany and Scandinavia, for assessing the veracity of a child's statement on the basis of verbal content. The overall SVA procedure involves (a) a semi structured interview, (b) a **criteria-based content analysis (CBCA)** of the statements made and (c) an evaluation of the CBCA outcome.

stress   emotional arousal induced in a victim or witness. High stress increases physiological arousal indicated by increased heart rate, faster respiration and increased muscle tone.

stress inoculation training   a form of therapy for post-traumatic stress disorder that attempts to inoculate the individual from future stressful situations.

substance misuse   an umbrella term to describe conditions such as intoxication, harmful use/abuse, dependence, withdrawal, and psychoses or amnesia associated with the use of the substance, typically associated with drugs and alcohol.

suggestibility   *see* **misinformation effect**.

suicidality   thoughts or behaviours associated with suicide.

symptomology   symptoms and syndromes associated with a particular condition or phenomenon.

system variables   factors that may affect the reliability of eyewitness memory, that are under the control of the criminal justice system. The selection of foils for a lineup is an example of a system variable (*see also* **estimator variables**).

Tamil Tigers (Liberation Tigers of Tamil Eelam)   a separatist organisation based in Northern Sri Lanka, seeking to create a separate state for the Tamil people. Founded in 1976, it conducted extensive terrorist attacks and had a very well developed military structure. In 2009, it was defeated by the Sri Lankan Army.

tertiary prevention   systematic attempt to reduce further offence recidivism by work with convicted offenders within the criminal justice system. (Primary prevention has a long-term focus; secondary prevention works with those at risk of delinquency.)

theory of mind (ToM)   the ability to attribute mental states (i.e. beliefs, intents, desires, pretending, knowledge, and so on) to oneself and others and to understand that others have beliefs, desires and intentions that are different from one's own.

trace alteration   misinformation that overwrites or amends the memory trace of the initially experienced event.

transfer of control   cognitive interview instruction designed to pass control of an interview to the interviewee.

traumatic brain injury (TBI)   occurs when an external force traumatically injures the brain.

Undeutsch hypothesis   hypothesis, first enunciated by Udo Undeutsch, that if a child's statement is based on the memory of an actual experience, it will differ in content and quality from a statement based on fabrication.

validity checklist   The final stage of the **statement validity analysis (SVA)**, in which alternative hypotheses are considered concerning a child's statement.

vicarious reinforcement/learning   learning to behave in a certain way as a result of observing the reinforcing and punishing consequences of that behaviour for other people.

video identification   a line-up in which the witness views successive video clips of the line-up members. It is used for the overwhelming majority of formal identification procedures in England and Wales, and has replaced the use of live line-ups.

video-recorded evidence-in-chief   usually an early investigative interview with a vulnerable witness by a trained practitioner. First introduced by the Criminal Justice Act 1991, and one of the special measures permitted by the YJCE Act 1999.

voice stress analysis   belief that by measuring the activity in the muscles responsible for producing speech, it may be possible to infer the speaker's mental state (e.g. experiences of stress).

voluntary false confession   a false confession offered by the suspect without any coercion from the investigator.

voyeurism   the derivation of sexual pleasure from observing other individuals involved in sexual acts. Non-consensual voyeurism is deemed to be an illegal act in England and Wales under section 67 of Sexual Offences Act 2003.

vulnerable witnesses a witness may be vulnerable due to their youth, incapacity or circumstances, for example, members of the following groups: children, elderly people, individuals with learning difficulties, physically impaired witnesses, victims of sexual offences and individuals with mental health problems.

Wahabi Wahabism is a radical branch of Islam developed by Muhammad ibn Abd al-Wahhab. It is the dominant form of Islam in Saudi Arabia and is characterised by an ultra-conservative interpretation of Islam.

working memory a temporary memory system that permits the simultaneous storage and manipulation of information prior to possible storage in long-term memory. Working memory is needed for complex tasks such as reasoning, comprehension and learning.

Index

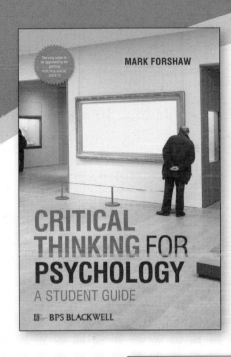
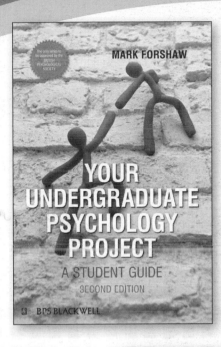

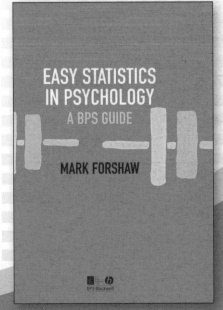

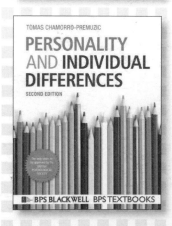
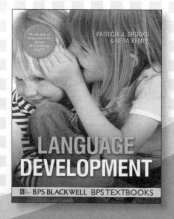
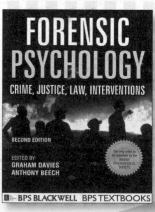
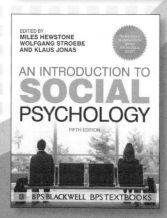